# THE DEVELOPMENT OF TRANSNATIONAL COMMERCIAL LAW

# The Development of Transnational Commercial Law

*Policies and Problems*

ROY GOODE

OXFORD
UNIVERSITY PRESS

OXFORD
UNIVERSITY PRESS

Great Clarendon Street, Oxford, OX2 6DP,
United Kingdom

Oxford University Press is a department of the University of Oxford.
It furthers the University's objective of excellence in research, scholarship,
and education by publishing worldwide. Oxford is a registered trade mark of
Oxford University Press in the UK and in certain other countries



First Edition published in 2018



Published in the United States of America by Oxford University Press
198 Madison Avenue, New York, NY 10016, United States of America

British Library Cataloguing in Publication Data
Data available

Library of Congress Control Number: 2018944715

ISBN 978–0–19–882581–4

For Naomi

# *Preface*

This is the second of my two volumes of collected writings over the past 57 years. The first, *Fundamental Concepts of Commercial Law: 50 Years of Reflection*, is devoted to English commercial law. The present volume gathers together essays on transnational commercial law and includes a chapter on the Hague Securities Convention not previously published. I have elsewhere defined transnational commercial law as 'that set of private law principles and rules, from whatever source, which governs international commercial transactions and is common to legal systems generally or to a significant number of legal systems'. While Philip Jessup is generally credited with coining the phrase 'transnational law' in his work, *Transnational Commercial Law*, published in 1956, and transnational commercial law was the subject of an excellent collection of essays, *The Transnational Law of Commercial Transactions*, edited by the late Professors Norbert Horn and Clive Schmitthoff, it appears that the postgraduate course on transnational commercial law which I introduced into the Oxford law curriculum in the mid-1990s was the first of its kind. Enthusiastically received by students because its focus was not on any particular national legal system but on the products and processes of harmonization, transnational commercial law is now taught by law schools around the world and there is an annual meeting of teachers of the subject held in different countries every year, the first being in Oxford in July 2009 and the most recent in Nijmegen in 2017. Four of us, Professors Kronke, McKendrick, Wool, and myself, together with specialist contributions from different experts, produced what is the first student text, cases, and materials book, now in its second edition, and the subject is flourishing.

My first serious incursion into transnational commercial law resulted from a chance discussion with Professor Ben Wortley, then Professor of Jurisprudence and International Law at the University of Manchester, at a meeting of the Board of Studies in Law at London University. He was then a member of the Governing Council of the International Institute for the Unification of Private Law (UNIDROIT) and suggested that I might like to become involved in the activities of UNIDROIT, an international, intergovernmental organization based in Rome and established in 1926 to promote the progressive harmonization of private law. There followed a meeting over lunch in 1974 with Martin Stanford, then a legal officer and later deputy Secretary-General of UNIDROIT, now retired. He was totally committed to the Institute and his enthusiasm was infectious. He involved me in two projects running in parallel, a proposed convention on international factoring and one on international financial leasing. So began a long association with UNIDROIT, a small but highly effective organization, to which I became devoted. I served on the Governing Council for 15 years and am still quite actively involved in some of its activities and in the Queen Mary-UNDROIT Institute of Transnational Commercial Law set up in 2016 within the Centre for Commercial Law Studies, a department of the School of Law I created in 1980, which has flourished under successive directors.

I have drawn a great deal of inspiration from the writings of legal academics from around the world and from working with them and with practitioners on many projects. These include the Principles of European Contract Law produced by the Commission on European Contract Law under the chairmanship of that great comparative lawyer Professor Ole Lando and, in its third stage, the UNIDROIT Principles of International Commercial Contracts, brilliantly driven by Professor Joachim Bonell. The number of people to whom I am indebted for their influence and friendship over the years is too great to enable me to identify them individually, but to all of them I express my deepest thanks.

I am indebted to the various publishers who have given copyright consent to re-publication in this volume of articles from their journals. Individual acknowledgements are contained at the foot of each reproduced article. My thanks also to an Oxford law undergraduate, Aleksandra Katholic, for her assistance in sending the letters seeking copyright consent.

Once again I should like to express my particular appreciation to Oxford University Press for all they have done to bring this publication to fruition. My thanks are due in particular to Rachel Mullaly, the Senior Commissioning Editor, her editorial assistant Amy Bartlett, the Senior Production Editor Clare Jones, the copy-editor Elissa Connor, the indexer Jane Ashley, the tabler Angela Foskett, and the proofreader Gillian Pickering.

Roy Goode

*Oxford*
*July 2018*

# *Table of Contents*

# *Table of Cases*

# Table of Legislation

TREATIES AND CONVENTIONS

## CODIFICATIONS



## NATIONAL LEGISLATION

### Argentina



### Belgium



### Canada



### China, Republic of



### Czech Republic



### Estonia



### France



### Germany



### Italy



### Lithuania



### Mexico



### Netherlands



### Russia



### Sweden



### Switzerland

## EUROPEAN SECONDARY LEGISLATION

# *Table of Other Instruments and Rules*

## RESTATEMENTS

# PART I

# HARMONISATION

There are four international organisations primarily concerned with harmonisation: UNIDROIT, the United Nations Convention on International Trade Law (UNCITRAL), the Hague Conference on Private International Law, and the International Chamber of Commerce (ICC). I have had the privilege of being involved in one way or another with all of them. UNIDROIT is concerned with the progressive harmonisation of private law, UNCITRAL with the development of the law of international trade, the Hague Conference with private international law across the board, and the International Chamber of Commerce with (among many other things) the production of uniform customs, practice, and rules which are given effect by incorporation into contracts. Such bodies utilise a variety of instruments, in particular international conventions, model laws, uniform rules, restatements of law, and legislative and other guides. Together these embrace both hard law and soft law.

The essays in this Part fall broadly into three groups: those that address problems of harmonisation of contract and commercial law generally (chapters 1 to 4), those devoted to harmonisation in specific subject areas, notably security and other interests in movable property (chapters 5 and 7 to 11), abstract payment undertakings in relation to uniform rules promulgated by the ICC (chapter 12); and the particular question of the attitude of the United Kingdom to the harmonisation of commercial law (chapter 6).

# 1

# Reflections on the Harmonisation of Commercial Law*,†

*by Roy Goode*

Norton Rose Professor of English Law, St. John's College, Oxford

## Introduction

Truly there is nothing new under the sun. Nearly two thousand years have elapsed since Cicero proclaimed the virtues of legal harmonisation: "… *nec erit alia lex Romae, alia Athenis, alia nunc, alia posthac, sed et omnes gentes et omni tempore una lex et sempiterna et immutabilis continebit* … ".[1]

The urge towards internal harmonisation of local laws and customs gave rise to the common law in England and to codification in Europe. Harmonisation spread geographically through colonisation and internationally through adoption by one State (typically a developing State) of codes conveniently in place elsewhere. But harmonisation of this kind remains purely internal. Colonisation involves merely a geographical extension of domestic law; adoption of another State's code is a short-cut route to the creation of the developing State's law and does not have as its objective the facilitation of a common market or of inter-State commerce.

The particular characteristic of twentieth century harmonisation lies in its motivation, which is to reduce the impact of national boundaries. But this overall objective encompasses two quite distinct purposes. The first is to create a special regime for international transactions while preserving the identity of national laws for domestic transactions, and is effected primarily by international Conventions. The second is to facilitate a common market or a political or economic grouping by harmonising national laws governing domestic transactions, so that State boundaries within the

* This paper, delivered at the Fifth Biennial Meeting* of the International Academy of Commercial and Consumer Law held in Oxford in 1990, is published with the kind permission of the Oxford University Press.

† Originally published as Reflections on the Harmonisation of Commercial Law. *Uniform Law Review* (1991-I): 54–74.

[1] Cicero, *De Republica*, 3. 22. 33.

geographical area covered by the members of the market lose much of their significance within the fields covered by the harmonising measures.

There is thus a fundamental distinction, both in objectives and in the character of the content, between, say, the Convention on Contracts for the International Sale of Goods on the one hand and the EEC Directive on Consumer Credit on the other. The Convention is concerned to facilitate inter-State trade, the Directive to promote the social aims of the Single European Market and to avoid distortion of the market. The provisions of the Convention are almost entirely dispositive, those of the Directive obligatory. The Convention is confined to international transactions, the Directive prescribes minimum rights and duties for parties to domestic transactions. The Convention excludes consumer sales contracts; the Directive is confined to consumer credit agreements. The Convention predicates the separateness of States, the Directive their integration in a common market.

Despite these differences between Convention law and Community law they possess a certain symbiosis. The influence of Community law is steadily expanding, so that each member State is increasingly having to adjust its thinking to accommodate principles and rules derived from other legal systems within the Community and thus to acclimatise itself to a less nationalistic approach to law. The harmonisation of laws affecting domestic transactions in member States has an effect on international transactions in that within the field covered by the harmonising measures these obviate the need to resort to conflict of laws rules and thus achieve one of the objectives of a Convention regulating international transactions.[2] The drive towards economic and political union has the tendency to convert what were previously international transactions into internal transactions, and thus reduces the sphere of influence of Conventional law within the EEC.

This paper is devoted primarily to harmonisation of legal rights and duties arising under[3] international transactions. It addresses certain key issues which continue to be troublesome: the selection of aspects of commercial law suitable for harmonisation; the level and scope of the harmonising measure and the extent to which it does or does not displace conflict of law rules; the factors relevant to the method of harmonisation and the likelihood of its success; the problem of language; the efficiency of the mechanism by which harmonising measures are brought into existence and implemented by national legislation, and, most crucial of all, the indifference, or even hostility, with which harmonisation proposals continue to be greeted. The principal vehicles for this analysis are the United Nations Convention on Contracts for the International Sale of Goods,[4] because of its major importance in private commercial law; the Unidroit Conventions on International Factoring and International Financial Leasing, with which the writer has been involved from

[2] But not all the objectives. For example, national laws governing domestic transactions, even if uniform, are not necessarily well suited to transactions involving an international element.

[3] I use this phrase in preference to the "the law relating to" in order to encompass harmonising instruments which do not in themselves constitute law but have effect by virtue of incorporation into contracts, the Uniform Customs and Practice for Documentary Credits and Incoterms, both promulgated by the International Chamber of Commerce.

[4] Referred to hereafter as the Vienna Sales Convention.

the early days of their conception; and the rules and trade terms promulgated by the International Chamber of Commerce, which demonstrate how much can be achieved by the contractual approach to the harmonisation of commercial law and practice, and which will be given particular attention later.

## Selecting the Field

### Genesis of a Proposal

By what process is the field of harmonisation selected? Typically, someone has a bright idea and decides to put it into play. He or she may be a member of an organisation involved with harmonisation—the EC Commission, Unidroit, UNCITRAL, for example—or an academic or other outsider who sends a proposal in to such an organisation for consideration. The idea may have been worked out with some care or, at the other extreme, it may have been put up spontaneously at a meeting convened to discuss the content of a future programme of activity. There is nothing wrong in this. Ideas have to begin somewhere, a point which tends to be overlooked by those who seize on leaked internal governmental memoranda floating a proposal at a formative stage of the idea and criticise both the content of the proposal and the secrecy which surrounds it, without reflecting that ideas have to be shaped by discussion and given preliminary approval as worthy of examination before they can go out under the imprimatur of the organising body.

### Is there a Problem?

Once an organisation has decided that a particular proposal falls within its remit and appears sufficiently meritorious to warrant further examination, what should happen next, before it is approved, is a testing process to see whether the problem which the proposal is designed to solve actually exists, and if so, whether it is sufficiently significant to warrant the labour and expense of a harmonising measure. It is far from clear that this essential step is always taken. For example, the earlier work of the EC Commission appeared to proceed on the untested assumption that any differences in national laws of member States within the field identified as potentially suitable for a Directive distorted the Common Market and justified the proposed Directive, without any fieldwork being undertaken to see whether there was in fact a problem. The tendency persists to this day. Thus the EC Commission and Council, not content with amending the Consumer Credit Directive to specify the equation which must be satisfied for a correct statement of the annual percentage rate of charge and the items that are to be excluded from computation of the total charge for credit, threaten a further Directive prescribing a single mathematical formula for calculating the APR. But why? Consumers do not in practice shop for credit outside their own country but simply use their home-based credit cards to make purchases abroad. The notion that an Englishman will cross the Channel to France to obtain credit in Calais because the formula under which French finance houses are allowed to quote APR enables them to advertise a cheaper rate than their English counterparts, and that the

Common Market is thereby distorted, is too ludicrous to warrant a moment's consideration. Yet it is just this kind of assumption, unsupported by any fieldwork, that is responsible for the proposal for the further Directive.

It is fair to say that international organisations are much more sensitive to this accusation than formerly. Unidroit, for example, goes to considerable trouble, by means of consultations with representative international organisations and by questionnaires to specialists and to Governments which in turn consult their national organisations, in order to establish that those practising in the field in question believe that differences in national laws create a problem and that harmonisation would bring benefits. UNCITRAL likewise engages in widespread consultation, drawing widely on the expertise of practising specialists. Projects least vulnerable to the accusation that they are dealing with non-problems are those initiated by the International Chamber of Commerce, the membership of whose Commissions is drawn preponderantly from the world of industry and commerce, banking, shipping, and arbitration.

The testing process is absolutely vital, not only to ensure that a significant problem exists which would be alleviated by a harmonising measure but also to identify it accurately. Case law, which is not infrequently relied on as an indication of problem areas, can be a very unreliable guide, since many cases are atypical and the real problems lie elsewhere.

## The Intruments of Harmonisation

### The Range of Available Instruments

There are at least nine methods[5] by which harmonisation may be either effected or in some measure induced, namely:

(1) a multilateral Convention without a Uniform Law as such;
(2) a multilateral Convention embodying a Uniform Law;
(3) a set of bilateral Treaties;
(4) Community legislation—typically, a Directive;
(5) a Model Law;
(6) a codification of custom and usage promulgated by an international nongovernmental organisation;
(7) international trade terms promulgated by such an organisation;
(8) model contracts and general contractual conditions;
(9) restatements by scholars and other experts.

[5] I exclude uncodified international trade usage because its *ad hoc* development and diffuse and variegated character severely limits its practical value, even on the assumption (which is certainly not true of English law) that such usage has normative force independent of contract, judicial reception, or legislative adoption.

The characteristic of the first four is that they have the force of law, subject to such constitutional acts as may be necessary to give them force in the territory of a particular Contracting State. The Model Law is, as its name implies, a model which can be adopted in its entirety, adapted, or simply used as the basis for ideas; it has no legal force as such. The next four instruments depend for their efficacy upon incorporation into contracts, though a codification of custom and usage could perhaps be relied on as the best evidence of custom and usage and as such be imported by implication into a contract, whilst the adoption of general contractual conditions is not the exclusive prerogative of private parties but can also be achieved by embodiment in bilateral or multilateral Conventions implemented by dispositive legislation in the various participating States.[6]

## Making the Choice

In an ideal world the choice of harmonising instrument would depend on what was most suitable for the particular project envisaged and carried with it the greatest prospect of successful implementation. In practice, the relative lack of co-ordination among the various harmonising agencies[7] means that the form of instrument is largely predetermined by the nature of the organisation initiating the measure. International intergovernmental organisations such as Unidroit and UNCITRAL and the specialist agencies could in theory select any of the available instruments but for practical reasons usually choose the route of a Convention (with or without Uniform Rules) or a Model Law. By contrast the International Chamber of Commerce, which is an international non-governmental organisation with national Chambers of Commerce as its members, promotes non-law instruments which depend for their effect upon contractual incorporation.

The advantages of the contract route are becoming increasingly appreciated.[8] Since Governments are not involved, the role of lawyers is reduced and the procedure is more flexible and informal, proposals can be implemented more rapidly, and rules found to cause difficulty can be changed more readily. The utility of contract rules increases as their use expands. The most striking example is provided by the Uniform Customs and Practice of the International Chamber of Commerce, which has been adopted by banks throughout the world. The beauty of the UCP is that since all relevant contracts involve a bank there is a ready mechanism for ensuring that all contracts are governed by the UCP. This applies to the account party's application to his bank to open the credit, the credit itself, the relationship between the beneficiary and advising and confirming banks, and the relationships of the banks *inter se*. Each of the relevant contract documents incorporates the provisions

[6] As was the case with the CMEA General Conditions of Delivery of Goods. See Ivan Szasz, *The CMEA Uniform Law for International Sales* (2nd ed.), chap. IV.

[7] See below, p. 9.

[8] They were observed by Professor Clive Schmitthoff many years ago. See "The Unification or Harmonisation of Law by Means of Standard Contracts and General Conditions" (1968) 17 ICLQ 551, reproduced in *Clive M. Schmitthoff's Selected Essays in International Trade Law* (ed. Chia-Jul Cheng), chap. 15.

of the UCP by reference. The result is to connect up a network of contracts by a uniform set of rules and thus give them multilateral force.

## Substantive Rules and Trade Terms

There is a close relationship between substantive rules embodied by contract and uniform trade terms so embodied. The latter constitute both a small dictionary of commercial abbreviations and a set of dispositive rules. Indeed, they differ from substantive rules only in that the latter have no dictionary function.

## Limits to the Contract Method

The International Chamber of Commerce has done valuable work in the formulation of uniform rules and trade terms effectuated by incorporation into contracts. But there are limits to what such an institution can achieve. First, since the ICC is not a lawmaking body it cannot formulate rules of a mandatory character; indeed, its rules are intended to encapsulate proper *practice*, rather than to distribute legal liability. So it would not have been the appropriate body to formulate rules of the kind embodied in the Vienna Sales Convention, though recommended contract *terms* might have been feasible. Secondly, since the ICC rules depend upon adoption by contract their success depends in large measure on the existence of an institutional structure sufficiently homogeneous and of contract terms sufficiently standardised to ensure the likelihood of such adoption. In the case of documentary credits and performance bonds and guarantees the banking mechanism provides the requisite homogeneity for the ICC Rules; the failure of the Uniform Rules for Guarantees[9] resulted from a different factor, namely too great a separation from commercial practice.[10] The ICC's Incoterms[11] are widely used by exporters and forwarders involved in the shipment of goods. But it is unlikely that the ICC could have successfully mounted an exercise to codify contract rules governing commercial agency agreements, though a Working Party of the ICC's Commission on International Commercial Practice under the chairmanship of Professor Fabio Bortolotti has successfully completed a model form of agency contract for international trade and is proceeding with work on a model distribution contract.

## Restatements

Insufficient attention has hitherto been given to the role that can be played by scholarly publications in influencing harmonisation. Of particular interest in this regard

[9] ICC No. 325, 1978.

[10] A new set of rules, the Uniform Rules for Demand Guarantees (ICC Publication No. 458), was adopted in December 1991. But ICC No. 325 is being retained for the time being for those who may still wish to use it. The former reflect more closely the documentary character of performance guarantees whilst at the same time providing safeguards against unfair calling.

[11] The current edition is *Incoterms 1990*.

are the various UNCITRAL Legal Guides and two projects on principles of contract law undertaken by Unidroit and the Commission on European Contract Law respectively. The latter are intended to offer a set of principles providing the best solutions to typical problems in contract law. Inspiration from these is drawn from a variety of sources, including national laws, the American *Restatement,* and the fertile minds of those engaged in the projects. It is hoped that these statements of principle will over time influence national courts by persuading them to look beyond their own, or indeed any one, legal system, particularly where the dispute is international and thus does not readily respond to national laws designed primarily for domestic transactions.

## Which Organisation?

There is a tendency to formulate proposals for uniform laws without adequate liaison among the various bodies involved in harmonisation to ensure that each is kept informed as to the other's projected programme of activity and that duplication of effort is avoided. In general, the organisation that conceives the idea retains the project, unless it is one which clearly falls outside its remit, and carries it through to completion. This is not to say that there is no collaboration between organisations. It is common for members of each to attend meetings of the others, at least as observers, and sometimes a project initiated by one body is subsequently brought to fruition under the aegis of another. Thus for practical reasons it has sometimes been found expedient for projects initiated by Unidroit to reach fruition at a Diplomatic Conference held under the aegis of UNCITRAL.

But much energy is expended fruitlessly by parallel work by different bodies, who by pooling their resources and expertise could have expedited the work and improved its quality. Thus while the EC Commission was working on its Draft Directive on Products Liability the Council of Europe was preparing a Convention on the very same subject. The Convention was the first to arrive, being opened for signature in January 1977, whilst the Directive did not appear until July 1985. But having done so it rendered the Convention otiose except in relation to non-EEC members of the Council of Europe.

Not all duplication can be avoided, for EC Directives are limited to members of the European Community, whilst the catchment area for bodies such as UNCITRAL and Unidroit extends across the world. But much more needs to be done to coordinate effort if limited resources are to be used to greatest effect.[12] The problem is less acute in specialist fields identified to one particular agency. Thus Conventions on conflicts of laws fall within the prerogative of the Hague Conference, matters relating to shipping within the domain of the IMO and the CMI, proposals concerning air transport within that of the ICAO and IATA, and those affecting intellectual property within the remit of WIPO. It is in the field of general international trade law—a

[12] UNCITRAL performs a valuable service in reporting each year on the activities of the numerous bodies involved in unification projects.

field in which three international organisations, Unidroit, UNCITRAL, and the ICC are particularly active—that the overlap is most prominent; and problems may also arise where work in such field is considered by specialist organisations to impact on their area of expertise.[13]

The question which organisation is best fitted to undertake a particular project should be determined not only by considerations of relative expertise and resources but also by reference to the type of instrument that is most likely to be effective. Should it be a Convention or simply a set of rules incorporated into contracts? If the former, it belongs to bodies such as UNCITRAL and Unidroit, if the latter, to the ICC. But the question seems rarely to be asked. In general, the approach is to leave a project to the first in the field without adequate consideration whether the type of instrument which that body's work will produce is necessarily the most appropriate.

## Scope of the Harmonising Measure

Determining the nature of the field to be covered is only the beginning. The next question is the scope of the proposed harmonising measure. How wide should its net be spread? At one end is the minimalist approach, which postulates that the narrower the field the greater the likelihood that the project will be successfully completed within a reasonable time. At the other is the maximalist approach, which predicates that the task is not worth undertaking unless all significant aspects of the field are covered. The former approach is usually expanded by ambition, the latter contracted by realism. What is achievable depends to some extent on whether the project is entirely new or is able to build on preceding work. In the latter case there is obviously scope for a harmonising measure of greater magnitude. What is difficult to judge in the early stages is the extent to which the project can be broadened without jeopardising the prospect of success. Just as the best is the enemy of the good, so also the largest is the enemy of the more modest. After all, earth was not made in a day and there is always scope for a second project once the first has been completed and shown to be a success.

There are a number of aspects of the scope issue. First, there is the range of substantive law issues to be covered. Next comes the question whether the harmonising measure should be confined to international transactions or should apply also to domestic transactions and, if the former, what tests of internationality should be applied. Thirdly, should the measure be confined to business transactions or apply to consumer transactions as well? Fourthly, what, if any, should be the connecting factor linking the subject-matter of the Convention to a Contracting State? Finally, to what extent is the harmonising measure to pre-empt national law and thus to

[13] Thus the CMI was opposed to the inclusion of ships in the Unidroit Convention on International Financial Leasing, concerned that this might encroach on their own work, but at the Diplomatic Conference in Ottawa in 1988 where the Convention was concluded and opened for signature the fifty-five participating countries were unanimous in their view that there was no good reason to exclude such an important subject of leasing activity. The problem is not new (see Kurt Gronfors, "Transport Law", in *International Uniform Law in Practice* 376 at p. 383), and calls for consultation and tact.

exclude conflict of laws issues? There is no special magic in the order in which these issues are taken.

They are so closely related that a provisional view on one may well be displaced as the result of conclusions reached on another. Each will be taken in turn.

## Coverage of Substantive Law

Let us take some concrete examples. The Vienna Sales Convention has been criticised for not dealing with the passing of property or with priority conflicts between the seller/buyer and a third party. Why were these important topics omitted? First, it would have made the project too large (as it is, the Convention runs to 101 articles). Secondly, it was felt that on issues of property law differences in legal policy and approach created a chasm too large to bridge. A particular stumbling-block is the significance of possession as a determinant of property rights. In a number of legal systems there is a presumption that the property in identified goods is intended to pass on the making of the contract, in others, only on delivery. The effect of an unauthorised disposition by a party in possession who has not yet acquired ownership also raises acute differences in approach. In particular, common law systems start from the position *nemo dat quod non habet,* civil law systems from the principle *en fait de meubles la possession vaut titre.* Both sets of systems have moved towards each other but a gulf remains. There is the additional problem that conflicting claims to tangible movables raise issues going well beyond sales law and that conflicts arising from sales transactions cannot sensibly be dealt with in isolation.

Much the same reasoning led to the steadfast refusal of the Unidroit study group to yield to pressures to extend the scope of the Convention on International Financial Leasing to cover general issues of priority of competing claims to leased equipment, though Article 7 does contain provisions preserving the lessor's real rights against the claims of the lessee's trustee in bankruptcy and execution and other creditors. What is interesting is that the provisions of Article 7 relating to mobile equipment have triggered a proposal to Unidroit by Canada[14] for a separate Convention on security interests in mobile equipment. Investigations into the extent of the problem raised by differences in national laws are being undertaken prior to the Governing Council deciding whether the project should proceed.

Questions of scope of subject-matter are not, of course, determined purely by feasibility; the scope of a project is also limited by its fundamental objectives. Again, the Unidroit Leasing Convention provides a case in point. The Convention is confined to international financial leasing, that is, to leasing which in economic terms is equivalent to a sale or purchase-money loan, the equipment being leased to a single lessee at whose request it was bought and the rentals being fixed not by reference to the use-value of the equipment as such but at a level which, taking into account cash-flows, tax-reliefs, and the like, will guarantee to the lessor the reimbursement

[14] Formulated by Professor Ron Cuming of the University of Saskatchewan.

of his capital costs and desired return on capital. There was much pressure to extend the scope of the Convention to cover operating leases, in which equipment is let at its market use-value to several lessees in succession. Again, this pressure was resisted by the study group and the ensuing committee of governmental experts, on the ground that whilst some provisions of the Convention would be appropriate to both types of lease, the primary function of the Convention was to recognise the particular financial nature of a finance lease by giving a substantial degree of immunity from suit to the lessor and transferring liability to the supplier. Such immunity would be entirely inappropriate in the case of an operating lease. Similarly, the International Chamber of Commerce has rightly refused to incorporate into the Uniform Customs and Practice for Documentary Credits (UCP) rules as to the effect of forgery or other fraud,[15] taking the position that the essential function of the UCP is to codify best banking practice in the handling of credits, not to provide a comprehensive legal text.

In essence, then, the scope of a harmonising measure is determined by the nature and extent of the problem to be tackled, the function of the particular body undertaking the measure, and the feasibility of the project in terms of ability to reach agreement within a reasonable time-frame. As regards time those involved in unification projects have learned to be patient and to think in decades rather than years. In general, a minimum of ten years is required to bring to fruition an initial proposal for an international Convention, though there are exceptions. Very often the period is much longer and securing the requisite number of ratifications may take a decade more, if, indeed, this is achieved at all. Projects of the International Chamber of Commerce can usually be completed much more quickly, since not only are they less formal but they are not legal instruments in themselves, simply rules or trade terms incorporated by contract, so that the legal issues are de-emphasised and, indeed, the product is primarily the work of non-lawyers. The size of the project is obviously a relevant factor in the time taken to complete it but length alone is not a reliable indicator. The UNCITRAL Model Law on International Commercial Arbitration, containing 36 Articles, was completed in a mere six years, the Convention on International Factoring, consisting of twelve articles,[16] took fourteen years from start to finish. The problem is not length as such but the infrequency and brevity of meetings at which the scientific work is conducted, a point to which I shall return towards the end of this paper.

## Internationality

Apart from harmonising measures formulated for the purpose of establishing a common market, whose regulators will have a keen interest in acts in one member State that can produce effects in others[17] most harmonisation instruments dealing

[15] Beyond making it clear that banks are concerned only with the *apparent* order of the documents presented and not with their genuineness, accuracy, or falsification (1983 Revision, art. 17).

[16] Excluding the relatively standard Final Provisions.

[17] This is particularly true of dealings within the field of competition law.

with contracts are confined to international transactions.[18] The reasons are not hard to find. National laws regulating domestic transactions are either considered adequate or, if not, are thought best changed by domestic legislation. Moreover, except in the context of a common market they are not thought to be of interest to outsiders. In the words of Professor John Honnold: "States can be expected to bind themselves to the same rules only in an area of shared interest—their international trade transactions". [19]

A further factor is that States feel more relaxed about harmonising measures which do not threaten (even though they may in some degree influence) long established concepts and traditions of their own legal systems governing domestic transactions.

Given that the harmonising measure is to be confined to international transactions, what test is to be applied to determine internationality? There are at least four possibilities:

(1) the transaction itself is cross-border in character in that it involves contractual activity in two or more States;
(2) the parties carry on business in different States;
(3) the transaction, even if internal and concluded between persons carrying on business in the same State, produces effects in another State;
(4) a combination of two or more of the above.

We can disregard (3), which is a prime concern of the EC but does not feature in international Conventions, and concentrate on the others. There is no uniformity of practice. The Hague Rules embodied in the 1924 Brussels Convention on Bills of Lading contain no express internationality requirement at all, though clearly directed at contracts for the carriage of goods by sea from one State to another, a point made explicit by the Visby amendments. The Uniform Law on the International Sale of Goods combines criteria (1) and (2) by a somewhat complex formula which requires, first; that the parties carry on business in different States and, secondly, that the transaction fulfil one of three alternative tests of cross-border activity.[20] This cumbersome formulation has been dropped in the Vienna Sales Convention, which substitutes as the sole criterion of internationality the fact that the parties carry on business in different States, a formulation adopted in the Unidroit Convention on Agency in the International Sale of Goods and the Unidroit Conventions on International Factoring and International Financial Leasing. Thus it is possible for one of these three Conventions to apply in relation to a purely internal supply

[18] Technically this is not true of the ICC's Uniform Customs and Practice for Documentary Credits, which in theory are just as applicable to intra-State as to inter-State dealings, but in practice the operation of the IJCP is almost entirely concerned with the financing of import/export transactions.

[19] *Uniform Law for International Sales*, para. 13.

[20] Art. 1(1), which specifies as the three alternative tests (a) that the goods are to be carried from the territory of one State to that of another, (b) that the acts constituting the offer and the acceptance have been effected in the territories of different States, and (c) that delivery is to be made in the territory of a State other than that within whose territory the acts constituting the offer and acceptance have been effected.

contract in which goods move from one place in a State to another place in the same State pursuant to a contract concluded by acts of offer and acceptance entirely within that State.[21]

It seems likely that the single criterion adopted by the Vienna Sales Convention will become the norm. It has the merit of simplicity and responds adequately to the desire of States to maintain control over purely domestic transactions, in that the laws of a State are enacted primarily for the benefit of its own residents, not for those situated abroad. Moreover, confinement of the test of internationality to a single factor enlarges the scope of the Convention, which is an important policy objective.

However, a complicating factor emerged in the preparation of the Leasing and Factoring Conventions. Previously, Conventions regulating contracts had been concerned with only one contractual relationship, for example, the relationship between shipper and carrier or between seller and buyer. The special feature of the two Unidroit Conventions is that they each deal with a transaction involving two distinct contracts. The Leasing Convention covers transactions in which equipment is sold by a supplier to an intending lessor who in turn lets it on lease to the lessee. The Factoring Convention embraces transactions in which goods are supplied under a contract of sale and the resulting receivables assigned by the supplier to the factor. Which, in each case, should be regarded as the relevant contract in order for the transaction as a whole to satisfy the internationality requirement? The solution adopted in both cases was to look to the transaction the parties to which typically carried on business in different States and to ignore the transaction which in the typical case was domestic. So the relevant contract for the Leasing Convention is the leasing agreement, not the supply contract, whereas for the Factoring Convention it is the sale contract, not the factoring agreement.

Mention has been made of two considerations relevant to the internationality test, namely simplicity and maximisation of the scope of the Convention. To these should be added a third consideration, transparency. It is important that each party to a prospective transaction should be able to ascertain readily whether or not his contract will be governed by the Convention. This point is sensibly picked up in the Vienna Sales Convention, which provides in Article 1(2) that: "The fact that the parties have their places of business in different States is to be disregarded whenever this fact does not appear from the contract or from any dealings between, or from information disclosed by, the parties at any time before or at the conclusion of the contract." For some reason (possibly through oversight) this provision is not reproduced in the Leasing and Factoring Conventions, which in other respects borrowed heavily from the scope provisions of the Sales Convention. It remains to be seen whether courts will be prepared to read such a provision into those Conventions, for example by reference to the requirement of good faith as a canon of interpretation.[22]

[21] Conversely the Conventions will not apply to a cross-border transaction between parties carrying on business in the same State, as where seller and buyer, both carrying on business in France, conclude a sale contract by which the goods are to be delivered by the seller to the buyer's sub-purchaser in Spain.

[22] Leasing Convention, Art. 6(1); Factoring Convention, Art. 4(1).

Bills of exchange raise special transparency considerations, for it is a tenet of the law relating to such instruments that the terms of payment are to be found exclusively in the instrument itself, without reference to extraneous facts. It is therefore logical that the 1988 UN Convention on International Bills of Exchange should adopt criteria of internationality which involve the form of the instrument rather than the place of business of the parties.[23]

## Restriction to Business Transactions?

Should the harmonising measure be confined to business transactions or should it embrace consumer transactions as well? Here again we can see a sharp distinction between the legislative acts of the European Communities on the one hand and conventional law on the other. Consumer protection represents an important plank in the evolving structure of Community law and several Directives have been issued in this field, including Directives relating to consumer credit and doorstep transactions. As previously noted, the purpose and effect of Directives is not to regulate international transactions but to impose uniform laws operating on domestic transactions within each member State. By contrast Conventions regulating transactions are concerned almost exclusively with business transactions. Such Conventions are seen primarily as facilitators of international trade rather than as instruments of social policy. There are good reasons for this approach. First, within the European Community the Treaty of Rome and subordinate legislation are the primary instruments of harmonisation at the consumer level and their implementation is mandatory for member States. Given the objectives of the Community and the fact that the Single European Market will constitute the most powerful trading bloc in the world, there is little point in extending conventional law into this field. Secondly, issues of social policy are peculiarly sensitive and dependent on domestic policy and prevailing social conditions, so that even within the European Community the best that can be hoped for is a set of minimum standards. It is for this reason that provisions in Conventions dealing with commercial contracts are almost entirely dispositive in nature, the parties being left free to exclude the relevant Convention entirely or to vary or derogate from its effects. This permissive attitude is generally acceptable to States in relation to business transactions[24] but is likely to meet strong objection if applied to consumer transactions. Hence the exclusion of these from the Convention.

[23] To be within the Convention the bill must contain by way of heading and in the text the words "International bill of exchange (Uncitral Convention)" and specify at least two of the following places with an indication that any two so specified are situated in different States, namely (a) the place where the bill is drawn; (b) the place indicated next to the signature of the drawer; (c) the place indicated next to the name of the drawer; (d) the place indicated next to the name of the payee; (e) the place of payment (Arts. 1, 2).

[24] Though even in relation to these difficulties can arise because of strongly felt policy views. Thus at the Diplomatic Conference to discuss the Unidroit Convention on International Leasing a group of States headed by France insisted on the inclusion of a power for a Contracting State to make a declaration preserving its domestic law prohibiting exclusion of a lessor's liability for default or negligence where this prohibition is wider than that provided by Art. 8(3) of the Convention (Art. 20).

## The Connection to a Contracting State

Should the scope of a Convention be limited to transactions in which there is some connection with a Contracting State, and if so, what should be the connecting factor? At first sight it seems inconceivable to apply a Convention to a transaction having no point of contact whatsoever with a Contracting State, yet that is precisely the effect which ULIS sought to achieve. Not only is there no requirement of connection with a Contracting State but Article 2 of the Uniform Rules provides in terms that: "Rules of private international law shall be excluded for the purposes of the application of the present Law, subject to any provision to the contrary in the said Law."

As if this remarkable provision[25] were not enough, Article 4 goes on to provide that:

> The present Law shall also apply where it has been chosen as the law of the contract by the parties, whether or not their places of business or their habitual residences are in different States and whether or not such States are parties to the Convention dated the 1st day of July 1964 relating to a Uniform Law on the International Sale of Goods, to the extent that it does not affect the application of any mandatory provisions of law which would have been applicable if the parties had not chosen the Uniform Law.

This bold attempt both to exclude private international law and to make ULIS applicable in Contracting States even if there were no point of contact with a Contracting State[26] had its supporters but attracted such fierce criticism that no organisation concerned with unification has had the temerity to repeat the experiment. All subsequent Conventions have required as a condition of their applicability not only internationality of the transaction but also a connection with a Contracting State. What should suffice as the connecting factor remains a matter of controversy. The Vienna Sales Convention prescribes two alternative methods of satisfying the connection test. The first is that both parties to the contract carry on business in a Contracting State,[27] the second, that rules of private international law lead to the application of the law of a Contracting State.[28] The first limb is universally accepted as legitimate; the second, though having the merit of expanding the scope of the Convention, has been criticised on various grounds. Where the parties have not chosen the law which is to govern their contract the applicability of the Convention will depend upon the law governing the contract as determined by the conflict rules of the forum, which, of course, may vary from State to State. This runs counter to at least two objectives of the Convention, namely transparency and removal of the advantages of forum shopping. A second objection is that where both parties carry on business in Contracting States they can reasonably be subjected to the Convention automatically since it forms part of their national law, whereas parties carrying on business in different non-Contracting States who agree that their contract is to be governed by the law of a third State which is a Contracting State may well have in mind only the domestic

[25] Discussed further below.

[26] Subject only to the power of a Contracting State to make a declaration under Art. 3 of the Convention enabling it to insert "Contracting" before "States" where the latter word first occurs in Art. 1 of the Uniform Law.

[27] Art. 1(1)(a). [28] Art. 1(1)(b).

law of that State and arguably ought not to be bound by the Convention unless they contract into it. In acknowledgment of the concerns expressed by various States the Vienna Sales Convention confers a power on Contracting States to make reservations excluding the second form of connecting factor.[29]

Again, the position under the Leasing and Factoring Conventions was complicated by the existence of two contracts. Accordingly, these Conventions apply in the first instance only when all three parties involved (supplier/lessor/ lessee and supplier/debtor/factor) carry on business in Contracting States. This, of course, is a much more significant limitation on scope than exists in single-contract Conventions such as the Sales Convention, and in consequence the authors of those Conventions decided not to allow a reservation in respect of the second limb of application.

## The Role of the Conflict of Laws

The relationship between the scope and substantive provisions of a Convention and rules of private international law is highly complex and can be treated only briefly here. First, to the extent that an issue is expressly covered by the Convention it displaces rules of national law that might otherwise apply and thereby renders otiose conflict of laws rules designed to lead to the selection of the applicable national law. Secondly, the Convention may itself prescribe a conflicts rule and thus displace the normal conflicts rules of the forum. This prescription may be made both in the scope provisions of the Convention and in its substantive provisions. Thirdly, the Convention may be silent both as to the substance of a particular issue and as to the law by which it is to be determined, in which case it is a question of construction whether the Convention covers the point or merely leaves it to be dealt with under the law applicable under the conflicts rules of the forum. The last two points raise difficult issues both of law and of policy.

### Use of the Conflict of Laws to Determine Scope

Reference has already been made to three Conventions under which the requirement of connection to a Contracting State is satisfied where the rules of private international law lead to the application of the law of a Contracting State. This, of course, is not in itself a prescription of a conflict rule, merely a reference to general conflicts rules. In most cases the same result would probably be reached even without a provision to this effect, given that in international commercial transactions the application of mandatory rules is likely to be limited, so that courts will usually respect the autonomy of the parties in choosing the law which is to govern their relationship. The principal effect of referring to rules of private international law to extend the scope of a Convention would seem to be to displace a possible

[29] Such a reservation would appear to have no greater effect than the removal of a Convention choice of law rule which would otherwise be applicable, thus leaving the field free for the conflict rules of the forum to operate. See below.

presumption that the parties, in choosing the law of a Contracting State, intended only its domestic law to apply (that is, without the Convention) and to impose on them the onus of displacing the Convention.[30]

The effect of a reservation against such a provision by the State of the forum where the conflict rules of that State lead to the application of the law of another Contracting State which has not made such a reservation is unclear. The better view would seem to be that the court must respect the intention of the legislature of the State whose law governs the transaction and apply the Convention despite the reservation made by its own State.[31] On this view the only reservation that is relevant is that made by the State whose law is applicable to the transaction, and reservations made by the State in which the forum is located have no significance as such and operate only if the conflict rules of that State lead to the application of its own law.

## Prescription of a Conflicts Rule in Lieu of a Substantive Rule

In what circumstances is it appropriate for a Convention to prescribe a conflicts rule in relation to an issue rather than settling it directly by a substantive rule? At least three cases suggest themselves:

(1) where agreement cannot be reached on the substantive rule but can be reached on the conflicts rule;
(2) where a particular State, though not opposed to the proposed rule *per se,* has such a strong policy interest in the particular issue that it would be reluctant to cede control directly to the Convention, though willing to submit to a conflicts rule;
(3) where the issue is tangential and raises considerations going beyond the scope of the Convention too complex to be covered in it.

The Unidroit Convention on International Financial Leasing provides a good example of all three cases. The study group at one stage contemplated the inclusion of a provision by which the lessor's title would have priority against even *a bona fide* purchaser from the lessee. This met with opposition from representatives from civil law jurisdictions on the ground that it was incompatible with the *possession vaut titre* principle and had implications going beyond the field of leasing, and the study group eventually concluded that no progress could be made on this issue and limited the statement of priority to conflicts between the lessor and the lessee's general creditors, subject to perfection of the lessor's title in accordance with any public notice requirements of the applicable law.[32] A similar problem arose in relation to priority

[30] For a powerfully argued protest against the modern practice of including in a Convention a provision which permits the parties to exclude the Convention without specifying what law is to apply in its place, see Professor Joachim Bonell's article "Uniform Law and Party Autonomy" in *International Uniform Law in Practice,* 433.

[31] The point is discussed by Malcolm Evans in his "Comment to Article 95 of the Vienna Sales Convention" in *Commentary on the International Sales Convention* (ed. Bianca and Bonen).

[32] Art. 7. See the Explanatory Report by Martin Stanford (1987) 1 *Uniform Law Review,* para. 89.

as between the lessor of equipment that becomes a fixture to land and the owner or encumbrancer of the land. Again, the solution finally adopted was to leave this to be dealt with by the *lex situs*.[33]

The prescription of a conflicts rule, though more readily agreed than a substantive rule, is very much the second best solution. Apart from the obvious point that it fails to produce uniformity its principal defect is that it leads to the application of a particular national law which is likely to have been devised for domestic transactions and may well be ill-suited to those which are international in character.

## Silence of Convention on Particular Issues

Since a Convention rule covering an issue displaces the need for resort to the conflicts of laws whilst the non-coverage of an issue necessitates recourse to the applicable law as determined by the conflicts rules of the forum[34] it may become necessary to decide whether an issue on which the Convention contains no express provision is covered by implication, applying any canons of interpretation laid down by the Convention itself, and if not, whether recourse is to be had to general conflict of law rules or to any particular conflict rules laid down by the Convention. It is not always easy to distinguish cases in which a Convention rule is to be treated as precluding the solution to a question that might otherwise be available under the applicable national law from cases in which the Convention rule is to be interpreted as not covering the question at all. Thus it is often erroneously supposed that a provision of the Convention which merely prevents it from displacing or affecting a particular legal right thereby effectuates that right, whereas in truth the sole consequence of the provision is to leave the matter to be determined under the applicable national law. So Article 7(5) of the Leasing Convention, which provides that nothing in Article 7 is to affect the priority of any lien creditor, does not mean that lien creditors are to have priority over the lessor, merely that Article 7 itself is not to be treated as dealing with the issue, so that resort must be had to the applicable law.

A rather more subtle case of silence on a point which appears to be dealt with exhaustively in the Convention is to be found in Article 7(3), which prescribes a conflict rule to determine the law governing public notice requirements (if any) needed to perfect the lessor's title against a trustee in bankruptcy and creditors. This provides that:

> For the purpose of the previous paragraph the applicable law is the law of the State which, at the time when a person referred to in paragraph 1 [that is trustee in bankruptcy or creditor] becomes entitled to invoke the rules [of public notice] referred to in the preceding paragraph, is...

[33] Art. 4(2); Explanatory Report, para. 99.

[34] This, of course, predicates that no Convention can be regarded as the exclusive determinant of issues within its field, in other words, that in contrast to national law every Convention has at least some gaps which cannot be filled solely by reference to the Convention itself and require resort to national law. This is rendered necessary by the unfortunate fact that, as Professor John Honnold has pointed out, "[i]nternational unifying Conventions, unlike true, (civil law) codes, lack a general framework from which general principles can be derived" ("The United States Uniform Commercial Code: Interpretation by the Courts of the United States", in *International Uniform Law in Practice*, 181 at 190).

There follows a set of four rules specifying which law is to apply, depending on the nature of the equipment. There would seem to be no gaps here. But consider the phrase "at the time when a person referred to in paragraph 1 becomes entitled to invoke the rules referred to in the preceding paragraph". What law determines the time of such entitlement? The answer is not to be found in the express provisions of Article 7. Two solutions are possible. The first is that this is a gap which must be filled by reference to the applicable law under general conflict of law rules. The second is that one applies the conflict rule laid down in Article 7(3) itself on the assumption that its conditions have been satisfied. This seems preferable. No doubt it is open to the objection that it presupposes the very point in issue, namely the law which is to be applied, but such a solution seems just as sensible in this context as the rule that the law governing the validity of a contract is determined by the law which would govern the contract if one assumed it to be valid.

## The Input of the Commercial Community

There has been a tendency for international intergovernmental organisations to lean too exclusively on the expertise of scholars in the preparation of instruments of unification and to obtain inadequate input from organisations of businessmen engaged in the particular field under consideration. Since international trade law is largely dispositive and is designed primarily to facilitate international transactions between business enterprises it is only sensible to try out proposals on those who will be affected by them to see whether they will really work. Happily attitudes are changing. Unidroit gave an admirable lead in this respect many years ago in relation to the Leasing and Factoring Conventions, not merely by involving the requisite international leasing and factoring organisations in its deliberations from an early stage but also by exposing drafts of the proposed Conventions to critical examination at seminars for professionals in a number of different countries. The exercise proved valuable not only in securing support for the projects but also in identifying issues requiring clarification or more closely reasoned argument. This is a procedure which should become standard in future work by intergovernmental organisations.

## Organisation of Work

Attention has already been drawn to the fact that a single harmonisation proposal can take decades to come to fruition. This is perhaps not so surprising when one bears in mind that the same can happen even with domestic legislation, which is infinitely simpler to enact. But more thought needs to be given to the organisational method. The expense in promoting a project is considerable, since every meeting involves the outlay of travelling expenses, accommodation, and subsistence for substantial numbers of participants from many parts of the world. Project management is therefore a matter which should begin to occupy the attention of the various bodies involved in harmonisation.

There are many reasons for the slow pace of a proposal, but if we leave on one side the lack of enthusiasm which can itself defer a project for years, the three key factors are:

(1) the expense, and thus the infrequency and relative brevity, of meetings of those engaged in the scientific work;

(2) the pressure of work on already overburdened secretariats of the institutions involved;

(3) the discontinuity which results from the interval between meetings and constant changes in the membership of the relevant study group or working party.

The problem, of course, is that experts and national representatives are busy people,[35] as are the members of the secretariat, upon whom the organisational burden of sending out questionnaires, sifting the answers, preparing reports, and arranging meetings is considerable, particularly since this is likely to involve the reproduction of all documents in at least two languages.[36]

An obvious answer is to have this basic groundwork done by a much smaller group who would meet more regularly and for longer periods at a stretch. Expenditure on research assistants might also save a significant degree of time and money in the long run. When meetings are held only once a year, or even less frequently, it is all too easy to forget why a particular provision was formulated and on what grounds one supported or opposed it. The frailty of human memory is such that it is by no means uncommon for a delegate to criticise fiercely the very rule for which he himself was responsible a year or two before! There is also much to be said for having a target for completion from the outset and for planning in advance the sequence of meetings that will result in that target being met. Of course, any plan that is made is liable to be disrupted by supervening events, but at least there will be a plan and a more systematic approach to the management of the project.

Finally, it is important for those involved in the work of harmonisation to appreciate that with the making of the Convention their work is only half completed. It is then necessary to market it, through lectures, seminars, and meetings with Governments, business interests, and lawyers, in order to generate a groundswell of support which will help to ensure ratification. Only then can the work be regarded as done. An example to us all in this respect is Professor John Honnold, who was responsible for the creation of UNCITRAL and was its first Secretary. His peripatetic labours contributed greatly both to the making of the Vienna Sales Convention and to its ratification in the years that followed.

[35] The calibre of those who are not is likely to be suspect!

[36] The problem of language in the formulation of instruments of harmonisation deserves a publication to itself. Considerations of space preclude its discussion here, except to note the extreme difficulty not only in translating concepts that have no exact legal equivalent in the other system but also in converting the structure and syntax of one language into the quite different structure and syntax of another. This can lead to an unenviable choice between precise adherence to the original text in the translation, with the risk that the rendering of the translation is inelegant or out of harmony with linguistic usage, or a freer rendering which responds to the structure and usage of the second language but at the sacrifice of legal accuracy.

## Attitudes towards Harmonisation

The advantages of harmonising law relating to international transactions would seem fairly evident even to the layman. But given the reluctance of businessmen, their legal advisers, and their legislatures to modify their national law in favour of harmonisation measures it is perhaps worthwhile restating the advantages of harmonisation. The harmonising measure:

(1) may fill a legal vacuum by providing rules in a field where national law was previously non-existent or obscure;

(2) substitutes a single law for a proliferation of national laws and thus within the given field dispenses with the need to resort to conflict of laws rules and the opportunity these give for forum shopping;

(3) is usually available in several languages, official or unofficial, and is therefore more readily accessible than a national law;

(4) by reason of (1) and (2), facilitates conversance with its provisions and saves time and expense;

(5) provides a neutral law for parties to a contract neither of whom is willing to accept the law of the other's country;

(6) offers a legal regime more attuned to international transactions than domestic law, since it reflects the influence of many legal systems, whereas domestic law is focused on internal transactions and may thus be less accommodating of international dealings;

(7) operates as part of the law of each ratifying State, so that the courts of each such State take judicial notice of it and it is established by legal argument, not by the expensive and time-consuming process of adducing expert evidence, often from a different jurisdiction;

(8) facilitates a common market.

Despite these manifold advantages it is often hard to persuade the commercial community even to take an interest in proposals for harmonisation affecting their sphere of business, still less to give the proposals their support.[37] Why is this so? Numerous reasons possessing varying degrees of persuasiveness are advanced.

Traditionally the first and principal line of attack is that existing domestic law is better or, if not better, is at least well known and understood. This may be true but presupposes that the law in question is the one which will govern the contract, whereas the reality is that for every contract governed by that law there will be

[37] For recent illustrations, see the note by Hobhouse, J., "International Conventions and Commercial Law: The Pursuit of Uniformity" (1990) 106 *LQR* 530 and the article by Derek Wheatley QC, "Why I Oppose the Winds of Change", *The Times*, 27 March 1990, expressing strong opposition to the ratification of the Vienna Sales Convention by the United Kingdom. For the writer's reply to the latter (unhappily mutilated by the editing process!) see R.M. Goode, "Why Compromise Makes Sense", *The Times*, 22 May 1990.

another contract governed by a foreign law with which the party concerned may be unfamiliar, which is in a foreign language he does not understand, and which, when put to the test, may prove demonstrably inferior not only to his own law but to the proposed uniform law.

A second line of attack is that the proposed harmonising measure is inadequate in scope. Thus the Vienna Sales Convention has been criticised for excluding questions relating to the validity of the contract of sale, the transfer of property, or the resolution of property disputes between the seller or buyer and a third party. The response of those engaged in the arduous labours which led to the conclusion of the Convention is no doubt not dissimilar to that of the scholar who writes a book on the doctrine of unconscionability in contract law and is then taken to task by a reviewer for his failure to cover breach and termination—in other words, for not writing a different book. Some limits have to be set to any project. How they are set is a difficult question to which I shall return, but those who decry as too narrow the scope of a Convention running to over a hundred articles must surely embody the resuscitated spirit of Oliver Twist who will always cry for more!

Then, of course, there is the inevitable criticism of the drafting. If ever I get to Heaven (which my friends tell me is unlikely) one of my first requests will be to witness The Perfect Draft. Such a thing is certainly not to be found on this earth; yet those who pick to pieces the open texture or verbal infelicities of an international Convention rarely pause to consider how, when legislation prepared in a single legal system is generally so verbose, obscure, and generally badly drafted, one can reasonably expect more of the product of many hands drawn from widely differing legal systems with different cultures, legal structures, and methods of legal reasoning and decision making, entailing maximum flexibility, co-operation, and compromise.

This is not to say that all criticism is unjustified. There are good Conventions and bad Conventions. The goods ones are those which, for all their rough edges, are found to work and are widely used. The bad ones do not work and are rightly neglected. The Geneva Convention on Bills of Exchange is an example of an excellent Convention which has functioned extremely effectively and has been widely adopted. By contrast, the Uniform Law for International Sales, the forlorn predecessor of the Vienna Sales Convention, is an indifferent product which has not attracted support.

But behind the expressed reasons for antagonism or inertia in the face of proposals for harmonisation lies a more fundamental consideration. It is human nature to be antipathetic to change. Let me render this more accurately. It is human nature to advocate change in someone else's affairs whilst vigorously opposing its necessity in one's own. The force of this NIMBY approach, as it has become known in England,[38] should not be underestimated. Few individuals or institutions are truly resistant to it. Even academics, who are supposed to embody the quintessence of

[38] Not in my backyard—a syndrome strikingly illustrated by a former Secretary of State for the Environment who urged on local authorities the importance of freeing land for housing development whilst at the same time vigorously opposing a proper development near his own country home.

detached assessment, somehow respond with a lack of enthusiasm[39] when it is suggested that their own methods of teaching, research, or organisation might benefit from review.

This inherent resistance to change is exacerbated by the low priority accorded by our law schools to the teaching of comparative law[40] and, in England, by an unwillingness to grapple with foreign languages, itself both a cause and a consequence of English becoming the new *lingua franca.* If the harmonisation process is to have any hope of acceleration it is essential for law schools to reduce their preoccupation with national law and their assumption of its superiority over other legal systems and to revert at least in some degree to the internationalism of medieval law teaching. It is primarily by the spreading of awareness of foreign legal systems among our students that we can hope to accelerate the process of harmonisation and to produce practitioners and judges of the future prepared to look beyond the horizon of their own legal system. In his outstanding study of unification[41] that great French comparativist the late Professor Rend David exposed the kernel of the matter with his customary elegance and felicity:

> Legal theory suffocates within the frontiers of a State. Like all science its prosperity requires a cosmopolitan atmosphere; only schools of a low intellectual level can exist in a country with closed frontiers, training narrow-minded practitioners, mere pawns to carry out the decrees of power. Universality is necessary to legal theory, and it is a factor favourable to the unification of law.

[39] This is an Englishman's euphemism for manic rage.

[40] A point made forcefully by a leading City of London solicitor, Mr Jeremy Carver, "The Experience of The Legal Profession", in *International Uniform Law in Practice,* 411 at p. 428.

[41] *The International Unification of Private Law,* II Int. Ency. Comp. Law, chap. 5, p. 16.

# 2

# International Restatements of Contract and English Contract Law*

*Roy Goode*

Generations of academic and practising lawyers in the United Kingdom and abroad have cause to be grateful to Professor Tony Guest for the immense contribution he has made to our understanding of contract law, commercial law, and consumer credit, and to the participation of the United Kingdom in the work of the United Nations Commission on International Trade Law. In his twenty years as general editor of *Chitty on Contracts*, building on the work of his predecessor John Morris and supported by a strong editorial team, Tony Guest has transformed what was for long a mediocre and ill-organised work into a first class textbook equally valued by academic and practising lawyers. Over the same period he has performed the same signal service as general editor of *Benjamin's Sale of Goods*.

The influence of scholarly writing on the development of law has consistently been under-acknowledged in this country and is only now beginning to regain recognition. In the United States this has been powered by the enormously influential Restatements, including the *Restatement of Contracts*, now in its second edition, which has been cited in literally tens of thousands of cases. Now we have two ambitious international equivalents, *Principles of International Commercial Contracts* ("UNIDROIT Principles"), promulgated by Unidroit[1] and directed by Professor Joachim Bonell,[2] and *Principles of European Contract Law* ("PECL"), formulated by the Commission on European Contract Law[3] under the leadership of Professor Ole Lando and designed specifically for contract law in Europe.[4] These will be referred

* Originally published as R Goode: "International Restatements of Contract and English Contract Law" in Lomnicka & Morse: "Contemporary Issues in Commercial Law: Festschrift in Honour of Tony Guest" (1997). Copyright Thomson Reuters (Professional) UK Limited. Reproduced with permission of the Licensor through PLSclear.

[1] The international, inter-governmental organisation established in 1926 for the purpose of promoting the progressive harmonisation of private law.

[2] Published by Unidroit in 1994. For a detailed guide, see M.J. BONELL, *An International Restatement of Contract Law*, 1994 (Irvington, New York).

[3] A private organisation consisting of scholars from all the member States of what is now the European Union. Three members of the Lando Group also participated in the Unidroit project.

[4] See Ole LANDO and Hugh BEALE (eds.), *Principles of European Contract Law, Part I: Performance, Non-Performance and Remedies*, 1995 (Dordrecht/Boston/London).

to together as "the Principles". The UNIDROIT Principles, prepared by leading scholars from many parts of the world, were the first to appear, in 1994. Part I of the PECL was published the following year. Work on a new text combining the rearranged Part I with Part II will be completed shortly.[5] Work on a third and final part will begin towards the end of 1997. Both sets of principles are divided into Articles, each of which is followed by comments and illustrations. The PECL also contain detailed notes identifying EU legislative and other sources utilised in their preparation. Though somewhat differently formulated, the UNIDROIT Principles and the PECL are very similar in their approaches. It is also striking that while concessions and compromises had to be made in relation to the different national legal systems, the various participants felt that with some exceptions the product of their work broadly reflected the principles of their own national legal systems. The present paper, after giving a brief overview of the Principles, focuses on those provisions relating to performance and remedies for non-performance which currently have no counterpart in English contract law and considers what benefits they have to offer.

The UNIDROIT Principles have, in a remarkably short space of time, attracted a degree of interest and influence surpassing even the most optimistic hopes of their progenitors. They have been the subject of a great many articles and have already been applied in several arbitral awards and at least one or two court judgments.[6] The response has been overwhelmingly favourable. The PECL, published more recently, have so far received rather less attention, but they too have been welcomed and are the subject of a growing volume of literature.

## Harmonisation through Non-Normative Instruments

If we leave on one side the special case of the European Union, whose legal measures constitute supranational law penetrating directly into the legal systems of its Member States, the traditional method of harmonising private law is through international instruments such as international conventions, uniform rules, and model laws, which on adoption have the force of law within the adopting State. Their binding nature leads to the paradox that while many States participate in the work leading to a convention, for fear of losing the opportunity to influence its terms, most of them are likely to drag their feet for many years before ratifying the convention, if, indeed, they ever get round to ratifying it at all. The result is that the treaty collections are littered with conventions that have never come into force, for want of the number of required ratifications, or have been eschewed by the major trading States. There are several reasons for this: failure to establish from potential interest groups at the outset that there is a serious problem which the proposed

[5] All references to the PECL are to the renumbered version, the equivalent references in the original text being shown in parenthesis.

[6] See M.J. BONELL, "The UNIDROIT Principles of International Commercial Contracts and the Principles of European Contract Law: Similar Rules for the Same Purposes?", *Uniform Law Review*, 1996–2, 229; and "The UNIDROIT Principles in Practice: The Experience of the First Two Years", *Uniform Law Review*, 1997–1, 34.

convention will help to resolve; hostility from powerful pressure groups; lack of sufficient interest of, or pressure on, governments to induce them to burden still further an already over-crowded legislative timetable; mutual hold-backs, each State waiting to see what others will do, so that in the end none of them does anything.

> Unification can only be achieved by lengthy and patient efforts which will ultimately convince those in all countries, who are in a position to sponsor and carry through changes in the law, that it is a matter of urgent necessity to take steps in order to remove sources of inconvenience and friction in the international sphere. Unification cannot be achieved by a stroke of the pen, nor can it be carried out within the four walls of law libraries, practitioner's offices or professorial studies. The ground must be very carefully surveyed, and the interests concerned must be won over before any action is undertaken. It is necessary, for our present purpose, to underline the fact that many of the woes from which the movement for unification suffers are undoubtedly due to premature and ill-advised attempts to draft schemes for unified law which have little or no prospect of acceptance. Apart from these errors of judgment which are largely responsible for the setbacks hitherto experienced, it is beyond doubt that unification is, in any circumstances, confronted by other obstacles of a psychological character. National pride makes itself felt in the realm of the law as well as in other spheres. The abandonment of national rules of law seems to imply that there is something amiss with the rules which are to be displaced, and national *amour propre* suffers accordingly.[7]

Little has changed since those wise words were penned a half century ago. Frustration with the relatively small return for the huge outlay of intellectual and other resources involved in the conclusion of international conventions, coupled with their inherent lack of susceptibility to change, has led increasingly to reliance on non-normative instruments ("soft law") to bring about the desired harmonisation in a given field. These instruments take a variety of forms: model laws, which States are free to adopt to whatever degree and in whatever form they choose;[8] uniform rules, trade terms and model forms promulgated by non-governmental international organisations, such as the International Chamber of Commerce, which are effectuated by incorporation into contracts;[9] and guides designed to harmonise contract practice and documentation.[10] To this range must now be added the UNIDROIT Principles and the PECL, the international and European equivalents of the American *Restatement of Contracts*.

The characteristic common to all these instruments is that they are not issued, endorsed, or implemented by lawmaking bodies. They are essentially non-binding tools made available to the international community for adoption in contracts and use by judges and legislatures. Their influence depends on their quality, on the standing of the individuals preparing them and the institutions sponsoring them and the vigour with which they are promoted. Thus in contrast to its practice in relation to its conventions, Unidroit deliberately refrained from seeking endorsement of the UNIDROIT Principles by the governments of its member States. In the case of

7 H.C. GUTTERIDGE, *Comparative Law* (2nd edn.), 1949 (Cambridge), 157–8.

8 For example, the influential *UNCITRAL Model Law on International Commercial Arbitration.*

9 For example, the *ICC Incoterms, Uniform Customs and Practice for Documentary Credits and Standard Documentary Credit Forms.*

10 See, for example, the *UNCITRAL Legal Guide on Drawing Up International Contracts for the Construction of Industrial Works* (1988).

the PECL the question did not, of course, arise, since the Commission on European Contract Law is a private body of scholars, not an international organisation.

Yet paradoxically the impact of the two sets of principles may prove to be greater than that of an international convention, for a convention has no force at the time it is concluded and represents at most a provisional indication of support by participating States which may or may not crystallise, whereas the Principles represent the unconditional commitment and consensus of scholars of international repute from all over the world.

## The Nature of Restatements

It is a characteristic of all harmonising measures, whether normative or non-normative, that they do not merely reproduce the existing rules or usages but also change them. This is inevitable. For one thing, since national laws (and in federal systems, state or provincial laws) differ from each other, any harmonisation necessarily changes them in some respects. For another, the task of those engaged in the work of harmonisation, whether it takes the form of a convention, a set of uniform rules to be incorporated by contract, a model law, or a scholarly restatement, is to find the best solutions to typical problems, and thus to improve the law, not merely to reproduce it. This is as true of the Principles as it is of the American Restatements. It is, of course, necessary to proceed judiciously. If the new rules are to have a reasonable prospect of acceptance they must advance thinking to some extent but not move too far ahead of prevailing rules or usage. The draftsmen of the Principles were very alive to the dangers of being too revolutionary. Accordingly, while observance of the Principles involves some departure from the existing rules of every legal system, and in certain cases the introduction of novel concepts, the Principles for the most part reproduce rules that will be familiar to legal systems generally.

## Purposes of the UNIDROIT Principles

The two sets of principles have overlapping, but in certain respects different, purposes. The stated purposes of the UNIDROIT Principles as indicated in the Preamble are:

- to serve as general rules for international commercial contracts;
- to identify "general principles of law" or "the *lex mercatoria*" where selected in contracts;
- to fill gaps in the relevant domestic law;
- to interpret or supplement existing international uniform law instruments, such as the 1980 Vienna Convention on Contracts for the International Sale of Goods ("CISG");
- to serve as a model for legislation by national and international legislators.

The UNIDROIT Principles can also be used to provide a guide and checklist in the drawing up of international contracts and to furnish a foreign language glossary through the translations that have been made into different languages.

## Purposes of the PECL

The stated purposes of the PECL are:

- to facilitate cross-border transactions within Europe;
- to strengthen the Single European Market;
- to create an infrastructure for Community laws governing contracts;
- to provide guidelines for national courts and legislatures and fill gaps in national laws;
- to construct a linkage between the civil law and the common law;
- to provide a modern formulation of "general principles of law" or "*lex mercatoria*" relating to contracts.

## Scope of the Principles

The UNIDROIT Principles are at once wider and narrower than the PECL in the range of transactions to which they are addressed. They are wider in that they are intended to be universal, whereas the PECL are designed for contracts within Europe; they are narrower in being confined to international commercial contracts (a phrase deliberately left undefined), while the PECL apply to contracts generally, whether domestic or international and whether commercial or non-commercial. However, it is a feature of international instruments, whether they are conventions, model laws, or contractually incorporated trade usages, that they can never exhaustively define the scope of their own application. For one thing, parties are always free to incorporate their provisions as contract terms, whether or not the contract is one which falls within the sphere of application of the incorporated instrument. For another, courts and arbitrators may choose to apply them by analogy. So a rule in the UNIDROIT Principles could be invoked in relation to a purely domestic transaction as evidence of what is now perceived to be the best rule for the situation under consideration. Similarly, the parties or a court or arbitrator could resort to the PECL even in relation to a transaction one of the parties to which carries on business in a State which is not within the European Union.

The UNIDROIT Principles, in addition to general provisions, contain rules governing most of the main aspects of contract law: formation, validity, interpretation, content, performance, and non-performance of contracts. Parts I and II of the PECL will cover broadly the same ground but will also include a chapter on the third-party aspects of agency, that is, relations between the third party and the agent or principal, while Part III will be devoted to assignment, subrogation, delegation, and prescription.

## Applicability to a Particular Contract

When will one or other of the sets of principles apply to a given contract? Both the UNIDROIT Principles and the PECL embody party autonomy as a primary principle.[11] It follows that, subject to any mandatory rules of the applicable law, the relevant set of principles *will* apply if expressly incorporated into the contract[12] and will *not* apply if and in so far as expressly excluded.[13] Where the contract is silent, both sets of principles state that they *may* be applied where the parties have agreed that their contract is to be governed by "general principles of law" or "the *lex mercatoria*".[14] The PECL are also expressed to be applicable if the parties have not chosen any system or rules of law to govern their contract,[15] while the UNIDROIT Principles would leave the contract to be governed by the applicable law under conflict of laws rules and would be an available reference point only if it proved impossible to establish the relevant rule of the applicable law[16] or by way of amplification of a more general provision in an applicable international convention.[17]

## Common Approaches

Though there are both technical and policy divergences between the UNIDROIT Principles and the PECL, the two formulations have much in common.[18] Both have been strongly influenced by the CISG, which, indeed, has become the prototype for general provisions in almost all subsequent international trade conventions. Both are intended to fill gaps in the existing legal framework, either by supplying a rule where none exists or is readily identifiable in national law or by supplementing existing international instruments. For example, one of the most litigated provisions of the Vienna Sales Convention is the seemingly innocuous Article 78, one of the shortest articles in the whole Convention:

> If a party fails to pay the price or any other sum that is in arrears, the other party is entitled to interest on it, without prejudice to any claim for damages recoverable under article 74.

Article 78 is silent as to the time from which interest runs, the method of determining the rate of interest applicable, and the currency in which and the place at which such rate is to be ascertained. By contrast, both sets of principles provide for interest from the time when payment is due at the average bank short-term lending

[11] UNIDROIT Principles, art. 1.1; PECL art. 1.102.
[12] UNIDROIT Principles, Preamble; PECL art. 1.101(2).
[13] UNIDROIT Principles, art. 1.5; PECL art. 1.102(2).
[14] UNIDROIT Principles, Preamble; PECL art. 1.101(3)(a).
[15] PECL art. 1.101(3)(b).
[16] UNIDROIT Principles, Preamble. This might be the case where the applicable law was relatively undeveloped, either because the country concerned was a less developed country or because the law was primarily religious rather than secular, as with some Middle Eastern countries.
[17] *Ibid.* [18] See M.J. BONELL, *loc. cit., supra*, n. 6.

rate to prime borrowers prevailing for the (contractual) currency of payment at the place for payment.[19] Courts and arbitrators can thus resort to the Principles to complement Article 78. This gap-filling function is particularly appropriate for cross-border transactions, since it allows the tribunal to avoid imposing a purely national rule in relation to an international contract. Similarly, both sets of principles embody approaches not currently reflected in English law. Some of these are pervasive: the duty of good faith and fair dealing, the duty to co-operate. Others relate to formation: the binding force of promises intended to be binding without acceptance,[20] the irrevocability of offers expressed to be irrevocable or stating a fixed time for acceptance, the avoidance of a contract for mistake of law. Others (and those with which this contribution is primarily concerned) concern performance and the effect of non-performance: the right to demand assurance of performance, the primacy of the remedy of specific performance; a general right of cure by a party whose non-conforming tender of performance is not accepted; the remedy of price reduction where a non-conforming tender is accepted; the adaptation of contract terms in case of change of circumstances causing hardship; the effect of impediments to performance on the duty to perform. In all these matters the Principles either reflect the approaches of civil law jurisdictions or, in a few cases, break new ground. On the other hand, the Principles also embody a number of themes characteristic of the common law, including party autonomy, the freedom of choice of remedies, the cumulation of remedies, and the preservation of accrued rights on termination for breach.

## Good Faith and Fair Dealing

English contract law is increasingly isolated in its refusal to recognise a general duty of good faith.[21] In the civil law subjective good faith, together with its objective counterpart, fair dealing, is a fundamental tenet of the law of contract, affecting every phase, from negotiation to performance and enforcement.

The principle of good faith and fair dealing is recognised or at least appears to be acted on as a guideline for contractual behaviour in all EC countries. There is, however, a considerable difference between the legal systems as to how extensive and how powerful the penetration of the principle has been. At the one end of the spectrum figures a system where the principle has revolutionized the contract law (and other parts of the law as well) and added a special feature to the style of that system (GERMANY). At the other end we find systems which do not recognize a general obligation of the parties to conform to good faith in the performance of a

[19] UNIDROIT Principles, art. 7.4.9; PECL art. 9.508(1) (*ex* art. 4.507(1)).

[20] Even English law, for all its formalism, recognises such contracts, the most typical examples being the letter of credit and the demand guarantee.

[21] A refusal which was lamented extra-judicially by STEYN J. (now Lord Steyn) in "The Role of Good Faith and Fair Dealing in Contract Law: A Hair-Shirt Philosophy?" [1991] *Denning LJ* 131. Good faith is now the subject of an enormous volume of literature. For an excellent collection of comparative essays, see Jack BEATSON and Daniel FRIEDMANN (eds.), *Good Faith and Fault in Contract Law*, 1995 (Oxford).

contract, but which in many cases by specific rules reach the results which the other systems have reached by the principle of good faith (ENGLAND and IRELAND).[22]

American contract law has also embraced a general duty of good faith, though it begins only on conclusion of the contract and does not extend to pre-contractual negotiations.[23]

Every contract imposes upon each party a duty of good faith and fair dealing in its performance and its enforcement.[24]

The PECL are even more succinct:

Each party must act in accordance with good faith and fair dealing.[25]

Further, the parties may not exclude or limit this duty,[26] which also finds expression in specific provisions in the definition of reasonableness[27] and in the rules relating to co-operation,[28] the conduct of negotiations,[29] fraud,[30] adaptation of the contract on the ground of excessive benefit or unfair advantage,[31] contract terms not individually negotiated,[32] change of circumstances,[33] and clauses excluding or limiting liability.[34]

There are several reasons why English law has been reluctant to embrace a generalised concept of good faith.[35] In the first place, we do not quite know what the concept means. Is it, for example, contrary to good faith to negotiate concurrently with

[22] *Principles of European Contract Law*, note 1 to art. 1.106 (now art. 1.201).

[23] See E. Allan FARNSWORTH, "The Concept of Good Faith in American Law" (1993) Saggi, Conferenze e Seminari 10 (Centro di studi e ricerche di diritto comparato e straniero, Roma).

[24] Restatement (2d) of Contracts, s. 205. *Cf.* Uniform Commercial Code, s. 1-203: "Every contract or duty within this Act imposes an obligation of good faith in its performance or enforcement." See also E. Allan FARNSWORTH, "Good Faith in Contract Performance" in BEATSON and FRIEDMANN (eds.), *op. cit.*, Chapter 6.

[25] Art. 1.201(1). Art. 1.7 of the UNIDROIT Principles is in the same terms except that it adds the qualifying words "in international trade", reflecting the fact that the Principles are concerned with international commercial contracts.

[26] Art. 1.201(2).

[27] Art. 1.302 (*ex* art. 1.108): "Under these Principles reasonableness is to be judged by what persons acting in good faith and in the same situation as the parties would consider to be reasonable."

[28] Art. 1.201(2): "Each party owes the other a duty to co-operate in order to give full effect to the contract."

[29] Art. 2.301 (*ex* art. 5.301), which provides that a party is free to negotiate and is not liable for failure to reach an agreement but that a party who has negotiated or broken off negotiations in good faith is liable for the losses caused to the other party, and that it is contrary to good faith, in particular, for a party to enter into or continue negotiations with no real intention of reaching an agreement with the other party.

[30] Art. 4.107 (*ex* art. 6.107): "(1) A party may avoid a contract when he has been led to conclude it by the other party's fraudulent representation, whether by words or conduct, or fraudulent non-disclosure of any circumstances which according to reasonable standards of good faith and fair dealing he should have disclosed ...".

[31] Art. 4.110 (*ex* art. 6.110). *Cf.* UNIDROIT Principles, art. 3.10, which gives the aggrieved party the option of avoiding the contract.

[32] Art. 4.110 (*ex* art. 6.110), paragraph (1) of which reproduces the effect of art. 3(1) of the EC Directive on Unfair Terms in Consumer Contracts (93/13/EEC), as to which see below.

[33] Art. 6.111 (*ex* art. 2.117). See below, p. 36.

[34] Art. 8.109 (*ex* art. 3.109): "A clause which limits or excludes one party's liability for non-performance may not be invoked if it would be grossly unfair to do so."

[35] See Roy GOODE, "The Concept of 'Good Faith' in English Law" (1992) Saggi, Conferenze e Seminari (Centro di studi e ricerche di diritto comparato e straniero, Roma), 3, 9.

several parties in relation to the same contract without disclosing that fact to each of them? Or to exercise a contractual right to terminate a contract when this would cause hardship to the other party? Or to sell a house without disclosing structural defects? The concern engendered by open-textured rules such as a duty of good faith is, perhaps, not entirely unjustified when one considers the huge volume of litigation generated by section 242 of the German Civil Code, the principal source of the duty of good faith in German contract law which has provided the foundation for the creation or elaboration of a whole network of contractual theories,[36] including *culpa in contrahendo, clausula rebus sic stantibus*, contracts for the benefit of third parties, and the duty to provide information needed to invoke rights. Secondly, judges adjudicating in one of the world's leading financial centres rightly sense that for the commercial enterprise the predictability of the legal outcome is more important than absolute justice. Thirdly, English law takes the view that in general it is for the parties themselves to allocate risk through the terms of their contract, and it is not the role of the courts to do it for them.

But with the advent of the Directive on Unfair Terms in Consumer Contracts, and its implementation in the Unfair Terms in Consumer Contracts Regulations 1994,[37] English courts will for the first time be faced with the problem of deciding whether a term which has not been individually negotiated and which is contained in a contract for the supply of goods or services to a consumer is unfair, and therefore of no effect, because, contrary to the requirement of good faith, it causes a significant imbalance in the parties' rights and obligations arising under the contract, to the detriment of the consumer.[38] It is true that the Directive and Regulations apply only to consumer contracts. But once the courts have become accustomed to applying this open-textured concept of good faith, they may well find that to utilise it on a broader basis is not as difficult or unsatisfactory as might have been supposed. The fact that two separate groups of scholars working largely independently of each other, and including lawyers from the United Kingdom, the United States, and Ireland, produced restatements embodying in almost identical terms a general requirement of good faith should give a powerful spur to reconsideration of the traditional perspective of English law, at least in international transactions.

## Adequate Assurance of Performance

The parents of a young woman who is about to be married make arrangements with a catering firm to provide a reception and dinner after the ceremony. A month before the wedding is due to take place, the mother of the bride-to-be contacts the

[36] "The doctrine of good faith (*Treu und Glauben*) is now a favorite subject in German contract law. Growing from little more than a legislative acorn [s. 242 of the German Civil Code], the doctrine of good faith has ripened into a judicial oak that overshadows the contractual relationship of private parties" (Werner EBKE and Bettina M. STEINHAUER, "The Doctrine of Good Faith in German Contract Law" in BEATSON and FRIEDMANN (eds.), *op. cit.*, Chapter 7. *Cf.* Basil MARKESINIS, Werner LORENZ and Gerhard DANNEMANN, *The German Law of Contract and Restitution*, Chapter VII (publication pending).

[37] SI 1994/3159. [38] Art. 3(1).

caterers to check that all the arrangements are in order, and is told: "Well, we are in the middle of a strike at the moment, but though I can't give an absolute guarantee I'm almost sure we shall be all right on the night." Are the parents still bound by the contract and obliged to run the risk of a ruined celebration and a huge social embarrassment? Is there any other step they can take for their protection? Astonishingly, English law does not yet provide any satisfactory answers to these questions. The case is not one of anticipatory breach, or of disablement from future performance, for the caterers have affirmed both their intention to perform and the strong likelihood of their ability to do so.[39] Nor does English law appear to provide a right to demand an adequate assurance of performance. Such a right, with an ability to terminate the contract if the assurance is not forthcoming within a reasonable time, is given by the Principles,[40] so that in the example given the devoted parents would have a remedy.[41]

## Specific Performance as a Primary Remedy

In both sets of principles, specific performance is available as the primary remedy.[42] The UNIDROIT Principles further provide for the imposition of a judicial penalty in default of performance, the penalty to be paid to the aggrieved party.[43] However, whereas CISG defers to the sensitivities of common law jurisdictions (where specific performance in relation to contracts not involving land is the exception rather than the rule) by providing that a court is not bound to enter a judgment for specific performance unless it would do so under its own law in respect of similar contracts of sale not governed by CISG,[44] neither the UNIDROIT Principles nor the PECL allow for judicial discretion. It will be interesting to see how far English courts will be prepared to modify their traditional approach in the light of the Principles. In general, businessmen accept that it is futile to seek to impose performance on an unwilling party, and most breaches can be adequately remedied by the soothing unguent of damages, coupled in appropriate cases with termination of the contract. Moreover, the provision of a penalty to be paid to the aggrieved party (as opposed to a fine for contempt of court payable to the State) would require legislation. But the remedy of specific performance does have one great advantage over damages, in that it provides a means of discouraging profitable contract-breaking, conduct which is not adequately sanctioned by the English law of restitution, which allows recovery of benefits only upon a total failure of consideration. For example:

[39] See *Chitty on Contracts* (27th edn.), vol. I, paras. 24-016 *et seq.*

[40] PECL art. 8.105 (*ex* art. 3.105); UNIDROIT Principles, art. 7.3.4. Both texts were inspired by the American Restatement (2d) of Contracts, s. 251, the Uniform Commercial Code, s. 2-609 and CISG art. 71.

[41] See LANDO and BEALE (eds.), *op. cit.*, p. 132, Illustration 1. However, this might be of limited consolation if the assurance were not given and another caterer could not be found in time!

[42] PECL art. 9.102 (*ex* art. 4.102); UNIDROIT Principles, art. 7.2.2.

[43] Art. 7.2.4. This corresponds to the remedy of *astreinte* given by French law.

[44] CISG art. 28.

> B contracts to build a house for O for £500,000. Under the contract 50% of the contract sum is payable in advance, and O accordingly pays B £250,000. When B has done a quarter of the work he is offered a more profitable contract by T and walks off the site. O is able to find another builder with considerably lower overheads who is willing to complete the house on time for £250,000, so that O suffers no loss and is only entitled to nominal damages. Since there has been partial performance by B he is entitled to keep the 50% of the price paid to him even though he carried out only a quarter of the work, and to retain the extra profit earned from the contract with T.

Though arguments have been advanced that to allow deliberate contract-breaking promotes economic efficiency, it seems wrong that the party in breach should be allowed to keep what he has not earned. The remedy of specific performance, backed up by financial penalties, helps to address this problem. Even so, English courts are likely to adhere to the view that such cases should be dealt with on an individual basis as a matter of equitable discretion rather than that the plaintiff should have a right to specific performance in every case not covered by the stated exceptions.[45]

## Cure

Following the precedent set by American law, the Principles confer on a party whose non-conforming tender of performance is rejected a right to cure the non-conformity by a fresh and conforming tender.[46] However, the Principles diverge as to the circumstances in which the right to cure is not available. The UNIDROIT Principles, which are more elaborate, require that notice of intended cure be given without undue delay, that cure be appropriate in the circumstances, and that the aggrieved party have no legitimate interest in refusing cure, but subject to these exceptions allow cure even after notice of termination by the aggrieved party; the PECL are silent on all these points, providing merely that a new and conforming tender may be made where the time for performance has not yet arrived or the delay would not be such as to constitute a fundamental non-performance. Whether English contract possesses a general principle as to cure is controversial; in the writer's view it does, and article 8.104 of the PECL mirrors it pretty accurately. A rejected tender of performance results in non-performance; except where this is repudiatory there is no reason to deny the validity of a fresh and conforming tender if made within the time open for the original tender.

## Price Reduction

Where a party accepts a non-conforming tender of performance, English law allows him to recover by way of damages the difference between the value of the

[45] For example, where performance would be unlawful or impossible or would impose an unreasonable burden on the obligor or performance involves work or services of a personal character.

[46] UNIDROIT Principles, art. 7.1.4; PECL art. 8.104 (*ex* art. 3.104).

performance as promised and its value as delivered. A specific illustration of this principle is found in the Sale of Goods Act 1979, section 53(3) of which specifies as the measure of damages for breach of the warranty of quality on the sale of goods the difference between the actual value of the goods at the time of delivery to the buyer and the value they would have had if they had fulfilled the warranty. As an alternative to claiming damages the buyer may set up the breach of warranty in diminution or extinction of the price.[47] However, English law has no equivalent of the *actio quanti minoris*, by which a party, instead of claiming damages for breach of warranty or off-setting the difference in value against the price, may claim adjustment of the price itself so as to reduce it in proportion to the reduction in the value of the promised performance. This is a better remedy where the aggrieved party made a bad bargain, though not if he made a good one. For example, S contracts to sell goods to B for £1,000. B has struck a bad bargain in that the goods, even if answering to their warranted quality, would only be worth £750, but because of S's breach of warranty are in fact worth a mere £500. Section 53 entitles B, on accepting the goods, to set up his loss of £250 in reduction of the price. The *actio quanti minoris*, however, would give him the option of reducing the price by a third, *i.e.* £333. This is an option he would not wish to exercise if the value of the goods as warranted had been £1,500, for the proportionate reduction would do no more than bring the contract price down to £1,000, the actual price under the contract. The PECL provide the remedy of the *actio quanti minoris*,[48] though this does not feature in the UNIDROIT Principles.

## Change of Circumstances

The most radical provisions of the Principles are those which impose on the parties a duty to re-negotiate the contract terms where "performance of the contract becomes excessively onerous because of a change of circumstances"[49] or where "the occurrence of events fundamentally alters the equilibrium of the contract either because the cost of a party's performance has increased or because the value of the performance a party receives is diminished".[50] The re-negotiation provisions are confined to cases where the change of circumstances occurred (or alternatively, under the UNIDROIT Principles, became known to the disadvantaged party) after the conclusion of the contract, could not reasonably have been taken into account by the disadvantaged party and were not a risk assumed by him. If the parties fail to reach agreement the court may terminate the contract at a date on terms to be fixed or may alternatively adapt the contract with a view to restoring the balance between the parties. The PECL also empower the court to award damages against a party who causes the other loss by refusing to negotiate or breaking off negotiations contrary to good faith and fair dealing.

[47] Sale of Goods Act 1979, s. 53(1)(a).

[48] PECL art. 9.401 (*ex* art. 4.401), following CISG art. 50.

[49] PECL art. 6.111 (*ex* art. 2.117).

[50] UNIDROIT Principles, art. 6.2.1.

These provisions, though finding their echo in certain civil law systems, and in particular in the French law concept of *imprévision* (which is, however, limited to administrative contracts), are unknown in others and have no counterpart in English law, which adopts the all-or-nothing approach of the frustration doctrine. On the other hand, the re-negotiation provisions do track hardship clauses to be found in many international standard-term contracts, and may thus be said to reflect a well developed, though far from universal, market practice. They are particularly suitable for long-term[51] relational contracts, as opposed to one-shot transactions in which the parties' relationship begins and ends with each discrete deal. Relational contracts build up a pattern of practices, co-operation, and expectations which may make it unreasonable to expect one party to bear the whole impact of an adverse change of circumstances simply because he failed to have these provided for in the contract. English courts are likely to be slow to assume powers to adapt contracts or to terminate contracts because of a change of circumstances falling short of frustration. Their view is likely to remain that it is for the parties themselves to make suitable provision in their contract. The fact that this is often done, far from giving support to the assumption of such powers by the court, may produce exactly the opposite effect, for it may lead the court to conclude that if parties choose not to insert into their contract hardship clauses which are common form in other contracts, they cannot complain if they are held to their bargain and may, indeed, be considered to have impliedly accepted the risks involved.

## Effect of Impediments to Performance

The Principles broadly track Article 79 of CISG in dealing with the effect of impediments to performance. A party's non-performance is excused if he proves that it was due to an impediment beyond his control and that he could not reasonably have been expected to take the impediment into account at the time of the conclusion of the contract, or to have avoided or overcome the impediment or its consequences.[52] Where the impediment is only temporary, performance is likewise excused only temporarily except where the delay amounts to a fundamental non-performance.[53] Hence the Principles follow Article 79 in adopting the civil law concept of *force majeure* rather than the common law doctrine of frustration. The differences are significant. The effect of frustration is to terminate the entire contract automatically by force of law, irrespective of the will of the parties or their knowledge of the salient facts; the effect of *force majeure* is simply to excuse non-performance of the obligation to which the impediment relates. The contract is not automatically brought to an end, though the non-performing party is immune from claims for

[51] In this context "long-term" is used to embrace not only contracts which by their terms are for a lengthy fixed period but those which in fact are operated by the parties on a continuing basis even though for an indefinite period and terminable at short notice.

[52] PECL art. 8.108(1) (*ex* art. 3.108); UNIDROIT Principles, 7.1.7(1).

[53] PECL art. 8.108(2); UNIDROIT Principles, art. 7.1.7(2).

damages or specific performance.[54] Apart from this, the rights of both parties continue in force. So the non-performance by one party entitles the other to withhold his own performance,[55] and also to terminate the contract if the non-performance is fundamental.[56]

## Mandatory Rules and Selection of the Principles as the Governing Law

The parties to a contract are, of course, free to incorporate the Principles as terms of the contract, in which case they yield to mandatory provisions of the applicable law, that is, to those rules of the applicable law, as determined by the conflict rules of the forum, which cannot be displaced by agreement. But can the parties choose the Principles as the applicable law itself? Clearly, neither the UNIDROIT Principles nor the PECL constitute a comprehensive contract code, still less a complete legal system, and their selection as the governing law, even if otherwise effective, will not dispense with the need to resort to the applicable law under conflict of laws rules to resolve questions not answered by the Principles. But both the UNIDROIT Principles and the PECL provide for their application where the parties have agreed that their contract is to be governed by "general principles of law", the "*lex mercatoria*", or the like,[57] and there now seems no obstacle to English courts recognising the parties' selection of the Principles, rather than a national legal system, to govern their contract, on the basis that they embody or evidence general principles of law[58] or alternatively international commercial usage.[59] Where the Principles are applied as rules of law, they may be effective to displace mandatory rules of the applicable law in the sense used above, on the basis that these are rules which are bounded by the conflict of laws and can thus be excluded by choice of some other law. By contrast, super-mandatory (or overriding) rules, that is, rules of the *lex fori* or (if the *lex fori*

[54] Rather curiously, art. 79 of CISG preserves all remedies other than damages, thus on the face of it leaving open the remedy of specific performance. The issue was hotly debated, and the outcome appears to have been influenced by the misconception that exclusion of the *remedy* of specific performance would somehow obliterate the ***obligation*** to perform and thus preclude termination of the contract for failure to perform. But the express preservation of other rights based on non-performance made this fear entirely groundless. The Principles avoid this error.

[55] PECL art. 9.201 (*ex* art. 4.201); UNIDROIT Principles, art. 7.1.3.

[56] PECL art. 9.301(1) (*ex* art. 4.301(1)); UNIDROIT Principles, art. 7.3.1(1). The phrase "fundamental non-performance" is more accurate than "fundamental breach", which is used in CISG but is plainly intended to cover any fundamental non-performance, whether or not excused under art. 79.

[57] UNIDROIT Principles, Preamble; PECL art. 1.101(3)(a).

[58] See the landmark decision of the English Court of Appeal in *Deutsche Schachtbau- und Tiefbohrgesellschaft mbH v. R'As al-Khaimah National Oil Co* [1987] 3 WLR 1023.

[59] These are, indeed, the two constituents of the *lex mercatoria*, to which a number of arbitral tribunals in international commercial arbitration have resorted as an alternative to determining or relying on the applicable law even where the parties have not expressly chosen the *lex mercatoria* or adopted any equivalent expression. An English court would be unlikely to go so far, since judges would generally regard themselves as bound to apply the national legal system determined by rules of the English conflict of laws as the *lex fori*, whereas there is now a respectable body of opinion which holds that there is no *lex fori* in arbitration. See Roy GOODE, "Usage and Its Reception in Transnational Commercial Law" (1997) 46 *The International and Comparative Law Quarterly*, 1 at pp. 27 *et seq.*

so provides) of a third State closely connected with the contract which have such a strong social or economic imperative that they apply even in relation to a contract otherwise governed by a foreign law, will always override the Principles, which, indeed, expressly defer to them.[60] The distinction between ordinary mandatory rules and super-mandatory rules is very clearly brought out in article 1.103 of the PECL:

> (1) Where the otherwise applicable law so allows, the parties may choose to have their contract governed by the Principles, with the effect that national mandatory rules are not applicable.
> (2) However, effect should be given to those mandatory rules of national, supranational and international law which, according to the relevant rules of private international law, are applicable irrespective of the law governing the contract.

## Mandatory Rules within the Principles

The Principles themselves contain a number of mandatory rules, which will thus apply even if the parties purport to exclude them. These include the duty of good faith,[61] the reduction of a grossly excessive stipulated payment for non-performance,[62] and curbs on contractual provisions excluding or limiting liability.[63] In addition, the UNIDROIT Principles provide that where the price is to be determined by one party and that determination is manifestly unreasonable, a reasonable price shall be substituted notwithstanding any contract term to the contrary,[64] while the PECL extend this to cover all contractual terms to be determined by one party.[65]

It may be asked how it is possible for Principles which do not themselves have the force of law to incorporate mandatory rules of any kind. But this is not as strange as it seems. In the first place, where the parties select the Principles as rules of law governing their contract,[66] they thereby subject themselves to the binding force of the mandatory rules. Secondly, in stating what rules are to be considered mandatory, the Principles provide evidence of a general acceptation of what is to be considered, or ought to be considered, mandatory. Thirdly, even where the Principles are merely incorporated as terms of the contract, rather than being selected as the applicable law, their adoption will indicate an intention to give overriding effect to those rules expressed as mandatory to the extent that this is not incompatible with the construction of the contract as a whole.

[60] PECL art. 1.103(2); UNIDROIT Principles, art. 1.4.
[61] PECL art. 1.201 (*ex* art. 1.106); UNIDROIT Principles, art. 1.7.
[62] PECL art. 9.509 (*ex* art. 4.508); UNIDROIT Principles, art. 7.4.13.
[63] PECL art. 8.109 (*ex* art. 3.109); UNIDROIT Principles, art. 3.109.
[64] Art. 5.7(2).
[65] Art. 6.105 (*ex* art. 2.102).
[66] As opposed to merely incorporating them as contract terms, in which case they are, of course, entirely free to pick and choose. Whether the parties *can* choose the Principles as the applicable law will, of course, depend on the *lex fori* or, in the case of arbitration, the approach taken by the arbitrators.

## Conclusions

The UNIDROIT Principles and the PECL can be expected to exert an increasingly powerful influence on the development of modern contract law. Arbitral tribunals in international commercial arbitration will find them a valuable resource as a neutral set of rules which avoids the need to rely, or rely exclusively, on the national law of one of the parties or on conflict of laws rules; and courts and legislatures may also find them helpful, not least in countries where contract law is relatively undeveloped or where as the result of political changes they are moving from a planned to a market economy. The House of Lords as currently constituted is now much readier than it was to look beyond the United Kingdom and, indeed, beyond the common law, to find solutions to difficult questions of legal policy.[67] More generally, the Principles serve to rekindle an awareness of the contribution of scholars and of doctrine to the development and enrichment of jurisprudence. English law, like other legal systems, will benefit from their publication.

[67] A good example is the decision of the House of Lords in *White v. Jones* [1995] 2 AC 207, where in the course of his speech Lord Goff referred to the laws of Australia, Canada, France, Germany, the Netherlands, and the United States in reaching the conclusion that a person who would have benefited from a testator's will but for the want of care of the solicitors in failing to have it drawn up before the death of the intending testator had a claim in tort against them for negligence.

# 3

# International Restatements and National Law*

*Roy Goode*

It is indeed a privilege to be invited to contribute to this collection of essays in honour of Lord Goff, who has made his impress on law and lawyers in so many ways. His profound legal knowledge has never inhibited Robert Goff from blazing a trail, from overthrowing the dead hand of precedent where a new approach was required. This has been particularly evident in the field of unjust enrichment, a subject which, with Professors Gareth Jones and Peter Birks, he made into an established branch of English law, in (no doubt respectful) defiance of the views of Lord Diplock, who was not prepared to recognize any general doctrine of unjust enrichment in English law.[1] Yet Lord Goff remains protective of the purity of law and legal reasoning, which he is prepared to uphold however inconvenient the practical consequences[2] and however unpopular the outcome.[3] He greatly enjoys vigorous debate with academic lawyers, and it is in no small measure due to his practice of citing scholarly writings where these are considered to illuminate the problem under discussion that the work of academics has come to receive more frequent public acknowledgement in judgments. His quiet, somewhat languid, style of speaking conceals a mind of rapier quality, and at academic gatherings of comparative lawyers his gentle, courteously phrased questions have more than once unsettled a speaker on some aspect of foreign law who found that on the point in issue Lord Goff appeared to be the better informed. It was thus with profound regret that we received the news of his decision to retire in September 1998.

* Originally published as pp 45–58 Ch.3 'International Restatements and National Law' by Roy Goode from *Search for Principle: Essays in Honour of Lord Goff of Chieveley* edited by Jones, Gareth & Swadling, William (2006). Copyright Oxford University Press. By permission of Oxford University Press.

[1] *Orakpo v Manson Investments Ltd* [1978] AC 95 at p 104.

[2] See eg *R v Preddy* [1996] AC 815; *Kleinwort Benson Ltd v Lincoln City Council* [1998] 3 WLR 1095.

[3] Lord Goff was the sole dissenter in the ruling of the majority of the seven-member panel of the Judicial Committee of the House of Lords in *R v Bow Street Metropolitan Stipendiary Magistrate, ex parte Pinochet Ugarte (No 2)* [1999] 2 WLR 827 that Senator Pinochet could be extradited for crimes against humanity.

## The Revival of Internationalism

As we approach the twenty-first century it is becoming clear that profound changes are taking place in perceptions as to the role of national law in international relations. International law itself, at one time centred on the law of war and even until recently conceived as regulating relations between states, has enlarged its ambit and shifted its focus. It is now recognized that even private concerns and individuals enjoy in some degree the protection of international law. The sovereignty of states within their own borders is qualified by the concept of crimes against humanity, as exemplified in the recent decision of the House of Lords in the *Pinochet* case.[4] The centre of gravity of international law has moved sharply in the direction of international economic law, a shift accentuated by the creation of the powerful World Trade Organization. Increasingly we are looking to internationally accepted principles and standards to make good perceived deficiencies in domestic law.

These developments are matched in commercial law by a return from the nationalism of the past three centuries to the internationalism of the medieval *lex mercatoria.* Private international law, which thrives on differences among national legal systems, is now under threat as dissatisfaction grows with the application of national law to cross-border transactions and efforts are intensified to develop principles and rules of transnational commercial law. And as the role of transnational commercial law expands, so that of private international law diminishes.

International commercial arbitration is proving a remarkably powerful motive force in these developments. While courts remain for the most part committed to determining disputes involving a foreign element by applying a national law determined by their conflict of laws rules, international arbitrators are taking an altogether more independent line. This manifests itself in a variety of ways: the reduced dependence of international arbitral tribunals on a *lex arbitri* to determine the appropriate national law to apply; their willingness, in some cases, to choose a national law directly without reference to a conflicts rule at all; and an increasing tendency to look beyond the applicable 'law' in the sense of the law of a state and to have resort instead to the wider 'rules of law', including internationally accepted general principles and international trade usages. It is therefore no exaggeration to say that we are beginning to see the evolution of a new *lex mercatoria,* albeit one the boundaries and content of which are uncertain and controversial.

## International Restatements of Private Law

The most recent phenomenon, and that to which the present contribution is addressed, is the appearance of the international 'restatement', the formulation of a set of principles and rules common to different jurisdictions and designed to fulfil at the

[4] n 3 above.

international level the unifying function performed in America by the Restatements published by the American Law Institute. In the field of contract law there are already two major published texts, the UNIDROIT Principles of International Commercial Contracts ('UNIDROIT Principles'),[5] produced by a Study Group under the direction of a leading Italian scholar, Professor Michael Bonell, and the Principles of European Contract Law ('European Principles'), prepared by the Commission on European Contract Law,[6] a group of scholars from every member state of the European Union under the chairmanship of a distinguished Danish comparative lawyer, Professor Ole Lando. These restatements,[7] though as yet incomplete, have already had a considerable influence, not only on scholars but on arbitrators. Another European group, in which Professor David Hayton of King's College London played a prominent role, has just produced a statement of principles of European trust law.[8] But there are even grander ambitions. For some years there has been an increasing interest in the preparation of a European civil code.[9] Now a huge research project, masterminded by a renowned German scholar, Professor Christian von Bar, is under way which has as its objective the production of just such a code.

It is natural that the first field of law selected for an international restatement should be the law of contract, for the almost universal principle of party autonomy allows parties, if not to select such a restatement as the applicable law, then at least to incorporate its provisions into their contract, whilst tort, property, and trust law all involve third-party rights and duties which for the most part can be provided for only by law, not by contract. Moreover, arbitral tribunals have greater power than courts to look outside national law for the sources of parties' rights, and it is contract law which lies at the heart of international commercial arbitration.

## The Principles

The two sets of Principles have much in common, in their membership (which consists predominantly of academic scholars), their objectives, and their drafting.[10]

[5] Published by the International Institute for the Unification of Private Law (UNIDROIT), Rome, 1994. For a detailed account of the background, purposes, and applications of the UNIDROIT Principles, see Michael Joachim Bonell, *An International Restatement of Contract Law*, 2nd edn (New York, 1997).

[6] O Lando and H Beale (eds), *The Principles of European Contract Law, Part I* (Dordrecht, 1995).

[7] Which are hereafter collectively referred to as 'the Principles'. The word 'restatement' is, of course, a misnomer, for any formulation which draws on a number of different legal systems and aspires to go beyond the pointless exercise of providing the lowest common denominator is bound to change them all to some degree, and, indeed, to offer certain solutions not to be found in any of them. But the term is convenient and finds some justification in the fact that all restatements contain a common core of propositions which *do* reflect the existing law in the jurisdictions surveyed.

[8] D J Hayton, S C J J Kortmann, and H L E Verhagen (eds), *Principles of European Trust Law* (The Hague, 1999).

[9] See A S Hartkamp *et al*, *Towards a European Civil Code*, 2nd edn (The Hague, 1998).

[10] For comparisons and contrasts, see Michael J Bonell, 'The UNIDROIT Principles of International Commercial Contracts and the Principles of European Contract Law: Similar Rules for the Same Purposes?' Uniform Law Review 1996, 229; Roy Goode, 'International Restatements of Contract and English Contract Law' Uniform Law Review 1997, 231.

Both are designed to identify general principles of law and '*lex mercatoria*'. Both are offered to contracting parties as rules they may choose to incorporate into their contracts; to courts and arbitrators as anational rules reflecting a common understanding of best solutions to typical problems; and to legislatures as a model contract law. Both can be used to fill gaps in national laws or in international conventions. Each has been strongly influenced by the 1980 Vienna Convention on Contracts for the International Sale of Goods, which has become the essential reference point for all private law conventions relating to commercial transactions. While each of the Principles embodies rules common to a number of states, they also advance contract law in some degree to reflect commercial practice, for example, in providing for renegotiation where a change of circumstances brings about a major shift in the equilibrium of the contract falling short of frustration. The Principles differ in scope in that the UNIDROIT Principles apply both within and outside Europe but are confined to international transactions, while the European Principles are designed primarily for contracting parties in member states of the European Union (though obviously they can be adopted by others) but apply equally to commercial and non-commercial contracts. The impact of these differences is in practice likely to be relatively small. Moreover, while there are some divergences in the coverage and content of the rules,[11] there is a high degree of common ground. What is more remarkable is that those participating in these two projects have been able to reach agreement without feeling that the Principles as a whole represent a substantial departure from the principles of their own legal systems.

## The Status of the Principles

It is not easy to place these international restatements within the traditional framework of legal norms. In one sense they are not normative at all, merely a particular form of 'soft' law which can be given effect by contractual incorporation. Yet like international treaties, which also lack legal effect until ratified, restatements such as the Principles have a force independent of contract. Not only are they a tool for lawmakers, they can be resorted to as evidence of general principles common to states or alternatively of international commercial usage by reference to which the parties can be taken to have contracted and standards of reasonableness can be determined. Indeed, in a curious way the Principles are proving to have an even greater effect than unratified conventions, for, as I have remarked elsewhere,[12] a convention has no force at the time of its conclusion and signifies no more than a provisional indication of support by participating states, whereas the Principles together represent the unconditional commitment of scholars of international repute from all five continents.

[11] Bonell, loc cit 236–41.

[12] Loc cit (n 10 above), at p 234.

## Some Conflict of Laws Problems[13]

Paradoxically, while recourse to international restatements reduces dependence on national law, and thus on conflicts rules, it poses new problems for private international law itself. Can parties choose such a restatement, or even an international convention such as the Vienna Sales Convention, as the law which is to govern their contract? Does such a choice displace national law altogether? Is it open to the parties to do this? Alternatively, are they free to select particular parts of a national legal system or to select a national law but exclude those parts they do not like, using the provisions of international restatements as a supplementary applicable law?

Of course, even if clauses selecting the Vienna Sales Convention or the Principles to govern the contract are not valid as choice of law clauses, they remain effective as contractual incorporations of the Principles or the Sales Convention, as the case may be. The distinction is significant in that rules incorporated by contract have the status of ordinary contract terms and are thus controlled by mandatory rules of the applicable law, whereas rules which themselves constitute the applicable law are not so controlled.

In proceedings before a court, such questions have to be resolved by reference to the conflict of laws rules of the forum, including rules resulting from the adoption of a convention. It is clear, for example, that in the Rome Convention on the Law Applicable to Contracts references to the applicable law are to the law of a state and do not include possible sources of law outside a particular national legal system or systems. In other words, 'law' is to be distinguished from the broader 'rules of law', which are not so confined. Again, where English law is the *lex arbitri* then in the absence of a contrary agreement between the parties (who are free to agree on the application of legal rules which do not form part of a national legal system[14]) the Arbitration Act 1996 follows the UNCITRAL Model Law on Arbitration[15] in requiring the court to find the applicable 'law' by reference to conflict of laws rules,[16] albeit these need not be rules of the English conflict of laws but are what conflict rules the tribunal considers applicable.[17] On the other hand, in an arbitration conducted under the rules of the International Chamber of Commerce the arbitral tribunal is empowered, in the absence of party choice, to apply 'the rules of law which it determines to be appropriate',[18] and the same is true of an arbitration under the rules of the London Court of International Arbitration,[19] so that where

[13] See the short but illuminating contribution by Ulrich Drobnig, 'The UNIDROIT Principles in the Conflict of Laws', to the *Uniform Law Studies in Memory of Malcolm Evans*, Uniform Law Review 1998, 385.

[14] Arbitration Act 1996, s 46(1)(b).

[15] Art 28(2).

[16] The position is otherwise, however, where an English court is called on to recognize an award based on the application of rules of law such as general principles where the *lex arbitri* is a foreign law which accepts the validity of a choice of such rules as the governing law. See the decision of the Court of Appeal in *Deutsche Schachtbau- und Tiefbohrgesellschaft mbH v R'As al-Khaimah National Oil Co* [1990] 1 AC 295.

[17] Arbitration Act 1986, s 46(3).

[18] ICC Rules of Arbitration 1998, art 17.

[19] LCIA Rules 1998, art 22.3, which refers to 'law(s) or rules of law'.

either such rules apply the tribunal can look beyond the law of a national legal system even in an English arbitration.

But while courts of member states of the European Union are bound by the Rome Convention to apply a national law and to do so through the conflict rules of the Convention, the same is not necessarily true of other states, whose laws may well see nothing odd in selecting the Vienna Sales Convention[20] or the Principles as the governing law. There are three possible objections. The first is that the rules referred to may not furnish an answer to all the issues arising in the dispute. This, however, is not a sufficient answer for in a number of legal systems there are, in theory as well as in practice, gaps in the law, which may (though not necessarily will) make it necessary for the judge to refer to other law to resolve the dispute. Moreover, since dépeçage is freely admitted in the conflict of laws, there seems no reason why (subject to the two further objections to be considered) parties should not be free to select non-national rules as the law governing issues within the scope of the rules, leaving the appropriate national law to determine other issues arising in the dispute.

A second objection to the selection of non-national law as the applicable law is a policy one. At first sight, a state whose law would otherwise be applicable would appear to have a legitimate interest in ensuring that the mandatory provisions of that law are not overridden by principles or rules which do not have the approval of the legislature of a sovereign state. To put the matter another way, state courts are generally willing to accept that mandatory provisions of their own law[21] should operate only where that law is the applicable law and that the choice of a foreign law which is bona fide (a requirement which in some systems may require a reasonable connection with the state whose law is selected) can safely be given effect on the basis that states generally act responsibly in enacting their laws, whereas the same considerations might not apply to usages fashioned by merchants or to rules the formulation of which has not had to undergo the purifying fire of political and parliamentary debate. The choice of a multilateral convention which has come into force (or, possibly, which has been ratified by at least one state) would not appear to be open to this objection, since this has been subject to the dual process of debate and negotiation among representatives of governments from different states and, later, parliamentary scrutiny when the resultant convention is brought before the legislature for ratification. It has to be admitted that this feature is lacking in the preparation of restatements, such as the Principles, and this may make it difficult for national courts, at least, to accept the validity of a clause selecting the Principles as the applicable law, and thereby displacing national mandatory rules, despite the encouragement to do so in Article 1.103(1) of the Principles of European Contract Law (there is no comparable provision in the UNIDROIT Principles).

Thus far, there would seem to be a reasonable case for allowing parties to choose, say, the Vienna Sales Convention as the applicable law but not the

[20] See eg Peter Schlechtriem (ed), *Commentary on the UN Convention on the International Sale of Goods (CISG)*, trans Geoffrey Thomas (Oxford, 1998), art 6, para 31.

[21] That is, provisions which cannot be excluded by agreement of the parties, as opposed to overriding mandatory rules which have effect even where the contract is governed by a foreign law.

Principles, though these might be given effect as individual rules recognized by courts or arbitrators. There is, however, a third, and more formidable, objection to the selection even of an operative convention as the applicable law, which is that it does not constitute part of a legal system, and therefore lacks an essential attribute of *law*, namely the existence of machinery, provided or recognized by a state, to authenticate the normative force of the rules and to interpret and enforce them. This does not, of course, mean that the selection of a convention as the applicable law has no force whatsoever. It will still be effective, not as a choice of law but as a contractual incorporation of the provisions of the convention, and these will displace any inconsistent rules of the applicable law so far as these are purely dispositive in character. But, as incorporated terms, the provisions of the convention will give way to any mandatory rules which the court or arbitral tribunal finds applicable.

## Mandatory Rules

A particularly interesting feature of the Principles is that, in addition to deferring to super-mandatory rules (that is, mandatory rules which, under rules of private international law, apply whatever the governing law), they themselves embody ordinary mandatory rules, namely those which the parties, if they choose the Principles, cannot exclude by agreement. At first sight this seems extraordinary. How can rules which do not in themselves have legal force contain provisions which have effect notwithstanding the contrary agreement of the parties? But further thought shows that this is not as surprising as it seems. In the first place, the designation of certain rules as mandatory indicates the intention of the parties themselves to treat those rules as overriding in effect and to require other rules to be subordinate to them. Secondly, for those legal systems that recognize the efficacy of a choice of law clause adopting rules of law, rather than the law of a national legal system, the parties are simply accepting the normal consequences of choosing a governing law, one of which is that they thereby contract into the mandatory rules of that law. Thirdly, the inclusion of mandatory rules responds to the function of the Principles in offering international solutions to courts and arbitral tribunals irrespective of whether the parties have adopted them in their contract. Identification of such rules as mandatory conveys to the court or tribunal concerned the existence of an international consensus that those rules are of such fundamental importance that they ought not to be capable of displacement by agreement between the parties. Into this category fall (*inter alia*) the duty of good faith,[22] the reduction of a stipulated payment for non-performance which is grossly excessive,[23] and curbs on contractual provisions excluding or limiting liability.[24] These reflect the overwhelming trend of case law and legislation in national legal systems.

[22] UNIDROIT Principles, art 1.7; European Principles, art 1.201.
[23] UNIDROIT Principles, art 7.4.13; European Principles, art 9.509.
[24] UNIDROIT Principles, art 7.1.6; European Principles, art 8.109.

## Impact of the Principles

It is fair to say that in the earlier stages of work on the UNIDROIT Principles the Governing Council of UNIDROIT gave them a relatively low priority and, indeed, was at certain points in a state of indecision as to whether the project should proceed at all. The Governing Council was finally won over by the persistence of Professor Bonell, a decision that has been amply justified by subsequent events. The success of the UNIDROIT Principles, in particular, has astonished even their more constant supporters. They have been the subject of numerous conferences in different countries and have been discussed in a large number of articles in periodicals around the world; they have influenced the drafting or revision of civil and commercial codes in a number of countries;[25] and many arbitral awards, including awards given in arbitrations conducted under the rules of the International Chamber of Commerce and the London Court of International Arbitration, have applied the Principles, even in the absence of an express incorporation into the contract made by the parties.[26] Still more striking is the fact that the UNIDROIT Principles have been referred to by a Panel of the United Nations Compensation Commission as a source of general principles of international law/international commercial contract law governing the award of compensation in claims against Iraq for loss and damage resulting from its invasion of Kuwait.[27]

## The Implications for Harmonization Projects

From the experience of the Principles we can draw a number of lessons which are important to the work of harmonization of law. The first is that, for cross-border transactions, at any rate, there is a widespread desire to be able to have recourse to a code which is politically neutral, anational, and thus detached from the law of either of the contestants. The second is the importance of exposing drafts to outside scrutiny by practising lawyers, members of the business community (of particular importance in work on international *commercial* contracts), and other sectors. This should be done when the project is sufficiently advanced to allow of a text that has been properly thought out and is clearly and accurately drafted but is early enough to allow of the infusion of new ideas, including thoughts on structure, when the work is still in its formative stages. The third is that even excellent products do not sell themselves; they have to be vigorously promoted by every legitimate means at the disposal of their proponents. Much of the success of the UNIDROIT Principles is due to the indefatigable work and enthusiasm of Professor Bonell in

[25] Bonell records that the UNIDROIT Principles have already influenced the revised civil codes of The Netherlands and Quebec, the Russian Civil Code, the Estonian Law of Obligations, the drafting of the civil codes of Lithuania, the Czech Republic, and Argentina, the draft legislation on contracts of the Republic of China, and the draft new Commercial Code of Tunisia. See Bonell, op cit (n 5 above), 235–8.

[26] See ibid 240–53.

[27] Ibid 253–4.

fostering interest through his own writings and lectures and his ability to induce scholars and other experts around the world to produce articles and host conferences devoted to a discussion of the Principles, bringing them to the notice of an ever wider audience, and constantly urging the advantages of an international restatement of a modern law merchant. In this work of salesmanship he followed in the footsteps of a distinguished American academic, Professor John Honnold, a former Secretary of the United Nations Commission on International Trade Law, who brilliantly performed a similar service in promoting the Vienna Sales Convention, going from country to country urging its virtues on audiences which were sometimes sceptical at the outset but became converted by John Honnold's crusading zeal.[28] An important, and sometimes neglected, aspect of this promotional work is the monitoring of references to and use of the Principles. Publishing details of arbitral awards adopting the Principles and of the growing literature on them itself provides an impetus for an expansion of their influence.[29] The fourth is that international restatements, while lacking the binding force of ratified international conventions, nevertheless have certain advantages. They are free from political interference and obstruction; they do not depend for their efficacy on pressure from industry or commerce or other interest groups; and they do not involve any process of ratification or any requirement for a minimum number of ratifications before they can be used.

The final lesson is the virtue of patience and persistence. The idea of a restatement was first put forward by the then President of UNIDROIT, Professor Mario Matteucci, in 1968, and the preparation of a restatement of principles of contract law was included in the Institute's Work Programme three years later. A further twenty-three years were to elapse before the UNIDROIT Principles were finally completed and received the imprimatur of the Governing Council. Similarly, the preparation of a restatement of European contract law was first mooted by Professor Lando in 1976 at a conference at the European University Institute in Florence, but a further six years were to elapse before the start of work on the project by what became the (self-styled) Commission on European Contract Law under Professor Lando's chairmanship. Part I of the Principles of European Contract Law was published in 1995, the combined Parts I and II are currently in course of publication, and work is still proceeding on Part III. Again, the successful completion of a major part of the project was due in large measure to the driving force of its Chairman.

[28] I vividly recall a seminar he conducted at the Institute of Advanced Legal Studies in London, during which a Court of Appeal judge was incautious enough to ask why the Vienna Convention should be imposed upon parties when its predecessor, the Uniform Law on International Sales, allowed a Contracting State to ratify it on the basis that it would come into force in that State only where adopted by the parties in their contract. John Honnold, after pointing out that the Convention was dispositive in that the parties to a contract were free to derogate from or vary almost all its provisions, silenced his questioner by artlessly enquiring whether the United Kingdom Sale of Goods Act, of which he professed complete ignorance, operated only where chosen by the parties!

[29] Professor Bonell rightly devotes an entire chapter of his book *An International Restatement of Contract Law* (n 5 above) to an account of practical experiences with the UNIDROIT Principles.

## The Contribution of the International Restatement to the Influence of Scholars

In human affairs those who exert the greatest influence are the thinkers who project their ideas at the highest levels of abstraction and generality. The leading European jurists of the Middle Ages acquired an ascendancy which today seems quite remarkable but which stemmed from their achievement as glossators in adapting the principles of Roman law to form a new *ius commune.*

> The Glossators were the first to learn from the great Roman jurists the art of resolving the conflicts of communal living not by force or other old irrational means but by intelligent and objective discussion of the actual problem involved and by the application of a general rule based on such discussion of the facts. The jurist's insistence on this has resulted in a permanent justification and rationalization of public life, and has created in Europe the only civilization in the world which is legalistic in this sense. By finding a rational principle to replace the resolution of human conflicts by force, at any rate within states, lawyers satisfied one of the essential preconditions for the improvement of material culture, especially in the art of administration, the management of the economy, and even our own technological mastery of nature . . .
>
> In this sense the Glossators are the fathers of European jurisprudence. Medieval universities were vastly important both as centres of intellect and in public life; their political and social effects were immeasurable. In a few centuries the host of learned jurists educated by Italian and French teachers of law monopolized diplomacy and administration, not to mention the practice of law.[30]

The unifying force of the received Roman law was finally broken by new civil codes, which sought to combine general principles derived from Roman law with a responsiveness to the needs and aspirations of the ordinary citizen. It is only now, with the creation of the European Communities, and later the European Union, that we are beginning to rediscover the need for a common law of Europe and, indeed, an international common law of obligations. With this rediscovery has come a renewal of the status of the academic in the development of transnational civil and commercial law. The standing of the scholar in civil law jurisdictions has always been higher relative to that of the judge than in common law jurisdictions. If this is true of the individual scholar of international repute, how much more so of an international group of scholars representative of the world's leading families of law, who while vigorously promoting the virtues of their own law nevertheless come to restatement projects with an open mind, determined to find solutions to common problems which represent the best modern thinking and most closely reflect the legitimate needs of interested parties.

[30] Franz Wieacker, *A History of Private Law in Europe* (trans Tony Weir, Oxford, 1995), p 46.

## The Influence of Restatements in England

England's legal history has not shown English law to be readily receptive to international influence. From the early Middle Ages the combination of the common law and strong central government made us relatively self-sufficient in the development of our legal system. Our island status, coupled with the absence of any successful foreign invasion in nearly a thousand years, has given us an independence of mind and spirit which is at once this country's blessing and its bane.

This fortress built by Nature for herself
Against infection and the hand of war;
This happy breed of men, this little world;
This precious stone set in the silver sea,
Which serves it in the office of a wall,
Or as a moat defensive to a house,
Against the envy of less happier lands;
This blessed plot, this earth, this realm, this England . . .[31]

The fortress, the wall, and the moat may provide admirable defences against invasion, but they do little to promote the free flow of ideas either to or from our island. The medieval *lex mercatoria* owed little to the English; rather it was the genius of the Italian mercantile community that gave birth to the international law merchant of the Middle Ages. Roman law, which in the form received by the civilians was to prove so powerful a unifying force in Europe, had only a modest impact here; the great European codes, annealed in the fire of revolution, found no counterpart in England except in very specific fields of law such as bills of exchange and the sale of goods. And while in the eighteenth century English lawyers kept abreast of developments in international law, Holdsworth records that 'the English literature on the subject is inconsiderable'.[32] Building our law brick by brick on specific cases, we found little occasion to examine fundamental questions of principle, policy, or organization of our law. In the absence of legislation this had perforce to be left, at the philosophical level, to the masters of jurisprudence and, at the more detailed subject level, to the writers of textbooks and encyclopedic works. We make invaluable contributions to the preparation of international conventions and then walk away from them when they have been successfully concluded. Ratification is blocked either on the ground of absence of pressure from industry or, if this is forthcoming, on the fall-back defence of lack of parliamentary time. We dallied so long before applying to join the European Communities that we were halted in our tracks for several years and, when we were finally admitted, lost at least some of the influence we would have had as a founding member.

While several English scholars have contributed to the three international restatements previously mentioned—the UNIDROIT Principles, the European

[31] Shakespeare, *The Life and Death of King Richard II*, Act II, Scene 1.
[32] *A History of English Law* (London 1938; repr 1966), xii, 638.

Principles, and the Principles of European Trust Law—it remains the case that our teaching and our textbooks continue by and large to reflect the insularity of English legal education. Because England is not part of a federal state, so that there is no pressure to take a broad view of legal developments, we have the luxury, in which we freely indulge, of teaching the minutiae of domestic law rather than focusing on principles and policies. Our student texts and courses, other than those devoted to comparative law, remain largely impervious to foreign influence. The United Kingdom has not ratified the 1980 Vienna Convention on Contracts for the International Sale of Goods. So our books say little or nothing about what has become one of the most important instruments of harmonization in international trade law. Our contract textbooks, with the odd honourable exception, continue to trawl exclusively through familiar waters. One will search in vain for any mention of the Principles of European Contract Law or the UNIDROIT Principles of International Commercial Contracts, despite the attention lavished on them overseas.

It is rather ironic that it should be the practising lawyers who are making the running. Seeking ways of overcoming jurisprudential or doctrinal obstacles to their clients' cases, they increasingly call on comparative lawyers and other scholars for information about legal developments overseas and for assistance in fashioning their arguments. It is by this means, coupled with the growing interchange between academics and judges, and between English judges and their counterparts in continental Europe, that the courts become more familiar with international conventions and with foreign case law and doctrine. But how much easier it would be if, in the law of obligations at least, our students were weaned away from preoccupation with the latest case and the fine detail of our domestic law and exposed to other ways of thinking and to the policy considerations that have influenced the international restatements.[33] Then our law graduates would enter the practising profession not only with a sharper picture of the distinctive characteristics of their own legal system but also with a broader foundation of knowledge in the principles and policies underlying the law of obligations.

## The Denationalization of General Law

It would be a Utopian view to conclude that fundamental principles of general law will be fused into a harmonious whole. Moreover, it is likely that for the foreseeable future the influence of international restatements will continue to be in international commercial arbitration rather than in litigation before national courts or in disputes involving purely domestic transactions. Judges of national courts will

[33] It is not necessary for this purpose that every course should be converted into a comparative law course (though some move in this direction would be welcome, since comparative law is still very much the Cinderella of English legal studies); it suffices that at certain key points students should be alerted to different perceptions and alternative solutions offered by the relevant restatement or by a particular foreign law and that restatements such as the Principles should be included in course materials.

usually be reluctant to use restatements to displace the national law applicable under their conflict of laws rules. Similarly, in domestic disputes there is little incentive to look beyond domestic law for solutions which that law already provides. Yet some progress has already been made. National courts are today much readier than once they were to apply more liberal approaches to international transactions than to those which do not involve any foreign element. It is increasingly recognized that principles and rules devised primarily for domestic consumption do not necessarily meet the legitimate expectations of parties from different jurisdictions, particularly where the *lex fori* is the applicable law but is not the law of either party. An infrastructure of general principles is seen by many as particularly important to the development of European Community law, and provided a strong motive power for the preparation of the European Principles.

The drive towards a European civil code is becoming stronger every year and is not lightly to be dismissed. Even if such a code were to remain purely in the form of a restatement, lacking any normative force, it could still prove influential in providing principles and rules supplemental to those of national law, and might over time influence judicial thinking even in disputes of a purely domestic character. This process is likely to be accelerated by triangular co-operation: between academics and judges within the same jurisdiction; between academics from a number of legal families and systems; and between judges of national courts at the highest level from different countries who increasingly come together to obtain an understanding of the principles, practices, and traditions of other legal systems. In this country Lord Goff has been at the forefront of successful endeavours to establish a rapport between the judicial members of the House of Lords and their counterparts in Europe. It is not too much to hope that this will lead to the enrichment of the jurisprudence of all the countries thus represented.

# 4

# Contract and Commercial Law

## The Logic and Limits of Harmonisation*

*Roy Goode*

I begin with the pleasant duty of thanking you for the privilege you have conferred on me in appointing me this year's G.J. Wiarda Visiting Professor at this distinguished University and Law Faculty. I should like to express my particular appreciation to my hosts, Professors Ewoud Hondius and Patrick Honnebier, and to Mrs Ellen Hondius, for all their kindness and hospitality, to the secretaries who with cheerful efficiency dealt with my seemingly endless requests for photocopies and to my postgraduate class in transnational commercial law, whose intelligence and enthusiasm made my teaching such a pleasure, even if perhaps some of them had what might be described as a balanced attitude to study! And I am delighted to see here tonight several other old friends: Professor Pieter Sanders, the doyen of international commercial arbitration; Judge Rosalyn Higgins of the International Court of Justice; and Professor Teun Struycken, President of the International Private Law Association.

Gerard Wiarda was a distinguished member of a family that can trace its lineage back 600 years. Beginning as an advocate, he became beguiled by academe and in 1947 was appointed professor of administrative law in Utrecht. It is a testament to his outstanding qualities that, although he was at Utrecht for no more than three years, after which he accepted an invitation to become a judge of the Supreme Court and eventually President, his influence as a scholar of enormous range was such that the G.J. Wiarda Institute was set up in his honour as an umbrella for the research departments within the Law Faculty. He had an absorbing interest in human rights, and it was therefore no great surprise when he was later appointed a judge of the European Court of Human Rights, of which he eventually became President. So I feel honoured to be asked to deliver this year's Wiarda inaugural lecture, and I am conscious of doing so in the shadow of one of Utrecht's outstanding commercial lawyers and a former *rector magnificus* of this University, Willem Molengraaff.

* Originally published as "Contract and Commercial Law: The Logic and Limits of Harmonisation", in *International Contract Law* (ed F Willem Grosheide, Ewoud Hondius and Katharina Boele-Woelki, 2004) 309.

My talk this afternoon is concerned with the harmonisation of contract and commercial law. The subject is vast and there are members of this law faculty possessing remarkable language skills which I lack and a knowledge of comparative law and of foreign legal systems vastly exceeding my own. My focus is therefore less on the broad theoretical underpinnings of the harmonisation debate and more on practical aspects of the harmonisation process, which I believe are all too often neglected and on the need to back up common assumptions with empirical evidence.

My talk will be in two halves. The first concerns harmonisation at the international level in a strictly limited field and by means of hard law, namely international conventions; the second addresses an altogether more ambitious project at regional level, namely the harmonisation of European private law with particular reference to a proposed European Contract Code, and in this context discusses the relative merits of hard law and soft law, that is, rules which do not in themselves have the force of law.

## I Harmonisation at the International Level

Fascination with the idea of some great universal law which would transcend the boundaries of empire and state is of long standing. Some 2,000 years ago Cicero wrote: "There shall not be one law at Rome, another at Athens, one now, another hereafter, but one everlasting and unalterable law shall govern all nations for all time."[1] It is a tribute to the power of Cicero's language that this passage was relied on by the founder of English commercial law, Lord Mansfield, in a case decided in 1759,[2] to resolve a disputed question of Admiralty law. Of course, Cicero's dream was never realised or realisable. Nevertheless, we came astonishingly close to a pan-European law in that remarkable period in the High Middle Ages when Roman law was rediscovered, reshaped by the Glossators and taught in the University of Bologna, to which flocked students from all over Europe in such numbers that by 1160 AD this one university is estimated to have had between 10,000 and 13,000 law students. And from the teaching at Bologna and later elsewhere there developed a relatively unified approach to the science of law, with Roman law as its base and Latin as the universal legal language. This *ius commune,* as we know, eventually succumbed to the rise of the nation state and national laws. The question for us in the 21st century is whether we are in the course of establishing a new European, or even international, *ius commune.*

The process of harmonisation through an international instrument is almost always lengthy and arduous and involves the infusion of a prodigious amount of expertise, time, and money. It is thus a process not lightly to be undertaken. I do not myself subscribe to the view that the existence of different national laws governing commercial transactions is self-evidently injurious to international trade. Rather I share the approach of that great commercial and comparative lawyer, Harold

[1] *De Republica,* 3.22.33. [2] *Luke v. Lyde* (1759) 2 Burr 882.

Gutteridge, who combined deep scholarship with a down-to-earth approach to his subject. In the second edition of his famous book *Comparative Law,* published in 1949 and still unsurpassed in its clarity and wisdom, he wrote in these terms of the limited progress in the unification of law: "It would seem that much of the blame for the failure to achieve more definite and permanent results must be attributed to an excess of zeal fostered by an exaggerated belief in the need for unification and over-confidence in its feasibility."[3] And there, in this simple, elegant statement, we find what I regard as even now the sole criteria which justify a harmonisation project: the existence of a problem sufficiently serious to justify the labour and expense involved and the feasibility of the harmonisation proposed. I shall return to the grand idea of a modern *ius commune* in the context of European private law. At this stage, I would merely offer the reminder that the mediaeval *ius commune* was developed by scholars, not by legislators, and the question who produces the law is fundamental.

The globalisation of international trade and finance over the past 20 years has led to an upsurge in conventions on different aspects of private law governing commercial transactions. Among these may be mentioned the 1980 Vienna Convention on Contracts for the International Sale of Goods, the 1988 UNIDROIT Conventions on International Financial Leasing and International Factoring, the 2001 Cape Town Convention on International Interests in Mobile Equipment with its associated Aircraft Equipment Protocol, the UNCITRAL Convention on the Assignment of Receivables in International Trade, also concluded in 2001, and the 2002 Hague Convention on the law applicable to certain rights in respect of securities held with an intermediary. Time allows me to talk of only two of these Conventions, the Cape Town Convention and the Hague Convention, in both of which I was one of those involved from the early origins to their conclusion.

## I.1 The Cape Town Convention

The Cape Town Convention is by any standards ambitious. It provides an international regime covering the financing of interests in aircraft objects, railway rolling stock, and space assets by means of secured loans, sales under reservation of title, and leases. A financier taking security over these classes of asset faces serious problems arising from the fact that the assets in question are either earth-bound but constantly on the move, so that a financier has no guarantee that a security or title-retention interest created under its own law will be recognized and enforced elsewhere, or, in the case of satellites and other space assets, is not on earth at all. Huge sums of money are invested in the acquisition of aircraft, satellites, and railway rolling stock. Yet there are countries whose law is hostile to the whole idea of non-possessory security or embodies restrictions and requirements which place obstacles to entry into a valid agreement and even more obstacles in enforcing security interests and giving them protection against the debtor's bankruptcy creditors. In consequence, developing countries either find it difficult or even impossible to obtain finance

[3] H.C. Gutteridge, *Comparative Law*, 2nd edn. (Cambridge University Press, 1949) p. 157.

for the acquisition of such objects or, if they do obtain finance, it is expensive. So a key objective of the Convention is to provide a legal regime which will make creditors feel comfortable, open to developing countries access to funds and bring down borrowing costs.

The central features of the Cape Town Convention are the easy creation of an international interest, by security or title retention, with a set of basic default remedies and the ability to secure fast provisional relief; the establishment of an international public register to record these interests, operated by a Registrar under the supervision of a Supervisory Authority; and a simple set of priority rules based on the principle that a registered interest has priority over a subsequently registered interest or an unregistered interest and is protected from the general body of creditors in the debtor's insolvency. The Convention does not come into force as regards any class of object unless and until there is a Protocol in force for that class and it then takes effect subject to the Protocol. So far, only one Protocol has been concluded, namely the Aircraft Equipment Protocol, and this both modifies and supplements the Convention to accommodate the particular requirements of the aviation industry and its financiers.

The Convention and Protocol are complex instruments which together run to 99 Articles, only two fewer than the Vienna Sales Convention and infinitely more complex. Nevertheless, the Convention and Protocol were signed on the spot at the Diplomatic Conference by no fewer than 20 States, and others have since signed. To come into force, the Convention and Protocol require eight ratifications. There is every expectation that these will materialise during the present year or shortly thereafter and that the Convention will be a considerable success.

## I.2 The Hague Convention

This Convention, concluded at The Hague in December 2002 under the presidency of Professor Struycken and with Professor Stefania Bariatti as Chair, deals with the law governing the proprietary effects of the holding and transfer or pledge of securities through a custodian or other intermediary rather than directly from the issuer. Under traditional conflict of laws rules, issues relating to the transfer of securities are governed, in the case of registered securities, by the law of the place where the issuer is incorporated or alternatively keeps its register and, in the case of bearer securities, by the *lex situs* of the certificates at the time of the transfer in question. These rules do not, however, work well in the case of securities held through an account with an intermediary, since the root of title is not the register or the physical location of bearer securities but the securities account with the intermediary, and the law best suited to determine proprietary issues is the law of the place of business of the relevant intermediary. This "place of the relevant intermediary" approach (PRIMA) is already embodied in a restricted way in Article 9(2) of the EC Settlement Finality Directive. What the Hague Convention does is to extend the concept, in modified form, to the international plane and in a relatively unrestricted way. The principal modification is that, to promote predictability, the law governing proprietary issues, whether as between the parties or in relation to third-party rights and priorities, will be that selected by the account holder and the intermediary to govern the account agreement. This is subject to a so-called "reality test", which in essence requires that the selected law is that of a state or territorial unit of a State in which the intermediary carries on the business of maintaining securities accounts, though without necessarily maintaining the particular account in question in that State.

Though the Hague Convention is very much shorter than the Cape Town Convention and a good deal less complex, it nevertheless raised a host of difficult issues stemming in no small measure from the wide diversity of institutions and practices involved in the securities industries in different countries. Yet the Convention was concluded a mere 2.5 years after work first began, an astonishing achievement. The existence of a major problem was quickly established. In world financial centres, dealings in securities may amount to billions of dollars *every night.* It is therefore of vital importance to the parties to know what law governs proprietary issues. Yet apart from the conflict rule in Article 9(2) of the EC Settlement Finality Directive, which is of limited application, and decrees in Belgium and Luxembourg, where the two international central securities depositories, Euroclear and Clearstream, are respectively based, there are few national laws laying down clear conflict rules.

## I.3 The ingredients of success

What can we learn from the working methods adopted in the preparation of these instruments? I would identify four crucial factors:

### *(1) The avoidance of excessive ambition*

It is better to have a limited target that is achievable than a grand design that is not. Three factors are common to the five conventions to which I referred earlier. First, they are confined to commercial transactions, because consumer transactions are already highly regulated and strongly overlaid with mandatory laws. Second, they are limited to cross-border transactions, because it is primarily in international trade that problems of differences in national laws are likely to cause the most acute problems and because of a perception that states who have a strong sense of the superiority of their own laws will feel less sensitive to changes where these are confined to transactions between businesses in different states. Third, their *raison d'être* is not simply the existence of differences in national laws but the fact that these were wholly inadequate to cater for the needs of those engaged in international trade.

### *(2) Participation of all interested parties from the outset*

The traditional method of preparing international conventions is for a study group or working party consisting of scholars and/or lawyers in government to prepare draft texts and send these out for comment. But consultation is not the same as participation. The quality of a project improves dramatically if from the very outset those who have first-hand knowledge and experience of the practices of the sectors affected are involved—not necessarily as members of the Study Group but as people committed to work together to produce proposals, criticisms, and suggestions for the improvement of texts. Early participation of interested sectors is necessary in order to show that there *is* a serious problem to be addressed and that it is capable of solution. If the major players give an affirmative answer on these two points, then at least the case for harmonisation has been properly made, and the project can proceed.

A huge impetus was given to work on the Cape Town Convention by the massive input of the aviation industry, different groups holding meeting after meeting, preparing paper after paper, and organising seminar after seminar. Not only did this help to ensure that the resultant texts reflected commercial practices and needs, it also reduced the financial and administrative burdens on the hard-pressed UNIDROIT Secretariat and, equally important, generated a high level of interest in the project and support for it which in turn influenced the thinking of governments. In addition, an economic impact assessment was commissioned from two economists working under the auspices of INSEAD, whose report estimated that if a stable international legal environment could be provided for the creation, enforcement, perfection, and priority of security and title-retention interests, the leading credit-rating agencies would upgrade the rating of aircraft receivables and the consequent reduction in borrowing costs could lead to savings of up to $4 billion a year. There were those who viewed this estimate with a considerable measure of scepticism. But a mere ten days ago, Ex-im Bank—the Export-Import Bank of the United States—issued a press release offering a reduction of one third in its exposure fee on the financing of large US aircraft for all buyers in foreign countries that ratify and implement the Cape Town Convention. This announcement shows in dramatic form the enormous potential value of a sound international legal regime for the protection of international interests in aircraft.

The participatory approach was also strongly present in the Hague Convention project. The securities industry is highly complex and diversified. The major players include issuers, registrars and transfer agents, central banks, international and national central securities depositories operating clearing and settlement systems, custodians and sub-custodians, and broker-dealers, and the indirect holding system sets up what is often a long chain of intermediaries and account holders, each of which may be based in a different jurisdiction. As with aircraft, there was intense participation by the numerous international and regional organisations, essential if one was to obtain a complete picture, since no one group or individual could be expected to have a detailed knowledge of the whole industry. At least one of the rules, namely the rule that a choice of law agreed between parties A and B, would also govern third-party rights, was counter-intuitive and would have been rejected outright by the traditional conflicts lawyer but has been found essential in order to promote predictability.

### *(3) Continuity of effort*

One of the major problems in preparing international conventions is that full-scale meetings are expensive and involve a lot of organisation. Thus a year or more may elapse between meetings, by which time the participants may have changed and memories may have faded. Under the old-style not a great deal was expected to happen between meetings. The drafting committee, if it had not already produced a text at the meeting itself, would prepare one on the basis of the decisions taken; some participants might send in papers; but otherwise it was left to the next meeting to carry the project forward. This process was largely responsible for the fact that work on a convention could take one or even two decades. A quite different approach was adopted for the two conventions to which I have referred. A great deal of work was undertaken between meetings with a view to focusing thoughts and saving time at the next meeting. In the case of the Hague Convention, a novel accelerating process was introduced. The Permanent Bureau and certain other key figures actively promoted discussion and debate among all the members of the Commission between meetings on key issues with a view to securing a consensus and the Drafting Committee was authorised to reflect any such consensus in drafting the text for the next meeting, instead of confining itself to decisions already taken. In this way, much of the groundwork for dealing with disputes issues was laid before the ensuing meeting took place.

### *(4) A driver*

There is one final element that contributed hugely to the preparation and successful conclusion both of the Cape Town Convention and Protocol and of the Hague Convention, namely the enthusiasm and commitment of a single individual, whose self-appointed task is to generate interest and support for the project, draw in participants, and secure their active and continuous involvement in the work. We were fortunate in that for each of the two projects there was just such a person. In the case of the Cape Town Convention, this was undertaken by Jeffrey Wool, who was UNIDROIT's consultant on aviation finance and whose energy and commitment almost single-handedly brought the aviation industry into the project, operating through a great driving force, the Aviation Working Group. Jeffrey Wool's counterpart for the Hague project was Richard Potok, who spurred academic, industry experts and governments into action, organised international conferences calls and seminars, and brought about a marked change in attitude on the part of those who were originally either uninterested or actively hostile, using the members of an extended Drafting Committee as the engine. Every project should, wherever possible, have a Jeffrey or a Richard.

## II Regional Harmonisation: The Proposal for a European Contract/Civil Code

### II.1 The work of the Lando Commission and the UNIDROIT Group

The legislation of the European Community affecting contracts has hitherto been confined almost exclusively to supranational mandatory rules, particularly in the fields of competition and consumer protection. But these rules represented a superstructure imposed on foundations of general contract law which varied widely from one Member State to another. This led Professor Ole Lando to establish his Commission on European Contract Law, with participants from each Member State, to seek to formulate a set of contract principles for Europe. The work was done in three phases. Part I was published in 1995, and was republished with Part II in the year 2000. Part III was completed last year, ending the work of the Commission, and its publication is imminent. In parallel, UNIDROIT produced some years ago the first part of its Principles of International Commercial Contracts under the direction of Professor Joachim Bonell, and work on the second and final part is proceeding. There was a certain degree of common membership of the two groups and a high degree of similarity in the two texts, both of which have attracted much interest and support and have been applied in numerous arbitrations and even in some judicial decisions. The two sets of principles are not, of course, legally binding instruments, they are restatements which have influence rather than authority, though they are frequently used as an indication of the best rule for a particular situation. The work of the Lando Commission has now been absorbed into the wider project being undertaken by the Study Group on a European Civil Code under the leadership of Professor Christian von Bar.

### II.2 The initiatives of the European Parliament and the European Commission

The European Parliament was clearly captivated by the idea of the harmonisation of European private law. In 1989[4] and again in 1994,[5] it called for the preparation of a European civil code. In April 2000 it commissioned a report by Dr Klaus-Heiner Lehne on the subject which was presented the following year. In July 2001, the European Commission issued a Communication on European contract law[6] in which it examined four options relating to the harmonisation of European contract

[4] Resolution A2-157/89, OJ C 158, 26.6.1989, p. 400.

[5] Resolution A3-0329/94, OJ C 205, 25/7/94, p. 518.

[6] Communication of the Commission to the Council and the European Parliament on European contract law, COM (2001) 398 (final), 11.7.2001, OJC 255, 13.9.2001, p. 1. For an interesting set of academic comments on the Commission's Communication, see the ERA-Forum Special Issue European Contract Law 2-2002, reproducing the papers presented at a conference on European Contract Law at Trier in March 2002. The most comprehensive academic examination of the Commission's proposals is to be found in the Joint Response of the Commission on European Contract Law and the Study Group on a European Civil Code.

law: no action; promotion of the development of common contract law principles leading to more convergence of national laws; improvement of the quality of existing Community legislation; and the adoption of comprehensive legislation at Community level. The Commission consulted widely on its paper. There was widespread agreement that to do nothing was unacceptable, and considerable support for the second and third options. By contrast, the fourth option, comprehensive Community legislation, proved very controversial. Academic opinion was divided; most governments that responded did not view it with favour and those that did felt that an essential prerequisite was to establish the need for a binding code; business interests for the most part felt it was unnecessary; and consumer organisations differed in their views. Many legal practitioners favoured a code but most who did so seemed to favour a non-binding or opt-in approach.

The European Parliament, in responding to the Commission's Communication, passed a resolution in November 2001[7] underlining what it described as "the need to pursue a *targeted* harmonisation of contract law where mutual recognition of national rules cannot be applied and where divergence of these rules leads to obstacles to the functioning of the internal market as defined by the Court of Justice". The resolution can fairly be criticised as reflecting a high-minded idealism rather than a coherent statement of objectives, and for lawyers some of the tasks allotted to the Commission seem neither feasible nor useful, for example, the compilation of a data base of contract cases and legislation from every Member State to be translated into all eleven Community languages within three years—a task which would leave the Commission's Translation Service no time for anything else and would in my opinion serve little useful purpose. Nevertheless, one cannot but applaud the Parliament's interest in this very important project and its strong support for the work of the Lando Commission and the von Bar Study Group. For its part, the European Commission has gone to a great deal of trouble to lay out the various options in a relatively neutral way and has provided a very fair summary of the responses.

## II.3 Which way to go?

I shall assume that there is widespread agreement on the value of a restatement of European contract law, as, indeed, there is in a restatement of European civil law if this can be achieved. The Community does not need to invest time and money to prepare such a contract restatement because we already have one in the shape of the Principles of European Contract Law. In fact, if we extend the exercise beyond Europe we have not one restatement but three: the PECL, the UNIDROIT Principles, and the European Contract Code prepared by the Academy of European Private Lawyers (also known as the Pavia Group) under the chairmanship of Professor Giuseppe Gandolfi. We certainly do not need any more. The question is not whether such restatements are useful—they have already proved their value—but whether Member

[7] Resolution on the approximation of the civil and commercial law of the Member States, COM (2001) 398 final, C5-0471/2001-2001/2187 (COS), OJ C 140E, 13.6.2001, p. 538.

States should be obliged to replace their existing contract laws with a European Contract Code. I shall not enter the controversy as to whether the Community has legal competence at all in this area; for the purposes of this presentation I shall assume that it does and that we can disregard the concept of subsidiarity. I do not propose to express a concluded view on this subject. In relation to the preparation of a European civil code, Professor Hondius, one of the most eminent authorities in this field and an ardent exponent of harmonisation, nevertheless urges caution in his contribution to that excellent work *Towards a European Civil Code*.[8] And where the course is thus charted by a direct descendant of the famous map engraver Jodicus Hondius, what can I do but follow it? What I should like to do is to return to the two key criteria mentioned so long ago by Gutteridge: Is there a problem? and are the means proposed feasible? But first I should like to make the point that there is a great deal of EC regulation of consumer contracts, which could certainly do with codification, but that outside consumer protection and competition issues the laws governing commercial contracts are almost entirely dispositive. An EC regulation would thus impose on courts of Member States the duty to apply a uniform contract law which the parties themselves would be free to vary or exclude. It would also impose on the parties the onus of so doing if they wished to retain the legal system with which they were familiar; in default, the rules with which they were wholly unfamiliar would apply. It has to be asked whether the citizenry of Europe regard such a major incursion into their long-established legal systems as meeting the test of legitimacy on which the need for the observance of law is based.

### *(1) Is there a problem?*

There is a curiosity here. It is assumed, mostly by academics, that differences in national contract and commercial laws are detrimental to business. As far as I can judge, in relation to dispositive law little or no empirical work has been done to substantiate this assumption, which, ironically, is disputed by the very sector on whose behalf it is made. Multinational enterprises are well used to dealing with different national laws. Differences in mandatory laws can, of course, be a problem; differences in dispositive rules are not, because *ex hypothesi* they can be varied or excluded by the contract so as to produce a standard set of terms. Moreover, to unify contract law would not obviate the necessity of consulting local lawyers on other issues, for example, the impact of specific rules governing sales, construction contracts, and all the other special classes of contract which would remain within the purview of domestic law. Yet uniformity is what Europe has always been about—hence the ploughing-up in England of orchards of apples in huge varieties because they did not fit the sizing standards prescribed by the bureaucrats in Brussels.

A further assumption is that "consumers avoid buying in another state just because of the fact that they do not know the law". This conjures up a vision of

[8] A. Hartkamp et al. (eds.), *Towards a European Civil Code*, 2nd rev. and exp. edn. (Nijmegen: Ars Aequi Libri / The Hague [etc.]: Kluwer Law International, 1998), at p. 8.

a woman from, say, Ruritania, who visits Rome and there, in the Via Condotti, sees a fabulous dress, a dress to die for. She is about to buy it but then caution prevails: I must not buy this dress because I am not familiar with Italian law. Clearly a very sophisticated consumer and one who by inference *is* familiar with Ruritanian law. Perhaps in the interests of legal science the scholar who espouses this view should take his wife shopping in the Via Condotti and see what happens.

### *(2) Is a binding Code feasible?*

Again, I will not offer an answer to this question, being mindful of the fact that when law schools in England were asked whether property law could be taught in the first year half said it couldn't be done while the other half were doing it! But I should like to offer a few practical considerations. First, if law is to be responsive to the social, cultural, and economic background of its citizens, then a binding European Contract Code presupposes a social, cultural, and economic background common to the Member States. I believe that at present this is demonstrably not the case. Can it seriously be said that a contract law suitable for a country with a relatively small volume of international financial transactions is equally suitable for one of the world's leading financial centres? Can it be the case that a legal system based very strongly on the concept of *laissez-faire* and self-help in commercial transactions shares the same philosophy as a legal system which is opposed to self-help remedies? These differences are of limited significance in a restatement, which offers a resource to legislators, courts, and arbitrators but not a threat to existing national laws. The assertion that the similarities in European legal systems are greater than the differences seems to me a somewhat facile way of brushing aside the very different methods of legal reasoning and of interpretation of contracts, even if in many cases the end results are similar. Second, who is to do the work? Surely not the Commission, which lacks both the time and the technical expertise to do it. But binding law cannot be left to scholars, since the democratic process requires the involvement of all interest sectors, including, of course, government and the Community institutions. So the nature of the product changes from a work of scholarship couched in clear and comprehensible terms to a product derived from political pressures and compromises which will result in complete distortion. And then, of course, it passes through the Translation Service, by which time it will be barely recognisable as the offspring of the PECL.

This brings me to my third point, language. Language is a serious problem. Parallel texts of high quality can be produced only by those who work together in the different languages and who are experts not only in their own language but in their own law. And they need to work together. The production of a parallel text by a drafting committee produces something wholly different in quality from a translation done by a translation agency. This is not intended to imply any criticism of the Commission's highly professional Translation Service, which possesses not only well-qualified staff but also access to powerful data bases. But quite apart from the fact that the Service works under great pressure, its translation skills lie in language, not in the substantive law content of what is being translated.

My own experience as chairman of different drafting committees of Study Groups and Diplomatic Conferences over a period of many years is that a drafting committee can handle two parallel texts at most in the time available to it. Given the absence of the time pressure imposed on a study group meeting or a Diplomatic Conference it might be possible to add a third language, though this alone would produce an exponential increase in the work. Any collaborative drafting work in more than three languages would in my view be impossible.

Finally, let us consider the huge implications of enactment of the Code. Every textbook, every encyclopaedic work would have to be rewritten. Every scholar, every practitioner, every judge would have to be retrained in a major field of law, and would have to be prepared to surrender a substantial slice of hard-won knowledge and experience and return to the law school; good for the law schools, of course, but at what cost to national legal systems, let alone national cultures and traditions! As Julius Hermann von Kirchner so aptly remarked 155 years ago: "... three amending words from the lawgiver and an entire library becomes waste paper ...".[9] Do we really want to consign to the dustbin of history the elegant prose of Portalis in the French Code Civil or the limpid clarity of Huber in the Swiss Civil Code? Did Germany wish to jettison its BGB when it underwent a major revision coming into effect only a year ago? And what of the relatively recently revised Dutch Civil Code? We might also ask: why are some of our leading scholars of European comparative contract law so keen to destroy European comparative contract law?

## III Envoi

I would summarise my conclusions as follows. First, every proposal for a harmonisation project must be rigorously tested against two criteria: the existence of a serious problem and the feasibility of a proposed solution. These factors having been established, thought must be given from the outset to the working methods, and in particular the need for participation, continuity of effort, and the assumption of responsibility by a dynamic and committed individual for carrying the project forward. At the international level, the successful conclusion of recent Conventions and, equally important, the strong likelihood of their early adoption, results in large measure from the presence of these various features.

In the case of the proposed European Contract Code, we have yet to establish either that there is a need for a general European contract law to replace the largely dispositive rules of national laws of Member States or that the project is feasible. But I am strongly in favour of adapting our conflict of laws rules to allow the parties to choose the PECL as the applicable law, though this would involve identifying criteria for giving such status to the work of a private body. I am equally supportive of the hugely ambitious and imaginative project for a European Civil Code *as a restatement.* I agree with Professor von Bar that only the community of European scholars

[9] In a lecture in 1848 on *Die Wertlosigkeit der Jurisprudenz als Wissenschaft:* "... drei berichtigende Worte des Gesetzgebers and ganze Bibliotheken werden zu Makulatur."

in the field of private law has the knowledge and the independence to undertake this and that there is an urgent need for a European Law Institute. Though I am strongly disinclined to see a restatement that has been crafted with meticulous care and accuracy taken over and wrecked by politicians and translators, yet as a restatement the project is of enormous interest and importance; and while the bulk of the funding has come from a German foundation, others too have contributed, including the NWO here in the Netherlands, which is supporting the study of sales and services law by a group of fine young scholars under the direction of Professor Hondius.

And why is this project so important? Because it responds to the desire of law students everywhere to learn more about other legal systems; because it gives further impetus to what the European Community has done so much to promote, the reappearance of the wandering scholar, who goes from a law school in one country to that in another and, perhaps, a third, always acquiring new experiences and stimulated by fresh ideas; because in understanding other legal systems, and in testing our own against a European restatement, we come to see more readily both the strengths and the weaknesses of our own civil law; and because it is through the work of scholars rather than legislators, and through finding unity of solutions in diversity of legal cultures, that we can best recreate the spirit of the European legal tradition.

## Postcript

The very next day after this lecture was delivered, the European Commission produced its Action Plan.[10] It acknowledged that a majority was against Option IV, which was aimed at a new instrument on European contract law, while noting that an important number of contributors suggested that further thought might be given to this in the light of future developments in pursuance of Options II and III. The Action Plan suggests a mix of non-regulatory and regulatory measures, including measures to increase the coherence of the EC *acquis* in the area of contract law, to promote the elaboration of European-wide general contract terms, and to examine further whether problems in the European contract law area may require non-sector-specific solutions such as an optional instrument. The first of these objectives is particularly to be welcomed. There is widespread agreement that the drafting of consumer Directives is of indifferent quality, lacks adequate definitions, is too vague and abstract, and is fragmented and inconsistent. Beyond dealing with this, the target is to establish a common frame of reference, establishing common principles and terminology in the area of European contract law. There is no reference to the Principles of European Contract Law in this context, nor are we told why the PECL do not already provide the required statement of common principles and terminology. Given that the Lando Commission devoted over 20 years to the three phases of its project, it may reasonably be asked why it is necessary to reinvent the wheel. But perhaps that is what lawmaking is all about!

[10] Communication from the Commission to the European Parliament and the Council, *A More Coherent European Contract Law*, COM(2003) 68 final, 12.2.2003.

# 5

# The Protection of Interests in Movables in Transnational Commercial Law*

*Roy Goode*[†]

## I. Introduction

The untimely death of Malcolm Evans robbed his family of a devoted husband and father and UNIDROIT of a Secretary General whose labours and wise counsel had taken the Institute to new levels of activity and influence. Malcolm carried lightly his immense knowledge and experience, combining modesty with determination and scholarship with realism, and infecting his many friends and colleagues with his warmth and enthusiasm. Ever diligent in promoting the Institute's standing and its scientific work, Malcolm was nonetheless respectful of other international organisations engaged in the harmonisation of private law and firmly committed to collaboration with them. Under his stewardship several significant UNIDROIT projects were brought to fruition: the Convention on Agency in the International Sale of Goods; the UNIDROIT Conventions on International Factoring and International Financial Leasing; the UNIDROIT Convention on Stolen or Illicitly Exported Cultural Objects; and the UNIDROIT Principles of International Commercial Contracts. Sadly, he did not live to see the culmination of work on the Guide to Franchising and the draft Convention on International Interests in Mobile Equipment, though he continued to the end to give the benefit of his guidance and good judgement. He will be greatly missed.

Until quite recently, international efforts to harmonise commercial law have focused on the law of obligations in general and contract law in particular. The proprietary effects of commercial dealings have largely been ignored.[1] A seminal

* Originally published as "The Protection of Interests in Movables in Transnational Commercial Law" *Uniform Law Review* (1998) 3 (2–3): 453–65.

[1] However, there are numerous points at which contract law and property law overlap. For example, the assignment of contract rights is primarily a transfer of property but is treated in all standard texts on contract law and will feature in the UNIDROIT Principles of International Commercial Contracts and the Principles of European Contract Law prepared by the Commission on European Contract Law. In common law systems an agreement to transfer property is treated in equity as a transfer. Moreover, the effects of *in rem* security can be produced by contractual mechanisms, such as the netting of mutual obligations and the novation to a clearing house of contracts between traders.

event in private international lawmaking was the conclusion in 1980 of the Vienna Convention on Contracts for the International Sale of Goods (CISG). This Convention has been hugely successful, having been adopted by 52 States, and with the likelihood of the United Kingdom acceding to it in the near future. But a deliberate decision was taken to exclude from CISG the property aspects of sales law in view of the wide divergences in approach among legal systems and the perceived difficulty of finding solutions. So CISG is silent on matters relating to the passing of property from seller to buyer, reservation of title to goods and proceeds, and the proprietary effects of a sale by a buyer who has not yet acquired the property or by a seller who has already sold the goods to an earlier buyer.

Where attempts were made to tackle some aspects of the law relating to property in movables they usually foundered, sooner or later, because the goal was over-ambitious and the task too daunting. This was the fate that befell the heroic endeavours of Professor Ulrich DROBNIG, who presented a comprehensive comparative study of security laws to the United Nations in 1975;[2] the 1973 draft EC Directive on non-possessory security in movables and reservation of title,[3] a project later taken over by the Council of Europe but ultimately abandoned; and the 1974 UNIDROIT draft Convention on the acquisition of goods in good faith.[4] Such successes as there were in the adoption of conventions on rights in movables lay in the sphere of transport law, notably through conventions relating to rights in ships and aircraft. These types of equipment are the most readily susceptible to the creation of internationally recognised security interests and other real rights because of their uniquely identifiable character and the systems of nationality registration that have developed in relation to them.

This paper seeks to identify the causes of the initial lack of progress and to depict the impetus for change that has led over the past ten years to intensive new efforts to tackle at least some of the proprietary aspects of commercial transactions. Reference will be made in particular to the 1988 UNIDROIT Conventions on International Factoring and International Financial Leasing,[5] the UNCITRAL draft Convention on Assignment in Receivables Financing, the 1994 Model Law on Secured Transactions

[2] *International Payments: Study on Security Interests* (ST/LEG/11), reproduced in the Appendix to the Report of the Secretary-General A/CN.9/131 dated 16 May 1980 (UNCITRAL Year Book 1981, vol. XI). The instrument envisaged by the Commission was not a uniform law embodied in a convention, which was considered an unrealistic objective, but a model law which would apply to domestic as well as international transactions. However, though the project never appears to have been formally abandoned, no further work was undertaken after the presentation of the above report.

[3] *Draft Directive on the recognition of securities over movables without dispossession and of clauses providing for retention of ownership upon sale of movables*, XL/466/73-E.

[4] *Draft Convention Providing a Uniform Law on the Acquisition in Good Faith of Corporeal Movables.* This draft, based on an earlier UNIDROIT project, the 1968 draft Uniform Law on the protection of the *bona fide* purchaser of corporeal movables, was approved by a Committee of Governmental Experts in June 1974 for submission to a Diplomatic Conference for adoption, and over several years negotiations were conducted with a Member State with a view to its hosting the Conference. Ultimately these came to nothing and the project was abandoned in 1981.

[5] See Franco FERRARI, "General Principles and International Uniform Commercial Law Conventions: A Study of the 1980 Vienna Sales Convention and the 1988 UNIDROIT Conventions", *Uniform Law Review* 1997, p. 451.

prepared by the European Bank for Reconstruction and Development, and the (preliminary) draft UNIDROIT Convention on International Interests in Mobile Equipment.[6]

## II. Obstacles to Progress

There is little doubt that the harmonisation of the law governing the proprietary aspects of dealings in movables is a great deal more complex than that of the law relating to the contractual aspects. There are several reasons for this.

In the first place, the range of harmonisation techniques is more restricted in the field of property law than in the field of contract. Leaving aside consumer protection legislation, contract law is founded on the principle of party autonomy. This allows parties the freedom to subject themselves to institutional rules and contract forms, such as those of domestic and international markets or the rules of the International Chamber of Commerce relating to documentary credits and demand guarantees. It also enables arbitrators in international commercial arbitration to resort to sources of law other than national legal systems, for example, scholarly "restatements" such as the Principles of International Commercial Contracts promulgated by UNIDROIT and the Principles of European Contract Law prepared by the Commission on European Contract Law. But property rights involve third parties and not infrequently State-backed systems for the registration of proprietary interests. Neither the parties to a contract nor arbitrators dealing with disputes between contracting parties have the power to make agreements or decisions affecting third-party rights or institutions established under public law. Accordingly, contract-based rules cannot operate in this field; only States or entities acting under powers delegated by States[7] have the ability to make legal instruments directly affecting property rights. It follows that of the numerous types of instrument available for the harmonisation of contract rights, only three are suited to the harmonisation of property rights, namely an international convention, a model law, and a law promulgated by the organs of a supranational body such as the European Union. Community law rules on private property rights have centred on intellectual property. It has been left to States to act directly to adopt harmonising measures in relation to dealings in other types of commercial asset, in particular goods and claims.

Secondly, there has been a reluctance to formulate rules which might be seen as encroaching on a State's bankruptcy policy. Property rights are of particular significance in a bankruptcy. Where all relevant parties are solvent, the role of property law is substantially diminished, since most of the desired effects can be achieved through the law of obligations. The common law trust of property is of significance

[6] See Roy GOODE, "Transcending the Boundaries of Earth and Space: The UNIDROIT Convention on International Interests in Mobile Equipment", *Uniform Law Review* 1998, p. 52; R.C.C. CUMING, "The Draft UNIDROIT Convention on International Interests in Mobile Equipment", 30 *UCC Law Journal*, p. 365; and Professor Cuming's background study "International Regulation of Aspects of Security Interests in Mobile Equipment", *Uniform Law Review* 1990–I, p. 63.

[7] This includes supranational entities such as the European Union.

primarily because of the protection it gives against the trustee's bankruptcy, in that the trust assets do not form part of the bankrupt's estate divisible among his creditors. In legal systems which do not recognise the trust, it would be possible to give broadly equivalent protection through a system of personal rights and remedies while the fiduciary is solvent coupled with a rule that in the event of his bankruptcy the property entrusted to him is ring-fenced from his creditors and is to be held for those who entrusted it.[8] Similarly, the denial of proprietary effect to an agreement for the assignment of future property would be of no great moment as long as the assignor were solvent and his contractual obligation to make over the property when acquired or its money value were enforceable against him by an order *in personam*. In the commercial world, ownership as such is less prized than among private citizens; what matters is recoverable value.[9] It is bankruptcy that provides the acid test of the efficacy of real rights in general and security interests in particular, and it is the protection of such rights from bankruptcy creditors that is a primary concern of the holders of such rights. It is paradoxical that the very event which should have been the driving force behind the move to harmonise property rights is that which until recently has been treated as off-limits in any harmonisation project.

Thirdly, there are profound philosophical differences between legal families, and even between legal systems in the same family, as to the extent to which real rights in general and security interests in particular should be encouraged, and these bring in their train differences in legal concepts and characterisations. Of all legal constructs property rights are the most particular to a given legal system. The harmonisation of laws governing the creation, perfection, and priority of real rights was thus perceived as an exceptionally daunting task.

The restrictive approach of civil law systems to the grant of security appears to have been motivated by three main concerns: the risk of fraud on creditors; the desire to avoid undue hardship for debtors; and the need to inhibit enforcement measures that might lead to a breach of public order.

## 1. Fraud on creditors

Both the common law and the civil law were concerned about the possibility of frauds on creditors. Hence the starting point for both legal families was hostility to non-possessory security rights. To allow a creditor to take security over goods while leaving the debtor in possession was to create the false impression among other creditors that the debtor was still the owner of the asset given in security. This "false wealth" doctrine required in principle that the creditor should take

[8] See "PM" [Paul Mousel] in (1996) 9 *Butterworths Journal of International Banking and Finance Law*, p. 410 at pp. 415–16. Of course, efficacy in a bankruptcy is not the whole story. Where a debtor defaults, the creditor will want to be able to take speedy remedial action. Enforcement of a security, particularly in legal systems allowing self-help, may be a quicker and more efficacious remedy than legal proceedings leading to a money judgment.

[9] It is assumed that the property is not required for use by the assignee in his business, in which case, of course, different considerations would apply. But in most transactions involving security (*e.g.* a mortgage or hypothecation) or quasi-security (*e.g.* sale under reservation of title) it is the debtor, not the creditor, who will be using the asset.

possession of the goods in order to perfect his security.[10] The doctrine was then applied by analogy in a number of legal systems to the assignment of claims. Such an assignment would be effective against third parties, including the assignor's general creditors, only after notification to the debtor. To common law eyes this requirement, which still applies in a number of civil law jurisdictions, seems strange. Notice is obviously required in order to bind the debtor, but why should it be necessary in order to make the assignment effective as between the assignor (and his trustee in bankruptcy) and the assignee? One answer to this was that actual possession was impossible in the case of intangibles and the giving of such notice was the nearest equivalent to possession. Another was that the notice constituted an overt act which would help to establish the existence of the assignment and preclude collusion between the assignor and the assignee in fabricating an instrument of assignment and giving it a false date. The same consideration influenced formal requirements such as the *date certaine* in French law, the authentication of a dated instrument by some legally approved method, such as registration, in order to make it effective against third parties, such as creditors in a bankruptcy.[11] A somewhat different concern was that one creditor might tie up the entirety of the debtor's assets, present and future. This could be avoided by the twin requirements of specificity—or individualisation of the items given in security—and the denial of proprietary effect to interests in future property in the absence of a separate post-acquisition act of transfer.

Fairness to general creditors might also lead to the adjustment of a particular creditor's real rights upon the debtor's bankruptcy—the very eventuality for which such rights were primarily designed.

## 2. Hardship to the debtor

By the same token, global security would bear harshly on the debtor, for what would be left to him as the means of subsistence? Accordingly, in various jurisdictions transactions that would have this effect were made invalid. Again, harsh contract terms or enforcement measures could be controlled, at least in some degree, by the prohibition of self-help remedies and the requirement of a court order to enforce a security.

## 3. Preservation of the peace

Certain forms of self-help, such as seizure of an asset given in security, were considered to risk a breach of the peace and thus constitute a threat to public order, another reason for barring self-help remedies and requiring creditors to resort to judicial procedures to enforce their rights.

10 However, rules in civil codes requiring possession were surmounted in some jurisdictions by invoking the concept of indirect, or mediate, possession (*constitutum possessorium*) by which the debtor could pledge an asset by agreeing to hold possession for his creditor. See, for example, s. 930 of the German BGB (Civil Code).

11 Code civil, art. 1328.

The cumulative effect of rules designed to meet these concerns was considerable. Had they been confined to the private transactions of individuals they could have been accommodated without too much difficulty. But as rules of general application governing commercial as well as private transactions they came increasingly to be seen as creating serious obstacles to business.[12] The introduction of systems for the registration of security interests in a public register provided a means of reconciling the needs of the secured creditor for a flexible form of non-possessory security with the needs of third parties for a means of acquiring knowledge of the secured creditor's interest, but in many jurisdictions such systems were either non-existent or incomplete.

It is fair to say that at one time the common law reflected the same concerns about real rights as those which continue to trouble the civilians. What changed the position in England and other parts of the British Commonwealth was the growth of secured lending to companies, which led to the development of highly flexible equitable proprietary rights (rights of a kind unknown to the civil law) and, later, a system of registration in a public register. Much later, the American states broke free from the shackles of the past by adopting Article 9 of the Uniform Commercial Code, an extremely innovative and successful synthesis of the previously different forms of personal property security, with the requirement of a public notice filing at the heart of its perfection and priority rules.[13]

## III. The Changing Scene

Over the past decade there has been a radical shift in thinking and renewed efforts have been made to introduce at least some measure of harmonisation into the legal treatment of real rights in commercial assets. Several factors appear to have contributed to this. At the domestic level, the World Bank has been urging on developing countries the economic importance of a sound system of security over movables. Countries which restrict chargeable assets to land, or to land and physical pledges of tangible movables, are likely to find that access to inward investment is limited and that economic growth is stultified by the reluctance of credit institutions to provide finance on an unsecured basis. Hence the Bank's concern to ensure, before releasing funds for development, that the country concerned has or will put in place an effective legal regime permitting non-possessory security in tangible and intangible movables. Hence also the importance of the EBRD's model law on secured transactions, the introduction to which neatly captures the significance of effective security rights.

> Secured transactions play a vital role in financing in emerging and transitional markets. Every commercial investor is interested in making a profit from his investment but in many cases

[12] See below, p. 75.

[13] We should also note the importance of the trust in commercial dealings. The trust, by which legal title to an asset is held by one person, the trustee, to manage on behalf of another, the beneficiary, has attracted growing interest in non-common law legal systems. It has been given a significant impetus by the 1986 Hague Convention on the law applicable to trusts and their recognition, though this is designed primarily for the traditional family trust rather than the commercial trust.

the first fundamental concern is to obtain protection against loss of the investment. A legal framework for secured transactions is a key requirement in creating an investor-friendly climate. An investor who knows that he has legally recognised rights to turn to his debtor's assets in case of non-payment may assess the investment risk quite differently. It may influence his decision whether to invest or not; it may also change the terms on which he is prepared to invest (typically by lowering the interest rate on a loan).[14]

At the international level, the growth of cross-border finance has made creditors acutely aware of the risks they face when dealing in assets based in a jurisdiction that is hostile to real rights, whether in its general law or in its bankruptcy legislation. These risks are particularly significant in transactions involving equipment of high unit value, such as ships and aircraft, or dealt with in large numbers at a time, such as containers, or involving global transfers, such as are entailed in receivables financing or in loans against international securities. Finally, the security of transactions has been profoundly influenced by political change, in particular from planned economies to market economies and from public ownership of industries to ownership by the private sector, in both cases leading to a shift from sovereign risk to enterprise risk.

These factors, and the ever-increasing pressure from banking and commercial interests to facilitate the grant of credit and the taking of security in cross-border transactions, have led country after country to review its laws governing interests in movables and to relax or sweep away principles of property law that had previously been regarded as fundamental.[15] Suddenly it was found that the world would not collapse if the rules requiring specificity in security agreements and precluding the grant of real rights in future property were jettisoned, and that global assignments, far from being oppressive to the debtor and unfair to general creditors, were a commercial necessity in modern business life. The introduction of public registration systems allowed non-possessory security interests to be taken while avoiding the false wealth problem.[16]

## IV. Surmounting the Problems of the Past

If it was a change of perception that led to a relaxation of the rules of national law concerning the grant of proprietary rights, the process at international level also drew on the lessons of the past. Several of the techniques used to address the concerns described earlier are not peculiar to property aspects but are particularly useful in relation to them.

[14] A recent economic impact study commissioned by the Aircraft Protocol Group engaged in work on the proposed aircraft equipment protocol to the UNIDROIT draft Convention on interests in mobile equipment, and conducted by Professors Saunders and Walter on behalf of INSEAD and the New York University Salomon Center, reached similar conclusions.

[15] See, for example, Guido FERRARINI, "Changes to Personal Property Security Law in Italy: A Comparative and Functional Approach", in *Making Commercial Law* (ed. Ross Cranston), Chapter 21.

[16] Lip-service was paid to the requirement of possession by treating registration as equivalent to possession. This explains why the civilians feel no difficulty in speaking of a pledge of non-documentary intangibles, a phenomenon unknown to the common law.

## 1. Restricting the scope of the work

Over the years many projects have foundered because they were overly ambitious and there was an inadequate appreciation of the need for a proper focus. In the preparation of a private law convention in international trade[17] three limitations on the scope of a project have been found helpful. The first is to confine the convention to commercial dealings. Private transactions are likely to be controlled locally by special consumer protection legislation, and the economic interests involved in such transactions will typically be relatively small.[18] So most of the modern commercial law conventions exclude consumer transactions. The second is to concentrate on a specific type of commercial dealing, selected for its importance in terms of the unit value of the subject-matter or the continuity of dealings involving property transfers. Examples are the 1988 UNIDROIT Conventions on International Factoring and International Financial Leasing, the draft UNCITRAL Convention on Assignments in Receivables Financing, and the draft UNIDROIT Convention on International Interests in Mobile Equipment. So the field of commercial property rights is carved up slice by slice like a salami, and when enough slices have been processed they can be reassembled to provide a corpus of law covering the field as a whole. The Factoring Convention was seen as a first step, on which the UNCITRAL draft Receivables Convention will build. The third limitation is to confine the convention to cross-border transactions. This is now standard. It reflects the view that States which are sensitive about interference with their legal policy in domestic transactions will be more responsive to instruments limited to international dealings, for which there is anyway a greater need for harmonisation.

Restrictions of the kind described above are not, of course, germane only to the property aspects of commercial dealings; they apply equally to the contractual aspects. But where property rights are involved it is particularly necessary to resist the temptation to expand the project beyond what is needed to achieve its objectives. Again, the draft Mobile Equipment Convention furnishes an illustration. This Convention is intended to facilitate security, conditional sale, and leasing agreements relating to equipment of high-unit value normally moving from one country to another in the course of business – for example, aircraft, space objects, oil rigs, railway rolling stock. It provides for a new form of international interest which can be created with relatively little formality and perfected by registration in a specially created international register. It also contains rules governing the priority of competing interests.[19] When the UNIDROIT Study Group first began work on the project, it envisaged an instrument that would reflect some of the key ideas in Article 9 of the American Uniform Commercial Code. In particular,

[17] Different considerations apply to a model law; and European Community law is, of course, a special case, being supranational and mandatory in character.

[18] This restriction is not without its disadvantages, as was pointed out by Professor GUTTERIDGE many years ago in his work *Comparative Law* at p. 158 *et seq*. While the force of these arguments must be admitted, the extension of conventions to domestic transactions would, in this sphere at least, pose insurmountable problems. It must be better to have a limited project which is adopted than a more comprehensive one which falls at the first fence.

[19] See below, p. 79.

transactions would be characterised on a functional, rather than a formal basis (so that, for example, a conditional sale agreement would be treated as a form of security agreement), registration would be against the name of the debtor and the security interest would extend to future property and to proceeds. But it became apparent at an early stage not only that such a project was altogether too ambitious but that it went well beyond the objectives conceived for it. To assimilate security, conditional sale and certain types of lease was too great a leap for systems outside North America, including other common law systems. The inclusion of rights to proceeds would take the Convention far outside interests in mobile equipment and into the realms of general receivables financing. This was not the objective and would bring the Convention into competition with UNIDROIT's own Convention on International Factoring and in possible conflict with the broader project for a Convention on the Assignment of Receivables in which UNCITRAL has been engaged for some years. So the decision was taken to change to an asset-based system of registration and, as a necessary corollary, to confine the Convention to interests in existing equipment capable of unique identification, and exclude altogether interests in proceeds other than insurance proceeds. This necessary step has kept the focus of the Convention on those issues which provided the motive power for the project in the first place.

## 2. Aiming for commercially desirable solutions

In other words, the dictates of doctrine should give way to the realities and needs of business life. It is commonly supposed that the aim of harmonisation is to make rules reflecting the lowest common denominator among legal systems. This is not the case. It is obvious that if a single set of rules is to be extracted from the divergent rules of national legal systems, changes in at least some national laws are inevitable, and changes in all of them highly probable. Indeed, even within a monolithic regime where a pure restatement might be possible, it would usually be undesirable, for it would simply perpetuate weaknesses in the existing law. Nor does the process of harmonisation involve simply the identification of factors common to the legal systems under review. If it did, then the formulation of uniform rules governing proprietary rights in commercial assets would indeed be a daunting task, for of all legal constructs the concept of property is the most specific to a given legal system. But the primary aim of those engaged in the scientific work is to produce a good product. While they will, of course, draw on their knowledge of comparative law and test formulations against the rules of their own legal systems, their task in the preparation of commercial law instruments is to provide rules which meet the legitimate concerns and expectations of the business community. This may lead to solutions which are not to be found in any legal system.

A good example, though not in the field of property rights, is furnished by the UNIDROIT Convention on International Financial Leasing. One of the problems addressed by that Convention was that in almost all legal systems the supplier's obligation to supply conforming goods is owed not to the lessee, by whom they are selected and to whom they are to be delivered, but to the lessor, who typically will have no involvement in the choice of the goods or the supplier and no control over the supplier's performance. The solution provided by the Convention was to cut through the legal formalism of the contractual relationships and to provide that in principle the lessor was not to be responsible for non-conformity of the goods, whilst the lessee would have a direct right of action against the supplier as if the lessee itself had been the buyer under the contract of sale.[20]

Once agreement has been reached on the results to be achieved, doctrinal differences between legal systems become of secondary importance and it will usually be possible to frame rules with which the various participants can feel comfortable even if these involve concepts unfamiliar to their particular legal systems or, indeed, to any legal system. The task is easier where, as in the case of the draft Convention on Mobile Equipment, a new type of interest is being fashioned as an international interest by the Convention itself, for since this does not derive from national law it need not carry with it the accumulated baggage of national law rules and concepts. Thus both the UNIDROIT Factoring Convention and the UNCITRAL draft Receivables Convention dispense with the requirement of specificity in assignments and allow an assignment of future receivables to take effect upon their acquisition without the need for any new act of transfer.[21]

## 3. Allowing a wide measure of party autonomy

Cross-border transactions in a particular sphere of business activity usually take place within the context of established market practice and of contract terms which contain a large amount of "boiler plate" clauses. Most modern commercial law conventions thus allow the parties, in the relations between themselves, a large measure of freedom to vary or exclude the convention provisions, while designating a small number of provisions as mandatory. It is not, of course, open to the parties to derogate from rights conferred on third parties. So in a convention dealing with real rights the power of derogation is necessarily confined to the relations between the grantor and the grantee of those rights, for example, as to additional conditions for the vesting of such rights in the grantee or as to the exercise of real remedies for default, such as a secured party's remedies of possession and sale of collateral in the event of the debtor's default. Even here, however, respect for national legal traditions means that some limits have to be set to party autonomy. There are different ways of doing this. One is to designate as mandatory those rules which are designed to provide essential rights or protections to a given party. Thus the UNIDROIT Leasing Convention limits the ability of a lessor to exclude the warranty of quiet possession[22] and renders ineffective a liquidated damages provision that would result in the lessor being substantially better off as the result of default than if the lessee had properly performed.[23] Similarly the UNIDROIT draft Mobile Equipment Convention

[20] Arts. 10, 12(5).

[21] Under the Factoring Convention, the receivables vest upon their coming into existence. Under the draft Receivables Convention, the vesting is retrospective to the time of assignment unless the parties have agreed to defer it to a later date.

[22] Art. 8(3).

[23] Art. 13(3)(b).

precludes forfeiture of an asset given in security without the consent of the court or the agreement of all interested parties. Another approach is to allow a contracting State to make a reservation excluding or modifying certain convention rules which its concepts of *ordre public* might make difficult to swallow. So the draft Mobile Equipment Convention enables a State which is opposed to self-help remedies to make a declaration requiring recourse to the court.[24]

## 4. Keeping the rules simple

Simplicity is, of course, a relative concept. Conventions are generally drafted with a broad brush, in the style of a European code rather than a statute, so that those not involved in the work will almost certainly need recourse to the *travaux préparatoires* not simply to catch the nuances of the drafting but even, on occasion, to acquire an understanding of the *raison d'être* of a particular provision. Rules in national legal systems governing property rights are usually detailed, subtle, and complex. In an international instrument it is better to have rules that are tough and simple than those which seek to do equity through a myriad of finely tuned detail. It is the fear of complexity that may in the past have deterred transnational commercial lawyers from tackling the proprietary aspects of commercial dealings. But if those engaged in the scientific work can liberate themselves from the detail of their own systems they will find it possible to come up with solutions of great simplicity.

Take, for example, the rules on the priority of competing interests. In any legal system priority rules are usually a nightmare; and the more voluminous and sophisticated the commercial activity, the greater the profusion of the rules. Article 9 of the American Uniform Commercial Code is admired the world over for its responsiveness to commercial needs and its preference for substance over form. But in the recently completed revision the priority rules, omitting Official Comments, run to 23 detailed sections occupying no fewer than 18 pages of typescript. This observation is not intended as a criticism. The rules have to encompass a wide variety of situations and to deal with them in a manner considered fair and equitable. However, in an international instrument focused on very specific types of transaction it is possible to adopt a broad-brush approach which dramatically reduces the detail.

A striking example is to be found in the priority rules of the UNIDROIT draft Convention on International Interests in Mobile Equipment. These appear in a single article consisting of five paragraphs. In the interests of simplicity a number of refinements found in national legal systems have been abandoned. Registered interests rank among themselves in order of registration and have priority over unregistered interests. A special rule is made in favour of outright buyers to reflect the fact that their interests are not registrable, so that they lack the means to protect themselves against subsequent interests. The priority rules, which may be varied by agreement, extend to insurance proceeds. A separate provision permits registration of a prospective international interest which, on coming into being and

[24] Art. Y(2) of the draft current in September 1998.

being registered as an actual interest, has effect from the time of registration of the prospective interest. And that, in substance, is the sum total of the rules! There are no provisions limiting the priority of future advances or giving special protection to purchase-money security interests; the integrity of the registration system is not diluted by rules subordinating the party who is the first to register to a prior interest of which that party had constructive notice or even actual knowledge. Earlier drafts containing provisions of these kinds were jettisoned because they were not only complex but in addressing one range of problems raised others which could be solved only by rules of still greater complexity.

Simplicity is one of the great merits of the EBRD Model Law on Secured Transactions, which is designed specifically for the needs of Central and Eastern European countries and provides a set of rules for the creation, attachment, and perfection of security interests which are drafted clearly and concisely and make no attempt to imitate the sophistication of rules in developed capitalist legal systems.[25]

## 5. Prescribing or deferring to a conflict rule

While the purpose of harmonisation is to avoid dependence on the conflict of laws, it is impossible to dispense with conflict rules altogether. There will always be issues not covered by the convention or ascertainable from the principles on which it is based; and even where a substantive convention provision on a particular topic might be expected, the differences in approach between legal systems might prevent agreement on the appropriate rule. In such cases it is preferable, where possible, for the convention itself to lay down a conflict rule. Where this is not possible, there is no alternative but to defer (expressly or by silence) to the applicable law under the *lex fori*. Thus in the UNIDROIT draft Mobile Equipment Convention the question whether an agreement is to be characterised as a security agreement, a title reservation agreement, or a leasing agreement is left to be determined by the applicable law under conflict of laws rules; and since in the United States and some Canadian provinces title conditional sales and certain types of leasing agreement are treated as security interests, it was also necessary to provide in the draft Convention that an interest constituting a security interest would not fall within either of the other two categories.

## 6. Recognising the limits of bankruptcy law

The reluctance to interfere with the policies of domestic bankruptcy law is understandable. But the role of bankruptcy law should not be exaggerated. Most bankruptcy laws take as their starting point a recognition of pre-bankruptcy entitlements under the applicable law. So convention rules which fix those entitlements and provide for their continued effectiveness in the event of the

[25] Remarkably, this project was completed in a mere 18 months by two experts, John L. Simpson and Jan-Hendrick M. Röver, aided by an Advisory Board and members of the Office of the General Counsel of the EBRD.

debtor's bankruptcy do not constitute any significant invasion of local bankruptcy policy, which typically is directed to questions such as the ranking of claims and the avoidance of unfair preferences and the like. This division between the recognition in bankruptcy of real rights established under the law of another State prior to the bankruptcy and the modification of those rights in accordance with the bankruptcy laws of the forum is a well-established feature of modern international instruments dealing with cross-border insolvency, such as the 1990 Istanbul Convention on Certain Aspects of International Bankruptcy, prepared by the Council of Europe, and the 1995 European Community Convention on Insolvency Proceedings.[26]

## V. The Way Ahead

There is little doubt that the drive towards harmonisation of the property aspects of commercial dealings will be intensified as comparative lawyers begin to focus on this field and expose the problems caused by outmoded property rules.[27] The UNIDROIT Conventions on International Factoring and International Financial Leasing are in place and simply await more widespread adoption. The EBRD Model Law, the UNCITRAL draft Receivables Financing Convention, and the UNIDROIT draft Mobile Equipment Convention are all ambitious and imaginative projects which, if successful, have the potential for significantly expanding the availability of credit in international trade and reducing the risk and cost of trade finance. If current efforts to provide an international regime for cross-border insolvency are successful, so that conventions emerge which provide for the mutual recognition of real rights created under the applicable law prior to bankruptcy, we can expect to see as great a consensus on the legal treatment of real rights in commercial transactions as has begun to emerge in the field of contractual rights. Property and bankruptcy will no longer be viewed as falling within the exclusive province of domestic law, and we shall have taken a further major step towards the progressive harmonisation of commercial law as we enter the third millennium.

[26] Signed by all the member States of the European Union except for the United Kingdom, which declined to do so as part of its then policy of non-co-operation in European Community matters because of what the U.K. Government saw as the intransigence of the Commission and other member States in resolving the dispute concerning BSE in British beef! The time for signature has now expired and other member States will need to give a fresh consent in order to bring the Convention into force.

[27] See, for example, the magisterial six-volume work by a leading English practising lawyer, Philip R. WOOD, *Law and Practice of International Finance*, London (1995).

# 6

# Insularity or Leadership? The Role of the United Kingdom in the Harmonisation of Commercial Law*

*Roy Goode*

## I. Introduction

THE last few decades have seen a substantial growth in what has become known as transnational commercial law, by which I mean that body of commercial law principles and rules, from whatever source, which is common to a number of legal systems. The various types of harmonisation fall broadly into four groups, each possessing its own implementing agency:

- Legislation—the task of governments and legislatures
- Judicial parallelism and judicial co-operation—the task of judges
- Business practices, codes, and model forms, including contractually incorporated uniform rules published by international bodies—the task of the international business community and its national and international organisations
- International restatements—the task of scholars.

In the limited space available I shall address only the first and last of these and confine myself to private, transactional law. I am not concerned here, except at the margins, with public law regulating transactions or institutions. My focus is the contribution to the development of transnational commercial law by United Kingdom judges, practising lawyers, businessmen, and legal scholars. My thesis is that we make a major input into the fashioning of international instruments of different kinds but all too often walk away from the finished product, so that if we adopt the instrument at all we come in very much later than our major competitors and lose the opportunity to give leadership to the international community and to gain the influence which that leadership would bring in its train. After explaining why

* Originally published as R Goode: "Insularity or leadership? The role of the United Kingdom in the harmonisation of commercial law" in (2001) 50 I.C.L.Q. 751–65.

I regard transnational commercial law as important in an era of globalisation I shall attempt to analyse the reasons for our failure to become more international in our approach to a legal regime for cross-border transactions, the consequences of that failure, and various ways in which we might restore the vision and influence which at the beginning of the century led to the adoption of UK commercial law statutes almost verbatim throughout the common law world.

## II. Harmonisation through Legislation

Harmonisation through legislation has two aspects. The first is the implementation of international instruments: the ratification of international conventions and the adoption, wholly or in part, of model laws. The second is the enactment of legislation which is domestic in character but which may nevertheless exert a two-way influence on transnational commercial law, because it draws on the laws of other countries and/or because it is itself used as a model or source of ideas by foreign governments and legislatures. This second aspect, which may be termed legislative parallelism, is often overlooked in discussions of transnational commercial law. It is, however, highly significant both for the improvement of our own law and for the exportability of our law to other countries, particularly developing countries and those that have moved or are in transition from a planned economy to a market economy, thereby extending the influence of the common law in general and English law in particular.

### A. International Conventions

#### *1. Why International Commercial Law Conventions are Important*

Those engaged in international commerce have become increasingly aware of the need to ensure that national laws are adequately adapted to the needs of global markets and cross-border transactions. The time has long passed when domestic legislation shaped for internal trade can provide sensible solutions to the problems of international commerce. Even within the field of contract law, where parties to an international agreement should be, and usually are, given a wide measure of freedom to make their own rules and choose their own law, there may be substantial advantages in uniform law within a restricted field. The parties are able to sing from the same hymn sheet, to become familiar with the text, to read it in their own language, and to reduce their dependency on local experts in every jurisdiction in which they transact business. Moreover, uniform rules provide a neutral legal regime for the many cases where the parties do not select the applicable law and, indeed, conclude their agreement informally—for example, on the telephone—and settle only the most essential terms. The success of the carriage of goods conventions provides a striking illustration of the advantages of uniform rules in cross-border commerce. So too does the Convention on Contracts for the International Sale of Goods.

In any event, the progressive move towards the globalisation of commerce and finance has resulted in a much greater awareness of the need to go beyond contractual relationships and to harmonise at least some of the rules relating to the acquisition and transfer of rights *in rem* in movable commercial assets, tangible or intangible, in order to enhance the security of transactions. Let us consider the following:

- Cross-border dealings in receivables, which may themselves be international in character
- The need for an adequate security regime to protect the financing of mobile equipment of high unit value
- The legal efficacy of cross-border settlement and payment system rules
- The creation and protection of ownership and security interests in pools of indirectly held investment securities which may involve an issuer and tiers of securities intermediaries, all in different countries
- The implications, yet to be worked out, of cross-border electronic commerce
- The growth of cross-border insolvency of multinational groups of enterprises.

These are matters which, in the light of the magnitude of the interests at stake, can no longer be left exclusively to individual national laws, though these will always retain a prominent role except, in the case of the European Union, where the field is occupied by European Community law. So the importance of harmonising at least some rules of substantive law by international convention should not be under-estimated. We are not here talking of a mere academic desire for a greater convergence of legal systems; we are talking of matters which industry, commerce, and banking regard as of immense importance to them.

Two illustrations will serve to underline this point. At a seminar in London to discuss a uniform conflict of laws rule to govern dealings in indirectly held investment securities we were told by a representative from one participant that systemic risk was a constant topic of discussion, there had been a drastic increase in the use of collateral, and the figures were in billions of dollars. The industry urgently needed a conflicts rule which adopted the place of the relevant intermediary approach (PRIMA). Moves are now under way both for a new European Directive and for a Hague Conference private international law convention on the subject. Happily, as I shall mention, the UK is playing a leading role in both of these initiatives, through the intensive efforts of two practitioners, Richard Potok (the driving force behind the project) and Guy Morton, and led on the government side by the Treasury.

My second example relates to certain types of mobile equipment of high unit value, notably aircraft, railway rolling stock, and space property. The financing of such equipment involves huge outlays. It is estimated that over the next 10 years more than 1,000 commercial satellites will be launched valued at $US 5 billion and that over the next 20 years expenditure on the financing of new aircraft alone will exceed $US 1 trillion. So security over the financed object is of crucial importance to the financier. But how do we protect security interests in objects that move daily from one country to another or, in the case of satellites, are not on earth at all? How do we ensure that an interest created under one legal regime will be recognised and enforced in others? The ambitious project initiated by UNIDROIT is the creation of an entirely new type of interest in such mobile equipment, an international security or title-retention interest which will be able to be created with very simple formalities, will confer on the secured party a range of essential default remedies, and will be perfected by entry in an international register, having priority over unregistered and subsequently registered interests in accordance with a short and simple set of priority rules. A study conducted under the auspices of INSEAD suggests that in relation to aircraft financing international acceptance of a legal regime of this kind, by increasing the security of aircraft receivables, could significantly raise their credit rating and reduce borrowing costs by as much several billion US dollars a year.[1] This important Convention, which in relation to aircraft is being co-sponsored by UNIDROIT and the International Civil Aviation Organization, is expected to be concluded at a Diplomatic Conference to be held in Cape Town at the end of October 2001.

## 2. *The Need for Limited Objectives*

Just as no one—at least, no one of sound mind—enters the academic world because of the pay, so also no one who has experience of the time, hard work, and sheer frustration involved in the preparation of instruments of harmonisation embarks lightly on a uniform law project. I am not one of those who believes that harmonisation is *per se* a good thing. Even if it were feasible (which plainly it is not) to harmonise all private law, whether at the international level or at the regional level—for example, within the European Community—I do not think it would be sensible to do so. In the European context Lord Goff has recently observed:

> We have today in Europe a whole range of legal cultures ... We should be profoundly grateful for this diversity. We can learn far more from these diverse systems than we could have ever have derived from a single monolithic regime.[2]

In his slim but classic work *Comparative Law,* that distinguished Cambridge scholar Professor Harold Gutteridge warned of the damages of over-ambition in the face of fierce loyalties to domestic law:

> The citizens of many countries are deeply attached to their national law; at one extreme we have, for instance, the Frenchman who carries in his pocket the *Code Civil,* the dog-eared leaves of which bear testimony to the frequency with which it is consulted, and, at the other end of the line, the Englishman who never looks at a law book but is nevertheless convinced that his common law is the quintessence of human wisdom and justice.[3]

[1] Anthony Saunders and Ingo Walter, *Proposed UNIDROIT Convention on International Interests in Mobile Equipment as applicable to Aircraft Equipment through the Aircraft Equipment Protocol: Economic Impact Assessment* (Sept. 1998) p. 32.

[2] 'Coming Together—The Future' in *The Clifford Chance Millennium Lectures,* B. S. Markesinis (ed) (Hart Publishing, 2000) at p. 239.

[3] *Comparative Law* (Cambridge University Press, 1949), pp. 157–8. It is not without interest that in the index to the English edition of a leading French textbook on international commercial arbitration the entry under '*Kompetenz-Kompetenz*' reads: 'see *Competence-Competence*'.

Yet Gutteridge remained firmly committed to the process of harmonisation. The point he was making was that it is necessary to be selective and to keep any harmonising project within manageable limits. During the last 25 years international organisations involved in the harmonisation of private law and private international law have become keenly aware of the need to proceed with circumspection, and in particular, not to embark on a project of harmonisation before satisfying themselves that the differences in national laws create a serious impediment to cross-border trade; to limit the scope of the project to what is both necessary and acceptable to States with widely differing legal philosophies; and to involve the relevant interest sectors not merely through consultation on a finished product but in the creation of the product itself.

## 3. *The Approach of the United Kingdom to the Harmonisation of Commercial Law*

Writing in 1949 Gutteridge observed that Great Britain's reputation for obstructing uniform law from selfish motives was undeserved and that with limited exceptions the movement for unification owed much to British initiative and collaboration. He instanced such unifying measures as the York-Antwerp Rules of General Average, the various Brussels Conventions on Maritime Law, the 1921 Hague Rules on the Liability of Shipowners, and the Foreign Judgments (Reciprocal Enforcement) Act 1933.

It remains the case that the United Kingdom makes a major contribution to the production of international instruments of various kinds. Our academic and practising lawyers, and lawyers and others in the civil service, participate prominently as chairpersons or members of study groups, working parties, and as rapporteurs; our government departments make an important input through the submission of papers, the organisation of seminars and conferences, and participation as members of UK delegations to diplomatic conferences; our national trade organisations contribute submissions through the international bodies of which they are members. And the UK is highly regarded for its commitment to support of the world's leading general harmonisation institutions, notably UNIDROIT, UNCITRAL, the Hague Conference, and the International Chamber of Commerce. But in the field of transnational commercial law our record of implementation has so far been rather dismal.

One could give a number of illustrations. The most striking is the inertia in regard to the 1980 UN Convention on Contracts for the International Sale of Goods (CISG). This is a major gap-filling convention consisting of some 101 Articles and dealing with the contractual (but not the property) aspects of sale. A number of its rules are undoubtedly better than those found in our own Sale of Goods Act, for example, the rule that risk passes with control (i.e. the delivery of actual or constructive possession) rather than with ownership, which is the rule in the Sale of Goods Act and which our courts in practice avoid by inferring a contrary intention on the part of the parties. Now the Convention offers no threat whatsoever to party autonomy. It is essentially a gap-filler designed to make provision where, as is not at all uncommon in international trade, the parties have failed to do so because their contract has been concluded informally on the telephone or on the basis of a brief description of the essential terms. The parties are free to exclude the convention almost in its entirety or to exclude or vary particular provisions, either directly or by selecting the domestic law of a particular country to govern their contract. The Convention has been ratified by no fewer than 57 States. They include virtually all our major competitors except Japan and India, the latter awaiting ratification by the UK. Government is not opposed to ratification of the convention; it is simply that it has not been found possible to provide legislative time. Now it is undoubtedly true that the volume and complexity of modern legislation are vastly greater than they were in Gutteridge's time. Even so, one has to say that the excuse of lack of parliamentary time begins to wear a little thin after 20 years!

Even where we do ratify a convention we can take an unconscionably long time to do it. One of the most successful international conventions of all time is the 1958 New York Convention on the Enforcement of Arbitral Awards, which 123 States have now adopted and which has made a huge contribution to the growth of international commercial arbitration. Now you might think that as one of the world's leading arbitration centres the United Kingdom would have been one of the first to ratify the New York Convention. In fact it took us no less than 17 years. Far from being the first we were 48th in line, coming in several years after most of our major competitors, including, this time, India. Happily we were not the last. Malta ratified the convention in September 2000, some 43 years after the event. So it's never too late to repent!

When we make such a major contribution to the fashioning of an international instrument, is it not sensible to adopt it and to give our courts the same opportunity as is eagerly seized by their counterparts from overseas to offer their own interpretative guidance which will then be available to courts and jurists in other jurisdictions? Would not this also have the effect of increasing still further the influence of English law and English courts?

### *4. Some Reasons for Non-Implementation of International Instruments*

Why does the UK find it so difficult to give leadership in the adoption of international instruments? Leaving aside sheer bloody-mindedness—as where the UK alone refused to sign the European Insolvency Proceedings Convention because of the row over BSE in British beef—the reasons appear to be a combination of policy considerations and perceived practical difficulties.

As regards policy, there are those who consider that English law in all its majesty is greatly superior to anything that could be devised at international level. For lawyers in this category the Sale of Goods Act is the quintessence of perfection, and the notion that we might benefit from CISG in any way at all is anathema. The fact is that our commercial law did once influence the whole of the common law world but our neglect to service it has cost us dear, as one common law country after another has abandoned the old UK legislation in favour of new enactments tailored to the needs of modern commerce. Allied to this notion of the superiority of English law is the implicit assumption that in an international contract it is English law that will be the governing law. But for every contract governed by English law there will be others governed by a foreign law in a contract of which the language or primary knowledge will not necessarily be English and which may be much less favourable to the English party than the rules of an international convention. Is there not merit in at least allowing UK parties to avail themselves, if they so wish, of rules designed specifically for international transactions and available in English language texts?

A further factor in the past has been the lack of industry pressure. It is naive to believe that the only relevant factor is the quality of the measure proposed. Faced with a crowded legislative timetable no government is likely to find time for a measure for which there is no pressure from at least one powerful interest group. Nowadays we recognise that it is crucial to secure the vigorous support of the relevant interest groups so that they in turn can put pressure on government and persuade Ministers that there really is a serious problem which the new measure will properly address. This involves raising the general level of interest and awareness. The Department of Trade and Industry's Business Law Unit here deserves an accolade for its hosting of several seminars to discuss the Leasing and Factoring Conventions and successive drafts of the UNIDROIT Mobile Equipment Convention.

Then there is the familiar problem of lack of parliamentary time, a problem that affects most, if not all, legislatures around the world. This affects our ability to implement domestic legislation as well as international conventions and I shall examine it in more detail in that context. Suffice it to say at this stage that the enactment of legislation as a prelude to ratification of an international instrument[4] can usually be expected to consume a quite short amount of time. The normal practice is to annex the text of the convention as a schedule to the Bill. No line-by-line analysis is involved, because apart from reservations permitted by the convention (which in modern conventions are usually the only reservations allowed) it cannot be changed; it must be enacted as it stands or not at all. This makes the inability to find time for the Vienna Sales Convention all the more mystifying.

But perhaps the most potent factor of all is that apart from the valiant work of the Law Commission we have long ago ceased to take an interest in servicing even our own general law. The Victorians had the foresight to expend large amounts of time, energy and money in providing an infrastructure that would last 100 years. We do not have this vision. Our commercial legislation, like our water pipes, our railways, and our underground, suffers from underinvestment and patchwork adjustments which in the end cost more than if we had done a proper job. It is therefore scarcely surprising that we are so inert when it comes to adopting international instruments.

[4] This article is concerned with private commercial law conventions which are intended to confer rights and duties within the UK and thus have to be carried into effect in the UK by legislation. Ratification is invariably deferred until after such legislation in order to avoid the risk of the Bill not being passed, resulting in the UK government being in breach of its international obligations, and takes effect at the same time as the Act comes into force. There are, of course, international treaties which are intended to take effect solely in international law. These do not require legislation but UK constitutional practice as crystallised by the 1924 Ponsonby Rule is to lay before both Houses of Parliament for a period of 21 days after signature and before ratification every treaty which is not intended to be enacted or dealt with under some alternative parliamentary procedure.

This is, I believe, a matter of the utmost gravity, and I shall say more about it when I come to discuss ideas for a UK commercial code.

## B. Model Laws

Just a brief word about model laws—instruments that will not in themselves acquire legal force at international level but are available to be adopted by States if and to the extent that they desire to do so. A good example in the field of commercial law is the UNCITRAL Model Law on International Commercial Arbitration. The initial response to this from the DTI Advisory Committee on Arbitration Law (DAC) in its 1989 Report was decidedly lukewarm. A new Arbitration Act was certainly needed. No doubt the Model Law provisions should be adopted where possible; but while the Model Law was good enough for countries whose arbitration law was relatively undeveloped—which included Scotland—it did not appear to have a great deal to offer the English. In those early days we were still wedded to concepts that had long been discarded in continental Europe: the dependence of the arbitration clause on the validity of the underlying agreement; the application of English rules of evidence and English conflict of laws rules in an English arbitration; and, of course, the vital importance of judicial review of arbitral awards. But by the time the DAC came to issue its final consultation paper six years later its views had undergone something of a sea-change. On the majority of issues where English law had been felt superior to the Model Law, it now fell into line. The resulting Arbitration Act 1996, drafted with admirable clarity and precision by Mr. Geoffrey Sellers, does, indeed, embody much of the philosophy of the Model Law.

But what is particularly significant about the Arbitration Act is that, lacking government interest, it started as a purely private enterprise in which one of our leading arbitrators, Mr. Arthur Marriott, persuaded private organisations and individuals to contribute funds for the preparation of an unofficial Bill, which was in due course produced. Eventually the DTI agreed to take over the Bill and the result was the excellent product we have today. But we might not have had it at all if there had been no private initiative. Is this the way to carry our commercial law forward? Perhaps it is!

## C. Legislative Parallelism

As I have previously explained, even domestic legislation has the potential to contribute to the harmonisation of commercial law, by a process of borrowing and lending. A proper reform of our commercial law requires a careful study of developments in other jurisdictions, both civil law and common law, though naturally in the field of commercial law America has pride of place. Where we borrow concepts from others we contribute to the harmonisation process, even if only at the level of ideas and concepts rather than detail. By the same token, if we frame a commercial law statute which is responsive to the needs of modern commerce, including cross-border commerce, then we have an exportable product which will help to spread the influence of English law and resort by foreign lawyers to English academic and practising lawyers.

The sad fact is that we no longer take seriously the review and reform of our commercial law; minor tinkering is all we seem able to achieve. Almost every statute governing commercial transactions is in substance, and in most cases in form, well over a century old. Instances are the Bills of Sale Acts 1878–91, the Bills of Exchange Act 1882, the Factors Act 1889, and the Sale of Goods Act, which though dated 1979 is not substantially changed from the Sale of Goods Act 1893. So we find ourselves in the twenty-first century with legislation enacted in the nineteenth—a shocking indictment of our approach to the modernisation of our law.

In the field of commercial law we seem to be particularly resistant to legislative change except at the margins. Successive governments have largely opted out of the field, leaving it to the courts to fill the vacuum. Our judges do a splendid job, but even though we now recognise that judges do not merely declare law, they also create it, there is a clear limit to what can be achieved through the common law, particularly where it is encumbered by archaic statutes. Our law of personal property security remains rooted in 19th century concepts and legislation despite the fact that no fewer than three official reports—the Crowther Report on Consumer Credit in 1971, the Cork Insolvency Law Review in 1982, and the Diamond Report on Security Interests in Property 1988—recommended the adoption of a functional approach to personal property security law along the lines of Article 9 of the American Uniform Commercial Code.

Again, the review of company law, which was launched in 1998 as a project designed to provide a strategic framework for a modern company law, seems to have moved away from its stated purpose and to have focused on a series of smaller and detailed changes which, though useful in themselves, do not represent a fundamental review starting from first principles. Nevertheless the Final Report, *Modern Company Law*, shows a welcome awareness of the wider issues arising from the review and includes a recommendation that the question of security interests in personal property should be referred to the Law Commission for a deeper study. The American experience over decades is that by simplifying and modernising commercial law, costs can be significantly reduced and business procedures streamlined.

There are other, equally pressing, concerns. A leading international financial lawyer, Mr. Hugh Pigott, in an article focusing attention on a marked increase in the cross-border use of securities as collateral, has noted the lack of legal certainty in identifying which laws apply to which parts of a transaction.

This lack of legal certainty is compounded by the fact that the laws of the Member States of the European Union relating to the use of collateral are in many cases complex, inconsistent, and impractical. The resulting uncertainties seriously impede the efficient use of collateral. This in turn restricts access to financial services and raises costs.[5]

[5] Hugh S. Pigott, 'Steps Towards the Harmonisation of Collateral Law in Europe' (2000) JIBFL 347.

In March of this year the Collateral Law Reform Group of the International Swaps and Derivatives Association published a report identifying the main legal impediments to the efficient use of collateral and urging, not an international convention, but a reform of national laws so as to embody certain key principles that would result in practical harmonisation across Europe—in other words, convergence through legislative parallelism. This is a warning call we simply cannot afford to ignore.

The fault does not lie with the civil service, which, though labouring under huge pressures exacerbated by years of diminution, neglect, and denigration, tries very hard to ensure that our law keeps abreast of developments. But it is, perhaps excessively, constrained in its thinking by the difficulties of securing a slot in the legislative timetable. In any event, there are certain fields of law which are best reviewed outside government, whether by a departmental committee or Royal Commission, the Law Commission, or some other expert group. Government departments are at their best in tackling issues high in political content. But the review and reform of technical general law are matters for outside specialists, working in extensive consultation with the various interest sectors and, of course, with participation from them and from the relevant government departments. Only the outsiders have the knowledge, experience, and time to undertake the work and to review developments in other countries and lessons to be learned from these.

The fundamental problem is that our parliamentary machinery is wholly inadequate for the needs of modern commerce. It is this fact above all that has inhibited a more broad-brush approach by government and the Law Commissions. The concerns I have expressed are echoed, in the field of company law, in a thoughtful and imaginative report by the Law Society's Company Law Committee, *The Reform of Company Law,* published in February 2000 and endorsed by the Law Reform Committee of the Bar Council. That report repeated criticisms expressed by the committee nine years previously that company law reform was failing because of inadequate resource, inadequate consultation, lack of political commitment to make Parliamentary time available, and a Parliamentary process which was no longer delivering sound technical legislation, so that recommendations in reports of the highest quality from bodies such as the Law Commission remained unimplemented. It also stressed the need for regular review of the state of company law, saying that 38 years (the period since the Jenkins Report) was too long, particularly when change in the business sector is more rapid than was previously the case. Every word of this excellent report is equally true of commercial law; and if 38 years is too long to wait for a new review, what are we to say of our commercial law, which has not been the subject of review for over a century?

The only reason our commercial law continues to enjoy regard, both here and abroad, is because of the quality of our judges, their sensitivity to legitimate commercial needs, and their receptiveness to new legal instruments and concepts fashioned to serve those needs. As an American professor once remarked to Lord Wilberforce:

> The elegance, style and analytical powers of the British legal community have survived the decline of the British Empire intact.

The combination of well-informed judges and generations of textbook writers has masked the fragmentation, obscurity, and inaccessibility of our commercial law. These deficiencies are not always evident to judges, for by the time they come to hear a difficult case a great deal of work will have been done by counsel and solicitors for all parties, so that the facts are winnowed, the relevant issues identified and sharply defined, and the case cogently presented. But the cost of the legal research involved in the preparatory process and of taking complex issues of law through the hierarchy of courts must run to tens of millions of pounds *every year*—and that is only the cost of the lawyers, not the value of the time of their clients or the cost of impediments to legitimate business.

Hence the proposal which I have ventured to put into play for a United Kingdom commercial code. Now let me be clear about what is envisaged. It is not the codification of our entire commercial law. In his lecture at the British Academy in November 2000 the Lord Chancellor, Lord Irvine, observed that no code can be entirely comprehensive.[6] I entirely agree. To seek to codify the whole of commercial law would be a preposterous undertaking. It would not even be sensible to cover all the main types of commercial contract. In fact, the code can literally be restricted to a handful of topics where review and, if appropriate, reform are really necessary. So I see no reason to include a treatment of negotiable instruments other than those issued on a market as investment securities. The Bills of Exchange Act is not perfect but nowadays creates few problems. For the same reason paper-based payment systems do not need to feature in a commercial code, nor do documentary credits or demand guarantees, which are perfectly well covered by contractual incorporation of uniform rules published by the International Chamber of Commerce. Again, there is no need to deal with marine or even nonmarine insurance or with carriage of goods. In fact, the great bulk of the work of our specialist Commercial Court can be readily handled within our existing law.

What, then, does qualify for inclusion in a commercial code? First, a few general principles relevant to commercial contracts, including electronic commerce. Then, the sale of goods, which is the central commercial contract. Sir Mackenzie Chalmers' Sale of Goods Act was a brilliant codification but now needs updating. After all, what was enacted in the nineteenth century is scarcely likely to be adequate for the twenty-first. Professor Hugh Beale, a Law Commissioner, has identified in a very preliminary study at least 28 matters which call for reconsideration. I have already referred to the state of our personal property security law, which is a disgrace. We urgently need a modern law covering dealings in investment securities, including market-responsive rules governing indirectly held securities and their use as collateral, along the lines of Article 8 of the Uniform Commercial Code, and a statement of the principles and rules governing electronic funds transfers, which involve the turnover of vast sums every night. Finally, there is much to be said for a restatement of the law relating to suretyship guarantees, which even if generally satisfactory is hard to access.

6 'The Law: An Engine for Trade', a lecture delivered at the British Academy on 22 Nov. 2000.

A code has several advantages over ordinary legislation. It gathers together in one place the main principles and rules in the selected field. It is prepared by or in collaboration with experts in that field, who, free from the pressures imposed on parliamentary draftsmen in the preparation of ordinary legislation, can take the time to consult practitioners in the field, to examine developments in other jurisdictions and to produce a structured text in plain English and logical sequence. An excellent modern example is the Arbitration Act 1996, where parliamentary draftsmen worked in close collaboration with the Chairman and members of the DAC to produce a text which is widely admired for its clarity as well as its content. The Act does not attempt to codify the whole of English arbitration law. It focuses on those principles and rules which are central to arbitration, leaving leeway for the courts to accommodate the Act to new developments. As Lord Wilberforce pointed out many years ago when speaking to the Law Commissions Bill, codification is not the enemy of the development of the common law but rather its enhancer.

> . . . by presenting to the courts legislation drafted in a simple way by definitions and principles we may restore to the judges what they may have lost for many years, to their great regret, the task of interpreting law according to statements of principle, rather than by painfully hacking their way through the jungle of detailed and intricate legislation. So I believe that a process of codification, intelligently carried out, will revive the spirit of the Common Law rather than militate against it.[7]

Lord Wilberforce went on to describe the export value of a code:

> As our friends the French know very well indeed, and apply in practice, legal institutions and legal ideas are a cement of great value in holding together the exporting country and the other countries in pursuit of common values.[8]

In 2000 the Department of Trade and Industry kindly hosted a seminar to test the response to the idea of a commercial code. Of the 60 people who attended, including academic and practising lawyers, representatives of banks and multinational companies, all who spoke strongly supported the code and not one participant dissented. Moreover, there was a clear consensus in favour of legislation, not merely a kind of Highway Code, which it was thought would simply add another layer of uncertainty. The Law Commission has indicated its willingness, subject to the Lord Chancellor's approval, to examine two topics in detail over a two-year period. It is hoped that the DTI will be the sponsoring department and provide the additional resources needed. It is envisaged that the project will be in the nature of a public-private partnership in which the professionals will play an active role. Professor Christian von Bar, who is directing the European civil code project, has indicated that a UK commercial code could exercise considerable influence in the development of commercial law in continental Europe. So it is doubly important for this project to proceed.

[7] HL Deb 1964–5, vol 264, cols 1175–6. [8] Ibid.

## III. Harmonisation through International Restatements

This brings me to the last of my topics, harmonisation not through any normative instrument but through 'restatements' by international groups of scholars. Two of these have attained particular prominence: the UNIDROIT Principles of International Commercial Contracts and the Principles of European Contract Law produced by a private group, the Commission on European Contract Law. These sets of principles are not, of course, restatements, for since national laws differ from one to another they necessarily change at least some of the rules in each of the legal systems represented. The search was not for the lowest common denominator but rather for best solutions to typical problems. The impact of the two sets of Principles has exceeded the wildest expectations of their progenitors, particularly in the field of international commercial arbitration. They demonstrate the immense persuasive power of rules produced by groups of independent scholars of international repute which are non-normative and therefore pose no threat to national law but are available as a resource to courts, arbitral tribunals, and legislators. Even more striking is the fact that all the participants were satisfied that for the most part the Principles reflected rules already embodied in their own legal systems.

Plainly the Principles, which are the product of extensive debate on policy issues, concepts, and technical considerations, should feature significantly in university student texts and contract courses. Unhappily in England, at any rate, they do not. Most of our contract textbooks make no mention of them at all. Nor, with a very limited number of exceptions, do the Principles appear to feature in undergraduate or postgraduate courses. This is a reflection of a wider problem, namely the inadequate, though gradually increasing, attention to comparative law in our law schools. All this is a pity, because quite apart from exposing our students to ways of thinking that in some respects are different from our own, discussion of other systems and other rules helps us to see more clearly the characteristics of our own legal system. Where we do find prominence and support given to the Principles of European Contract Law is not in the student textbook but in an essay contributed by the then Lord Chief Justice and current Senior Law Lord, Lord Bingham, in his important contribution to the Clifford Chance Millennium Lectures.[9]

## IV. The Way Ahead

In the light of this rather lamentable state of affairs in our commercial law, what is to be done? First, we need to become much more aware of the benefits to be derived from implementation of international instruments to the preparation of which we contribute so much. Secondly, we need to take the servicing of our own commercial law much more seriously than we have until now, recognising that a good modern

[9] 'A New Common Law for Europe' in *The Clifford Chance Millennium Lectures*, B. S. Markesinis (ed) 27.

code which focuses on those aspects of commercial life crucial to the smooth functioning of business and markets can not only produce better results but also save a huge expenditure of time and money currently devoted to ascertaining the law and, in addition, provide us with a product which we can export to other countries. In this task the members of the Commercial Bar Association, with their long expertise in handling commercial disputes, can play an invaluable role.

Thirdly, we in the law schools must engage the interest of our students in international instruments relevant to their fields of study in domestic law, so that they can see how there may be several ways of tackling a common problem and can have a keener appreciation of the characteristics of their own law. There are welcome indications that this is now beginning to happen.

Finally, there is an urgent need to review our parliamentary procedure in order to find time to implement international commercial law instruments with which we are in sympathy and to provide the framework of a modern commercial law. One way is to reduce not only the volume but also the complexity of modern legislation. Is it really necessary to add several hundred pages of text to our tax law every year? Should we be so preoccupied with trying to cover every eventuality and stop up every loophole? And could we not have a mechanism by which a Bill that is technical rather than political and has secured a consensus within the sectors affected can be presented to Parliament to approve the principles on which it is based and then amended as necessary and brought into force by statutory instrument? This was one of the many useful proposals advanced by the Law Society's Company Law Committee in the report to which I have previously referred. Such a procedure would enable us to simplify and modernise our commercial law and to make it accessible and exportable and worthy of a country whose capital is the world's leading financial centre.

This article is an updated version of a lecture given on 30 November 2000 (the COMBAR Lecture).

Emeritus Professor of Law, University of Oxford.

# 7

# The Treatment of Intangible Assets Under the Cape Town Convention and Protocols*

*Roy Goode*†

*The Cape Town Convention and its associated Protocols are primarily concerned with the protection of interests in tangible movables, namely aircraft objects, railway rolling stock, and space assets. However, these instruments also contain important provisions on intangible assets related to such objects; indeed, in relation to space assets such rights, in the form of obligations owed to the debtor by third parties ('debtor's rights') and assigned to the creditor as additional security are potentially more valuable as collateral than the space asset itself. Yet national laws are ill-equipped to deal with such assignments in an international setting, since not only do they vary from country to country but there are fundamental disagreements as to the appropriate choice of law rule. This article analyses the complex provisions of the Convention and Space Protocol concerning the protection of dealings in intangible assets. Roy Goode acted as Rapporteur at the diplomatic Conference in Berlin in 2012 to adopt the Space Protocol. His Official Commentary on the Convention and Space Protocol was published by UNIDROIT in May 2013 and the third edition of his Official Commentary on the Convention and Aircraft Protocol in July 2013.*

## 1. Introduction

The Convention on International Interests in Mobile Equipment, adopted in Cape Town in November 2001 and generally known as the Cape Town Convention, has three sets of rules affecting intangible assets:

(1) Rules governing interests in proceeds of objects to the extent that they take the form of intangibles—discussed in Section 2.

* Originally published as R Goode: "The treatment of intangible assets under the Cape Town Convention and Protocols", Cape Town Convention Journal Volume 2, 2013—Issue 1.

† Professor Sir Roy Goode QC is Emeritus Professor of Law in the University of Oxford and Emeritus Fellow of St John's College, Oxford.

(2) Rules governing the assignment of associated rights or their acquisition by subrogation—discussed in Section 3.

(3) Rules regarding the exercise of remedies relating to intangibles, examined in Section 4.

To these sets of rules the Space Protocol adds a fourth, namely rules relating to the assignment and reassignment of debtor's rights and the recording of such assignment and reassignments. These are examined in Section 5.

## 2. Claims to Intangible Proceeds

Article 2(5) provides that an international interest in an object[1] extends to proceeds of that object, while under Article 29(6) any priority given to an interest by Article 29 extends to proceeds. But proceeds are narrowly defined, being limited to money or non-money proceeds of an object arising from its total or partial loss or destruction or its total or partial confiscation, condemnation, or requisition.[2] So the term does not extend to general proceeds, such as receivables arising from sale of an object which is governed by an international interest, for this would take the Convention outside its primary focus, physical objects, and could lead to the application of the Convention to proceeds having no continuing linkage with the object from which they were derived. Proceeds as so defined will almost always take the form of a money payment that will end up in the creditor's bank account and will thus constitute a claim against the bank. So if insurance proceeds are paid into the debtor's bank account the creditor's international interest extends to the claim on the bank and enjoys the same priority as in relation to the original object. However, even if the creditor holds the senior interest its right to the proceeds is not absolute. In particular, any right of setoff the bank may have under the applicable law is not controlled by Article 29, and the creditor will therefore take subject to the right of set-off if the applicable law so provides.

## 3. The Assignment of Associated Rights; Subrogation

### The nature of associated rights

Associated rights are all rights to payment or other performance by a debtor under an agreement[3] which are secured by or associated with the object.[4] Rights are 'secured by' a security agreement or 'associated with' a title reservation or leasing agreement.

[1] An international interest is an interest granted in an object (i.e. an aircraft object, railway rolling stock, or a space asset) which is uniquely identifiable, the interest being granted by the chargor under a security agreement or vested in a person who is the conditional seller under a title reservation agreement or the lessor under a leasing agreement (Articles 1(o) and 2).

[2] Article 1(w).

[3] That is, a security agreement, a title reservation agreement, or a leasing agreement (Article 1(a)).

[4] Article 1(c).

Included among associated rights are the right to repayment of a secured loan, instalments of a purchase price, and lease rentals, as well as rights to non-monetary performance, such as repair, insurance, and the observance of negative obligations, including a prohibition against sale or lease of the object. Obligations of the debtor under other contracts with the creditor are not associated rights, even if secured by the agreement, unless the debtor also undertakes in the agreement itself to perform such obligations. Similarly obligations of third parties to the creditor, whether under the agreement or some other contract, are not associated rights in the hands of the creditor unless the debtor too undertakes performance in the agreement. The Convention rules cover the effects of assignment, the formalities for assignment, the position of the debtor vis-à-vis the assignee, and the priority of assignments.[5]

## Debtor's consent

Under national laws an assignment does not usually require the consent of the debtor, and the Convention takes the same approach, but to avoid disputes as to the efficacy of an assignment the Aircraft and Space Protocols require that the debtor consent to the assignment, though such consent may be given in advance and may be general in nature.[6]

## The tail wags the dog

The treatment of associated rights is in some respects confusing. This results from the fact that while earlier drafts of the Convention provided that the effect of an assignment of an interest was to transfer the associated rights as well, an approach supported by several commentators,[7] conceptual purity was allowed to take precedence over observance of the fundamental purpose of the Convention, which is to protect international interests in physical assets, not to promote receivables financing as such. The logical course would have been to provide for the assignment of international interests and the registration of such assignments, coupled with a provision that an assignment of the international interest would carry with it the associated rights.

But purists objected that this contravened a basic principle that a security interest was an accessory to the obligation secured, not the other way round.[8] So we ended up with a situation in which the focus of Chapter IX of the Convention is the assignment of associated rights, which are intangibles and as such are not capable of

[5] The formalities (Article 32) and the default remedies of the assignee in the event of default by the assignor track those laid down for international interests in Articles 7 and Chapter III of the Convention respectively.

[6] Aircraft Protocol, Article XV; Space Protocol, Article XXIV. No such requirement is contained in the Luxembourg Protocol.

[7] See, for example, the comment on what was then Article 31 by the International Bar Association Sub-Committee E8 on International Financial Law Reform, reproduced in the Acts and Proceedings of the diplomatic Conference, page 112. See also pages 20, 54, 83, 163 of the Acts and Proceedings.

[8] See Acts and Proceedings, pages 839, 880.

independent registration, while the assignment of the related international interest is left trailing in the wake of the intangible.[9]

There is little doubt that the result has been to make the provisions more complex than they should have been. It became necessary to include provisions as to the effect of assignment of associated rights independently of the related international interest—which are rightly taken outside the Convention—and of the assignment of an international interest independently of the related associated rights. The drafting itself slipped into references to a registered assignment of associated rights when in fact these are incapable of registration, despite the oddity of Article 16(2), which refers inappropriately to associated rights. Indeed 'assignment' is defined as an assignment of associated rights; nothing is said about the international interest. These problems could have been avoided by a simple provision that the assignment of an international interest carried with it the associated rights. Instead, we have exactly the reverse. Fortunately, with proper interpretative techniques the provisions work out surprisingly well. While Part 3 is devoted to remedies these are not couched in terms of enforcement of associated rights; indeed, these are dealt with only in the provisions on assignment and subrogation and, in the Protocols, on choice of law, though not there referred to as associated rights.

## 'Assignment'

This is defined as 'a contract which, whether by way of security or otherwise, confers on the assignee associated rights with or without a transfer of the related international interest.'[10] So any conferment of associated rights by the creditor on a third party by agreement falls within the definition, whether it is absolute or by way of security and whether it takes the form of an assignment (in the sense of a transfer) or a charge, that is, a mere encumbrance not involving any transfer. It is usually clear whether a transaction is an assignment, but it is necessary to distinguish it from a novation, that is, a new agreement in which a new creditor is substituted for the old. This contrasts with an assignment, where the assignor-creditor remains in a contractual relationship with the debtor, whilst the assignee has no such relationship, incurs no positive obligations under the agreement and merely has a right to enforce the associated rights, subject to available defences and rights of setoff. Whether a transaction is an assignment or a novation is to be determined by reference to the Convention itself, not the applicable law.

There are hybrid transactions in which the creditor assigns its rights and also, with the consent of the debtor, transfers its obligations, wholly or in part, to another party. Such a transaction may be characterised as a novation under the applicable law but for the purposes of the Convention, which is concerned only with the transfer of the benefit of the associated rights, it is an assignment.

[9] An intermediate draft had provided that an assignment of the international interest would transfer the associated rights and an assignment of the associated rights would transfer the international interest, but this was not adopted.

[10] Article 1(b).

## Categories of assignment of associated rights

Chapter IX of the Convention deals with two entirely distinct categories of assignment which attract different priority rules.[11] The first concerns the assignment of different sets of associated rights related to different international interests held by different creditors in the same object, as where the debtor grants an international interest to A and B in succession, A assigns its rights to X and B assigns its rights to Y. Priority issues arising from this type of assignment are governed by Article 31(1)(b). The second concerns successive assignments of the same associated rights related to a single international interest to different assignees. The priority of these competing assignments is governed by Articles 35 and 36. The two sets of priority rules are discussed below.

## Assignment of unregistered international interest

An assignment can be taken of an unregistered international interest and the assignment can be registered and enforced against the debtor but the assignee will lose out to the holder of a subsequently registered international interest or that holder's assignee and creditors in the debtor's insolvency.[12]

## Splitting the associated rights from the related international interest

Provided that the relative simple formalities for assignment are complied with[13] an assignment of associated rights, unless otherwise agreed, also transfers to the assignee the related international interest and all the rights and priorities of the assignor under the Convention.[14] The priorities referred to are those of the international interest vis-à-vis other interests under the priority rules in Article 29, whether or not such other interests are themselves international interests. An assignment of associated rights does not, however, carry the international interest if the parties otherwise agree or if the formal requirements laid down by Article 32(1) are not complied with. In either such case the Convention is inapplicable to the assignment of the associated rights,[15] the effect of which is in general governed by the applicable law, though the Convention priority rules apply to the extent of subordinating such assignment to an assignment which is effective to transfer the international interest where the latter assignment is registered.[16] By contrast a purported assignment of an international interest created or provided for by a security agreement is not valid unless some or all related associated rights are also

[11] See below, p. 102. [12] Article 29(1). [13] See Article 32. [14] Article 31(1).

[15] Article 32(3).

[16] Article 35(1). The fact that an interest is not one to which the Convention applies does not mean that it is unaffected by the Convention, only that the interest does not qualify for protection under the Convention. So Article 29(1) provides that a registered interest (i.e. an interest registered under the Convention) has priority over an unregistered interest, and this is so even if the latter is incapable of registration because it is outside the scope of the Convention. The same rule applies to an assignment (Article 35(1)).

assigned.[17] The reason is that a security interest which does not secure any obligations of the debtor to the secured party is without content. This principle does not apply to an international interest held by a seller or lessor, who could in theory transfer title to the object without assigning the associated rights to the transferee but this would be of little value to the transferee unless the debtor defaulted, enabling the object to be repossessed.

## Competing assignments derived from different international interests

Suppose that Debtor grants A an international interest, which is registered, after which Debtor grants B an international interest, which is also registered, and that B then assigns its associated rights and related international interest to Y,[18] who registers the assignment, after which A assigns its associated rights and the related international interest to X, who registers it. In this case the competition is not between the successive assignments but between the assigned international interests. Accordingly X has priority by virtue of the priority of the international interest acquired from A as the first to register,[19] and this despite the fact that the assignment to B was taken and registered first. The same principle applies if one of the two international interests is unregistered.

## Competing assignments derived from the same international interest

In this scenario Debtor grants A an international interest, which is registered, after which A assigns its associated rights and the related international interest, first, to X, and, secondly, to Y, who registers the assignment in its favour before the assignment to X has been registered. Here there is no competing international interest; the competition is between the assignments and priority goes to Y as the first to register.[20] However, this is subject to two important qualifications.[21] First, the contract under which the associated rights arise must state that they are secured by

[17] Article 32(2).

[18] So long as the assignment of the associated rights conforms to Article 32 it is not necessary for the assignment to refer to the related international interest, which will pass automatically under Article 31(1).

[19] Article 29(1). Though in general registration is confined to consensual interests, Article 40 empowers a Contracting State by declaration deposited with the Depositary (UNIDROIT) to list the categories of nonconsensual right or interest which are to be registrable under the Convention as if these were international interests. Most States have made a declaration under Article 40, typically covering judgments or orders permitting attachment of equipment covered by the relevant Protocol and State liens for taxes or unpaid charges.

[20] Article 35, which applies the first-to-register rule in Article 29(1). For an analysis of the drafting deficiencies in Article 35 see the writer's *Official Commentary on the Convention on International Interests in Mobile Equipment and Protocol thereto on Matters Specific to Aircraft Objects* (3rd edition, 2013, UNIDROIT) ('Official Commentary'), paras 2.202(2) and 4.252.

[21] Article 35(1). However, if neither assignment had included the international interest (either because it was excluded by the agreement of the parties or because the formalities of Article 32 had not been complied with) Article 35 would not apply, there being nothing to register.

or associated with the object.[22] This requirement is aimed at an agreement under which the debtor has an obligation to perform not only the obligations under that agreement but also those incurred to the creditor under any other contract. The latter obligations become part of the associated rights under the original agreement and are secured by that agreement but if the later contract contained no reference to security an assignee of that contract would have no way of knowing that the obligations of the debtor under that contract were secured. So the first creditor's priority is dependent on the later contract stating that the associated rights are secured by the object. Secondly, the priority applies only to the extent that the associated rights are related to an object[23] in one of the ways specified in Article 36(2)—broadly where the associated rights represent payment of the price of the object, the advance of a loan for the purchase of the object (or in some cases the purchase of another object), the rental of an object or other obligations arising from the agreement and related to the object, such as maintenance, repair and insurance. The reason for this is that the Convention is not concerned to regulate priorities between general receivables financiers. The priority between two assignees of non-object-related associated rights is governed not by the Convention but by the applicable law.

### Acquisition of rights by subrogation

Nothing in the Convention affects the acquisition of associated rights and the related international insurance by legal or contractual subrogation under the applicable law.[24] Typical cases are where a surety discharges the debt of the principal debtor and becomes subrogated to the creditor's securities or an insurer pays out a claim to its insured for loss or damage caused by a third party and becomes subrogated to the insured's claim against the third party. There seems no reason why in a Contracting State rights of subrogation under the Convention itself[25] should not fall within Article 38 as being part of the applicable law.

## 4. Remedies Relating to Intangibles

The provisions of the Convention confer remedies on chargees and assignees which include rights to intangible property and the ability to earn intangible property. Leaving aside sale of a charged object, which is a one-off transaction, Article 8(1) empowers a chargee, on default by the chargor and to the extent that the chargor has at any time so agreed, to grant a lease of the charged object and/or to collect or receive any income or profits arising from its management or use.[26] Alternatively the chargee

[22] Article 36(1)(a). [23] Article 36(1)(b). [24] Article 38.

[25] Under Article 9(4) any 'interested person' (as defined by Article 1(m) of the Convention) other than the debtor who discharges a security interest by paying the creditor in full becomes subrogated to the rights of the chargee.

[26] Article 8(1). For a detailed analysis of Article 8 see the Official Commentary, Goode (n 20) paras 2.84 *et seq.*, 4.78 *et seq.*

can apply for a court order directing any of such acts.[27] Where the chargor has itself granted a lease or sub-lease of the object the creditor can take over the chargor's right to rentals under the lease or sub-lease lease and give notice to the lessee or sub-lessee to pay the rentals to the chargee instead of to the chargor. The creditor can also recover from the chargor any rentals collected by the chargor after the chargee has given notice of its intention to collect such rentals. Similar remedies are conferred on an assignee of associated rights against the assignor under a security assignment.[28]

## 5. Assignments and Reassignments of Debtor's Rights

The most innovative of the provisions relating to dealings in intangible property are to be found not in the Convention but in the Space Protocol. Though the Convention is primarily concerned with asset-based finance, the practical difficulties of enforcing an international interest against an asset in outer space severely limit the value of the physical asset. Potentially more valuable to the creditor is the revenue stream accruing to the debtor from its claims against third parties ('debtor's rights') arising, for example, from the grant of leases and licences of space assets, which the debtor then assigns to the creditor as additional collateral under a 'rights assignment.' So space financing is regarded as more in the nature of project finance than asset-based finance. There is no problem about making a rights assignment enforceable as between the parties and as against the (account) debtor. The key question that arose was how to protect the priority of the assignee under a rights assignment. The original proposal was to treat the rights assignment as if it were itself an international interest and to register it accordingly. That was rightly rejected as running counter to the central pillar of the Convention, namely to protect interests in uniquely identifiable physical assets. To allow independent registration of rights assignments would be to extend the Convention to general receivables financing, for which there was already a separate convention,[29] and to apply it to intangibles which were in no sense uniquely identifiable.

The neat solution was to require a right assignment in favour of a creditor to identify both the debtor's rights and the space asset to which those rights relate,[30] thereby linking the rights assignment to an international interest concurrently or previously granted to the creditor, and to provide for the assignment to be recorded against registration of the international interest. This, of course, presupposes that the international interest has been registered. This linkage of the rights assignment to an international interest in the International Registry is fundamental to the priority of the rights assignment, for it enables third parties, by searching against the space asset in the International Registry, to discover the recording of the rights assignment, which would have been impossible if rights assignments had been made registrable in isolation from the international interest. For example, the debtor gives a security interest over a satellite to the creditor and, at the same time or subsequently, assigns debtor's

[27] Article 8(2). [28] Article 34.

[29] The United Nations Convention on the Assignment of Receivables in International Trade, 2001.

[30] Space Protocol, Article IX.

rights to the creditor, who registers the international interest and, upon taking the rights assignment, records it against registration of the international interest, with the priority effects described below. The Protocol extends the provisions on rights assignments to cover onward assignment ('rights reassignments') by the creditor to a new assignee. The link between the rights assignment and the registered international interest must be maintained. Accordingly discharge of the registration of the international interest also discharges any recording forming part of that registration.[31]

The provisions relating to the assignment of debtor's rights constitute a most valuable element in space financing, because the assignment of receivables and other debts is one of the most complex areas of law on which national legal systems differ to the point where there is not even an agreed conflict of laws rule to determine the applicable law. So in the context of assignments linked to a space asset the Protocol brings certainty to an area hitherto bedevilled by insecurity.

## Debtor's rights

These are defined as 'rights to payment or other performance due or to become due to a debtor by another person with respect to a space asset.'[32] The definition is very wide, covering not only the debtor's contractual rights against third parties but other sources of rights relating to a space asset, including claims in tort and unjust enrichment, rights derived from assignment or subrogation and even government licences to the extent that these are capable of transfer. Moreover, it is not necessary that the space asset should be in existence at the time the rights arise. So debtor's rights include the rights of the debtor under a contract for the manufacture and sale of a space asset or as operator under a contract with a services provider or as customer under a contract for the provision of ground services relating to an existing or projected space asset, as well as the debtor's rights as 'lessor' under a lease capacity agreement[33] or indefeasible right of use, any intellectual property rights it may have been granted, and its rights as insured under a contract of insurance covering the space asset. But the rights must relate to a space asset, whether in regard to its construction, purchase, launch, or operation. Sums due to the debtor in respect of loans advanced or goods or services supplied which are unconnected to the space asset are not debtor's rights and are incapable of being recorded against the registration of the international interest.

## Rights assignment

This is defined by Article I(2)(h) of the Protocol as:

a contract by which the debtor confers on the creditor an interest (including an ownership interest) in or over the whole or part of existing or future debtor's rights to secure

[31] Article XII(5). [32] Article I(2)(a).

[33] It is not usual for space assets such as transponders to be leased. Instead, the 'lessee' enters into a 'lease capacity agreement' giving it an exclusive or limited access to transponder bandwidth. Such an agreement is not a true lease, the rights of the 'lessee' under it are purely contractual and the 'lessor' does not hold an international interest.

the performance of, or in reduction or discharge of, any existing or future obligation of the debtor to the creditor which under the agreement creating or providing for the international interest is secured by or associated with the space asset to which the agreement relates.

It will be seen that the definition does not cover all assignments, only those typically effected pursuant to a debtor-creditor relationship, namely assignments by way of security and outright assignments in reduction or discharge of the debtor's obligations to the creditor. So the sale of debtor's rights falls outside the definition. This is a necessary limitation because otherwise there could be a situation in which the obligations secured by the international interest were discharged but the creditor would continue to hold the assigned rights as security for other obligations, so that the linkage with the space asset giving rise to the assigned rights would be lost.

## Effects of a rights assignment

A rights assignment made in conformity with Article IX[34] transfers to the creditor the debtor's rights the subject of the assignment to the extent permitted by the applicable law.[35] This may raise questions as to the validity of the assignment where, for example, the assigned rights arise under a contract prohibiting assignment. The effectiveness of the assignment is not dependent on registration of the international interest or on the recording of the assignment against that registration, these being required solely to preserve the priority of the assignment. So the assignment is effective on its own as between the parties and against the debtor. The obligor (i.e. the debtor's debtor) then comes under an obligation to make payment or give other performance to the creditor if, though only if, the obligor has been given notice of the rights assignment in writing by or with the authority of the debtor and the notice identifies the debtor's rights.[36] The applicable law determines the defences and rights of set-off available to the obligor against the creditor.[37] Future debtor's rights may also be assigned and take effect when they come into existence.[38]

## Recording of the rights assignment

The holder of an international interest or prospective international interest in a space asset who has acquired an interest in or over debtor's rights under a rights assignment or by subrogation may, when registering the international interest or prospective international interest or subsequently by amendment to such registration, record

[34] Which requires that the debtor's rights and the space asset to which they relate be identified and, in the case of a rights assignment by way of security, that the obligations secured by the agreement be determined but without the need to state a sum or maximum sum secured.

[35] Article X. [36] Article XIV(1). [37] Article X(2).

[38] Article XI, which is taken from Article 5(b) of the UNIDROIT Convention on International Factoring, 1988.

the rights assignment or acquisition by subrogation.[39] However, where what has been registered is only a prospective international interest the rights assignment will be treated as unrecorded until the international interest comes into existence, in which case the rights assignment has priority as from the time it was recorded so long as the registration of the prospective international interest was still current immediately before the international interest was constituted.[40] This tracks the provisions of Article 19(4) of the Convention as to the deemed time of registration of an international interest into which a prospective international interest has ripened. The recording need not specify the assigned rights individually. It could be expressed to cover all the debtor's rights but if it relates to only some of them they will need to be identifiable.

## Priority of rights assignment

Rights assignments[41] have priority over any other transfer of debtor's rights (whether or not a rights assignment) except a rights assignment previously recorded.[42] Priority is thus determined according to the date of recording, not according to the date of registration of the international interest against which the recording is made. So if an international interest in a space asset is granted to A and registered and is followed by registration of an interest in the same space asset in favour of B, who takes and records an assignment of debtor's rights before A has recorded a similar assignment, B, though holding the junior international interest, has priority over A as to the debtor's rights. Where the competing assignment is not accompanied by a grant of an international interest in the asset itself the creditor/assignee will be subordinated to a creditor/assignee who has also taken and registered an international interest in the space asset and recorded its assignment against the registration, and this despite the fact that the other creditor, having no international interest, had no means of recording the assignment in its favour. For example, creditor A takes from the debtor an assignment of rental payable to the debtor under lease capacity but does not negotiate the grant of an international interest. Subsequently creditor B takes an international interest and a rights assignment, registers the international interest and records the assignment. Creditor B has priority. This is deliberate policy. Since the assignment to creditor A does not feature in the register creditor B had no means of knowing of its existence. Moreover, a prudent creditor will not take an assignment of revenue derived from an asset without taking an interest in the asset itself, for its right to the revenue is lost once the debtor loses control to another creditor. Where the revenues assigned do not relate to the space asset at all the assignment is not a rights assignment and is incapable of protection under the Protocol.

The priority rules are qualified in one important respect. Among the rights that may be assigned under a rights assignment are the debtor's rights under a policy of

[39] Article X. [40] Article XIII(2).

[41] In what follows this should be taken to include rights acquired by subrogation.

[42] Article XIII(1), which follows *mutatis mutandis* Article 29(1) of the Convention as to the priority of a registered international interest.

insurance covering loss of or damage to the space asset. But the creditor's priority in respect of its international interest applies also to insurance proceeds,[43] and the creditor may be in a better position relying on this priority than if it claims in its capacity of assignee under a rights assignment.

## Rights reassignment

A rights reassignment can take one of two forms. The first, as the label suggests, is a contract by which the creditor transfers to the assignee, or an assignee transfers to a subsequent assignee, the whole or part of its rights and interest under a rights assignment.[44] The second is where a rights assignment has been recorded as part of the registration of an international interest which is subsequently transferred in accordance with Articles 31 and 32 of the Convention.[45] This operates as an automatic reassignment of debtor's rights[46] without the need of any contractual assignment, and carries with it the right to be shown in the record as assignee under the rights assignment,[47] which in this context means the rights reassignee under the rights reassignment.[48] This form of reassignment has more powerful effects than an assignment under Article X in that the reassignment is not controlled by the applicable law.

A reassignee, whether under Article X or under Article XII(4), can record the rights reassignment, though only as part of the registration of the assignment of the international interest to the person to whom the rights reassignment was made.[49] So a reassignee who does not also acquire the related international interest cannot record the reassignment. This is in line with the policy that an assignment or reassignment cannot be recorded in isolation but must always be linked to the international interest to which the assigned rights relate.

[43] Article 29(6). [44] Article I(2)(i)(i). [45] Articles I(2)(i)(ii), XII(4).
[46] It therefore more properly belongs to Article XV than to Article XII.
[47] Article XII(4)(b). [48] Article XV(1). [49] Article XV(2).

# 8

# From Acorn to Oak Tree: The Development of the Cape Town Convention and Protocols*

*Roy Goode*†

The preparation of any international uniform law is a long and arduous business. The Cape Town project began as a relatively modest venture on a proposal made in June 1988 by Mr T.B. Smith QC, the Canadian member of the UNIDROIT Governing Council, to build on the *UNIDROIT Convention on International Financial Leasing*, which had been adopted the same year, and prepare an instrument focused on mobile equipment but otherwise broader in scope than the Leasing Convention. The new instrument would deal with security interests in mobile equipment, covering not only security in the traditional sense but also the interests of conditional sellers and lessors.

Now experience over the years has shown the vital importance of establishing three key factors before embarking on a project of uniform law. First, is there a problem? That may seem an obvious question but I can recall the time when UNIDROIT was very much influenced by academics—which, of course, is an excellent thing, there can never be too many academics—and the Governing Council had on its work programme a large range of projects most of which had appeared in the programme because a member of the Governing Council had had a bright idea! The existence of a problem was assumed to arise simply from differences in national laws. That rather happy-go-lucky approach was long ago abandoned, and the Governing Council will not approve a project unless at least three questions receive a satisfactory answer: is

* Originally published as Roy Goode: "From Acorn to Oak Tree: the Development of the Cape Town Convention and Protocols". *Uniform Law Review* (2012) 17 (4): 599–607.

† Emeritus Professor of Law in the University of Oxford and Emeritus Fellow of St John's College, Oxford (United Kingdom). The writer was Chairman of the UNIDROIT Study Group that developed the text of the Convention and subsequently chaired the Drafting Committee at the diplomatic Conference in Cape Town in 2001 and served as Rapporteur at the diplomatic Conference in Luxembourg in 2007 which adopted the Luxembourg Protocol on railway rolling stock and the diplomatic Conference in Berlin in 2012 which adopted the Space Protocol. His Official Commentary on the Convention and Space Protocol, together with a new edition of the Official Commentary on the Convention and earlier Protocols, is due to be published in the first half of 2013. This article is a revised and updated version of the author's contribution to the international seminar held at the seat of UNIDROIT in Rome on 30 November 2011 to commemorate the 10th anniversary of the adoption of the Cape Town Convention and Aircraft Protocol.

there a problem? is there a feasible solution? and is the project likely to receive a substantial measure of support not only from governments but from industry and other interested sectors?

This was where Professor Ron Cuming of the University of Saskatchewan came in. An international expert on secured transactions, Professor Cuming sent a letter to academic experts in 11 different countries setting out the possible parameters of the project and a set of assumptions which his enquiry to the experts was designed to test. This was followed by a detailed study[1] which, from the responses received, showed that there were indeed serious problems in the taking of security over mobile equipment and that it was desirable to have an international Convention to address these.

However, Professor Cuming was careful to point out that he had not had the time to undertake empirical research. Accordingly, a questionnaire was sent out by UNIDROIT to approximately 1,000 business and financial institutions designed to elicit the requisite empirical information. The responses indicated that from the perspective of legal practitioners and industry interests there were indeed a range of quite serious problems in the financing of mobile equipment such as aircraft objects, railway rolling stock, and space assets for the resolution of which an international Convention was desirable.

The most serious problem concerned the international protection of security and related interests in mobile equipment. A security interest may be effective for this purpose if perfected under its law of origin but this is no guarantee that its efficacy will be recognised in other jurisdictions. The widely adopted conflict of laws rule is that property rights in tangible movables are governed by the *lex rei sitae*, or, as we would say in England, *lex situs*. (It will be noted that English Latin is different from European and even Scottish Latin. We are very fond of Latin in the English legal world; we put things into Latin when they are too banal to say in English.) So we looked at the *lex rei sitae* but fairly quickly concluded that it was not well suited to equipment that has no fixed *situs*, for example, aircraft flying from one jurisdiction to another in the course of its daily life or railway rolling stock crossing national boundaries every day. Nor does it work for space assets, for when in outer space these are not within the territorial boundaries of any jurisdiction. Not so long ago there was a case in New York[2] involving half a billion dollars of collateral, including satellites in outer space, and the secured creditor's claim to priority was met by unsecured creditors with the argument that in the absence of any law governing priorities of assets in space there was no basis for giving priority to a secured creditor over an unsecured creditor. Everyone was flummoxed by the question how to determine the applicable law and in the end the case was settled, though there were other factors involved. It was stated in one of the filed documents that the problems created by the issue of the applicable law would have been avoided if the Space Protocol had been in place.

[1] R.C.C. CUMING, International Regulation of Aspects of Security Interests in Mobile Equipment (UNIDROIT Study LXXI – Doc. 1, December 1989).

[2] *In Re ProtoStar Ltd.*, Case No. 09-12659 (MFW), US Bankruptcy Court for the District of Delaware.

Then there were problems about default remedies. A secured creditor[3] might find that while the laws of his own country provided a range of effective and efficient remedies for default, the laws of other jurisdictions in which the creditor might wish to take enforcement action could be strongly debtor-oriented, and even a successful outcome might take months, or even years, to achieve. That, indeed, was a factor strongly influencing the question whether institutions in a particular jurisdiction could get access to credit at all and, if they could, whether it would be available at a reasonable cost. An international regime providing strong creditor protection could thus increase the availability of credit and reduce its cost.

So there was clear support for a uniform law project. Even so, we proceeded cautiously. A restricted exploratory group was set up which would take as its starting point a rule of recognition as regards the validity of security interests but would formulate substantive priority rules. A broad view was to be taken of the concept of security, embracing not only security in the traditional sense but also sales under reservation of title and leases. The group concluded that the project was both useful and feasible. It favoured the creation of a *sui generis* international interest derived from the Convention itself and constituting a right *in rem*. If this were found not to be feasible there should be a rule of recognition of a security interest created either under the law of the nationality registration of the equipment (as for aircraft) or under the law of the debtor's principal place of business. The Convention should include some basic default remedies and priority rules.

The Governing Council then established a Study Group to carry the project forward. The group appointed a two-person sub-committee consisting of Professor Hervé Synvet of the University of Paris II and myself to produce an initial draft of a few key aspects of the proposed Convention, namely the sphere of application, the creation of a new international interest, the establishment of an international register, and the recognition of international interests in mobile equipment created under the Convention. We were quite proud of the succinctness of our draft, which sought to cover these basic issues in a mere five articles! That has become my definition of an optimist! We were not to know that, as the range of issues to be considered multiplied exponentially, we would end up with a Convention of 62 articles and an Aircraft Protocol of a further 77 articles—99 articles in total.

## The Project Develops

As so often happens, the project started with one vision and ended up with something radically different and altogether more ambitious. The conflict of laws approach was abandoned and the decision taken to proceed with provisions for the creation of an international interest in mobile equipment derived solely from the Convention, not from national law. The categories of equipment to be covered were narrowed to three: aircraft objects, railway rolling stock, and

[3] For brevity, "secured creditor" is used throughout to include a conditional seller and a lessor.

space assets. Ships were excluded because of a perception (or as I subsequently concluded, a misconception) that these were already catered for by existing Conventions, though in respect of consensual security interests all of these were confined to rules of recognition and none of them had been very successful.[4] The generic concept of a security interest was quickly abandoned in the light of opposition and instead three separate categories of international interest were specified, namely a security interest, the interest vested in a conditional seller, and the interest vested in a lessor. What was originally planned as a debtor-based registration system was replaced by an asset-based system requiring, for the purposes of registration, unique identifiability of the object. Provision was made for the protection of non-consensual rights or interests without registration pursuant to a Contracting State's declaration. Registrable interests were extended to include prospective international interests, registrable non-consensual rights or interests (again pursuant to a declaration), assignments and prospective assignments of international interests, acquisitions of international interests by legal or contractual subrogation, notices of national interests for internal transactions, and subordinations.

With these extensions it soon became clear that the problems were formidable. Prior international commercial law instruments had steered clear of what were regarded as taboo subjects: property rights, priority rules, rules affecting insolvency law in some degree. Now we were proposing to invade all these areas and, to that end, not only to create a brand-new type of interest but also to establish an international registry for its protection. Even definitions presented a problem. How to define an aircraft? an aircraft engine? How to deal with the concepts of internationality and mobility (interestingly, the Convention is entirely silent on these two issues, treating them as inherent in the categories of equipment covered).

What transformed the entire process was the involvement of Airbus Industrie and The Boeing Company, which together established the Aviation Working Group under the leadership of Jeffrey Wool, a specialist aviation finance lawyer who had already been engaged as consultant to UNIDROIT. The AWG, which is now a semi-permanent organisation and a great driving force in the project, began to come up with a series of papers, including detailed drafts, which were of inestimable value. Even so, some of the nuts were hard to crack. The aviation industry spent six months working out definitions of aircraft objects and aircraft engines and even then did not get it right the first time. Then default remedies had to be fashioned, provisions devised for the International Registry and priorities. In fact, the priority rules governing international interests are remarkably simple and are all gathered together in a single article, Article 29. The drafters eschewed the complexity of national laws and went for simplicity. More complex are the priority rules governing assignments of associated rights, that is, rights to payment or other performance under the security, etc., agreement. The rules for the International Registry proved to be complex. There had

[4] See R. GOODE, "Battening Down Your Security Interests: How the Shipping Industry Can Benefit from the UNIDROIT Convention on International Interests in Mobile Equipment", the 1999 *Donald O'May Lecture, Lloyd's Maritime and Commercial Law Quarterly* (2000), 161–91.

to be provisions for a Supervisory Authority to control the International Registry, the immunity of the Supervisory Authority, the liability of the registrar (strict), and provisions for insurance.

The next question arose from the fact that work on aircraft objects, railway rolling stock, and space assets was proceeding under different working groups operating at different speeds. How, for example, was the work on aircraft objects to avoid being held up pending progress with railway rolling stock and space assets? That was where Lorne Clark, General Counsel of the International Air Transport Association (IATA), came up with a brilliant solution. Why not adopt a two-instrument approach: a framework Convention which would apply to all three categories of assets without differentiation and then separate Protocols for each category of asset, which would, unusually, control the Convention, adapting it to the needs of the particular industry sector affected, while allowing each group to proceed at its own pace. Interestingly, this proved quite controversial. There were those who argued for a series of stand-alone Conventions, and the argument was so fierce that it was only on the first day of the diplomatic Conference in Cape Town that opponents of the two-instrument approach finally bowed to the will of the vast majority of delegates speaking on the issue. The advantages are manifest: a single Convention allowing of uniform interpretation of provisions not specific to a particular category of equipment, as opposed to a series of Conventions drafted by different hands; a text not cluttered by detailed technical definitions of the assets covered or the varying requirements of the different sector; and the avoidance of the need for two, or even three, diplomatic Conferences or alternatively one enormous Conference lasting for several weeks.

In collaboration with the AWG UNIDROIT advanced the project through the Study Group and various specialist groups, in particular an Insolvency Working Group, a Public International Law Working Group and an International Registry Task Force. Meanwhile UNIDROIT had been joined by IATA and finally, as co-sponsor of the project and co-organiser of the diplomatic Conference, by the International Civil Aviation Organization. Innovative features were added: a system of declarations which enabled States for whom a particular provision might run counter to its basic legal philosophy to opt into or opt out of the provision; a new default remedy of de-registration and export of aircraft; an extension of the Convention registration and priority rules to cover outright sales of aircraft objects and, later, of space assets. The AWG, IATA, and ICAO also commissioned an economic impact assessment from INSEAD in Paris and the New York University Salomon Center, and the resulting report estimated that on conservative assumptions the economic gains that could be expected to result from the Convention and Aircraft Protocol would run to several billion U.S. dollars a year and would be widely shared among airlines and manufacturers, their employees, suppliers, shareholders, and customers, and the national economies in which they are located.[5]

[5] A. SAUNDERS and I. WALTER, *Proposed UNIDROIT Convention on International Interests in Mobile Equipment as applicable to aircraft equipment through the Aircraft Equipment Protocol: Economic Impact Assessment* (September 1998).

Two further developments resulted from the diplomatic Conference. First, the Conference passed a resolution requesting the Chairman of the Drafting Committee to prepare an Official Commentary in collaboration with the two Secretariats, Chairmen of Conference committees, and participating governments and observer organisations. The unique feature here was that instead of an Explanatory Report submitted for approval by the diplomatic Conference, which would be the normal procedure, the Official Commentary was to be prepared afterwards and the text prepared and finalised in the light of comments received. This had two great advantages. In the first place, it enabled the preparation of a much fuller and more well-informed commentary than would have been possible for a text prepared in advance. Next, if similar Official Commentaries were called for by resolutions of subsequent diplomatic Conferences (as proved to be the case at both the Luxembourg and the Berlin conferences on railway rolling stock and space assets respectively) then these could reflect new knowledge and thinking and allow the prior Official Commentaries to be revised so as to align the three texts.[6]

The second development was that UNIDROIT for the first time assumed the unique role of Depositary of instruments of ratification and the like, a particularly arduous role because of the complex system of declarations but one which it has performed to perfection.

There is no question that this vast effort has been crowned with success. We now have a Convention and Protocols for all three categories of object.[7] The Convention itself has been ratified by 51 States plus the European Community (now the European Union) and the Aircraft Protocol by 45 States plus the European Community. In the United Kingdom the Minister for Business and Enterprise has publicly announced that the UK Government is committed to ratification of the Cape Town Convention and Aircraft Protocol, subject to some more work on costs and benefits, the aim being to complete the process as soon as possible. It is expected that a final decision will have been announced by the time this article appears. A positive statement may encourage other European States to ratify. Australia has now announced its intention to ratify.

What are the lessons to be learned from the Cape Town experience? First, the effort involved is very substantial and should never be under-estimated. If we had known at the outset the prodigious labours that would be entailed we probably would never have embarked on the project in the first place. However, the other side of the coin is that if a uniform law project is really important it can be made to happen through a combination of expertise and sheer determination. The UNIDROIT Secretariat played a pivotal role in carrying the project forward and

[6] The Official Commentary on the Convention and Space Protocol will be published in the first half of 2013; the third edition of the Official Commentary on the Aircraft Protocol and the second edition of the Official Commentary on the Convention and Luxembourg Protocol have been prepared and await only the formal approval by the Council of ICAO of new regulations for the aircraft registry, to which the regulations for the registry of railway rolling stock will be closely tied. These Official Commentaries will be published towards the end of 2013.

[7] The Luxembourg Protocol, relating to railway rolling stock, was adopted in Luxembourg in February 2007; the Space Protocol in Berlin in March 2012.

working indefatigably towards its conclusion. Secondly, it is critically important to involve industry experts, and building up their support, from the very outset. It would not have been possible to bring such a major project to fruition without the active participation of the various industry sectors affected, as well as government and academic experts, and bodies such as the AWG and IATA and, of course, the co-sponsor, ICAO. Thirdly, it is often assumed that the work has been completed with the adoption of the relevant international instrument and that it will secure ratification by its own self-evident quality. That is far from the case. Adoption is merely the halfway point. What is then needed is a major campaign for ratification and its implementation in domestic legislation where ratification is not self-executing. Here again, the AWG has played a major role, presenting the case for ratification to governments around the world and offering advice and assistance as to the form of ratification. Finally, I have come to realise over the years that a project is unlikely to make progress unless there is a single individual external to the Secretariat acting as a driving force to harness support and input, working with the Secretariat. In the case of Cape Town the driving force has been Jeffrey Wool, the Secretary-General of the AWG, who has worked tirelessly to bring all this about. Without his labours and his negotiating skills I doubt whether we could ever have brought this project to fruition. He has also been responsible for setting up the Cape Town Academic Project, a collaboration between the law schools of Oxford University and the University of Washington, with the co-operation of UNIDROIT and ICAO. The Project has four limbs: an annual conference devoted to Cape Town; an annual electronic Cape Town Convention Journal; a comprehensive database of Cape Town materials held at the two law schools, with an on-line reporting system; and the collation of materials on the teaching of the Cape Town Convention, whether on its own or as a component of courses on transnational commercial law, comparative law, and the like.

Within UNIDROIT's dedicated Secretariat I should like to pay particular tribute to the former Deputy Secretary-General, Martin Stanford, who has recently retired from UNIDROIT after more than 40 years of devoted service and who played a crucial role in the development of the Cape Town Convention from start to finish.

It would not be right to end without paying tribute to the Government of South Africa. The three-week diplomatic Conference in Cape Town to adopt the Convention was, to the best of my knowledge, the first diplomatic Conference ever to have been held in the African continent. Not only was it superbly organised but the hospitality was overwhelming, generating a convivial atmosphere that significantly contributed to the success of the Conference. So, *floreat* Cape Town!

# 9

# The Priority Rules under the Cape Town Convention and Protocols*

*Roy Goode*[†]

*The 2001 Cape Town Convention and associated Protocols relating to aircraft objects, railway rolling stock, and space assets are among the most ambitious international instruments ever to have been concluded in the field of commercial transactional law. The Convention and Aircraft Protocol, which together consist of no fewer than 99 Articles, have been widely adopted and more ratifications are in train. Central to the Convention is the International Registry in which international interests, and, in the case of aircraft objects and space assets, sales, can be registered and secure priority over subsequently registered interests and unregistered interests. By the end of 2011, in under six years since it came into operation, the International Registry for aircraft objects in Dublin had processed 313,000 registrations. The priority rules constitute key provisions of the Convention. In this article Roy Goode, who chaired the UNIDROIT Study Group and Drafting Committee and the Drafting Committee at the Diplomatic Conference on the Convention and Aircraft Protocol in Ottawa, and acted as Rapporteur at the Diplomatic Conferences in Luxembourg in 2007 to adopt the Rail Protocol and Berlin in 2012 to adopt the Space Protocol, provides a detailed analysis of the priority rules.*

## 1. Introduction

The general rule in the conflict of laws is that proprietary rights and priority issues are governed by the law of the location of the object (*lex situs*) at the time of the relevant dealing, though in some jurisdictions interests in aircraft are subject to the law of the State of nationality registration (*lex registri*). The *lex situs* rule is singularly ill-adapted to mobile equipment such as aircraft objects, where the validity of the creation of a mortgage may be determined by the temporary presence of the aircraft in one jurisdiction while en route to another, as was held to be the position in the

* Originally published as R Goode: "The priority rules under the Cape Town Convention and Protocols" in Cape Town Convention Journal, Volume 1, 2012—Issue 1.

† Professor Sir Roy Goode QC, Emeritus Professor of Law at the University of Oxford and Emeritus Fellow of St John's College, Oxford.

*Blue Sky* case,[1] and even where there is a uniform conflict rule such as the *lex registri* the substantive content of the applicable law will vary from jurisdiction to jurisdiction, creating uncertainty and legal risk and reducing the availability of finance, increasing its cost and raising the level of premiums for credit insurance.

Only a uniform set of substantive rules governing creation, perfection and priority can resolve these problems. That is what is provided by the Cape Town instruments, which lay down a set of basic default remedies, with speedy relief pending final determination, an International Registry for the registration of international interests, a set of priority rules, and a provision for recognition of a registered international interest in the event of the debtor going into insolvency proceedings. The present article focuses on the priority rules of the Cape Town Convention on International Interests in Mobile Equipment (hereafter the 'Convention') and the Protocol to the Convention on International Interests in Mobile Equipment on Matters Specific to Aircraft Equipment (the 'Aircraft Protocol'). The rules for the other two Protocols are similar except that the Luxembourg Protocol does not cover outright sales, while the Space Protocol has a quasi-priority rule concerning physically linked space assets.[2]

## 2. The Priority Rules: International Interests

### (a) Introduction

All priority rules provide exceptions to the principle *nemo dat quod non habet*. One might, for example, think that if the owner of an asset sells it to A and then purports to sell the same asset to B the second sale is void because A has nothing to give. But like national legal systems the Convention treats the question as one of priority, not of validity, so that it is perfectly possibly for the sale to B to displace A's title, as where B is the first to register.

The priority rules in the Convention and Aircraft Protocol are of four kinds. First, there are rules in Article 29 governing the priority of registered interests, whether international interests or otherwise. These are remarkably simple for an area which in national legal systems tends to be complex. Nevertheless there are some underlying complexities. Secondly, under Article 31 the priority of assignments of associated rights[3] related to different international interests is determined by the priority of those interests themselves under Article 29. So the two go together and the order of registration of the assignments is irrelevant. Thirdly, there are rules in Article 35 relating to the priority of competing assignments of associated rights related to the same international interest. These rules are more complex and are discussed separately in Section 3. Under Article 35 the question of priority of international interests does not arise, there being only one. Instead, the priority rules of Article 29 are

[1] *Blue Sky One Ltd & ors v Mahan Air & anor* [2010] EWHC 631 (Comm) (Beatson J).

[2] See Section 2(i) below.

[3] That is, rights to payment or other performance under the agreement creating or providing for the international interest (Article 1(c)).

applied to the competing assignments themselves. However, Article 36 qualifies the extent of any priority under Article 29. The rules governing the priority of competing interests acquired by subrogation follow those relating to competing assignments. Fourthly, there are provisions relating to certain non-consensual rights or interests the subject of declarations by Contracting States. These are of two kinds: declarations the effect of which will be to give priority to specified non-consensual rights or interests without registration[4] and declarations by which specified non-consensual rights or interests can be registered as if they were international interests,[5] so that they will be governed by the ordinary priority rules. Finally, there are provisions governing the priority of competing sales. Such provisions apply priority rules similar to those governing international interests.[6] Linked to the priority rules are rules in the Aircraft Protocol determining the persons against whom a debtor or buyer is entitled to quiet possession.[7] For the most part the Aircraft Protocol leaves the Convention priority rules intact. However, Article 29(3) is disapplied[8] and there is a modification of the rule as to the effect of installation in or removal from an aircraft object of an item which is not an aircraft object.[9]

Fractional interests in an aircraft object—for example, a 20% interest in an airframe or aircraft engine—are not uncommon in the aviation industry and constitute a special case in that among themselves they do not usually fall within the priority rules at all, for the simple reason that they are not in competition with each other.[10]

## (b) The International Registry

A core feature of the Convention is the International Registry. There will be a separate registry for each of the three categories of equipment. So far only one registry is in existence, for aircraft objects, established and maintained by the registrar, Aviareto Ltd, in Dublin. The International Registry registers not only international interests and prospective international interests but a variety of other interests and transactions affecting interests, including certain nonconsensual rights or interests, assignments and prospective assignments of associated rights together with the related international interest, acquisitions of international interests by legal or contractual subrogation, and subordinations of interests. The registry system is asset-based, not debtor-based, so that it can only accept registrations of uniquely identified objects. It is wholly electronic, involving no human intervention at the registry end, and except when suspended for maintenance is operational 24 hours day, seven days a week. The Registrar operates under the guidance of a Supervisory Authority, which appoints the Registrar, sets fees and makes the regulations governing the registry. At present there is only one supervisory authority, the Council of the International Civil Aviation Organization (ICAO), which supervises the aircraft registry in Dublin, though under the Luxembourg Protocol a Preparatory Commission currently

[4] Article 39. See Section 4(d)(vii) below. [5] Article 40.
[6] Aircraft Protocol, Articles III and XIV. [7] Article XVI.
[8] See Section 2(e)(ii) below. [9] See Section 2(d)(v) below.
[10] See Section 2(h) below.

functions as the provisional Supervisory Authority until such time as the registry for railway rolling stock, which will be based in Luxembourg, becomes operative, and is currently negotiating a contract for the establishment of the International Registry. In most cases registration is the key to priority, hence its importance in the Cape Town scheme.

### (c) The basic rule: Article 29(1)

The primary rule, laid down in Article 29(1), is that a registered interest has priority over an interest subsequently registered and over an unregistered interest.[11] 'Registered' means registered in the International Registry pursuant to Chapter V of the Convention[12] and 'registered interest' means a registered international interest, a non-consensual right or interest registrable and registered under Article 40, or a registered national interest specified in a notice of a national interest.[13] An unregistered interest is a consensual interest or a non-consensual right or interest falling outside Article 39[14] which has not been registered, whether or not it is registrable.[15]

The rule in Article 29(1) is a strong rule. It usually applies to give priority over an unregistered interest even if it is not one capable of registration under the Convention. Examples of non-registrable consensual interests are the interest of an outright buyer (except under the Aircraft Protocol) or of a lessee from a party other than the debtor (a lessee from the debtor can shield behind the priority of his lessor, as discussed below). Non-consensual interests, such as liens given by law over stored or repaired objects to secure charges due to the warehouse or repairer, and attachments under court order, are non-registrable unless covered by a declaration under Article 40 and will be displaced by a registered interest except so far as within the scope of a declaration under Article 39. The interest first registered has priority even if acquired or registered with knowledge of the earlier unregistered interest and even as regards value given with such knowledge.[16] The purpose of this rule is twofold: to avoid transaction costs that would be incurred by pursuing lines of enquiry and to avoid factual disputes as to whether a party did or did not have knowledge. The aim of the rule, as indeed of Article 29 as a whole, is simplicity and predictability of outcomes.

Article 29 applies to assignments of competing international interests but not to competing assignments of the same international interest.[17]

### (d) Specified exceptions to the basic rule

Most exceptions to the general rule laid down in Article 29 are laid down in the Convention itself. These are set out below. There are also, however, some special cases in which exceptions from the general rule have to be inferred from general principles. These will be dealt with a little later.

[11] The priority of competing assignments of associated rights is discussed below, Section 3(c) below.
[12] Article 1(bb). [13] Article 1(cc), (dd). [14] See Section 2(d)(vii) below.
[15] Article 1(mm). [16] Article 29(2). [17] See Section 3(c) below.

### *(i) Proceeds*

An international interest in an object extends to proceeds of that object[18] and any priority given by Article 29 to an interest in an object extends to its proceeds[19]even though an interest in proceeds is not independently registrable. However, proceeds are narrowly defined, being limited to money or non-money proceeds of an object arising from its total or partial loss or physical destruction or its total or partial confiscation, condemnation, or requisition. Insurance proceeds are an example. So if successive international interests in an aircraft object which is insured against loss or damage are registered, first, in favour of A and then in favour of B, A has the first claim on the insurance proceeds and B's interest in the insurance proceeds is limited to any surplus remaining after A has been paid out. But in its application to proceeds Article 29(6) is limited to competing claims to proceeds both of which are derived from the object whose loss or compulsory acquisition gave rise to them. So Article 29(6) does not determine priority between the holder of an international interest claiming the proceeds of an insurance claim and a receivables financier who did not have an international interest in the object and claims the proceeds as original collateral or as proceeds of debts purchased by or charged to the financier.

### *(ii) Outright buyer*

The second exception concerns an outright buyer of an object, who acquires its interest in it free from an unregistered interest even if it has notice of it. The reason for this is not simply that outright sales are not registrable under the Convention (though they are under the Aircraft Protocol) but also that sales are such common transactions that it was considered necessary to give special protection to a buyer who takes before registration of the international interest.

### *(iii) Conditional buyer or lessee*

A somewhat different protection is given to conditional buyers and lessees. They too do not have registrable interests but they can rely on any priority enjoyed by the conditional seller or lessor against a third party claimant. For example, if a lessor grants a lease of an airframe, registers its interest as an international interest and then charges the airframe to a creditor, who registers the charge as an international interest, the lessee takes free from the chargee's interest because the interest of the lessor was registered before that of the chargee. The Aircraft Protocol buttresses this protection by giving the conditional buyer or lessee a right of quiet enjoyment against the chargee.[20] The position would be otherwise if the chargee was the first to register.

[18] Article 2(5). [19] Article 29(6). [20] Aircraft Protocol, Article XVI.

### (iv) *Contractual variation*

The priority of competing interests or rights under Article 29 may be varied by agreement between the parties.[21] Inter-creditor priority agreements are common in the financial world and this is reflected in Article 29. Typically a subordination agreement will provide for the subordination of an interest which begins as the senior of the two competing interests but it is also possible to have a variation which subordinates an interest previously ranking *pari passu* with the competing interest. It is not necessary to obtain the debtor's consent to a variation, which concerns only the holders of the parties to it and does not affect the debtor. The subordination agreement does not affect an assignee of the subordinated creditor unless the subordination has been registered in the International Registry at the time of the assignment,[22] for if this is not done the assignee is entitled to assume that it is dealing with the senior creditor. Article 29(5) does not deal with the effect of the assignee's knowledge of the subordination agreement but if this had been material Article 29(5) would surely have so provided, and in the light of the general policy of treating knowledge as irrelevant in order to avoid factual disputes as to the existence of knowledge[23] it may be assumed that the intention is that the assignee should not be bound by a subordination agreement even if taking the assignment with knowledge of the agreement. A subordination agreement may be registered even if the interest subordinated by it has not itself been registered, but there will usually be little point in seeking to procure subordination of an interest if that does not start as the senior or equal-ranking interest.

### (v) *Exclusion of doctrine of accession*

Article 29(7)(a) provides that the Convention does not affect the rights of a person in an item, other than an object, held prior to its installation on an object if under the applicable law those rights continue to exist after the installation. Under Article 29(7)(b) the Convention does not prevent the creation of rights in an item, other than an object, which has previously been installed on an object where under the applicable law those rights are created. This provision is designed to make it clear that the Convention does not implicitly embody a doctrine of accession by which, in many legal systems, ownership of an object which becomes incorporated in a larger object passes to the owner of the principal object.[24] So Article 29(7)(a) leaves it to the applicable law to determine whether the installation of an item affects prior rights in it or whether those rights continue to exist. Article 29(7)(b) deals with the case where an item previously installed is then removed from the object. Again, the purpose of this provision is to make it clear that even though in principle accessories form part of the object on which they are installed the Convention is not to be taken to mean that the interest a person has in the installed item as part of the object continues after the removal of the item.

[21] Convention, Article 29(5). [22] Article 29(5). [23] See Article 29(2), (3).

[24] It may be noted that in Article I(2) of the Aircraft Protocol 'aircraft engines', 'airframes' and 'helicopters' are all defined as including all installed, incorporated or attached accessories, parts and equipment.

Article 29(7) does not apply to items which are themselves objects governed by the Convention. So in the case of aircraft objects it does not apply to the installation of an aircraft engine, which is treated as a distinct object, not as part of the airframe on which it is installed. Examples of items within Article 29(7) are computers, other equipment, and components of various kinds.

Article 29(7) is not strictly a priority rule in itself but it can have priority effects in precluding the holder of a registered international interest from asserting the doctrine of accession to extinguish another creditor's rights in the installed item or to preclude that other creditor from granting new rights after the installed item has been removed. Article 29(7) is replicated in Article XIV(4) of the Aircraft Protocol. However, it does not apply to installed or removed aircraft engines, for these are not mere items but distinct Convention objects that do not form part of the airframe on which they are installed, interests in them being separately registrable. Article XIV(3), unlike Article XIV(4), does not leave ownership or other rights in installed engines to be dealt with by the applicable law; it lays down a positive rule that such rights are not affected by the aircraft engine's installation or removal from the airframe.

### *(vi) International interest following registration of a prospective international interest*

The priority of international interests which come into existence after the registration of a prospective international interest departs from the normal rule only in the sense that the international interest itself is never actually registered, it is merely treated as registered as from the time of registration of the prospective international interest.[25]

### *(vii) Non-consensual right or interest covered by Article 39*

Where a Contracting State makes a declaration under Article 39 declaring that non-consensual rights or interests which under its law have priority over an interest equivalent to an international interest are to have priority over registered international interests the priority ordinarily given to a registered international interest does not apply. In many national legal systems, lien creditors exercising repairers' liens or warehouse liens over objects in their possession have priority even over a perfected security interest. The policy reason is that they are adding value to or preserving the collateral and it would be unfair to allow the secured creditor to benefit from this without payment. So most declarations under Article 39 relate to such liens, while others also include liens in favour of employees for unpaid wages, either generally or for wages due to airline employees. Though Article 39 refers only to the priority of declared non-consensual rights or interests over *registered* international interests it must follow *a fortiori* that the non-consensual rights or interests also have priority over *unregistered* interests as well.

[25] Article 19(4).

### *(viii) Registered non-consensual rights or interests*

Non-consensual rights or interests registered pursuant to Article 40 are not international interests at all, but for priority purposes they are treated as if they were registered international interests.

### *(ix) Pre-existing rights or interests*

In general the Convention does not apply to a pre-existing right or interest, which retains the priority it enjoyed under the applicable law before the effective date of the Convention.[26] A pre-existing right or interest is a right or interest of any kind in or over an object created or arising before the effective date of the Convention,[27] which for this purpose means in relation to a debtor the date when the Convention enters into force or the time when the State in which the debtor is situated becomes a Contracting State, whichever is the later.[28]

### *(x) Special case: debtor cannot trump own creditor*

A debtor cannot use Article 29(1) to trump his own creditor. So if A grants a lease to L who in turn sub-leases to SL, L cannot, by registering his interest as sub-lessor before A registers his own interest as head lessor, jump ahead of A. This exception is not to be found in the text of the Convention. It follows from the general legal principle that a person cannot act inconsistently with the obligations he has undertaken to another to the detriment of that other. To give L priority over his own creditor, A, would be inconsistent with L's obligations to A and a denial of A's title.

## (e) Extension of the priority rules to outright sales

### *(i) Adoption of the Convention priority rules*

Article III of the Aircraft Protocol and Article IV of the Space Protocol extend the registration and priority rules of the Convention to outright sales. Sales are outside the scope of the Convention and do not constitute international interests. Nevertheless Article 41 of the Convention provides for extension of the Convention to sales as provided for in the Protocol with any modifications therein, and the above Protocols implement that extension. The two sets of provisions follow the same pattern, so only those of the Aircraft Protocol will be discussed. The Luxembourg

[26] Article 60(1). [27] Article 1(v).

[28] Article 60(2)(a). For the difficulties with this provision see Roy Goode, *Official Commentary on the Convention on International Interests in Mobile Equipment and Protocol thereto on Matters Specific to Aircraft Equipment* (revised edn, UNIDROIT 2008), paras 4.343–4.354. When the Luxembourg Protocol was under discussion these difficulties were felt to be sufficiently significant to justify departure from the general policy of avoiding pure drafting improvements in subsequent Protocols, so that Article XXVI of the Luxembourg Protocol amends Article 60 of the Convention. However, the *Official Commentary on the Luxembourg Protocol* (revised edn, UNIDROIT 2008) paras 2.172, 5.80 makes it clear that these amendments are designed purely to make explicit what was previously implicit and do not alter the substantive effect of Article 60 as set out in the Convention.

Protocol does not apply the Convention to sales. Instead it provides for registration of notices of sale, which however, is for information purposes only and has no effect under the Convention or Protocol,[29] its purpose being to serve as notice with a view to giving or preserving priority under national law.

Article XIV(1) of the Aircraft Protocol provides the same priority rule for competing sales *by the same seller* as does Article 29(1) of the Convention for competing international interests.[30] The effect is that if S sells an aircraft engine to B1 who registers the sale in the International Registry, and S then sells the same engine to B2, B1 retains its interest free from that of B2. Suppose that B1 had failed to register its purchase and B2 registered its own purchase. B2 now has priority even if acquiring the engine with knowledge of the unregistered sale to B1. However, successive sales do not raise a priority issue at all unless made by the same seller. For example, S sells an aircraft object to A and then wrongfully makes a second sale, to B. Priority goes to the first buyer to register its purchase. By contrast, in a chain of sales S→B1→B2→B3 there is no priority issue as the buyers are not in competition with each other, so that Article 29 does not apply. The position is simply that each buyer in the chain succeeds to the rights of its predecessor. Assuming that the sales are registered, each registration is independent of the others and because the International Registry is not a title registry nothing turns on the order of registrations. However, if registrations follow the order of sales it will be apparent that it is the *last* registration that will indicate the current holder. If we exclude the case of sales by different sellers in succession, Article 29(1) applies to give a registered sale priority over (a) a second sale by the same seller; (b) a subsequently registered or unregistered international interest; (c) a registrable but subsequently registered or unregistered non-consensual right or interest; (d) a non-registrable non-consensual right or interest not protected by a declaration by a Contracting State under Article 39; (e) any other interest which is not registrable; and (f) a national interest notice of which is registered after the registration of the sale or is not registered.

### *(ii) Disapplication of Article 29(3)*

Article III of the Aircraft Protocol disapplies Article 29(3) of the Convention[31] for the simple reason that the outright buyer of an aircraft object can protect

[29] Luxembourg Protocol, Article XVII.

[30] However, the astute reader will have observed that Article XIV(2), which is designed to be the converse of Article XIV(1), does not quite match it because instead of referring to the time of the second buyer's *registration* it refers to the time of its *acquisition*. In the ordinary way this would not matter, because a buyer cannot register a purchase until it has been made, but what the text does not allow for on a literal reading is the registration of a prospective sale with retrospective effect upon crystallising into a sale (Article 18(3)), an effect which on a strict construction Article XIV(2) overrides. But Article XIV(2) has to be construed to be consistent with Article XIV(1), which applies the order of registration, and should therefore be interpreted as if it read: 'A buyer of an aircraft object under a registered sale acquires its interest in the object subject to an interest previously registered.' See Official Commentary, Goode (n 28) para 5.72.

[31] Article 29(3) provides that '[T]he buyer of an object acquires its interest in it: (a) subject to an interest registered at the time of its acquisition of that interest; and (b) free from an unregistered interest even if it has actual knowledge of such an interest.'

its interest by registration, so there is no need for the special rule provided by Article 29(3) and priorities are determined as stated above. Article XIV of the Protocol follows Article 29(2) of the Convention in making it clear that B2's knowledge of B1's prior interest does not affect B2's priority. There are two provisions under which a buyer acquires priority without the need to register. Where the creditor exercises a power of sale under Article 8(1)(b) or under Article 13(1)(d) as added by Article X(3) of the Aircraft Protocol ownership or any other interest of the debtor passes to the buyer free from any other interest over which the creditor's international interest has priority under Article 29 of the Convention.[32]

### (f) Installed and removed engines

While Article XIV(4) applies Article 29(7) of the Convention[33] to an item, other than an object, installed on an airframe, aircraft engine or helicopter, Article XIV(3) applies a different rule to aircraft engines. An aircraft engine is not a mere 'item' but an 'object' and as such is the subject of independent treatment and is separately registrable. Article XIV(3) does not leave the effect of installation or removal of an aircraft engine to be dealt with by the applicable law; instead it provides that ownership of or another right or interest in an aircraft engine shall not be affected by its installation on or removal from an aircraft. This is consistent with the treatment of airframes and aircraft engines as distinct objects in the Convention and the Aircraft Protocol. It is not possible to take an international interest in an aircraft as such unless it is a helicopter, only in an airframe or aircraft engine. Accordingly, though the definition of an airframe in Article I(2)(e) of the Protocol includes accessories it does not include aircraft engines, which even without Article XIV(3) would retain their distinct identity, so that an international interest in them would not be affected by their installation or removal.

Helicopters represent the exceptional case, because an installed engine is treated as part of the helicopter itself, with the result that an international interest cannot be taken over a helicopter engine while so installed, because it is not an aircraft object at all.[34] The solution for the financier is to register not only an international interest in the helicopter but a prospective international interest in the helicopter engine which will crystallise into an actual international interest the moment the engine is removed, registration of the international interest being retrospective under Article 18(3). On the other hand, prior to its installation a helicopter engine is an aircraft object, not a mere item such as a component, so that if an international interest is taken in an aircraft engine prior to its installation on a helicopter Article XIV(3) ensures that such installation does not affect the creditor's rights.

[32] Convention, Article 10(5); Aircraft Protocol, Article X(4).

[33] See Section 2(d)(5) above.

[34] This view is not accepted by all representatives of the aviation industry but the arguments in favour of it are overwhelming. See the Official Commentary, Goode (n 28) paras 3.8, 3.10, 5.3–5.5.

### (g) The need for dual registration: no crossover protection

A person may have a registrable interest in an aircraft object in two different capacities. For example B buys an aircraft engine from S and leases it to L. B can register both its interest under the sale and an international interest arising from the grant of the lease. Again, if a lessee under a leasing agreement containing an option to purchase grants a sub-lease it can register both a prospective sale and an international interest as sub-lessor. In such cases there need to be two registrations, one of the sale, the other of the international interest. In the first example, registration of the sale will protect B against a wrongful double sale by S but not against a wrongful sale by L to T. It is true that under Article XIV(2) a buyer's registered interest is overridden by a previously registered interest, which might suggest that T is bound by B's registered interest but that is not the case. Article XIV(2) is concerned with cases where the registered interest is a Protocol interest, ie a sale, not an international interest arising under the Convention the purpose of the registration being to protect B against a wrongful second sale by S. So B's registration of the sale in order to protect itself against a subsequent sale by S does not dispense with the need for B to protect its separate international interest arising from the lease by registering the international interest so as to bind T as a purchaser from L. Registration of the sale protects B only *as buyer*; registration of the leasing agreement as an international interest is needed to protect B *as lessor*. The two interests are quite distinct.

Conversely, the purpose of registration of an international interest is to protect the creditor from a wrongful disposition by the debtor. So B's registration of its international interest, though protecting B in its capacity of creditor, does not protect it against a subsequent wrongful sale by S to B2, which requires registration of the sale to B. In short, the two interests to be protected are distinct, the purposes of registration are different, and each has to be registered in accordance with the rules applicable to it. Thus, there can be no 'cross-over' protection.

### (h) Fractional interests

As stated earlier, it is not uncommon in the aviation industry for a buyer to take a fractional interest in an aircraft object, for example, a 20% interest, and for that interest to be given in security as an international interest. Fractional interests are not expressly dealt with by the Convention and initially the International Registry was not geared up to accept them but as the technology developed they became registrable as separate international interests. So if an aircraft object is sold as to 40% to A, 20% to B, and 30% to C three sales are registrable in the International Registry. Similarly each purchase of a fractional interest may be financed by a different creditor which takes security over that fractional interest, and each security constitutes a distinct international interest and is registrable as such. Fractional interests normally fall outside the priority rules in Article 29 because they are not in competition with each other. If, however, sellers sell or debtors charge by way of security fractional interests exceeding 100% of an aircraft object a priority issue arises and is determined by the order of registration.

### (i) *Physically linked assets*

A provision unique to the Space Protocol is that dealing with physically linked assets. Article XVII(3) of the Protocol provides that, unless otherwise agreed, a creditor may not enforce an international interest in a space asset that is physically linked with another space asset so as to impair or interfere with the operation of the other space asset if an international interest has been registered with respect to the other space asset prior to the registration of the international interest being enforced. This is not strictly a priority rule since the two international interests relate to different assets. Nevertheless the underlying idea is similar. If the international interest in the physically linked space asset against which enforcement is sought was the first to be registered the enforcing creditor cannot proceed against the space asset in which he has an international interest if this would impair or interfere with the operation of the other space asset, for example by disabling a bank of transponders so as to interfere with the operation of other transponders. This restriction does not apply to an enforcing creditor who registers its international interest first, but that does not necessarily render the creditor immune from action under the applicable law.

## 3. The Priority Rules: Associated Rights

### (a) *The nature of associated rights*

Chapter IX of the Convention is devoted to the assignment of associated rights, that is, all rights to payment or other performance by a debtor under an agreement[35] which are secured by or associated with the agreement. Associated rights are 'secured by' a security agreement or 'associated with' a title reservation or leasing agreement. The concept of associated rights is limited by three factors. First, associated rights are confined to rights to performance of obligations due from the debtor. Obligations due from third parties do not fall within the definition unless the debtor itself has undertaken in the agreement to procure their performance. Second, it is only performance due from the debtor 'under the agreement' that is relevant. Rights to performance by the debtor under other contracts do not qualify unless in the agreement itself the debtor undertakes to perform its obligations under the other contracts, whether these are individually specified or are referred to in generic terms. Where the debtor does agree to perform obligations under other contracts then subject to the third requirement the rights to performance under those contracts also become associated rights under the agreement. So if the debtor enters into a loan agreement and a separate security agreement which secures performance under the loan agreement, the rights to such performance constitute associated rights. Third, the performance must be secured on or associated with the agreement. So in the case of a security

[35] That is, a security agreement, a title reservation agreement or a leasing agreement (Article 1(a)).

agreement the relevant obligations are those covered by the security. Other obligations which are unsecured do not count. In the case of a title reservation agreement all obligations the performance of which is necessary for the transfer of title to the debtor qualify. These will obviously include the price and typically other obligations, such as insurance, repair, indemnities of different kinds and the observance of negative obligations, such as prohibition on sale or the grant of a security interest in the object.

Associated rights are of two kinds: those that are related to the financing or leasing of an object as described in Article 36(2) (hereafter referred to as 'object-related rights') and those that are not. As will be seen, the distinction is of importance in that any priority under Article 35 is limited to object-related rights.

### (b) Assignment of associated rights

It is unfortunate that in the drafting of Chapter IX conceptual purity was allowed to obscure the true focus of the Convention, which is the registration and assignment of international interests in physical assets. The original draft provided that the transfer of an international interest would carry with it the associated rights. In the view of the writer, who as Chairman of the Drafting Committee was heavily involved in the drafting, this was the correct approach, because associated rights, being intangible, are not in themselves susceptible to registration, nor can an assignment of associated rights be registered. However, the diplomatic Conference succumbed to the argument that in legal theory a security interest is an accessory right and therefore follows the destination of the contract creating the secured obligations, not the other way round. As a matter of doctrine this cannot be faulted, but its application in the context of the Convention led to drafting complications, for the priority of competing assignments then had to be framed not along traditional lines (first to give notice of assignment to the debtor, or first to register, in a legal system providing for registration) but according to the priority of the assignment of the international interest to which the associated rights were related. In consequence, for the provisions to operate at all the assignment of associated rights can be effected only as part of the assignment of the related international interest. So Article 31 provides that except as otherwise agreed by the parties the assignment of associated rights transfers the related international interest and all the priorities of the assignor under the Convention; and where the assignment of associated rights is not effective to transfer the related international interest, eg because the parties have agreed that it should not be, the Convention does not apply to the assignment at all,[36] the reason being that associated rights are not in themselves capable of registration. As a corollary, an assignment of an international interest created or provided for by a security agreement is not valid unless

[36] Article 32(3).

some or all related associated rights also are assigned.[37] This is, of course, because the function of a security agreement is to secure payment or other performance, and if none of the associated rights secured are assigned the security agreement is not securing anything.

### (c) Priority of competing assignments

It follows from what has been said before that what the Convention is really doing is laying down rules for the priority of competing assignments of international interests, from which flows the priority of competing assignments of associated rights. That is why it would have been better to ignore traditional doctrine and to provide that the assignment of the international interest carries with it the assignment of associated rights, rather than the other way round.

The rules on the priority of competing assignments of associated rights are rather more complex than those governing the assignment of the related international interest. In the first place it is necessary to distinguish the position of assignees of associated rights related to different international interests from that of competing assignees of the same international interest. Article 31 deals with the former and in essence applies the priority rules of Article 29 to the competing international interests, on the basis that the competing assignees stand in the shoes of their assignors as described below, while Articles 35 and 36 deal with the latter and are concerned not with the priorities of the assigned international interests but with those of the assignments themselves, where the priority is based on the order of registration of the assignments, not of the assigned international interests. Secondly, the priority given by Article 35 is heavily qualified by Article 36.

#### *(i) Assignments of different international interests and associated rights*

The rules here are relatively simple. Where there are competing international interests the assignee of associated rights succeeds to the priority of its assignor.[38] What is relevant is the order of registration of the assigned international interests, not of the assignments themselves. Whether the assignments are registered, and if so the order of registration, is irrelevant because the assignments relate to different associated rights linked to different international interests and are therefore not in competition with each other at all. So if international interests granted successively to A and B are registered in that order, A and B assign their respective interests and associated rights to C and D and D's assignment is registered first, C nevertheless has priority because it succeeds to the priority of A, while D succeeds to B's junior international interest. The two assignments do not relate to the same international interest and therefore do not attract an independent priority rule governing competing assignments of associated rights; their status stems entirely from the priority of the international interests to which they are related.

[37] Article 32(2). [38] Article 31(1)(b).

### *(ii) Competing assignments of the same associated rights*

The position discussed here is the very different one in which there is a single international interest and either that interest, with its associated rights, is assigned first to A and then to B or it is assigned to A alone while the assignment to B is only of the associated rights. In this case the priority issue is not between competing international interests but between competing assignments of associated rights. This priority is governed not by Article 31 but by Article 35. The starting position under Article 35 is that the references in Article 29 to a registered interest are to be applied as if they were references to a registered assignment. So a registered assignment has priority over a subsequently registered assignment or an unregistered assignment.

In order for Article 35 to apply at least one of the assignments must include the international interest (for otherwise there would be nothing against which to effect a registration), the associated rights passing under that assignment must retain their linkage with the international interest[39] and at least one of the assignments of the international interest must be registered (because Article 29(1) does not regulate priorities between competing unregistered interests, this being left to the applicable law).

Article 36 contains two qualifications to the general priority rule. First, it is necessary for the contract under which the associated rights arise to state that they are secured by or associated with the object. This is to deal with the situation where the security agreement secures not only the obligations for which it provides but the obligations under a later agreement which does not refer to the security, so that an assignee of associated rights under the later agreement has no way of knowing that those obligations are secured. In such a case it would be unfair to expose the assignee to the Convention's priority rules. Second, the priority of the first assignment to be registered is given only to the extent that the associated rights are object-related as provided by Article 36(2). This broadly covers obligations for the repayment of purchase-money loans,[40] and the payment of the price and rentals of objects, together with all ancillary obligations under the financing transaction documents, such as contract and default charges and interest, funding breakage costs, enforcement costs, and the like. In all other cases priority is determined by the applicable law.[41]

[39] See the Official Commentary, Goode (n 28) para 4.246. It is not necessary that the international interest should itself be registered in order to become the subject of a registered assignment, but the assignee will be displaced by the holder of a subsequent international interest who registers, and thus obtains priority over the unregistered interest, by the assignee of such a holder and by the debtor's bankruptcy creditors unless the applicable bankruptcy law treats the unregistered interest as effective (see Article 30(2)).

[40] Whether of the same object or of another object in which the assignor held another international interest if the assignor transferred that interest to the assignee and the assignment has been registered (Article 36(2)(b)). This is designed to cover cross-collaterisation. See Official Commentary, Goode (n 28) para 4.253.

[41] Article 36(3).

*(iii) Pre-existing rights or interests*

As mentioned above, pre-existing rights or interests fall outside the Convention except so far as covered by a declaration under Article 60(3). It follows that, with the same exception, the Convention does not apply to the assignment of pre-existing rights or interests.

## 4. Modes of Transfer Other than Assignment

### (a) Subrogation

The Convention contains various provisions relating to the acquisition of interests and rights by subrogation under the applicable law. Typical cases of subrogation under national law are where a surety discharges the debt and becomes subrogated to the creditor's rights or where an insurer meets a claim for loss or damage caused to its insured by a third party and becomes subrogated to the insured's rights against a third party. So Article 16(1)(c) provides for the registration of the acquisition of international interests by legal or contractual subrogation under the applicable law, while Article 38(1) provides that nothing in the Convention affects the acquisition of associated rights and the related international interest by legal or contractual subrogation under the applicable law.

The priority rules here follow those relating to assignments. As with assignments, a competing interest can arise in one of two ways. The first is where there are two subrogees whose subrogatory rights relate to *different* international interests. So it is the international interests, not the subrogatory rights as such, that are in competition with each other. In this case each subrogee stands in the shoes of the original holder of the international interest to whom it has become subrogated and will succeed to any priority enjoyed by that international interest over the competing interest, irrespective whether the acquisition by subrogation is registered. So it is necessary to see whether under Article 29(1) the international interest has priority over the competing interest. For example, if international interests granted to A and B are registered in that order, S1 and S2 become subrogated to A and B respectively and S2 is the first to register its acquisition of the international interest by subrogation, S1 nevertheless has priority because it is subrogated to the interest of the senior creditor, A. Again, if an international interest is held by X, B buys the equipment before X has registered its international interest and S becomes subrogated to X, B takes free of the international interest, so that S acquires no interest in the equipment. A second possibility is that the subrogee is in competition with another subrogee in respect of *the same* international interest. In this case the competition is not between international interests but between rights of subrogation and priority goes to the first subrogee to have its acquisition registered. This is not expressly provided by the Convention but must follow from the general principle that the order of registration determines priorities. The parties can vary the priority of any such subrogatory interest and a competing interest by an agreement in writing but this will not bind an assignee of the junior interest unless at the time of the assignment the subordination had been registered.[42] The priority is in any event qualified by Article 36.

In short, the priority rules governing rights acquired by subrogation follow those applicable to assignments.

There is one right of subrogation given by the Convention itself. Article 9(4) provides that where, after default by the debtor and before sale of a charged object or its vesting in the creditor, an interested person other than the debtor[43] discharges the debt in full that person becomes subrogated to the creditor's rights. There seems no reason why, in a Contracting State, the right of subrogation given by Article 9(4) should not be considered to be given by the applicable law and be registrable accordingly.

### (b) Assignment by operation of law

The Convention provisions on assignment are confined to contractual assignments and do not apply to transfers taking effect by operation of law, for example, transfers under statutory provisions or on a statutory merger of two corporations.

## 5. Effect of Debtor's Insolvency

The courts of a Contracting State are obliged to recognise the effectiveness of an international interest registered before the commencement of insolvency proceedings against the debtor,[44] though this does not impair the effectiveness of an unregistered interest where that interest is effective under the applicable law.[45] The near-universal conflicts rule is that the acquisition of an interest in an object is governed by the *lex situs* of the object at the time of the relevant dealing. Where under that law the creditor's interest has been duly perfected the insolvency courts of a Contracting State are obliged to treat the interest as perfected for the purpose of the insolvency proceedings even though the interest has not been registered in the International Registry. There are two qualifications. First, nothing in Article 30 affects any rules of law applicable in insolvency proceedings relating to the avoidance of a transaction as a preference or a transfer in fraud of creditors.[46] But only those grounds of avoidance can be invoked in a Contracting State. For example, the fact that the international interest was not registered in the domestic registry prescribed by that State's law and would ordinarily be void on that ground is not a legitimate ground for refusing to recognise the effectiveness of the international interest. Similarly the priority rules applicable under the Convention cannot be displaced

[42] Article 38(2), which corresponds to Article 29(5) governing the variation of priorities of international interests.

[43] That is, a surety, an issuer of a demand guarantee or standby letter of credit or other form of credit insurance or any other person having rights in or over the object (Article 1(m)(ii), (iii)).

[44] Article 30(1). [45] Article 30(2). [46] Article 30(3)(a).

by a rule of the *lex concursus* subordinating the registered international interest to the claims of preferential creditors, eg for taxes or unpaid wages. Secondly, nothing in Article 30 affects any rules of procedure relating to the enforcement of rights to property which is under the control or supervision of the insolvency administrator.[47] So it remains open to the insolvency court to suspend or restrict the enforcement of a security interest or the institution of other proceedings against the debtor pursuant to an insolvency regime such as a UK administration or a US Chapter 11 in collective proceedings designed to facilitate a rescue of the debtor or a scheme of arrangement with creditors or to place the debtor in a better position than would result from an immediate liquidation. But in a Contracting State which ratifies the Aircraft Protocol and makes a declaration adopting Alternative A of Article XI[48] the provisions of Article 30(3)(b) are displaced.

## 6. Conclusions

The rules governing the priority of competing interests at least one of which is registrable in the International Registry are remarkably simple, being contained in a single Article of the Convention, Article 29. Equally simple are the rules governing a competition between assignments of associated rights arising under different international interests, because these follow the priority of the international interests to which they relate and thus apply Article 29. More complex are the provisions relating to competing assignments of associated rights arising under the same international interest, for these are hedged with rather intricate conditions and qualifications. Nevertheless they stand up surprisingly well to rigorous analysis. No doubt problems will arise which have not been foreseen but these are for the future. The key point is that the Convention and Protocols are concerned with security and quasi-security interests in, and sales of, physical, uniquely identifiable assets, and with rights to payment or other performance linked to registered international interests and sales, not with general receivables financing. For that there is a separate convention, the 2001 United Nations Convention on the financing of receivables in international trade, which was concluded soon after the Cape Town Convention, though so far it has secured only a single ratification.

If those who initiated the Cape Town Convention had realised the ambitious character of the project at the outset it is doubtful if they would have had the courage to embark upon it. As it is, the Convention and Aircraft Protocol, trenching on areas previously considered taboo and devising a range of innovative instruments and techniques, have proved a resounding success, to which the priority rules have made a major contribution.

[47] Article 30(3)(b).

[48] Which gives the creditor the right to recover the aircraft object without judicial interference if the insolvency administrator fails within the declared waiting period to cure all default and to undertake to perform the debtor's future obligations.

# 10

# Battening Down Your Security Interests*

## How the Shipping Industry Can Benefit from the UNIDROIT Convention on International Interests in Mobile Equipment

*Sir Roy Goode*†

It is a privilege to be invited to deliver this year's Donald O'May lecture here at Southampton University's Institute of Maritime Law, which has done so much not only to promote maritime law as a subject of academic study but also to foster collaboration between scholars and practising maritime lawyers and other shipping specialists and provoke critical enquiry into the state of maritime law internationally. This lecture series began in 1983 but was retitled in 1989 in memory of Donald O'May. For many years senior partner of Ince & Co., Donald O'May, who had himself given the fourth of these annual lectures, was not only a leading shipping lawyer but also a powerful protagonist of efforts to harmonize shipping law, and was a major influence in the work leading to the 1989 Salvage Convention. He would, I am sure, have been extremely happy to witness the contribution which the Institute, under its various directors and currently under the leadership of Professor Nick Gaskell, continues to make to the advancement of maritime law.

## I. Introduction

Let me come clean from the start and confess to you now what will readily become apparent in the course of my talk. I am not a maritime lawyer, though I have the

* Originally published as "Battening down your security interests: How the shipping industry can benefit from the UNIDROIT Convention on International Interests in Mobile Equipment" [2000] LMCLQ 161 (pages 161–91).This article first appeared in Lloyd's Maritime and Commercial Law Quarterly, [2000] LMCLQ 161. Published by Informa Law, London. Reproduced with permission of Informa Law.

† Emeritus Professor of Law in the University of Oxford and Emeritus Fellow of St John"s College, Oxford. This paper reproduces the 1999 Donald O"May Lecture, delivered at the Institute of Maritime Law, University of Southampton, on 10 November 1999, updated to take account of the revised text resulting from the third Joint Session convened by UNIDROIT and ICAO and held in Rome in March 2000.

profoundest admiration for those who are. If I had previously thought that commercial law, national and transnational, was complex, I am comforted to find that it is of stark simplicity when examined against the arcane mysteries of Admiralty law. Indeed, my impression is that the quickest way of grasping the fundamental concepts of Admiralty law is to take a basic, long-established principle of the general law and stand it on its head. For example, maritime liens, which are secret, are almost everywhere given priority over mortgages, which are required to be made public by registration. In the general law a non-possessory lien is displaced by a transfer to a bona fide purchaser for value without notice; by contrast a maritime lien binds the bona fide purchaser. At common law a junior incumbrancer may sell the charged asset without the consent of the senior incumbrancer, the sale taking effect subject to the latter's interest; in maritime law the consent of the senior incumbrancer is required. The general rule of the common law is that security interests rank in order of time; by contrast maritime liens generally rank in *reverse* chronological order. Again, in the general law the phrases "*in rem*" and "*in personam*" are used to distinguish real, or proprietary, rights from purely personal rights; in English maritime law they are employed to describe a type of action, and to differentiate between an Admiralty claim against a ship—or, perhaps more accurately, a claim against its owner restricted to the ship—and a claim based on the personal liability of the defendant which, though labelled "*in personam*", may encompass proprietary as well as personal rights. In the general law you normally have to find your defendant in order to get your action under way; in maritime law you name your defendant and then simply go after the vessel. As Professor Rhidian Thomas puts it:[1]

> The maritime law as developed by the High Court of Admiralty and its successor, the High Court of Justice, is liberally sprinkled with concepts peculiar to the *droit maritime* and which are unfamiliar to the jurisprudence of terrestrial systems of law.

Similarly, whereas in the general law issues of priority are considered matters of substantive law to be governed by the *lex situs* (or, as the civilians say, the *lex rei sitae*), in English Admiralty law they are regarded as procedural and remedial and are to be determined by the *lex fori*. Add to this the vast number of maritime and statutory liens now to be found in every jurisdiction—and how many even of the *cognoscenti* could claim to know and rank them all?—and you can begin to understand the despair of a general commercial lawyer at ever being able to grasp the intricacies of maritime law. And, of course, I shall not attempt to do so. My purpose is a rather different one, namely to underscore the lack of any uniform substantive law rules, or even uniform conflict of laws rules, governing ship mortgages and related types of consensual interest, to depict the serious problems this creates for shipping finance and fleet expansion, particularly in developing countries, and to show how the UNIDROIT Convention on International Interests in Mobile Equipment, which is now at an advanced stage of preparation, can offer the same kind of benefits in relation to ship financing as the aviation industry worldwide recognizes it can offer for aircraft financing. My focus is not on maritime or statutory liens and their priorities among

[1] *Maritime Liens* (Stevens & Sons, London 1980), para. I.

themselves or in relation to ship mortgages but rather on consensual security and quasi-security instruments, namely mortgage and charge, sale under retention of title and lease, all of them important tools for facilitating the acquisition and use of ships.

## II. The Internationality of Maritime Law in History and Today

The *lex maritima* is of a noble and ancient lineage. The Rhodian Maritime Code was promulgated as far back as the 2nd or 3rd century BC and a thousand years were to elapse before the preparation of the next, and more ambitious, Rhodes codification, the Rhodian Sea Laws. Later codifications of the laws of the sea included two that were to prove of enormous influence, laying the foundations of modern maritime law. The first was the Rolls of Oleron, dating back to the 11th or 12th century, exported to England and embodied in the Black Book of the Admiralty at the behest, so it is said, of that remarkable queen, Eleanor of Aquitaine, whose tomb lies in Fontevrault Abbey. Among the more striking provisions of the Rolls of Oleron was that under which a pilot who negligently grounded his ship was to suffer instant decapitation. No less significant was a later compilation, the Consulate of the Sea, published in the 14th or 15th century. Throughout this period maritime law was truly international, forming an integral part of the wider mediaeval *lex mercatoria.* Later, for a variety of reasons, both general commercial law and maritime law lost a good deal of their internationality, becoming increasingly domesticated with the rise of the nation State, the gradual usurpation by the central courts of jurisdiction previously exercised by the Courts of Admiralty, the consequent displacement in England of the influence of the civil law and civilian lawyers, and the development of national maritime legislation. This was in turn followed by a revival as the *in personam* jurisdiction of the Admiralty Court, which had largely disappeared, was revived by statute. During the present century the huge expansion in international trade, coupled with more recent concerns over pollution and drugs, has focused attention on the necessity of at least some measure of harmonization. This has been particularly notable in relation to such matters as the international law of the sea, the carriage of goods by sea (with the Hague Rules and later the Hague-Visby and Hamburg Rules), civil liability to passengers and liability for pollution damage.

Unfortunately this drive towards harmonization has not been equally successful in other fields, including in particular the field of maritime mortgages and liens. Here we have three Conventions, the 1926, 1967, and 1993 Conventions. Only the 1926 Convention has ever come into force. Of the 24 countries parties to the Convention, none is a common law country. The 1926 Convention provides for recognition in all Contracting States of mortgages, hypothecations, and other similar charges on a vessel created in accordance with the law of the Contracting State where the vessel is registered, provided that the mortgage, etc., is registered in a public register. The Convention also subordinates ship mortgages to the maritime liens listed in Art. 2. That is as far as the Convention goes in relation to ship mortgages, and it is not very far. It does not, for example, prescribe even a conflict rule for the priority of competing mortgages, nor does it unify any substantive rules of law governing ship mortgages other than their subordination to the listed maritime liens. The 1967 Convention, and its intended successor, the 1993 Convention, provide that the ranking of mortgages as between themselves and, without prejudice to the Convention provisions, their effect in regard to third parties, is to be determined by the law of the State of registration, while all matters relating to the procedure of enforcement are left to the law of the enforcing State. Neither Convention is in force.

Where does that leave us? In countries to which the 1926 Convention applies (which, as I have said, does not include any common law country), mortgages registered in a Contracting State must be recognized in other Contracting States, but the effect of an unregistered mortgage is left to be determined by its governing law, which will vary from State to State. Where the 1926 Convention does not apply, there is no uniform rule of recognition; it is for the conflict of laws rules of each State to determine the conditions upon which it will recognize a mortgage created under the law of another jurisdiction. The conditions for the creation, enforcement, and perfection of a ship mortgage, and of its priority as against competing mortgages, differ widely from one jurisdiction to another. The applicable law will again depend on the conflict rules of the forum. Matters relating to creation and perfection will usually be governed by the law of the State of registration as the legally attributed *situs* of the ship. Matters relating to enforcement will be controlled by the law of the State of enforcement. Priorities will, under the conflict rules of some countries, be treated as substantive and be governed by the law of the place of registration or alternatively the law of the actual situation of the vessel at a particular time, while in others they will be regarded as procedural and be determined by the *lex fori.* In short, not only are there no uniform substantive rules governing ship mortgages, there are almost no operative conflicts rules. It is scarcely surprising, then, that as far back as 1936 Mr Griffith Price, like David upon the death of Saul, lamented with great lamentation over the state of affairs as he perceived them:[2]

> As a result of the conflict of laws in the matter of maritime liens and mortgages, this particular sphere of jurisprudence has been in a state bordering on chaos.

It will be seen that the *lex fori* is of enormous influence in relation to ship mortgages. Not only does the *lex fori* apply its own conflict rules to determine the applicable law—which is the almost universal rule in the conflict of laws—but it controls enforcement and even, in many jurisdictions, the ranking of ship mortgages among themselves. Accordingly the powers of arrest conferred under the Arrest Conventions of 1952 and 1999 are potentially of great importance to the rights of mortgagees of ships, particularly since under Art. 57 of the Brussels Convention, and our enactment of it, that Convention defers to the 1952 Arrest Convention where the ship is actually arrested, so that the general rule that a defendant must be sued in the country of his domicile does not apply.

Moreover, both Conventions expressly confer on the arresting court the power to determine the case upon its merits in stated conditions, which in the 1999

[2] *The International Unification of the Law of Maritime Liens and Mortgages* (Sweet & Maxwell, London, 1936), 8.

Convention are somewhat different from those of the 1952 Convention. It may be noted that the 1952 Arrest Convention, which attracted widespread support, is the only Convention of all those mentioned to which the United Kingdom and a few other common law jurisdictions have become parties, though in their illuminating article on the 1999 Convention Professor Gaskell and Mr Shaw were critical of the mode of enactment of the 1952 Convention in the United Kingdom.[3] Finally, all five Conventions, insofar as they regulate consensual interests, are concerned exclusively with security interests in the sense in which that is understood outside North America, that is to say, with mortgages, charges and hypotheques, and the like. None of them deals with the rights of conditional sellers or lessors, though conditional sales and leases are enormously important in ship finance.

It is not unreasonable to conclude that the *lex maritima,* which in earlier times was an integral part of the *lex mercatoria,* has somehow become detached from the general law merchant and has insulated itself from current trends in the development of what has become known as transnational commercial law, that corpus of law which, through various sources of harmonization, written and unwritten, has become common to a substantial number of States. So my talk tonight, though directed primarily to the advantages for shipping of the Draft UNIDROIT Convention on International Interests in Mobile Equipment, has also a wider purpose, namely to urge a return of maritime law to the main body of transnational commercial law which would thereby be greatly enriched and would in turn provide a strong unifying force in the future development of maritime law itself.

## III. Shipping Development Needs

If we look today at the world of international trade and finance we can identify a number of characteristics affecting ships and shipping:

(1) the universal use of containers;
(2) connected to this, the huge growth in multimodal transport operations, and thus the need, as regards secured financing, for a legal regime which covers the principal types of transport equipment used in the different stages of transit, instead of a regime confined to a single category of equipment;
(3) the variety and sophistication of modern financing tools, so that we have not only mortgages and charges but also the use of conditional sales, finance leases, and subleases, often of considerable complexity;
(4) the vast sums involved in building and equipping a modern fleet;
(5) the concern of many developing countries that, because of lack of a legal infrastructure supportive of security and quasi-security interests (conditional sale, leases, and the like), they are unable to obtain the finance necessary to construct their fleets of ships—a fact which also, of course, affects the ability

[3] See Nicholas Gaskell and Richard Shaw, "The Arrest Convention 1999" [1999] LMCLQ 470, 472.

of shipbuilders to export ships into those countries and of banks to finance such exports.

So what are the current needs for an international legal regime for ship finance? These were very clearly identified by the International Sub-Committee of the CMI in the early stages of its work on the revision of the 1967 Convention on Maritime Liens and Mortgages, and have been summarized by Professor Francesco Berlingieri in the following terms:[4]

> The Sub-Committee agreed that the primary purpose of a Convention should be that of improving the security level of mortgages and *hypotheques*. In particular, it agreed that:
> (a) long-term financing is essential for the development of merchant marine;
> (b) the more readily available and less expensive security is the vessel itself;
> (c) the need for uniform rules is increasing, for ship financing is becoming more and more international;
> (d) the essential features of a satisfactory security are: (i) the possibility of enforcement wherever the vessel may be found, and to this effect the security must be recognized in as many countries as possible through an international Convention; (ii) the possibility of sale of the vessel at the market price, and to this effect it is necessary to offer the prospective buyer a valid title wherever the ship may go after the forced sale; (iii) the possibility of recovering the outstanding portion of the loan from the proceeds of the forced sale, and to this effect the claim of the lender must be granted the highest possible priority.

To this list one might add the need to encompass not only mortgages and charges but other forms of non-possessory interest, notably conditional sales and leases. All these objectives, and others besides, are intended to be realized by the UNIDROIT Convention on International Interests in Mobile Equipment, to which I now turn.

## IV. The UNIDROIT Draft Convention: An Outline

### About UNIDROIT

UNIDROIT, the short name for the International Institute for the Unification of Private Law, is an international, intergovernmental organization founded in 1926 to foster the progressive harmonization of private law. Based in Rome it was originally set up under the auspices of the League of Nations but later became an independent body. Some 58 States are currently members of UNIDROIT. Over the 73 years of its existence UNIDROIT has played a major role, both on its own and in collaboration with other bodies, such as UNCITRAL (the United Nations Commission on International Trade Law) and the Hague Conference on Private International Law, in preparing and promoting international Conventions in a variety of fields, including transport.

[4] "The 1993 Convention on Maritime Liens and Mortgages" [1995] LMCLQ 57.

## The need for a Convention

Preparatory work to evaluate the need for a Convention on international interests in mobile equipment began some 10 years ago. A careful study was conducted by Professor Ron Cuming of Canada to establish that a need did indeed exist, and only when it became clear that this was so did the Governing Council authorize the work to proceed. The impetus for such a Convention was recognition of the fact that attitudes toward security over tangible movables vary widely from one country to another, and while some legal regimes, such as English law, are very liberal towards the creation and enforcement of security rights of all kinds, and give great weight to the concept of party autonomy, others are hostile and either do not recognize non-possessory security at all or limit it to security in land. Accordingly, the secured creditor has no assurance that a security interest validly created under the law of one jurisdiction will be recognized and enforced in another, nor that it will necessarily have priority over subsequent interests. So, even if a uniform conflict of laws rule could be devised—and the traditional *lex situs* rule is not well suited to objects constantly on the move—it would not address the fundamental problem of dependence of a security interest on a law of a State of enforcement which might view it with disfavour or which might so constrict its scope and limit party autonomy as to render the security of doubtful value. It was no longer sensible to try to deal with these problems through the conflict of laws; what was needed was a Convention laying down substantive rules which would apply in all Contracting States. I will explain a little later the interesting institutional mechanisms through which equipment-specific Protocols relating to aircraft, space property, and railway rolling stock have been developed—a striking example of institutional collaboration and partnership embracing international non-governmental organizations as well as international governmental bodies.

## The purposes of the Convention

These are reflected in the Preamble, the current text of which reads as follows:

THE STATES PARTIES TO THIS CONVENTION

AWARE of the need to acquire and use mobile equipment of high value or particular economic significance and to facilitate the financing of the acquisition and use of such equipment in an efficient manner,

RECOGNISING the advantages of asset-based financing and leasing for this purpose and desiring to facilitate these types of transaction by establishing clear rules to govern them,

MINDFUL of the need to ensure that interests in such equipment are recognised and protected universally,

DESIRING to provide broad economic benefits for all interested parties,

BELIEVING that such rules must reflect the principles underlying asset-based financing and leasing and promote the autonomy of the parties necessary in these transactions,

CONSCIOUS of the need to establish a legal framework for international interests in such equipment and for that purpose to create an international registration system for their protection, HAVE AGREED upon the following provisions ...

It will be apparent that the Convention has a much broader purpose than the legislation of private rights. What it seeks to do is to ensure that finance that would not otherwise be available because of lack of adequate security and related rights becomes available, that through the existence of strong security rights the cost of borrowing is significantly reduced, to the benefit both of borrowers and of end-users, and that developing countries whose legal regime is not adequately equipped to cater for the needs of secured financiers will have greater access to markets in capital goods than hitherto.

## Nature and scope of the Convention

The UNIDROIT Convention differs in a number of important respects from the maritime lien Conventions. First, it is not a conflict of laws Convention but an instrument which provides a set of uniform substantive law rules governing international interests in mobile equipment. An international interest acquired and perfected in accordance with the Convention rules is thus not in principle dependent on rules of national law governing the creation, perfection, and priority of security interests, though national law is relevant for some purposes, for example, whether there is a contract at all under the general law, whether it falls within one of the categories of agreement covered by the Convention and whether it relates to equipment of which the chargor, seller, or lessor has power to dispose. The Convention possess its own set of default remedies, including provisions for speedy interim judicial relief, as well as provisions for assignment, and recognition of the secured party's rights in bankruptcy, and two Articles dealing with non-consensual rights and interests.

Secondly, the Convention is not confined to a single category of objects but covers airframes, aircraft engines, helicopters, railway rolling stock, and space property. Other categories of uniquely identifiable object may be added if this is found appropriate. The Convention itself is not equipment-specific; for each distinct category it will be supplemented by a Protocol as described later.

Thirdly, the definition of "international interest" covers not only the interest of a chargee under a security agreement but also the interest vested in a person who is the conditional seller under a title reservation agreement or a lessor under a leasing agreement. For brevity I will use the terms "security agreement", "chargee" and "debtor" to include conditional sale and leasing agreements and the parties to them.

Finally, the Convention provides for the creation of something unique, namely an international register to receive registrations of international interests, the sole method of perfection required to give international efficacy to the international interest.

So what the Convention aims to do is to replace at the international level the multiplicity of national laws governing security and related interest created under national law and to provide a single regime of rights and duties and a single system of protection and priorities, coupled with recognition of rights in bankruptcy. This does not mean that national interests will disappear; on the contrary most national interests in mobile equipment will simultaneously be international interests. Their status as national interests will continue to be governed by national law, but a national interest not registered as an international interest in the international registry will be subordinate to a registered international interest.

As indicated in the Preamble, the Convention is designed for equipment which is mobile, in the sense that it regularly moves from one country to another in the course of business. That is the first limiting factor, though it is not expressly stated in the Convention itself. The second limiting factor is that the equipment is of high unit value (for example, aircraft and space property) or is of particular economic significance in cross-border transactions. That, too, is not stated in the text of the Convention but it features in the Preamble and will be picked up in the equipment-specific Protocols to which I shall shortly refer. The third limiting factor is that, since entries in the international registry are against the asset, not against the debtor, the Convention is confined to equipment that is uniquely identifiable, typically by serial number. In short, the Convention is aimed at high-value or high-volume business dealings in uniquely identifiable assets that are mobile in the sense I have described.

## The two-instrument approach

It became evident from an early stage of work on the Convention that, while its provisions were designed to cover all the categories of object I have mentioned, these would need to be supplemented by at least some equipment-specific provisions and that these could only be worked out through specialists and specialist agencies. At the suggestion of the Aviation Working Group, set up to explore the application of the Convention to airframes and aircraft engines, the decision was taken to keep the Convention itself general in terms and to embody equipment-specific provisions in a series of Protocols, one for aircraft, one for space property, one for railway rolling stock, and so on.

It would have been possible to deal with the matter in other ways. One would have been to place such provisions in the Convention itself, but that would have two major drawbacks. In the first place, it would delay the completion of the Convention until each sector had made its input. The aviation industry, through a small Aviation Working Group, later expanded as IATA and ICAO, had become keenly interested in the project, in which it was investing considerable time and resources, and it was reluctant to be held up while similar groups in other sectors were being assembled. Secondly, inclusion of equipment-specific provisions would encumber the text with a great deal of detail, some of it highly technical, which would not be appropriate for such an instrument.

Another option would have been to have a series of stand-alone Conventions, each devoted to a separate category of equipment. Though some initially favoured such an approach, others were strongly opposed, seeing a number of disadvantages. The single-instrument process would involve a substantial duplication of work. Moreover, since each Convention would be drafted at different times and by different hands, the uniformity of the provisions that were not equipment-specific would be lost. The resulting fragmentation would mean, for example, that those involved in two or more categories of equipment would have to become familiar with two or more Conventions framed in different language. Further, judicial interpretations of provisions of one Convention would not necessarily be applicable to the different wording of another. An additional drawback would be the need to hold a Diplomatic Conference for each Convention, a time-consuming and expensive process. The Convention/Protocol approach avoids these disadvantages. It allows the aviation sector to press ahead with work on the Aircraft Protocol without being held up by other sectors that are not yet quite so advanced in their work. It leaves those provisions of the Convention not requiring modification for particular types of equipment to apply as a general framework to all categories of equipment. It affords States the opportunity of choosing from a menu of options, so that, for example, those interested only in aircraft and space property would be able to ratify the Convention and the aircraft and space property Protocols without having to ratify any others. Finally, the two-instrument approach permits the possibility of additional categories of equipment being brought under the Convention by virtue of further Protocols to be adopted by fast-track procedures which would avoid the need for additional Diplomatic Conferences; and it provides the newcomers with the opportunity to negotiate modifications of the Convention as regards their equipment sector in order to meet their particular needs. At the end of the third Joint Session opinion swung strongly behind the two-instrument approach.

Accordingly, as currently structured, the Convention will apply only to a category of object designated in a Protocol and will come into force as regards such category only when the requisite Protocol has come into force. Rather more unusually, the Protocol controls the Convention. The usual function of a Protocol is to supplement a Convention rather than displace any of its provisions. But it came to be seen that the needs of particular sectors made it imperative to allow provisions of the Convention to be overridden to the extent that they were incompatible with those needs. So the two-instrument approach, while providing a general framework, also allows a considerable measure of flexibility.

Let me give some examples of problems that have been resolved through this method in relation to aircraft. First, there is the apparently simple question of definitions. What is an airframe? How should one define an aircraft engine? Even at the technical level these questions require a good deal of thought. For example, an early draft of the Aircraft Protocol defined aircraft engines in terms of engines powered by jet propulsion or turbine technology. At the first Joint Session of the UNIDROIT Committee of governmental experts and the Sub-Committee of the Legal Committee of ICAO in February 1999 it was pointed out by one delegate that this formulation did not cover engines powered by piston technology, and the definition was amended accordingly. It was also necessary for the definition to be so framed as to exclude aircraft not of high unit value. This was done by specifying a combination of minimum thrust or power of engines and minimum passenger or goods capacity for airframes. Modules, manuals, and other accessories also had to be considered. Again, it was necessary to set out the criteria for unique identifiability of the object. For aircraft objects that will be by serial number; but, since apparently a manufacturer may use different types of serial number for the same engine or airframe, further work will have to be done on this. Then there were policy questions, such as whether aircraft used in military, Customs, or police services should be excluded. One can imagine very similar problems of definition and scope arising in relation to ships, which could only be resolved through the work of CMI and IMO.

The Protocol approach must, of course, be disciplined, as, indeed, it has been with aircraft objects, space property, and railway rolling stock. The function of the Protocol is not to rewrite the Convention but rather to make such modifications, and only such modifications, as are needed to meet the particular practices of the sector concerned. The Aircraft Protocol amends various provisions, particularly those relating to remedies, and applies a provision of the Convention enabling it to be extended to outright sales, but leaves the great bulk of the Convention untouched. That is the proper approach.

## The principles underlying the Convention

There are certain key principles which shape the Convention.[5] They reflect the fact that it is concerned with commercial transactions, not consumer transactions; with equipment that regularly crosses national boundaries or, in the case of space property, is outside terrestrial jurisdiction altogether; and with high-value or high-volume dealings entered into by sophisticated enterprises well versed in the art of negotiation and possessing the necessary economic muscle to do so. Accordingly, the Convention embodies five fundamental principles:

### *(i) Party autonomy*

The Convention attaches great importance to the right of the parties, within certain outer limits, to set their own agenda and agree on their own rights and default remedies.

### *(ii) Predictability*

Prospective lenders, and rating agencies asked to rate equipment receivables, need as high an assurance as possible that the legal regime will enforce bargains and provide a prompt and efficient method of asset recovery. That is brought out in Article 6(1):

> In the interpretation of this Convention regard shall be had to its purposes as set forth in the Preamble, to its international character and to the need to promote uniformity and predictability[6] in its application.

This is a significant departure from the standard formulation established by the UN Convention on Contracts for the International Sale of Goods 1980, in that it substitutes predictability for good faith as an interpretative element, because it was considered that in large-scale business dealings the introduction of good faith as an aspect of interpretation would generate an unacceptable degree of uncertainty, when what was required above all was predictability.

[5] See also Lorne Clarke and Jeffrey Wool, "Proposed Unidroit Convention and Aircraft Protocol" 1998/99 *Airfinance Annual* 42.

[6] Emphasis added.

### *(iii) Transparency of priority rules*

As will be seen, the Convention priority rules are strikingly clear and concise.

### *(iv) A strong enforcement regime*

Those engaged in asset financing and leasing in large cross-border transactions involving mobile equipment need to feel that the legal regimes in which they operate around the world will provide an enforcement regime which accords a high degree of autonomy to the parties in the selection and mode of enforcement of default remedies and which facilitates speedy and efficient enforcement while at the same time providing a facility for rapid interim relief to safeguard the chargee's interests in equipment pending the determination of the substantive dispute. But it is not only the lenders and lessors themselves who feel such a need. The existence of a strong enforcement regime is also of great importance to the rating of equipment receivables by rating agencies such as Moody's and Standard and Poor. I shall return to this later.

### *(v) A responsive insolvency regime*

By this I mean an insolvency regime which respects the title of the secured party and imposes only limited restrictions on the recovery of the equipment where the insolvency administrator decides not to meet the obligations under the security agreement.

## Creation of the international interest

How is an international interest created? All that is required is that the agreement creating or providing for the interest is in writing, relates to an object of which the chargor, conditional seller, or lessor has power to dispose, enables the object to be identified in accordance with the Protocol, and in the case of a security agreement enables the secured obligations to be determined but without the need to state a sum or maximum sum secured. It is envisaged that in the great majority of cases a security agreement made in conformity with national law will simultaneously meet the Convention requirements for an international interest. Registration is not an element in the creation of an international interest, merely a requirement if it is to be protected against third-party claims.

## Perfection of the international interest

This is achieved by registration in the International Registry. It is envisaged that in the ordinary way registration and searching will be electronic and automatic and that existing national registration systems will be the required entry points for registration. Though conceptually there is a single Registry for all types of equipment, it is likely that operationally there will be different registries for different categories of equipment, and the Convention provides for this. A useful provision is included allowing registration of a *prospective* international interest where the equipment exists but the interest has not yet attached under the security agreement. When attachment occurs the prospective interest can be converted into an actual interest with priority retrospective to the date of its registration as a prospective interest. Compensation would be payable for loss suffered through Registry errors or system malfunction.

## Priorities

On the basis that clarity was preferable to sophistication, the Convention provides a remarkably succinct set of priority rules within a single Article. The primary rule is that a registered interest has priority over any other interest subsequently registered and over an unregistered interest. The priority over an unregistered interest applies even if the registered interest was acquired or registered with actual knowledge of it. The priority of the first registered interest over the later registered interest applies even as regards value given by the holder of the former with actual knowledge of the latter. This displaces, in the interests of simplicity, the normal common law restriction against the tacking of further advances. The second rule is that the outright buyer of an object takes subject to an interest registered at the time of the buyer's acquisition but free from an unregistered interest even if he has actual knowledge of it. The primary rule cannot fairly be applied to an outright buyer, since the Convention does not apply to outright sales so that he has no ability to protect himself by registration. By contrast, the Aircraft Protocol extends the Convention to outright sales of aircraft, so that the special rule for the protection of the buyer is not needed and is disapplied. The third rule is that priorities may be varied by agreement.

## Effects of insolvency

The general principle is that the title of the chargee, conditional seller, or lessor is to be respected in the event of the insolvency of the other party, but without prejudice to special insolvency rules, such as unfair preferences, transactions in fraud of creditors, and the like.

## Assignments

The provisions of the Convention are carried over, *mutatis mutandis,* into assignments of international interests.

## Non-consensual rights and interests

The last substantive part of the Convention deals with non-consensual rights and interests. These are typically of two kinds. The first is a right of interest which can be identified as arising at a particular time, for example, a lien for storage or repair or for airport dues, or an attachment by an execution creditor. The second is the preferential right, usually conferred by statute, for certain types of debt, such as wages and taxes. Here the preferential right is usually inchoate until the occurrence of an event such as bankruptcy and is restricted in time and amount. Non-consensual interests of the first kind lend themselves to registration, those of the second usually do not. It is interests of the first kind that are envisaged by the Convention provision enabling a Contracting State to list in a deposited instrument the categories of non-consensual right or interest which are to be registrable under the Convention as if they were international interests. Upon such registration a non-consensual right or interest would rank accordingly. A separate provision of the Convention, which is particularly designed for the second category, but is capable of accommodating the first, provides for a Contracting State to declare those categories of right or interest which under that State's law would have priority over an interest equivalent to that held by the holder of the international interest and which are to have priority even over a registered international interest. This would safeguard, among other things, the traditional priority of maritime liens. Furthermore, the declaration would not have to specify individual categories, nor would it have to be confined to existing categories. It would be sufficient if it stated that all non-consensual rights or interest currently enjoying, or to enjoy in the future, priority over an interest equivalent to that held by the holder of the international interest would have priority over that interest even if registered.

## V. The Institutional Collaboration

### The aviation industry

It was clear from an early stage that, while UNIDROIT was well-equipped to formulate the general provisions of a Convention on international interests in mobile equipment, a task undertaken by a Study Group established by the Governing Council, specialist expertise would be needed to identify the needs and concerns of particular business sectors. The first to show interest, and the most advanced with its Protocol, was the aviation industry, which has already concluded that the 1948 Geneva Convention on the recognition of rights in aircraft was not adequate for the needs of modern aviation finance. Beginning with an initiative taken by UNIDROIT's aviation consultant, Mr Jeffrey Wool, and two leading aircraft manufacturers, Boeing and Airbus Industrie, an Aviation Working Group was formed to make an input into the process while it was still in its formative stage and to ensure that the principles of the Convention were consistent with the requirements of aviation finance. The AWG in turn urged IATA to give its support to the project and later, at the invitation of UNIDROIT, the International Civil Aviation Organization (ICAO) agreed to participate in the work. An Aircraft Protocol Group was then formed to prepare the draft of an Aircraft Protocol. The three international organizations, UNIDROIT, ICAO, and IATA, together with the other members of the Aircraft Working Group, are working in tandem to advance the project, which as regards aircraft is being jointly sponsored by UNIDROIT and

ICAO. This has now gained a strong momentum. Already two Joint Sessions of the UNIDROIT Committee of Governmental Experts and the ICAO Legal Sub-Committee have met, in Rome and Montreal, to conduct a detailed examination of the draft Convention and Protocol. A third and final Joint Session took place in March 2000, and, if agreed by the UNIDROIT Governing Council, will be followed by a Diplomatic Conference in 2001.

At an earlier stage of the work the Aircraft Protocol Group commissioned a study by economists at INSEAD and the New York University Salomon Center to assess the economic effects of the Convention as modified by the Protocol. Their conclusion was that there were substantial benefits to all interests concerned. It was estimated that a strengthened legal regime for international security interests could have a very significant effect on risk assessment and credit ratings and save several *billion* dollars a year, the benefits of which would flow to airlines, aircraft manufacturers, airlines, shareholders, and customers.

Now things are moving ahead with space property and railway rolling stock. A Space Working Group has produced the first draft of a Protocol on space property, tailoring the provisions of the Convention to the particular requirements of the space industry,[7] and the United Nations Office for Outer Space Affairs has now become involved. Similarly, a Rail Working Group has been hard at work producing a draft Protocol on railway rolling stock,[8] and OTIF, the European organization for international transport by rail, is closely involved in the project.

Much work remains to be done, particularly in relation to the structure and supervision of the International Registry, which raise both technical and policy issues; but the ground has been well prepared. Moreover, from the outset there have been extensive consultations with outside organizations in the private sector and with individual experts, and we have had the benefit of ideas thrown up at numerous seminars in different countries to discuss the Convention and Protocol. This was essential if the product of the work was to reflect the real needs of industry and finance, rather than those merely perceived as necessary by academic lawyers, albeit of great international standing. The input of legal and other specialists and of the suppliers and operators of aircraft and other equipment has been a major factor in attracting such widespread interest and support for the draft Convention from a relatively early stage. This is amply attested by the contributions to the second issue of the 1999 volume of UNIDROIT's legal periodical *Uniform Law Review,* an issue devoted exclusively to the UNIDROIT Convention and Protocols, as well as by highly supportive articles in specialist journals, all of which, in supporting the Convention, indicate that it should not cause problems of compatibility with national law in the jurisdictions discussed.

[7] See Paul B. Larsen and Juergen A. Heilbock, "UNIDROIT Project on Security Interests: How the Project Affects Space Objects" (1999) 64 J. Air. L. & Co. 703; Dara A. Panahy and Raman Mittal, "The prospective UNIDROIT Convention on international interests in mobile equipment as applied to space property" [1999] (2) Uniform Law Rev. 303.

[8] See Howard Rosen, "Creating an international security structure for railway rolling stock: an idea ahead of its time?" [1999] (2) Uniform Law Rev. 313.

## VI. The Convention and the Shipping Industry

And now we ask: what of our friends in the shipping industry? Can they be persuaded to see the prospect of shipping and shipping finance securing benefits from the Convention, with a maritime Protocol, similar to those perceived by the other three sectors I have mentioned? The world already owes an immense debt to bodies such as the CMI and the IMO, which have laboured prodigiously to advance the cause of unification. Here they have an opportunity, in collaboration with UNIDROIT, to create a product of lasting value. The work is hard but the prize is great. I would suggest that the three-cornered partnership in place for aircraft—UNIDROIT, ICAO, and IATA—could very easily be replicated for ships, with UNIDROIT and IMO co-sponsoring the marine Protocol, while CMI would bring its long experience and the enormous expertise of its members to bear on issues affecting ships and help to ensure that the Convention works for the shipping industry and its financiers and that any necessary adjustments and additional provisions are made. And that is the thought on which I should like to end this, the 17th Annual Lecture of the Institute of Maritime Studies and the 11th lecture bearing the name of Donald O'May. It remains only to express my warm thanks to you for coming here tonight and for listening with such patience to one whose lack of knowledge of your field will by now have become all too apparent.

# 11

# The Power to Dispose Under the Cape Town Convention and Aircraft Protocol*

*Roy Goode*

The 2001 Cape Town Convention on international interests in mobile equipment, together with its associated Aircraft Protocol, contains a set of uniform rules governing, among other things, the creation, perfection, and priority of international interests in aircraft. An international interest is an interest granted by a chargor under a security agreement or vested in a person who is the conditional seller under a title reservation agreement or a lessor under a leasing agreement (collectively "the debtor"). An aircraft object is an airframe, aircraft engine, or a helicopter. The Aircraft Protocol extends the Convention, other than the default provisions, to outright sales.[1] The primary method of perfecting an international interest or an outright purchase is by registration in the International Registry, which is based in Dublin, operated by Aviareto and supervised by the Council of the International Civil Aviation Organization (ICAO), which at a later stage joined the initiating organisation, the International Institute for the Unification of Private Law (UNIDROIT) in sponsoring the Cape Town Project.

The conditions for constituting an international interest are prescribed by Article 7 of the Convention and for a sale by Article V of the Protocol.

* First published in [2018] CTCJ 2.

[1] This is true also of the Space Protocol. By contrast the Luxembourg Protocol, covering railway rolling stock, and the draft mining, agriculture, and construction ("MAC") Protocol do not apply to outright sales and merely permit registration of a notice of sale having no Convention effects but designed to give notice of the existence of the sale for the purpose of priority rules under national law. I am indebted to Kenneth Gray for his comments on an earlier draft of this paper, "The Power to Dispose under the Cape Town Convention and Protocol: A Reply". I have accepted Mr Gray's point on the protection of the sub-lessee under Article 29(4) of the Convention—indeed, his position was that taken in my Official Commentary, para 2.166, a point that he was too polite to mention—and have expanded the treatment of power to dispose to reinforce my reasoning, disputed by Mr Gray, that a power to dispose can arise not only under national law but under the Convention.

Article 7 provides as follows:

**Article 7—Formal requirements**

An interest is constituted as an international interest under this Convention where the agreement creating or providing for the interest:

(a) is in writing;
(b) relates to an object of which the chargor, conditional seller or lessor has power to dispose;
(c) enables the object to be identified in conformity with the Protocol; and
(d) in the case of a security agreement, enables the secured obligations to be determined, but without the need to state a sum or maximum sum secured.

Article V is in similar terms except that it states the necessary elements of a contract of sale instead of the constitution of an international interest.

Non-compliance with any of these provisions means that no international interest comes into existence and registration of the purported interest will be of no effect. Indeed, insofar as such registration casts a shadow on the title of the owner or of another, lawful, registrant it may be actionable. For example, under English law a wrongful registration made maliciously, that is, without an honest belief of entitlement to make it, and causing pecuniary loss to the claimant constitutes the tort of slander of title, attracting a right to damages and, in the case of a Cape Town Convention registration, an order requiring the defendant to procure discharge of the registration. Irish law is similar, and in the absence of an order from a court outside Ireland, and to overcome lacunae in Article 44 of the Convention,[2] the Irish High Court has invoked its general jurisdiction rules as regards torts committed in Ireland to make an order *in personam* against the registrant to discharge the registration and then, in exercise of its Convention jurisdiction under Article 44(1), has directed the Registrar to discharge the registration.[3]

The requirements of paragraphs (a), (c), and (d) are reasonably clear, but there has been much discussion of the meaning of "power to dispose" under paragraph (b) and it is to this issue that the present article is directed.

## "Dispose"

The word "dispose" has a wide meaning, covering every form of grant of a property interest by the debtor or outright seller, including a sale (whether outright or under reservation of title), a lease, a sub-lease, an assignment of a lease or sub-lease, a charge or sub-charge (whether by a transfer of title under a mortgage or sub-mortgage or by a hypothecation or sub-hypothecation[4]), an assignment of a

[2] See Roy Goode, *Official Commentary on International Interests in Mobile Equipment and Protocol thereto on Matters Specific to Aircraft Objects* (3rd edn), paras 2.226–2.228.

[3] *Transfin-M v Stream Aero Instruments SA and Aviareto Ltd* 2013 No 112 MCA. See *Official Commentary* (n 1 above), para 2.228.

[4] See the definition of "security agreement" in Article 1(ii) read with that of "debtor" in Article 1(j).

charge or sub-charge, or the delivery of possession under a pledge, contractual lien, or other kind of bailment. For this purpose delivery of possession may be actual (direct, physical) or constructive (indirect), for example, by giving control of the contents of a warehouse through possession of the keys or the delivery of possession to a third party who agrees to hold the object to the order of the grantee. But the grant must confer a property interest of some kind; the conferment of a mere contractual right to buy, take a lease, etc, unaccompanied by the delivery of possession is not a disposition.

The only relevant disposition is one by the debtor or outright seller, but the debtor may also be a creditor, as where a lessee grants a sub-lease or a chargor grants a sub-charge.

## Power to Dispose and Right to Dispose

The phrase "power to dispose" includes but is wider than a right to dispose, extending to the legal power to dispose even where there is no right to do so. A power to dispose exists either where there is a right to dispose or where the applicable law or the Convention gives effect to the disposition even though the person making it has no right to do so.

## Right to Dispose

The right to dispose exists where the grantor, whether the debtor or an outright seller, either transfers no greater interest than it has or, if transferring more, obtains the consent of the party or parties whose interests would be affected by the disposition. There are two main cases:

(1) The debtor or seller is the unencumbered owner
(2) Though the debtor or seller is not the unencumbered owner the disposition is made with the consent of the owner and of the holder of any other interest which the disposition, if effective, would override.

Case (1) needs no explanation. Examples of case (2) are dispositions by an agent acting within his actual authority, express or implied; sales by a mortgagee pursuant to a power of sale contained in the mortgage; transfers of a mortgage; and sub-mortgages or sub-charges by a mortgagee or chargee. Further, a right of disposal suspended while the holder has granted an interest to another which is incompatible with exercise of the holder's rights[5] if not made subject to those rights may be revived

[5] As on the grant of a lease, where the lessee has a right of quiet enjoyment against its lessor and any person whose interest was not registered prior to the registration of the lessor's interest (Protocol, Article XVI(1)(a); Convention, Article 29(4)(b)).

by the termination of that interest under the applicable law.[6] Also within case (2) are dispositions of no greater interest than the grantor has, for example, second and subsequent mortgages or charges by a mortgagor or chargor and assignments or sub-leases by a lessee where not prohibited by the lease.

Examples under the Convention are dispositions by a chargee[7] who has exercised a right of repossession, sale, or grant of a lease under Article 8 (a right which under that Article is dependent on the chargor's agreement), the vesting of ownership in the chargee under Article 9 (which requires the agreement of the debtor as an interested person[8]), and lawful termination of the agreement by a conditional seller or lessor under Article 10 in accordance with an agreement concluded under Article 11. In all these cases the right of disposal is consensual and the disposition does not transfer greater rights than those of the person by whom or on whose behalf it is made.

## Power to Dispose

A power to dispose goes much wider than a right to dispose, covering every case in which, by exception to the *nemo dat* rule,[9] the debtor or seller can confer an interest greater than that which it holds and without the consent of the holder of superior interests. Such an exception may arise either under the applicable law or, by necessary implication, under the Convention as extended by the Protocol.

## Exceptions to the *Nemo Dat* Rule under the Applicable Law

Most common law systems, while taking the *nemo dat* rule as their starting point, provide exceptions. English law examples include dispositions by: an agent beyond his actual authority but within the scope of his ostensible authority; a non-owner who is held out as the owner by the true owner; a mercantile agent in possession with the consent of the owner;[10] a seller who remains in possession with the consent of the buyer;[11] and a buyer who obtains possession with the consent of the owner.[12]

[6] An interesting question arising under English law is the effect on an authorised sub-lease of termination of the head lease. Curiously there appears to have been no reported case on this question, nor is it discussed in textbooks on bailment or personal property. The writer has expressed the view that, subject to any conditions imposed by the lessor on the right to grant a sub-lease this continues in force, the sub-lessee becoming the direct lessee of the lessor on the terms of the sub-lease. See *Goode on Commercial Law* (5th edn, ed Ewan McKendrick), para 28.28 and fn 50. This conclusion derives support from the decision of the Privy Council in *The Pioneer Container* [1994] 2 AC 324 dealing with the binding effect of a sub-lease on the head lessor. On this basis termination of the lessor's power of disposal would remain in suspense despite termination of the head lease in the absence of conditions attached to the grant of the sub-lease.

[7] Which under Article 1(ii) includes a mortgagee.

[8] Article 1(m).

[9] *Nemo dat quod non habet*, also rendered in civil law jurisdictions as *nemo plus juris ad alium transferre potest quam ipse habet.*

[10] Factors Act 1889, s 2(1).

[11] *ibid*, s 7; Sale of Goods Act 1979, s 24.

[12] Factors Act 1889, s 9; Sale of Goods Act 1979, s 25. See generally *Goode on Commercial Law* (5th edn 2016, ed Ewan McKendrick), chapter 16; Michael Bridge, *The Sale of Goods* (3rd edn 2014), chapter 5.

In almost all these cases[13] the effectiveness of the disposition is dependent on its being made to one who takes in good faith and without notice of the prior title. Outside these exceptions the *nemo dat* rule prevails. So a lessee has no power to sell or even to grant a sub-lease where this would be in breach of the leasing agreement. Civil law systems by contrast have a different starting point, adopting the general principle that *en fait de meubles, la possession vaut titre*,[14] pursuant to which a person who is not the owner but holds possession with the consent of the owner can transfer title to one taking possession in good faith. Here the effect of the applicable law is that the person effecting the transfer has a power of disposal within s 7 of the Convention and this includes power to make an outright sale, grant a mortgage or charge, or assign a lease or grant a sub-lease despite a prohibition in the lease agreement.

## What Is the Applicable Law?

This question is not answered by the Convention, which leaves the matter to be determined by the domestic rules of private international law of the forum State.[15] Under most legal systems, including English law, the proprietary effects of a dealing in tangible movables are governed by the *lex situs* (*lex rei sitae*), that is, the law of the situation of the asset at the time of the disposition in question.[16]

## Exceptions to the *Nemo Dat* Rule under the Convention and Protocol

A power to dispose can also arise under the Convention as extended by the Protocol. Under Article 29 the first to register an interest acquires priority[17] and this is so even if the registrant of the second, unauthorised, interest took with actual knowledge of the prior unregistered interest.[18] Similarly a second buyer from a seller in possession who registers its purchase before registration by the first buyer has priority even if taking with actual knowledge of the prior sale.[19] This rule is designed to protect the integrity of the registry system and to avoid factual disputes as to whether a party did or did not have knowledge. In national legal systems such knowledge would almost always make the second disposition ineffective except in the case of successive charges.[20] It is thus implicit in the registration and priority provisions that a debtor

[13] Mortgages of registered ships and aircraft constitute an exception. See n 20 below.

[14] See, for example, the French code civil, Article 2279.

[15] Article 5(3). This reflects an almost universal rule that conflict of laws issues are to be determined by the *lex fori*, which in this context means its domestic rules, excluding *renvoi*.

[16] For English law, the latest case, concerning the law applicable to an aircraft mortgage, is *Blue Sky One Ltd v Mahan Air, PK Airfinance US Inc v Blue Sky Two Ltd* [2010] EWHC 631 (Comm).

[17] Article 29(1). [18] Article 29(2). [19] Protocol, Article XIV(1).

[20] Since the chargor always remains free to deal with his reversionary interest. Moreover, registration systems governing aircraft mortgages may provide priority by registration regardless of actual or constructive notice of an unregistered mortgage. But Article 29 also applies to title reservation and leasing agreements, which in most countries (the US, Canada, New Zealand, and Australia being the exceptions) are not registrable, so that a disposition to a third party taking with knowledge of a prior interest will have no effect.

in possession and a seller remaining in possession have power to dispose under the Convention, because otherwise Article 29(2) would be deprived of effect and Article 29(1) would be rendered otiose, at least as regards conditional sale and leasing agreements, since there would be no point in providing a facility for the conditional seller or lessor to register its international interest or the buyer to register its purchase in order to protect its priority.[21] Three simple illustrations will demonstrate this.

*Illustration 1*
Under an agreement governed by English law and falling within the Cape Town Convention A leases an airframe to B, who wrongfully sells the airframe to C. B has no power to make the disposition under English law. A fails to register its international interest. If B were not to be considered to have a power of disposal under the Convention there would be only one international interest, that held by A. In this situation A would have priority over C, not under Article 29(1), which applies only if there is at least one registered interest, but because there is no valid competing interest either under the Convention or under the applicable law. So a conflict between competing international interests, the outcome of which is intended to be determined by Article 29, could never arise and Article 29(1) would be rendered otiose.

*Illustration 2*
The facts are as Illustration 1 except that B, instead of selling the airframe to C, grants C a sub-lease in breach of the leasing agreement. Again, B has no power under English law to grant the sub-lease, so if it were not to be considered to have a power of disposal under the Convention there would be no point in A registering its international interest as it would have priority anyway, making Article 29(1) redundant.

*Illustration 3*
A supplies goods to B under a conditional sale agreement which reserves title until payment but fails to register the title reservation as an international interest in the International Registry. B wrongfully sells the goods to C who, knowing of A's title, registers the sale in the International Registry. C has priority over A under Article 29(1), and under Article 29(2) this is the case despite C's knowledge of A's prior interest and despite the fact that such knowledge renders the disposition to C ineffective under the applicable law.

So it is clear that a lessee in possession has a power of disposition under the Convention and if the lessee sells or charges the leased equipment to a third party who registers the sale or charge before the lessor has registered its international interest the third party has priority under Article 29(1) of the Convention. Similarly a sub-lease by the lessee not only creates an international interest in favour of the lessee[22] but also confers rights on the sub-lessee against both the sub-lessor and the head lessor[23] even

[21] See Roy Goode, *Official Commentary on the Convention on International Interests in Mobile Equipment and Protocol Thereto on Matters Specific to Aircraft Equipment* (3rd edn, UNIDROIT 2013), para 2.65(4). It may be noted that this conclusion has been widely accepted. It was the position taken in the Official Commentary from the very first edition published in 2002 after extensive consultation with delegations and with the aviation industry, which has indorsed it. See, for example, *Practitioners' Guide to the Cape Town Convention and the Aircraft Protocol* published by the Legal Advisory Panel of the Aviation Working Group, September 2015, p 18.

[22] Though not one which, on registration, will give him priority over his own lessor. See below.

[23] Convention, Article 29(4); Protocol, Article XVI(a). But see below, p. 157.

if the sub-lease is in breach of a provision of the lease agreement. Again, a seller who is allowed by its buyer to remain in possession, perhaps for the purpose of remedying minor defects in the aircraft object, retains a power of disposal and if the seller makes a wrongful second sale to another buyer who is the first to register its purchase the second buyer has priority under Article 29(1) as applied to sales by Article III of the Aircraft Protocol.[24] In a Contracting State the law of which possesses the institution of trust it is the trustee, not the beneficiary, who has the power to dispose.[25]

There is one exception to this general priority principle, namely that a debtor cannot use the priority rules to impeach its own creditor's title and renounce its obligations under the agreement. So where an aircraft object is supplied under a title reservation agreement and the supplier registers its international interest and then charges the equipment to a third party, the supplier cannot rely on its registration to obtain priority over the chargee. Similarly, a lessee who grants a sub-lease cannot secure priority over his own lessor by registering his interest as sub-lessor before the lessor has effected registration of its own international interest. As the Official Commentary explains,[26] for the conditional seller to assert its prior registration would be inconsistent with the security interest it has granted to the chargee, while a lessee's claim to priority over its own lessor by virtue of having registered its international interest before the registration of the lessor's international interest would be inconsistent with its obligations under the lease and a denial of the lessor's title. However, its sub-lessee is protected by Article 29(4) of the Convention and Article XVI(1)(a) of the Protocol. Nevertheless the sub-lessee's position is not necessarily secure because if the head lease is terminated, whether by reason of the lessee's breach of its obligations under the head lease or otherwise, then it may be that its rights under the sub-lease come to an end.[27] That is a matter governed not by the Convention or Protocol but by the applicable law.

## Disposition of an Aircraft Engine Installed on a Helicopter

An international interest can only be constituted and registered in relation to an aircraft object, that is, an airframe, an aircraft engine, or a helicopter. There can be no separate registration of a component of one of these objects. An aircraft engine which is uninstalled or is or becomes installed on an airframe is a separate object for the purpose of the Convention and therefore capable of being the subject of an international interest. By contrast a purported disposition of an engine while installed on a helicopter has no Convention effects. This is because, as is clear from Article I(2) of the Protocol, such an engine is merely a component of the helicopter, not an aircraft object.[28] Article I(2)(a) defines aircraft as "aircraft as defined for the purposes

[24] Article 29(1) applies only where the two interests are in competition. So it has no application to a chain of sales where each buyer acquires its seller's title, which is thus displaced, so that it is usually the last buyer in the chain that acquires title.

[25] Official Commentary, paras 2.67, 5.33; Aircraft Protocol, Article VI.

[26] Para 2.171.

[27] As to the position under English law see above, n 6.

[28] Official Commentary, paras 3.8, 3.10.

of the Chicago Convention which are either airframes with aircraft engines installed thereon or helicopters", no reference being made either to helicopter airframes or to helicopter engines, while the definition of airframes in Article I(2)(e) the reference to installed accessories expressly excludes aircraft engines but there is no such exclusion in the definition of helicopters. The practical solution to this problem is for the creditor to take and register an international interest over the helicopter, which includes the engine as a component, and at the same time to take and register a prospective international interest in the engine which will become a completed interest the moment it leaves the helicopter, registration (and accordingly priority) dating back to the time of registration of the prospective international interest with no requirement of further registration.[29]

## Party Having Neither a Right to Dispose nor Possession

A party who has neither a *right* to dispose nor actual or constructive possession has no power of disposal under the Convention and any purported grant of an international interest or sale under the Convention will be ineffective unless a power of disposal arises under the applicable law. So a lessee who has not yet taken delivery of an aircraft object and thus has no right *in rem*, merely a contractual right to delivery under the terms of the leasing agreement, has no power of disposal under the Convention, the power remaining with the lessor, while the power of disposal of a seller who delivers possession to the buyer is extinguished. In such cases the power of disposal of a party not in possession depends on the applicable law. For example, under many systems disposal by an agent within the scope of his apparent authority will be effective even if the agent is not in possession and this power will meet the Convention requirement.

On the other hand it is not necessary for the aircraft object to have been delivered to the buyer from a lessee in possession or the second buyer from a seller in possession in order to secure priority for the buyer under the first-to-register rule. Delivery of possession may be necessary for an effective disposition under the applicable law, as with some of the exceptions to the *nemo dat* rule under English law described above, but it is not an element of a disposition in exercise of a power to dispose under the Convention.

[29] Articles 16(1)(a), 18(3), 19(4). See Official Commentary, para 3.10.

# 12

# Abstract Payment Undertakings and the Rules of the International Chamber of Commerce*

*Roy Goode*†

## I. Introduction

The first half of the 1990s witnessed an unprecedented level of activity on the part of the International Chamber of Commerce (ICC) in the promulgation of uniform rules governing bank payment undertakings.[1] In 1992 it issued its Uniform Rules for Demand Guarantees (URDG).[2] The following year saw the publication of a new revision of the ICC's outstandingly successful Uniform Customs and Practice for Documentary Credits (UCP),[3] first published 60 years before and now in universal use for international trade transactions, together with Standard Documentary Credit Forms for the UCP 500,[4] and Uniform Rules for Contract Bonds (UCB),[5] the first set of ICC rules dealing with suretyship bonds. Due to appear shortly are the Model Forms for Issuing Demand Guarantees[6] and Model Forms for Contract

* Originally published as R Goode: "Abstract Payment Undertakings and the Rules of the International Chamber of Commerce", 1995) 39 Saint Louis U.L.J., p. 740. Reprinted with permission of the Saint Louis University Law Journal © 1995 St. Louis University School of Law, St. Louis, Missouri.

† Norton Rose Professor of English Law in the University of Oxford, Fellow of St. John's College, Oxford.

1 The ICC, an international, non-governmental organization consisting of thousands of companies and business associations in more than 130 countries, represents the diverse interests of the world business community, operating through its numerous specialist Commissions based in Paris and its National Committees throughout the world. One of its most important functions is to harmonize international trade practices through uniform rules and trade terms incorporated into contracts, and through publications of guides devoted to specific fields of activity or specific problem areas.

2 Int'l Chamber of Commerce, Pub. No. 458, *ICC Uniform Rules for Demand Guarantees* (1992) [hereinafter URDG].

3 Int'l Chamber of Commerce, Pub. No. 500, *ICC Uniform Customs and Practice for Documentary Credits* (1993) [hereinafter UCP 500].

4 Int'l Chamber of Commerce, Pub. No. 516, *The New Standard Documentary Credit Forms for the UCP 500* (Charles del Busto ed., 1993).

5 Int'l Chamber of Commerce, Pub. No. 524, *ICC Uniform Rules for Contract Bonds* (1993) (effective Jan. 1, 1994).

6 Int'l Chamber of Commerce, Pub. No. 503, *ICC Model Forms for Issuing Demand Guarantees* (1995).

Bonds,[7] and a revision of the Uniform Rules for Collections.[8] Running in parallel with these activities is the work of the United Nations Commission on International Trade Law (UNCITRAL), whose work on a draft Convention on Independent Guarantees and Stand-By Letters of Credit is gradually approaching completion.

There are now no fewer than four sets of ICC Rules dealing with bank payment undertakings. The first, the ill-fated Uniform Rules for Contract Guarantees,[9] was in theory designed to cover performance bonds and demand guarantees. However, its requirement for a judgment or arbitral award as a condition of entitlement to payment was too far removed from international practice to be acceptable, coming close to crossing the line between a documentary guarantee and a suretyship guarantee. The second is the URDG, which covers bank payment undertakings that are primary in form but secondary in intent in that as between principal and beneficiary they are invoked only in the event of actual default by the principal.[10] The final text of the URDG results from the activities of a joint working group set up by the Banking Commission and the International Commercial Practice Commission, and, when the members of that group were unable to reach agreement on certain provisions, a Drafting Group set up to finalize the text. The third is the UCP, governing undertakings that are primary both in form and in intent, in that the beneficiary is both entitled and obliged to look to the bank in the first instance as the source of payment, and can only resort to the buyer if the bank defaults on its payment obligation. The Banking Commission entrusted the revision of the 1983 text to a working group, and a huge effort went into the revision, culminating in what has on the whole been a very successful new text, the UCP 500. The last set of rules on payment undertakings is the UCB, a set of rules governing suretyship bonds, a fact unhappily concealed by its ambiguous title. The suretyship bond is the classical guarantee: a payment (alternatively payment or performance) obligation triggered only by actual default on the part of the principal. Since the ICC is a private organization, not a lawmaking body, these rules have no independent force of their own; they take effect by incorporation into contracts. By contrast, if the UNCITRAL Convention is adopted it will acquire the force of law in contracting states.

This article is concerned only with the UCP and the URDG, both of which are concerned with a particular type of promise, the abstract payment undertaking, which is conditioned solely by reference to the presentation of specified documents conforming to the terms of the undertaking and is independent of the underlying trade transaction. These formulations by the ICC are not only of practical importance;[11] they also raise some interesting academic questions. First, what precisely are

[7] Int'l Chamber of Commerce, *ICC Model Forms for Contract Bonds* (forthcoming 1995).

[8] Int'l Chamber of Commerce, *ICC Uniform Rules for Collections* (forthcoming 1995).

[9] Int'l Chamber of Commerce, Pub. No. 325, *ICC Uniform Rules for Contract Guarantees* (1978).

[10] *See infra* Section II.

[11] The UCP are used in a huge volume of international trade transactions; the URDG, as a recent publication, is not yet in widespread use but is slowly gaining acceptance.

the legal status and scope of the UCP and the URDG and their relationship to substantive law? This involves, among other things, distinguishing issues of documentary credit law,[12] to be determined (inter alia) by interpreting the UCP or URDG, from issues governed by rules of law outside the UCP or URDG or, indeed, outside documentary credit law altogether. Second, what is the legal character of credits and guarantees within the UCP and the URDG respectively, and what makes them enforceable? What limits are there to their independence from the underlying transaction? Third, how is uniformity of the interpretation of the rules to be achieved? What is the legal effect of interpretive rulings on the rules by the relevant ICC Commission or other ICC body entrusted with that task? To what extent would it be sensible for parties to give such rulings contractual force?

## II. The Status and Scope of the UCP and the URDG

### A. The Function of ICC Uniform Rules

Both the content and the interpretation of ICC uniform rules are influenced by the fact that their function is to serve as rules of best banking practice, not rules of law, a point which is sometimes overlooked. That is why the UCP and the URDG contain on the one hand peremptory instructions ("[b]anks must examine all documents ... with reasonable care")[13] and on the other hand expressions which are purely precatory (e.g. "banks should discourage any attempt ... to include excessive detail in the Credit").[14] It is also why the UCP and URDG usually avoid touching on issues which are considered the province of the applicable law and of the courts of the forum, such as the effect of fraud on the bank's duty to pay.[15] In this respect the provisions of the URDG as to governing law and jurisdiction[16] represent something of a departure from precedent, though one which should prove useful.

### B. When Do the UCP and URDG Apply?

A question of some uncertainty is what brings about the application of the UCP to a particular documentary credit relationship? Article 1 of UCP 500 brings out more sharply than its predecessor the need for textual incorporation:

> The Uniform Customs and Practice for Documentary Credits ... shall apply to all Documentary Credits (including to the extent to which they may be applicable, Standby Letter(s) of Credit) where they are incorporated into the text of the Credit. They are binding on all parties thereto, unless otherwise expressly stipulated in the Credit.

The terms "documentary credit" and "standby credit" are defined in Article 2, which does not distinguish between them but applies a single definition to both, a point

[12] Including, in this context, the law on demand guarantees and standby credits.
[13] UCP 500, *supra* note 3, art. 13(a).
[14] UCP 500, *supra* note 3, art. 5(a).
[15] UCP 500, *supra* note 3, art. 18(d).
[16] URDG, *supra* note 2, arts. 27–28.

addressed further in this article. Accordingly, if one applies the scope provisions of the UCP, two conditions are necessary for their application: the bank's undertaking must fall within the definition of a documentary/standby credit in Article 2, and it must expressly incorporate the UCP.

However, it is a feature of institutional contractual rules, as opposed to statutes and international Conventions, that they cannot fully control the scope of their own application. This is because there is nothing to prevent the parties from subjecting themselves to the rules by any method whatsoever having contractual force, even if the method they select or the transaction to which they apply the rules is not one for which the rules themselves provide. For example, parties can agree by some entirely independent contract that their rights and duties under a documentary credit should be governed by the UCP, even if the UCP were not incorporated into the text of the credit itself. By the same token, a court can find that the parties had adopted the UCP by implication, for example from a prior and consistent course of dealing incorporating the UCP, or even from the fact that the UCP are of such universal application that their intention to apply them could be assumed. Accordingly, the effect of the UCP is not at all like that of a statute or a Convention, which can set its own boundaries.[17] Moreover, there is nothing to prevent a legislative enactment from explicitly providing that the UCP apply to all transactions governed by the applicable law unless expressly excluded.

Similar considerations apply to the URDG. The definition of a demand guarantee differs from that of a documentary credit,[18] and the provisions requiring express incorporation are differently worded. But the technique is the same, and as with the UCP, there is nothing to prevent the parties from agreeing to be bound by the URDG, even if the transaction is one which otherwise would be outside the scope of its terms.[19]

[17] Contracting parties may, of course, incorporate statutory provisions or Convention rules by reference, as a form of shorthand which avoids the need to set them out as contractual terms. But this does not produce the same effects as if the statute or Convention applied directly within a given State, where the courts would be obliged to apply it. However, since the UCP do not themselves have the force of law and is contractual in character, any method by which they are given contractual effect is as good in law as any other method, and no special sanctity applies to the method laid down by the UCP themselves, though if parties applied the UCP to a transaction different in kind from those for which they are designed, they might experience considerable difficulty in making them work.

[18] Interestingly, the definition of "demand guarantee" in article 2 of the URDG remained influenced by the definition of "documentary credit" in the UCP to the extent that nowhere in article 2 is there an indication of the essential difference between them, namely the fact that as between principal and beneficiary a demand guarantee is intended to serve as a standby form of recourse in the event of the principal's default. It is only through article 20 of the URDG that this distinction is brought out, and then somewhat obliquely. In this respect, article 2 of the URDG masks the distinction between demand guarantees and documentary credits in much the same way that article 2 of the UCP masks the distinction between standby credits and documentary credits. *See* URDG, *supra* note 2, arts. 2 and 20; UCP 500, *supra* note 3, art. 2.

[19] Roy Goode, Int'l Chamber of Commerce, Pub. No. 510, *Guide to the ICC Uniform Rules for Demand Guarantees* 39 (1992) [hereinafter *Guide to the URDG*].

## C. Application of the UCP to Standby Credits

Until the 1983 revision, the UCP were confined to documentary credits in the strict sense, that is, credits in which the bank's undertaking to pay is primary both in form and in intent. The typical case is a letter of credit covering the price of a shipment of goods under a documentary sale transaction. The agreed method of payment of the price is not payment by the buyer but payment by the bank pursuant to its independent undertaking. The bank is the first port of call for payment, and the buyer's direct payment obligation under the contract of sale is suspended pending presentation of the documents and payment by the bank. Only if the documents are duly presented and the bank declines to pay does the buyer's own duty of payment revive. If the credit is honored, that duty is extinguished, while if the bank refuses to pay because of the seller's failure to tender conforming documents, the buyer is entitled to withhold payment and, indeed, to treat the sale contract as repudiated in the absence of a fresh and conforming tender within the period of the credit.

However, the 1983 revision, UCP 400, introduced an innovation by extending the UCP to standby credits. This was retained in UCP 500.[20] This extension was motivated by a concern on the part of American banks that their courts might confuse a standby credit with a suretyship guarantee, which most banks in the United States are legally prohibited from issuing. Therefore, American banks naturally pressed for standby credits to be included in the UCP, so that they would be visibly equated with documentary credits, to which the prohibition did not apply, and the appropriate signal would thus be sent to their courts.

Understandable though the reasons for it may be, the assimilation of standby credits to documentary credits in the UCP is not a happy one, for its effect is to apply a set of rules designed specifically for primary payment undertakings to credits which, though primary in form, are secondary in intent and cannot properly be invoked by the beneficiary unless there has been actual default by the principal, or at the very least an honest belief that such default has occurred. It is true that the standby credit has certain important features in common with the documentary credit. In particular, it is independent of the underlying trade transaction and is documentary in character in that the payment obligation is triggered solely by a written demand and any other specified documents presented in conformity with the credit. But there the resemblance ends. In the case of the documentary credit, the beneficiary is the party who has the duty to perform the underlying contract, and he receives payment on tendering the prescribed documentary evidence of performance. By contrast, the beneficiary of the standby credit is not a performing party to the underlying transaction, but the party entitled to receive performance, and his entitlement to make a demand for payment arises not because of his own performance, but because of the other party's failure to perform. The result of this

[20] And accordingly to demand guarantees, since these, though not mentioned in the UCP, are the same from a legal viewpoint as standby credits. See *Guide to the URDG*, *supra* note 19, at 8.

fundamental distinction is that most of the provisions of the UCP are simply not applicable to standby credits.[21]

## D. Standby Credits, Demand Guarantees, and the URDG

There is a widespread misconception that standby credits and demand guarantees are different legal animals. This is not the case.[22] Both are undertakings for the payment of money which are independent of the underlying transaction; both are documentary in character; and both are primary in form but secondary in intent. The distinction between them is not one of legal characterization, but of business use. From a commercial standpoint, the standby credit is a different product, for it is used to support not only non-money performance (sale of goods, construction, and the like), but also an extremely diverse range of financial performances, and is governed by banking practices which in many respects are more akin to documentary credits than to demand guarantees.[23] But as a matter of law, there is no distinction between the two forms of credit.

Conceptually, therefore, the URDG are a more appropriate home for standby credits than the UCP, being specifically designed for undertakings which are properly invoked by the beneficiary only when he honestly believes that the principal has committed a breach of the underlying transaction. Why, therefore, do the URDG contain no reference to standby credits in the Introduction?

There is an interesting history to the treatment of standby credits in successive drafts of the URDG. The last draft produced by the Joint Working Party set up by the ICC's Banking Commission and International Commercial Practices, a draft on which the members of the Joint Working Party were ultimately unable to reach agreement, retained a provision expressly excluding standby credits from their scope. The Drafting Group set up to resolve the impasse not only deleted this provision as one that was likely to be incomprehensible to courts, given that in law demand guarantees and standby credits were the same, but in its own first revision of the text made it explicit that standby credits were covered by the URDG. Though the legal reasoning which led to this action was not disputed, there was concern that if standby credits were explicitly equated with demand guarantees this might send the wrong signal to American courts about their legal nature. Having succeeded in getting the UCP extended to standby credits the American banks, and indeed the Banking Commission itself, were insistent that they should continue to be governed by the UCP. Moreover, it was undoubtedly the case that in certain respects the UCP, which are much longer and more detailed than the URDG, catered more effectively for standby credit practices.

[21] Except for the misleadingly labelled "direct pay" standby, which in reality is not a standby credit at all but a clean or documentary credit.

[22] The Banking Commission, understandably, has declined to frame the UCP in such a way as to identify those provisions which apply solely to documentary credits and those which apply solely to standby credits.

[23] E.g., banks may issue standby credits for their own account as well as for that of their customers, may arrange for payment by a third bank rather than their own, etc.

The compromise was to recognize in the Introduction to the URDG that technically they were applicable to standby credits, so that banks had the option of selecting either set of rules to govern their standby and demand guarantee transactions, but to draw attention to the advisability of continuing to use the UCP for standby credits and to avoid any specific reference to these in the text of the URDG.

## III. The Principle of Abstraction

### A. The Nature of the Bank's Undertaking

The documentary credit and the demand guarantee do not fit into the traditional rules governing formation of contracts. In mercantile usage they take effect from the moment of issue,[24] and are therefore not dependent for their validity on acceptance, consideration, or reliance by the beneficiary. They are best regarded as a modem form of specialty, an abstract payment undertaking binding solely by virtue of its issue. The disagreement among experts as to whether a letter of credit or demand guarantee is a contract is part of a wider, and often rather sterile, debate about the ambit of contract law and the characterization of promises which are considered binding despite the absence of consideration or bargain. For our purposes, it is sufficient to note that all parties proceed on the basis that what the beneficiary is entitled to is performance, that is, the protection of his expectation interest, as opposed to a reliance interest or a restitution interest, and that remedies for breach are analyzed under conventional contract law. Accordingly, whether the letter of credit is referred to as a promise, an undertaking, an engagement, or a contract, it is not inappropriate to treat it as contractual in nature, even though possessing distinctive features which make it *sui generis.*

### B. The Principle of Autonomy of the Credit

It is a characteristic of documentary credit law that the payment undertaking embodied in the letter of credit or demand guarantee is independent of performance of the underlying transaction. In the case of documentary credits this autonomy of the credit manifests itself in two distinct rules in the UCP. One is the principle of separation contained in Article 3(a), and the other is the documentary character of the credit as stated in Article 4. There are, of course, exceptions to the autonomy principle, of which the most important relates to fraud in the documents presented under the credit. But these exceptions do not derive from the UCP. They are rules

[24] Rather curiously, UCP 500 states this principle in relation to amendments but says nothing about the time when the original credit takes effect. *See* UCP 500, *supra* note 3, art. 9(d)(ii). However, what is true for amendments is equally true of the original letter of credit itself. Article 6 of the URDG states in terms that a guarantee enters into effect as from the date of its issue unless its terms expressly provide that such entry into effect is to be at a later date or is to be subject to conditions specified in the guarantee and determinable by the guarantor on the basis of any documents therein specified. *See* URDG, *supra* note 2, art. 6.

of law applied by courts in accordance with the law applicable to the credit, and will not be discussed in the present paper.[25] The questions addressed at this point are whether any of the changes introduced by UCP 500 modify, whether by enlarging or contracting, the principle of the autonomy of the credit which is a cornerstone of documentary credits law, and how far the same principles apply to demand guarantees under the URDG.

## C. The Principle of Separation

Article 3(a) of the UCP provides:

> Credits, by their nature, are separate transactions from the sales or other contract(s) on which they may be based and banks are in no way concerned with or bound by such contract(s), even if any reference whatsoever to such contract(s) is included in the Credit. Consequently, the undertaking of a bank to pay, accept and pay Draft(s) or negotiate and/or to fulfil any other obligation under the Credit, is not subject to claims or defences by the Applicant resulting from his relationships with the Issuing Bank or the Beneficiary.

The second sentence of Article 3(a) was not incorporated in UCP 400 and is designed to emphasize that any complaint the applicant for the credit may have against the beneficiary under the contract of sale (e.g. for shipment of nonconforming goods) has no effect on the bank's obligation to make payment under the credit.

In a three-party situation, where the bank's undertaking is given for the account of a third party, its customer, and not for itself, the independence of the letter of credit engagement from the underlying trade transaction should be self-evident, for the parties to the two transactions are different. There is also no basis in contract law by which the banker's duty to pay the beneficiary under the credit should be dependent on the fulfillment of the beneficiary's duty to the applicant for the credit under the separate contract of sale. Thus, the autonomy of the letter of credit is not simply to be ascribed to the distinctive character of documentary credit law, it also reflects principles of general contract law.

The extension of the UCP to cover credits issued by a bank for its own account, that is, to discharge an obligation incurred by the bank to the beneficiary, raises a question whether in this two-party situation, the letter of credit engagement still remains independent of the underlying transaction. Here the parties to the two contracts are identical, so that the doctrinal case for treating the one as independent of the other is less compelling. Nevertheless the general principle must still apply. There is no reason why a letter of credit in a two-party situation should require support by consideration any more than in a three-party relationship, because mercantile usage recognizes that the bank's promise is binding by virtue of

[25] *See* Raymond Jack, *Documentary Credits* (2d ed.), Chapter 9; John F. Dolan, *The Law of Letters of Credit* (2d ed.), Chapter 7 (1993 & Cum. Supp. No. 2); Brook Wunnicke & Diane B. Wunnicke, *Standby Letters of Credit*, ch. 10 (1989 & Supp. 1993); Roeland F. Bertrams, *Bank Guarantees in International Trade*, ch. 14 (1990); Roy Goode, 'Abstract Payment Undertakings', in *Essays for Patrick Atiyah* 209, 228–34 (Peter Cane & Jane Stapleton eds., 1990).

its issue. It follows that since consideration is not required, no question of failure of consideration through nonperformance of the underlying contract can arise. In this respect, the autonomy of the credit, like that of the medieval bond, is of a different order than the more qualified autonomy of a negotiable instrument, which requires consideration between the parties to the underlying transaction and can, as between them, be defeated wholly or in part by a total or partial failure of consideration.[26] Even so, the degree of autonomy is unlikely in practice to be as high as in the three-party credit transaction. In a two-party case, the bank may well have a right of set-off against the beneficiary, whereas in the three-party situation, this can arise only where by coincidence the beneficiary is a customer of the bank.[27]

The abstract nature of the payment undertaking in a demand guarantee is of the same degree, and manifests itself in the same way, as in a documentary credit.[28] Indeed, in practical terms, the demand guarantee could be said to be even more abstract. Whereas in documentary credits the beneficiary must almost always present trade and transport documents, frequently quite voluminous, so that more often than not the tender does not conform with the credit, most demand guarantees require no more than the presentation of a written demand for payment, so that the scope for rejection is greatly reduced.

The URDG, unlike the UCP, are confined to undertakings issued at the request or on the instructions of another party,[29] and do not cover guarantees issued for the issuing bank's own account. Accordingly, the question whether the autonomy of a credit applies in the situation where the bank is also party to the underlying transaction cannot normally arise. The issue is capable of surfacing, however, in the context of a counter-guarantee given by the principal's bank (termed "the Instructing Party") to a local bank in the intended beneficiary's country when instructing that bank to issue a guarantee to the beneficiary. In carrying out that instruction, the local bank is required to act in accordance with its mandate from the Instructing Party, and in so doing is entitled to reimbursement for any payment it makes to the beneficiary and to be paid its customary charges.

However, just as the guarantee is independent of the underlying trade transaction, so also the counter-guarantee is independent of the mandate, except so far as the counter-guarantee incorporates the terms of the mandate. The counter-guarantee is purely documentary in form and is triggered primarily by a written demand on the Instructing Party.[30] So long as the documentary conditions are satisfied and the demand made within the period of the counter-guarantee, the guarantor bank is

[26] *See* Goode, *supra* note 25, at 217, 233.

[27] *See Hongkong and Shanghai Banking Corp. v. Kloeckner & Co. AG* [1989] 3 All E.R. 513 (upholding set-off defence in two-party situation).

[28] *See* URDG, *supra* note 2, art. 2(b) (stating that demand guarantees are by nature separate transactions from the contracts or tender conditions on which they may be based).

[29] URDG, *supra* note 2, art. 2(a).

[30] Article 20 of the URDG requires that demands under the counter-guarantee be supported by a written statement setting forth that the principal is in breach of his obligations and the nature of such breach. *See* URDG, *supra* note 2, art. 20(b).

entitled to be paid even if it has committed a breach of the underlying mandate,[31] for example, by issuing the guarantee for a longer period than that authorized by the Instructing Party or by failing to include a documentary condition which it was instructed to include. Thus, the guarantor has two independent sources of entitlement: a right of reimbursement, which is controlled by the mandate, and a right to be paid the specific sum set out in its demand, which is independent of the mandate, so long as that sum is within the unexhausted limit of the counter-guarantee, and the demand and other specified documents are presented in conformity with the counter-guarantee. The remedy of the Instructing Bank, thus forced to pay out under the counter-guarantee, is to bring separate proceedings for recovery of the payment on the ground of breach of the mandate.

## D. The Documentary Character of the Credit

The other aspect of the autonomy principle is the documentary character of the credit or demand guarantee. The bank's duty is to pay against specified documents which are presented within the period and in accordance with the other conditions of the credit, without regard to external facts such as whether the beneficiary has fulfilled his obligations under the underlying contract. Thus, Article 4 of the UCP, repeating almost verbatim the language of their predecessor, states that "WTI Credit operations all parties concerned deal with documents, and not with goods, services and/or other performances to which the documents may relate." The function of this Article is to complement Article 3 by making it clear that in determining whether the beneficiary is entitled to be paid, banks are concerned with one question only: whether the documents presented to them conform to the credit. The same idea is expressed, though in different language, in Article 2(b) of the URDG.[32] Conceptually, non-documentary conditions are alien to documentary credits and demand guarantees. Their inclusion may give rise to serious problems, particularly in relation to documentary credits.

Unfortunately, many applicants for a credit do not understand the importance of adhering to the rule that banks deal only with documents, not with goods, services or other performances, and instruct their banks to incorporate into the credit conditions which are non-documentary in character. Frequently the banks, which should know better, act on these instructions, when they should of course explain to their customers that non-documentary conditions are unacceptable, for such conditions are outside the scope of the UCP altogether, and if literally construed compel the banks to satisfy themselves that the specified conditions have been satisfied, a task for which banks are ill-equipped and which they are reluctant to undertake. In practice, the problem is not quite as great as it might have been, because banks have sensibly tended to convert apparently non-documentary conditions into documentary

[31] *Guide to the URDG*, *supra* note 19, at 20.

[32] URDG, *supra* note 2, art. 2(b) ("The duty of a Guarantor ... is to pay the sum ... on the presentation of a written demand for the payment and other documents ...").

conditions by construing them as requiring the production of a document reasonable evidencing fulfillment of the state condition, and in so doing they have generally been supported by the courts, at least in England.[33] For example, if the letter of credit specifies that the quality of the goods is to be verified by a surveyor, it is likely to be construed as a requirement that the beneficiary include a satisfactory survey report in the documents presented under the credit.

All this may now change as the result of a new and highly controversial rule introduced by Article 13(c) of the UCP, which states in peremptory terms that "[i]f a Credit contains conditions without stating the document(s) to be presented in compliance therewith, banks will deem such conditions as not stated and will disregard them." It remains to be seen whether the Working Group's laudable endeavor to impose discipline in the marketplace will have its desired effect. No doubt many an applicant, who through failing to observe the rule loses the benefit of a condition to which he had attached importance, will learn to be a good deal more careful next time. Even so, Article 13(a) of the UCP poses potentially serious problems. First, it leaves little leeway to banks or to courts to continue their previous beneficent practice of looking to the presumed intent of the stated condition rather than its formulation. If Article 13(a) had simply said that "non-documentary" conditions would be ignored, that might have enabled banks to continue to construe apparently non-documentary conditions as calling for production of a document, and thus to avoid Article 13(a) except where it was clear beyond peradventure that the stated condition meant exactly what it said. But such a technique cannot be applied to an Article which requires the document or documents to be stated.

Moreover, it is not at all clear how in contractual terms Article 13(c) can be made to work in the manner intended. It is, after all, open to parties to contract out of provisions of the UCP which would otherwise be binding. The very first article states that the UCP are "binding on all parties thereto, unless otherwise expressly stipulated in the Credit."[34] Thus, it would be open to the parties to exclude Article 13(a) altogether. Furthermore, there is nothing to stop the parties from agreeing to terms which operate outside the UCP. If the issuing bank itself is willing to include a non-documentary condition in its letter of credit, and agrees with its customer to do so, what power do the UCP have to interfere with their agreement? Indeed, if a bank accedes to its customer's request to include a non-documentary condition, what right has the bank to breach that agreement with its own customer and treat as a nullity a condition which the bank itself imposed? It is one thing to allow other banks to disregard a non-documentary condition inserted by the issuing bank. But how can the issuing bank itself be permitted to ignore its own stipulation? Further, does not the issuing bank owe a duty to its customer to warn him that any non-documentary condition it includes in the credit at his request will be null and void? Moreover, why should the beneficiary be allowed to treat as a nullity a condition which may go to the root of the transaction with the applicant for the credit? It seems likely that

[33] *See, e.g., Banque de l'Indochine et de Suez S.A. v. J.H. Rayner (Mincing Lane) Ltd.* [1983] 1 Lloyd's Rep. 228; *Esal (Commodities) Ltd. v. Oriental Credit Ltd.* [1985] 2 Lloyd's Rep. 546.

[34] UCP 500, *supra* note 3, art. 1.

Article 13(a), well-intentioned though it is, will lead to problems more serious than those it was designed to prevent. Only time will tell.

## IV. The Documentary Requirements

### A. The Nature of the Documents to be Presented

Though credits and demand guarantees are documentary in character, it would be erroneous to assume that the documents to be presented under a letter of credit or demand guarantee can be determined exclusively from the language of the credit. In the case of documentary credits, the UCP themselves contain provisions, which have become increasingly elaborate with each revision, as to the documents that are or are not acceptable to banks. Accordingly, these provisions, as varied by the terms of the credit, must be read in conjunction with the credit to get the full picture of the documentary requirements. The principal documents presented under a credit are the commercial invoice, insurance documents and transport documents. The new UCP devote no fewer than eleven articles, nearly a quarter of the total, to the requirements for different categories of transport document.[35] Seven different categories of transport document are dealt with in separate articles: marine/ocean bills of lading, non-negotiable sea waybills, charter party bills of lading, multimodal transport documents, air transport documents, road, rail or inland waterway transport documents, and courier and post receipts.[36] In addition, an eighth article is devoted to transport documents issued by freight forwarders.[37]

The problems confronting the Working Group in revising the rules relating to the transport documents were formidable. The UCP cannot operate in isolation. It has to reflect, so far as possible, the documents and practices of carriers which are constantly evolving and being modified and refined. One solution to the problem, which has indeed been advocated recently,[38] is for the UCP to keep their provisions on transport documents short and simple and leave it to the applicant for the credit to specify his requirements. This does, of course, have the great merit of simplifying the task of drafting the UCP. Its effect, however, is not so much to solve the overall problem as to shift the detailed specification of documents from the UCP rules to the letter of credit itself. Since many applicants are unlikely to possess the degree of expertise necessary to frame such specifications, with all the variations that may be involved from one transaction to the next, it is doubtful whether this approach is practicable. Moreover, the great merit of laying down the rules through the UCP rather than having all the detail set out in the credit itself is that the letter of credit is kept to a reasonable length and the transport document requirements for those presenting credits, are standardized, having been worked out by experts in the field.

[35] UCP 500, *supra* note 3, arts. 23–33.

[36] UCP 500, *supra* note 3, arts. 23–29.

[37] UCP 500, *supra* note 3, art. 30.

[38] Angelo J. Schiraldi, *Going Beyond The Call of Duty*, Letter of Credit Update, June 1994, at 29.

Even so, the undertaking is not without hazard, and fierce controversy has arisen over certain aspects of the new requirements of Article 23(a)(i) relating to the signature and authentication of the carrier or master. On a natural construction, these appear to require that where the named agent signs a bill of lading covering port-to-port shipment for the carrier, he must state the name of the carrier as part of the signature even if the carrier's name is shown elsewhere on the bill of lading, and that where he signs as agent for the master he must name the master, even though the master's identity may not be known at the time and the master may change before or during the voyage, and even though if the master signed personally he would only have to sign as "Master" without the need to add his name. These requirements have been heavily criticized as contrary to established practice and as both impracticable and pointless—impracticable because, as stated above, the information is not necessarily known, and pointless because it is in any event of no interest to banks.

The Banking Commission initially took the position that Article 23(a)(i) did not mean what it appeared to mean, that the name of the carrier did not need to be shown twice and that it was not necessary for the Master to be named even where the agent signed on his behalf. Whereas the views of the Banking Commission generally command great respect, in this instance many bankers and national associations are not prepared to accept an interpretation which appears to fly in the face of the language of the Article and might well be ignored by courts. The Banking Commission has now set up a group of experts to examine this and a few other issues with a view to issuing a definitive interpretation.[39]

The commotion generated by this Article, among others, lends force to the view that it is not enough for the Banking Commission to receive input from national Committees and trade interests, and that the membership of the Working Groups, instead of being confined to bankers, should include shipping and trade interests with current expertise in the issues addressed.

There is much less of a problem with demand guarantees, which rarely involve transport documents and, indeed, in most cases require no more than the presentation of a simple demand in writing. Again, however, it would be a mistake to assume that the documentary requirements can be gleaned solely from the language of the guarantee. Article 20(a) introduces an innovation into the requirements for demand guarantees by requiring that:

> Any demand for payment under the Guarantee shall be in writing and shall (in addition to such other documents as may be satisfied in the Guarantee) be supported by a written statement (whether in the demand itself or in a separate document or documents accompanying the demand and referred to in it) stating:
>
> (i) that the Principal is in breach of his obligation(s) under the underlying contract(s) or, in the case of a tender guarantee, the tender conditions; and
> (ii) the respect in which the Principal is in breach.

[39] *See infra* Section V.

The purpose of this provision is to give some measure of protection against the unfair calling of the guarantee without interfering with the documentary character of the guarantee and the need of the beneficiary to have speedy recourse in the event of a perceived breach. It is true that the protection is rather limited in that it is the beneficiary himself, rather than an independent third party, who has to issue the statement of breach, but the effect of this should not be too lightly dismissed. Beneficiaries who may be quite ready to make an unjustified demand, if this is all that is required, may be more reluctant to commit themselves to a false statement of breach, particularly where the general nature of this has to be identified.

There is a similar provision relating to counter-guarantees. Under Article 20(b) any demand under the counter-guarantee is to be supported by a written statement that the guarantor has received a demand for payment under the guarantee in accordance with its terms *and with Article 20 itself.* In other words, the guarantor, when claiming under the counter-guarantee, is in effect required to certify that the beneficiary's demand was accompanied by the statement of breach required by Article 20.

These provisions do not affect the documentary character of the demand guarantee. The guarantor is not required to investigate the truth of the beneficiary's statement that the principal is in breach, and the instructing party receiving a demand under the counter-guarantee is not concerned with establishing whether the guarantor has in fact received a demand from the beneficiary, or whether that demand was accompanied by the statement of breach which Article 20 requires.

Article 20 proved to be the most controversial in the entire set of rules. At one stage it was removed altogether, but was restored after protests. One particular ground of criticism was that it adversely affected the transparency of the guarantee by incorporating an additional documentary requirement not apparent on the face of the guarantee. However, as pointed out above, the same is true of the documentary requirements of the UCP, so that the idea can hardly be described as novel. Moreover, there is nothing to prevent a bank from setting out the text of Article 20 in its guarantee, or alternatively the additional documentary requirement it embodies. Article 20, in fact, proved crucial to the agreement of the final text of the URDG, since it went some way towards meeting the concern over unfair calling, while not weakening the documentary character of the guarantee or the speed with which it could be invoked.

## B. The Compliance Standard

English courts and the majority of courts in the United States apply a doctrine of strict compliance to documents tendered in conformity with a credit. This does not mean that a document will be treated as non-conforming if it fails to dot every "i" or cross every "t" or contains obvious typographical errors.[40] The standard must be applied with a measure of common sense. Nevertheless it is in principle strict.

[40] *See generally Hing Yip Hing Fat Co. v. The Diawa Bank Ltd.* [1991] 2 H.K.L.R. 35 (holding that the use of word "industrial" rather than "industries" on a letter of credit application was an obvious typographical error and could not be relied on by defendant as a discrepancy to reject the plaintiff's application).

A minority of courts in the United States apply a lower standard, that of "substantial compliance." This allows greater leeway for discrepant documents, but at the expense of raising problems for the paying bank as to whether it should or should not pay. The preponderant view supports a principle of strict compliance sensibly applied.[41]

In addition to retaining certain built-in tolerances,[42] UCP 500 introduces for the first time a rule that compliance of the stipulated documents on their face with the terms and conditions of the credit is to be determined by "international standard banking practice as reflected in these Articles."[43] It is hard to know what the effect of this provision will be. On the one hand, it is intended to deter courts from being too ritualistic in treating documents as non-conforming where the defects are trivial and obvious. On the other hand, it is intended to discourage courts from being too liberal by invoking considerations such as good faith or the lack of commercial importance of the discrepancy. The difficulty, as with international commercial usage generally, is to determine where international standard banking practice is to be found. It is always easier to identify local practices than international ones, even in relation to international transactions. Just as the law of international trade is not truly international, but consists in England of the English law of international trade, in France the French law, and so on, banking practice in international transactions is likely to vary in certain respects from one part of the world to another. What is done in London and New York is not necessarily what is done in Sydney or Tokyo. Certainly the new rule has the merit of facilitating the admission of evidence against the adoption of too extreme a view one way or the other as to the standard of compliance. The difficulty is likely to be locating a practice sufficiently uniform in international banking transactions to enable identification as international standard banking practice.

## C. Rejection: Only One Bite at the Discrepancy Cherry

A small but important change of wording requires a bank that rejects documents for non-conformity to state "all" discrepancies in respect of which the bank refuses the documents.[44] In some jurisdictions that was already considered the rule, in the sense that if the beneficiary, having been notified of one defect, was led to assume that there were no others, the bank might be estopped from relying on the other defects, particularly if by the time it sought to do so the beneficiary no longer had time to cure them. Under English law, courts have been reluctant to find a duty to state all defects when the documents are first rejected, and instead allow a defect not relied on at the first presentation to be invoked at a subsequent presentation.[45] The new rule is therefore a welcome change.

[41] *See* WUNNICKE & WUNNICKE, *supra* note 25, at 284; DOLAN, *supra* note 25, 6.02 *et seq.*

[42] *See, e.g.,* UCP 500, *supra* note 3, art. 39 (providing for allowances in credit amount, quantity, and unit price).

[43] UCP 500, *supra* note 3, art. 13(a).

[44] UCP 500, *supra* note 3, art. 14(d)(ii).

[45] *See e.g., The Lena* [1989] 1 Lloyd's Rep. 68; *Hing Yip Hing Fat Co. v. The Diawa Bank Ltd.* [1991] 2 H.K.L.R. 35.

## V. Resolving Disputes Issues of Interpretation of the UCP and URDG

The concern caused by the wording of some of the provisions of UCP 500 raises the question whether some way might be found to resolve difficulties that arise without having to await the usual decennial revision. To some extent this happens already, in that Opinions of the Banking Commission are from time to time published by the ICC, recording particular problems put to the Commission, points made in the discussion of the problem, and conclusions as to whether the problem does in fact lie within the UCP at all, and if so, the meaning and effect of the relevant UCP provision.[46] Though some of the queries presented to the Commission are fairly basic, the Opinions of the Commission have over the years been very helpful in clarifying points on which the UCP provisions have been unclear. Moreover, the Opinions have an independent value in helping to ensure that the UCP are applied in a consistent manner from one country to another.

The Opinions of the Banking Commission, though influential, do not, of course, bind courts or arbitrators, and the same applies to any views expressed by the Group of Experts recently established to look at Article 20(i)(a) and certain other provisions on which queries have been raised. It is open to parties in documentary operations to stipulate that UCP 500 is to be applied on the basis of the interpretation in an identified Opinion or, more generally, as from time to time interpreted by the Banking Commission or other bodies appointed for that purpose by the ICC. But there are dangers in such an approach. In the first place, such Opinions cannot safely be relied on to the extent that they contradict the clear words of the UCP. The Banking Commission can express a view as to what the words mean, but one cannot change contractually incorporated terms by a ruling that though they say one thing they were actually intended to mean something else. Second, Opinions of this kind, resulting from discussions among a small number of Commission members appointed for the purpose, are not forged in the fire of the same intensive and prolonged debate, by national committees, trade associations, and individual experts around the world, as that attendant on the formulation of the UCP themselves. The members of the Commission have always recognized the need to be circumspect in their interpretations and in giving views on best practice on matters on which the UCP are not explicit.

An avenue that might be explored is the preparation and promulgation of interim protocols amending or supplementing the UCP (and the URDG) on points on which the need for clarification or amendment is urgent, and which can be dealt with in relative isolation from the general fabric of the UCP. Such protocols, being limited to a few key provisions, could be prepared relatively quickly. They would have the same status as the UCP themselves and would be effective to supplement or amend the UCP, but would be seen as urgent interim measures, not necessarily final solutions.

[46] *See Opinions of the Banking Commission* 1984-86 (ICC No. 434), 1987–88 (ICC No. 469), 1989–91 (ICC No. 494).

# PART II

# PRIVATE AND PUBLIC INTERNATIONAL LAW

One of the hazards of being a writer on commercial law is that it links up with so many cognate subjects, so that one has to familiarise oneself, at least temporarily, with fields of law outside one's central expertise. One such field is the conflict of laws, or private international law, a subject of endless fascination on which great tomes of have been written. Yet in every case, I have found that my endless intellectual curiosity has led me to examine such subjects from the viewpoint of one who was for many years a practising lawyer and thus problem-oriented; and where traditional theory does not seem to produce a commercially sensible result when applied to business practice and documentation it seems necessary to refine the theory. So in the words of the map-maker John Speed, in a graceful tribute to the splendid Elizabethan surveyor Christopher Saxton, "I have put my sickle into other mens corne."

The first three essays in this Part are devoted to the conflict of laws aspects of intermediated securities, an immensely complex subject which gave rise to two international conventions, the Hague Convention on the Law Relating to Certain Aspects of Intermediated Securities and the UNIDROIT Convention on Substantive Rules for Intermediated Securities. The former was triggered by a colloquium in Oxford in 1998, and Chapter 13 is a paper derived from that colloquium. Chapter 14 is a new paper which examines the Hague Convention in some detail. The Convention on International Interests in Mobile Equipment, with its associated Aircraft Protocol, one of the most successful private conventions on commercial law ever concluded and which raises numerous conflict of laws issues, is the subject of Chapter 15, which reproduces a contribution to a collection of essays in honour of Dr Hans van Loon, former Secretary General of the Hague Conference. Chapter 16 results from an approach by my former colleagues at the Centre for Commercial Law Studies at Queen Mary, who asked if they could establish an annual lecture in my honour. Being ever responsive to flattery I was happy to agree, but I was unprepared for the next question, which was: "Would you give the first lecture?" So after some hesitation I decided to embark on an examination of public and private international law when applied to private commercial law conventions. Chapter 16 reproduces the lecture, given at a meeting under the chairmanship of Lord Collins of Mapesbury. This Part concludes with a chapter on the rules governing the assignment of claims, to which the European Commission has recently returned.

# 13

# Security Entitlements as Collateral and the Conflict of Laws*

*Roy Goode*†

*Where physical securities are deposited with a depository institution or other securities intermediary in exchange for an entitlement to equivalent securities from the pool of fungible securities held by the intermediary, the question arises what law governs the nature of that entitlement and dealings with it. In this paper the writer argues that it is fully in accordance with the concept of the lex situs in the English conflict of laws to treat the entitlement as located at the place of business of the intermediary but that such a concept is artificial when applied to intangibles and serves no useful purpose. Instead, the conflict of laws should embody a direct rule applying the law of the intermediary's place of business.*

The multi-tiered systems of indirect holdings of securities, and the immobilisation of physical securities[1] with a custodian,[2] are well described and illustrated in the

* Originally Published as R. Goode: "Security Entitlements as Collateral and the Conflict of Laws" [1998] 9 Butterworths Journal of International Banking and Financial Law (special supplement) 22.


† Norton Rose Professor of English Law in the University of Oxford, Fellow of St. John's College, Oxford.

[1] Under English law these are equated with bearer securities, since certificates relating to registered securities are not as such transferable, so that registered securities are by their nature intangible. This is not true of all legal systems. For example, in America any certificated security, even if not negotiable in the full sense, is transferable. This paper is confined to indirect holdings of physical securities, in order to underline the distinction between claims *in specie* and claims to an undivided interest. Under English law an interest in a registered security, even if identified by serial number and evidenced by a certificate, is not specific but is simply a fractional interest in an undivided share capital. This was the basis of the Court ruling in *Hunter v Moss* [1994] 1 WLR 452, in which the Court of Appeal, affirming the decision at first instance, upheld the validity of a declaration of trust of five per cent of the issued share capital of a company. The decision has been criticised by certain commentators as incompatible with the requirement of certainty, and analogies have been drawn with claims to an unascertained part of a bulk of goods. In my view these criticisms are misconceived on two counts. In the first place, even in the case of goods a declaration of trust of five per cent of an identified bulk (as opposed to a given number of unsegregated units in the bulk) would be valid, since the subject-matter is the bulk itself, not the units. Secondly, registered shares are intangible and thus incapable of segregation, each share being indistinguishable from the others. English law, imperfect though it may be, does not require the impossible!

[2] In relation to a particular investor the custodian is the securities intermediary with which the investor has a custody agreement. The securities themselves will usually be physically deposited with the custodian's local agent or sub-custodian in the country of the place of issue.

papers by Richard Potok and Mark Moshinsky.[3] Multi-tiering, in addition to its other advantages, makes for market efficiency, creating a pyramid structure, with the CSDs at the apex, in which issuers can deal with a limited number of large players, who in turn will deal with a greater number of smaller participants, and so on down through the pyramid. The aggregation of holdings of securities in undesignated pools of fungibles held by a securities intermediary facilitates book-entry transfers and reduces expense and, in the case of physical securities, the risk of loss or theft.[4]

Immobilisation can occur from either of two ends: at the point of issue of a new security in the form of a global note deposited with the ICSDs and representing the entirety of the issue; or by an investor's choosing to deposit its certificates to existing securities with a securities intermediary or to buy securities through the intermediary and have its securities account credited with the purchase. The effect is that the investor either does not acquire or ceases to have a direct claim on the issuer in relation to specific securities and instead acquires a proportionate interest in the securities pool of like securities held by the intermediary, this interest deriving from its securities account with its securities intermediary. It is thus the account rather than the certificate which is or becomes the source of the investor's entitlement. An investor can usually have its indirect holding converted or reconverted into a direct holding simply by giving the necessary instruction to the securities intermediary with which it has its account. Implementation of this instruction restores the investor's relationship with the issuer. However, this is not possible in the case of an issue represented by a permanent global note. In this case the note is permanently retained by the ICSDs through their common depository and except in extreme circumstances (for example, the bankruptcy of a depository) the investor can never acquire a direct holding from the issuer and can deal with its interest only by transfer through the books of its securities intermediary.

Mark Moshinsky's separate paper[5] sets out the various steps by which a court will reach a conclusion on the law applicable to security interests in a security entitlement (as it is conveniently termed in the revised Article 8 of the American Uniform Commercial Code) recorded in an account held by an investor with a securities intermediary. The purpose of the present paper is to examine in a little more detail the nature of the investor's entitlement under English law, and to show that the location of this interest at the place where the intermediary is situated[6] is fully consistent with the approach of the English conflict of laws to determination of the *situs* of an asset. But I shall urge the advantages of a rule which dispenses with the concept of a *situs* and directly selects the *intermediary's* law. I also have a few comments on the

[3] Richard Potok and Mark Moshinsky, "Cross-Border Securities Collateral: A Conceptual Framework for Choice of Law Situations"; Mark Moshinsky, "Securities Held Through a Securities Custodian—Conflict of Laws Issues."

[4] One should add the cautionary comment that the pooling of funds does not bring universal joy. Auditors and liquidators, in particular, view them with less than whole-hearted enthusiasm because of the difficulty of tracking the securities entitlement of an individual investor where the custodian has not kept proper records, coupled with the risk of one investor's account being used to fund that of another.

[5] "Securities Held Through a Securities Custodian—Conflict of Laws Issues".

[6] This could be identified in various ways, for example, its place of incorporation, its seat or principal place of business, or the place of the particular office where the record is kept.

provisions of Article 8 enabling the parties to a securities account agreement to select the law which is to govern not only their contractual relationship but the proprietary effects of their agreement.

I should like at the outset to pay tribute to the distinguished American scholars whose creative thinking and commercial awareness have led to the adoption, in the new Article 8, of a revolutionary approach to the legal treatment of indirect holdings. This skilfully combines a coherent conceptual structure with the modification of certain long-established principles of the law of trusts and commercial law in order to respond to commercial needs and realities. These scholars include Professor Charles Mooney, of the University of Pennsylvania Law School, who initiated the whole debate with a pioneering article in the Cardozo Law Review,[7] and Professor James Steven Rogers, Professor at the Boston College Law School, who served as Reporter to the drafting committee responsible for revising Article 8.[8] Valuable insights have also been provided by Randolph Guynn of Davis Polk & Wardwell in his discussion paper prepared for the Capital Markets Forum of the Section on Business Law of the International Bar Association.[9]

The present discussion paper is concerned with only one aspect, albeit an important aspect, of the debate, namely the treatment of security interests in security entitlements in the conflict of laws.[10] This requires a careful analysis of the legal nature of such entitlements. Since English law has no equivalent of Article 8, or indeed any legislation whatever on the characterisation question, we have to work within the existing framework of equitable property rights. In most cases the investor's interest is that of a beneficiary under a trust. But, like the unit trust, it is a trust with very distinctive features to which I shall draw attention and which need to be kept in mind if error is to be avoided. The trust concept is not in general recognised in civil law jurisdictions[11] but they can achieve, and in several cases have achieved, the desired result by different means through legislation.[12]

[7] Charles W Mooney, Jr, "Beyond Negotiability: A New Model for Transfer and Pledge of Interests in Securities Controlled by Intermediaries", 12 Cardozo Law Rev 305 (1990).

[8] Of which he has given an illuminating analysis in his lengthy article in 43 UCLA Law Rev 1431 (1996).

[9] "Modernizing Securities Ownership, Transfer and Pledging Laws" (IBA, 1996).

[10] One of these days some genius will come up with a generic term to describe security which does not lead to confusion with investment securities.

[11] Though states which have ratified the 1986 Hague Convention on the law applicable to trusts are obliged to respect trusts created in jurisdictions which do possess the trust concept, and to apply the governing law of the trust as determined by application of the rules of the convention. For the purposes of the convention a trust is a legal relationship created by a person, the settlor, whose assets have been placed under the control of a trustee for the benefit of a beneficiary or for a specified purpose (art 2(1)). This definition appears to exclude trusts arising from the investor-securities intermediary relationship, which are not created by a settlor at all. See n 36, below.

[12] Luxembourg law is particularly interesting in that the investor has two alternative and entirely different forms of protection available to him. The first is to be given a co-ownership interest from the outset. The second is to make an outright transfer to the intermediary as a fiduciary transfer and invoke the provisions of article 3 of the 1983 Luxembourg decree under which the pool of fungibles held by the securities intermediary is ring-fenced from the intermediary's bankruptcy creditors and made available for distribution *pro rata* among investors. See "PM" [Paul Mousel] in (1996) 9 JIFBL 410 at pp 415–16.

I think the draftsmen of the new Article 8 were wise to avoid reference to the trust, not merely because of the special characteristics of the trust relationship but also because the adoption of trust law *en bloc* would have risked the adoption of long-established trust law principles of notice and priorities that are inimical to the efficient functioning of dealings in indirect holdings and need to be displaced by specific rules. Article 8 is in its way as trail-blazing in its treatment of investment securities as was Article 9 in its assimilation of the treatment of security in personal property. Accordingly this paper does not seek to argue that English law on indirect holdings is satisfactory and requires no legislation, merely that the existing legal concepts are fully compatible with selection of the law of place of record of an entitlement as the applicable law under English conflict of laws rules. The several advantages of this approach, and conversely the very serious problems that would be caused by looking to the location of each underlying security, are documented in the above paper by Richard Potok and Mark Moshinsky.

## Conflict of Laws Issues

In discussing the conflict of laws issues that can arise in the use of an investor's securities entitlements as collateral[13] the starting point must be the legal nature of the security entitlement and its enforceability against the trustee in bankruptcy of the securities intermediary. These matters having been established, we can then go on to consider the law applicable to the different facets of the security transaction. These include the characterisation of the creditor's interest, the creation (or in American terminology, the attachment) of that interest as a proprietary interest, its perfection,[14] its priority in relation to competing claims to the same collateral, and its efficacy in the investor's bankruptcy. In the case of a claim to a specific security all these diverse issues will usually be governed by the same applicable law (traditionally the *lex situs*), except that in the event of a party's bankruptcy it is the law of the bankruptcy jurisdiction that will determine the efficacy of a security interest validly created under the applicable law.[15] Whether the approach adopted for interests in a pool of fungible securities[16] is to refine the *lex situs* concept so as to encompass book-entry transfers or to fashion a new rule which directly selects the law of the place of the securities intermediary, there is, fortunately, no reason why the same law should not govern all these diverse issues, since the securities intermediary's place of business forms the natural focal point of the rights of all interested parties.

[13] For this purpose the terms "collateral" and "security" are used loosely to embrace not only security *stricto sensu* but title transfers intended to fulfil a security function (and in some legal systems characterised as security).

[14] That is, the step legally necessary to protect the interest against the subsequent claims of secured and unsecured creditors, including creditors in a bankruptcy. The traditional method of perfecting security over an intangible is registration.

[15] Bankruptcy law can usually be expected to respect prebankruptcy entitlements under the law governing them in order to determine a creditor's starting point, but will then apply its own rules to determine the impact of the bankruptcy, such as whether the interest is voidable as an unfair preference.

[16] It is for the moment assumed that under the applicable law the investor has a co-ownership interest, not merely a personal entitlement. The question is discussed below in the context of English law.

In the discussion that follows it is assumed that certificates to the underlying securities remain immobilised. Where this is not the case it may become necessary to characterise separately the certificate and the underlying security, particularly where the certificate is transferred by pledge or sale in a jurisdiction other than where the issuer is incorporated. It is also necessary to distinguish relations between the company and a claimant and relations between competing claimants.[17] The position under English law is now somewhat confused as the result of the divergent views of Staughton LJ and Auld LJ in the decision of the Court of Appeal in *Macmillan Inc v Bishopsgate Investment Trust plc (No 3)*,[18] affirming on different grounds the decision of Millett J at first instance, whose approach (though not the end result) differed from that of both members of the Court of Appeal.[19] Suppose, for example, that certificates to registered shares in a company incorporated in England and held by an intermediary on behalf of A are wrongfully removed to New York and there pledged to B. What law determines the conflict between the rights of A and those of B? It seems clear that the question whether the shares are negotiable or non-negotiable is governed by English law as the law of incorporation. It is also evident that the best right to the certificates as pieces of paper is governed by New York law, the *lex situs* at the time of the pledge.[20] More difficult is the remaining question whether B is entitled to be substituted for A on the register. In principle it is the *lex societatis* which governs relations between a company and its members and the conditions that have to be met in order to be placed on the company's register. At the same time, it is a well-established principle of the conflict of laws that whether a title vested in one person under the law of State X is displaced by a dealing in State Y is determined by the law of State Y. This suggests that in our example the duty of the company is to deal with the matter on the basis that, while A is the registered member, B has acquired the better right to be placed on the register.

## Characterisation Issues

As indicated above, the question of characterisation arises at two levels. First, there is the characterisation of the security entitlement itself. Is this a purely personal right, a purely proprietary interest, or a combination of the two? And what law should be applied to determine this question? Secondly, where a security entitlement is transferred under arrangements designed for the security of the transferee, how is that transfer to be characterised? Is it an outright title transfer under an agreement providing for the transfer back of an equivalent? Or is it to be characterised as a transfer by way of security? Again, by what law should this question be determined? In either case, is there is a risk of recharacterisation by the court of a jurisdiction other than that of the law so determined? This risk is particularly significant where the obligor is bankrupt and the question of recharacterisation comes

[17] *Macmillan Inc v Bishopsgate Investments Trust plc (No 3)* [1995] 3 All ER 747, *per* Millett J at p 762.
[18] [1996] 1 All ER 585. [19] [1995] 3 All ER 947.
[20] *Colonial Bank v Cady* (1890) 15 App Cas 267.

before the court of the bankruptcy.[21] Recharacterisation will be discussed by other speakers and is not referred to further in this paper.

## Characterisation of Rights to Securities under Traditional Trust Law

Under English law the deposit of physical securities with a securities intermediary is capable of creating any one of at least three different relationships. At one extreme, the depositor retains legal ownership of its investment and the intermediary acts purely as bailee, or physical custodian. This case is outside the scope of the present paper, for it involves an investor who retains a direct relationship with the issuer. At the other extreme, the depositor transfers full title to the securities intermediary and acquires no rights *in rem* in exchange, merely a personal right to the delivery of the equivalent of what was transferred[22] and various ancillary personal rights. In this case the securities intermediary acts as a banker and the deposit is the securities equivalent of a deposit of money with a bank. Except where legislation otherwise provides,[23] the investor takes the risk of its intermediary's insolvency. This case too will not be discussed. Intermediate between these extremes lies the trust.

## Identifying the Subject-matter of the Trust

Under English law it is not necessary to the validity of a trust that the beneficiary should have an interest *in specie* in any particular asset; it suffices that the subject-matter of the trust is identifiable. English law therefore has no problem with the concept of equitable co-ownership of a pool of fungible securities under a trust or equitable co-ownership under a sub-trust of a security intermediary's security entitlement against a higher-tier intermediary. When an investor deposits a security with his securities intermediary and has his securities account credited with the deposit, the subject-matter of his entitlement becomes completely different from what it was before. Ownership of the deposited security is transferred to the securities intermediary and the investor loses all rights in it.[24] What he acquires in its place is a combination of personal and proprietary rights. The former include the right to call

[21] See Ian Jameson, "Cross-Border Securities Collateralisation—Lenders Beware" (1996) 10 JIFBL 465 at pp 466–7.

[22] This is often conveniently referred to as "re-delivery", but the term is inexact, since what is being given to the depositor is not the same as what it deposited.

[23] There are various ways in which this might be done by legislation. One is by a statutory deposit insurance fund, another is by deeming depositors to be co-owners of the fungible pool, a third is by ring-fencing the securities held by the depository in the event of the latter's bankruptcy. See further n 12 above.

[24] Either by delivery with intent to transfer ownership, in the case of a tangible security, or by the intermediary's replacing the depositor in the issuer's register as the holder of the security. Where the deposit is by way of security the investor could alternatively charge the security to its intermediary. In this case the investor retains ownership, but the advantages of pooling described earlier are lost, in addition to which there are certain unusual situations in which the charge might be registrable under s 395 of the Companies Act 1985.

for redelivery of equivalent securities;[25] the latter include equitable co-ownership, in common with other depositors of securities of the same kind, of the pool of fungible securities of that kind from time to time held by the securities intermediary. At any given moment this pool may or may not include the particular securities deposited by the investor. Over time it is likely that these will be turned over and replaced by other securities of the same kind, so that the security originally deposited disappears from the scene.

The disconnection between the investor and the underlying security, which precludes any "look-through" to the issuer,[26] becomes even more pronounced where his securities intermediary does not hold directly from the issuer but has a security entitlement against a higher-tier intermediary who is the direct holder. In this case there is no relationship between the investor and the higher-tier intermediary, and the investor's co-ownership rights subsist not in the pool of securities themselves but rather in such part of his intermediary's own security entitlement[27] as that intermediary is holding for its investors rather than on its own account. Again, there can be no look-through to the higher-tier intermediary. As under Article 8 of the Uniform Commercial Code, the investor's rights are available only against the securities intermediary with which he has his account. There is no ability to leap-frog as there might be in the case of a bare sub-trust of an asset to which the beneficiary had an *in specie* entitlement. Accordingly the investor's interest is best seen as an original trust interest created by his agreement with his intermediary rather than as a derivative interest arising by way of sub-trust.

The fact that the investor has a co-proprietary interest in whatever is held for him by his securities intermediary has the incidental effect of strengthening his personal right to delivery of equivalents. In the ordinary way a personal right becomes unenforceable on the bankruptcy of the obligor and becomes converted into a right to prove for a dividend. But since the asset pool from which the intermediary's duty of delivery is to be satisfied is not the property of the intermediary, each co-owner remains entitled in principle to performance of that duty by the intermediary through its trustee in bankruptcy or liquidator. In practice, things may work out differently, since there may be doubts as to who owns what, in which case the prudent trustee or liquidator will obtain an order from the court directing sale of the asset pool and distribution of the net proceeds among those found to be entitled, to the extent of their respective interest.

## Characterisation of the Transfer

There is a marked distinction between English law and American law as to what constitutes a secured transaction. Under Article 9 of the Uniform Commercial Code the emphasis is on intention and substance, not on form. So a transfer of title to a

[25] Except in the case of an issue of securities represented by a permanent global note. See above, p. 178.

[26] There is now American authority to that effect. See *Fidelity Partners Inc v First Trust Corp of New York* (1997) 1 Dec, a decision of the US District Court for the Southern District of New York.

[27] Ie against the higher-tier intermediary.

security under an agreement providing for retransfer of that security or its equivalent, for example, under a repo, runs the risk of being characterised as a secured transaction despite the absolute nature of the transfer according to its form. By contrast English law adopts a more form-oriented approach. The court will look behind the document to see whether it genuinely represents the intention of the parties or is a sham. If satisfied that the purported transaction is not a sham the court will then determine whether its terms are consistent with the legal effect claimed for it.[28] If they are, the court will adopt the characterisation given by the parties in their document. So even a sale and repurchase of the identical will not be treated as a secured transaction if the parties genuinely intend the transferee to acquire outright ownership. *A fortiori* this is the case where the repurchase entitlement is not to the same asset but only to its equivalent.

## Conflict of Laws: Possible Approaches

### The Alternatives

The traditional approach in the English conflict of laws is to treat rights to securities as determined by the *lex situs.* Since legal title to registered securities derives from entry in the issuer's register, such securities are considered situated at the place where the register is kept, while the *situs* of bearer securities is wherever at the relevant time the securities certificate is physically located.[29] The case law establishing these principles was based on the assumption of an entitlement to an interest in a specific security transferred either by entry of a transfer in the issuer's register, where the security is intangible, or by delivery of a certificate where the security is tangible. It did not envisage modern mechanisms for holding interests in a pool of fungible securities held in and transferred through the books of the investor's securities intermediary. It is therefore necessary to amplify the conflict rules to accommodate interests of this kind. There are two ways of doing this. The first is through the traditional *lex situs* approach. No change would be necessary to the underlying concept of the *lex situs*, which for both of the traditional methods of transfer is the law of the place where the document from which the title is derived (ie the register for registered securities and the bearer certificate for bearer securities) is located. All that is needed is to elaborate the rule so as to cater for a third mode of transfer, ie through the books of the securities intermediary, and substitute the place of the intermediary's location for that of the issuer. The uniform connecting factor, the *situs* of the document constituting the root of title, remains untouched. The alternative approach, and that advocated in the present paper, is to dispense with the concept of a *situs* altogether and instead to select the intermediary's seat or place of incorporation directly as the

[28] *Welsh Development Agency v Export Finance Co Ltd* [1992] BCC 270.
[29] Dicey & Morris, *The Conflict of Laws* (12th edn), pp 931–2.

connecting factor.[30] Both approaches yield the same result. The apparent merit of the former is that of intellectual elegance in preserving a connecting factor that is equally applicable to all modes of dealing. However, the supposed unity of treatment is spurious, since the *situs* will vary according to whether the asset is tangible or intangible and, in the latter case, on whether it is a pure debt, a holding of securities or some other special type of intangible. The advantages of a direct rule which bypasses reference to the *situs* are that it avoids artificiality and the complexities of characterisation and eliminates an unnecessary step in the choice of law process.[31]

## The *Lex Situs*

The transmutation of the investor's interest from the physical security deposited with his securities intermediary to co-ownership of a fungible pool makes the location of the physical security irrelevant in determining the *situs* of the investor's entitlement.[32] By the same token, even if the security deposited was a registered security, the detachment of the investor from any relationship with the issuer would make the issuer's place of incorporation irrelevant. This point seems to have been overlooked in the decision of the Court of Appeal in the *Macmillan* case, where it was assumed throughout that the subject-matter of the entitlement was the underlying security rather than the interest in the account, though in the end nothing turned on this. By contrast in *Fidelity Partners Inc v First Trust Co of New York*,[33] in an admirably concise judgment, the court held that the investor's interest is located at the place where the books in which it is denominated are located.

As pointed out earlier, the *lex situs* rule can be amplified to accommodate book-entry transfers without any interference with the underlying concept, namely the *situs* of the document (the register, the certificate, or the account) from which the investor's title is derived. The co-ownership interest is located at the place of the securities intermediary, for being a chose in action it is enforceable only by proceedings against the securities intermediary as trustee.[34]

While no individual investor has a claim *in specie* to any physical security held by the securities intermediary in the pool, the question arises whether it could be argued that the collective interest of all investors, being an interest in the entire

[30] A plausible alternative is the *lex loci actus*, which will almost invariably coincide with the *lex situs*. The *lex loci actus*, which was adopted as the applicable law by Millett J in *Macmillan* but rejected by the Court of Appeal in that case, has much more to be said for it than the Court of Appeal was prepared to recognise, particularly since it works for all three forms of transfer and, moreover, the place of the act of transfer can be factually determined and does not need to be artificially attributed by law. But the *lex loci actus* suffers the disadvantage of being less stable than the location of the intermediary, since with computer networking the place of record, and thus of transfer, can be quite arbitrary and changeable. See Roy Goode, "The Nature and Transfer of Rights in Dematerialised and Immobilised Securities" (1996) 4 JIFBL 167 at p 172.

[31] See below, p. 186.

[32] See generally on this Joanna Benjamin, "Immobilised Securities: Where Are They?" (1996) JIFBL 85.

[33] (1997) WL 752725 (S.D.N.Y).

[34] Dicey and Morris, *The Conflict of Laws* (12th edn), pp 922 *et seq.*

pool of deposited securities of the same class, is an interest *in specie* in the totality of the certificates which all co-owners, acting together and being of full capacity, could require to be handed over *in specie* and distributed among them according to their respective interests under the rule in *Saunders v Vautier*,[35] thus making the location of the individual securities the relevant factor. The short answer to this argument,[36] which is purely theoretical while the custodian is still in business, is that the collective holding has no common physical *situs*; its location has therefore to be attributed by law, and can only be based at the common point of recovery, namely the place of the securities intermediary.

## The Intermediary's Law

Though the *lex situs*, refined as suggested above, produces a commercially workable result, it does possess certain disadvantages. It is hard to see what is gained by attributing a fictitious *situs* to an intangible right,[37] a *situs* which can only be determined after first engaging in a sometimes elaborate exercise to characterise the nature of the right under consideration. Moreover, it is desirable to place the selection of the applicable law on a broader basis so as to have an alignment with those jurisdictions which do not recognise the trust. There is much to be said for a rule directly applying the intermediary's law. Examples are readily to hand. Both Belgium and Luxembourg have passed decrees to this effect, and these form the basis of the protection of investors holding accounts with MGT as operator of Euroclear and Cedel Bank. Article 8-110 of the Uniform Commercial Code applies the local law of the securities intermediary to the acquisition of a security entitlement and the treatment of adverse claims, while Article 9-103(6)(d) applies the same law to the perfection and priority of a security interest in a security entitlement. Similarly, Article 9(2) of the EU Directive on Settlement Finality in Payment and Securities Systems[38] provides that where securities are provided as collateral to participants whose right is legally recorded on a register, account, or centralised deposit system located in a Member State, the determination of their rights in regard to the securities shall be governed by the law of that Member State.[39] So the prevailing trend of legislation is uniformly in this direction.

If I may make a slight digression at this point, there is what is to me one rather surprising feature of Article 8, namely the provisions that empower the parties to

[35] (1841) Cr & Ph 240.

[36] Though not the only one. Another is that the rule in *Saunders v Vautier* is concerned with trusts by way of gift by a settlor, not with commercial trusts established by trustees and managers in advance of the receipt of funds, so that there is no settlor. See the useful discussion by Dr Kam Fan Sin in *The Legal Nature of Unit Trusts*, pp 114–20.

[37] *Cheshire and North's Private International Law* (12th edn) expresses serious reservations as to the utility of attributing a *situs* to intangibles.

[38] Directive 98/26/EC (OJL166, 11.6.1998, p 45), adopted on 19 May 1998.

[39] Rather curiously paragraph (21) of the Preamble provides that the provisions of Article 9(2) are not intended to prejudice the operation and effect of the law of the Member State under which the securities are constituted or of the law of the Member State where they may otherwise be located. This does not feature in the text and it is hard to know how it is to be reconciled with the objectives of Article 9(2).

a securities account agreement to select the law to govern not only the contractual aspects of their relationship but also the proprietary aspects, including competition with adverse claimants.[40] These provisions are carried a stage further in Article 9, which applies the law thus selected even to the perfection and priority of a security interest in a security entitlement.[41] The implication of these provisions seems to be that as long as all relevant issues are governed by the same law it does not very much matter which law it is. What is surprising to me, and is no doubt due to my ignorance of the background, is that it should be competent to parties to a private agreement to determine the law which is to apply to the proprietary rights and priorities of third parties who have not participated in that agreement and have no means of discovering its terms. The law thus selected may have no relationship to the securities intermediary or the place of record, either of which would be a natural place by the law of which third parties might reasonably expect to be governed. I look forward to enlightenment!

Whichever of the two approaches—*lex situs* or direct rule—is adopted, the fact that the investor has a personal right to delivery against the securities intermediary which survives the latter's bankruptcy[42] reinforces the case for applying to the rights of the parties the law of the place of the intermediary, which is where those rights are enforceable.

## Mandatory Perfection Requirements of Third States

Finally, while the intermediary's law may apply, it is not possible to displace the mandatory requirements of the law of another jurisdiction. For example, there may be exceptional cases where a charge given by an English company over a security entitlement with Cedel Bank or MSG would be characterised as a floating charge and would be void against the liquidator if not registered in conformity with section 395 of the Companies Act 1985. In practical terms, however, the chargee's entitlement would be based in Luxembourg or Brussels, as the case may be, and would fall under the control of its courts, which would apply the local law. This may provide some comfort to the chargee in enabling it to collect and liquidate the collateral; whether it will be able to retain the proceeds is another question.[43]

40 Uniform Commercial Code, §8-110(b), (e)(1).

41 UCC §9-103(6)(d). This provision is retained in §9-305(a)(3) of the newly revised text of Article 9.

42 See above, p. 182.

43 See the response by Kathleen Tyson-Quah in (1996) 10 JIFBL at p 469 to the article by Ian Jameson, "Cross-Border Securities Collateralisation—Lenders Beware", (1996) 10 JIFBL at p 465, which had rightly drawn attention to the fact that perfection under local law does not guarantee the lender complete protection.

# 14

# The Hague Convention on Intermediated Securities

*Roy Goode*

## I Introduction to Intermediated Securities

### Classes of security

Securities are broadly of two kinds: debt securities (bonds and loan stock) and equities (shares). The traditional investor held its securities direct from the issuer, whether as bearer securities transferable by delivery or as registered securities (those in which the investor was registered with the issuer as a shareholder, bondholder, or holder of a given amount of stock). These in turn might be certificated or uncertificated, delivery of the certificate pursuant to a share transfer agreement being effective to transfer beneficial ownership to the transferee, though completion of the transfer would depend on entry in the company's register. But the inconvenience, expense and, in the case of bearer securities, risk of loss or theft, of large volumes of securities has for many years displaced direct holdings of securities and has led to indirect, or intermediated, holdings in which the securities are held on behalf of the ultimate investor by a custodian or other intermediary and are transferred by entry across the books of the intermediary ("book-entry securities").

### Holding patterns

In a domestic issue the securities are held by a national central securities depository (CSD), with whom participants maintain accounts.[1] Typically they will hold such accounts both on their own behalf and on behalf of others, who in turn may hold for customers of their own, so that there is a chain of intermediaries, the CSD being at the top of the chain and the ultimate investor at the bottom, with, sometimes, several

[1] In the United Kingdom this function is performed by CREST, with whom issues are held in wholly dematerialised form.

layers of intermediary (banks, broker-dealers, etc) between them. International securities, issued on different markets, will be issued through and deposited with a common depository of one of the two international central securities depositories (ICSDs), Clearstream Banking and Euroclear Bank. Typically an entire issue will be embodied in a global (or jumbo) note deposited with the ICSD which, though it may be described as negotiable, is never intended to be transferred and thus lacks the essential quality of negotiability.

There are many different holding structures but they fall broadly into three groups: transparent systems, in which the investor's entitlement is recorded all the way up the chain to the relevant CSD;[2] non-transparent systems, in which each investor's account is held solely with its own intermediary, usually in common with other account holders holding accounts in relation to the same issue (non-segregated, or fungible, accounts), and does not feature in the books of a higher-tier intermediary; and semi-transparent systems, in which the investor's interest is recorded in the books of its own intermediary and one or more higher-tier intermediaries but not in the records of the CSD, which merely holds an omnibus account for its intermediary customer without designation of, or sub-accounts for, that intermediary's own customers.

In a transparent system intermediaries in the chain between the ultimate investor and the CSD are merely account operators and do not themselves act as principals or have any rights in the securities. By contrast, in non-transparent systems each intermediary acts as a principal, being a customer of its immediate higher-tier intermediary and holding securities for its own customers. In each case the account holder's relationship is solely with its own intermediary, not with a higher-tier intermediary or with the issuer.

Where an investor holds a fungible account with its intermediary its interest will not be identified in the books of that intermediary's intermediary. But there are also segregated accounts, where the higher-tier intermediary, though holding an account for its customer the lower-tier intermediary, also records that this is held for that intermediary's customer. Such an account is a non-fungible account and does not form part of the pool held for investors holding fungible accounts.

There are also mixed systems, with one part of the chain being in a jurisdiction that operates a transparent system while another part is in a jurisdiction operating a non-transparent chain.[3] In each case the question is where the relevant account is held. So if the ultimate investor, A, holds an account with intermediary B in a non-transparent system while B holds its account with its own intermediary, C, in a transparent system then A's relationship will be solely with B, not with C or any higher-tier intermediary or with the issuer, while B's rights will be recorded right up the chain to the CSD.

[2] In some systems the securities are held only in the books of the CSD's intermediary customer in the first instance but details are periodically transmitted to the CSD.

[3] For a detailed description of holding patterns, with diagrams, see the UNIDROIT Legislative Guide on Intermediated Securities (UNIDROIT 2017), pp 17–27.

Intermediation has many advantages. Risk and cost are reduced, securities can be rapidly sold or given as collateral both domestically and across national borders, and efficiency is further enhanced though multilateral netting. A further advantage is that the issuer typically has to deal with only one entity, a CSD or ICSD, which itself holds accounts for a relatively small number of major players acting as second-tier intermediaries. Each link in the chain draws in more account holders, so that, as stated above, what is created is a pyramid structure with the CSD/ICSD at the top and the ultimate investor at the bottom. Yet increasingly, non-transparent systems are coming under attack as concealing the derivation of the investor's title[4] and as subjecting the ultimate investor to the risk not only of the issuer's insolvency but of that of all intermediaries in the chain.[5] Further, voting through multiple tiers of intermediary is cumbersome and votes may be lost.[6]

## The two conventions

There are two international conventions governing intermediated securities both of which have been examined in detail by Official Commentaries.[7] The first is the 2006[8] Convention on the law applicable to certain rights in respect of securities held with an intermediary (the Hague Securities Convention). This Convention, organised by the Permanent Bureau of the Hague Conference on Private International Law, is a pure conflict of laws convention and does not prescribe substantive rights or obligations, these being the subject of the 2009 UNIDROIT Convention on substantive rules for intermediated securities, organised by the Secretariat of UNIDROIT, which is not yet in force. But the two conventions have much in common in their approach, as do the two Official Commentaries on them.[9] This paper is confined to the first of these conventions. Also of interest is the work of the International Insolvency Institute in preparing for consideration by States model provisions on secured transactions for intermediated securities.[10]

[4] See below, n. 5.

[5] This is one of the major issues that will be explored in a forthcoming publication *Intermediation and Beyond* (ed Louise Gullifer and Jennifer Payne, Hart Publishing 2018) based on a series of seminars held at Harris Manchester College, which will also offer solutions.

[6] Nona Rachman and Maria Vermaas, "Corporate Actions in the Intermediated System: Bridging the Gap between Issuer and Investor" in Keijser (ed), below, n 8, at paras 6-14 *et seq*.

[7] Roy Goode, Hideki Kanda, and Karl Kreuzer, with assistance from Christophe Bernasconi, *Hague Securities Convention: Explanatory Report* (Hague Conference 2005, republished in a new format 2017); Hideki Kanda, Charles Mooney, Luc Thévenoz, and Stéphane Beraud, assisted by Thomas Keijser, *Official Commentary on the UNIDROIT Convention on Substantive Rules for Intermediated Securities* (Oxford University Press 2012).

[8] The Hague Convention was in fact adopted in December 2002 and after *toilettage* was issued in final form in February 2003 but under the then practice of the Hague Conference was undated at the time of adoption and treated only as a draft until the first signature, which in this case was by Switzerland in 2006.

[9] Above, n 6. See also Francisco Garcimartîn and Florence Guillaume, "Conflict of Laws Rules" in Thomas Keijser (ed), *Transnational Securities Law* (Oxford University Press 2014), Chapter 10. This book contains a valuable collection of papers on the legal aspects of intermediated securities.

[10] See Charles W Mooney Jr., *Model Provisions for Secured Transactions for Intermediated Securities* (draft 11 January 2018).

## II The Hague Securities Convention

### A little history

The genesis of the project leading to the Hague Convention was a colloquium at St John's College, Oxford, in May 1998, organised by an Australian lawyer, Richard Potok, who acted as *rapporteur* to the colloquium. The colloquium was attended by practitioners and academics from a number of jurisdictions and it quickly became clear that the existing international legal framework was quite inadequate.[11] The traditional *lex situs* rule under which dealings in property are governed by the law of the situation of the asset at the time of the dealing was simply inappropriate when applied to intangible property. The outcome of the meeting was an approach by Potok to the Permanent Bureau of the Hague Conference to engage their interest in a project to draft an international convention on intermediated securities and the idea was vigorously taken up by Christophe Bernasconi, then First Secretary of the Bureau and now its Secretary General.[12] In the result the Permanent Bureau agreed to expedite the project, Potok becoming Legal Adviser to the project. The initial drafts were based on the concept of the place of the relevant intermediary (PRIMA), reflecting the rule in Article 9(2) of the EC Settlement Finality Directive[13] and Article 9(1) of the Financial Collateral Directive,[14] both of which provide that the applicable law is the law of the country in which the relevant account is located or maintained.

The project was characterised by a remarkably open, informal, and flexible approach, much aided by the Permanent Bureau. There were intensive contacts with industry bodies and no fewer than 17 regional discussion workshops. The committee of experts mandated the drafting committee to draft for a consensus emerging from intersessional discussions organised by Potok and typically consisting of

[11] See *The Oxford Colloquium on Collateral and Conflict of Laws* (1998) Butterworths Journal of International Banking and Financial Law: Special supplement.

[12] See Christophe Bernasconi, *The Law Applicable to Dispositions of Securities Held Through Indirect Holdings Systems* (Permanent Bureau Preliminary Document No 1 of November 2000). The literature is now vast but particularly helpful on the operation of the intermediated system and on the rationale of rules governing are Richard Potok, *Cross Border Collateral: Legal Risks and the Conflict of Laws* (Butterworths/LexisNexis 2002); Keijser (ed), above, n 9; Randall Guynn, "Modernising Securities Ownership, Transfer and Pledging Laws: in *A Discussion Paper on the Need for International* Harmonization, Capital Markets Forum, Section on Business Law of the International Bar Association, 1996), p 16; James Steven Rogers (the reporter for the revised UCC art 8), "Conflict of Laws for Transactions Held Through Intermediaries" 39 Cornell Int'l LJ 285, 2006; Maisie Oui, "The Choice of Choice of Law Rule" in Louise Gullifer and Jennifer Payne (eds), *Legal Problems and Practical Issues* (Hart Publishing 2010), Chapter 9; Luc Thévenoz, "Intermediated Securities, Legal Risk, and the International Harmonization of Commercial Law" 13 Stanford Journal of Law, Business and Finance 384, 2007–8; Louise Gullifer (ed), *Goode & Gullifer on Legal Problems of Credit and Security* ($6^{th}$ edn, Sweet & Maxwell 2017), paras 6-08 *et seq.* For a comprehensive bibliography, see Keijser (ed), above, n 6, pp 313 *et seq.*

[13] Directive 98/26/EC of the European Parliament and of the Council of 19 May 1998 on settlement finality in payment and securities settlement systems, OJ 166, 11.10.1998, pp 45–50.

[14] Directive 2002/47/EC of the European Parliament and of the Council of 6 June 2002 on financial collateral arrangements, OJ 168, 27.06.2002, pp 43–50.

three-hour telephone conference calls which left some of us in a state of *rigor mortis* but in which Potok, the driving force behind the project, drew in all participants to ensure that all views were heard. This saved much time because the ensuing meeting of the experts committee, instead of being confined to the draft adopted at its previous meeting, could work on the revised text produced by the drafting committee and based on consensus. This is a technique which could usefully be adopted in work on future private law conventions.

There was a change of course six months before the diplomatic Conference when, on the suggestion of experts from the United States, the PRIMA approach was modified to take account of the fact that the maintenance of securities accounts might be dispersed among different offices of the intermediary—for example, the office where the account is opened, that from which statements are sent, a central office from which securities accounts are monitored—giving rise to uncertainty. So PRIMA in its original form was abandoned and instead the primary rule became the law expressly agreed by the parties as governing the account agreement or such other law as the parties expressly agreed.[15]

Though there is no doubt that such a rule gives greater certainty than PRIMA it is at least arguable that this was a case of the best being the enemy of the good, because although the idea became embodied in the convention, which was strongly supported by the European Commission, it encountered fierce opposition from some European countries as well as reservations by the European Central Bank; and the Commission's legal assessment of four areas of concern[16] led to the conclusion that three of the four issues raised by the Council did not pose major difficulties and the fourth could be addressed by a modification the Settlement Finality Directive, so that adoption of the Convention was the best way to address uncertainty, opposition continued. In the end the Commission had to withdraw its proposal to adopt the Convention. There is little doubt that but for this change the convention, brought to fruition a mere two and a half years after the Oxford Colloquium, would have come into force within a year or so thereafter. But now the Convention is in force there are hopes that the EU will proceed to adopt it. In 2017 the European Commission appointed an Expert Group to advise on what law should apply to securities and claims and issued a consultation document on the subject.[17] The Group has completed its work and the outcome is awaited.

The present paper is confined to identifying a selection of key issues arising under the Convention. For a comprehensive analysis with illustrations reference should be made to the Explanatory Report.[18]

[15] There was an intervening text in which the PRIMA concept was maintained but the place of the relevant intermediary was determine by selection of the parties, subject to satisfaction of the qualifying office test. But in the end it was rightly decided that the reference to PRIMA was meaningless and it was dropped.

[16] Commission Staff Working Document, "Legal assessment of certain aspects of the Hague Securities Convention", Brussels, 02.97.2006, SEC(2006) 910.

[17] *Consultation document on conflict of laws rules for third party effects of transactions in securities and claims*, 7 April 2017.

[18] Above, n 6. For a detailed treatment of fact patterns of intermediated securities and the applicable law in 25 jurisdictions, see Richard Potok (ed), above, n 9.

## Purpose of the Convention

The purpose of the Convention is to provide rules to determine the law applicable to all issues arising from the holding and dealing with securities credited to a securities account with an intermediary. By "the law" is meant the domestic law of the State concerned, excluding its conflict of laws rules.[19] As stated earlier, the Convention contains no substantive law rules, these being the subject of the UNIDROIT Geneva Convention.

## Sphere of application

The Convention applies where the following conditions are satisfied:

(1) *Securities have entered the intermediated system by being credited to a securities account.* What constitutes a credit to an account is governed by the Convention law.[20] In some legal systems the account must record a credit; in others it suffices that the intermediary has taken a decision to make the credit and all that remains is for this to be processed. Once securities have entered the intermediated system so as to render the Convention applicable all dealings will be governed by the Convention, whether or not the rights of a particular claimant have been recorded in a securities account.

(2) *The account is maintained by an intermediary.* Who constitutes an intermediary is discussed below.

(3) *The issue to be decided falls within Article 2(1).* The list of issues falling within the Convention is comprehensive and only issues that are purely contractual or otherwise purely personal are excluded.

(4) *The case involves a choice between the laws of different States.* The Convention applies whether or not the law determined by its provisions is that of a Contracting State. In this sense the Convention is universal in application. So where the above conditions are fulfilled the Convention applies in a Contracting State even if its conflict of laws rules would lead to the application of the law of a non-Contracting State.[21]

The Convention does not govern the relationship between investor and issuer and takes a neutral position on holding structures, applying equally to transparent, non-transparent, and semi-transparent systems. But the applicable structure determines who is to be regarded as the relevant intermediary.

## Some key definitions

Article 1 contains a series of definitions which need to be understood when reading the Convention.

[19] Art 10. So *renvoi* is excluded. [20] See below, text to n 28.

[21] In this respect the Hague Convention differs from the Geneva Convention, which, unusually, does not specify its own connecting factor. See Francisco J Garcimartín Alférez, "The Geneva Convention on Intermediated Securities: A Conflict-of-Laws Approach" 2010 3/4 Unif L Rev 751 at 752.

### *"Securities"*

This is widely defined to denote any shares, bonds, or other financial instruments or financial assets (other than cash) or any interest therein. The term covers both registered and bearer debt and equity securities, whether or not listed on an exchange, including securities that are dematerialised, and the definition will also pick up any new types of financial instrument that may be created. But cash, which includes bank deposits, is excluded, so that cash paid to an intermediary to acquire securities is outside the scope of the Convention and this is so whether the cash is credited to a cash account or to the securities account. On the other hand an entitlement to dividends, income, or other distributions *is* within the scope of the Convention.

### *"Securities account"*

This is an account maintained by an intermediary to which securities may be credited or debited. It is not necessary for any securities to be credited at any particular time.

### *"Intermediary"*

An intermediary is a person that in the course of a business or other regular activity maintains securities accounts for others or for itself and others and is acting in that capacity. Excluded from the definition are (a) a registrar or transfer agent (its function being purely administrative), and (b) a bank arranging for a securities account to be opened with a third party, the bank maintaining a parallel account for record purposes but not effecting transfers across its books. A CSD or other person (eg a central bank) across whose books securities are transferable by book entry falls within the definition but a Contracting State may exclude the operator of a system for the holding and transfer of securities whose records constitute the primary record of entitlement. This is the position, for example, with CREST, whose records of issues it holds constitute the primary record of entitlement as opposed to the register of the issuing companies.

### *"Relevant intermediary"*

This is the intermediary that maintains the securities account for the account holder. In a transparent system this will usually be the CSD, in a non-transparent system the particular intermediary with whom the investor opens the securities account, and in a semi-transparent the highest-tier intermediary with whom the investor holds a securities account. Where an account holder makes a disposition in favour of its own intermediary who effects the transfer not in its own books but in the books of its (higher-tier) intermediary, it is the account holder's (lower-tier) intermediary that is the relevant intermediary.

### *"Securities held with an intermediary"*

This denotes the rights of an account holder resulting from a credit of securities to a securities account. For any securities account there can be only one relevant intermediary. In the case of a disposition of securities by an account holder to its own intermediary, that is the relevant intermediary.[22] In other words, it is the intermediary at the bottom of the chain between the account holder and the issuer.

*"Disposition"*

This denotes any transfer of title, whether outright or by way of security, and any grant of a security interest, possessory or non-possessory. The disposition may cover the entire account as it exists from time to time or merely some or all of the securities credited to the account at the time of the disposition. Also included are a disposition in favour of the intermediary itself and a lien by operation of law in favour of the intermediary to secure an advance by the intermediary for the acquisition of securities.

## Underlying principles

Five principles underlie the Convention:

(1) The securities account is the account holder's root of title to an interest in the securities, this interest usually being a co-proprietary interest in the pool of securities of the same kind held for investors by the intermediary in a pooled (omnibus) account.[23] The investors collectively cannot enjoy a greater interest than what is held in the pool, any shortfall usually being borne proportionately by account holders. So long as the securities remain credited to the account the Convention law governs all entitlements to that account. But transfer of the securities to a new account, whether with the same or a different intermediary, creates a new root of title which in principle is unaffected by transactions effected in relation to the old account.

(2) Each account holder's relationship is solely with its own intermediary. The account holder has no relationship with a higher-tier intermediary or with the issuer. This principle is particularly important in a non-transparent system, where the higher-tier intermediary will usually have no knowledge of any person lower in the chain other than its own customer.

(3) As a corollary of the second principle, each account is governed by its own law.

(4) As a further corollary of the second principle, neither the account holder nor a creditor of the account holder has a right to look through the account holder's own intermediary to a higher-tier intermediary or to the issuer. In consequence, while an execution creditor can attach the debtor's securities account with its own intermediary the creditor cannot attach securities held by that intermediary's own intermediary or a higher-tier intermediary.

[22] Art 4(3)(a).

[23] This assumes that the account holder does indeed have a property right. In some jurisdictions the right may be contractual but that does not affect the application of the Convention (art 2(2)). See further below, p. 199.

This prohibition of upper-tier attachment also features in the UNIDROIT Convention on Substantive Rules for Intermediated Securities.[24]

(4) An additional consequence of the second principle is that the holder of a securities account is not affected by claims of a third party based on an alleged wrongful transfer from that party's securities account.[25]

(5) All issues covered by the Convention are governed by the same law.[26] The primary rule is contained in Article 4(1) and derives from the parties' express agreement, though this is effective only if the intermediary has a qualifying office in the designated State at the time of the agreement.[27] Where Article 4(1) does not apply Article 5 provides fall-back rules applied in cascade order.[28]

## Issues governed by the Convention

Article 2(1) sets out the issues governed by the Convention ("the Article 2(1) issues"), while Article 2(3) contains the exclusions.

### *Article 2 Scope of the Convention and of the applicable law*

1. This Convention determines the law applicable to the following issues in respect of securities held with an intermediary—
   a) the legal nature and effects against the intermediary and third parties of the rights resulting from a credit of securities to a securities account;
   b) the legal nature and effects against the intermediary and third parties of a disposition of securities held with an intermediary;
   c) the requirements, if any, for perfection of a disposition of securities held with an intermediary;
   d) whether a person's interest in securities held with an intermediary extinguishes or has priority over another person's interest;
   e) the duties, if any, of an intermediary to a person other than the account holder who asserts in competition with the account holder or another person an interest in securities held with that intermediary;
   f) the requirements, if any, for the realisation of an interest in securities held with an intermediary;
   g) whether a disposition of securities held with an intermediary extends to entitlements to dividends, income, or other distributions, or to redemption, sale or other proceeds.
2. This Convention determines the law applicable to the issues specified in paragraph (1) in relation to a disposition of or an interest in securities held with an intermediary even if the rights resulting from the credit of those securities to a securities account are determined in accordance with paragraph (1)(a) to be contractual in nature.
3. Subject to paragraph (2), this Convention does not determine the law applicable to—
   a) the rights and duties arising from the credit of securities to a securities account to the extent that such rights or duties are purely contractual or otherwise purely personal;

[24] Art 22(1).
[25] The so-called "page 37" problem. See below, p. 202.
[26] See below, p. 199.
[27] See below, p. 200.
[28] See below, p. 201.

b) the contractual or other personal rights and duties of parties to a disposition of securities held with an intermediary; or
c) the rights and duties of an issuer of securities or of an issuer's registrar or transfer agent, whether in relation to the holder of the securities or any other person.

In general this Article is self-explanatory. There are, however, some points which need explanation. The starting point is, of course, the credit of securities to a securities account, for it is from this that all the relationships within Article 2(1) flow. Whether or not securities *have* been credited to an account is itself a matter governed by the applicable law. In other words, the putative Convention law is to be applied to determine whether there has been a credit of securities resulting in the application of the Convention.[29] This may seem to be a *petitio principi* but the concept is well established in the conflict of laws. For example, whether a contract has been validly formed is determined by the putative law, that is, the law that would be applicable if the contract had been validly formed. As regards the right to securities credited to an account the Convention applies to relations between (a) the account holder and its intermediary, (b) the intermediary and a transferee, (c) the account holder and its transferee, and (d) the account holder any other claimant to the account, as well as the efficacy of a disposition in the account holder's insolvency.

Paragraph (2)(1)(a) deals with the effect of the credit of securities to the account prior to any disposition by the account holder and thus governs relations between the intermediary and the account holder and the latter's attachment and execution creditors. It is the Convention law that will determine whether the account holder's rights against the intermediary are a purely personal right to delivery or transfer of the credited securities or arise under a trust, securities entitlement, or other form of proprietary or co-proprietary interest. Paragraph 2(1)(b) refers to the legal nature and effects *against the intermediary and third parties* of a disposition of securities held with an intermediary. Through a drafting slip it says nothing about the effects as between transferor and transferee but the paragraph clearly applies to this too by implication. So the Convention law will apply to determine, for example, whether a two-leg transaction in the form of a sale and repurchase of securities ("repo") is indeed what it purports to be or is on the other hand to be characterised as a transaction creating a security interest. Again, the question whether a secured creditor enjoys a right of use entitling it to deal with the securities as owner even if there has been no default, with a personal obligation to replace the collateral, is to be determined by the Convention law. Paragraph 2(1)(c) covers perfection requirements (eg control or registration) as well as priority issues and is particularly relevant to a competition between successive secured creditors. Paragraph 2(1)(e) applies the Convention law to the duties, if any, of an intermediary to a person asserting an interest in the account against the account holder or another claimant, while paragraph 2(1)(g) subjects to the Convention law the question whether a disposition of securities held with an intermediary extends to entitlements to dividends, income, or other distributions or to redemption, sale, or other proceeds.

[29] See the Explanatory Report, paras 2-15 and 2-16.

While paragraph 2(2) makes it clear that the Convention applies to rights resulting from a credit to a securities account even if those rights are determined by the Convention law to be contractual, paragraph 2(3)(a) states that subject to paragraph 2(2) the Convention does not determine the law applicable to such rights if they are *purely* contractual or otherwise *purely* personal (emphasis added). Perhaps the text could have made clearer the relationship between these two provisions, which are intended to convey that the Convention applies to rights *in or to the securities* even if they are only contractual but not to rights that are purely contractual or otherwise purely personal in that they do not affect the securities entitlement, for example, those under provisions of the account agreement relating to the supply of statements, the exercising of voting rights, the collection of dividends, the standard of care required of the intermediary and its responsibility or lack of responsibility for the acts and omissions of its agent or sub-custodian. Similarly, the Convention law does not determine the contractual or other personal rights of parties to a disposition of securities credited to an account, only the proprietary effects of the disposition. Also excluded from the Convention law are the rights and duties of an issuer or its registrar or transfer agent. The issuer is excluded because the Convention provisions are confined to dealings with intermediaries, while registrars and transfers agents perform purely administrative functions and are not intermediaries.[30]

## Determining the applicable law: the primary rule

The primary rule, embodied in Article 4(1), is based on the express agreement of the parties. Under Article 4(1) the law governing all the Article 2(1) issues is the law in force in the State expressly agreed in the account agreement as the law governing that agreement to govern *all* the Article 2(1) issues or, if the account agreement expressly applies that another law is applicable to all such issues, that law. But in either case the selected law applies only if the relevant intermediary has, at the time of the agreement, an office in that State. This "qualifying office" test is discussed below. Two points should be noted. First, to be effective the law chosen by the agreement must be expressed to cover *all* the Article 2(1) issues. The parties cannot select one law for some issues and another law for the rest. The reason for this is to ensure that the same law governs all relationships. Second, the applicable law is not the law "of" the selected State but the law "in force" in that State. In a federal or other multi-unit State[31] the law in force in a territorial unit includes both the law of that unit and, to the extent applicable in that unit, the law of the multi-unit State itself.[32]

It is at first sight counter-intuitive that parties to an account agreement A and B should be able to choose the law governing not only their own relationship but the relationship of either to a third party C and even that between competing claimants

[30] Art 1(3)(a).

[31] Examples of federal States are the United States, Canada, and Australia. By contrast the United Kingdom, for example, is a multi-unit State in which sovereign power is vested in the Parliament in Westminster, the parliaments of Scotland, Wales, and Northern Island acting under delegated powers.

[32] Art 12(2)(a).

to the account C and D. But the solution, first adopted by the United States in its own law,[33] provides the certainty that the PRIMA rule lacks and has the advantage of applying the same law to all transactions relating to the same account. It may be objected that the rule lacks transparency because the account agreement is not visible to third parties, but this is more a theoretical than a practical problem because any third party with whom the account holder intends to call will call for a copy of the account agreement.

## The qualifying office test[34]

In order to avoid a purely arbitrary or capricious choice of law Article 4(1) imposing a "reality" test by providing that choice of a law of a particular State in an account agreement is not effective unless the relevant intermediary has, at the time of the agreement, an office in that State (the "qualifying office") which:

(a) alone or together with other offices of the relevant intermediary or with other persons acting for the intermediary in that or another State –
  (i) effects or monitors entries to securities accounts;
  (ii) administers payments or corporate actions relating to securities held with the intermediary;[35] or
  (iii) is otherwise engaged in a business or other regulatory activity of maintaining securities accounts; or

(b) is identified by an account number, bank code or other specific means of identification as maintaining securities accounts in that State.

There are two points to be made about this part of Article 4. First, while the intermediary must have an office in the designated State it is not necessary that such office should conduct any of the above activities on behalf of the particular account holder of the relevant intermediary, merely that at least one of the activities is conducted on behalf of account holders. For this purpose an activity listed in Article 4(2) must be disregarded. Secondly, the time when the qualifying office test applies is when the account agreement is concluded. If the test is not satisfied at that time Article 4 does not apply even if subsequently the test becomes satisfied. Conversely, if the test *is* satisfied at the time of the agreement the fact that it ceases to be subsequently does not result in the disapplication of Article 4.

Article 4(2) sets out, for the avoidance of doubt, activities of an office which do not constitute in its engagement in a business or other regular activity of maintaining securities activities.

[33] UCC § 8-119(e)(i), (ii).

[34] For a particularly instructive analysis, see Rogers (above, n 10, at 308 *et seq*. See also the Explanatory Report, paras 4-21 *et seq*.

[35] Corporate actions are acts of an issuer which affect the issued securities, such as the payment of dividends or other distributions, buy-backs, corporate restructuring, and the like.

## Determining the applicable law: the fall-back rules

In cases outside Article 4 a set of fall-back rules is provided by Article 5. This Article comes into play where:

(1) the qualifying test is not met; or
(2) the account agreement fails to expressly state either the law governing the account agreement or some other law to govern *all* the Article 4(1) issues.

The fall-back rules are arranged as a cascade and are thus to be applied in descending order.

### *Rule 1*

The law of the State in which is located the office of the intermediary expressly and unambiguously stated in a written account agreement as the office through which the agreement was entered, provided that such office is a qualifying office. Failing this, then

### *Rule 2*

The law of the State where the relevant intermediary is incorporated or is otherwise organised in the sense that though not having a distinct legal personality it is formed in accordance with specified legal rules and thus enjoys a legal status.[36] Where neither of these conditions is satisfied it is necessary to resort to the ultimate fall-back rule

### *Rule 3*

The law in force in the State, or the territorial unit of a multi-unit State, in which the relevant intermediary has its place of business or, if more than once such place, its principal place of business at the time the written account agreement is entered into or, if there is no such agreement, at the time the securities account was opened. Article 6 sets out factors to be disregarded in determining the Convention law. Article 6 is designed, to discourage courts, first, from applying rules appropriate only for direct holdings and, second, from adopting a look-through approach that would lead to the application of a law other than that prescribed by Article 4 or Article 5. So to be disregarded are the place of the issuer's incorporation or organisation or the place where it has its statutory seat, registered office, central administration, or place or principal place of business; the place where securities certificates are located; the place where the register of holders of securities is located; or the place where any intermediary other than the relevant intermediary is to be located.

[36] *Explanatory Report*, above, n 6, para 5.8.

## Competing laws: the "page 37" problem

What is the position where securities are improperly transferred from A's securities account with intermediary 1 in Ruritania to B's securities account with intermediary 2 in Urbania, and under Ruritanian law the transfer is invalid and A is entitled to recover the transferred securities while under Urbanian law B acquires an independent and overriding title? This became known as the page 37 problem because it was first raised on page 37 of the Permanent Bureau's Preliminary Document No 1.[37]

The first point to note is that this situation will hardly ever happen. Whereas goods can be transferred from A to B by physical delivery, the transfer initiated by A in Ruritania will lead to transfers through a series of intermediaries, each transfer typically being included as one of a batch of transfers going through clearing and settlement, so that although, if all goes well, there should ultimately be a credit to B's account with intermediary 2 in Urbania, there is no way in which the credit to B's account can be ordinarily be traced back to the debit to A's account in Ruritania. Apart from anything else, an intermediary who credits to a customer's account securities acquired from a variety of sources will not necessarily know from which particular source it took the securities credited to the account, and usually the chain will be much longer.

But let us imagine that there is a direct transfer from A's account with intermediary 1 to B's account with intermediary 2. Is it the case that A may be able to recover the securities improperly debited by intermediary B while at the same time B may be able to assert title to the securities to his account with intermediary 2? This is a problem well known in the conflict of laws, particularly when applied to goods, and it is resolved by applying the "last event" rule. The last event in our example was the credit to B's account in Urbania. It is therefore for Urbanian law to determine the effect of that credit. If under Urbanian law B as a good faith transferee acquires an overriding title, that is the end of the matter and it is unnecessary to resort to Ruritanian law. If, on the other hand, Urbanian law provides that a transferee acquires no better title than its transferor then reference will be made to Ruritanian law under which, *ex hypothesi*, the transfer was invalid, so that B does not acquire any title.

## Change of law

What happens if the parties to the account agreement decide to change the law previously determined by that agreement? This is the subject of Article 7, which is designed to ensure that the effect of the change is prospective only and does not affect accrued rights, which will continue to be governed by the old law except as regards a person who has consented to the change. So the old law will still govern issues such as the creation and perfection of an interest in securities as well as priorities as between parties whose interests arose before the change of law. The same applies to Article 2(1) issues arising with respect to an insolvency administrator in an insolvency proceeding opened after the change of law. So the advent of insolvency after

[37] Above, n 9.

the change in law does not affect an interest in securities held with an intermediary arising before the change of law. On the other hand, priority as between the holder of an interest governed by the old law and that of a person derived from a dealing under the new law will be determined by the new law, and this may also be applied to an old law interest created but not perfected under the old law but perfected under the new law. However, if the interest was both created and perfected under the old law the Article 2(1) issues will continue to be determined by the old law even if the interest is re-perfected under the new law.

## Impact of insolvency

Notwithstanding the opening of an insolvency proceeding, the Convention law continues to govern all the issues specified in Article 2(1) in respect of any event occurring before the opening of the insolvency proceedings.[38] But this does not affect the application of any substantive or procedural rules insolvency rules, including any relating to (a) the ranking of categories of claim or the avoidance of a disposition as a preference or a transfer in fraud of creditors, or (b) the enforcement of rights after the opening of an insolvency proceeding.[39] This reflects a general principle in national legal systems that the starting point of insolvency law is respect for pre-insolvency entitlements but that for the protection of the general body of creditors these rights may be curtailed[40] or become subject to avoidance, though in the latter case only as a preference or transfer in fraud of creditors.[41]

## Public policy

Article 11 contains important provisions on public policy. Application of the Convention may be refused:

(1) where the effect of its application would be manifestly contrary to the public policy of the forum, or

(2) as regards internationally mandatory rules of the forum, that is, those rules that apply regardless of the otherwise applicable law.

However, requirements of the *lex fori* governing perfection (eg registration requirements) or priorities may not be applied, even in insolvency, unless the *lex fori* is that applicable under the Convention. So if, prior to the opening of insolvency proceedings, a security interest in intermediated securities is created in respect of which

[38] Art 8(1).

[39] Art 8(2). For a detailed discussion see Charles W Mooney Jr and Guy Morton, "Harmonizing Insolvency Law for Intermediated Securities" in Keijser (ed), above, n 6, Chapter 8.

[40] For example, by restraining enforcement by secured creditors in order to allow restructuring of a debtor company or by subordinating claims to those of preferential creditors.

[41] This follows art 30(3) of the 2001 Convention on International Interests in Mobile Equipment (the Cape Town Convention). So other grounds of avoidance that would ordinarily be applicable, such as the avoidance of transactions at an undervalue or non-registration (as to which see also art 10(3) of the Hague Convention) cannot be invoked.

the Article 2(1) issues, including perfection, are governed by the law of Ruritania which has no registration requirement and the account holder becomes subject to insolvency proceedings in Urbania, under the law of which an unregistered security interest becomes invalid in the debtor's insolvency, this rule of Urbanian law may not be applied, the security interest having been validly perfected under Ruritanian law. This rule is designed to ensure predictability and the stability of transactions.

## Transition provisions

These somewhat complex provisions are contained in Chapter IV of the Convention and are not discussed here.

## Regional Economic Integration Organisations

Article 18 provides that a regional economic integration organisation constituted by sovereign states to which competence has been transferred by its Member States may adopt the Convention. A prime example is the European Union. Article 18 is taken directly from Article 48 of the Cape Town Convention on International Interests in Mobile Equipment, most of which relates to matters outside the competence of the EU, so that in EU terms it is a mixed convention. Nevertheless the division of competence is a matter for regional law and does not operate on the international plane, so that the Depositary[42] will accept the deposit of instruments of ratification which conform to the Convention even if they are in breach of the rules of the EU or other REIO. By the same token an REIO, even though its competence may be limited, has to ratify the entire Convention, since partial ratification is permitted only to the extent allowed by the Convention itself. In the case of the Hague Convention Article 21 precludes reservations, though declarations may be made under those articles that provide for them.

## Conclusion

Like most private law conventions the Hague Convention has had a slow take-up and has still received only three ratifications, the minimum number to bring it into force. But now that it is in force, and particularly because one of the ratifying States is the United States, it is to be hoped that following its current review the European Commission will again recommend adoption by the EU and that this time the recommendation will be accepted by Member States, recognising that the fragmentary provisions of the Settlement Finality Directive and the Financial Collateral Directive, useful though they have been, are no substitute for the comprehensive set of provisions contained in the Hague Convention.

[42] In the case of the Hague Convention the Ministry of Foreign Affairs of the Kingdom of the Netherlands.

# 15

# The Cape Town Convention and Protocols and the Conflict of Laws*

*Roy Goode QC*†

It is both a pleasure and a privilege to be invited to contribute to a Liber Amicorum for Dr Hans van Loon, though I do so with considerable trepidation as a general commercial lawyer whose ignorance of private international law is about to be revealed and who accepted the invitation only in the knowledge of the generosity of private international lawyers to outsiders wandering on to their patch. Like the great 17th-century mapmaker John Speed "I have put my sickle into other mens corne."

As Secretary General of the Hague Conference on Private International Law for 16 years, Hans has guided it with humour, skill, and commitment through sometimes choppy waters, greatly enhancing the influence of the Conference and its Permanent Bureau, negotiating the accession of the European Community, steering the Conference's work on a wide range of conflict of laws conventions on which he has published widely and lectured extensively around the world and, most recently, setting up the Conference's Asia Pacific Regional Office in Hong Kong. Despite the pressures of work Hans always managed to appear relaxed, offering afternoon tea and a congenial chat to visitors who like myself dropped in without appointment, as if he had all the time in the world. He has achieved much and will be greatly missed.

The increasing international harmonisation of commercial law has from time to time led to speculation that in this area at least the role of private international law will be seriously diminished. That has not proved to be the case. Private international law continues to flourish, and one of the reasons is that no international convention can cover the entire field related to its subject-matter. There will always be an important role for the conflict of laws in international lawmaking. What is interesting is the interplay between a convention's substantive provisions and the conflict of laws, an issue which the present paper examines in the context of the 2001 Cape

* Originally published as R Goode: 'The Cape Town Convention and Protocols and the Conflict of Laws' in The Permanent Bureau of the Hague Conference on Private International Law (ed), *A Commitment to Private International Law: Essays in Honour of Hans van Loon* (Intersentia Publishing Ltd 2013), pp 221–34. Reproduced by kind permission of the publisher.

† Emeritus Professor of Law in the University of Oxford, Emeritus Fellow of St John's College, Oxford.

Town Convention on international interests in mobile equipment and its associated Aircraft Protocol, this being a complex pair of instruments which entered into force on 1 March 2006 and are rich in conflict of laws issues. The Convention has already secured 55 ratifications and the Aircraft Protocol 49 ratifications, with more in train and promises to be one of the most important private commercial law conventions ever to be concluded. The Luxembourg Protocol, concluded in February 2007 and devoted to railway rolling stock, will not be discussed. Brief reference will, however, be made to some special features of the Space Protocol, concluded in March 2012.

## Introducing the Cape Town Convention

The international harmonisation of commercial law can take one of two forms: the harmonisation of substantive law or the less ambitious and more readily attainable harmonisation of conflict of laws rules. The purpose of the latter is to ensure that in whatever Contracting State proceedings are brought the same choice of law rules will be applied. This helps to avoid that form of forum shopping which seeks to have proceedings brought in the State whose conflict of laws rules lead to the application of the law most favourable to the claimant. For claims involving proprietary rights the law almost universally applied by the conflict of laws is the location of the object in question at the time of the relevant dealing, that is the *lex situs*, or *lex rei sitae.*[1] This works well enough as a conflicts rule for assets that typically remain in one place but is unsuited to high value tangible movables that typically cross national borders in everyday use, in particular aircraft and railway rolling stock. But even if a suitable conflicts rule could be devised for such assets there would remain the serious disadvantage that the substantive law varies from State to State or, in the case of space assets when no longer on Earth, is not governed by any readily determinable rules of private law. In some States the creditor is given strong protection, in others the law is debtor-oriented, while in relation to priorities there is not even an agreed conflicts rule, so that priorities will depend on the applicable law selected by the *lex fori* and are likely to vary from State to State. The resulting uncertainties create risk for creditors and may lead either to the refusal of credit or to an increase in the cost.

It was these considerations that led to the adoption of the Cape Town Convention on international interests in mobile equipment and its associated Protocols. The purpose of the Convention is to introduce a set of uniform rules governing the creation, registration, and priority of competing security and related interests in such mobile equipment and thereby to reduce uncertainty and consequential risk, open capital markets to financing that would otherwise be unavailable, and lower borrowing costs and fees for credit insurance. It has been estimated that in relation to aircraft objects implementation of the Convention with a particular set of declarations under it could save billions of dollars a year, and for several years a significant Cape Town discount from credit exposure fees has been able to be provided

[1] It will be observed that English law (and the writer is an English lawyer) differs from civil law systems not only in its law but also in its Latin!

throughout the OECD, whilst in States that have a bankruptcy-immune provision under or comparable to what is provided by Alternative A of Article 11 of the Aircraft Protocol companies are often able to raise money in the capital markets against the issue of enhanced equipment trust certificates on terms significantly cheaper than are available for bank loans.

The Convention covers three categories of equipment: aircraft objects (that is, airframes, aircraft engines, and helicopters), railway rolling stock and space assets (spacecraft, payloads, and parts thereof). The Convention provisions are equipment-neutral but for each category of equipment there is a separate Protocol, which not only supplements the Convention but, unusually, controls its entry into force and adapts it to meet the specific needs of the relevant industry sector. The Convention establishes a unique type of interest, the international interest, defined as the interest of the chargee under a security agreement or the interest vested in a person who is the conditional seller under a title reservation agreement or a lessor under a leasing agreement. Compliance with the relatively simple formalities for an agreement establishes the international interest, which can then be registered in the International Registry for the type of equipment in question.

The Convention provides a set of basic default remedies which must be made available in each Contracting State and contains a set of simple priority rules based on the order of registration in the International Registry. With certain exceptions an international interest has priority over any other interest subsequently registered and over an unregistered interest, whether or not capable of registration. Registration is against the object, not the debtor, and is therefore available only for uniquely identified objects.[2] One effect of these provisions is that though they do not preclude the grant of interests under national law these will usually be overridden by a registered international interest even if earlier in time. Also provided by the Convention are rules governing the creation and priority of assignments of "associated rights" (rights to payment and other performance under the agreement).

Both the Aircraft Protocol and the Space Protocol extend the registration and priority provisions of the Convention to outright sales and supplement or modify the Convention in other ways, most notably by providing strong creditor protection in the event of the debtor's insolvency.[3]

## Sphere of Application

Some international Conventions are bounded by the conflict of laws in that they do not apply in a Contracting State unless the rules of private international law of the

[2] In the case of aircraft objects the identification criteria are the manufacturer's name, generic model, and serial number. These must be satisfied not only for registration but for the constitution of the international interest, whereas in the other two Protocols requirements for the latter are very flexible.

[3] For a comprehensive analysis of the Convention and Aircraft Protocol, see Roy Goode, Official Commentary on the Convention on International Interests in Mobile Equipment and the Protocol thereto on Matters Specific to Aircraft Equipment (Revised Edition 2008). The third edition of this Official Commentary will be published in the summer of 2013.

forum State lead to their application. Examples are the 1980 Vienna Convention on Contracts for the International Sale of Goods where applicable by virtue of Article 1(1)(b) of the Convention[4] and the 2009 UNIDROIT Convention on substantive rules for intermediated securities. The Cape Town Convention is not of this kind. Once incorporated into the law of a Contracting State it takes effect according to its own terms and the fact that such State's rules of private international law would otherwise lead the issue to be governed by a foreign law is irrelevant. All that is required to trigger the application of the Convention and Aircraft Protocol is that the parties have entered into an agreement falling within one of the three categories referred to above and relating to a uniquely identifiable aircraft object, that the agreement is duly constituted under Article 7 of the Convention and that the requisite connecting factor exists, namely situation of the debtor in a Contracting State or, in the case of aircraft objects, registration of the aircraft in the nationality register of a Contracting State, at the time of the agreement. A court in a non-Contracting State could also apply the Convention if its conflict of laws rules lead to the application of the law of a Contracting State and the other conditions for the application of the Convention are satisfied.

## The Convention Treatment of the Conflict of Laws

The Convention and Aircraft Protocol treat conflict of laws rules in a variety of ways:

(1) Occasionally they prescribe a positive conflicts rule. So under Article 5(4), where a State comprises several territorial units, each of which has its own rule of law in respect of the matter to be decided, and where there is no indication of the relevant territorial unit, it is for the law of that State to decide which is the territorial unit whose laws are to govern, or in the absence of any such rule, the law of the territorial unit with which the case is most closely connected. Again, Article VIII of the Aircraft Protocol allows the parties to an agreement or a contract of sale to choose the law which is to govern their contractual rights and obligations, wholly or in part. I shall return to this Article a little later.

(2) More commonly the Convention and the Aircraft Protocol make a reference to the applicable law in specific provisions without specifying how that law is to be determined. References to the applicable law are to the domestic rules of the law applicable by virtue of the rules of private international law of the forum State (Article 5(4)). In other words, *renvoi* is excluded. In at least one case the applicable law could, unusually, be the Convention itself.

(3) The two instruments contain several apparently simple but in reality quite complex provisions on jurisdiction which are not discussed here.

[4] The effect of which is that the Convention applies to contracts of sale between parties whose places of business are in different States when the rules of private international law lead to the application of the law of a Contracting State. The scope of Article 1(1)(b) when read with Article 95 remains controversial.

(4) Where the Convention makes no reference to the applicable law, it may nevertheless apply by virtue of Article 5(2), which prescribes the applicable law as the residual rule to determine matters governed by the Convention which are not expressly settled in it and are not deducible from the general principles on which it is based.

## Nature and Constitution of the International Interest

The international interest established by the Convention is an autonomous *sui generis* interest the characteristics of which derive solely from the Convention itself, not from national law. Further, it is constituted as such where the agreement creating or providing for it is in writing, relates to an object of which the chargor, conditional seller, or lessor has power to dispose, enables the object to be identified in accordance with the Protocol, and, in the case of a security agreement, enables the secured obligations to be determined, but without the need to state a sum or maximum sum secured (Article 7). An international interest so constituted is effective under the Convention whether or not it is an interest of a kind recognised by the applicable law and whether or not it conforms to the formal requirements of the applicable law. This is not to say that the applicable law is entirely irrelevant to the creation of an international interest. Matters of substantive validity, such as the existence of a *consensus ad idem* or the impact of illegality, are governed by the applicable law. This is nowhere expressly stated in the Convention but is implicit in the requirement that there be an agreement. The applicable law may also confer the requisite power of disposal, though the Convention itself implies a power of disposal on the part of a debtor by virtue of its registration requirements, which would otherwise not be necessary to preserve priority against a subsequent international interest wrongfully granted by the debtor.

## Characterisation

As stated above, the Convention applies to three types of agreement: a security agreement, a title reservation agreement, and a leasing agreement. There is an important distinction between a security agreement and the other two agreements in that the default remedies available to a secured creditor are set out more extensively than for a conditional seller or lessor, reflecting the traditional view in many legal systems that the conditional seller or lessor is the owner and on termination of the agreement for default and repossession should be free to deal with the repossessed object as it pleases. However, in the United States, Canada, New Zealand, Australia, and certain other American jurisdictions a conditional sale agreement and certain types of leasing agreement are characterised as security agreements. So, sensibly, the Convention leaves characterisation to be dealt with by the applicable law.

"Article 2—The international interest

1. This Convention provides for the constitution and effects of an international interest in certain categories of mobile equipment and associated rights.
2. For the purposes of this Convention, an international interest in mobile equipment is an interest, constituted under Article 7, in a uniquely identifiable object of a category of such objects listed in paragraph 3 and designated in the Protocol:
   (a) granted by the chargor under a security agreement;
   (b) vested in a person who is the conditional seller under a title reservation agreement; or
   (c) vested in a person who is the lessor under a leasing agreement.
   An interest falling within sub-paragraph (a) does not also fall within sub-paragraph (b) or (c).
3. The categories referred to in the preceding paragraphs are:
   (a) airframes, aircraft engines and helicopters;
   (b) railway rolling stock; and
   (c) space assets.
4. The applicable law determines whether an interest to which paragraph 2 applies falls within subparagraph (a), (b) or (c) of that paragraph.
5. An international interest in an object extends to proceeds of that object."

It is important to note that Article 2(4) goes only to characterisation, not to the sphere of application. So the effect is not to subject to the Convention all interests that constitute security interests under the applicable law but simply to leave it to the applicable law to characterise an agreement which falls within the Convention definition of a security agreement, a title reservation agreement, or a leasing agreement. For example, while a consignment agreement structured in a particular way may constitute a security agreement under Article 9 of the Uniform Commercial Code it does not fall within any of the above Convention definitions, so that the Convention does not apply.

## Party Choice of Law

In international commercial contracts a high degree of autonomy is given to the parties in choosing the law which is to govern their contractual relations. The limits on this vary from jurisdiction to jurisdiction. But if one leaves on one side for the moment mandatory rules of a legal system which cannot be excluded by agreement but are applicable only if the contract is governed by the legal system and can therefore be excluded by a choice of foreign law, and overriding (supermandatory) rules which are of such policy importance that they apply regardless of the otherwise applicable law, the constraints on choice of law are quite limited. Article VIII of the Aircraft Protocol, which applies only where a Contracting State makes a declaration under Article XXX(1) opting into it, includes the following provision:

"The parties to an agreement or a contract of sale, or a related guarantee or subordination agreement, may agree on the law which is to govern their contractual rights and obligations, wholly or in part."

The questions for consideration are what Article VIII(2) adds to the general principle of party autonomy and what constraints remain. The conflict of laws rules of some States limit party choice by requiring that the chosen law has some connection with the parties or the transaction or by restricting the power of choice to agreements with an international element, thus excluding party choice in the case of purely domestic agreements in which all the elements of the situation are based in one State. In a Contracting State opting into Article VIII such limits on party choice cannot be imposed. The parties are, of course, bound by any applicable mandatory and overriding rules but these do not limit party choice, they merely impose themselves on the transaction, leaving the law selected by the parties to govern other matters. Member States of the European Community (now the European Union) are precluded from making a declaration under Article XXX(1) applying Article VIII, since the EC has declared that it will make no declaration under Article XXX(1), leaving Member States bound by the Rome regulation on the law applicable to contractual obligations (Rome I).

## Matters Referred to the Applicable Law

The Convention expressly leaves it to the applicable law to determine a whole range of matters, only a few of which can be examined here. Several of the items, particularly those dealing with remedies, the installation on and removal from an object of an item which is not itself an object but may be an accession, defences and rights of set-off against an assignee, are capable of ready resolution by reference to well-established conflict of laws principles. But there are some that cause more difficulty, because it is not immediately clear how a well-known principle is to be applied to the facts or because they raise the question whether the issue is to be resolved by reference to the language of the Convention and the principles on which it is based or by the applicable law, or because the question relates to priority issues falling outside the provisions of the Convention or the relevant Protocol. Space allows only a few of these to be examined here.

## Insolvency and the Applicable Law

Unusually for a private commercial law convention the Cape Town Convention intrudes on insolvency law, an area previously regarded as taboo. Article 30(1) provides that an international interest registered in conformity with the Convention prior to the commencement of the insolvency proceedings is effective in those proceedings, that is, it must be recognised by the insolvency administrator as having proprietary effects. But under Article 30(2) nothing in Article 30 impairs the effectiveness of an (unregistered) international interest in the insolvency proceedings where that interest is effective under the applicable law. Since the international interest is the creation of the Convention, not of national law, the reference to "international interest" must be construed as referring to the national equivalent, namely a security interest or interest held by a conditional seller under a title reservation agreement or a lessor under a leasing agreement.

The applicable law will depend on the conflict of laws rules of the forum, which will typically be the rules of the *lex concursus* itself but could be those of another State in which proceedings are brought, *e.g.*, for recovery of the aircraft object where it is situated outside the insolvency State. In most jurisdictions the law to be applied to property claims in the first instance is the *lex situs* of the object at the time of the relevant dealing, though this may be displaced (a) by a subsequent dealing when the object is in a different *situs*, in which case it is for the law of that *situs* to determine the impact of that dealing on any prior rights, and (b) by special avoidance provisions of insolvency law. This is straightforward as regards security interests, where one applies the law of the place of the object at the time of the grant of the security interest, but the analysis requires some refinement as regards title reservation and leasing agreements, because the title of the conditional seller or lessor derives not from the agreement but from an antecedent manufacture or acquisition by the conditional seller or lessor. Nevertheless the international interest, and thus its national law equivalent, is created by entry into the title reservation agreement or leasing agreement, and it is therefore the *lex situs* at the time of that agreement that is the applicable law.

Under Article 30(3)(a) nothing in Article 30 affects any rules of insolvency law applicable in insolvency proceedings relating to the avoidance of a transaction as a preference or a transfer in fraud of creditors, though no other grounds of avoidance in insolvency may be asserted against a registered international interest. Nor does the Convention affect any rules of procedure relating to the enforcement of rights to property under the control or supervision of an insolvency administrator, *e.g.*, for the purpose of a restructuring of the debtor or an arrangement with creditors.

## Assignment and Novation

The Convention provides for the assignment of associated rights (that is, rights to payment or other performance under the agreement) and such an assignment carries with it the related international interest unless the parties so agree. An assignment of the international interest is registrable in the International Registry under Article 16(1)(b). "Assignment" is defined by Article 1(b) as "a contract which, whether by way of security or otherwise, confers on the assignee associated rights with or without a transfer of the related international interest." Sometimes transactions by which a new party acquires the creditor's rights take a form which some legal systems would regard as a new agreement (novation), not an assignment, and if, as I at one time believed, the characterisation of the transaction were governed by the applicable law this could lead to the need for a fresh registration with a new priority point.

But given the wide variety of approaches in national legal systems to the distinction between assignment and novation, and the need for predictability as well as the protection of third parties, I have concluded that "assignment" has an autonomous meaning under the Convention and that national law characterisations do not come into play. On this basis an assignment which, for example, also involves the assumption by the assignee of the assignor's accrued and/or accruing liability to the debtor is to be treated as an assignment so far as it involves the transfer of the creditor's rights and a novation to the extent that the transfer of obligations is treated as such by the applicable law.

## Subrogation

Article 38(1) provides that nothing in the Convention affects the acquisition of associated rights and the related international interest by legal or contractual subrogation under the applicable law, and such acquisitions too are registrable in the International Registry under Article 16(1)(c). Of course the reference to the applicable law is primarily to non-Convention law. However, Article 9(4) provides that a person who, after the debtor's default under a security agreement, discharges the secured debt becomes subrogated to the rights of the chargee. There seems no reason why this right of subrogation should not be treated as arising under "the applicable law" even though it is the law embodied in the Convention itself.

## Pre-Existing Rights or Interests

Article 60(1) provides as follows:

> "Unless otherwise declared by a Contracting State at any time, the Convention does not apply to a pre-existing right or interest, which retains the priority it enjoyed under the applicable law before the effective date of this Convention."

By a pre-existing right or interest is meant one of any kind in or over an object created or arising before the effective date of the Convention, which is the time the Convention enters into force or the time when the State in which the debtor is situated becomes a Contracting State, whichever is the later. The pre-existing right or interest need not be of a kind equivalent to an international interest. It could be a right or interest arising under a different kind of contract or, indeed, a right or interest arising by operation of law, such as a non-consensual lien. Of all the Articles in the Convention Article 60 is the most difficult, because various elements necessary to make it work are not made explicit. By "the applicable law" is meant the domestic rules of law applicable by virtue of the rules of private international law of the forum State (Article 5(3)). As stated earlier, conflict rules will usually lead to the application of the law of the situation of the asset at the time of the agreement. Again, the applicable law in a State which was not a Contracting State at the time the pre-existing right or interest arose will have no concept of an international interest, so that the priority contest is between the pre-existing right or interest and an interest equivalent to an international interest where the conditions of priority (*e.g.*, registration) under the applicable law have been satisfied.

It is open to a Contracting State to make a declaration applying the Convention to pre-existing rights or interests arising under an agreement (that is, a security agreement, title reservation agreement, or leasing agreement) as from a date not earlier than three years after the declaration becomes effective, so that during the period allowed by the declaration the holder of a pre-existing right or interest which is of a registrable kind can preserve its interest by registration. Article 60 is silent on the question who is entitled to make the declaration but it seems clear that it can be made only by the Contracting State where the debtor was situated at the time of conclusion of the agreement under which the pre-existing right or interest arose, which is the same connecting factor as that governing the application of the Convention as a whole under Article 3(1).

## The Space Protocol

The secured financing of satellites and other space assets gives rise to distinctive problems of private international law which the Space Protocol is designed to alleviate. In the first place, though the normal rules on the law applicable to contracts apply, matters are more difficult when it comes to property rights between private parties. That is because for a long time space activity was the prerogative of governments, so that all international treaties in this area deal with matters of public international law concerning the rights and responsibilities of States and the State regulation of space activity, so that there have been no uniform private law rules in the area. There has been at least one court case[5] in which it was contended that a security interest in a satellite in outer space, even if validly perfected under the applicable law (which was disputed), was not subject to the priority rules of any determinable national law, so that secured and unsecured creditors were to be treated a ranking *pari passu*. Secondly, the value of a satellite as collateral is limited because of the obvious practical difficulties in enforcing the security, so that financiers attach much greater value to the debtor's receivables derived from the grant of licences and lease capacity which can be assigned to the creditor as additional collateral. In other words, satellite finance is seen as more in the nature of project finance than asset-based finance.

It was thus considered essential to bring the assignment of these "debtor's rights" into the Space Protocol and to provide a means of securing their priority. The initial suggestion to permit their registration as international interests in themselves was discarded, since the whole Convention and registry system is based on uniquely identifiable physical assets. The solution was to provide for recording of debtor's rights against the registration of the related international interest granted by the debtor, so that there would always be a searchable association between the registered international interest

[5] *In Re ProtoStar Ltd.*, Case No. 09–12659 (MFW), US Bankruptcy Court for the District of Delaware. The case was eventually settled.

and the assignment of debtor's rights. This aspect of the Space Protocol has generally been underestimated, but it solves a serious problem in receivables financing in that there are not only no uniform rules governing the priority of successive assignments of receivables but there is not even an agreed conflicts rule, though both aspects are addressed in some detail in the UNCITRAL Legislative Guide on Secured Transactions. It is true that the UN Convention on the assignment of receivables in international trade contains a conflicts rule in Article 30(1) applying the law of the assignor's location to the priority of competing claimants, together with an Annex in different sections by any of which a State can declare itself bound and dealing with priority on the alternative bases of registration and absence of registration, but so far only one State, Liberia, has ratified the Convention. So for satellite financing the Space Protocol fills a major gap.

## The Law Applicable in Relation to Space Assets

Most of the proprietary aspects of dealings in space assets, whether pre-launch or post-launch, are covered by the substantive rules of the Convention and the Space Protocol. This is fortunate because the space law treaties are concerned essentially with public law rights and duties, not with concepts of property in private law. Moreover, space assets receive little or no mention in our otherwise admirable textbooks on private international law. Reference to the *lex situs* as the applicable law is unhelpful if by *situs* one means the physical location of a space asset which has reached Earth orbit, because there is no *lex* in space.

Since the rationale of the *lex situs* rule is that the law governing property rights should be that of the jurisdiction which has control of the asset, the concept of control should replace that of physical location in the case of assets in space, and Article VIII of the 1967 Outer Space Treaty gives control to the State which is the State of registry of the object under the 1975 Registration Treaty. So for registered objects the appropriate law to govern dealings is the *lex registri*. However, space objects are not registrable until they are at Earth orbit or beyond. Moreover, not all registrable objects are registered. This is not a significant problem as regards the pre-launch phase, in which most of the financing is provided, because the Convention, in combination with the Space Protocol, applies to pre-launch as well as post-launch agreements and its provisions cover most of the property issues likely to arise. There are two principal exceptions. The first is the acquisition of an international interest by legal or contractual subrogation, as where a surety pays the amount necessary to discharge the debtor's obligations under a security agreement. Article 38 of the Convention preserves such rights of subrogation, and Article 16(1)(c) provides for their registration in the International Registry. The second relates to pre-existing rights or interests. Both of these involve resort to the applicable law. But it is highly unlikely that subrogation will occur before the asset is in space, so that leaves for consideration only the treatment of assets in space but unregistered and pre-existing rights or interests. For these assets the most appropriate law would seem to be the law of the State which has international responsibility for space activities in relation to the space asset under Article VI of the Outer Space Treaty.

## The Law Applicable to Debtor's Rights

The Space Protocol governs the formalities, effects, and priority of an assignment of debtor's rights to the creditor and for the most part its provisions avoid the need to resort to national law. But there remain some issues left to be determined by the applicable law, including the extent to which a transfer of debtor's rights to the creditor is permitted (Article X(1)) and the availability of defences and rights of set-off against the creditor as assignee (Article X(2)). Questions of transferability are most likely to arise where the agreement under which the debtor's rights arise contains a prohibition against assignment. Most legal systems give effect to this at least to the point of laying down that the debtor does not have to recognise the title of the assignee, but some override the prohibition in the interests of protecting the free flow of receivables in the stream of trade. The applicable law will usually be that governing the assigned obligation, as exemplified by Article 14(2) of Rome I. Where this is the law of a State that has ratified the 1988 UNIDROIT Convention on International Factoring the assignment of debtor's rights will have effect notwithstanding any prohibition against assignment (Factoring Convention, Article 6(1)) unless at the time of conclusion of the contract of sale of goods under which the debts arise the debtor has its place of business in a Contracting State which has made a declaration under Article 18 (Article 6(2)). Defences and rights of set-off will typically be governed by the law applicable to the claim against which the defence or right of set-off is asserted. See, for example, Rome I, Articles 12 and 17.

## Conclusion

The application of the conflict of laws rules under the Cape Town Convention and Protocols is at certain points not free from difficulty. But the extensive references to the applicable law[6] vividly illustrate the continuing importance of conflict of laws in international instruments dealing with the substantive harmonisation of private law. Also of interest is the need to resort to instruments of public international law, such as the Outer Space Treaties, in order to determine the applicable law concerning international interests relating to space assets. So private international law continues to flourish and with it the Hague Conference and the Permanent Bureau. Long may that continue!

[6] There are approximately 20 provisions of the Convention and Aircraft Protocol referring to the applicable law.

# 16

# Private Commercial Law Conventions and Public and Private International Law

## The Radical Approach of the Cape Town Convention 2001 and Its Protocols*

*Roy Goode*

## I. Introduction

It is a remarkable circumstance that with a few honourable exceptions[1] all writers on international law in general and treaty law in particular focus exclusively on public law treaties. Private law conventions, including those involving commercial law and the conflict of laws, simply do not come into consideration. Yet such conventions, like public law conventions, are treaties between States and are governed by the 1969 Vienna Convention on the Law of Treaties and many of them are of great significance. Their distinguishing feature is, of course, that while only States are parties, private law conventions deal primarily, and often exclusively, with the rights and obligations of non-State parties. So while the treaty is international it does not for the most part commit a Contracting State to any obligation other than that of implementing the treaty in domestic law by whatever method that State's law provides, if it has not already done so prior to ratification.

Yet some private law conventions are capable of making significant innovations in the methods and effects of international law-making. This article focuses, by way of illustration, on the 2001 Convention on International Interests in Mobile Equipment ("the Cape Town Convention")[2] and its associated Protocols dealing respectively with security interests and title-retention rights in aircraft objects,[3]

* Originally published as R Goode: "Private commercial law conventions and public and private international law: the radical approach of the Cape Town Convention 2001 and its Protocols" in I.C.L.Q. 2016, 65(3), 523–40.

[1] For example, JG Sprankling, *The International Law of Property* (OUP 2014); J Basedow, "Uniform Private Law Conventions and the Law of Treaties" (2006) 11(4) UniflRev 731.

[2] Adopted 16 November 2001.

[3] Protocol to the Convention on International Interests in Mobile Equipment on Matters Specific to Aircraft Equipment (adopted 16 November 2001, entered into force 1 March 2006) (the Aircraft Protocol).

railway rolling stock,[4] and space assets.[5] The Convention and Aircraft Protocol came into force on 1 March 2006;[6] the 2007 Luxembourg Protocol, dealing with railway rolling stock, and the 2012 Space Protocol have yet to enter into force. The Convention and Aircraft Protocol have achieved remarkable success in a relatively short space of time, the Convention having received 72 ratifications and the Aircraft Protocol 65, the United Kingdom being one of the last to ratify with effect from 1 November 2015.

It is not proposed to examine any of these instruments in detail, merely to set the scene with an outline of their provisions and then go on to describe the radical, and in various respects revolutionary, features of the Convention and Protocols, the substantial benefits they are already producing in the field of aviation finance, and the technical and organizational challenges that had to be overcome.

Professor Sir Andrew Wiles, now Royal Society Research Professor of Mathematics at the University of Oxford, devoted seven years of his life to providing a proof of Fermat's last theorem, a task which had evaded top mathematicians for 350 years. Fermat's last theorem is not in itself considered of great importance.[7] What is of huge value is the range of new mathematical techniques Andrew Wiles had to devise to overcome otherwise insurmountable problems with the proof. The Cape Town instruments, though in fact important in themselves, also bring a new dimension to international law-making through the range of devices that evolved to overcome what sometimes appeared to be intractable problems. They deal with areas of private law previously regarded as exclusively for national law, recognizing that it is necessary to think outside the boundaries of national law in devising new solutions to international problems. In particular, one of the key features of the international interest which the Convention and Protocols create is that it constitutes a right *in rem* and is a creature of the Convention, not of national law. However, the public interest both in national security and in the continuance of public services also means that there are likely to be more areas in which what is primarily a private law convention will also contain public law provisions. The Convention and Final Act also contain novel and innovative procedures to address practical difficulties in achieving international agreement, for example, the novel procedure for linguistic alignment of different language texts.

The instruments are also of interest in that, though primarily regulating the rights and obligations of private parties, they also impose duties on Contracting States. As regards aircraft objects they resulted from collaboration between the International

[4] Protocol to the Convention on International Interests in Mobile Equipment on Matters Specific to Rolling Stock (adopted 23 February 2007) (the Luxembourg Protocol).

[5] Protocol to the Convention on International Interests in Mobile Equipment on Matters Specific to Space Assets (adopted 9 March 2012) (the Space Protocol).

[6] The UN Treaty Series (2307 UNTS 285) wrongly gives the date of entry into force as 1 April 2004 by reference to the deposit of the third instrument of ratification but this overlooks art 49(1)(a) of the Convention under which all the provisions apart from those that become operative under the Vienna Convention before entry into force of the Convention as a whole come into force only when the relevant Protocol comes into force.

[7] Fermat's last theorem postulates that $x^n + y^n = z^n$ is an equation having no solutions in positive integers greater than 0 for any integer value of $n$ greater than two.

Institute for the Unification of Private Law (UNIDROIT), an international, intergovernmental body, and the International Civil Aviation Organization (ICAO), which was established by the United Nations to manage the administration and governance of the 1944 Chicago Convention[8] regulating international air travel. The International Air Transport Association (IATA) also played an important role as the international private organization representing the worldwide aviation industry.

## II. An Outline of the Cape Town Convention

The Cape Town Convention is concerned with three categories of equipment: aircraft objects, railway rolling stock, and space assets. Aircraft objects divide into airframes, aircraft engines (which are often separately financed), and helicopters.[9] Railway rolling stock consist primarily of locomotives and passenger and freight wagons but the definition in Article I(2)(e) of the Luxembourg Protocol covers a wide range of additional objects.[10] Space assets subdivide into spacecraft, payloads, and parts of a spacecraft or payload,[11] though anything which is not a complete spacecraft must be capable of registration under the space registry regulations. They share the characteristics that they regularly cross national borders or orbit round the Earth and they are generally of high-unit value. This poses problems for those financing the acquisition or use of such objects through secured loans, title reservation agreements, or leases. Default remedies exercisable against the debtor in one jurisdiction may be more restricted than in another or may take much longer to exercise. Security rights created under the law of a particular jurisdiction may not be recognized in others and even if they are their priority cannot be guaranteed, being dependent both on the conflict of laws rules of the forum and the content of the applicable law as determined by those rules.

The consequence of these risks for creditors is that prospective buyers or lessees of such items of equipment either cannot secure the necessary finance or have to pay significantly more for it than they would in a stable legal environment. The Cape Town Convention addresses these concerns in ways that are radical, even revolutionary. Instead of having to rely on a national interest the creditor is provided with a new animal, the international interest, which derives its force from the Convention, not from national law and can be created with the minimum of formalities.[12] The Convention applies where the debtor is situated in a Contracting State at the time of the agreement[13] or alternatively, in the case of aircraft, the agreement relates to a helicopter, or an airframe pertaining to an aircraft, registered in a Contracting State which is the State of registry at that time.[14]

[8] Convention on International Civil Aviation (adopted 7 December 1944, entered into force 4 April 1947).

[9] Art I Aircraft Protocol.

[10] See Sir Roy Goode, *Official Commentary on the Convention on International Interests in Mobile Equipment as Applied to Railway Rolling Stock* (2nd edn, UNIDROIT 2014) para 3.8.

[11] Art I Space Protocol.

[12] Arts 2, 7 Cape Town Convention.

[13] Arts 3(1), 4 Cape Town Convention.

[14] Art IV Aircraft Protocol.

The Convention gives the creditor a set of basic default remedies (repossession, sale, collection of income),[15] including speedy advance relief on the production of evidence of default,[16] while the Aircraft and Luxembourg Protocols confer additional remedies of deregistration (aircraft),[17] export, and physical delivery.[18] The creditor's international interest is protected by registration in the international registry, created under the provisions of the Convention.[19] Registration gives that interest priority over subsequently registered interests and over unregistered interests,[20] whether registrable or not, with exceptions in favour of non-consensual rights or interests which under a Contracting State's laws give priority over the equivalent of an international interest and are declared by that State to have priority over a registered international interest.[21] Finally, the Convention and the Aircraft Protocol contain rules to protect the creditor against the consequences of the debtor's insolvency, subject to avoidance of transactions in fraud of creditors and preferences.[22]

The benefits of these instruments are considerable. US airlines have for some time been able to securitize their receivables by the issue of enhanced equipment trust certificates because of the strong creditor protection given by Section 1110 of the Federal Bankruptcy Code.[23] In Contracting States that ratify the Cape Town Convention and Protocols such benefits will now be available to non-US airlines, making borrowing from the market significantly cheaper than bank borrowing.[24] Economic assessments estimating that such ratification would save billions of dollars a year in the cost of borrowing and in premiums for export credit insurance have been borne out by experience. For example, the Organisation for Economic Co-operation and Development permits member States of the OECD to offer a so-called Cape Town Convention discount from the minimum premium rate they are required to charge for credit insurance provided that they make a prescribed set of declarations.[25] It has been estimated that the cost savings will amount to an average of between USD 7 billion and USD 8 billion over a period of 20 years, repaying the substantial resources that went into the making of the Convention many times over.[26]

[15] Art 8(1) Cape Town Convention. [16] Art 13 Cape Town Convention.

[17] Art IX(1) Aircraft Protocol.

[18] Art IX(1) Aircraft Protocol, art VII(1) Luxembourg Protocol.

[19] Pursuant to art 16 Cape Town Convention. [20] Art 29(1).

[21] Art 39. The same article preserves the right of arrest or detention of an object enjoyed by a State or State entity, intergovernmental organization, or private provider of public services, for payment of amounts directly relating to those services in respect of the object in question or another object (eg the so-called "fleet lien" enjoyed in the UK by Eurocontrol).

[22] Art 30 Cape Town Convention, art XI Aircraft Protocol.

[23] US Bankruptcy Code Chapter 11, Title 11.

[24] For example on 25 June 2013 "British Airways raised funds through its first-ever enhanced equipment trust certificates (EETCs) offering to finance the purchase of 14 new Airbus and Boeing aircraft", Reuters. "British Airways launches debut EETC offering to finance planes" available at <http://uk.reuters.com/article/newstory-idUSL2N0F11TH20130625>.

[25] The latest set of rules prescribing the qualifying declarations is contained in the Arrangement on Officially Supported Credits (TAD/PG (2016) 1, dated 1 February 2016) Annex III, Sector Understanding on Export Credits for Civil Aircraft (ASU), Appendix II, Annex 1.

[26] Such was the impact of the Convention and Aircraft Protocol that one of the first States to ratify, in the middle of a war, was—Afghanistan!

The Convention is an umbrella instrument the provisions of which apply indifferently to all three categories of equipment but have been modified by each Protocol to meet the particular needs of the industry—aviation, railways, or space—with which the Protocol is concerned. The Convention and Protocols are governed by five underlying principles: practicality, party autonomy, predictability, transparency, and sensitivity to national legal cultures. The rules have to be workable; the provisions attach high importance to party autonomy, since the parties know best what is necessary to achieve their aims; with the high sums involved, predictability is of the utmost importance, displacing good faith as a usual canon of interpretation; the registration system is designed to ensure transparency, so that third parties are not affected by hidden liens; and the Convention and Protocols give protection to the creditor in the event of the debtor's insolvency. Finally the Convention respects the sensitivity of States to its basic legal philosophy by providing for declarations by which certain provisions apply only if States make an opt-in declaration,[27] while for certain others a State may opt out.[28]

## III. Some Unique Features

Just as the proof of Fermat's last theorem led Andrew Wiles to devise a range of groundbreaking mathematic techniques, so also obstacles to the creation and protection of the international interest, and the need to meet the differing requirements of aviation, railways, and space, forced the progenitors of the Cape Town project to enter into fields of law previously regarded as taboo in international conventions and to invent a range of novel techniques in international law-making. In the following section, nine distinctive features will be briefly described.

### 1. Definition

Article 2(2) of the Convention defines an international interest in mobile equipment falling within one of the three categories as "an interest . . . in a uniquely identifiable object granted by the chargor under a security agreement, vested in a person who is the conditional seller under a title reservation agreement or vested in a person who is the lessor under a leasing agreement". The interest acquired by an outright purchaser is not an international interest and is not registrable under the Convention but the Aircraft Protocol and Space Protocols extend the third-party effects of the Convention to outright sales, which accordingly fall within the registration and priority rules as regards aircraft objects and space assets.

27 See, for example, Aircraft Protocol art XXX (1)–(3).
28 See, for example, Convention, art 55, Aircraft Protocol art XXX(5).

## 2. Constitution

The key point about the international interest is that it constitutes a right *in rem* and is the creature of the Convention, not of national law. Not only does it trump national law interests it must be given effect in a Contracting State even if it is of a kind not known to the law of that State or of another State whose law is applicable. In his book *The International Law of Property* Professor John G Sprankling writes:

> The concept that private actors can obtain direct property rights in objects that are located within the territory of sovereign states—solely as a matter of international law—is revolutionary.[29]

The requirements for the constitution of an international interest are set out in Article 7 of the Convention and are relatively simple. The agreement creating or providing for[30] the interest must be one which (a) is in writing, (b) relates to an object of which the chargor, conditional seller, or lessor has power to dispose,[31] (c) enables the object to be identified in conformity with the Protocol,[32] and (d) in the case of a security agreement, enables the secured obligations to be determined, but without the need to specify a sum or maximum sum secured.

## 3. Relationship with national law

In most cases a security agreement, title reservation agreement, or leasing agreement created in conformity with the applicable national law will also be constituted in accordance with the Convention so as to give rise to an international interest. But the international interest is the creature of the Convention and is not dependent on national law except, of course, that the agreement must be a valid contract under the applicable law (the interaction with private international law is discussed further below). Given this, the fact that the applicable law does not recognize an interest of the kind created by the Convention is irrelevant. The national law interest continues to subsist but in most cases is subordinate to a registered international interest. There will, however, be cases where it may be necessary to rely on the national law interest. For example, while the Convention covers the proceeds of an object, "proceeds" is narrowly defined as money or non-money proceeds of an object arising from its total or partial destruction, confiscation, condemnation or requisition.[33] So it may be

[29] Sprankling, *The International Law of Property* (n 1) 63.

[30] "Creating' in the case of a security agreement, "providing for' in the case of a title reservation or leasing agreement, since in these last two cases the interest of the seller or lessor does not derive from the agreement but typically precedes it.

[31] This may arise under the applicable or by inference from the provisions of the Convention. The provision for registration of an interest held by a conditional seller or lessor implies that the conditional buyer or lessee has a power of disposal, for only the conditional seller or lessee in possession is likely to be in a position to dispose of the object, so that it is only against such a disposal that registration serves any purpose.

[32] In the case of an aircraft object the identification criteria are the manufacturer's serial number, the name of the manufacturer and the (generic) model designation (art VII).

[33] Art 1(w).

necessary to invoke national law to capture general proceeds, such as the proceeds of wrongful disposition of the object by the debtor.

## 4. The International Registry and the Supervisory Authority

Equally striking are the provisions establishing an International Registry to record the grant, assignment, subordination, and discharge of international interests.[34] To quote Professor Sprankling again:

> The registration system established under the convention is a remarkable achievement - an international mechanism for defining and coordinating security interests among private actors, independent of municipal laws. It is the first global title system for any form of property rights.[35]

The only registry currently in operation is the International Registry of Mobile Assets run by Aviareto,[36] a joint venture company of SITA[37] and the Irish government based in Dublin and operating the registry of interests in aircraft objects. The International Registry was established by the Council of the International Civil Aviation Organization (ICAO), which acts as the Supervisory Authority and as such is responsible for the appointment of the Registrar and the effective functioning of the Registry.[38]

The registration system is asset-based, so that interests can be registered only against a uniquely identified asset. As the result of meticulous planning by the industry and the Registrar and the development of advanced technology this has become a highly efficient and sophisticated registry system, which is wholly electronic and has recorded some 650,000 registrations and 720,000 searches in the 10 years of its operation. There is no human intervention at the Registry end and on average an international interest becomes searchable within 38 seconds of receipt of the data by the Registry. There are stringent controls on registration but anyone can make a search. ICAO, as a specialized agency of the United Nations, enjoys immunity from legal and administrative process, while the assets, documents, databases, and archives of the International Registry are also inviolable,[39] subject to a right of access of a claimant against the Registry to such information and documents as are necessary to enable the claimant to pursue its claim.[40] The Registry is strictly liable not only for its own errors but for system malfunction, yet despite this, no claim has ever been made against the Registrar except for the purpose of procuring discharge of a registration wrongfully made by a party having no registrable interest, the Registrar fulfilling a neutral function and abiding by the court's decision.

34 Ch IV Cape Town Convention.
35 Sprankling, *The International Law of Property* (n 1) 61.
36 See <https://www.internationalregistry.aero/ir-web/>.
37 Société Internationale de Télécommunications Aéronautiques.
38 See art 17(1)–(4) Cape Town Convention.
39 Art 27 Cape Town Convention.
40 Art 27(5) Cape Town Convention.

## 5. The Two-Instrument Approach

Work on the three Cape Town Protocols proceeded concurrently but at different speeds. The substantial resources put into the project by the Aviation Working Group (referred to further below) meant that aviation was well ahead of rail and space. Naturally the aviation industry did not wish to be held up by the other two industry sectors. How was the problem to be overcome? There were two possibilities. One was to have a separate convention for each of the three industries. That, of course, would overcome the three-speed problem but it also had several disadvantages. First, there would be much duplication of effort, since most of the provisions in the draft Convention were equally applicable to all three categories of object. Secondly, this approach would entail a substantial degree of additional expenditure in that the substance of such provisions would have to be addressed at three separate diplomatic Conferences. Thirdly, the representation of States at such conferences would be likely to be different and the drafting would be in different hands, thus producing a serious risk that the uniformity flowing from a single convention would be lost. Finally, each convention would be encumbered with a considerable amount of technical detail, for example, the definitions of airframes, aircraft engines, and helicopters and the limitation of the convention to exclude light aircraft.

The novel solution propounded by Mr Lorne Clarke, then General Counsel of IATA, was to have a single convention applicable to all three categories of equipment supplemented by separate Protocols for each category.[41] The benefits of this speedily became apparent. The unity of the equipment-neutral provisions could be maintained, whilst technical data could be left to the relevant protocol. Yet there were those who continued to press for separate conventions and the issue was not finally resolved until the opening day of the diplomatic Conference.[42] In the event the structure of an equipment-neutral umbrella Convention and equipment-specific protocols has proved of the utmost utility.

## 6. The Controlling Force of the Protocol

The other innovative aspect of Lorne Clarke's solution was that the Protocol would not fulfil the normal function of supplementing the main Convention, it would in fact control it. By the terms of the Convention itself, not only would its entry into force be dependent on the coming into force of the related protocol but its provisions would also take effect subject to the protocol, which could thus modify the Convention to meet the particular needs of the industry in question. This is a revolutionary approach in international law which has been remarkably effective in resolving what otherwise might have been insoluble problems.

[41] See generally L Clark, "The 2001 Cape Town Convention on International Interests in Mobile Equipment and Aircraft Equipment Protocol: Internationalising Asset-Based Financing Principles for the Acquisition of Aircraft and Engines" (2004) 69 Journal of Air Law and Commerce 3.

[42] 16 November 2001.

## 7. The Invasion of Areas Previously Taboo

Another radical feature of the Convention is that it has invaded areas of law previously regarded as taboo, that is, matters which should be exclusively for national domestic law, in particular substantive rules on property rights, the priority of competing interests, and the impact of insolvency. Property was thought too embedded in domestic law to be suitable for substantive provisions, matters relating to property being governed by national law under the *lex situs* rule. Thus the 1980 Vienna Convention on Contracts for the Sale of Goods[43] says nothing about property and is confined to contractual relationships, while the 1988 UNIDROIT conventions on international factoring[44] and international financial leasing,[45] though covering the acquisition of rights *in rem*, still shy clear of priorities and insolvency. By contrast the provisions of the Convention dealing with the priority of interests are contained in a single article, Article 29, which adopts the basic rule previously referred to that a registered interest has priority over any other interest subsequently registered and over an unregistered interest, even if it is of a kind not capable of registration. The Convention also provides that the *in rem* rights conferred by a registered international interest are to be respected in the debtor's insolvency,[46] while the Aircraft Protocol includes an option for a Contracting State to adopt by declaration powerful creditor remedies which exclude interference by the court.[47] All Contracting States except one have made such a declaration, which is a condition of securing the economic benefits conferred by the Convention.

## 8. The Declaration System

Reservations are not allowed under the Convention and Protocols[48] but the two instruments embody a facility to make declarations which, though not entirely unique, differ both in character and extent from those found in other treaties. Under this facility Convention rules contrary to the settled legal philosophy of a Contracting State do not apply unless that State makes an opt-in declaration, while certain other provisions can be the subject of an opt-out declaration. For example, a Contracting State may choose not to allow self-help remedies[49] and may opt out of the provisions which entitle a creditor who adduces evidence of default to speedy advance relief,[50] while the

[43] Adopted 11 April 1980, entered into force 1 January 1988.

[44] Convention on International Factoring (adopted 28 May 1988, entered into force 1 May 1995).

[45] Convention on International Financial Leasing (adopted 28 May 1988, entered into force 1 May 1995).

[46] Art 30 Cape Town Convention. [47] Art XI (Alternative A) and XII Aircraft Protocol.

[48] The Vienna Convention is rather inconsistent in its concept of a reservation. Art 2(1)(d) defines a reservation as "a unilateral statement, however, phrased or named, made by a State, when signing, ratifying, accepting, approving or acceding to a treaty, whereby it purports to exclude or to modify the legal effect of certain provisions of the treaty in their application to that State", and it is a reservation as so defined that is prohibited by the Cape Town Convention. On the other hand, as an exception to the general rule that a State may formulate a reservation, art 19(b) precludes this where "the treaty provides that only specified reservations, which do not include the reservation in question, may be made", which indicates that a reservation is not necessarily unilateral but may be provided by the treaty itself.

[49] Art 54(2). [50] Art 55.

Protocol provisions on insolvency, including a strong option designed to avoid judicial intervention,[51] depend on an opt-in declaration by a Contracting State. The declarations feature was designed to ensure that States otherwise favouring the Convention might feel obliged to refuse to ratify it. Further, a Contracting State can make a declaration preserving the priority of non-consensual rights or interests given by its national law without the need to register in the International Registry or can designate non-consensual rights or interests as registrable as if they were international interests.

There is a further aspect. In its capacity as a Regional Economic Integration Organisation the European Community (EC) was and the European Union (EU) is for most purposes treated as if it were a Contracting State. As regards matters within its competence the EC/EU was/is able to control the making and content of declarations made by Member States to ensure conformity with EC/EU law.[52] That, however, has no effect on the international plane, so that UNIDROIT as depositary must accept the deposit of instruments of ratification conforming to the Convention and relevant Protocol whether or not these are in compliance with EU law. Thus Ireland ratified long before the European Community[53] and because it was chosen as the site of the International Registry the European Commission had the good sense not to intervene. The same happened with Luxembourg's ratification of the Rail Protocol.[54]

## 9. Post-Adoption Changes

A further striking feature of the Convention is the insertion of provisions designed to allow certain limited changes to be made to the text without the need for further consultation with negotiating States. The changes in question relate to the different language versions of the text and the need to ensure that, as regards the assignment of associated rights,[55] the Convention provisions would prevail over those of the slightly later UN Convention on the Assignment of Receivables in International Trade.[56]

### *(a) Linguistic alignment*

The question of linguistic alignment arose in the following way. UNIDROIT usually works in two languages, English and French, and its drafting committees produce

[51] Protocol, art XI, Alternative A, which provides the debtor or insolvency administrator, as the case may, a grace period for remedying existing defaults and undertaking to perform future obligations, failing which the creditor is entitled to repossess the aircraft object without judicial intervention, delay, or modification of the debtor's obligations.

[52] See the Declaration lodged by The European Union under the Cape Town Convention at the Time of the Deposit of its Instrument of Accession, para 5.

[53] The ingenuity of the Irish knows no bounds. Many years ago Irish bank staff went on strike. In almost every other country in the world this would have caused mayhem. Not in Ireland. The pubs offered their services as clearing houses for the trading of unpresented cheques, which were thus used to settle debts, contingently on their being met when the strike came to an end, as most of them were.

[54] Which ratified the Luxembourg Protocol 31 January 2012, while the EU did so 18 December 2014.

[55] Arts 31–37. "Associated rights" mean "all rights to payment or other performance by a debtor under an agreement which are secured by or associated with the object" (art 1(c)).

[56] (Adopted 12 December 2001) 41 ILM 777.

parallel texts (not *translations*). However, ICAO had five working languages at the time and decided to add Chinese as a sixth language of the diplomatic Conference. While a drafting Committee can cope with two languages, even one extra language would produce an exponential complexity and the work would never be completed. The solution adopted was to draft in English and then send the text down the wire from Cape Town to ICAO's bank of highly professional translators in Montreal for translation into the five other languages and transmission back to Cape Town. But the work of translators, however well qualified, cannot compare with that of a draft committee consisting of trained lawyers and, moreover, those thoroughly versed in the substantive subject-matter. The result was predictable, delegation after delegation rising to criticize the parallel texts. However, diplomatic protocol required the signature of texts in all six languages of the Conference. The neat solution adopted was to include a provision in the Final Act of the diplomatic Conference making the texts subject to verification by the Joint Secretariat of the Conference under the authority of the President of the Conference within a period of 90 days as to the linguistic changes required to bring the texts in the different languages into conformity with one another. This was done and the same technique adopted for the Luxembourg and Space Protocols.

### *(b) How to override a later Convention*

The second problem arose from the fact that although the UN Convention on the Assignment of Receivables in International Trade which had certain provisions on the assignment of rights that overlapped and were potentially inconsistent with those of the Cape Town Convention, was envisaged as reaching a diplomatic Conference first, as things worked out it was not to be adopted until a month later. How then could the Cape Town diplomatic Conference ensure that its own provisions prevailed? The solution adopted was a resolution of the diplomatic Conference that upon the deposit of the UN Convention with the Secretary General of the United Nations a new article, Article 45 *bis,* should be inserted into the Cape Town Convention providing that in case of conflict that Convention should prevail. This was a novel and ingenious method by which a convention can be made to override a subsequent convention and effective for that purpose (provided that the later diplomatic Conference does not pass a similar resolution).

Finally, the Convention, though primarily a private law convention, also contains a number of public law elements which are discussed in the following section.

## IV. The Confluence of Public Law and Private Law

Most private commercial law conventions neither confer protections nor impose obligations on Contracting States. A striking exemption is to be found in certain provisions of the Cape Town Convention and the Luxembourg and Space Protocols. These arise partly from the institutional structure set up for the

International Registry, partly from the nature of some of the remedies and partly from the perceived need to protect national security and the continuity of public services.

## 1. Duties Imposed on Contracting States

What is striking about the Convention and Aircraft Protocol is that though these instruments are designed as private law instruments they nevertheless include provisions that impose obligations on a Contracting State, though these can be avoided by reliance on the rules governing declarations. These duties are: the availability of speedy advance relief for a creditor who adduces evidence of default;[57] the provision of the remedy of de-registration and export and delivery of aircraft at the behest of the creditor where there has been default, with a requirement of expeditious administrative action, all these being subject to applicable safety laws;[58] and, under the Aircraft Protocol, timely relief to the creditor on the debtor's insolvency and the provision of insolvency assistance to foreign courts in carrying out the provisions for the protection of the creditor on the debtor's insolvency.[59] What happens if a Contracting State fails to carry out any of these treaty obligations? In contrast to the position under the Convention on the Settlement of Investment Disputes (ICSID)[60] as regards rights of investors under a bilateral investment treaty, the Cape Town Convention confers no rights of enforcement on the aggrieved creditor against the offending State, who is dependent on the willingness of its own State (if it is not the offending State) to secure redress by way of diplomatic protection after local remedies have been exhausted.

## 2. The Protection of the Public Interest

The Protocols have a set of provisions which are rarely found in private commercial law instruments. These are designed to protect the public interest. The Aircraft Protocol preserves rights of arrest and detention under national law, while the Luxembourg and Space Controls limit the exercise of default remedies so as to ensure the continuance of public services.[61] It is not difficult to imagine the chaos that could result from repossession of public service railway rolling stock or the termination of access to public service satellite communications. So the two Protocols restrict, albeit in different ways, the exercise of remedies that could affect the provision of public services, whilst containing provisions designed to safeguard creditors' interests.[62]

[57] Art 13 Cape Town Convention.

[58] Arts IX and X(6) and (7) Aircraft Protocol.

[59] Arts X and XII Aircraft Protocol.

[60] Convention on the Settlement of Investment Disputes between States and Nationals of Other States (adopted 18 March 1965, entered into force 14 October 1966) 575 UNTS 159.

[61] Art XXVII Space Protocol, art XXV Luxembourg Protocol.

[62] Art XXV Luxembourg Protocol, art XXVIII Space Protocol.

## V. Private International Law and the Cape Town Convention

It was at one time thought by a number of experts that with the growth in the harmonization of substantive law the conflict of laws would tend to wither away. That, of course, was never likely and has not happened. Indeed, what we have seen is the growth of conflict of laws conventions. But quite apart from that, the sphere of every convention is limited, so that matters falling outside its provisions or the general principles on which it is based must necessarily be left to the applicable law as determined by the conflict of laws rules of the forum. The Cape Town Convention is no exception.

### 1. The Traditional Approach to Property Rights

The long-established rule in many jurisdictions is that dealings in goods are governed by the law of the country in which the goods are situated at the time of the dealing in question (the *lex situs* rule).[63] This works well enough in many cases but it is quite inappropriate for dealings in mobile equipment, which by its nature is regularly crossing national borders and the location of which at any given time may be quite fleeting. This was brought out in the famous *Blue Sky* case[64] where mortgagees of aircraft registered in the United Kingdom but mortgaged while temporarily in The Netherlands sought their recovery in proceedings in the English High Court. Under Dutch domestic law the mortgages would have been invalid but under Dutch conflict of laws rules the validity of the mortgages was governed by the *lex registri*, ie English law, under which they were valid. Naturally the mortgagees argued that the appropriate law under English conflict of laws rules was the *lex registri*, or alternatively, if it was the *lex situs*, that the application of the doctrine of *renvoi* from Dutch law would lead to the same result, while the defendants contended that Dutch domestic law as the *lex situs* had to be applied.[65] Beatson J (now Beatson LJ) held that the *lex situs* principle had to be observed and rejected the application of *renvoi*.[66] Though this result was in line with prior decisions of the High Court it caused consternation to UK aircraft financiers, who resorted to desperate expedients, such as bringing the aircraft into UK airspace for the brief time it took to sign the documents and then flying off again. This exercise apparently cost some £70,000 a time and led to suggestions that aircraft mortgages should be made subject to New York law, which was thought (probably erroneously) to be more favourable to the mortgagee.

Satellites and other space assets gave rise to special problems, including the question of what law governs dealings in assets in outer space. Here the *lex situs* rule

[63] See, for example, Dicey, Morris, and Collins, *The Conflict of Laws* (15th edn, Sweet & Maxwell 2015) Rule 133.

[64] *Blue Sky One Ltd v Mahan Air PK Airfinance US Inc* [2010] EWHC 631 (Comm).

[65] Paras 73 and 152.

[66] See paras 151–85 for discussion of these issues.

leads to the conclusion that there is no law governing dealings in such assets. That, indeed, was one of the arguments advanced in the ProtoStar Chapter 11 proceedings in Delaware,[67] where creditors claiming to hold security over satellites in space were met by the argument that since the priority of secured creditors depended on the applicable national law and since there was none, all creditors ranked *pari passu.* In the end a compromise was reached which involved the secured creditors giving up a significant proportion of the value of their collateral. No doubt if it had come to the crunch the court could have fashioned a deemed *situs* rule, for example, by treating the satellites as situated in their State of registry under the 1975 Convention on the Registration of Objects Launched into Outer Space.[68] But where the Cape Town Convention applies resort to such devices is unnecessary, because the substantive rules laid down by the Convention largely displace the need to have regard to the otherwise applicable law. This is because in terms of its application the Convention is not bounded by the conflict of laws but applies in a Contracting State regardless of the otherwise applicable law.

So strong has been the hold of the *lex situs* that it has been extended to intangibles by ascribing to them an artificial *situs.* This extension has been criticized:[69] not only do intangibles not possess a physical location but since the deemed *situs* varies according to the nature of the intangible the *lex situs* does not provide any organizing principle nor is it simple to apply. The Convention expressly deals with the assignment of rights to payment under a security agreement. In the case of space assets the main collateral relied on is not the physical object in outer space, which for obvious reasons is of limited value, but so-called "debtor's rights", that is, the rights of the debtor against third parties for licence fees, etc, which are assigned to the creditor as additional collateral.[70] Since the registration regime is based on physical assets, the Space Protocol does not permit the independent registration of assignments of debtor's rights, but where the related international interest has been registered it enables such assignments to be recorded against the registration of the international interest, priority among competing assignments being given by order of recording rather than by order of registration of the related competing international interests. This facility is a recognition of the fact that the financing of space assets is essentially project finance rather than asset-based finance.

Nevertheless, the conflict of laws still has a role to play. Leaving aside some rather complex rules on jurisdiction, once an agreement is shown to fall within the definition of a security agreement a title retention agreement or a leasing agreement it falls

[67] *Re ProtoStar Ltd* US Bankruptcy Court for the District of Delaware, Case No 09-12659 (MFW), motion of Official Committee of Unsecured Creditors dated 21 October 2009, para 28.

[68] Convention on Registration of Objects Launched into Outer Space (adopted 12 November 1974, entered into force 15 September 1976).

[69] See, for example, Sir Roy Goode, "The assignment of pure intangibles in the conflict of laws" [2015] LMCLQ 289, 292–3; P Rogerson "The Situs of Debts in the Conflict of Laws—Illogical, Unnecessary and Misleading" (1990) 49 CLJ 441; Dicey, Morris and Collins, *The Conflict of Laws* (n 63) 22–5.

[70] See arts I, IX–XV.

to be recharacterized according to the domestic law of the forum. So a conditional sale agreement would be treated by New York law as a security agreement but by English law as merely a title reservation agreement. On the other hand, a consignment agreement, which under New York law will in some cases be characterized as a security agreement, falls outside the Convention altogether. The Protocols allow the parties to an agreement to choose the law governing their relations, though this provision does not apply in an EU Member State.[71] There are altogether some 20 provisions of the Convention which refer to the applicable law,[72] so that conflict rules remain indispensable.

## 2. The European Community/European Union as a Player

The status of the EC, now the EU, under the Convention has already been referred to. There are also provisions of the Convention and Aircraft Protocol which Member States are precluded from adopting by declaration or which they can adopt only in a limited form. The freedom of the parties to choose the forum for their disputes is exercisable only in conformity with the Brussels I Regulation (recast)[73] as interpreted by the Court of Justice of the European Union. As regards the insolvency provisions in Article XI of the Aircraft Protocol the Commission, asserting that the EC had competence because of a possible effect on the Insolvency Regulation, initially took the view that they did not mind which declarations Member States made as long as they all made the same. I persuaded the UK government that the EC had no competence over substantive insolvency law and that the Insolvency Regulation, as a conflict of laws regulation, was unaffected, and initially several other Member States took the same view. Eventually, the Commission having secured a rather weak Opinion from the EC Legal Services, that the Regulation was capable of being affected, the Member States in question withdrew their opposition as part of a deal by which they preserved their competence over substantive insolvency law and, though not able to make a declaration under Article XI, were free to enact legislation to the same effect. This the UK has done, so it has ended well, though I remain of the view that the assertion of competence was a political matter and did not rest on any sound legal foundation. Finally, Article VIII of the Aircraft Protocol gives the parties freedom to choose the applicable law to govern their relations with each other, but this applies only where a Contracting State has made a declaration, and the EU (as a deemed Contracting State) declined to do so on the basis that this could conflict with the Rome I Regulation,[74] so that EU Member States are precluded from making the declaration.

[71] See below.

[72] See R Goode, "The Cape Town Convention and Protocols and the Conflict of Laws" in *A Commitment to Private International Law: Essays in Honour of Hans van Loon* (Intersentia 2013) 221.

[73] Reg No 1215/2012.

[74] Regulation (EU) No 593/2008.

## VI. Final Reflections

Those involved in the work of harmonization know all too well the perils of embarking on a major project and the huge effort and resources needed to bring it to fruition. That great comparative lawyer Harold Gutteridge, whose book on comparative law still provides, after 65 years, the most authoritative description of the practical aspects of harmonization, expressed the point succinctly in the following terms:

> Unification can only be achieved by lengthy and patient efforts which will ultimately convince those in all countries, who are in a position to sponsor and carry through changes in the law, that it is a matter of urgent necessity to take steps in order to remove sources of inconvenience and friction in the international sphere. Unification cannot be achieved by a stroke of the pen, nor can it be carried out within the four walls of law libraries, practitioners' offices or professorial studies. The ground must be very carefully surveyed, and the interests concerned must be won over before any action is undertaken.[75]

It is therefore important to have clear objectives and to establish at an early stage the likelihood of substantial benefits for interested parties. In the field of commercial law this means securing the involvement of the relevant industry sectors, in the case of the Cape Town Convention, aviation, rail, and space. At an early stage three support groups were established, the Aviation Working Group, the Rail Working Group, and the Space Working Group.

For a private law convention the Cape Town Convention, with its associated Protocols, was unusually complex. It was only when the Aviation Working Group, directed by Professor Jeffrey Wool (as he now is), came on the scene that the project really began to take off. Realizing the potentially large benefits to be obtained from a good Convention and Aircraft Protocol the Aviation Working Group invested a substantial amount of time and resources in the project and without their efforts, and those of the other working groups, the project would not have succeeded.

As explained, the Cape Town Convention and Protocols involve private law, public international law, and the conflict of laws. The range of private law fields was extensive: the creation, perfection, and priority of consensual security interests and title-retention rights and the interests of outright buyers; the provision of default remedies; the protection of non-consensual rights and interests arising under national law; the assignment of claims; the creditor's rights on insolvency. The jurisdictional questions were complex. There was also a range of difficult technical issues. How were the different types of equipment within the Convention and Protocol to be defined and limited to items of high value? What fast-track mechanism could be provided for amendments to the Convention? On what basis was the International Registry to be established? How should the insolvency provisions be structured? And what was to be the relationship between the Convention and Aircraft Protocol and the Geneva and Chicago Conventions

[75] HC Gutteridge, *Comparative Law* (2nd edn, Cambridge University Press 1949) 157.

and UNIDROIT's own Convention on International Financial Leasing? Finally, there were great technological challenges in the establishment of the Aircraft Registry, based in Dublin.

To deal with all these issues paper succeeded paper, report succeeded report, meeting succeeded meeting, and in a variety of venues: Rome, of course, Oxford, London, New York, Paris, Montreal, Cape Town, Berne, Berlin, and it was necessary to call on a wide range of expertise. There were specialist groups on public international law, insolvency law, the operation of the registry and the immunities to be given to the Supervisory Authority, and the jurisdiction provisions. Finally, the two sponsoring organizations, UNIDROIT and ICAO, worked in different fields, the former in private law, the latter in public law governing aviation safety, and each had its distinctive working methods. It was therefore important to hold joint sessions of the UNIDROIT committee of governmental experts and a Sub-Committee of the Legal Committee of ICAO to ensure that both organizations were satisfied with the result, particularly important in that the Council of ICAO was to be the Supervising Authority of the Registry.

But that was not the end of the story. What is often overlooked is that when an international instrument is adopted one is only halfway there; it is necessary to procure ratifications. And here too the Aviation Working Group (AWG) supporting the work of UNIDROIT, engaged with governments around the world urging them to ratify the Convention and Protocol and providing advice and assistance.[76] The success of these instruments is thus due not only to their intrinsic quality and economic value but also to the continuing efforts of the AWG. Finally, the meaning of the Convention and its three Protocols has been elucidated in three Official Commentaries, for aircraft, rail, and space respectively, that for aircraft being now in its third edition and for rail in its second edition.[77]

What conclusions can be drawn from these instruments? First, no area of private law should any longer be regarded as taboo. Second, it is necessary to think outside the boundaries of national commercial laws in devising new solutions to international problems. Third, the public interest both in national security and in the continuance of public services means that there are likely to be more areas in which what is primarily a private law convention will also contain public law provisions. Fourth, the novel procedure for linguistic alignment of different language texts has much to commend it. Finally, it is to be hoped that in future private law conventions will be recognized as a form of treaty law!

[76] Cape Town Convention on International Interests in Mobile Equipment and its Aircraft Protocol Summary of National Implementation (February 2015) available on the AWG website.

[77] Sir Roy Goode, *Convention on International Interests in Mobile Equipment and Protocol Thereto on Matters Specific to Aircraft Equipment: Official Commentary* (3rd edn, UNIDROIT 2013); Sir Roy Goode, *Convention on International Interests in Mobile Equipment and Luxembourg Protocol Thereto on Matters Specific to Railway Rolling Stock: Official Commentary* (2nd edn, UNIDROIT 2014); Sir Roy Goode, *Convention on International Interests in Mobile Equipment and Protocol Thereto on Matters Specific to Space Assets: Official Commentary* (UNIDROIT 2013).

Emeritus Professor of Law in the University of Oxford and Emeritus Fellow of St John's College, Oxford. This is a revised and slightly expanded version of the inaugural Roy Goode annual lecture established by the Centre for Commercial Law Studies, Queen Mary, University of London, and delivered at the Inner Temple 1 March 2016. The writer would like to thank Claire Jervis for her helpful editorial assistance.

# 17

# The Assignment of Pure Intangibles in the Conflict of Laws*

*Roy Goode*†

*Within the EU the law governing the assignment of contract rights is governed by Rome I, Art.14, which, however, does not apply to third-party issues. Several years ago the European Commission suggested an addition to Art.14 to the effect that third-party conflicts, such as those between competing assignees, be governed by the law of the assignor's place of business. This attracted much support but also opposition from the securitisation industry, which urged the law governing the assigned obligation. A report from the British Institute of International and Comparative Law reached no firm conclusion. This paper supports the Commission's proposal and argues that selection of the law of the obligation for issues that are no concern of the debtor has nothing to commend it.*

* Originally published as 'The assignment of pure intangibles in the conflict of laws' [2015] LMCLQ 289 (pages 289–313). This article first appeared in Lloyd's Maritime and Commercial Law Quarterly, [2015] LMCLQ 289. Published by Informa Law, London. Reproduced with permission of Informa Law.

† Emeritus Professor of Law, University of Oxford, and Emeritus Fellow of St John's College, Oxford.

This article first appeared in L Gullifer and S Vogenauer (eds), *English and European Perspectives on Contract and Commercial Law: Essay in Honour of Hugh Beale* (Hart, Oxford, 2014) and is reproduced here by kind courtesy of Hart Publishing.

The following abbreviations are used:

BIICL: British Institute of International and Comparative Law;
BIICL Final Report/the Report: see *infra*, fn.33;
Explanatory Report: R Goode, H Kanda, and K Kreuzer, assisted by C Bernasconi, *Hague Securities Convention: Explanatory Report* (Koninklijk Brill NV, Leiden, 2005);
Rome Convention: Rome Convention on the Law applicable to Contractual Obligations 1980;
Rome I/Rome I Regulation: Regulation No 593/2008 of the European Parliament and of the Council of 11 July 2007 on the law applicable to contractual obligations [2008] OJ L177/6;
Rome II Regulation: Council Regulation (EC) 864/2007 of 11 July 2007 on the law applicable to non-contractual obligations [2007] OJ L 199/40;
*UNCITRAL Guide: UNCITRAL Legislative Guide on Secured Transactions* (UN, New York, 2010).

## Introduction

Despite the growing volume of international Conventions designed to harmonise substantive rules of commercial law, it is clear that private international law continues to flourish. In the case of the transfer of goods the rules governing the applicable law have been tolerably well worked out.[1] It is necessary to describe these briefly in order to highlight the problems involved in seeking to apply the same principles to the assignment of intangible movables, a topic that is the subject of extensive literature, only a very small selection of which can be noted here.

## Law Applicable to Dealings in Goods

The general rule applicable to dealings in goods[2] is that the validity of a transfer of goods, including a security interest, is governed by the *lex situs* (*lex rei sitae*) of the goods at the time of the relevant dealing. This applies not only to security interests in the traditional sense but also to reservation of title under conditional sale agreements, which has given rise to a good deal of case law.

Validity as between the parties is not to be confused with efficacy against third parties. Where, for example, D grants C1 a security interest in goods while they are in Ruritania, under the law of which a security interest must be registered in order to be effective against a subsequent secured creditor, this perfection requirement is entirely irrelevant to the validity of the security interest as between D and C1. It comes into play only if there is a further dealing in the goods by D, as by granting a second security interest, to C2, while they are still in Ruritania, and then it is a question not of validity but of priorities. An English court would recognise C1 as having a valid security interest but one which, if C1 had failed to register under Ruritanian law, would be subordinated to the security interest of C2. The same applies where S agrees to sell goods situated in Ruritania to B, who wrongfully disposes of them to T while they are still in Ruritania. If under Ruritanian law a title reservation is ineffective against a subsequent purchaser unless registered and S failed to register, an English court would hold that T acquires an overriding title under Ruritanian law.

[1] Some 50 years ago, one of Canada's leading commercial lawyers, Professor Jacob Ziegel, teamed up with me to write a comparative survey of hire-purchase and conditional sales law, of which one chapter was devoted to the conflict of laws. In this we took issue with several leading scholars on what was then thought to be established doctrine on the effect of a change of *situs*. Half a century later our analysis, which was well received, still seems to hold good. See RM Goode and JS Ziegel, *Hire-Purchase and Conditional Sale: A Comparative Survey of Commonwealth and American Law* (British Institute of International and Comparative Law, London, 1965), Part V. The subject was further developed by Ziegel in "Conditional Sales and the Conflict of Laws" (1967) 45 Can Bar Rev 284. However, the traditional *lex situs* rule is not well suited to mobile equipment regularly moving across national borders and makes no sense at all when applied to pure intangibles. See *post*, p. 237.

[2] For this purpose, documentary intangibles such as documents of title, negotiable instruments and negotiable securities are equated with goods, so that the *lex situs* is the location of the document of title, negotiable instrument or negotiable bond or certificate at the time of the relevant dealing.

Things become a little more complex where there is a change of *situs*, as where D, instead of granting a second security interest to C2, takes the goods to Urbania and sells them to T, a bona fide purchaser for value, or where B does the same in relation to the goods acquired from S. Here the rule of the law of last dealing applies. An English court will treat the perfection requirements of Ruritanian law as of no relevance to a dealing in the goods after they have left Ruritania. So the court will look to Urbanian law to determine the impact of the sale on C1's security interest or on S's reservation of title. If under Urbanian law T acquires an overriding title, no reference to Ruritanian law is necessary. If, on the other hand, Urbanian law applies the principle *nemo dat quod non habet*, then T will be considered by an English court as taking the goods subject to C1's security interest validly created, or S's title validly reserved, under the law of Ruritania.

The rule of the last dealing also applies to a wrongful double sale by the seller and, indeed, to theft. So in *Winkworth* v *Christie, Manson & Woods Ltd*,[3] certain works of art were stolen from the plaintiff in England and taken to Italy where they were sold to the second defendant, who subsequently delivered them for sale to the first defendants, auctioneers in England. The plaintiff claimed the works of art as his property but the second defendant successfully established his overriding title under Italian law, being the law of the new *situs*, as a purchaser in good faith without knowledge of his vendor's defect in title.

In general the *lex situs* rule, though not immune from criticism,[4] works well enough for tangible movables. It is, however, unsatisfactory when applied to goods in transit or to dealings in mobile equipment of a kind regularly moving from one jurisdiction to another, as in the case of aircraft. The location of an aircraft at any given time may be quite unrelated to the state with which it has its closest connection. For example, in the famous *Blue Sky* case,[5] the dispute concerned the validity of mortgages of two aircraft, one of which was registered in the United Kingdom but grounded at Schiphol airport in the Netherlands at the time of execution of the mortgage. The mortgage was valid under English law but invalid under Dutch domestic law. However, a Dutch court would have applied English law as the *lex registri*[6] and it was argued that this was more satisfactory than the *lex situs* because it would mirror the position under the Geneva Convention on the International Recognition of Rights in Aircraft 1948, Art.1. This was rejected by Beatson J on the ground that the application of the *lex situs* was well established and that reference to the *lex registri* would not by itself secure uniformity, because

[3] [1980] Ch 496.

[4] Primarily on the ground that the parties will not necessarily know where the goods are situated. The most detailed analysis is by JM Carruthers, *The Transfer of Property in the Conflict of Laws* (OUP, 2005), chs 8 and 9. Dr Carruthers concluded that "the legitimate interests of the law of the *situs* must be protected" in order to preserve predictability but with exceptions to allow flexibility in appropriate cases, eg where the transfer of property issue concerns only the parties themselves: *ibid*, [9.48–9.49].

[5] *Blue Sky One Ltd* v *Mahan Air PK Airfinance US Inc* [2010] EWHC 631 (Comm).

[6] The judgment adopts the language of counsel in referring throughout to the *lex registrii*, though it is not clear where the second 'i' comes from. The word "registrum" does not feature in classical Latin, in which the word for "registry" is *tabularium*, but it is found in mediaeval Latin.

the conflict rules of other jurisdictions might be different. Further, the reference back to English law under Dutch conflict of laws rules would involve resort to *renvoi*, a doctrine which is nowadays rejected by the English conflict of laws in most situations. The mortgage was therefore invalid as being contrary to Dutch domestic law.

It was this kind of problem that led to the Cape Town Convention on International Interests in Mobile Equipment 2001 and its associated Protocols, which establish an international legal regime for international interests (security interests and interests held by conditional sellers and lessors) in aircraft objects, railway rolling stock, and space assets, with a set of basic default remedies, an International Registry for the registration of such interests, and priority largely determined by the order of registration.[7]

## Law Applicable to Assignments of Non-Documentary Intangibles: General Considerations

### Assignment by way of security and absolute assignments

The common use of title reservation clauses in contracts for the sale of goods, coupled with the requirements in many jurisdictions of registration of chattel mortgages, has led to a focus on rules for the recognition and displacement of security and quasi-security devices in goods. Under English law, where title is reserved to the seller, the buyer acquires neither legal nor equitable ownership of the goods. By contrast, there are many agreements for the assignment of non-documentary intangibles where the transfer of legal title by a statutory assignment is deferred, and indeed may never take place at all, but beneficial ownership vests in the assignee from the outset. Moreover, despite the well-understood distinction between security assignments and outright assignments of debts, it is not always easy to distinguish the economic effects of the two types of transaction; and in a number of jurisdictions registration and priority rules apply alike to outright and security assignments.

Consistently with this, Art.14(3) of the Rome I Regulation[8] is expressed to cover both security and outright assignments, while the UNCITRAL legislative guide on secured transactions (the "*UNCITRAL Guide*") explains in detail why, exceptionally, its proposals as to creation, third-party effectiveness, and priorities apply equally to security assignments and absolute assignments of receivables.[9] None of the suggested changes to the Rome I Regulation is based on a distinction between outright and security assignments of non-documentary intangibles and no distinction is drawn between the two in the analysis which follows.

[7] The Convention and Aircraft Protocol are the only ones yet in force. There have so far been 67 ratifications of the Convention and 57 of the Aircraft Protocol, with ratification by the UK pending.

[8] Regulation No 593/2008 of the European Parliament and of the Council of 11 July 2007 on the law applicable to contractual obligations [2008] OJ L177/6 ("Rome I Regulation").

[9] *UNCITRAL Legislative Guide on Secured Transactions* (UN, New York, 2010), [25].

## Decline and fall of the *lex situs*

Attempts to determine the law applicable to the proprietary effects of a security assignment of non-documentary (or "pure") intangibles have mainly led to confusion. So strong has been the influence of the *lex situs* rule that conflict of laws lawyers have been driven to ascribe an artificial *situs* to intangibles, namely, the location of the debtor, being the place where the debt can be recovered. This, however, meets difficulties as soon as it is sought to be applied to particular facts. In the first place, non-documentary intangibles have no physical location, so what is provided is a purely legal construct which is not axiomatic but needs justification. Secondly, the appropriate applicable law depends on the relationship under examination and cannot sensibly be ascertained by reference to a single determinant, the *lex situs*.[10] Thirdly, since the notional *situs* varies according to the type of intangible under consideration, reference to the *lex situs* does not serve as an organising principle at all. That is why our conflict textbooks, having gone to some trouble to define the *situs* of intangibles, then tend to avoid applying it except in relation to documentary intangibles. This exposes the futility of the *lex situs* approach, which has, indeed, been disavowed by more recent decisions.[11] Why go through the two-stage process of designating the *lex situs* as the applicable law and then seeking to determine the *situs* of a particular pure intangible? Why not simply lay down a direct rule appropriate to the type of relationship under consideration? It is therefore not surprising that the *lex situs* has been discredited as a choice of law rule for the assignment of debts, contract rights and other pure intangibles, and that the various options put forward by the consultees of the British Institute of International and Comparative Law ("BIICL")[12] did not include the *lex situs* rule, which accordingly now serves no useful function except in relation to documentary intangibles.

## Special cases

There are certain rights in respect of which the problem either does not arise at present, namely, recorded rights to financial collateral,[13] or will cease to arise once the Space Protocol to the Cape Town Convention is in force, namely, recorded assignments of rights to payment or other performance due to a debtor by any person with respect to a space asset ("debtor's rights").

[10] See *post*, p. 254.

[11] *Macmillan Inc* v *Bishopsgate Investment Trust Plc (No 3)* [1996] 1 WLR 387, 401; *Raffeisen Zentralbank Österreich* v *Five Star General Trading LLC* [2001] EWCA Civ 68; [2001] QB 825; [2001] 1 Lloyd's Rep 597; Carruthers, *The Transfer of Property in the Conflict of Laws* (2005), chs 8 and 9. See to similar effect the *UNCITRAL Guide*, [20]: "as intangible assets are not capable of physical possession, adopting the *lex situs* as the applicable conflict-of-laws rule would require the development of special rules and legal fictions for the determination of the actual location of various types of intangible asset. For this reason, the *Guide* does not consider the location of the asset as being the appropriate connecting factor for intangible assets and favours an approach generally based on the law of the location of the grantor".

[12] For details of the consultation by the British Institute of International and Comparative Law. See *post*.

[13] See *post*, p. 249.

*Financial collateral*

For financial collateral the right to which is recorded in a register or account located in a Member State of what is now the European Union, the ordinary conflict rules in the Rome I Regulation are displaced by the Financial Collateral Directive,[14] Art.9(2) of which applies the law of the place where the register or securities account is maintained.

The Hague Convention on the Law Applicable to Intermediated Securities 2006 initially adopted the same approach but moved away from this because of the perceived problem that the functions of maintaining securities accounts were often distributed among different offices of the same bank situated in different jurisdictions. The *Explanatory Report* on the Convention[15] gave as an illustration an account initially opened in Tokyo, where the first credit to the account was effected; the dispatch of all account statements from an office in Dublin; the administration and remittance of dividends from an office in Hong Kong; the obtaining of advice as to the ongoing status of the account from an office near the client's main office in Singapore; and the backing-up and monitoring of each securities account by two computer systems run from the bank's New Delhi and San Francisco offices, respectively. Accordingly the solution adopted was to select as the law governing all issues, except purely contractual or purely personal issues,[16] the law expressly provided by the account agreement to govern that account agreement or, if the account agreement expressly provided for the application of another law, that law,[17] provided that in either case the relevant intermediary had at the time of the agreement a qualifying office in the designated state.[18] The Convention is not yet in force.

*Assignments of "debtor's rights"*

The Space Protocol to the Cape Town Convention provides a regime under which a creditor holding a registered international interest in a space asset may, either at the time of that registration or subsequently, record against the registration an assignment of debtor's rights to the creditor. Of the three categories of equipment covered by the Cape Town Convention, space assets are unique in that once launched they cease to be readily susceptible to the exercise of default remedies, though it is possible for an enforcing creditor to exercise some control, for example, by taking control of the command codes or by exercising a contractual right to terminate the debtor's access to the space asset and blocking such access. But the value of these remedies is limited. Greater importance is attached to the provision of debtor's rights

[14] Council Directive 2002/47/EC of 6 June 2002 on financial collateral arrangements as regards linked systems and credit claims [2002] OJ L168/43 as amended by Council Directive 2009/44/EC of 6 May 2009 [2009] OJ L146/37.

[15] R Goode, H Kanda, and K Kreuzer, assisted by C Bernasconi, *Hague Securities Convention: Explanatory Report* (Koninklijk Brill NV, Leiden, 2005) (the "*Explanatory Report*"), 20.

[16] Hague Convention 2006, Art.2.

[17] *Ibid*, Art.4(1).

[18] This was the shorthand expression used by the authors of the *Explanatory Report* to denote an office fulfilling the requirements of Art.4 as to the maintenance of securities accounts in the designated state. See the *Explanatory Report*, 68, para 1-45. Where the requirements of Art.4 are not fulfilled, then one of the cascade of fallback rules in Art.5 has to be applied.

as additional collateral, since these may be enforced against the account debtors (the debtor's debtors). In other words, funding for space assets is considered to be more in the nature of project finance than asset-based finance.

However, security interests in debtor's rights cannot be registered in isolation, because the registration system is based on the registration of interests in physical assets and requires that each asset be uniquely identified and registered separately. Debtor's rights, by contrast, are intangible and incapable of any standard system of unique identification. The Space Protocol overcomes this problem by allowing the creditor to protect this additional collateral by recording the assignment against the linked registered international interest, a recorded assignment having priority over a subsequently recorded assignment and over an unrecorded assignment.[19]

## Ordinary non-documentary intangibles

### *Matters affecting the debtor: the general rule*

When we come to ordinary non-documentary intangible movables (loans, sale, lease and credit card receivables, mortgage debts, contract rights, intellectual property rights, and the like), certain things are clear. In general, anything that affects the debtor—such as the assignability of the debt *vis-à-vis* the debtor (including the effect of a no-assignment clause),[20] defences to the creditor's claim, rights of set-off, and other grounds of discharge of the debtor—is governed by the law applicable to the debt, for the obvious reason that the debtor ought not to have its position affected by an assignment to which it is not a party. This is expressly provided by the Rome I Regulation, Art.14(2). On the other hand, the effect of a prohibition against assignment on the efficacy of the assignment as between assignor or its liquidator and assignee is of no concern to the debtor and will be governed not by Art.14(2) but by the law applicable to the assignment agreement under the Rome I Regulation, Art.14(1), as a matter going to performance.[21]

What if the purported assignee is asserting an assignment that was never made? The issue here is whether a debtor who pays a purported assignee obtains a good discharge. That is undoubtedly a matter governed by the law applicable to the debt, not, however, because of Art.14, which is plainly inapplicable, but under Art.12(1)(b).[22]

[19] UNIDROIT, Protocol to the Convention on International Interests in Mobile Equipment on Matters specific to Space Assets ("Space Protocol") (UNIDROIT, Berlin, 2011), Art.XIII. For a full analysis see the writer's Official Commentary on the Convention and Space Protocol (UNIDROIT, Rome, 2013), [3.45 *et seq*], [5.54 *et seq*].

[20] Certain assignability issues do not concern the debtor. For example, a legal system might treat an assignment as void if it is by way of security or relates to future debts. The law applicable to this issue is that governing the contract of assignment: Art.14(1).

[21] See F Garcimartín Alférez, "Assignment of Claims in the Rome I Regulation: Article 14", in F Ferrari and S Leible (eds), *Rome I Regulation: The Law Applicable to Contractual Obligations in Europe* (Sellier, Munich, 2009) 217, 231.

[22] So far as English law is concerned, the position of a debtor who in good faith pays a person wrongfully claiming to be an assignee is remarkably obscure. The question is which of two innocent parties should bear the risk, the creditor or the debtor. One of the few scholars to address the issue considers the risk is on the debtor, see G Tolhurst, *The Assignment of Contractual Rights* (Hart, Oxford, 2006), 387. This is almost certainly the position under English law. See to similar effect, from an American

### *Proprietary effects as between assignor and assignee*

To the above rule there is one qualification. It is now generally accepted that as Art.14 stands, the proprietary effects as between assignor and assignee as well as contractual effects are governed by the law applicable to the contract between them, [23] a principle embodied in Rome I, recital 38. That is no doubt why the rule in *Dicey, Morris & Collins: The Conflict of Laws*[24] is not formulated in property terms at all but refers merely to the mutual *obligations* of assignor and assignee. This rule applies even though the debtor is affected as well as the intended assignee in that the debtor is not obliged to recognise an assignment which is invalid under the law applicable to it. This is not a true exception, because in proceedings against the debtor the validity of the assignment is a preliminary question which has to be answered by reference to the law governing the assignment.[25]

A rather different case is where it is asserted that the assignment is invalid because the assignor never acquired the title to the assigned claim in the first place. This is not a matter for the law governing the agreement to assign; rather, it is a preliminary question which has to be answered by reference to its own applicable law.[26]

It has to be said that this focus in Rome I Regulation, Art.14(1) on the *contract* between assignor and assignee is wholly illogical. It is possibly predicated on the mistaken assumption that an assignment depends on the validity of the underlying contract. However, a more likely explanation is that the predecessor of Art.14(1)—namely, Art.12(1) of the Rome Convention on the Law applicable to Contractual Obligations 1980 (the "Rome Convention")—was conceived as purely contractual in character; and, when recital 38 was introduced into the Rome I Regulation to encompass proprietary effects, there was no corresponding change from the contract of assignment to the assignment itself in what is now Art.14(1).

The fallacy of ascribing proprietary effects to a contract that does not also constitute a conveyance was convincingly demonstrated many years ago by Mark Moshinsky.[27] It is necessary to distinguish an agreement for transfer from the

law perspective, G Gilmore, *Security Interests in Personal Property* (Little Brown & Co, Boston, MA and Toronto, 1965), 393, while drawing attention to what is now the Uniform Commercial Code, Art.9-416(c), which entitles the debtor to ask the assignee for reasonable proof of the assignment and, if this is not provided, to pay the assignor. The UNIDROIT Principles of International Commercial Contracts, Art.9.1.12 and the Principles of European Contract Law ("PECL"), Art.11:303(2) do not allow payment to the assignor, merely a right to withhold payment to the assignee, while PECL, Art.11:304 also entitles the debtor who pays the supposed assignee to a discharge unless the debtor could not have been unaware that such person was not the person entitled to performance. See to similar effect Dutch Civil Code, Art.6:34. The prudent course for a debtor who is unsure of the status of the person claiming to be an assignee is to consult the creditor and, if the latter denies there has been a valid assignment and calls for payment, to interplead.

[23] Namely, the law chosen by the parties (Rome I Regulation, Art.3(1)) or, in the absence of choice, the law determined by the applicable rule in Art.4.

[24] L Collins (gen. ed.), *Dicey, Morris & Collins: The Conflict of Laws*, 15th edn (Sweet & Maxwell, London, 2012), Rule 135(a).

[25] T Hartley, "Choice of Law regarding the Voluntary Assignment of Contractual Obligations under the Rome I Regulation" (2011) 60 ICLQ 29, 36–7.

[26] *Ibid*, 34.

[27] M Moshinsky, "The Assignment of Debts in the Conflict of Laws" (1992) 108 LQR 591.

transfer itself. Where the assignment is effected by a distinct act, as where an agreement to assign is subsequently followed by an assignment, or where in a given legal system there is a notional, abstract transfer distinct from the contract, the assignment is in no way dependent on the validity of the contract[28] and, indeed, may be governed by its own distinct law. Further, it is perfectly possible to have an assignment with no underlying contract to assign, a point made by Professors Hugh Beale and Wolf-Georg Ringe in a discussion of assignment in the context of the proposed European sales law.[29]

It is interesting that, in the case of a transfer of tangible movables, eg under a sale, the textbooks distinguish sharply between the contractual and the proprietary effects, the latter being governed by the *lex situs*. Why this distinction should be ignored in the case of intangible movables is not explained. However, since the rule is confined to relations between assignor and assignee and does not engage third parties, the point is of little importance in practice, and anyway it falls outside the remit given by the European Commission to the BIICL Study Group[30] and is not discussed further.

## Third party issues

Among the relationships not covered by Art.14 are disputes between an assignee and (a) the assignor's trustee or liquidator where occupying the position of a third party;[31] (b) an attachment creditor of the assignor; and (c) a competing assignee. Moreover, competing claims to proceeds which are not the subject of a contractual provision in the assignment agreement are governed not by the Rome I Regulation but by the Rome II Regulation.[32]

Some years ago, the European Commission proposed a sensible new rule that would subject these third party issues to the law of the assignor's habitual residence. The proposal received strong support but also determined opposition, particularly from UK lawyers acting in securitisation arrangements, who favour the law applicable to the assigned debts, while others favoured freedom of choice of the parties to the assignment.

In view of this division of opinion, the European Commission invited the British Institute of International and Comparative Law ("BIICL") to prepare a study on the question of the effectiveness of an assignment or subrogation of a claim against third parties and the priority of the assigned or subrogated claim over a right of another person. The BIICL team, coordinated by Dr Eva Lein of BIICL and Professor Andrew Dickinson then of the University of Sydney, undertook a major programme of comparative research, drawing on national rapporteurs from 12 European countries and working with an expert group of academic and practising lawyers and

28 See Garcimartín, "Assignment of Claims in the Rome I Regulation" (*supra*, fn.21), 225.

29 H Beale and W-G Ringe, "Transfer of Rights and Obligations", in G Danneman and S Vogenauer (eds), *The Common European Sales Law in Context* (OUP, Oxford, 2013), 524.

30 See *post*, p. 249.

31 See below, p. 244.

32 Council Regulation (EC) 864/2007 of 11 July 2007 on the law applicable to non-contractual obligations ("Rome II Regulation") [2007] OJ L 199/40. See *post*, p. 248.

representatives of ISDA and AFME. The *BIICL Final Report*,[33] presented to the Commission in December 2011, contains a wealth of statistical, empirical and legal analysis. Its recommendations are discussed below. [34]

## Specific Priority Issues

### Assignee versus assignor's liquidator

In an excellent article some three years ago,[35] Professor Trevor Hartley made the point that where the assignor (the creditor) goes into liquidation it is necessary to distinguish cases where the liquidator is not asserting rights greater than those of the creditor (the assignor) and cases where he is invoking an overriding right by virtue of a rule of insolvency law, for example, avoidance of the assignment as a preference or a transaction in fraud of creditors. In the former case the liquidator simply stands in the shoes of the insolvent assignor and is not a third party for the purpose of any proposed new rule, and the liquidation is of no significance in determining the applicable law, which is the law governing the assignment. By contrast, if the liquidator is asserting an overriding right by virtue of insolvency law, then he is a third party[36] and the applicable law will be the *lex concursus* and, where the assignor's centre of main interests is in an EU Member State and the insolvency proceedings are brought in a Member State other than Denmark, the EU Insolvency Regulation.[37] In this situation there seems no scope for the operation of any addition to Art.14.

The interrelationship between the Rome I Regulation and the Insolvency Regulation is not free from difficulty but the position would appear to be as follows. In the case mentioned above, the effects of insolvency, for example, grounds of avoidance of a transaction, are governed by the *lex concursus* under the Insolvency Regulation, Art.7 but, subject to this, Art.8(1) provides that rights *in rem* acquired by the assignee which are situated within the territory of another Member State at the time of opening of the insolvency proceedings are not affected.[38] For this purpose an assigned debt is situated in the Member State within the territory of which the obligor has its centre of main interests.[39] Article 8(1) is attracted if this is anywhere outside the Member State in which the insolvency proceedings are opened. However, this does not necessarily mean that the law of that Member State governs

[33] British Institute of International and Comparative Law, *Study on the Question of Effectiveness of an Assignment or Subrogation of a Claim against Third Parties and the Priority of the Assigned or Subrogated Claim over a Right of Another Person: Final Report* (British Institute of International and Comparative Law, London, 2011) ("*BIICL Final Report* "), available at *www.ec.europa.eu/justice/civil/fi les/report_assignment_en.pdf*.

[34] See *post*, pp. 249 *et seq*.

[35] T Hartley (2012) 60 ICLQ 29.

[36] *Ibid*, 38.

[37] The original regulation was Council Regulation (EC) 1346/2000 of 29 May 2000 on insolvency proceedings ("Insolvency Regulation") [2000] OJ L160/1, as amended This was replaced earlier this year by Regulation (EU) 2015/848 of the European Parliament and of the Council of 20 May 2015 on insolvency proceedings (recast) [2015] OJ L141/19. In the present context references to "debtor" in the Regulation denote the insolvent assignor, not the account debtor under an assigned claim, who to avoid confusion is here labelled the "obligor".

[38] Insolvency Regulation, Art.8(1).

[39] *Ibid*, Art.2(9)(viii).

the efficacy of the assignment. Article 8(1) does not lay down a conflict of laws rule; the applicable law remains determined by the conflict of laws rule of the forum,[40] which in a case within the Rome I Regulation, Art.14(1) leads to the law applicable to the agreement to assign.

The following example illustrates the points made above:

A, an English factoring company, enters into a factoring agreement with B for the purchase of B's ongoing stream of receivables arising from export transactions, these to vest automatically in A on coming into existence. The agreement, which is expressed to be governed by English law, provides for advance payments to be made to B by A. B's centre of main interests is in the Netherlands but the receivables are or will become due from customers in England. Various receivables arising from contracts already concluded at the time of the factoring agreement come into existence. B then goes into liquidation in the Netherlands. The liquidator challenges A's title to the receivables on the ground that (a) the formalities prescribed by Dutch law for perfection of an assignment of receivables were not observed; and (b) the assignment of some of the receivables was a fraudulent conveyance for the purposes of Dutch insolvency law.

Here, ground (a) is based on the general law, not on some overriding provision of insolvency law, so that the liquidator is not a third party but stands in the shoes of the assignor, the validity of the assignment is governed by English law under Rome I Regulation, Art.14(1), and A's claim is not affected by the insolvency proceedings against B in the Netherlands, the assigned debts being situated in England.[41] Ground (b), however, is a special rule of insolvency law, as regards which the liquidator is a third party, and the issue of fraudulent preference is in any event governed by Insolvency Regulation, Art.7(2)(m), and is not excluded under Art.16. The assignment will therefore be invalid if constituting a fraudulent conveyance under Dutch insolvency law.

Another example, given by Hartley, of an overriding right in the liquidator is avoidance of an assignment against insolvency creditors for want of the registration required by statute.

## Assignee versus assignor's attachment creditor

This case is more complex in that it depends on the basis of the attaching debtor's claim. If this is based on the invalidity of the assignment, that is a claim governed by the law applicable to the assignment. If the attachment is sought in the mistaken belief that the assignor is still the owner of the claim, it should be refused. Where, on the other hand, the question is whether the claim can be attached even against an

[40] R Goode, *Principles of Corporate Insolvency Law*, 4th edn (Sweet & Maxwell, London, 2011), [15.88].

[41] However, the application of Insolvency Regulation, Art.8(1) does not depend on this; it suffices if the assigned debts are situated anywhere outside the Netherlands. So if, for example, they were due from obligors having their centres of administration in France, this would suffice to ensure the application of Art.5(1) but the law governing the efficacy of the assignment as between assignor and assignee would be English law, not French law. See Goode, *Principles of Corporate Insolvency Law* (2011), 15.88.

assignee, the question is one of priorities. The distinction is well brought out in the decision of the Court of Appeal in *Raiffeisen Zentralbank Österreich AG* v *Five Star Trading LLC*,[42] a decision on the Rome Convention 1980.

In that case, Five Star borrowed money from RZB to finance the purchase of a ship, the loan being secured by a mortgage of the ship and an assignment of an insurance policy covering it and issued by French insurers, the insurance policy and the assignment being governed by English law. The assignment was notified to the insurers by fax, a mode of notification valid under English law but not under French law.

Subsequently the ship was involved in a collision. Among the claimants were cargo owners, who contended that they were entitled to attach the insurance policy as being an asset of Five Star. They were granted a provisional attachment by the Paris Tribunal de Grande Instance de Commerce, stayed to await the outcome of proceedings in England brought by RZB as assignee of the policy claiming a declaration of its entitlement, the cargo owners being subsequently joined in the proceedings.

RZB argued that the question was whether the claim was validly assigned to it, this being a contractual matter governed by English law. The cargo owners contended that the issue was one of priority as between them and RZB and fell outside the Convention, being a property law issue governed by the *lex situs* of the debt, ie French law. The Court of Appeal applied English law, holding that the question whom the insurer had to pay was a contractual matter governed by English law [43] and that the notified assignment was binding on the insurers.[44]

If the question had truly been one of priority, as contended by the cargo owners, then under English conflict of laws rules French law would have been applied to determine whether the attachment overrode RZB's title. But the evidence indicated that the French court had proceeded on the basis that the insurance policy was an asset of Five Star, whereas by reason of the assignment (governed by English law) it was not. So the issue was not a priority issue at all. As Hartley puts it, since the attachment creditors were not invoking a priority

[42] [2001] EWCA Civ 68; [2001] QB 825; [2001] 1 Lloyd's Rep 597.

[43] This is questionable. An assignment does not make the assignee a party to the contract; and the assignee acquires rights against the assignor's counterparty, not by virtue of the contract, but by virtue of the assignment itself. The issue is whether at a given time the contractual rights belonged to the assignor or to the assignee. That is a question of property. The fact that the subject matter of the assignment consists of contractual rights is not to the point. But on the facts of the case this characterisation made no difference, the assignment being expressed to be governed by English law, under which it was valid, so that title to the policy moneys passed to RZB, with the result that they were no longer an asset of Five Star. Mance LJ concluded that in any event the Rome Convention, Art.12(1) and (2) plainly covered the situation. It is now clear, from recital 38 to what is now the Rome I Regulation, that in the relations between assignor and assignee there is no distinction between contractual and proprietary aspects, both being governed by the law applicable to the agreement to assign. See further M Bridge, "The Proprietary Aspects of Assignment and Choice of Law" (2009) 125 LQR 671, esp 687, where Professor Bridge also takes the view that the assignee's acquisition of ownership of the contractual right to the insurance monies was a matter of property, not merely of contract.

[44] Presumably the Tribunal de Commerce then discharged the provisional attachment. However, I have not been able to verify this.

rule but only attaching on the basis that the asset was still vested in the assignor, they stood in no better position than the assignor itself. The position would have been otherwise if under French law the attachment had the effect of overriding the assignee's title.

## A competing assignee

It may be necessary to distinguish the assignment of a single debt from an assignment of multiple debts or future debts. This distinction is drawn by *Dicey, Morris and Collins in The Conflict of Laws*,[45] which, however, does not address the former in the Comment and simply provides in its Rule 135 that, *semble*, "the validity and effect of an assignment may be governed by the law with which the right assigned has its most significant connection". That is as far as the guidance goes and it makes no specific mention of any of the three specific priority issues identified above. Cheshire, North, and Fawcett, *Private International Law*,[46] at least propound a rule, albeit a controversial one:

> The law governing the right to which the assignment relates is the most satisfactory system by which to determine the ranking of competing claimants where the creditor has made more than one contractual assignment.

As will be seen from the BIICL study,[47] this view receives support from a substantial proportion of the securitisation industry who responded to the consultation paper, but is opposed by the factoring and invoice discounting industry and by some securitisers.

*Cheshire, North & Fawcett* does admit an exception, where both assignments are governed by the same law, in which case, it says, it is that law that should determine priorities. The problem with this apparently reasonable solution is that it lacks transparency *vis-à-vis* third parties; there is no external connecting factor, merely a couple of internal governing laws, which themselves may result from an express choice of law. It is not without significance that this did not feature as an option in the responses of consultees to the BIICL study.

Finally, by the time the dispute between the competing assignees surfaces, the debt may no longer exist; it may have been collected by one of the assignees, so that the dispute now concerns title to the proceeds. There is obviously no sense in applying the law governing a debt which has ceased to exist.[48]

What, then, should be the law governing the priority of competing assignments? Addressing this issue was one of the main tasks of the BIICL Study. The resulting report is discussed below.

[45] *Dicey, Morris & Collins: The Conflict of Laws* (*supra*, fn.24), [24.079].

[46] J Fawcett, J Carruthers, and P North (eds), *Cheshire, North and Fawcett: Private International Law*, 14th edn (OUP, Oxford, 2008), 1234.

[47] See *post*. See also, to similar effect, Carruthers, *The Transfer of Property in the Conflict of Laws* (2005), [6.40].

[48] See *post*, p.248 as to proceeds.

## Treatment of proceeds

### *As between assignor/assignor's liquidator and assignee*

In invoice discounting and other forms of non-notification finance, the account debtor is not notified of the assignment and it is left to the assignor to collect in the assigned debts and account for them to the assignee. In English assignment agreements, it is customary to include a provision that the assignor will hold the proceeds on trust for the assignee until handing them over; and this suffices to protect the assignee from the effects of the assignor's insolvency, since the proceeds will not form part of the assignor's assets—indeed, this would be so even without an express trust provision. Assuming that the agreement to assign is governed by English law, either because of an express provision to that effect or because of the rules in the Rome I Regulation,[49] the rights of the assignee in regard to the proceeds will be governed by English law as the law of the contract governing the assignment.[50]

Where, however, the contract makes no provision for the application of proceeds, the Rome I Regulation does not apply and the case falls within the Rome II Regulation as a claim based on unjust enrichment.[51] The Rome II Regulation, Art.10(1) applies the law governing a closely connected pre-existing relationship between assignor and assignee, namely, the relationship established by the agreement to assign. So the result under the Rome II Regulation is the same as where there is an express proceeds clause governed by the Rome I Regulation.

[49] The Rome I Regulation, Art.4(1) and (2) states that in general the law applicable to the sale of goods or the supply of services is governed by the law of the country where the seller or service provider has its habitual residence. However, Art.4 is curiously silent as to the law applicable to a contract for the assignment of intangible movables. In most cases this is likely to be the law of the habitual residence of the assignor, either by analogy with the sale of goods or the supply of services (Art.4(1)(a), (b)) or because it is the assignor whose performance is characteristic of the contract (Art.4(2)).

[50] Rome I Regulation, Art.14(1). It may be noted that an express trust of proceeds contained in the assignment agreement is governed by the Rome I Regulation, not by the Rome II Regulation, Art.1(2)(e) of which excludes non-contractual obligations arising out of the relations between the settlors, trustees and beneficiaries of a trust created voluntarily. It is thought that proceeds held on trust by an assignor under a trust provision in an assignment do not constitute "assets placed under the control of a trustee" so as to fall within the Hague Convention on the Law applicable to Trusts and their Recognition 1986, implemented in the United Kingdom by the Recognition of Trusts Act 1987; but, even if the Convention applies, the trust is governed by the law chosen by the parties (Art.6), which is that governing the contract as a whole, including the trust provision, so that the applicable law is the same as under Rome I Regulation, Art.14(1). For a detailed analysis, see A Dickinson, *The Rome II Regulation: The Law Applicable to Non-Contractual Obligations* (OUP, Oxford, 2008), chs 3 and 4 and *Updating Supplement* (2010).

[51] However, the *BIICL Final Report*, 18, 379, 382, 406, advocates extension of the Rome I Regulation to cover claims in unjust enrichment arising from a contractual relationship. The question has long been controversial. See, eg S Pitel, "Rome II and Choice of Law for Unjust Enrichment", in J Ahern and W Binchy (eds), *The Rome II Regulation on the Law Applicable to Non-Contractual Obligations* (Martinus Nijhoff, Leiden, 2009), 231, 239 and A Scott, "The Scope of Non-Contractual Obligations", in the same volume, at 57.

*As between competing assignees*

Where there are successive assignments to A and B and the proceeds are collected by B, any claim by A against B will normally be based on unjust enrichment. If both parties have their habitual residence in the same country, it is the law of that country that will determine priority.[52] If their habitual residence is in different countries, then the law of the country in which the unjust enrichment took place will apply,[53] or, if the unjust enrichment claim is manifestly more closely connected with another country, the law of that country. [54] It is for the applicable law to determine whether A's claim is proprietary, in which case it will survive B's insolvency, as under English law,[55] or is purely personal, in which event A will simply be an unsecured creditor, as under German law. There is much controversy as to these provisions and space does not allow them to be explored here.[56]

## BIICL Final Report

The BIICL Study, though handicapped by a very disappointing response rate, was a major research undertaking which included: a collection of statistical data; an EU-wide empirical analysis of practical problems encountered in different market sectors in cross-border assignment and subrogation cases; a legal analysis based on national reports from 12 EU Member States; and a comprehensive examination of the arguments for and against a new conflict of laws solution. The study was opposed to special rules for special types of transaction on the ground that this was likely to result in more uncertainty and characterisation issues.[57] However, it considered that the transfer of intermediated securities should be excluded as being governed by special rules.[58]

Some 80 per cent of responding stakeholders expressed a need for new legislation on the law applicable to third-party effects of an assignment. Of the various possible solutions, only three came into serious consideration, namely, the law applicable to the contract between assignor and assignee (11 per cent), the law applicable to the assigned claim (30 per cent), and the law of the assignor's habitual residence (44 per cent). As regards the second and third of these, the securitisation industry largely favoured the law of the assigned claim, while the factoring and invoice discounting industries were equally strongly supportive of the law of the assignor's habitual residence. The securitisers were content that, if the general rule adopted was the law of the assigned claim, there should be an exception for factoring and invoice discounting in favour of the law of the assignor's habitual residence.

[52] Rome II Regulation, Art.10(1). [53] *Ibid*, Art.10(3). [54] *Ibid*, Art.10(4).

[55] To similar effect is the (European) Draft Common Frame of Reference, Art.III 5.122, which provides that, where the debtor who pays the assignor is discharged, "the assignee's right against the assignor to the proceeds has priority over the right of a competing claimant so long as the proceeds are held by the assignor and are reasonably identifiable from the other assets of the assignor".

[56] For detailed analyses see Dickinson, *The Rome II Regulation* (2008); Pitel (*supra*, fn.51), 246–53; *Dicey, Morris & Collins: The Conflict of Laws*, [36.037–36.045].

[57] *BIICL Final Report*, 364. [58] *Ibid*. See *ante*.

## Solution 1: Law applicable to the contract between assignor and assignee

The Study describes the advantages and disadvantages as follows:[59]

*Advantages*

- flexibility for the different sectors;
- no evidence of abuse in practice in the Netherlands, where the solution has been implemented;
- avoidance or reduction of the need for sector-specific rules;
- synergy, reduction of applicable laws and of complexity;
- suitability for the assignment of future claims.

*Disadvantages*

- possible prejudice to third parties, however reduced by the suggested limited party autonomy approach;
- risk of the avoidance of publicity requirements.

## Solution 2: Law applicable to the assigned claim

The *BIICL Final Report* sets out the perceived advantages and disadvantages of the law applicable to the assigned claim as follows: [60]

*Advantages*

- consistency of the connecting factor;
- synergy and cost-effectiveness;
- suitability for financial claims.

*Disadvantages*

- unsuitability for future claims;
- complexity and inefficiency for bulk assignments;
- uncertainty as to the law applicable to the claim assigned.

[59] *BIICL Final Report*, 385 *et seq.* [60] *Ibid*, 390 *et seq.*

## Solution 3: Law of assignor's habitual residence

The BIICL Study summarises the advantages and disadvantages of the law of the assignor's habitual residence in the following terms:[61]

*Advantages*

- single connecting factor;
- suitability for bulk assignments, and for assignments of receivables under contracts not yet in existence;
- synergies with the Insolvency Regulation and the UN Convention on the Assignment of Receivables in International Trade;
- suitability for factoring transactions;
- suitability to resolve conflicts between competing right-holders.

*Disadvantages*

- problems in defining "habitual residence" as the connecting factor;
- increased transaction costs, complexity;
- conflict of connecting factors;
- problems in practice, in particular in Belgium and Luxembourg;
- unsuitability for financial claims;
- inflexibility.

## Recommendations

The Study Group advanced all three possible solutions, without stating a preference but on the basis that: (a) the law applicable to the contract of assignment should apply only where chosen by the parties and then only if the chosen law was that of the assigned claim or the law of the country in which the assignor has its habitual residence; and (b) whichever solution was adopted, the selected law should govern all property aspects of an assignment without distinguishing between whether they arise in the relationship between assignor and assignee or against third parties, with consideration being given to a moderate use of sector-specific rules.[62]

61 *Ibid*, 394 *et seq.*

62 *BIICL Final Report*, 402–3.

## Reflections on the Recommendations in the BIICL Final Report

### Overview

The BIICL Study Group engaged in Herculean efforts to produce its report and is to be congratulated on its compilations of statistical data, its national reports on the applicable law and its laying out of the issues. But at the end of the day one is left with a sense of disappointment. Asked to come up with a report providing the basis for a new conflict of laws solution on third party aspects of assignment, the BIICL felt unable to put forward an unequivocal set of rules because of differences of opinion among the members of the Expert Group and consultees. Instead, the Institute found itself with no alternative but to present to the Commission three options and no indication of preference, coupled with a recommendation that, whichever option was adopted, the conflict rule should govern all proprietary aspects regardless of the relationship under consideration.

There are three comments that can be made on these proposed alternative solutions.

First, solution 1 (law applicable to the contract of assignment) is not really a solution at all—it simply gives the parties a choice whether to adopt solution 2 (law of the assigned claim) or solution 3 (law of the assignor's habitual residence). But these alternatives are far apart. Why should it be open to the parties to an assignment to dictate third-party effects under a choice of law that will not be visible to third parties? Moreover, as the *BIICL Final Report* points out,[63]competing assignments may specify different laws. For example, assignment 1 specifies the law applicable to the assigned claim, while assignment 2 designates the law of the assignor's habitual residence. The Report refers to the "last event" rule as one way of resolving the problem but then goes on to say that it would seem preferable to have a single connecting factor, which seems to suggest a rule that is not based on party choice at all but on the second option, the third option or some other unstated option.

Secondly, the alleged merits and demerits of each of the remaining alternatives could have received rather more critical examination than they did. Instead, they are reproduced without significant comment.[64] Where the Report does offer some independent thinking— as instanced by its proposed "super conflict" rule to deal with cases where the primary rule is that of the assignor's habitual residence and the assignor changes its habitual residence between the first and the second assignments— the rule proposed makes little sense either in commercial or in conceptual terms.[65]

Thirdly, some of the conclusions of the Report do not match the preceding analysis. For example, the factors and invoice discounters want the habitual residence

[63] *Ibid*, 388–9.

[64] For example, a disadvantage of the rule applying the law of the assignor's habitual residence is said to be that it is inflexible, yet it is a key recommendation of the Report that, whichever rule is selected to determine the law applicable to third party effects, that law should govern *all* relationships.

[65] See *post*, p. 258.

rule; the securitisers and their lawyers want the law governing the assigned claim but are not opposed to a carve-out for the factoring and discounting industry.[66] So there is general agreement that, if the general rule were to be in favour of the law of the assigned claim, there should be a factor-specific exception. Yet the Report suggests exactly the opposite, stating that only one company representing 3 per cent of stake-holders supported a sector-specific solution and that the overwhelming majority advocated a single rule for all sectors;[67] and it goes on to set out what it sees as the *disadvantages* of such a carve-out, which the factors and invoice discounters want and to which the securitisers do not object. The overwhelming consideration seems to be to have a single law governing all proprietary aspects without differentiation.

It is worth looking in a little more detail at the primary ground on which a substantial part (but by no means all) of the securitisation industry wanted a conflict of laws rule based on the law of the assigned claim and opposed the European Commission's proposal that the applicable law for third party issues should be the law of the habitual residence of the assignor, and the perceived disadvantages of such a rule.

## Claimed advantage of applying the law of the assigned claim

The primary advantage claimed is that there would be a reduction in the number of laws applicable to the assignment, with a consequent reduction in cost. As the evidence submitted to the Study Group shows, it is the practice of securitisers, as part of their legal due diligence, to analyse each individual debt to seek to determine: the applicable law; the formalities prescribed by that law; the assignability of the claims; the proprietary effects of the assignment and the effectiveness of the assignment as between assignor and assignee; the enforceability of the assignment against the debtor; and its enforceability against third parties.[68] Accordingly, the securitisers say that selection of the law of the assignor's habitual residence to govern third-party effects would simply add one more legal system to those already examined as part of the legal due diligence. As will be seen,[69] this is a misconception; far from adding to the number of legal systems to be consulted on proprietary effects, the application of the law of the assignor's habitual residence reduces them. Securitisers are also concerned at what they see as the lack of legal certainty in determining the habitual residence of the assignor as defined in Rome I Regulation, Art.19. The Report addressed this concern by proposing that Rome I Regulation, Art.19(2) and (3) should be disapplied, leaving only the place of central administration as regards other bodies, corporate or unincorporated.

[66] *BIICL Final Report*, 117–18. [67] *Ibid*, 400.

[68] See, eg the response of an unidentified French company reproduced in *BIICL Final Report*, Annex, file 1.PDF. See also J Perkins, "Proprietary Issues arising from the Assignment of Debts: A New Rule?" (2010) 6 JIBFL 333.

[69] See *post*, pp. 257–8.

## Different viewpoints of the two main industries

When one examines the advantages and disadvantages perceived for each of the two primary alternatives, it is clear that they reflect the different needs and practices of the securitisation industry, on the one hand, and the factoring and invoice discount industry, on the other. As stated above, securitisers examine each assigned contract and check the applicable law and its effects as regards all relationships;[70] factors and invoice discounters are not geared up to do so, so that for the latter the application of the law of the assigned claim would entail a substantial additional burden, particularly since under a whole turnover agreement the assignment may cover debts not notified to the factor. So, for factors and discounters the law of the assignor's habitual residence provides a single law which is known at the outset without the need to examine individual assigned contracts and which, moreover, can be applied to the assignment of future debts arising under contracts not yet concluded and whose governing law will therefore not be known.[71] The Report concedes[72] that for such assignments the solution does not work and it would be necessary to specify that the relevant date for ascertaining each such future debt would be the date it came into existence. One would think that this solution is far from simple. In any event, there are other serious objections to the selection of the law of the assigned claim to govern priority between competing assignees. These are set out below.

## Report's final conclusions

The Report sensibly concludes that no general solution is perfect. There are in fact only two solutions receiving significant support and the third, the law applicable to the assignment, should be dropped, as suggested earlier. The Report does not indicate any preference for one solution over the others but strongly advocates a single rule covering *all* third-party proprietary interests, regardless of the relationship involved.

In other words, the same rule should apply to proprietary effects as between assignor and assignee, assignee and attachment creditors, assignee and the assignor's insolvency trustee or liquidator and competing assignees. That is a major change from existing conflict of laws rules and one would have thought should receive extended reasoning. Instead, this proposal is justified in just two sentences.[73] The first states simply that there would be only one applicable rule governing the proprietary aspects of assignment and the number of potentially applicable laws could be reduced from the outset. The second asserts that "the current artificial distinction between property aspects as between assignor and assignee and as against third parties could be removed". Neither of these arguments is in the slightest convincing.

[70] This legal due diligence is partly driven by the demands of rating agencies for information that will enable them to assess the rating of the notes or bonds issued on the market.

[71] See Garcimartín, "Assignment of Claims in the Rome I Regulation" (*supra* , fn.21), 249, arguing that the law-of-the-assignor approach offers an adequate solution for future and bulk assignments and one which should in principle be acceptable to the securitisation industry.

[72] *BIICL Final Report*, 391. [73] *Ibid*, 402.

## "One rule": the law of the assigned claim

Where a single debt is assigned, it would no doubt be feasible to apply the law of the assignor's place of business to all third-party relationships. However, if the law applicable to the assigned claims were to be adopted as the conflict of laws rule in relation to bulk assignments, there would not be a single law at all but a potential plethora of laws varying according to the law governing each particular assignment. In that scenario, only a preoccupation with legal tidiness could justify the argument in favour of applying the same law to proprietary effects regardless of the relationship under consideration and even without consideration of the question of what constitutes a third party. As between the assignor and the assignee, the effect of a valid assignment is to transfer ownership of the assigned debts to the assignee, a matter of great importance to the assignee if the assignor should become insolvent after collecting in the debts but before accounting for them to the assignee. What possible justification can there be for subjecting the efficacy of the assignment as between assignor and assignee, a matter of no concern to the debtor, to the law applicable to each assigned claim? What can be the rationality of a rule that would require a liquidator or trustee in bankruptcy of the assignor to examine every one of what may be hundreds or even thousands of contracts, identify the applicable law and then determine whether the collected proceeds of the assigned debts belong to the assignee or remain part of the assignor's estate? As we have seen, unless asserting an overriding right under insolvency law, a liquidator is not a third party but stands in the shoes of the assignor, so that an assignment effective as between assignor and assignee should be equally effective against the assignor's liquidator, subject to any overriding legislation of the *lex concursus*.[74]

The argument for the application of the law of the assigned claim may be based on the common misconception that the obligor's duty is to pay the assignee with the best title to the debt.[75] That is certainly not the case under English law. If the assignee fails to give the debtor notice of assignment, the debtor obtains a good discharge by paying the assignor, and the fact that as between assignor and assignee it

[74] For example, where a company registered in the United Kingdom grants a security assignment or charge which is registrable under Companies Act 2006, s.859A but is not registered, the assignment or charge is void against the liquidator, an administrator and a creditor in UK insolvency proceedings (Companies Act 2006, s.859H(3)) regardless of the law otherwise applicable to the assignment or charge.

[75] That seems to have been the thinking behind the approach taken by the Bank of England's Financial Markets Law Committee. See *Issue 121: European Commission Final Proposal for a Regulation on the Law Applicable to Contractual Obligations ("Rome I")* (April 2006, para.9.4; October 2006, 5), which stated that "Article 13(3) arguably ignores the important principle of debtor protection"; J Perkins, "A Question of Priorities: Choice of Law and Proprietary Aspects of the Assignment of Debts" (2008) *Law and Financial Markets Rev* 238, 240. However, in its later paper, *Issue 137: European Commission Review of Article 14: Assignment* (March 2010), the FMLC recognised the need to reach a compromise between the law of the assigned obligation and the law of the assignor's habitual residence (by exceptions in favour of the factoring and related industries and assignments by consumers), while still maintaining that the habitual residence rule "would unfairly prejudice the interests of the underlying debtor" and that it "is important for several reasons for the underlying debtor to be able to identify the person entitled to lay claim to the debt in priority to other assignees" (para.2.1.3).

is the latter who has best title to the debt is irrelevant.[76] Similarly, where there are two successive assignments, the debtor is entitled to pay the assignee who first gives notice of assignment and has no obligation to investigate which assignee has priority. Let us assume, for example, that, under two assignments governed by English law, C assigns first to A1 and then to A2 a debt due from D, A2 purchasing the debt with knowledge of the prior assignment to A1 but being the first to give written notice of assignment to D. It is clear that D obtains a good discharge on paying A2,[77] but it is equally clear that the best title to the debt is vested in A1, who has a proprietary claim for any monies received from D by A2. In other words, priority between competing assignees has no necessary connection with the question whether the debtor obtains a good discharge by paying one creditor rather than another and is not the debtor's concern.[78]

It would be hard to think of a more impracticable rule than that which applies the law of the assigned claim. The point was made with great clarity many years ago in a comprehensive article by Professor Catherine Walsh:[79]

> However, in modern financing practice, the assignment of multiple and future receivables in a single transaction is commonplace, whether the assignment involves the outright sale of receivables as in a factoring or securitization arrangement, or their assignment merely as collateral for a secured obligation. This practical reality makes application of the law governing the assigned debt a commercially inefficient solution. The assignee would need to scrutinise each of the assigned contracts to determine the applicable law and would then have to conform to the priority rules of all relevant states. Priority would vary for different receivables depending on their governing law, increasing the costs of dispute resolution and insolvency administration. If the assignment included future receivables owing by as-yet-unidentified debtors, the assignee might not even be able to predict which laws might potentially apply.
>
> It is the practical demands of modern receivables financing which ultimately led the [UNCITRAL] Commission to endorse the law of the assignor's location as the most appropriate choice of law rule for priority. It is the only approach capable of supplying a single predictable governing law for the global assignment of multiple receivables owing by debtors

[76] *Bence* v *Shearman* [1898] 2 Ch 582. See to the same effect *Principles of European Contract Law, Part 3* (Kluwer Law International, The Hague, 2003), Art.11:303(1), (3); *UNIDROIT Principles of International Commercial Contracts 2010* (UNIDROIT, Rome, 2010), Art.9.1.10.

[77] The reasoning is the same, namely, that in the absence of notice from the first assignee the debtor is entitled to assume from the second assignee's notice of assignment that the debt has become vested in the second assignee. See to the same effect the UNIDROIT Principles (*supra*, fn.76), Art.9.1.11, which states that the debtor is discharged if he pays the first assignee to give notice.

[78] In the illustration given by Perkins (*supra*, fn.75), the obligor receives notices from both assignees. In that situation, contrary to what is suggested, it is not necessary for the debtor to work out which of the assignees has priority. If he pays the second assignee before receiving notice of the first assignment, he obtains a good discharge. If he has not paid the second assignee before receiving notice of the first assignment, then, depending on the applicable law, he can either still pay the second assignee (the solution adopted by the UNIDROIT Principles, *supra* fn.76) or invoke appropriate procedures such as interpleader or a payment into court. But the case where only one notice of assignment is given makes the point more sharply that the party from whom the debtor can get a good discharge by payment does not have to be the one with the strongest title to the debt.

[79] C Walsh, "Receivables Financing and the Conflict of Laws: The UNCITRAL Draft Convention on the Assignment of Receivables in International Trade" (2001) 106 Dickinson L Rev 159, 174.

in different states and for the assignment of future receivables, thereby vastly reducing the inquiry and monitoring burden on the assignee.

The superiority of the assignor location rule has been recognised by analysts who have examined the issue with the practical realities of modern global assignment practices in mind.

To illustrate the point, let us suppose that an assignor based in London wishes to assign to an assignee also based in London, under an agreement expressed to be governed by English law, the assignor's rights under four sale contracts, one of which is governed by French law, one by German law, one by Spanish law, and the fourth by Italian law. Does it really make sense to have a rule that requires the validity of the assignment as between assignor and assignee to be separately tested against French law for the first assignment, German law for the second, Spanish law for the third, and Italian law for the fourth? By contrast, the case for adopting the law of the assignor's habitual residence has been convincingly demonstrated not only by Professor Walsh but by other scholars.[80]

## Supposed artificiality of the distinction

These considerations make it difficult to understand the desire to remove what the *BIICL Final Report* refers to as "the current artificial distinction between property aspects, as between assignor and assignee and against third parties".[81] There would be force in this observation in the case of the assignment of a single debt, which could sensibly be treated in the same way as the sale of goods, where the *lex situs* is applied both to the transfer of ownership as between seller and buyer and to the effects of the sale *vis-à-vis* third parties. But, in the case of assignments of multiple debts, the distinction between the assignor-assignee relationship and third-party relationships, far from being artificial, responds to commercial realities. What the parties want is one law to govern the effects of the assignment as between themselves. They do not want to find such effects dependent on a possible diverse range of laws governing different claims each of which can be determined only by examining the terms of each assigned contract.

## Law of the assignor's habitual residence

If there is to be one rule, it is surely clear that it cannot be the law applicable to the assigned claim. The factoring and invoice discounting industry would not be willing to accept it because of the substantial additional burdens imposed, while, on the other hand, the *BIICL Final Report* argues that there could be difficulty in defining factoring and invoice discounting for the purpose of a carve-out. That should not be beyond the wit of man. But the simpler solution is to say that all third-party proprietary effects are governed by the law of the assignor's habitual residence. The securitisers say that this would impose an additional burden on them. But that is surely to view the

[80] See *post*, pp. 258–9.

[81] *BIICL Final Report*, 402, 409.

matter from the wrong end of the telescope. We are only talking about third-party effects. It must be much easier and cheaper for securitisers to examine a single law, the law of the assignor's habitual residence, than it is to look at the variety of legal systems covering the securitised claims. Moreover, securitisers already have to look at the law of the assignor's place of business to see whether assignments of receivables are required to be registered and, if so, to search the register,[82] and, more generally, will conduct a due diligence exercise on the assignor as originator. For their part, factors and invoice discounters would face major additional burdens, and indeed have to change their systems, if they had to examine every assigned contract and then research each applicable law to determine the third-party effects of the assignment.

As noted above, the habitual residence rule is that adopted by the UN Convention on the Assignment of Receivables in International Trade 2001,[83] and its several advantages were trenchantly described by a Dutch scholar and practitioner in the following terms:[84]

> There are good reasons for adopting this conflicts rule. First of all, the place of business or residence of the assignor is the connecting factor that places the issues in their natural environment. That is where his wealth is showing, where he participates in trade and commerce, where third parties act on the appearance of solvency, where he is declared insolvent or bankrupt ...
>
> Secondly, the place of business of the assignee is an easily ascertainable connecting factor. It is stable and foreseeable for all parties involved ...
>
> Thirdly, the proposed conflicts rule does not incur the practical difficulties that would result from conflicting rules that apply the law governing the debt, or the law of the domicile of the debtor, it is practical both for global assignments of many debts in one transaction and for the assignment of future debts. It provides certainty from the start about the law that will govern the transaction.

To this one might add that, in those jurisdictions which require registration of assignments, it is against the assignor that registration will be effected and searches made.

## Change of habitual residence and competing connecting factors: the "super conflict" rule

*BIICL Final Report* also addressed the question of competing connecting factors. If, for example, the connecting factor were to be the assignor's habitual residence, what should be the position if there were successive assignments in favour of different assignees and the assignor's habitual residence changed between the two assignments?

The *Report* raises the possibility of a "super conflict" rule, by which the first assignee, by following a particular procedure such as the giving of written notice to the debtor,

82 A number of legal systems require registration not only of security assignments but also of outright assignments.

83 See Art.22. See to similar effect, see the *UNCITRAL Guide*, recommendation 208.

84 THD Struycken, "The Proprietary Aspects of International Assignment of Debts and the Rome Convention, Article 12" [1998] LMCLQ 345, 357.

could fix the applicable law once and for all by reference to the circumstances prevailing at the time of the first assignment.[85] But there are serious problems with this suggestion. For one thing, it totally overlooks the fact, of which the Study Group cannot have been unaware, that the vast proportion of receivables financing, including securitisation, takes the form of non-notification finance. There are several reasons for this, succinctly set out by Professor Philip Wood in his analysis of securitisation:[86]

> Notice will not normally be given to the debtors because of the inconvenience and expense, because it is preferable for the originator to continue collection (the originator has the data and the system), because the debtors might be confused by notice of an assignment and because the originator wishes to maintain its relationship with its customers.

To this one might add that it is not only the debtors who would be confused. What could the assignee be expected to make of a payment from a debtor for whom the assignee maintains no accounts and whose payment relates to a transaction in respect of which the data are held by the assignor, not by the assignee? And what of the assignor, whose accounts will show that the debtor appears to be in default? So the last thing any of the parties would want is for the obligor to be given notice of assignment purely to fix the applicable law.

Secondly, the proposed rule would run counter to the well-established "last event" rule in the conflict of laws, by which it is the law of the last dealing or event which determines whether the purchaser or assignee has acquired an overriding title or whether the *nemo dat* rule applies, so that the title of the purchaser or assignee depends on that of his own seller or assignor. So, if the connecting factor is the assignor's habitual residence, which is in Ruritania, and this changes to Urbania between the first and the second assignment, the court should apply Urbanian law in the first instance. Only if this does not give the second assignee an overriding title will it be necessary for the court to resort to Ruritanian law to determine the title of the first assignee.[87] There seems no good reason to depart from a rule that respects laws found in every jurisdiction by which, in given circumstances, a non-owner can pass a good title. Nor is it easy to see why such laws should be displaced by a law determined under a prior transaction to which one of the parties to the later transaction was not a party and of which it may have had no knowledge.

Thirdly, why should the position of a later assignee be fixed with a law applicable to a prior assignment of which it may have no knowledge by reason of a notice which will be equally invisible?

[85] *BIICL Final Report*, 401.

[86] P Wood, *Project Finance, Securitisations, Subordinated Debts* (Sweet & Maxwell, London, 2007), [6.045].

[87] The *Report* refers at different points to the last event rule but starts with the law governing the first assignment and then applies the law governing the second assignment to determine if the first assignee's title is overridden. This produces the same result but is less economical than beginning with the law of the second assignment, which may make it unnecessary to refer to the law governing the first assignment. Hartley (2011) 60 ICLQ 29 suggested that the problem of changing habitual residences made it difficult to decide which assignment should have priority and that this was best left to the law of the assigned obligation. However, in an exchange of views, Professor Hartley readily accepted that the solution I have proposed in the text is the correct one.

Finally, if prior to the giving of the notice by the first assignee the second assignee has already acquired priority under the last event rule or whatever other rule is applicable, why should that priority be retrospectively disturbed?

The BIICL was clearly not unaware of problems such as these and wisely omitted reference to the "super conflict" rule in its final recommendations.

## Conclusion

Neither the BIICL nor the Expert Group can be blamed for the inconclusive results of the study. These reflect a problem common in attempts at harmonisation, namely, that of securing consensus on a result when there is a sharp difference of opinion. Evidently the only way forward was the compromise solution recommended in the *BIICL Final Report*, a recognition that the best is often the enemy of the good. It is, however, to be hoped that in due course the European Commission will resuscitate its original proposal that third-party effects of an assignment should be governed by the law of the assignor's habitual residence, however defined. Such rules would allow for third-party effects to be governed by a single law without the need for a carve-out in favour of any particular industry sector. As the *Report* states, there is no single ideal solution. But we need to move on. To leave things in limbo to be dealt with by national conflict of laws rules is not a commercially sensible option.

# PART III

# USAGE AND THE *LEX MERCATORIA*

A scholar exploring certain fundamental concepts may find that as he or she drives down ever deeper there comes an issue at base that cannot readily be resolved by legal concepts alone. The *lex mercatoria* raises one such issue. The ever-growing trend towards convergence of national laws, and the expansion of transnational commercial law, as the result of the expansion of cross-border trade and consequent need for greater harmonisation, has led to the idea of a new *lex mercatoria* which in the view of some is an autonomous, a-national legal system based on international custom and usage and not dependent for its efficacy on any national legal system. The key issue, and one that remains heatedly debated by scholars, is what exactly converts business practice into binding usage. The traditional view in both public international law and transnational commercial law is that usage derives its binding force from consistent practice (*usus*) and observance of that practice from a sense of binding obligation (*opinio juris*). But this raises a paradox. If a belief that the obligation is binding is correct then it is unnecessary; and if on the other hand it is incorrect then how can it give rise to a legal obligation? I endeavoured to address these questions in Chapters 18 to 21, suggesting that it is necessary to distinguish business practices that are *de facto* binding because failure to observe them may attract criticism from the commercial community and possible sanctions, such as exclusion from an exchange or trade organisation, and those that become binding *de jure* because they receive endorsement from a court or arbitral tribunal, as they usually will because of the perceived importance of upholding contracts and of recognising reasonable trade usage. But in my view all contracts ultimately depend for their validity on satisfying criteria imposed by national law.

# 18

# Usage and Its Reception in Transnational Commercial Law*

*Roy M. Goode*[†]

## I. Introduction

The study of what has become known as transnational commercial law[1] is fraught with hazards. What do we mean by transnational commercial law? Is it the same as the *lex mercatoria* or something broader? What are its sources? Can we identify general principles of commercial law and, separately, uncodified international trade usage? If so, what happens to these principles when they become embodied in convention or contractually incorporated uniform rules? Do they disappear, maintain a parallel existence in their original form, or change their shape to match the convention or rules? And how far do conventions and rules either evidence preexisting principles and usages or influence the creation of new ones?

If one examines the literature on public international law, one finds an astonishing correlation between the kinds of issue discussed by the international lawyers and those that have perplexed the scholars of transnational commercial law. Indeed, international law provides a rich harvest for the commercial lawyer, not least because the International Court of Justice has on numerous occasions given rulings directly bearing on the relationships between the different sources of international law, and in particular between treaties and customary international law. Yet the two streams

* Originally published as R Goode "Usage and its reception in transnational commercial law" in I.C.L.Q. 1997, 46(1), 1–36.

† Norton Rose Professor of English Law in the University of Oxford, Fellow of St. John's College, Oxford. This article is a revised version of a paper presented at Bar-Ilan University, Israel, in August 1996, at the 8th Biennial Conference of the International Academy of Commercial and Consumer Law. The conference proceedings will be published by Hart Publications in 1997 (ed. Jacob S. Ziegel). I am indebted to Lady Fox and Professor Christine Chinkin for their very helpful comments and suggestions on the public international law aspects of this paper. I hope that I have accurately reflected these in the final text.

[1] The concept of transnational commercial law was pioneered by Professors Berthold Goldman, Clive Schmitthoff, and Aleksander Goldstajn in the early 1960s. There is now an enormous literature on the subject.

of literature, on international law and transnational commercial law, appear so far to have developed in almost total isolation from each other.

This article focuses on international trade usage: its nature, its normative force, the means by which its existence is established, and its relationship to other elements of transnational commercial law. In so doing it seeks to ascertain how far parallels may be drawn with principles of public international law. The article concludes with a discussion of the relationship between the *lex mercatoria* and the conflict of laws and the implications of the diversity of approaches adopted in international commercial arbitration.

## A. Terminology: Transnational Commercial Law and *Lex Mercatoria*

The phrase "transnational law" seems first to have been given prominence by Philip C. Jessup, whose work *Transnational Law* was published in 1956. Yet his conception of it seems markedly different from what we understand, in the field of commercial law, by the phrase "transnational commercial law". He considered the terms "international" and "international law" misleading since they suggested a concern only with relations between States. He therefore used transnational law, instead of international law, to embrace "all law which regulates actions or events that transcend national frontiers", including public and private international law and other rules not fitting wholly into such standard categories. But in relation to commercial law, at any rate, this description is too broad, for it includes the *national* law of international trade and *national* conflict of laws rules. By contrast, "transnational commercial law" is conceived as law which is not particular to or the product of any one legal system but represents a convergence of rules drawn from several legal systems or even, in the view of its more expansive exponents, a collection of rules which are entirely anational and have their force by virtue of international usage and its observance by the merchant community. In other words, it is the *rules,* not merely the actions or events, that cross national boundaries.

But there is no agreement as to the meaning or content of transnational commercial law. Some equate it with the new *lex mercatoria,*[2] though this too is given different meanings by different writers. If transnational commercial law is taken to mean the product of the convergence of rules of commercial law through all means, including conventions and other international instruments, then its ambit is plainly far wider than law fashioned by merchants. Yet that, surely, is the essence of the *lex mercatoria.* It is by nature uncodified, non-statutory, and non-conventional. Rules embodied in an international convention can legitimately be described as part of transnational commercial law but, *qua* conventional law, they are not part of the *lex mercatoria,* for the convention in which they are incorporated operates only by the will of States which become parties to it or otherwise adhere to it.

[2] See Ole Lando, "The *Lex Mercatoria* in International Commercial Arbitration" (1985) 34 I.C.L.Q. 747, 748 *et seq.*

Similarly, the codification of unwritten usages in a standard set of rules adopted by contract subjects them to national law, namely, the law governing the contract. Accordingly, an international convention or a contractually adopted codification is at most evidence of the uncodified rules previously existing; and by itself it is not very reliable evidence because the purpose of most conventions or contractual codifications is not to reproduce an existing set of universally adopted usages—for in truth no such universality exists—but, rather, to build on existing usage and to provide best solutions to current problems. It is in the nature of conventions and codifications that they do not simply reproduce the *status quo*; they change it, and sometimes quite radically. The extent to which they are evidence of pre-existing customary rules cannot be determined solely, or even primarily, from the instrument itself except where it expressly states that it is declaring existing custom (a declaration which is not always reliable) or where it replaces earlier codified rules; what is required is an examination of the *travaux préparatoires* and, if this is not sufficient, an analysis of other materials or the reception of oral or documentary evidence of practice to determine the content of the pre-existing rules.

So for the purpose of this article the phrase "transnational commercial law" is used to describe the totality of principles and rules, whether customary, conventional, contractual, or derived from any other source, which are common to a number of legal systems, while the phrase "*lex mercatoria* " is used to indicate that part of transnational commercial law which is uncodified and consists of customary commercial law, customary rules of evidence and procedure, and general principles of commercial law, including international public policy.[3]

## B. The Elements of Transnational Commercial Law

It has been said of the *lex mercatoria,* as of public international law, that it is not possible to provide an exhaustive list of elements or sources. In a widely cited article[4] Professor Ole Lando identified eight elements of the *lex mercatoria,* namely, public international law, uniform laws, the general principles of law, the rules of international organisations,[5] uncodified customs and usages,[6] codifications of customs and usages by international organisations, standard-form contracts, and reported arbitral awards. In the terminology adopted in this article only general principles and uncodified usages constitute the *lex mercatoria*; collectively the various elements make up transnational commercial law. Curiously, no reference is made to the decisions of the Court of Justice of the European Communities, which has itself

[3] See *infra* n.19 and main text. For a masterly comparative survey of the whole field of transnational commercial law see Filip De Ly, *International Business Law and Lex Mercatoria.*

[4] *Supra* n.2.

[5] In which are included formulations of general principles prepared by scholars and issued by an international organisation, such as the Principles of International Commercial Contracts published by Unidroit and the Principles of European Contract Law prepared by the Commission on European Contract Law.

[6] The two terms are nowadays used interchangeably, and for brevity are hereafter referred to as "usages". But see *infra,* n.20.

developed general principles, or of national courts when interpreting or applying international instruments or usage, though these obviously carry a much more general authority than arbitral awards and should be regarded as constituent elements of transnational commercial law.

It is not without significance that Professor Lando uses the term "elements" rather than the more usual "sources". "Elements" is more exact, since it is evident that the items in the shopping list are of very different kinds. Some create law, some declare law,[7] some are not themselves law but are sources of rights and some are evidence of law. Instruments that create law may also serve evidential purposes.[8] Transnational commercial law shares with public international law the characteristic that it raises fundamental jurisprudential questions such as "What is law?" and "What are the sources of law?" It is outside the scope of this article to examine issues of this kind. My concern is to examine briefly the nature of uncodified international trade usage, its role in transnational commercial law, the methods by which courts and arbitrators satisfy themselves of the existence of a usage, and the effect on uncodified usages of their reduction to a convention or to a set of uniform rules promulgated by international organisations and effectuated by incorporation into contracts.

## C. Hierarchy of Norms

As a matter of impression, if a commercial lawyer were asked to rank norms of transnational commerce in descending order of importance he or she would probably rank international trade conventions at the top and compilations of scholars at the bottom, with international trade usages somewhere in between. But things are not always what they seem, and a good case can be made for standing this ranking completely on its head. At the time of its making a convention is not law at all; at most its existence signifies that States are contemplating its adoption. By contrast, an international trade usage has normative force through the conjunction of *usus* and *opinio juris*.[9] Again, since conventions are effectuated only by ratification or some other adoptive act, the agreement of States to the text of a convention indicates a provisional view only of the acceptability of the text, whereas a compilation of scholars, such as the Unidroit Principles of International Commercial Contracts or the Principles of European Contract Law published by the Commission on European Contract Law, represents a commitment to the text by the scholars concerned and carries the weight appropriate to their international standing. Moreover, even in countries where a convention has become operative its dispositive provisions will be, and will very often be expressed to be, subordinate to the contrary agreement of the parties, which would include any contractually incorporated codifications of usages. So the UNCITRAL Convention on Independent Guarantees and Standby Letters of Credit, most of the provisions

[7] This is the theory of the common law, but it is recognised that in reality the existing law represents a framework within which the judge has a limited power to create law.

[8] See *infra* p.279.

[9] See *infra* p.270.

of which are purely dispositive,[10] will usually be displaced by the non-binding Uniform Customs and Practice for Documentary Credits (UCP) or Uniform Rules for Demand Guarantees (URDG) issued by the International Chamber of Commerce, one or other of which is likely to be incorporated into the relevant contract. Nor can we necessarily conclude that an apparently normative international usage takes precedence over, say, the Unidroit Principles or the Principles of European Contract Law, for it would be open to courts and arbitrators to say that this product of the collaboration of a group of internationally known scholars points the way to what should now be seen as the best rule of contract law on the relevant point and should be adopted in preference to existing rules or usages.

## D. The Impetus for the Concept of Transnational Commercial Law

The development in the past few decades of a theory of transnational commercial law represents in some degree a desire, part pragmatic, part intellectual, part emotional, to recreate the internationalism of the mediaeval law merchant. No doubt the usages of merchants, accepted by the mercantile community as binding and applied by the merchant courts, were a significant unifying factor in the regulation of international trade and transport. There is, however, a tendency to romanticise the law merchant and to treat it as an integrated corpus of universally applied law akin to the canon law, when in truth it was never an organised body of legal rules at all; rather, a diverse and constantly changing aggregation of mercantile customs which might from time to time be brought together in a more or less authoritative compilation. Most of these focused heavily on maritime customs rather than on general commercial usage, and they consisted of a collection of detailed rules which addressed very specific, albeit common, problems.[11] Nevertheless, a number of these rules can be regarded as indicative of broader principles of more general application. They thus represent an important source of general principles of law applicable to international trade.[12]

Though national courts and arbitral tribunals continue to make extensive use of conflict of laws rules to determine the law applicable to a transaction with a foreign element, arbitrators in international commercial arbitrations have shown a growing desire to throw off the shackles of private international law and to avoid dependence, or exclusive dependence, on any particular national law, however selected, and instead to resort to a modern *lex mercatoria*. The reasons for this are discussed later in this article.[13]

[10] See Art.1(1) and the various arts. (Arts.13. 14, 16) referring to generally accepted rules, usages, and accepted standards of international practices; and, for a general discussion, Rafael Illescas-Ortiz, "International Demand Guarantees: the Interaction of UNCITRAL Convention and the 458 Rules of the CCI", an as yet unpublished paper presented at the 8th Biennial Conference of the International Academy of Commercial and Consumer Law at Bar-Ilan University, Israel, Aug. 1996.

[11] See *infra*. [12] See n. 10 [13] See *infra* p.289.

## E. The Influence of the Dispute-Resolution Method on Substantive Rights

It is clear that while litigation and arbitration are alternative methods of dispute resolution, the difference between them is not purely procedural but has a significant effect on substantive rights. There is nothing new in this. Even in the Middle Ages the law merchant as administered by the merchant courts was significantly different from that administered by the courts of common law, and, indeed, was given pre-eminence over the common law within its legitimate sphere of application.[14] Necessarily, therefore, the principles of law to be applied varied with the tribunal. This is even more true today. Arbitrators undoubtedly have a greater freedom than national judges. While the requirements of the *lex loci arbitri* have to be observed in relation to matters such as capacity to act, jurisdiction and the conduct of the arbitration if the award is to be enforceable under the New York Convention, it is primarily for the arbitrators, within the limits agreed by the parties, to determine their own procedure and the admissibility of evidence; and it is widely (though far from universally) held that even in the absence of express authority from the arbitration agreement or any rules it incorporates[15] arbitrators may apply their own conflict of laws rules to determine the applicable law, in the absence of a choice of law by the parties,[16] or even choose directly the law or rules of law they consider appropriate,[17] and can more freely invoke general principles of law or international trade usage to define the rights and duties of the parties. Again, it is the view of some scholars that an arbitrator, unlike a national judge, is free to recognise the contractual adoption of an otherwise inapplicable convention as a valid choice of law, not merely a contractual incorporation of terms.[18]

Moreover, since finality is one of the key attractions of arbitration it is an almost universally accepted principle of national laws, as reflected in the UNCITRAL Model Law on Arbitration, that courts should be slow to interfere with arbitral awards, even if they appear to be erroneous in fact or law, with the result that it is inherently harder to upset an award than it is to reverse a judge on appeal. To the extent that national laws limit the ability of national courts to interfere with arbitral awards the arbitrators are in practice able to disregard any theoretical limitations on the way they reach their decisions and the law they apply. Even so, arbitral tribunals have a moral, as well as legal, obligation to act in a disciplined fashion and according to settled principles unless they are dispensed from such obligation by the agreement of the parties. So the fact that the control exercised over their functions is relatively light is not a ground for treating the legal basis for their decisions as unimportant.

[14] Statute of the Staple, 27 Ed. III, stat. 2 (1353) cc. 5, 6, 8, and 21.

[15] E.g. the ICC Rules of Conciliation and Arbitration. Art.13(3).

[16] Since, while a national judge is obliged to apply the conflict rules of his own jurisdiction as the *lex fori*. there is no particular *nexus* between an arbitrator and the place or seat of the arbitration and thus, on one view, no arbitral *lex fori*. However, views remain divided on this question. See further *infra* p.286, as to international trade usage and the conflict of laws.

[17] See *infra* p.287.

[18] See *infra* p.284.

## II. The Nature, Elements, and Scope of International Trade Usage

### A. The Nature of Unwritten International Trade Usage

Unwritten[19] trade usage is a practice or pattern of behaviour among merchants established by repetition which has in some degree acquired normative force. There are two theories as to the nature of unwritten trade usage. One is that it is a particular form of international customary law.[20] The other, adopted by (*inter alia*) English law and by Article 9(2) of the 1980 UN Convention on Contracts for the International Sale of Goods (the "Vienna Sales Convention"), is that it takes effect as an implied term of a contract. Though the contract theory has been criticised as artificial, in that it ascribes to the parties a knowledge of the usage which they may not possess, this is entirely consistent with the objective theory of contract by which terms are interpreted not according to the subjective intention of the parties but as a reasonable person would interpret them. Usages depend for their efficacy on the settled practices of parties to contracts; they are essentially contractual in nature. Proponents of the *lex mercatoria* tend to be hostile to the contract theory, seeing it as inconsistent with the status of international trade usage as "law". But the practical effect of the distinction between the two theories appears to be slight.

### B. The Normative Force of Unwritten International Trade Usage

Until relatively recently it has been widely accepted that for an international trade usage to have normative force it is not sufficient to establish a pattern of repetitive behaviour among merchants; it must also be shown that this pattern of behaviour is observed from a sense of legally binding obligation, not from mere courtesy, convenience or expediency:[21]

There is, however, the world of difference between a course of conduct that is frequently, or even habitually, followed in a particular commercial community as a matter of grace and a

[19] The term "unwritten" is here used to denote a principle or rule that has not been reduced to writing, whether in binding form (such as a judicial decision, statute or convention) or in nonbinding form (such as private codification or scholarly or mercantile publication).

[20] The subject of trade usage and custom is bedevilled with problems of linguistic ambiguity. Usage is sometimes used to denote practice or behaviour, sometimes to indicate a pattern of behaviour which has risen to the level of a norm. It has been traditional to distinguish custom from usage, but the distinctions have been drawn in widely differing ways. E.g. according to some authorities custom is the practice of a particular locality, usage the practice of a trade, profession, or vocation. Others consider that usage is merely a pattern of behaviour and that custom is the application of the usage from a sense of binding obligation. Others again divide custom into different categories, according to the degree of their antiquity or universality. The modern approach is to treat the two terms as interchangeable. In transnational commercial law the term "usage" or "usages" is that generally adopted; in international law the reference is usually to custom. For convenience, "usage" is the term adopted in this article to denote a settled practice which has acquired normative force and is thus equated with custom. But since "usage" does not have an adjectival form, reference will also be made to customary law or customary rules of law. Mere repetitive behaviour will be referred to as such or as practice.

[21] *General Reinsurance Corp.* v. *Forsakringsaktiebolaget Fennia Patria* [1983] Q.B. 856, 874 (*per* Slade LJ).

course which is habitually followed because it is considered that the parties concerned have a legally binding right to demand it.

The point was strikingly illustrated by the decision of Staughton J in *Libyan Arab Foreign Bank* v. *Bankers Trust Co.*,[22] in which the above passage was cited. In that case the plaintiffs maintained a Eurodollar deposit account with the defendants in London. The US government imposed a freeze on transfers by American banks from and to accounts of Libyan nationals. The plaintiffs contended that the freeze had no effect outside the United States and demanded repayment in cash in London or by any other means not involving activity in the United States. The defendants did not argue that the freeze order had extraterritorial effect but contended that it was a usage of the Eurodollar deposit market that transfers from an account outside the United States denominated in US dollars could be made only through a US clearing system, i.e. through CHIPS or Fedwire, and that this necessarily involved acts in New York on which the order would bite.

It was held by Staughton J that, while there might be a habitual practice of transferring Eurodollars through CHIPS or Fedwire, the evidence did not establish that this was because such methods of transfer were considered the only ones a depositor was legally entitled to demand. Accordingly, the plaintiffs were entitled to payment in cash[23] or by some other means which did not involve going through CHIPS or Fedwire.

This principle finds an exact parallel in international customary law, which requires a conjunction of *usus* and *opinio juris sive necessitatis* to establish a principle or rule of customary law.[24] Thus Article 38(1) of the Statute of the International Court of Justice identifies as one of the sources of international law the Court is required to apply: "b. international custom, as evidence of a general practice accepted as law". To much the same effect is the elegantly worded rule in the *American Restatement (Revised), Foreign Relations Law of the United States,* §102:

(1) A rule of international law is one that has been accepted as such by the international community of states
    (a) in the form of customary law;
    ...
(2) Customary international law results from a general and consistent practice of states followed by them from a sense of legal obligation.

The problem with the requirement of observance of custom from a sense of *legally* binding obligation is that it is based either on circularity or on paradox, for it presupposes a belief in an existing legal duty which if correct would make the belief

[22] [1989] Q.B. 728.

[23] A fairly dramatic finding, given that the amount of the demand was US$292 million! In the end, the US regulatory authorities agreed to authorise the transfer, thus obviating the need for an appeal against the decision.

[24] See generally Michael Akehurst. "Custom as a Source of International Law" (1974–75) XLVII B.Y.I.L. 1; G. M. Danilenko, *Law-Making in the International Community,* chaps.IV and V; G. J. H. van Hoof, *Rethinking the Sources of International Law,* chap.VI; Karol Wolfke, *Custom in Present International Law* (2nd revised edn).

itself superfluous and if erroneous would convert non-law into law through error. It is interesting to note that §1-205 of the American Uniform Commercial Code and Article 9(2) of the Vienna Sales Convention have jettisoned the *opinio juris* element. Under §1-205(2): "A usage of trade is any practice or method of dealing having such regularity of observance in a place, vocation or trade as to justify an expectation that it will be observed with respect to the transaction in question." Article 9(2) of the Vienna Sales Convention (which as previously mentioned attributes the binding force of usage to implied agreement)[25] takes the same position, though in rather more prolix terms:

> The parties are considered, unless otherwise agreed, to have impliedly made applicable to their contract or its formation a usage of which the parties knew or ought to have known and which in international trade is widely known to, and regularly observed by, parties to contracts of the type involved in the particular trade concerned.

Yet these two formulations are not without their problems either, for they fail to distinguish usage observed as binding from usage followed purely as a matter of habit, courtesy or convenience or simply a desire to accommodate one's business counterparty voluntarily where this is not detrimental to one's own interests. Clearly there must be some perception of obligation, even if it is not obligation in the full legal sense of that which has been ordained by law. Perhaps the most satisfactory way of capturing the element of obligation without reference to law is to say that the usage relied on must be one which is considered by the relevant mercantile community to bear on the making, proof, interpretation, performance or enforcement of the parties' commercial engagements towards each other.[26]

A vexed question, which has long been debated in discussions on the nature of customary law and, indeed, of the common law itself,[27] is whether the combination of *usus* and *opinio juris* suffices or whether it is also necessary that the customary rule contended for has received judicial, arbitral, or legislative recognition. What exactly is the status of an uncodified usage before it has been the subject of an adjudication in a dispute? There are at least two divergent views on this question. The first is that before the usage has been formally recognised it does not exist, for its normative force is dependent on satisfying certain criteria—consistency of practice, reasonableness, notoriety, and conformity with international public policy and any applicable national mandatory law—which are imposed externally by the law and

[25] See above, p.269.

[26] An alternative approach is to think in terms of the sanctions that the relevant sector of the mercantile community would consider an aggrieved party entitled to exact if the usage were not observed. But this would be appropriate only for usages governing performance, not those relevant to the interpretation of contract terms.

[27] Jeremy Bentham considered the common law to be "a fiction from beginning to end" (*Collected Works,* Vol.IV, p.483). Ewart (he of estoppel fame) took the same view of the law merchant, conceived as a body of law, in his splendidly iconoclastic article "What is the Law Merchant?" 3 Col.L.Rev. 135 (1903). See also A. W. B. Simpson, "The Common Law and Legal Theory", in *Oxford Essays in Jurisprudence* (2nd series, ed. A. W. B. Simpson), who favours the approach taken by Blackstone that the common law is a system of customary law. The question is less meaningful in public international law, where there is neither compulsory recourse to adjudication nor the expectation of adjudication.

which can be shown to be satisfied only by a decision of a court. This Austinian view of custom fails to address the paradox that if the function of the court or the arbitrator is to *declare* the law, including any rule of customary law, the rule contended for must exist already. The decision is the authority for the existence of the rule but is not the rule itself. Moreover, if the custom has no normative force until declared, how can it affect the rights of the parties under a contract necessarily made before the decision? The alternative position, advocated by Hart, Salmond, and others,[28] is that a ruling by the court in favour of a custom as meeting certain legally defined criteria is purely declaratory and is not the source of the custom's legal force any more than it is the source of, say, subordinate legislation that is challenged but upheld by the court as *intra vires.* This position, which is paralleled in the field of transnational commercial law by advocates of the new *lex mercatoria,* seems the preferable solution. It also surmounts another problem, namely, that a finding of usage in an arbitration binds only the parties to it and cannot be constitutive of the usage as regards third parties. Only a consistent upholding of the usage in a series of awards could have this effect. To a lesser degree this is true of decisions of national judges at first instance, for these too are not binding on anyone except the parties. And if this is the case as regards local usage, how much more so of international usage, which cannot be ruled on authoritatively by any national court so as to bind the courts of other jurisdictions. The problem, then, is to determine by whom or by what standards the external criteria against which the validity of an international trade usage must be tested are to be set.[29]

## C. Scope

Trade usage, like custom in public international law, may vary widely both in its sphere of influence and in its degree of specificity. Its sphere of influence may be delineated in a number of ways, for example:

(1) *geographically,* by reference to a particular town, port or region;
(2) *politically,* by reference to a particular political grouping or affinity;
(3) *economically,* by reference to a particular economic grouping or affinity;
(4) *legally,* by reference to a particular legal tradition;
(5) *commercially,* by reference to a particular trade or market.[30]

Each of these groupings is to some extent independent of the others, so that, for example, an international trade usage may be confined to a particular type of business activity (e.g. bank documentary payment undertakings) but may be near-universal

[28] For a sophisticated theory based on a distinction between a practical judgment as to what would be a desirable pattern of conduct to be adopted as an authoritative rule and a practical judgment that such a pattern has been adopted warranting treatment as an authoritative rule, see John Finnis, *Natural Law and Natural Rights,* pp.238 *et seq.*

[29] See *infra* p.276.

[30] Either geographical (as in the case of a commodities market) or organisational (as in the case of the financial markets).

in geographical scope, whilst on the other hand there may be usages which apply to business activities generally but only within a defined geographical area or a particular legal family.

In content the usage may express a very broad principle of required behaviour or a very specific one. Usages that express very broad norms of behaviour may, if extended beyond a given type of international contractual activity, become elevated into general principles of law or become embodied in international convention and lose their distinctive status as usages of trade. An example is the principle *pacta sunt servanda,* a principle common to domestic and international trade law and public international law, which can be said to have developed from customary law to become a general principle of law or, in the case of international law, a rule codified in Article 26 of the Vienna Convention on the Law of Treaties.[31]

Just as the sphere of application of each trade usage grouping has no necessary relationship with that of the others, so also the level of generality or specificity of a usage is not necessarily related to the generality or specificity of its sphere of application. For example, the principle that a party cannot take advantage of his own fault to escape from a contract on the ground of his own or the other party's inability to perform is a very broad principle which is not specific to a particular trade, location, or legal system. It is interesting to find that virtually every rule identified from arbitral awards as a rule of the *lex mercatoria* in the brilliant essay by Lord Justice Mustill (now Lord Mustill) on the new *lex mercatoria*[32] is of this broad character. Yet there are many widely adopted trade usages that are highly specific: for example, in the sphere of international banking, that a reasonable time for examination of documents presented under a letter of credit is no more than a few days,[33] or that banks are concerned only with the apparent good order of documents, not with their genuineness or authenticity.[34] The degree of specificity of an unwritten international trade usage may be relevant to the ease or difficulty with which its recognition before an arbitral tribunal can be secured, for the more general the asserted usage the greater its affinity with a general principle of law and the lower the burden of showing that it is generally known.

## III. How Uncodified Usage is Established

### A. The Nature of the Problem

The difficulty with uncodified usage, as with any other customary law, is to establish its existence. Individual members of the commercial community may have, or believe that they have, a broad perception of what a given usage is or means, but

[31] See further *infra* p.278.

[32] "The New *Lex Mercatoria* : The First Twenty-five Years", in Martin Bos and Ian Brownlie (Eds), *Liber Amicorum for Lord Wilberforce,* chap.11, at pp.174–7.

[33] *Bankers Trust Co.* v. *State Bank of India* [1991] 2 Lloyd's Rep. 443. See now UCP, Arts.13(b), 14(d)(i), allowing a maximum of seven days.

[34] UCP, Art.15.

typically the postulated usage will lack definition, its boundaries and qualifications will be hazy, and even its central core may prove to be a matter of debate.

That this is so can readily be demonstrated by everyday experience and by the process of litigation, and it applies with equal force to asserted but previously unexplored rules of the common law. A young lawyer practising in England and not familiar with the workings of English bank settlement systems attends a gathering of experienced bankers who are discussing problems of daylight exposure arising from a multilateral settlement system which nets out obligations only at the end of the day. The young lawyer is curious to know whether a payment order given by a customer to his bank can be countermanded after it has gone into the bank clearing but before the conclusion of the daily settlement. He would like to ask about this but is reluctant to expose his ignorance on what must obviously be such an elementary matter. Eventually he plucks up courage and poses the question. He may then quite possibly find to his surprise that half the assembly replies yes and the other half no. He would almost certainly have had a similar experience if, before the decision in the *Banque de l'Indochine* case,[35] he had enquired as to the meaning and effect of a payment "under reserve" to the beneficiary of a documentary credit. One group of bankers would have said that the paying bank could recover the payment from the beneficiary if the account party could demonstrate that the documents were not in conformity with the credit, whilst the other half would have answered (correctly, as it would turn out) that the bank could recover if the account party declined to take the documents, even if the reason for his refusal to take them was not legitimate.

In fact, every case in which there is a dispute between expert witnesses as to the fact and content of an unwritten trade usage makes the point that, not being reduced to writing, the usage is exposed to challenge as to its meaning or even its very existence. Precisely the same situation obtains where there is a dispute as to whether a right or remedy is given by the common law on a point not previously the subject of a judicial decision or scholarly writing. It is worth emphasising this point because there are arbitrators who seem willing to infer international trade usage on the flimsiest of evidence or even on no evidence at all beyond their own personal experience.

## B. Usage as It Exists and Usage as the Merchants Would Like It to Be

Before considering the various conditions in which an international trade usage may be received by a court or arbitral tribunal I should like to focus on a point which hitherto appears to have escaped attention, namely, whether so much emphasis should be placed on usage as it stands, and whether there is not a case for admitting evidence that the usage is no longer acceptable to the mercantile community and is observed solely because it has been given contractual force. In international law it is recognised that there may be a fine line between *lex lata* and *lex*

35 *Banque de l'Indochine et de Suez SA* v. *J. H. Rayner (Mincing Lane) Ltd* [1983] Q.B. 711.

*ferenda.*[36] Indeed, *lex ferenda* may quickly become *lex lata,* as in the case of scholarly compilations such as the Unidroit Principles of International Commercial Contracts where what are offered are in effect best solutions adapted from existing principles, solutions which within a year or two of publication of the Principles have already been applied in a number of arbitrations and at least one court decision.[37] What should a tribunal do when a rule of codified usage becomes seen as obstructive or unhelpful and in need of replacement and is observed solely because it is seen as having contractual force? The problem is less acute in the case of uncodified usage, for all the business community has to do is to abandon the usage and replace it with a new one.[38] But where a usage becomes embodied in a codification incorporated into contracts it acquires contractual force and, unless negated or modified by express contractual provision, can be changed only by altering the code. It might be said that the duty of the tribunal is to ignore dissatisfaction with the existing rule and to apply it. But in the typical case where a tribunal applies a codified rule as evidence of existing usage it is usually prompted to do so because the rule is seen to reflect what is desirable, not simply what is done.

By way of illustration, when the Uniform Customs and Practice for Documentary Credits was first published by the International Chamber of Commerce in 1933 it contained a rule that credits were to be deemed revocable unless otherwise indicated. Given the fact that a beneficiary under a revocable credit was almost wholly unprotected, it was not surprising that the vast majority of credits were issued as irrevocable credits. In other words, the rule, if it had ever reflected the needs and practices of the merchant community, long ago ceased to do so. Nevertheless the rule remained in force for 60 years; not until the 1993 revision was it changed to make credits irrevocable unless otherwise indicated.[39] Now suppose that in 1990 a documentary credit had been issued which was in traditional form and appearance in all respects except that it did not state whether it was revocable or irrevocable and omitted any reference to the UCP, and that an arbitral tribunal was called upon to decide whether, in mercantile usage, the credit was to be considered revocable or irrevocable. What position should it take? On the one hand there was a clear rule of the UCP that a credit was to be presumed revocable unless otherwise indicated; on the other a long-settled practice of calling for irrevocable, rather than revocable, credits. Should not the tribunal rely on the practice (if duly proved or capable of judicial notice) rather than treating the rule as evidence of usage or of a general principle of documentary credits law? To generalise the question, if parties to a set of contractually incorporated rules consistently exclude one of them, should that rule continue to be presumptive of the intention of business generally so as to bind

[36] See Danilenko, *op. cit. supra* n.24, at pp.16–22.

[37] M. J. Bonell, "The UNIDROIT Principles of International Commercial Contracts and the Principles of European Contract Law: Similar Rules for the Same Purposes?" (1996) II Uniform L.Rev. 229.

[38] The transition may, of course, raise intricate questions as to whether at a certain point there are two competing usages in operation or alternatively none at all.

[39] UCP, Art.6(c).

parties who have not adopted the rules and thus have no contractual commitment to apply the presumptive rule if they have not excluded it?

Unfortunately a negative answer to this question confronts an immediate difficulty, namely, that most parties do in fact adopt the UCP and therefore the presumptive rule. There is no argument about what the former rule was, merely about what it ought to be. It is not, therefore, a case where the parties decided to create a new usage by acting outside the former UCP; on the contrary, what they did was to apply the freedom given by the UCP itself to displace the presumptive rule by declaring the credit irrevocable. Thus, however much the commercial world might have thought the rule out of touch with commercial needs, there can be no doubt that they accepted its binding force. So while the *usus* of issuing irrevocable credits could readily have been established, there would have been no basis for inferring an *opinio juris* that the issue of a credit imposed an irrevocable commitment on the part of the issuer.

## C. The Reception of Usage by a Court or Tribunal

There are three principal conditions in which a court or an arbitral tribunal can be led to accept the existence of a trade usage. The first is where the usage is so well known that the tribunal can take judicial notice of it; the second, where written or oral testimony is given by expert witnesses; and the third, where the usage can be inferred from international conventions, uniform rules prepared by international organisations, standard contracts, scholarly writings, and the like. The first two of these require no particular comment here, except to note that international arbitrators appear much readier than courts to make confident statements about international trade usage and to take judicial notice of them. But the inference of usage from conventions and other international instruments and writings raises questions of acute difficulty both as to what can legitimately be inferred and as to the impact of such an instrument or writing on existing usage. Indeed, in many respects the role of international trade usage *vis-à-vis* other elements of transnational commercial law remains obscure, despite the considerable volume of literature devoted to the subject.

## D. Determining the Relevant Sphere of Influence

A usage may be international without being universal; indeed, there can be very few usages that are universal and finding them poses almost insurmountable difficulties. However, the application of an international usage presupposes that both parties are operating within its sphere of influence. This is relatively easy for transactions conducted on an organised market or exchange with an identified seat or location, for usually both parties will be bound. But in other cases the problem is more difficult. Trade usages are most highly developed in those parts of the world that have well-developed legal systems which attach importance to party autonomy. Suppose that one party to an international supply contract has its place of business in one such part of the world while the other party is based in a country in which law is relatively undeveloped or is subordinate to political and economic goals, so that the role of contract is diminished. An attempt by the former party (who will typically be the supplier) to invoke international usage is likely to be met by the other party's challenge: why should we be bound by a usage which our countries and others of like philosophy or stage of development had no part in shaping and which runs quite counter to that philosophy? If there is nothing else to indicate into which of the two possible spheres of influence the transaction falls, that of the supplier or that of the customer, there seems no alternative but to resort to the applicable law as determined by the conflict of laws rules of the forum.

## IV. The Interrelation of International Trade Usage and Other Elements of Transnational Commercial Law

### A. International Trade Usage and General Principles of Law

In my view it is an inherent feature of an international trade usage, and that which distinguishes it from a general principle of law, that it is particular to a given form of international trade, or to finance or other contractual activity linked to international trade. It may be a usage related, for example, to the international sale or carriage of goods, international construction contracts, or the provision of security for payment or performance through letters of credit and demand guarantees. But once a usage has acquired such general acceptance as to become independent of any particular form of international trading activity it ceases to be a usage and becomes elevated into a general principle of law. Examples are the principles *pacta sunt servanda* and *rebus sic stantibus.* It is not a great oversimplification to say that general principles of law, to the extent that they are not overriding rules of international public policy, are generalised (though not necessarily universal) expressions of former international trade usages or conventions. General principles of law recognised by civilised nations are also identified as a source of public international law in Article 38(1)(c) of the Statute of the International Court of Justice (and some writers contend that they can also be derived from international law itself), but in practice they are invoked relatively infrequently.

The various maritime codifications of the Middle Ages show, as one might expect, that merchants and mariners were not concerned with broad principles or sweeps of policy; what they wanted was a more or less consistent application of current usage by tribunals of their peers. A good example is provided by the fifteenth-century Catalonian compilation known as *The Consulate of the Sea,*[40] one of the most detailed and influential compilations of its time. This consists of no fewer than 334 articles covering almost every known eventuality, from the responsibility of a patron of a vessel to his partners and his merchants to the punishment of a sailor improperly

[40] Trans, by Stanley S. Jados (1975).

undressing for the night,[41] and from waterlogged cargo carried in an open boat to the liability of shareholders in a boat construction venture.

Yet it is also true that the detailed rules contained in *The Consulate of the Sea* have certain recurrent themes from which one may legitimately extract a surprising number of underlying principles. These include the duty of disclosure,[42] the binding force of agreements,[43] including informal and unwitnessed agreements concluded by a handshake,[44] the immunity from liability to pay for unrequested benefits,[45] the duty of care owed by the patron to merchants and passengers,[46] *force majeure* as an excuse for non-performance,[47] but no excuse where the inability to perform is self-induced,[48] immunity of a bailee of goods lost without fault,[49] the duty to account for profits or proceeds made from the joint-venture vessel,[50] and the buyer's right to damages for breach of warranty by the seller, measured by the difference between the value of the goods as warranted and their value as delivered.[51] The common thread that links all these rules is the duty to act reasonably and in good faith; and where life or limb is at stake a high degree of importance was attached to the exercise of proper care and skill.[52]

General principles of law, other than rules of international public policy, are so broad as to be of little practical utility except to give comfort to an arbitrator or respectability to his award. The principle *pacta sunt servanda* is everywhere accepted. What we need to know is the circumstances in which performance is excused. *Rebus sic stantibus* is all very well as a general principle but is too vague to be of great practical assistance and in the field of public international law appears never to have been successfully invoked, despite its embodiment in Article 62 of the Vienna Convention on the Law of Treaties. Increasingly issues of this kind are dealt with expressly in international conventions[53] and international restatements of contract.[54] General principles of law are still capable of being derived from conventions as well as from usage, but the scope for this source is shrinking with the increasing adoption of the rule of interpretation laid down in the Vienna Sales Convention requiring resort to general principles of the Convention itself and, where there is none, reference to the applicable law under conflict of laws rules. By contrast, there are principles of

[41] Which was, for each transgression, to be tied and dunked in the ocean three times while held by a rope (Art.170).

[42] Art.47, dealing with the duty of a patron to give certain information publicly to prospective investors.

[43] Arts.48, 89, 90, 102, 194.

[44] Arts.48, 89.

[45] Arts.50. 51 (no liability of shareholders to pay an additional sum to the patron for constructing a vessel larger than agreed).

[46] Arts.61, 69.

[47] Arts.66, 262, 282.

[48] Art.85 (inability of merchant to ship cargo by reason of sale to a third party).

[49] Arts.206, 255.

[50] Arts.241, 256, 287.

[51] Art.293.

[52] Some of the rules of the sea were of long standing. The 12th-century Sea-Laws of Oleron, for example, decreed that if a pilot failed to exercise due skill in bringing a vessel to port and was not able to make satisfaction he should lose his head. Three hundred years later the option of giving satisfaction had apparently disappeared; instant decapitation was the price of failure.

[53] E.g. the Vienna Sales Convention, Art.79.

[54] E.g. the Unidroit Principles of International Commercial Contracts and the Commission on European Contract Law Principles of European Contract Law.

international public policy or morality of such overriding importance that they will displace any contrary usage. For example, it is almost universally held that a contract procured by bribery is void or unenforceable, and it is not to the point that in the locality with which the transaction is connected bribery is an everyday occurrence of which all parties were likely to be aware.

## B. Trade Usage and International Conventions

The relationship of conventions to usages is as complex in transnational commercial law as it is in international law.[55] A convention may be evidence of a usage, so as to allow its admission where the convention would not as such be applicable; it may operate concurrently with the usage; it may displace the usage; and it may create or evidence new usage through consistent adoption in cross-border commercial transactions or by non-contracting States. Further, if a convention is evidence of usage it may equally be the case that its non-adoption negates its significance as evidence of usage.

### *1. International trade conventions as evidence of existing trade usage*

An international trade convention may legitimately be relied on in given conditions as evidence of pre-existing usage, in the same way as an international treaty may be relied on as evidence of international customary law.[56] It is a characteristic of conventions that they can never exhaustively determine the scope of their own application, which may be extended by contract, usage, or acquiescence.

The crucial question is whether the convention does in fact reflect pre-existing usage or whether, on the contrary, it changes the usage. It has been pointed out by a number of writers that it is impossible for *jus scriptum* accurately to capture any unwritten law, if only because the scope of the latter is inherently uncertain and changeable and may also, when reduced to writing, be found in some respects to be incomplete or unsatisfactory. The notion that "codifiers" sit down faithfully to reproduce rules of customary law is pure mythology, particularly at the international level, where there are likely to be significant differences between the rules of one legal system and those of another. When legal experts gather together to frame a convention or a set of uniform rules they will normally have the advantage of a report by the secretariat of the sponsoring international organisation setting out in broad terms the existing law and practice in selected jurisdictions. Each of the participating experts will bring to bear a knowledge of his or her own legal system and, understandably enough, can be expected to test each proposed rule against the rules of that system to see whether it overlooks a problem or, on the contrary, represents an improvement. But the drafters of the convention or uniform rules would make no progress at all if they conceived their task as being to assemble before them all the

[55] As to which see the citations *supra* n.24 and the North Sea Continental Shelf Cases, 1969 ICJ Reports 3.

[56] See above.

known rules and practices and strive to create an amalgam of them all. Even if such a task were feasible its product would negate any notion of mere reproduction of existing law, for necessarily the amalgam could be created only by changing in some degree the existing rules of its various constituents. In any event, that is simply not how the process of harmonisation works. What those involved in the project seek to achieve is best solutions to typical problems, being solutions which are not so far removed from existing practice as to make them unacceptable. Accordingly, change is inherent in any redaction of rules, whether written or unwritten. The resulting text will thus be a combination of rules that existed before, modifications of existing rules and entirely new rules.

How, then, is a court or arbitral tribunal to determine whether a convention or codification reproduces existing usage or changes it? If the usage has already been embodied in an earlier convention or codification the task is relatively easy, for all the tribunal has to do is to compare the two texts. But where the convention or codification is relied on as evidence of existing unwritten usage this resource is not available. If the alleged usage is disputed then unless it is of the near-universal kind of which judicial notice can be taken a national court is likely to require it to be established by evidence. Such evidence could take a variety of forms, of which the most compelling would be the *travaux préparatoires* and the rapporteur's report.[57] What is interesting is the readiness of some arbitral tribunals to assume, without any evidence whatsoever, that the best reflection of existing usage is the provisions of an international convention or codification.

A striking example of this is the award in an ICC arbitration, case no. 5713 of 1989.[58] The seller of goods under a contract of sale made in 1979 brought arbitration proceedings to recover the balance of the price. The buyer claimed the right to set off loss suffered from the fact that the goods did not conform to the contract of sale. An issue arose as to whether the buyer had given notice of the lack of conformity in due time. The tribunal applied generally accepted conflict of laws rules to decide that the law governing the contract was that of the seller's country. However, the applicable law as thus determined was considered by the tribunal to impose time requirements for the giving of notice of defects that were so short and specific as to run counter to generally accepted trade usages. The tribunal therefore declined to apply the law applicable under conflict of laws rules, and instead applied Articles 38 and 39 of the Vienna Sales Convention.

> The tribunal finds that there is no better source to determine the prevailing trade usages than the terms of the United Nations Convention on the International Sale of Goods of 11 April 1980, usually called "the Vienna Convention". This is so even though neither [the country of the buyer] nor [the country of the seller] are parties to that Convention. If they were, the

[57] It should be borne in mind that we are not here talking of *interpretation* of a convention or codification, for which reference to *travaux préparatoires* would normally be inadmissible unless the text to be interpreted was ambiguous or would lead to a manifestly absurd or unreasonable result (see e.g. the Vienna Convention on Treaties. Art.32), but its relationship to pre-existing usage, which cannot be determined solely from the text of the convention or codification itself except in those cases where it is expressed to be declaratory of existing usage.

[58] (1990) 15 YB Comm Arb 70; Jarvin *et al. Collection of ICC Arbitral Awards,* Vol.II, p.223.

Convention might be applicable to this case as a matter of law and not only as reflecting the trade usages.

The Vienna Convention, which has been given effect to in 17 countries, may be fairly taken to reflect the generally recognized usages regarding the matter of the nonconformity of goods in international sales.

The tribunal went on to hold that the buyer had given notice of non-conformity within the time laid down by Articles 38 and 39, that in any event the seller was debarred by Article 40 from invoking the time limits laid down in those Articles because he had known of the non-conformity and did not disclose it, and that accordingly the buyer was entitled to compensation which could be set off against the seller's claim. It can reasonably be inferred from the rather truncated report of the award that under the applicable law the buyer would have been held to have given notice of non-conformity out of time.

What is surprising about the award is not that it extended the scope of the Convention beyond its own stated boundaries—for this can happen in a variety of ways, including treatment of the Convention as the embodiment of existing usage—but that it completely disregarded the applicable law[59] and, in doing so, assumed without discussion that the Vienna Sales Convention did in fact embody relevant trade usage. On the latter point there are at least four matters which should have given the tribunal pause for thought.

(1) When the contract was concluded (which is accepted as the point where rights and duties are established) the Vienna Convention not merely lacked the necessary number of ratifications to bring it into force, it had not even been made! All the more curious, then, that the tribunal indicated that the Convention could have applied directly if both parties had carried on business in contracting States.

(2) There *was* a convention in force at the time of the contract, namely, Vienna's predecessor, the 1964 Uniform Law on International Sales. Why, then, did the tribunal not apply (or even refer to) ULIS? One can only speculate. Perhaps the tribunal considered that the ULIS rules on the time for examination were too rigid[60] and would have left the buyer remediless. Another answer might be that by 1979, 15 years after it was made, ULIS had attracted only eight ratifications and one accession, compared with the 17 ratifications, etc., referred to in the award, and that a total of nine adopting States was not considered strong enough evidence of prevailing international trade usage. But if this is true of ULIS, then how much more so of a convention that was still only in draft at the time of the contract and might conceivably have proved as unsuccessful as ULIS.

[59] A point developed *infra*, pp.287–8.

[60] See John Honnold, *Uniform Law for International Sales* (2nd edn), paras.250–2. Professor Honnold comments (in para.250): "In the UNCITRAL proceedings it was possible to make the rules on examination of goods more flexible and consistent with current commercial practice."

(3) At the 1980 Diplomatic Conference there was protracted debate on what became Article 39 and was then Article 37, and two delegates on separate occasions made the point that the article in question was one of the most controversial in the entire Convention[61]—hardly the strongest basis for treating the article as evidence of an internationally established usage! It is true that the UNCITRAL Commission text which came forward for consideration by the Diplomatic Conference and embodied what is now Article 39 could be given some weight as representing the views of the working group and the full UNCITRAL Commission, but why should it be accorded greater weight than the stricter provisions of a convention which had then already been in force for 14 years?

(4) International trade conventions are made by States, not by businessmen and accordingly are not formulated by the members of the community whose usages they are supposed to embody. Not uncommonly conventions fail to gain acceptance precisely because they do not reflect the practices or perceptions of the dominant commercial community. A good example is provided by the Hamburg Rules, which though technically operative have proved very much of a damp squib. Nowadays more determined efforts are made to consult business interests on a proposed international trade convention—indeed, their representative organisations may be involved in the preparatory work as observers—but the policy decisions and the drafting are undertaken almost entirely by lawyers, and it is primarily lawyers who will lead the representation of their governments at a diplomatic conference to conclude a convention.

Unfortunately there is no indication from the report of the award (which, as is customary, has been filleted to preserve the anonymity of the parties) as to whether any of the above arguments were placed before the tribunal or, indeed, whether there was any opportunity given, or any attempt made, to challenge the assumption that Article 39 of the Vienna Sales Convention reflected current usage at the time of the contract or, indeed, at the time of the making of the Convention. There is a further problem to be considered. A purely dispositive provision of an international trade convention, even if accurately reflecting existing usage, may be displaced by subsequent usage.[62] How can a tribunal be sure that the convention still reflects trade usage? No doubt there is a presumption in favour of continuing validity of a convention as evidence of usage but it should certainly be capable of being rebutted by evidence.

The drawing of inferences of uncodified usage from an international trade convention raises a number of other conundrums. How far is the tribunal entitled to rely on hindsight? In the arbitral award referred to above the tribunal, deciding a case ten years after the contract, relied on the fact that the Vienna Sales Convention had been

[61] Mr Khoo (Singapore) at the 16th meeting; Mr Inaamullah (Pakistan) at the 21st meeting. See John Honnold, *Documentary History for the Uniform Law on International Sales*, p.542, para.51, p.566, para.6.

[62] Whether in public international law a treaty may be displaced by subsequent State practice is highly controversial. See the citations *supra* n.24.

carried into effect in 17 countries. Suppose that the hearing had taken place not in 1989 but in 1981, when there had been no ratifications at all. Would that have made a difference? Certainly there would be no clear indication at that stage of the level of support the Convention would command. The absence of ratifications would have had no significance either, because it would have been too soon to draw any inferences. Suppose that, at the time when the case was in fact heard, there had still been no ratifications. That would be a clear indication that the Convention had attracted no support from Governments and was unlikely to do so. Should the tribunal take this fact into account in giving an award in 1989, when if it had made the adjudication in 1981 no real significance could have been attached to the lack of ratifications? If the adoption of a convention is to be relied on as evidence of usage, or its non-adoption as evidence to negate usage, do we not need to know why it gained acceptance or, on the contrary, did not? It is conceivable that the particular provision invoked in the dispute was highly controversial and considered out of touch with commercial reality[63] but that the benefits of the convention as a whole were considered to outweigh the drawbacks of this one provision. Conversely, States may have been unanimously in favour of the provision as reflecting current usage but opposed to the convention on other grounds.[64] Further, the fact that a convention may not have come into force does not necessarily deprive it of significance, for it may be sufficiently persuasive within the commercial community to generate new usages. Similarly, in the field of international law the ability of treaties to generate customary law prior to their coming into force is widely recognised, as in the case of recognition of the 200-mile exclusive economic zones in the course of negotiation and after adoption of the final text of the 1982 UN Convention on the Law of the Sea.

Reliance on conventions as evidence of international trade usage is at once a virtue and a danger. As previously indicated, the effect may be to extend the scope of the convention well beyond its stated sphere of application. Reference has already been made to an arbitral award which applied Article 39 of the Vienna Sales Convention to a case where the Convention was not in existence at the time of the contract, and even at the time of the award many years later the Convention would not have been applicable on its own terms, since neither of the parties carried on business in a country that had become party to the Convention. Extensions of this kind may not trouble arbitrators; they are of much graver concern to national judges, for their effect may be to impose on a national court the duty to apply the provisions of a convention which its own State has declined to ratify. The same objection applies to the theory advanced by some scholars that parties may subject their contract to the terms of a convention not as a method of incorporation of contractual terms but as the choice of an applicable law under conflict of laws rules. There is no objection to the former, for the incorporated terms of the convention become subject to the mandatory rules of the applicable law in just the same way as any other contract terms, but strong objection to the latter, which if valid would give private parties the

[63] As was the case on the provisions of ULIS for automatic termination of the contract on a fundamental breach.

[64] See Mark E. Villiger, *Customary International Law and Treaties*, p.164.

right to invoke the convention against the wishes of a non-ratifying State in which the dispute was tried. Again, however, it has been argued that while this is a valid argument as regards national judges it should have no application to arbitrators, who typically will not occupy any position of authority in, or indeed have any connection with, the State where they sit.[65]

Of course, it has to be recognised that courts and arbitral tribunals and the parties appearing before them are unlikely to have detailed knowledge of more than a very small number of legal systems and that they cannot be expected either to engage in a major comparative study or to expend huge effort in tracking the antecedents of conventions presented to them. In meeting the exigencies of dispute resolution they cannot be said to be acting unreasonably in assuming, in the absence of evidence or argument to the contrary, that a particular convention reflects pre-existing usage. But that is a matter of evidence and of onus of proof. The difficulty in using prior arbitral awards as precedents is that we know so little about the facts and arguments. Often the reports do not show even the date of the contract in dispute, though that may be highly relevant. The countries involved and the commercial background to the dispute will usually be omitted for reasons of confidentiality, and it can be difficult even to deduce the arguments advanced or to know to what extent the arbitral tribunal was relying on its own knowledge rather than on evidence.

### 2. *Effect of international trade convention on existing usage*

It may be equally difficult to determine the effect of an international trade convention on existing usage. To the extent that the convention indicates a change of direction it may establish a new usage, or induce courts and arbitrators to adopt a new rule, in place of the existing usage. It is also possible, however, for the existing usage to continue in force and to run in parallel with the convention as regards transactions to which the convention does not apply, or even to supplement the convention on matters on which the latter is silent.

### 3. *The expansion of the scope of international trade conventions through international trade usage*

Just as a convention may change unwritten international trade usage, so also usage may qualify or override the dispositive provisions of a convention. Moreover, in so far as the convention is evidence of usage its provisions may become applicable *qua* usage even where the connection to a contracting State prescribed by the convention is missing, e.g. where, in an international sale of goods, one of the parties does not have its place of business in a contracting State. Again, this finds a counterpart in international law, where a State may be taken to have adhered by practice to a convention to which it is not a party.[66]

[65] See the note by Yves Derains (1995) Clunet 1020, criticising the award in ICC case no.6754 of 1993.
[66] See Christine Chinkin, *Third Parties in International Law*, chap.3.

## C. Trade Usage and Formulations by International Organisations

Similar considerations apply where reliance is placed on a codification promulgated by an international organisation. Such codifications take a variety of forms: uniform rules or trade terms incorporated by contract, legal guides, formulations of legal principles by scholars, and the like.

Prominent among organisations publishing uniform rules and trade terms is the International Chamber of Commerce, which over the years has prepared and published numerous sets of uniform rules and trade terms which are carried into effect by incorporation into contracts. Examples are the Uniform Customs and Practice for Documentary Credits, the Uniform Rules for Demand Guarantees, the Uniform Rules for Contract Bonds—all of which lay down rules to be observed by participating banks and other parties to transactions of the types in question—and Incoterms, standard price and delivery terms for contracts of sale, each term carrying with it a defined set of duties for seller and buyer respectively. Such rules do not in themselves have normative force; indeed, even the contracts which incorporate them cannot be regarded in themselves as part of transnational commercial law, for though they are the source of entitlements they operate only as between the parties and do not constitute law in themselves but are dependent on law for their effect. It follows that if these contractually incorporated rules are to play any part in the scheme of transnational commercial law they do so as evidence of existing usage or as fashioners of new usage.

Of a different kind altogether are the Unidroit Principles of International Commercial Contracts and the Principles of European Contract Law prepared by the Commission on European Contract Law. These are formulations of general principles and rules of contract law prepared by two different (though overlapping) groups of scholars. They have no binding force as such, though it would be open to contracting parties to incorporate them by reference into their contracts. More significant is their availability as a tool for courts and arbitrators seeking to identify current norms of contract established by mercantile usage or general principles of law, to ascertain what in modern legal thinking are conceived as best solutions to typical contract problems and to fill gaps in existing conventions. Such formulations are likely to be particularly persuasive in relation to cross-border transactions where the tribunal, recognising that at least one of the parties is from another jurisdiction, may be more receptive to the application of principles or rules deviating in some degree from those of its own national law. Publications by outstanding scholars have long been influential in shaping legal principles, particularly (though not exclusively) in the field of public international law. In this field their status is now enshrined in Article 38(1)(d) of the Statute of the International Court of Justice, which includes among the materials the International Court of Justice is to apply "the teachings of the most highly qualified publicists of the various nations". The enormous interest attracted by the Unidroit Principles shows the impact of the fruits of top-level intellectual collaboration from distinguished scholars drawn from a number of different legal families and systems. More generally, the growing influence of non-formal "soft" law sources is to be seen in transnational commercial law as it is in public international law.

Both sets of principles defer to mandatory rules of the applicable law under conflict of laws rules, a realistic recognition of the fact that general principles of law and usages cannot wholly displace national law since they do not constitute complete systems of law. What is interesting is that both sets of principles also incorporate a few mandatory rules of their own, such as the requirement of good faith and the rules on unilateral price determination. It may be asked how principles which are themselves non-binding in character can sensibly include mandatory provisions. There are at least two reasons why this is not as strange as it may seem. First, the parties may choose to incorporate the principles into their contract, in which event they will be presumptively bound by the provisions declaring certain principles mandatory or non-excludable. Second, the stated mandatory principles provide strong evidence of a general acceptance of types of rule that are to be considered to have such a strong policy content that they should not be capable of exclusion by the parties, whatever the applicable law—i.e. they should be given the character of *jus cogens.*

## V. International Trade Usage and the Conflict of Laws

### A. The Antipathy Between the *Lex Mercatoria* and the Conflict of Laws

National conflict of laws rules developed as part and parcel of the overall process of nationalising law. To the extent that law was unified by the canon law, the *jus civile* and the mediaeval *lex mercatoria,* it was unnecessary to devise rules to determine which State's law applied. But with the gradual replacement of the merchant courts by the central courts and of international rules with national laws it became necessary for each legal system to develop its own rules for determining (among other things) what law was to govern disputes involving a foreign element.

In his essay on the *lex mercatoria*[67] Lord Justice Mustill pointed out that the purpose of the conflict of laws is antithetical to the premise of the *lex mercatoria,* in that the former seeks to identify the applicable national law whereas the latter is conceived as anational in character.

### B. The Application of Conflict of Laws Rules

National judges for the most part continue to regard themselves as bound to determine a dispute by reference to a national law determined by the conflict of laws rules of the forum. Arbitrators in international commercial arbitration also regularly resort to conflict rules to determine the applicable law.[68] Nevertheless,

[67] *Supra* n.32.

[68] An approach supported by the Resolution on Arbitration in Private International Law prepared by the XIVth Commission of the International Law Association and approved at its meeting in Amsterdam in 1957. However, a resolution adopted at the 1992 meeting of the Association in Cairo declared that the fact that an award was founded on transnational rules (general principles of law, principles common

the difference in approach between courts and arbitrators has perceptibly widened over the past two decades. There is a strong body of opinion which denies the existence of any arbitral *lex fori,* on the ground that the arbitrator is appointed by the parties, not by the State, and that the connection of an arbitrator with the seat of the arbitration is usually temporary and tenuous, so that there is no reason why the arbitrator should necessarily feel obliged to apply the conflict rules of the State in which the arbitration has its seat. So a number of arbitrators would feel free to decide which legal system's conflict of laws rules should be applied. Others go further still; they would not regard themselves as bound to apply the conflict rules of any *system* of law but (in the absence of an express choice of law by the parties) simply apply general principles of the conflict of laws or alternatively the conflict *rule* (i.e. the connecting factor) that seems to them appropriate, e.g. that in a contract of sale the rights of the parties are governed by the law of the seller's place of business. Such a power is enshrined in the 1988 ICC Rules on Conciliation and Arbitration,[69] though it would seem not to be exercisable where the Rome Convention applies.[70]

## C. The Supplementation or Disregard of the Applicable Law

These diverse routes to the selection of the applicable law can, of course, lead to strikingly different results. But we have not exhausted the possibilities. If not otherwise constrained by the *lex loci arbitri* or contractually adopted arbitration rules, the arbitrator may bypass conflict of laws rules altogether and go directly to the law, or rules of law, which he considers appropriate.[71] There have also been a number of arbitrations in which the arbitral tribunal has applied international trade usage or the *lex mercatoria* either to supplement or to displace the applicable law as determined by the arbitral tribunal. It is generally accepted that the tribunal cannot override the parties' own choice of law. More delicate is the question whether, in the absence of party choice, the arbitrator can invoke the *lex mercatoria* either in addition to or in

to several laws, international law, trade usage, etc.) should not by itself affect its validity if the parties (1) had agreed that the arbitrators might apply transnational rules or (2) had remained silent concerning the applicable law.

[69] Art.13(3) of which provides that "in the absence of any indication by the parties as to the applicable law, the arbitrator shall apply the law designated as the proper law by the rules of conflict which he considers appropriate". Even in English law, which has tended to take a restrictive view of the powers of arbitrators, the courts have accepted that the references to "law" and "proper law" in Article 13(3) embrace rules of law or general principles of law and do not require the application of a particular national law. See n.74 *infra.*

[70] Since this is generally taken to require reference to a legal system. However, if it be the case that arbitrators are not bound to apply the conflicts rules of the seat of the arbitration or, indeed, the conflicts rules of any particular national legal system (which is the position taken here), then it would seem to follow that they are not obliged to apply the Rome Convention, even if sitting in a Convention State. They are, however, obliged to respect rules of international public policy. For a masterly analysis of this complex topic see Pierre Lalive, "Transnational (or Truly International) Public Policy and International Arbitration" in *Comparative Arbitration Practice and Public Policy in Arbitration* (ICCA Congress series no.3) pp.256 *et seq.*

[71] The legislation of several jurisdictions now expressly confers the power to do this. See *infra.*

substitution for what he has found to be the applicable law.[72] As regards supplementation of the applicable law, Article 10 of the Organization of American States Inter-American Convention on the Law Applicable to International Contracts (1994) is of particular interest.

In addition to the provisions in the foregoing articles, the guidelines, customs and principles of international commercial law as well as commercial usage and practices generally accepted shall apply in order to discharge the requirements of justice and equity in the particular case.

The application of the *lex mercatoria* in disregard of the applicable law is the threshold objection to the approach taken by the arbitrators in the ICC award to which reference was made earlier. It is not clear why the tribunal found it necessary to disregard the applicable law in arriving at the result they wanted to reach. In general, legislative provisions regulating non-consumer sales are dispositive only; they can be displaced by contrary agreement and they can also be displaced by relevant trade usage, whether that usage be local or international. So in most cases it is unnecessary to reject the dispositive application of the law applicable under conflict of laws rules, for that law will also provide for its dispositive provisions to yield to contract and usage. It is only where the law in question is mandatory that there need be an urge to bypass it at all.

## D. The *Lex Mercatoria* as the Applicable Law

Assuming that for some reason the applicable law under traditional conflict of laws rules does not allow its provisions to be displaced by contrary international usage, the question is whether, instead of expressing itself as disregarding that law, the tribunal could not reach the same result more subtly by applying what it considers to be an appropriate rule of conflict to treat the *lex mercatoria* itself as the applicable law. To the extent that the *lex mercatoria* represents general principles of law common to relevant States[73] there seems no reason why it cannot be applied as the proper law governing the substantive rights of the parties. This approach has been adopted in case law.[74] Whether that part of the *lex mercatoria* represented by international trade usage that has not been expressly or impliedly incorporated into the parties' contract can be invoked in this way is a separate question. Before addressing it we need to see why a number of arbitral tribunals might wish to avoid reference to a national law to determine the dispute.

[72] Whether the arbitrator can choose the *lex mercatoria* as being itself the applicable law is a separate question, discussed *infra*.

[73] The question which States are relevant is not discussed here.

[74] See e.g. the landmark decision of the English Court of Appeal in *Deutsche Schachtbau-und Tiebohrgesellschaft mbH* v. *R'As al-Khaimah National Oil Co.* [1987] 3 W.L.R. 1023, upholding an award in which the arbitrators, under an agreement to arbitrate held to be governed by and valid under Swiss law, applied "internationally accepted principles of law governing contractual relations" to determine a dispute arising under an oil exploration agreement.

## E. The Reasons for Applying Anational Law

As the essay by Lord Mustill has shown, most of the reported cases in which the arbitrators chose to apply the *lex mercatoria* could just as well have been decided under the applicable law as determined by a conflict of laws rule. Why, then, should the parties or the arbitral tribunal strive to avoid applying the relevant national law? At the contract stage this may be done because the parties are unable to agree on a national law to govern their contract. Where the concern is to avoid choosing the law of one or other of them this is sometimes dealt with by subjecting the contract to general principles common to the two legal systems. This was the approach adopted in the Channel Tunnel agreements and is a recipe for uncertainty, since there is a high risk that common principles either cannot be identified at all or are applied in very different ways or are too general to be of help in resolving the particular issue. A better solution is to choose the law of a neutral State. But parties do sometimes elect to avoid any reference to national law, perhaps with a view to giving the arbitral tribunal greater flexibility and responsiveness to international trade usage.

At the arbitration stage there are at least seven possible reasons why the tribunal might wish to avoid determining the applicable law or relying on the law which would ordinarily be applicable. First, there may be cases where the putative applicable law is so undeveloped that it is incapable of furnishing a solution to the issue under consideration. No developed secular legal system would admit to such a possibility[75] but the problem has been experienced in Islamic countries, where the law is primarily religious in character, and with this in mind parties to contracts have sometimes made express provision for recourse to general principles of law or international trade usages in cases where the applicable law does not furnish an answer. In such a case disregard of the applicable law is seen as the only practical solution. Second, the laws of the two parties are in conflict and the use of conflict rules would lead to the selection of the law of the winner; recourse to the *lex mercatoria* is thus seen as a neutral method of resolving the dispute without offending the sensitivities of the loser. Third, the laws of the two parties, or of the different States with which the contract is closely connected, are the same as to the issue in contention, in which case the arbitral tribunal may understandably feel that no useful purpose is served by undergoing an exercise to determine which law should be treated as the applicable law. The identity of rule in the two systems provides the tribunal with a justification for declaring it to be a rule of the *lex mercatoria.* Fourth, the rules of the competing systems are different and the choice between one national law and another under conflict rules is so finely balanced that the tribunal finds it difficult to prefer one to the other,[76] in which case reference to

[75] It is thus surprising that in *SPP* v. *Arab Republic of Egypt,* ICC case no.233 of 1992, the arbitral tribunal found that Egyptian law did not furnish an answer to the question from what date interest should run, so that this had to be resolved by reference to international law, a ruling described by Professor Gaillard as "si caricatural qu'il suffit à discréditer la méthode" (Emmanuel Gaillard, "Trente ans de Lex Mercatoria" (1995) Clunet 5, 13).

[76] Consider e.g. a dispute between multinationals over a pipeline running through six different countries.

the *lex mercatoria* provides a way out of the problem. Fifth, choice of a national legal system, whether by recourse to the conflict of laws or otherwise, is seen by the tribunal as inherently unsatisfactory because it involves the application to an international transaction of a national law fashioned primarily for domestic transactions. Sixth, the tribunal simply does not like the rule of the applicable national law, or the result it would produce, and is determined to find a method of avoiding it. This was the case in the above-mentioned ICC award. Finally, the tribunal is wedded to the concept of the *lex mercatoria* and wishes to avail itself of every opportunity to apply it and to expand its influence.

## F. Applying the *Lex Mercatoria* as "Rules of Law"

Most of the reasons given above for seeking to bypass the conflict of laws have at least some merit,[77] and they suggest that it is fruitless to insist that arbitrators are obliged to apply conflict of laws rules[78] or a particular national legal system, or that an international usage must be shown to have received recognition in any particular national law before it can be accorded normative force. This conclusion is reinforced by the widespread recognition that arbitral awards should be set aside only in exceptional circumstances. The parties have made their bed; they must lie on it. To the extent that the arbitral award falls beyond the purview of judicial review under the *lex loci arbitri* or of grounds for refusal of enforcement under the New York Convention it will be enforceable, and any objections to its application of the *lex mercatoria* as the applicable law are largely of theoretical interest. In such cases the arbitral tribunal is effectively free to draw on whatever materials it chooses in order to reach the result it wants to reach. This is not because the failure of the parties to designate an applicable law constitutes an implied choice of the *lex mercatoria*[79] but because, having omitted to choose the applicable law, the parties cannot complain if the arbitral tribunal looks to what it regards as the best solution to the problem. So far, national courts have shown themselves reluctant to refuse enforcement of an award solely on the ground that the tribunal applied the *lex mercatoria*.[80] If this is so where the *lex loci arbitri* is silent on the *matter, a fortiori* it will be the case where the *lex loci arbitri* authorises selection of the *lex mercatoria* as the applicable law. It is considered to do

[77] Only the last two are in my view illegitimate, the one because having found the applicable law the arbitrators have no right to disregard it merely because they think another rule is better, the other because the parties should not serve as cannon fodder for an arbitrator's personal crusade.

[78] For a powerful attack on conflicts scholarship and its dedication to the concept of an applicable national law in every case see Frederick K. Juenger, "American Conflicts Scholarship and the Law Merchant" 28 Vand.J.Trans.L. 487 (1995).

[79] See K. P. Berger, *International Commercial Arbitration,* who argues persuasively (at p.561) that there is usually no way of knowing the exact reason for the omission of a choice of taw clause, so that it is dangerous to deduce from this an intention to be governed by the *lex mercatoria.*

[80] See e.g. the protracted and ultimately unsuccessful attempts in Austria and France to upset the award in the celebrated *Norsilor* case (*Pabalk Ticaret Sirketi* v. *Ugilor/Norsilor SA,* ICC case no.3131 of 1979): and, for a general discussion, David W. Rivkin, "Enforceability of Arbitral Awards Based on *Lex Mercatoria*" (1993) Arb.Int. 67.

this where, though not referring *eo nomine* to the *lex mercatoria,* it authorises the arbitrator to apply *rules of law* and does not constrain him to select a "law" in the sense of a legal *system.* Article 1496 of the French Code of Civil Procedure gives statutory blessing to such an approach:

> L'arbitre tranche le litige conformément aux règles de droit que les parties ont choisies; à défaut d'un tel choix, conformément à celles qu'il estime appropriées.

Provisions to similar effect are to be found in Article 1054(2) of the Netherlands Arbitration Act 1986 and in Article 42 of the 1965 Washington Convention governing investment disputes involving a State. But it appears that this option is not open in arbitral proceedings governed by the UNCITRAL Model Law, Article 28 of which requires the application of "the law determined by conflict of laws rules".

## G. Is the *Lex Mercatoria* Anational?

Does this mean, then, that the *lex mercatoria* is truly anational and autonomous? Put in this way the question is ambiguous, as becomes apparent when one considers the diversity of ways in which objections to the whole concept of *lex mercatoria* have been expressed.[81] The first objection is that the *lex mercatoria,* consisting of general principles of law and international trade usage, is not a complete legal system, so that it is futile for the parties to seek to designate it as the law applicable to their contract. It is certainly the case that the *lex mercatoria* is not a complete legal system. But that does not mean that to choose it as the applicable law is wholly ineffective, merely that so far as its principles do not cover the question in dispute it will be necessary to refer to some applicable national law. Whether they do cover the question is for the tribunal to decide, drawing on whatever materials are to hand. Second, it is objected that the *lex mercatoria* is not an autonomous body of principles, for it is controlled by rules of public policy and mandatory rules of national law. This also is true, but it does not follow that the *lex mercatoria* lacks normative force, merely that it is subordinate to higher norms, in much the same way as principles laid down by the courts may be affected by legislation. Third, it is contended that every international usage depends for its normative force on recognition by national law. To the extent that it consists of general principles of law common to States (or to relevant States, however these might be defined) this condition is met. More debatable is whether the usage has to be shown to have been received into national law. If by this is meant a particular national law then it necessarily predicates selection of a given legal system as the applicable law, for that is the national law that is relevant to the question. Since arbitrators do from time to time decide cases according to international trade usage without reference to a national law and have their awards upheld by courts it would be rather futile to deny the efficacy of awards made on this basis. Nor can we even say, conformably with arbitration practice, that international usage is necessarily to

[81] See the discussion in Craig, Park, and Paulsson, *International Chamber of Commerce Arbitration* (2nd edn) pp.603–9.

be found in a convergence of rules in different legal systems, for such usage can also be inferred from conventions which have not yet come into force or, if in force, have not yet been ratified by the relevant States.

It is everywhere admitted that the normative force of usage, whether domestic or international, depends on its satisfying certain essential criteria.[82] But where do we look to find what these are? The usage itself cannot speak as to its own validity. There are no doubt some usages that are so broad in character and so universal of application that they would be recognised in any developed legal system, and would, indeed, be likely to have lost their distinctive status as trade usages and to have acquired the status of a general principle of law.[83] But broad principles of this kind, such as *pacta sunt servanda,* are so hedged about with qualifications which vary from one legal system to another that they serve little purpose except as a device by which an arbitral tribunal can claim support for its conclusions without having to determine an applicable law.[84] Outside these broad principles we cannot point to some universal law against which to measure the validity of a usage, for such a law does not exist; both the character of a trade usage and the conditions of its validity vary from jurisdiction to jurisdiction.[85] How, then, can arbitral tribunals satisfy themselves that an international usage is valid without resorting to national law? A short answer to this is that if the usage is truly international it cannot depend for its existence on any particular national law or decisions of any particular national court. That would be to localise and domesticate what is *ex hypothesi* international.[86] But the admission of international usage as a determinant of rights *is* dependent on national law in a different sense in that (quite apart from mandatory rules and rules of public policy) the existence of international usage can be ruled upon only by a tribunal of competent jurisdiction—and in the case of an arbitral tribunal, jurisdiction is determined by the *lex loci arbitri.* It is everywhere the case that an award may be set aside where the arbitrators have exceeded their jurisdiction, and that is also a ground for refusing enforcement under the New York Convention.[87] It is primarily the *lex loci arbitri* which controls the conditions in which arbitrators can make valid awards. Within the limits set by those conditions, and in the absence of a choice of law by the parties, arbitrators can draw on whatever sources seem to them proper in order to determine the rights of the parties. Accordingly, the normative force of international trade usage depends not on what national law says about the usage but upon whether the power to decide on the existence and

[82] See *supra* p.271. [83] See *supra* p.277.

[84] Why arbitrators should want to do this is discussed *supra.*

[85] See Clive M. Schmitthoff, *Interpretation and Application of International Trade Usages*, a study prepared for the ICC.

[86] That is not to say that national law has nothing to say about it. See e.g. s.62(2) of the UK Sale of Goods Act 1979, which expressly preserves in relation to contracts of sale of goods "the rules of the common law, including the law merchant".

[87] New York Convention on the Recognition and Enforcement of Foreign Arbitral Awards, Art. V(1)(c).

content of such usage has been exercised by a tribunal having competence under the *lex loci arbitri* and conforming with its procedural requirements.[88] National laws, through their conferment of decision-making powers on arbitral tribunals, have delegated to them the power to decide whether the requisite criteria for recognising an international usage have been satisfied and for that purpose to draw on such materials as seem to them proper.[89] As Professor Clive Schmitthoff so perceptively observed many years ago: "... the new law merchant, as an autonomous legal regulation, is founded on the complementary interaction of party autonomy and arbitration."[90]

## VI. International Trade Usage and the Search for Uniformity

The underlying motive power for the new *lex mercatoria* is the desire to return to a perceived golden age when commercial law was relatively universal and the outcome of a dispute was likely to be the same in whichever country it was decided by the merchants according to international trade usage.

The first point to make is that such a golden age never truly existed. International usage was interwoven with local usage, each codification in a particular locale differed from its contemporaries and its predecessors, the rules were fragmented and in many cases uncertain in their content and ambit, and many of them were only transient. But even if we allow (as we must) that some unifying effects are created by an international law merchant the diversity of approaches now adopted tends to undermine it. First, we have noted the marked differences between the approaches and powers of courts and those of arbitrators, leading to the increased likelihood that the outcome of the dispute on contested issues of law will depend on the procedure adopted. Second, the widely diverse approaches to the inference of international trade usage from conventions that are not applicable according to their own terms means that in one group of cases the applicable law is applied and in another group its dispositive rules are treated as displaced by international trade usage applicable to the contract. Third, the difference in view as to whether there is an arbitral *lex fori* means that, unless otherwise agreed by the parties or provided by the arbitration rules to which they have subjected themselves, one arbitral tribunal will apply the conflict rules of the jurisdiction where the arbitration has its seat while another will resort to the conflict of laws rules of a different State and a third will determine the *rule* it considers appropriate without reference to the conflict rules of any particular legal *system.* Fourth, one arbitral tribunal will seek to find an applicable law under a conflict rule or system while another will choose a national law directly, without

88 It is the need for controls of this kind which makes the concept of a *lex loci arbitri* indispensable and is the most powerful argument against the notion of delocalised arbitration. Accordingly the provisions of art.177 of the Belgian Code Judiciaire depriving Belgian courts of the power of judicial review where neither party is a Belgian national are particularly unfortunate.

89 See e.g. Art.1496 of the French Code of Civil Procedure, *supra* p.291.

90 "International Business Law: A New Law Merchant" in *Clive M. Schmitthoff's Select Essays on International Trade Law* (ed. Chia-Jai Cheng) 20 at p.33.

reference to any conflict rule, and a third will disregard all national laws and simply apply what it perceives to be the *lex mercatoria.* Finally, while arbitral tribunals are trying to escape from the application of national conflict of laws rules, modern international trade conventions almost invariably include at least some provisions laying down a uniform conflict rule on a particular point or referring particular issues to the applicable law under rules of private international law.

Yet what some will see as anarchy will be stoutly defended by others on the ground that it is in the nature of arbitration that it is flexible and admits of a variety of approaches, and that whereas decisions of courts build up a pattern of principle and rule which contributes to the common law and to which resort may be had to predict or determine the outcome of future disputes, it is not the function of arbitral awards to develop international jurisprudence. All that matters at the end of the day is that the arbitral tribunal reaches a result that commends itself to the reasonable man as just *in the particular case.* That this is so is shown by the private nature of arbitration (which is inconsistent with its function as a law-making institution) and by the reluctance of parties to arbitration proceedings to allow the full text of awards to be published. So perhaps the growing recourse to international trade usage, to the exclusion of national law, is not such a bad thing after all.

# 19

# A New International *Lex Mercatoria*?*

*Roy Goode*[†]

I should like to express my deep sense of privilege that the Cassel Foundation, through the medium of that distinguished scholar and good friend, Professor Jan Hellner, should have invited me to deliver this year's Cassel lecture. I have happy memories of my earlier visits to Stockholm, and to its great university, and I have always been overwhelmed by the kindness and hospitality of my hosts. I should particularly like to thank Professor Jan Kleineman and his wife Maria for looking after me so well during my few days' stay here on the present occasion.

To speak of the *lex mercatoria* is to conjure up a vision of a corpus of law built up by the usages of merchants, having its roots in the Roman *ius gentium,* and developed in the Middle Ages as a body of principle and rule that crossed national boundaries and was common to civilized states in Europe. The fascination with the *lex mercatoria* is not due entirely to the fact that Latin phrases seem so much more beguiling and significant than those uttered in one's native tongue, though we can understand that the phrase "law merchant" is not so evocative as "*lex mercatoria*". I suspect that the reason why the Latin is so appealing is that it suggests the existence of a body of law that is independent of national law and of national courts, is based on the customs and usages of merchants and is available either to supplement or to replace the applicable domestic law as determined by the rules of private international law of the forum State.

Part of the difficulty we have in discussing the *lex mercatoria* is that no two writers are agreed on its meaning. To some it denotes the totality of law governing cross-border transactions, whether derived from usage, general principles of law, conventions, uniform rules effectuated by contractual incorporation, or even standard-term contracts. Used in this sense the *lex mercatoria* is simply a synonym for what has become known as transnational commercial law. But to treat the two terms as synonymous means that we give up a label which is useful in describing *unwritten*

* Originally published in Juridisk Tidskrift Nr 2 1999/00, s. 253. Reproduced by kind permission from the publisher.

† Emeritus Professor of Law, the University of Oxford and Emeritus Fellow of St John's College Oxford. This is a revised and slightly expanded version of the 1999 Cassel Lecture delivered at the University of Stockholm on Friday 28 May 1999.

commercial law, *ius non scriptum,* which to me is the essence of the *lex mercatoria.* So for my purposes I shall treat the *lex mercatoria* as consisting of customary commercial law, customary rules of evidence and procedure, and general principles of commercial law, including international public policy. All of these are unwritten in the sense that, though there may be compilations which provide evidence of them, they derive their force from the common understanding among commercial men, not from legal decisions or from incorporation into contracts, contractual codes, or international conventions. Transplantation of usages and general principles into written instruments possessing normative force changes the character of what is incorporated into rules which are binding by reason of contract law or legislation rather than by reason of common observance. Moreover, almost invariably the document substantially and intentionally changes the unwritten rules. I shall use the term *transnational commercial law* to describe the totality of principles and rules, whether customary, conventional, contractual, or derived from any other source, which are common to a number of legal systems.

Historically it is doubtful whether the *lex mercatoria* had any real connection with the Roman *ius gentium.* Rather it was spontaneously created by the consistent observance among merchants of practices which had evolved to overcome problems, to reduce risks, and to distribute burdens in an equitable manner. There has always been a close link between the *lex mercatoria* and the *lex maritima,* and codifications of mercantile custom have usually been in the maritime field. Examples are the Rhodian Maritime Code of the 2nd or 3rd century BC, accepted equally by Greeks and Romans and the first known code to adopt the principle of general average in maritime insurance; the Rhodian Sea Laws, which came a thousand years later; the Rolls of Oléron, an island commune off the coast of Aquitaine, produced in the 11th or 12th century; and the Consulate of the Sea, a 14th or 15th century code originating in Barcelona. All of these had an influence that went far beyond their city of origin. Thus the Rolls of Oléron were brought to England and incorporated into the Black Book of the Admiralty. The mediaeval law merchants were particularly effective in devising instruments to localize payment (the bill of exchange) and to facilitate dealings with goods while still in transit (the bill of lading), and their usages laid the foundations of the laws of partnership and of marine insurance. The Middle Ages also appears to have introduced a tightening of rules compared with ancient law. Under the Code of Hammurabi a pilot who carelessly lost his ship had to restore its equivalent to the owner. By the time of the Sea Laws of Oléron the penalty imposed on a negligent pilot was instant decapitation. This appears to have resulted in a marked improvement in the quality of service provided by pilots!

We know that with the development of the nation-state and a corresponding increase in nationalism and the power of the central courts the *lex mercatoria* went into decline. Increasingly it became superseded by national law, so that one ceased to speak of the international law of trade and spoke instead of the English law, or the Swedish law, or the Italian law, of international trade. The divergences in laws gave a wholly new meaning to private international law, which Martin Wolff had shown was originally not national law at all but—like the received Roman law of the Middle Ages—supra-national, the product of the Italian universities of the 13th century. But just as substantive law became state-based and lost its international character, so also private international law came to be seen as part of a state's national law which it was free to develop in its own way. Characteristically, the pragmatic English were slow in coming on board, and until the 17th century avoided all problems by a very simple rule: if an English court has jurisdiction, then English law applies!

I have referred to the two main branches of what I regard as the *lex mercatoria*, namely unwritten international trade usage (which may also be termed customary commercial law) and general principles of commercial law or, more broadly, general principles of law. These two branches of the *lex mercatoria* are usually discussed together and often treated by writers as if they were interchangeable. But in my view it is important to keep them separate, for they rest on different foundations and may have different legal effects. General principles operate at a higher level of abstraction, usages are specific. In my view general principles necessarily derive from national legal systems and from international law (which is applied by national legal systems), while international trade usages are created independently and spontaneously, though they may depend on courts for their validation. General principles are therefore law in the true sense. As law they embody mandatory rules. (I use the term "mandatory" here and hereafter to refer to rules which cannot be excluded by agreement). There is now a strong drive, to which I shall refer later, to capture these general principles in international restatements of private law within a given field. International trade usages rest on party autonomy (contract) and require external validation, so that their force is provisional only. But though the two branches of the *lex mercatoria* are, and should be kept, distinct, there are connections.

Both the *lex mercatoria* and international restatements have a creative power; the former is constantly evolving as practices change to meet new demands, the latter can never be a pure restatement but must inevitably embody divergences from the national laws of some, if not all, of the states represented.

Moreover, what starts as the usage of a particular form of international trade may become so broad in its application as to be converted into a general principle of commercial law. The obvious illustration is the principle *pacta sunt servanda*, which is the universal rallying cry of the hard-nosed merchant who wants his pound of flesh, though its utility is rather limited, since what we need to know is not that contracts are binding but the circumstances in which they can be set aside or modified. The party confronting the hard-nosed businessman will have a different rallying cry: *rebus sic stantibus.*

My talk tonight has a fourfold purpose:

1) to caution against romanticization of the law merchant and to ask whether it does, as is often claimed, constitute an independent set of norms of substantive law;
2) to say a few words on the much-discussed question whether in international commercial arbitration there is an independent set of norms of procedural law rendering the arbitration process anational and free from the constraints of any courts other than those of the place of enforcement;

3) to draw attention to the welcome resurgence of the scholar, and particularly of collaborative international restatements, as an influence in the shaping of transnational commercial law, with especial reference to the PICC and the PECL; and
4) to offer some thoughts on the future of transnational commercial law.

## Is the *Lex Mercatoria* a Body of Independent Norms of Substantive Law?

I should like to challenge the view that the *lex mercatoria* is some free-standing corpus of law, intangible, invisible but somehow pervading the commercial law world. My contention is, first, that so far as the *lex mercatoria* embodies international trade usage it is contractual in character and is not as such law at all, simply a set of superadded rights and obligations which are expressly or impliedly incorporated into contracts and are therefore no more immune from mandatory rules of an applicable law than any other contract terms; and, secondly, that insofar as the *lex mercatoria* consists of general principles of commercial law, or general principles of law, these are necessarily either drawn from national legal systems and shown to be common to legal systems or a substantial number of them or alternatively are formulated in the first instance by scholars or others and taken by judges of national courts into their own law.

Inevitably, any discussion of customary law, of which international trade usage is a particular manifestation, leads to the unanswerable question: what is law? I propose to leave that issue to the masters of higher jurisprudence. What I do want to suggest is that while international trade usage is undoubtedly a source of rights it is not in itself law. Law does not merely consist of rules; it presupposes a legal system, with the apparatus provided by a sovereign state for interpreting the law and for giving effect to decisions, whether by judges, arbitrators, or administrators. Parties are not bound by trade usage merely because it is there. They are bound because they have contracted, or are taken to have contracted, with reference to the usages of the particular market in which they are engaged. This point is very well brought out in what has become the central convention of international trade law, the 1980 Vienna Convention on Contracts for the International Sale of Goods. Article 9 says:

> (1) The parties are bound by any usage to which they have agreed and by any practices which they have established between themselves.
> (2) The parties are considered, unless otherwise agreed, to have impliedly made applicable to their contract or its formation a usage of which the parties knew or ought to have known and which in international trade is widely known to, and regularly observed by, parties to contracts of the type involved in the particular trade concerned.

Though the convention is confined to international sales, article 9 in my view correctly states the legal basis for the recognition and enforcement of international trade usage generally. Accordingly trade usage, being contractual in character, has no higher status than the express provisions of the contract and can only take effect so far as recognized by the applicable national law and subject to its mandatory rules and to the rules of international public policy which are to be applied by national courts and arbitral tribunals. A contract is not by itself law; it depends for its effectiveness on recognition and enforcement by a national legal system. This is true both of the express terms of the contract and of those implied from international trade usage. If the position were otherwise we should have an anarchic commercial world in which business interests were able to make their own law free from any constraints whatsoever. That, I suggest, is simply not acceptable.[1]

## Ascertaining and Applying International Trade Usage

As a slight digression from my central propositions, I should like to state once again a caution I have uttered elsewhere against what I perceive as too lax an approach by some arbitral tribunals to evidence of international trade usage. It is all too easy for arbitrators to conclude that international trade usage relevant to the point at issue is whatever will lead the arbitral tribunal to the result it wishes to reach. One of the more reliable ways of establishing the existence of an international trade usage is from the evidence of experts. Very often experts for the opposing sides will disagree, but that is no more of an obstacle for a tribunal than disagreement among witnesses of any other kinds of fact; the tribunal simply weighs the conflicting testimony and decides whose it prefers. Much more questionable is the readiness of certain arbitrators to infer the existence of customary commercial law from other sources such as standard-term contracts and international conventions. If, for example, it is found that standard-term contracts contain adjustment clauses requiring the parties to renegotiate the contract terms where a change of circumstances substantially alters the equilibrium of the contract, some arbitrators will take that as evidence of an international trade usage establishing a right of adaptation. But many contracts do not contain adjustment clauses. That would not preclude an arbitrator from finding, if it were the fact, that the right of adjustment was not simply a common usage but so well entrenched as to have become a general principle of commercial law, and thus a principle to be applied externally except where the contract excludes it. But the existence of a substantial number of contracts in the trade in question which do not contain an adjustment clause surely makes it impossible to infer a right of adjustment as a matter of consistently applied international trade usage.

[1] It is not necessary to revive the long-standing controversy as to whether a rule of law can be said to exist before it has been declared by the court. The declaratory theory of the common, reluctantly restated in the recent majority decision of the House of Lords in *Kleinwort Benson Ltd. v. Lincoln City Council* [1998] 3 WLR 1095, is that the judges do not create law, they merely declare it, so that once stated the new rule, even if previously unknown, must be taken always to have represented the law. The declaratory theory is widely regarded as a fiction. However, that criticism cannot be levelled with the same force at trade usage, for whereas there was no evidence for the existence of the common law rule before it was first enunciated, trade usage is an observable fact and needs only to possess the attributes required by law to entitle it to recognition.

Arbitral tribunals can be even bolder in inferring the existence of an international trade usage from an international convention. My favourite example is an arbitral award given in Paris in 1989 on a contract made in 1979. The question was whether the buyer of goods seeking to reject them for non-conformity with the contract had given notice of non-conformity in due time. The arbitrators, having determined that the applicable law was that of the seller's country, concluded that the time which that law allowed was too short and not in conformity with international trade usage as exemplified by the Vienna Sales Convention. They therefore declined to apply the applicable law and instead upheld the buyer's to reject on the basis that his notice was given within the time allowed by Articles 38 and 39 of the convention. There were several remarkable features about this conclusion. First, the Vienna Convention not only had not been ratified at the time the contract was made but was not even in existence at that time. Secondly, the arbitrators chose to disregard the applicable law—surely inadmissible—when with a little more subtlety they could have avoided by treating its provisions as dispositive and therefore able to be modified by express or implied agreement of the parties. Thirdly, the proposition that a convention restates international trade usage is far from self-evident. One needs evidence from *travaux preparatoires* as to whether it was intended to do so or to formulate an entirely new rule. Moreover, one has to look at the degree of acceptability of the convention relied on. Finally, there *was* a convention in force at the time of the contract, namely the Uniform Law on International Sales, so why was that not relied on? The answer, presumably, was that it had not gained acceptance and therefore would not be helpful in enabling the tribunal to reach the desired result. I should add that in making these comments I do not know the identity of the arbitrators; I only hope they are not good friends of mine, for perhaps they would no longer be good friends!

## Are General Principles of Law Independent Norms?

I have stated my view that international trade usages are not independent legal norms of substantive law. What of general principles of law? If these are principles of public international law they can certainly be accepted as law, for international law is incorporated into or otherwise recognized by the national laws of civilized nations and one of the sources of international law is customary international law. International law might therefore be prayed in aid for such principles as "no expropriation without compensation". But I do not feel able to accept that there are general principles of commercial law having effect as legal norms independent of national legal systems. The conclusion is therefore the same as for international trade usage, though for a different reason. General principles cannot simply be plucked out of the air; they have to come from somewhere. Typically they are derived from a convergence of legal doctrine in a multiplicity of legal systems. In such a case they derive from national law, without which this source of their derivation would not exist. It is, however, possible, to infer the existence of general principles of commercial law by other means, in particular, international scholarly restatements, such as the UNIDROIT Principles of International Commercial Contracts and its European counterpart, the

Principles of European Contract Law, prepared by the Commission on European Contract Law. But these Principles, influential though they are, do not in themselves possess normative force. They can be incorporated into contracts, in which case they take effect, as terms of the contract, which as previously observed are not law. Alternatively, they can be relied on by national courts and by arbitrators as the best evidence of a rule which finds international acceptance. However, this depends on the willingness of the court or arbitral tribunal to receive and apply them as law. Judges of national courts may do so if they feel that the stated rule is one which they can adopt as part of their own domestic law of international trade. But they are free to reject the Principles which in any event sensibly defer to external mandatory law, a point to which I shall return. The Principles have proved very influential with arbitrators; but arbitral tribunals should apply them not as independent legal norms but rather as *evidence* of a consensus as to what a sensible rule should be.

## Can the *Lex Mercatoria* be Selected by the Parties, or Relied on by Arbitral Tribunals, as the Applicable Law?

Under traditional conflict of laws rules parties can choose, and courts apply, a national legal system, that is to say, the law of a state, whether a fully sovereign state or one forming part of a federal system, such as the state of New York. However, the impatience with dependence on national legal systems to resolve international disputes has led to a re-evaluation of the traditional rules and to the question whether the parties are really obliged to select the law of state X or the law of state Y, and whether on the contrary they are not free to choose "the *lex mercatoria*" or "general principles of law" or "internationally accepted principles of law" as the law to govern their contract. The question is not answerable in this particular form. It is necessary to distinguish, first, general principles of law from international trade usage and, secondly, the validity of such a provision, in terms of public policy, from its effect as a matter of private international law. These distinctions are not commonly drawn, yet they should not be neglected.

When reference is made to "general principles of law" or "internationally accepted principles of law", the first question is: what does this mean? Does it require all countries of the world to adopt the principle? Clearly not. It is highly unlikely that all countries do in fact embody the principle in their law, and even if they did it would as a practical matter be impossible to research all the countries to find out. So what is involved is a selection. Does the principle have to be one common not only to a number of legal systems within the same family of laws—for example, common law or civil law or Scandinavian law—but also to at least some systems in different legal families? Such an exercise seems equally futile. If, for example, a French company and an English company enter into a contract for construction in works in France on the basis that the contract will be governed by "general principles of law", it would seem pointless to refer, say, to Chinese law to discover whether a principle contended for forms part of that legal system. So the only practical approach is to treat the relevant systems as those connected to the parties or the transaction in dispute. If that still leaves more legal systems to consider than the arbitrators are willing to manage, they will no doubt treat the relevant systems as those with which they themselves are familiar. But assuming that the principle is indeed common to the legal systems connected to the parties or the transaction, there is no problem in applying that principle, for *ex hypothesi* it forms part of one or other national legal system constituting the objectively determined applicable law under traditional conflict of laws rules. In short, the arbitrators are in fact applying a principle to be found in a relevant legal system; all that the choice of law clause does is to dispense with the need to identify the particular national legal system that is being applied. On this basis even a cautious English court in an arbitration of which the *lex arbitri* is English might be willing to uphold such a clause as a true choice of law clause. We have no authority on the question as yet. The closest we have come to it is in the *Deutsche Schachtbau* case, where the court declined to find any public policy objection to an award applying "internationally accepted principles of law governing contractual relations" in view of the fact that the *lex arbitri* was Swiss law and the expert evidence from Professor Pierre Lalive was that under Swiss law such a clause was considered perfectly legitimate.

But a clause purporting to apply "the usages of international trade" as the applicable law raises quite different considerations. I have already indicated my view that international trade usage is not law, and that a reference to international trade usage is not a reference to a legal system. Accordingly it would not in my view be possible to choose international trade usage as the governing law in such a way as to override the mandatory rules of law of the legal systems whose law, objectively determined, would otherwise be applicable. That does not mean that the clause is wholly ineffective; it may well have effect as a contractual incorporation of international trade usage and thus as a term of the contract. But, like any other contract term, it will be subject to the mandatory rules of the applicable law.

Is it open to parties to choose, say, the Vienna Sales Convention as the applicable law? One objection might be that this is ineffective because the convention is not a comprehensive code and covers only matters within its scope. That does not seem to me a valid objection. In the first place, the convention may be adequate to cover the particular issues before the tribunal. Secondly, so far as it is not, the tribunal can resort to the applicable law under traditional conflicts rules. Nor is it an objection that the result is to leave different issues to be governed by different laws, for the principle of dépeçage is widely accepted. The real objection to having the Vienna Sales Convention as the applicable law is that it does not represent part of a legal system. It may fall within the somewhat misleading phrase "rules of law" but it is not *law* for conflict of laws purposes. I am aware that this view is controversial, but it seems to me that to speak of law without legal system, including the machinery of a state for interpreting and enforcing the law, would be fallacious. However, there is no reason why the designation of the convention should not be effective to displace or supplement an applicable law whose provisions are (as they normally will be) purely dispositive. The parties are then simply exercising the right given under the applicable law to vary or exclude one or more of the dispositive provisions.

## Why the Urge to Avoid Applying National Law?

A few years ago I sought to identify the reasons why some international arbitrators were so keen to apply the *lex mercatoria* in place of national law.[2] I managed to come up with a list of seven reasons, five of which I considered to be entirely legitimate. They are: that the putative law is not sufficiently developed to furnish an answer to the point in issue; that if the competing applicable laws are those of the contestants, recourse to the *lex mercatoria* as a neutral system enable the arbitral tribunal to avoid causing offence or a sense of unfairness to the loser, who had not agreed to the law determined objectively under conflicts rules; that the laws of the relevant states are in all material respects the same, so that there is no point in deciding which of them applies (but of course there is then no need to use the *lex mercatoria* either); that the choice between one of two competing legal systems is so finely balanced as to make it difficult to come down on one side or the other, so that a useful way is to choose a third way; and that the application of a national law designed primarily for domestic disputes is seen by the tribunal as inherently unsatisfactory. The remaining two reasons are that (as in the French award previously referred to) the tribunal does not like the solution given by the applicable law; and that the tribunal is romantically attracted to the *lex mercatoria* and seeks to appeal to it on every conceivable occasion. These last two reasons, understandable though they may be, seem to me to be illegitimate.

I believe, though I have not had time to research the matter, that the concept of an autonomous *lex mercatoria* has been given a prominence out of all proportion to its practical significance, partly because of the influence of French courts, which have traditionally adopted a laudable non-nationalistic approach to issues of international trade law, and partly because in writings on arbitration and in reports of arbitral decisions the focus has been on those cases in which the *lex mercatoria* has been successfully invoked, and which are therefore more interesting and more supportive of the views of its exponents, rather than on the great bulk of cases where arbitrators apply traditional conflict of laws rules and the national law thereby determined. But that is not to decry the importance of the practice and usage of international trade as a source of legal rights. On the contrary, one of the most significant benefits to emerge from the debate is the growing recognition that it is time to move away from national laws of international trade and towards a modern transnational commercial law.

## Is there an Autonomous Body of Arbitral Procedural Law?

It is impossible to come to Stockholm without mentioning arbitration. Stockholm is one of the world's leading arbitration centres, and those not familiar with the

[2] Roy Goode, "Usage and its Reception in Transnational Commercial Law", (1997) 46 ICLQ 1.

admirable book by Dezalay and Garth called *Dealing in Virtue* will be gratified to know that an entire chapter is devoted to what they call "Vintage Arbitration in Stockholm". This seems to refer not only to the long-standing nature of the Swedish arbitration system but also the maturity (if one may so describe it) of Swedish arbitrators. It is apparently an unwritten rule in Swedish arbitration circles that at least grey hairs, if not grey beards, are an essential qualification for a Swedish arbitrator. That does not seem to have stopped distinguished colleagues such as Professor Jan Ramberg from receiving recognition as one of the world's leading arbitrators; likewise Professor Kleineman has no difficulty in attracting arbitration work. But at least a measure of seniority is needed here in Stockholm, as, indeed, tends to be looked for elsewhere.

No academic can resist the temptation to join the debate on the question whether arbitration proceedings are subject to a *lex arbitri* or whether on the other hand, in the graphic words of that distinguished international arbitrator Jan Paulsson, arbitration is "unbound", that is, anational and delocalized, i.e. detached from the law of the seat of the arbitration or, indeed, from any other law except that of the state of enforcement. It is, of course, accepted that within their own jurisdictional rules national courts have control over all acts taking place within the state of whose legal machinery they form part. The question is whether decisions of courts in the *lex loci arbitri* setting aside an award should be respected by courts of the state of enforcement, and whether the latter should have regard to the fact that a final award in the *lex loci arbitri* is subject to an as yet undecided judicial challenge.

There can be no doubt that within the limits of their own law, including the 1958 New York Convention in a state party to that convention, the courts of the state of enforcement have the last word on the enforcement of an arbitral award. Article V of the New York Convention limits the grounds on which enforcement may be refused but says nothing about whether a court in the state of enforcement can allow enforcement of an award even if it has been set aside by courts at the seat of the arbitration or is under challenge in those courts. One view is that such courts are free to do as they please and to disregard orders of courts under the *lex loci arbitri* setting aside awards. In a literal sense that, of course, is true. Courts of the state of enforcement have complete control over enforcement in their jurisdiction. The question, then, is not whether they *can* disregard orders made under the *lex loci arbitri* but whether they are acting appropriately in so doing. Of course, this depends on their municipal law and the view they take of it. Jan Paulsson's seminal article "Arbitration Unbound"[3] was prompted by the much-discussed decision of the Paris Court of Appeal in the *Gôtaverken* case declining to take jurisdiction in a claim set aside an arbitral award rendered in Paris in an arbitration governed by the rules of the International Chamber of Commerce where both parties were foreign and the contract had no connection with France. The Court of Appeal held that the award was not a French award and that parties to an arbitration were entitled

[3] "Arbitration Unbound: Award Detached from the Law of its Country of Origin" (1981) 30 ICLQ 358. See also the same writer's follow-up, "Delocalisation of International Commercial Arbitration: When and Why it Matters" (1983) 32 ICLQ 53.

to detach the arbitration from the national law of the seat of the arbitration. I hope I am not being presumptuous in saying that this is a perfectly legitimate conclusion. It is the prerogative of any national court to decide, within its perception of its own domestic law, whether in a given case it does or does not have jurisdiction.

Much more of a problem is created where an award is enforced despite a judgment of a court at the seat of the arbitration setting the award aside. What is the justification for this disregard of an order made under the *lex loci arbitri*? The proponents of the delocalization theory must be taken seriously. A number of them are eminent lawyers and arbitrators with a deep knowledge of all aspects of the subject. They quite rightly point out that an arbitrator is not like a judge; he is not an official of the state but an adjudicator appointed by private agreement. He has no duty (and this is now widely accepted) to apply the rules of procedure or evidence that would be applicable in litigation at the seat of the arbitration; he is not obliged to apply the conflict rules of the forum, though under the Rome Convention on the Law Applicable to Contractual Obligations, the UNCITRAL Model Law on Arbitration, and the law of a number of jurisdictions, including England, he is obliged to select a national legal system and to select it in accordance with conflict rules of some kind. The advocates of the delocalization theory also point out that the arbitrator, unlike the judge, has only a temporary connection with the seat of the arbitration, that the seat may have been selected for reasons of convenience rather than because of any connection with the dispute (though the basis of this assertion is unstated), that there is often no connection at all between the forum and the parties or the transaction; and that anyway there is no reason why a court in the country of enforcement should not be free to say that since its own law allows enforcement, and since it regards the reasons for discharge of the award by the courts of the seat as attributable to the peculiarities of the *lex loci arbitri,* it will enforce the award even if it has been set aside by a court of the forum.

These are powerful arguments but in my view are not in the end compelling ones. It is a universally accepted principle of the conflict of laws that a sovereign state has the exclusive power to control acts done within its borders, that the courts of that state have primary, and in many cases exclusive, jurisdiction to decide the validity of those acts under their law, and that their decisions should be respected by other states. It is upon these concepts of mutual recognition and comity that the maintenance of proper relations between states depends. Both the parties and the arbitral tribunal may need the assistance of courts of the seat to facilitate the arbitral process and to give coercive orders in support of rulings of the tribunal. It is surely a little rich for parties to want to have the state machinery available to them when it suits them and then to feel free to disregard adverse rulings when the award comes to be enforced in another state. It is, moreover, the parties themselves who choose the seat of the arbitration, directly or indirectly through the institution administering the arbitration, and who may well do so because of satisfaction with the legal framework of arbitration in the selected forum. Again, why should they not in principle be bound by judicial decisions of that forum? Similarly, if mandatory provisions of legislation at the seat impose public policy restrictions on the freedom of the parties to contract as to the conduct of their arbitration, should not these restrictions be respected by the courts of other states? For example, it is clear from the English Arbitration Act 1996 that while parties can exclude the right of appeal for error of law, they cannot exclude an application to review an award for want of substantive jurisdiction or serious procedural irregularity. If the tribunal goes beyond its mandate, its award should not be binding. If it commits a serious irregularity, for example, by hearing one party without having given notice of the hearing to the other, who in consequence fails to attend, the award should not be allowed to stand, notwithstanding a provision of the arbitration agreement purporting to exclude judicial review in such a case. Surely legislative provisions of this kind affecting arbitral proceedings within the state enacting them should be respected by other states. And surely it is the courts of the seat who are presumptively best placed to interpret and apply those provisions.

I do, of course, accept that at the end of the day it must be the court of the state of enforcement that has the final word, compatible with its own law and, in a New York Convention state, the provisions of the convention. Different courts allowing enforcement of an award despite the fact that it has been set aside by a court of the seat of the arbitration have given different justifications for so doing. One is that arbitral awards are anational and therefore should be unfettered by the *lex loci arbitri.* Another is Article V of the New York Convention, which sets out the sole grounds on which enforcement may be refused in language which suggests to many authorities that the court asked to enforce the award has a discretion to enforce even in a case within Article V.[4] A third route is Article VII of the convention, which empowers the court of the state of enforcement to enforce an award if its own law allows it to do so, notwithstanding other provisions of the convention. There are at least two leading cases in which, on different grounds, a court in the state in which enforcement was sought has allowed enforcement of an award even where it had been set aside by a court at the seat of the arbitration. In *Hilmarton*[5] the Paris Court of Appeal upheld the decision of a lower court enforcing an award rendered in Geneva even though it had been set aside by the Court of Justice of Geneva in a decision upheld by the Swiss Federal Tribunal. The reason given was that the award was an international award and had not been integrated into the Swiss legal system. A subsequent decision of the Paris Court of Appeal made it clear that this ruling was not case-specific but established a general principle of French law that an arbitral award in an international commercial arbitration was international in character and thus by definition not integrated into the legal system of the country where it was given.[6]

[4] It seems to be taken for granted that the discretion to allow enforcement despite the existence of a ground under Article V stems from the phrase "may be refused" in Article V imports a discretion. However, this ignores the context and the subtleties of the English language. The full phrase is: "Recognition and enforcement of the award may be refused ... only if ...". All this means is that a court at the place of enforcement is not to refuse enforcement except on one of the stated grounds. As a matter of language the discretionary effect would be the same even if "shall" were substituted for "may". It would be otherwise if Article V had said "if and only".

[5] *Hilmarton Ltd. v. Omnium de Traitement et de Valorisation (OTV), Cour de Cassation 1994, (1995) 20 YB Comm Arb 663.*

[6] The *Hilmarton* case eventually came before an English court (*Omnium de Traitement de Valorisation SA v. Hilmarton Ltd.,* Timothy Walker J., 24th May 1999), where OTV unsuccessfully sought to persuade the court to refuse enforcement of the award in favour of Hilmarton on the ground that in its

In the *Chromalloy* case[7] an Egyptian award was held enforceable in the United States although it had been set aside by the Cairo Court of Appeal. Reliance was placed on the discretionary character of Article V (1) (e) of the New York Convention and on Article VII.[8]

There can be no question that courts of the state where enforcement is sought have power to enforce an award even if it has been nullified under the *lex loci arbitri.* My point is that the court where enforcement proceedings are taken should as a matter of international co-operation and comity respect decisions of the court of the seat setting aside the award unless there are strong reasons for not doing so, for example that the state is one whose courts are under the domination of the government and whose decisions are therefore not judicial in the internationally accepted sense. It is not without significance that Article V (1)(d) of the New York Convention expressly provides as one of the grounds for refusing enforcement of an award that "the constitution of the arbitral tribunal or the arbitral procedure has not been carried out in accordance with the law of the State where the arbitration took place". Similarly, Article V (1)(e) allows refusal of enforcement where the arbitral award "has been annulled or suspended by a competent authority of the State in which, or according to the law of which, the decision has been made. Whether or not courts of the state of enforcement are *bound* to refuse enforcement in such a case or whether they have simply a discretion to do so, Article V (1)(d) and (e) seem to me to indicate a proper regard for and deference to the *lex loci arbitri.* A further argument in favour of this approach is that it helps to avoid exposing the party who succeeds in having the award set aside to the potentially oppressive burden of separate proceedings in every state where enforcement is sought and to the unpredictability of outcomes dependent on the particular law of each such state. If an award is set aside by a judicial decision under the *lex loci arbitri,* then a uniform presumption in favour of supporting that decision operates as a unifying factor which should lead to the same result in every enforcement state.

## International Restatements

In the concluding part of this lecture I wish to examine the role and influence of international restatements of law such as the UNIDROIT Principles of International Commercial Contracts and the Principles of European Contract Law. The UNIDROIT Principles represent something of an innovation for UNIDROIT, in that they lay out rules for international commercial contracts but they do so in

performance there was a breach of an Algerian statute and the domestic policy of Algerian law. The case was ultimately settled. This suggests that the parties might have done well to consider the virtues of alternative dispute resolution at the outset!

[7] *Chromalloy Aeroservices, A Division of Chromalloy Gas Turbine Corp. v. The Arab Republic of Egypt* 939 F.Supp. 907 (US District Court, DC, 1996).

[8] For a detailed discussion of these decisions, and more generally of the relationship between the law of the state of origin of an award and the law of the state of enforcement, see Georgios C. Petrochilos, "On the Mechanics and Rationale of Enforcing Awards Annulled in their State of Origin under the New York Convention" (1999) ICLQ (publication pending).

a form which is not that of an international convention, or indeed any kind of binding instrument, and they were deliberately not submitted to the governments of Member States for their approval. The Principles are the product of work by an international team of legal scholars from all five continents, under the overall leadership of Professor Michael Bonell, each an expert in contract law, the work being carried out over a lengthy period and undergoing many drafts. The Principles of European Contract were prepared by a private group under the chairmanship of Professor Ole Lando, a leading comparative and conflicts scholar. These Principles are both wider and narrower than the UNIDROIT Principles; they are wider in not being confined to international contracts or to commercial contracts; they are narrower in being designed specifically for parties in Member States of the European Union. The two groups of scholars worked independently but had an overlapping membership, borrowed from each other and ended up with a set of contract principles possessing a high degree of commonality.

It is fair to say that during the early stages of preparation of the UNIDROIT Principles many members of the Governing Council were rather sceptical about the value of the exercise. The Principles were not law; why would anyone apply them? In retrospect one can see that some relevant considerations were overlooked. One was the influence of scholars. In the Middle Ages scholars were the emperors of the law. There was little legislation prior to the civil codes, and the courts were profoundly influenced by doctrinal writings and by schools of thought developed by leading scholars of the day. The second consideration was that the Principles could be available as a neutral set of rules for parties neither of whom wished to be subjected to the law of the other party. The third consideration that was overlooked—or perhaps more accurately could not have been foreseen—was the enthusiasm with which international arbitrators would come to apply the Principles, even where not selected by the parties, precisely because of their neutrality and because of the high international standing of those involved in the work and, in the case of UNIDROIT, its own standing as an international, intergovernmental institute for the unification of private law.

The Principles, and particularly the UNIDROIT Principles, have been successful beyond the wildest dreams of UNIDROIT and of the two teams of scholars involved. They have been the subject of a large number of conferences around the world, as well as a considerable volume of legal literature, and have been applied in numerous international arbitrations as representing widely accepted principles of the law of contract. In fact, the hierarchy of sources of law, which would place an international convention at the top of the latter and a private restatement near the bottom, is in practice completely reversed. The reason is simple. The conclusion of a multilateral convention is at most a provisional indication by states of their interest in adopting the convention. By contrast, the Principles represent the unconditional commitment of internationally known scholars who, coming from widely varying legal backgrounds, cultures, and traditions, have nevertheless made common cause to produce a set of principles acceptable to all. Even more remarkably, all those engaged in the exercise found to their delight that while each legal system represented had to make some sacrifices, the resulting product was one which, taken across the board, did not involve a significant departure from their own laws of contract. Moreover, the principles thus fashioned came from a desire to reflect the best thinking on desired solutions to common problems and were not motivated by political considerations in the governmental or intergovernmental sense, though of course they did reflect a sensitivity to the differing legal traditions of the countries represented.

There are two features of both sets of Principles to which I wish to draw attention and which are particularly relevant to the issues I have presented to you. Both concern mandatory rules of law. The first is that both sets of Principles defer to external super-mandatory rules applicable to the contract. This reflects a manifestly sensible acceptance of the fact that no set of contract provisions can be freestanding or self-validating, any more than international usages can speak to their own validity. All rules must ultimately draw for their legitimacy on national legal systems. Thus the Principles do in my view support the basic proposition I have been advancing in tonight's lecture. The second point is that the Principles contain mandatory rules of their own, for example, requirements of good faith, which cannot be excluded by agreement. Now it may well be asked how on earth non-binding Principles can possibly possess mandatory rules. But this is not as strange as it seems. In the first place, where parties adopt the Principles they thereby adopt at the very least a rule of interpretation that the requirement of good faith is not intended to be affected by ordinary exemption clauses and must be treated as overriding in the absence of very clear language to the contrary. Secondly, the statement of certain rules as mandatory is an encouragement to courts and arbitrators to treat the mandatory character of those rules as general principles of law. Thirdly, in those legal systems which are prepared to accept the ability of contracting parties to choose the Principles as the applicable law (which in my view they should not do), the parties thereby subject themselves to the mandatory provisions of the Principles as part of the applicable law.

I have referred to the two sets of principles governing international contracts. But other restatements are either in being or in course of being undertaken. I refer in particular to the Restatement of European Trust Law, prepared under the direction of Professor David Hayton, and the huge project for a European Civil Code which is just being initiated under the leadership of Professor Christian von Bar. Both of these involve international teams of scholars.

## The Resurgence of the Influence of Scholars

What do these restatements indicate? I would like to think that they represent the first step in a programme of academic activity which will once again give the international scholar pride of place as the motive power for efforts to harmonize private law and to expand the role and compass of transnational commercial law. Of course, this will to some extent be at the expense of private international law; but we cannot harmonize all law, and I am sure that there will be enough work left for the private international lawyers to carry them through to the fourth millennium.

## The Future of Transnational Commercial Law

It is evident that, in some quarters at least, there is a growing dissatisfaction with national law as a means of resolving international disputes, and an increasing pressure to look to international trade usage and general principles of commercial law, including those evidenced by international restatements by groups of scholars from different legal families and systems. I welcome this trend, provided that decisions—and particularly those of arbitral tribunals—are disciplined and not self-indulgent and that findings of fact as to trade usage are supported by proper evidence, whether expert or documentary. I do not consider that what is not law can be made into law by calling it *lex mercatoria.* But in most cases this will not matter, as principles impliedly incorporated into contracts will usually be enforceable as ordinary contract terms. However, law in the true sense cannot be excluded. It is important to control party autonomy by reference to some concept of overriding mandatory law, and to require asserted international trade usages or general principles of commercial law to be validated by external sources of law forming part of a legal system.

Arbitrators are already on the move in contributing to the expansion of transnational commercial law. It remains to be seen whether, as one hopes, judges of national courts can be persuaded to interpret their own law to reflect the international character of the transaction and thus to receive into their legal systems principles shown to be common to other jurisdictions relevant to the parties or their dispute.

The last word can be left to Lord Justice Mustill (later Lord Mustill) in his celebrated essay on the *lex mercatoria*:

> Finally, the person whose interests lie at the heart of the *lex mercatoria,* as of all commercial arbitration, is the businessman. All the debates proceed upon rival assumptions about his opinion and wishes on this or that topic. Yet all the literature is written by lawyers. Perhaps the time has now arisen for the contestants to call a truce, and for the businessman to speak for himself.[9]

It only remains for me to express my thanks once again to the Board of the Cassel Foundation for inviting me to give the 1999 Cassel Lecture, an invitation which I thought prudent to accept extremely promptly before Lord Justice Mustill's wise comment had been recalled to the minds of my hosts.

[9] "The New *Lex Mercatoria*: The First Twenty-Five Years", in *Liber Amicorum for Lord Wilberforce* (ed. Maarten Bos and Ian Brownlie, Clarendon Press, Oxford, 1987), at pp. 182–3.

# 20

# Rule, Practice, and Pragmatism in Transnational Commercial Law*

*Roy Goode*†

I feel privileged to have been invited to deliver this year's FA Mann lecture in succession to a long line of distinguished lawyers who have paid their own tribute to one of the most outstanding German legal émigrés of the 1930s. Francis Mann became a legend in his lifetime for his profound scholarship and his expertise in international and commercial litigation. While still in Germany he had fallen under the spell of the legendary Martin Wolff, the great conflicts lawyer, with whom he was able to resume contact years later in England. Mann himself was to become a leading light in both private and public international law. He had strong views on everything, a few of them decidedly unorthodox. His work *The Legal Aspect of Money* became a classic, and he died in bed while correcting the proofs of the fifth edition. Happily, Charles Proctor has taken over the mantle of editing the sixth edition, which has now been published by Oxford University Press. Full details of the contributions to English law by Wolff, Mann, and other outstanding German émigré lawyers will be found in a collection of essays in a fine new publication, *Jurists Uprooted,* edited by Sir Jack Beatson and Professor Reinhard Zimmerman.

My talk tonight is about transnational commercial law, that is, the product of the various means—international conventions, model laws, contractually incorporated uniform rules, international restatements, and conscious or unconscious legislative or judicial parallelism—which lead to the harmonization of commercial law at the international level. My concern is primarily with the private law governing cross-border transactions, not with international economic law or regulatory law. Nevertheless, it is necessary to traverse some aspects of public international law, private international law and comparative law. In none of these fields can I claim to have particular expertise, being merely a general commercial law mongrel! But I am comforted by the fact that almost every aspect of public international law appears

* Originally published as R Goode: "Rule, Practice, and Pragmatism in Transnational Commercial Law" in *ICLQ* vol 54, July 2005 pp 539–62.

† Emeritus Professor of Law at Oxford University and Emeritus Fellow of St John's College, Oxford. This is a revised and slightly expanded version of the 28th FA Mann Annual Lecture delivered at the Old Hall, Lincoln's Inn, on 15 November 2004.

to be controversial, the role of private international law is declining with the drive towards harmonization and, as to comparative law, we have it on the authority of the great Gutteridge that the subject-matter defies definition because it does not exist.[1]

## I. The Changing Face of Transnational Commercial Law

In earlier times, life was so much simpler than it is today. Cross-border trade was at a relatively low level, differences in national laws were dealt with primarily through national conflict of laws rules to determine the applicable law and the primary form of harmonization was the international convention, an instrument which typically took at least a decade, and often a good deal longer, to bring to fruition, and even then was all too often left to moulder on the shelves of Departments of States, unwept, unhonoured, and unsung, without ever securing enough ratifications to come into force effectively, if at all. No one talked of transnational commercial law; indeed, such a thing scarcely existed. Instead, we spoke—and still speak—of the law of international trade, which is not international at all but simply national law as it affects cross-border transactions.

Commerce and finance have always been dependent for their vitality on constant change. But the last quarter of the 20th century has witnessed change on an unprecedented scale. The advent of global trading, in which national markets are interconnected and modern technology linked to large clearing and settlement systems enables vast amounts of money and securities to be transferred across national boundaries, has led to highly developed settlement arrangements in which the sources of acquisitions and payments are lost through multilateral netting. The huge growth, both in the value and volume of transactions and in their diversity and complexity, has resulted in increased specialization with ever more complex and sophisticated contracts, contract structures, and markets, which only specialists fully understand. New trade associations have emerged which are heavily involved in the standardization of contracts and procedures. Many business disputes are settled not by litigation but by international commercial arbitration, a process which in form may appear purely procedural but which also has a profound effect on the substantive determination of disputes. The move from planned economies to market economies has enhanced the importance of private law and translated sovereign risk into enterprise risk. Old certainties such as the place of performance of an act or the location of an asset have given way to doubts and difficulties as we wrestle with the legal implications of contracts concluded on the internet, the maintenance of securities accounts through centralized accounting systems and 'virtual' offices, the daily movement of aircraft subject to security or leasing agreements from one country to another, and the location of satellites in space. The dominance of New York and London as world financial centres, coupled with the emergence of China, India, and Japan as major trading nations, has led to the displacement of the Eurocentric

[1] *Comparative Law* (2nd edn CUP 1949) 2.

model of international law-making and a much broader basis for agreement on international instruments, albeit with a strong shift towards the use of the English language as the *lingua franca* and to common law principles of *laissez-faire*.

All these developments have had a profound effect on both the content of transnational commercial law and the harmonization process. The conception of sources of commercial law governing international transactions is much broader than it was, encompassing the so-called *lex mercatoria* and a variety of forms of soft law, including model laws, legislative guides, contractually incorporated uniform rules, trade terms promulgated by international business organizations, and international restatements prepared by scholars from different legal families and jurisdictions.

In work on international conventions the complexity of modern cross-border business and finance has inevitably resulted in a certain reduction in the influence of scholars and a corresponding increase in that of legal practitioners and industry experts, and this in turn has led to an awareness that general rules in an international instrument are no longer sufficient and need to be supplemented by rules which in varying degrees are problem-oriented and fact-specific. Yet in another way the role of the scholar has been enhanced with the emergence of international and regional restatements, such as the UNIDROIT Principles of International Commercial Contracts and the Principles of European Contract Law prepared by the Commission on European Contract Law. Finally, non-governmental organizations are increasingly prominent as players in the preparation of international instruments.

I propose to examine four issues: some problems confronting private international law in this field; international trade practice and the reality of the *lex mercatoria;* the status of international restatements such as the UNIDROIT Principles of International Commercial Contracts as a source of transnational commercial law; and the process of harmonization through international conventions and the various kinds of tension that have to be addressed, including the impact of the European Community as a negotiating partner.

## II. Some Problems of Private International Law

It is self-evident that every substantive law harmonization reduces the scope of the conflict of laws. Indeed, it is the desire to escape from the conflict of laws that has powered the drive to assert the existence of the *lex mercatoria* as an autonomous international legal order, detached from all national laws and existing by its own force. It is clear, however, that since there are practical limits to what can be harmonized, private international law will remain of considerable importance in the resolution of cross-border disputes for the foreseeable future.

Yet the techniques for the development of private international law are not without their problems. To start with, there is the formulation of doctrine. The difficulties confronting conflicts textbook writers have not always been appreciated. In order for them to formulate sensible rules they need to have a good understanding of the substantive law of all the different subjects they are covering. Given the breadth of law, this is a formidable task in which they have achieved an astonishing degree of success. However, there are limits to what can be done without the involvement of substantive law specialists, whose participation will help to ensure that rules formulated in relation to commercial transactions are responsive to legitimate market needs and practices. But at this point we encounter the problem to which I referred earlier, namely the increasing sophistication of commercial activity, which leads to what I would describe as the special-situations syndrome calling for a highly specialist input. Traditional theory in the game of chess held, among other things, that certain types of pawn structure were inherently weak and should be avoided and that in a given opening it was unwise to capture a particular pawn, termed the poisoned pawn. But with the advent of modern analysis backed up by computing power it became clear that the general theory did not cater for specific board positions where the correct move involved creating the very pawn structure, or capturing the very pawn, which theory had previously condemned. In his book *The Evolution of Chess Opening Theory*,[2] the international grandmaster Raymond Keene recorded:

> the triumph of practicality over abstract theorising in contemporary competitive chess ... Any generalised discussion of the PP [poisoned pawn] is virtually worthless for anyone who intends to play it, for either colour. It is a razor-sharp undertaking, where inaccuracies can spell immediate disaster, where theory is in a state of constant flux ...

This is true of modern commercial law as it is of chess and it applies as much to private international law as to substantive law. One example will suffice. In *Macmillan v Bishopsgate Investment Trust plc (No* 3),[3] which arose from Robert Maxwell's fraudulent dealings in securities which one of his companies held as nominee, the court had to consider the law applicable to the competing claims to priority of securities held indirectly through an account with an intermediary. At first instance Millett J focused on the act of transfer and identified the place of this, correctly in my view, as the place where the book entry effecting the transfer took place. In the Court of Appeal, however, the Court applied the law of the place where the issuer was incorporated. Since all routes led to New York the outcome was the same and the appeal was dismissed.

With all respect to the Court of Appeal, application of the law of the place of incorporation fails to take account of the indirect holding system, where the account holder's relationship is solely with its own intermediary, not with the issuer, who will have no knowledge of his existence. Both academic and practitioner opinion supported a different rule, the place of the relevant intermediary approach (PRIMA), which looks to the place of the particular intermediary with which the account in question is held. It is a tribute to the progressive approach of the learned editors of *Dicey and Morris* that despite the Court of Appeal decision they were willing to go along with PRIMA,[4] a rule which became embodied in Article 9 of the EC settlement finality directive. So when work began on the Hague draft Convention on the law applicable to securities held with an intermediary, PRIMA was adopted,

[2] At 202. [3] [1995] 1 WLR 978; on appeal [1996] 1 WLR 387.
[4] *Conflict of Laws* (13th edn Sweet & Maxwell London 2003), para 24-064.

reflecting what was then seen to be a particular application of the *lex situs* principle. Yet further examination by industry experts revealed that this approach itself needed modification, because the maintenance of securities is a function frequently distributed over the offices of an intermediary in different countries or even carried out electronically in a 'virtual' office having no physical existence at all. Moreover, account maintenance could at the press of a button be switched to some central recording unit having no connection with the parties' relationship. In my view there was a further difficulty and one of more general application. The attribution of a *situs* to an intangible asset, which has no physical location, is a purely legal construct and, moreover, one which serves no useful purpose, for the deemed *situs* varies according to the nature of the intangible, so that the *lex situs* rule does not represent an organizing principle and is thus an unnecessary step which should be discarded in favour of a direct rule fashioned for the particular type of intangible in question.

The upshot of the debate was that the Hague Convention retained as its central concept the account with the relevant intermediary but jettisoned the place of the intermediary. The primary rule finally adopted was that the law governing the account agreement between investor and intermediary, or such other law as they choose, should govern not only their relations *inter se* but effects against third parties and even priorities. This is certainly counter-intuitive. The notion that an agreement between A and B should govern the law applicable to a priority contest between C and D seems remarkable and, indeed, astonished me when I first heard of its appearance in Article 8 of the American Uniform Commercial Code. But it turns out to have many advantages. Conflicts forum shopping is avoided and all issues relating to a securities account are routed to the same law. Those intending to acquire an interest in the securities will as a matter of course call for a copy of the account agreement to see what law applies and can obtain confirmation from the intermediary. The transfer from one account to another creates a new relationship with its own governing law. The rule has been in place in the United States for a decade and has been found to work successfully.

That is a good example of what I would call a special rule which is not susceptible to the traditional conflicts approach and is highly fact-specific. Indeed, the best way of testing the efficacy of a set of such rules is to avoid mechanical conceptual reasoning, throw at the rules as many typical fact situations as one can imagine and see if the rules produce the desired effect. The judiciary, too, has recognized the need to avoid a mechanical approach to the conflict of laws, a point forcefully made by Mance LJ in *Raffeisen Zentralbank Osterreich AG v Five Star Trading LLC*:[5]

> **26** Both parties accept that, at common law, the identification of the appropriate law may be viewed as involving a three-stage process: (1) characterisation of the relevant issue; (2) selection of the rule of conflict of laws which lays down a connecting factor for that issue; and (3) identification of the system of law which is tied by that connecting factor to that issue: see *Macmillan Inc v Bishopsgate Investment Trust plc (No* 3) [1996] 1 WLR 387, 391-392 per

[5] [2001] 2 WLR 1344 at 1355–6.

Staughton LJ. The process falls to be undertaken in a broad internationalist spirit in accordance with the principles of conflict of laws of the forum, here England.

27 While it is convenient to identify this three-stage process, it does not follow that courts, at the first stage, can or should ignore the effect at the second stage of characterising an issue in a particular way. The overall aim is to identify the most *appropriate law* to govern a particular issue. The classes or categories of issue which the law recognises at the first stage are man-made, not natural. They have no inherent value, beyond their purpose in assisting to select the most appropriate law. A mechanistic application, without regard to the consequences, would conflict with the purpose for which they were conceived. They may require redefinition or modification, or new categories may have to be recognised accompanied by new rules at stage 2, if this is necessary to achieve the overall aim of identifying the most appropriate law . . .

However, the fact that general principles do not work in all situations, and that it may be necessary to have some rules that are very fact-specific, does not mean that general concepts can be abandoned. On the contrary, if the conflict of laws were to become no more than a collection of rules geared to very particular situations it would lose all coherence. Without a conceptual framework the courts would be deprived of the tools for applying existing rules to new situations. Hence it has rightly been argued that a strong case can be made for an international restatement of the principles of the conflict of laws.[6]

There are other conflict of laws issues which are currently under review. One of these arises in the context of the proposed conversion into an EC regulation of the Rome Convention on the law applicable to contractual obligations. Should the regulation permit choice of rules which are not those of a national legal system? In a number of countries this is now permitted in international commercial arbitration where the parties so agree or, in some places, where they have not reached a contrary agreement.[7] The European Commission has posed the question whether, for example, the parties could choose the Vienna Convention on Contracts for the International Sale of Goods (CISG) or the UNIDROIT Principles of International Commercial Contracts as the applicable law. The first of these does not seem to me to be problematic. It is true that to allow the parties to choose CISG would be to impose on a national court the duty to apply CISG as the governing law even if the court were situated in a non-Contracting State, but they could do that anyway by choosing the law of a Contracting State. It is also true that CISG is not a complete legal system, but that too is not a real objection, for to the extent that its provisions do not resolve the issue resort may be had to the otherwise applicable law. By contrast, to permit selection of the Principles of International Commercial Contracts as the applicable law raises an issue of legitimacy, for its effect would be to enable the parties to displace the domestic mandatory rules of the forum State by a set of rules in the preparation of which neither business interests nor governments were involved and which were not subject to any legislative scrutiny.

[6] Herbert Kronke 'Most Significant Relationship, Governmental Interests Cultural Identity, Integration: "Rules" at Will and the Case for Principles of Conflict of Laws' [2004] 3 Uniform Law Rev 467.

[7] As to the choice of 'the lex mercatoria' as the applicable law, see below, p.323.

In separate proposals relating to the preparation of a European contract code the Commission has sought to address the legitimacy question by the novel idea of incorporating the contract code into a regulation which would take effect only in relation to contracts in which the parties had chosen to opt into it. At the same time the Commission has also said that there is a strong case for incorporating into the opt-in code a set of internationally mandatory rules. I should myself have thought it was by definition impossible to have internationally mandatory rules in an optional code but I have no pretensions to be a conflicts lawyer. One thing is clear, though, and that is that the disappearance of some of the old certainties afflicts private international law every bit as much as it afflicts substantive law.

## III. International Trade Usage and the *Lex Mercatoria*

Just as the hegemony of States has been eroded with the growth of international organizations, so also we have seen the emergence of a theory of the autonomy of international trade law, motivated by a strong desire by its proponents to free international transactions from the perceived shackles of national law. In cases where the parties have not chosen a national law, a reference to transnational rules is seen as possessing a number of advantages. It avoids applying to an international contract rules of national law designed primarily for domestic transactions, though this is of limited significance in that most developed countries have laws well able to accommodate cross-border transactions, and scholars have noted that there is a remarkable degree of similarity in the laws of different jurisdictions relating to international trade. Secondly, and more importantly, recourse to principles of substantive transnational law avoids the need to deal with what are sometimes complex issues of private international law and the consequential opportunities for forum shopping to select the jurisdiction whose conflict of laws rules lead to the application of the law most favourable to the claimant. It thus becomes unnecessary to engage in characterization for conflicts purposes, identification of the connecting factor and other conflicts issues or to incur the expense of engaging experts on foreign law. Thirdly, transnational commercial law is seen as party-neutral.

The idea of a new autonomous *lex mercatoria,* reviving the traditions of the mediaeval law merchant based on the practices of merchants and administered by powerful, largely independent, bodies such as the Italian *Mercanzia,* has gripped the imagination of modern scholars. It is not a new idea—the great Leone Levi published a draft international commercial law code as far back as 1863—but is much in vogue among scholars. Many years ago, at a conference on international commercial arbitration organized by the School of International Arbitration within the Centre for Commercial Law Studies at Queen Mary College, that remarkable French scholar Professor Berthold Goldman, sitting as a member of a distinguished group of panellists, commented: 'I think that here, in London, it would not be prudent for me to speak of the *lex mercatoria*!'

Since Goldman was rightly considered one of the founding fathers of the subject, this was self-restraint of truly heroic proportions. Happily it did not last, and he went on to give a paper of crystal clarity on general principles of law and the *lex mercatoria*.[8] The concept of the *lex mercatoria*, initially propounded by Fragistas, Goldstajn, Goldman, and Schmitthoff, has been powerfully developed by modern scholars, in particular Filip De Ly,[9] Ole Lando,[10] Klaus Peter Berger,[11] and Emmanuel Gaillard,[12] to name only a few. But what is the *lex mercatoria?* And is it truly autonomous?

## A. The nature of the *lex mercatoria*

Unfortunately there is no agreement on what the *lex mercatoria* comprises. To some it is merely another label for transnational commercial law and thus encompasses all kinds of harmonization, formal and informal. To others, it is the product of so-called spontaneous international law-making through international trade usage as evidenced by rules of trade associations, standard-term contracts, and general principles and rules and restatements formulated by international agencies. The *lex mercatoria* is propounded as a set of rules which can not only be applied by arbitrators after the event but selected as the applicable law in contracts.

My own preference is to confine the *lex mercatoria* to international trade practice. To equate the *lex mercatoria* with the entirety of transnational commercial law deprives us of a useful label to denote that part of transnational commercial law which derives from the international practice of merchants. To treat as part of the *lex mercatoria* standard-term contracts, codes of practice promulgated by international business organizations, and even international conventions seems to me to confuse customary law, which is surely the essence of the *lex mercatoria,* with contract and treaty law, and to treat as a homogeneous mass things that are quite different in character.[13] In a brilliant essay many years ago[14] Lord Justice Mustill (as he then was) pointed out that the *lex mercatoria* is not intentionally fashioned as an instrument of harmonization; it simply exists as a product of spontaneous generation, whereas international conventions and standard-term international contracts have as their objective the harmonization of rights, duties, and practices. International conventions derive their force from the exercise of sovereign power through the process of ratification and thus form part of national law, not of some independent legal order.

[8] 'The applicable law: general principles of law—the lex mercatoria', in Julian DM Lew (ed) *Contemporary Problems in International Arbitration* (Centre for Commercial Law Studies London 1986) 113.

[9] *International Business Law and the* Lex Mercatoria (North Holland Amsterdam, 1992).

[10] Klaus Peter Berger *The Lex Mercatoria in International Commercial Arbitration* (North Holland Amsterdam 1992).

[11] *The Creeping Codification of the* Lex Mercatoria (2nd edn, Wolters Kluwer, The Netherlands, 2010).

[12] KP Berger (ed) 'Transnational Law: A Legal System or a System of Decision-Making', in *The Practice of Transnational Law* (Kluwer International The Hague 2001) 53.

[13] For a similar criticism of the tendency to lump together legalized and non-legalized rules in international law, see Anne-Marie Slaughter 'International law and international relations theory: a prospectus', in Eyal Benvenisti and Moshe Hirsch (eds) *The Impact of International Law on International Cooperation* (CUP 2004) 16 at 41. I am indebted to Lady Fox for drawing my attention to this paper.

[14] 'The New Lex Mercatoria: The First Twenty-five Years', in Maarten Bos and Ian Brownlie (eds) *Liber Amicorum for Lord Wilberforce* (Clarendon Press Oxford 1987) 149 at 152–3.

In principle, private law conventions, like private contracts, bind only those who become parties to them, in sharp contrast to customary law, which is more general in character. As to the utility of standard-term contracts as a source of law it would be helpful to be given some specifics of the rules to be extracted from such contracts so that we could form a judgment on whether they were sufficiently precise to be useful and how far they could be said to represent a generally adopted market approach.[15]

Though a number of scholars claim that contracts create law, my view is that contracts cannot by themselves constitute a source of law; they have effect only by virtue of recognition by a national legal system. Clive Schmitthoff, who was one of the leading exponents of the modern *lex mercatoria*, is regularly invoked as a progenitor of the idea that there is an autonomous law of international trade created by spontaneous generation and owing nothing to national laws or sovereign powers, and that an important aspect of this was the international contract. What is often overlooked is that while Schmitthoff accepted that parties to international contracts were largely free to make their own law, his clearly stated view was that the parties enjoyed this power only by the will of sovereign States, alone or acting in concert, and it was subject to important exceptions, for example, those based on public policy or overriding mandatory rules. It is true that Schmitthoff frequently referred to the autonomous law of international trade but it is clear that by that he meant only that, *under the authority given by States,* parties were free to subject themselves by contract to sources of law other than national laws and to organise their relations as they thought fit.[16]

No contract can speak to its own validity and no legal system allows complete freedom to contracting parties, whose agreement is everywhere bounded by rules of public policy and mandatory rules. Accordingly, though a valid contract is undoubtedly a source of legal rights, every contract is required to satisfy certain external criteria of validity. Nor can the arbitration process elevate the status of contracts, as some have claimed, for it is everywhere accepted that unless otherwise agreed arbitrators must decide in accordance with legal rules. In Mann's words, *lex facit arbitrum.*[17]

What of general principles of law? Though it is common to treat the *lex mercatoria* as including general principles of law, and I myself used to follow this approach, it seems to me on further reflection that these principles—for example, *pacta sunt servanda*, the *nemo dat* rule, and the duty to mitigate loss suffered from a breach of contract—are not particular to international trade or even to commercial contracts, are qualified by numerous exceptions and tell us nothing about the process of spontaneous lawmaking which is said to be the hallmark of the *lex mercatoria.* If we look

[15] To illustrate some of the difficulties, Mustill observes (n 14, above, at 158–9) that 'a single institution within a single trade may publish a repertoire of different and mutually inconsistent documents from which the contracting parties may choose the most suitable to reflect the balance of their bargain; there coexist in many trades a number of institutions, each offering its own standard form, and is, of course, a commonplace that parties alter the standard forms to suit their own purposes. Thus there is no guarantee of homogeneity even within a single trade.'

[16] *The Sources of the Law of International Trade* 4–5.

[17] The title of his famous contribution to *a Liber Amicorum* for Martin Domke.

at the lists of rules of the *lex mercatoria* propounded by modern scholars and remove from it general principles of law, we find that almost nothing is left, while on the other hand there is a conspicuous absence of references to important modern usages in relation to documentary credits, demand guarantees, and clearing and settlement systems for the transfer of funds and investment securities. Professor Jan Dalhuisen is one of the few scholars to draw attention to the fact that usages of the financial markets are every bit as important as usages of trade.[18] It would be different if we had general principles of *international trade* law, but these are never mentioned, for what is to me the self-evident reason that they do not exist; we simply have usages of a particular trade or locality. So I would follow the international lawyers in treating general principles of law as a separate source, thus confining the *lex mercatoria* to international trade usage, which is surely the epitome of spontaneous law-creation.

## B. Is the *lex mercatoria* autonomous?

The concept of autonomy means different things to different people. There is *de facto* autonomy in that for the most part the business community is left free to develop its own practices and give effect to them through its own rules, contracts and dispute resolution procedures. Since the legality of what is done and decided is not usually questioned, we can say that as a practical matter the custom of merchants and the rules they formulate for the future conduct of transactions do operate as law within the business community, whether or not they have the force of law. I believe that the failure to distinguish *lex mercatoria as law* from its observance as a matter of *practice* accounts for much of the misunderstanding that exists between those who propound the existence of a *lex mercatoria* and those who deny it. As law the *lex mercatoria* consists of binding usage and depends in the last resort on recognition by national law. As observed practice the *lex mercatoria* is not dependent on external legal recognition at all, for it is not truly *lex*. It simply exists, and it is effective because business people in the relevant community perceive its observance as necessary to the fair and efficient conduct of business, so that the sanction for failure to follow the practice is not a legal sanction but opprobrium from fellow businessmen, their unwillingness to deal with the culprit and, in the last resort, expulsion from the relevant mercantile community. *Lex mercatoria* as practice is thus almost as potent as a true law, and this is why it has been described by some leading scholars as operating at the periphery of the legal process[19] and as soft law but not weak law.[20]

There is also de jure autonomy to the extent that merchants are left free by sovereign authority to make their own laws and settle their own disputes without regard to the ordinary laws of the land. But while the parties to a contract may to a large degree subject themselves to rules which do not depend on any particular national

[18] *Dalhuisen on International Commercial, Financial and Trade Law* (2nd edn Hart Publishing Oxford 2004) 27.

[19] Gunther Teubner '"Global Bukowina": Legal Pluralism in the World Society', in *Global Law Without a State* (Dartmouth Ashurst Aldershot 1997) 3 at 12.

[20] ibid at 21.

legal system, their autonomy is not absolute, since it is universally recognised that contracts must give way to internationally mandatory rules and *lois de police.* As Montesquieu pointed out long ago, in his great work *De L'Esprit des Lois,* it is necessary to distinguish freedom of contract from freedom of commerce:

> The freedom of commerce is not power granted to the merchants to do what they please; this would be more properly its slavery. The constraint of the merchant is not the constraint of commerce ... The English constrain the merchant, but it is in favour of commerce.

## C. Usages and codes of practice

Usages (in the sense of practices that have acquired normative force) are to be distinguished from rules set out in codes of practice promulgated by trade and professional organizations for the benefit of their members or for a particular business sector, which take effect in the first instance by express or implied incorporation into contracts. Take as an example the widely adopted Uniform Customs and Practice for Documentary Credits. These *may* be evidence of pre-existing usage but this will not be true of all the terms, since there will inevitably be some departures in order to improve current practice; indeed, some of the 'rules' are merely precatory indications of desirable practice, such as the avoidance of excessive detail in a credit. Again, a codification *may* in due course establish new usages, but only when it becomes generally known and widely adopted. The UCP were first published in the year I was born and are now undergoing yet another revision. Each revision introduces changes, and it usually takes several years for some sectors of the banking community even to wake up to the existence of a new revision. So there is always a period in which changes effected by a new revision take effect solely by express or implied incorporation into a contract, binding on the parties to the contract but not on participants generally, as in the case of usage.

There is no question that codes of practice, though contractual in origin, may make a powerful contribution to transnational commercial law by engendering new usages which do not depend for their force on express contractual incorporation. For example, there are certain concepts underlying every revision of the UCP which are so fundamental that they can be regarded as basic principles of documentary credits law, derived from the UCP but no longer dependent on them. I refer to the principle that a letter of credit creates a commitment independent of the underlying contract; that banks deal in documents, not in goods; that a bank acting in good faith can safely pay against documents which on a reasonable examination appear to conform to the credit, even if they are forged or otherwise fraudulent. Also of great importance are usages of financial markets relating to the irrevocability of payment and securities transfer instructions and the finality of transfers.

## D. Uncodified usages

Uncodified usages are inherently more difficult to establish, for they generally depend on expert evidence. It is hard enough to satisfy a court of the existence of a local usage, let alone a usage prevalent on an international market. When does international commercial practice acquire normative force as a usage? Here there are striking parallels between usage in private law and customary international law. The traditional principle of public international law has been that State practice, even if consistently adopted, does not by itself create a rule of customary international law; *usus* must be conjoined with *opinio juris,* that is, observance of the practice not as a matter of courtesy or convenience but in the belief that it is legally binding. A similar rule has been held to obtain in private law as regards the binding force of usage, which requires a consistently adopted practice observed from a sense of binding obligation.

However, there is much difficulty in the supposed requirement that the practice be observed from a belief in its legally binding nature, for if the belief is true it is unnecessary, whereas if it is false that is a strange basis for giving the practice binding force. Moreover, the *opinio juris* requirement would seem to make it impossible for a new usage to develop. One could substitute a collective intention or a collective will to be bound which looks to the future, but this would be to ascribe to the business community a collective mental state which is rather unreal.[21] It is therefore interesting to see that despite a not insignificant line of authority which appeared to be to the contrary, the International Law Association, in its Resolution 16/2000,[22] robustly rejected the requirement of *opinio juris,* adopting the Report of its Committee[23] and of the Committee's Chairman Professor Maurice Mendelson in his Hague lectures,[24] that while *opinio juris* may be a sufficient basis for a rule of international customary law it is not a requirement. It suffices that the practice is uniform, extensive, and representative of States whose interests are specially affected.[25] This view is not uncontroversial. However, it is also significant that no subjective element is to be found in §1-205 of the American Uniform Commercial Code or in Article 9 of the Vienna Convention on Contracts for the International Sale of Goods (CISG). The former adopts the helpful test that the usage must have such regularity of observance as to justify an expectation that it will be observed with respect to the transaction in question. This would place on the party challenging the binding nature of the usage the onus of showing that it was followed purely for convenience or by way of a voluntary accommodation of a customer's wishes. And on this basis there is no reason why minor or occasional departures from a settled practice should displace its binding nature.

That approach would have avoided the difficulties that arose in *Libyan Arab Foreign Bank v Bankers Trust* Co.[26] In that case, which arose out of a dispute between

[21] See to the same effect in relation to international customary law Philip Allott 'The Concept of International Law', in Michael Byers (ed) *The Role of Law in International Politics* (OUP Oxford 2000) 69 at 77.

[22] Formation of General Customary International Law.

[23] The Committee on the Formation of Customary (General) International Law: Final Report of the Committee (2000).

[24] Maurice H Mendelson *The Formation of Customary International Law* (Martins Nijhoff The Hague 1999) 285 ff.

[25] Final Report (above, n 23), pp 20 ff.

[26] [1989] QB 728.

the United States and Libya, a claim for repayment of a Eurodollar deposit with the London branch of an American bank was resisted on the ground that it was a usage of the Eurodollar market that withdrawals could be made only by transfer through a clearing system in the country of the denominated currency, which in the instant case was CHIPS in New York, where the transfer would have been blocked by a Presidential order prohibiting transfers to Libyan nationals. Staughton J held that the expert evidence did not establish such a usage and that the plaintiff was entitled to payment in a variety of other ways not involving a step in the United States, and went on to hold, perhaps more surprisingly, that this included cash, notwithstanding the slight practical difficulty in that the amount involved was some $292 million!

That part of the decision in the *Libyan Arab Foreign Bank* case dealing with international trade usage was probably inevitable given the traditional approach then prevailing and the way the expert evidence turned out. It is interesting to re-examine the case in the light of the suggested new approach. The fact that the vast majority in number and value of withdrawals from the Eurodollar account were made through CHIPS would suffice to establish the asserted usage. The relatively small number and value of transactions effected otherwise than through CHIPS would be discounted as being done to help a customer and not because it was a settled practice. The huge cost and inconvenience created for both parties by large withdrawals in cash compared with inter-bank transfers would not only support the usage of inter-bank transfer through CHIPS but also justify the implication of a term against the right to cash withdrawals which, as Francis Mann himself pointed out, could not seriously have been contemplated by either party.[27]

## E. Choice of the *lex mercatoria* as the applicable law

Connected to the question of the autonomy of the *lex mercatoria* is its suitability for selection as the applicable law. It is not an objection that the *lex mercatoria* is not a complete legal system for its rules, so far as identifiable, may suffice to solve the question in issue and, where they do not, recourse may be had to the otherwise applicable law. A more serious objection is their indeterminacy. It was this that led most of the respondents to a worldwide survey carried out by the Center for Transnational Law (CENTER)[28] to say that as international lawyers they were strongly opposed to the selection of the *lex mercatoria* as the governing law.[29] I agree with this. No doubt it is possible after the event for an arbitrator, armed with all the relevant facts, to identify a rule of the *lex mercatoria* applicable to the case in hand. It is quite another to extrapolate from this *ex post* identifiability the *ex ante* ability to determine that the *lex mercatoria* would be suitable as a governing law for a dispute that has not yet arisen and the nature of which may be difficult, if not impossible, to foresee.

[27] *The Legal Aspect of Money* (5th edn Clarendon Press Oxford 1992), 201. See now 6th edn (Prosser ed OUP Oxford 2005) para 7.10.

[28] Then based at Miinster University but now relocated in the University of Cologne.

[29] Klaus Peter Berger 'The New Law Merchant and the Global Market Place', in Berger (ed) *The Practice of Transnational Law* (above n 2) 1 at 1-2.

## IV. The International Restatement

This brings me to what is perhaps the most interesting development of the last quarter of the 20th century, the international restatement of contract law. I refer, of course, to the UNIDROIT Principles of International Commercial Contracts, completed earlier this year and paralleled at the regional level by the Principles of European Contract Law, an initiative of the Commission on European Contract Law. The idea is borrowed from the American Restatements published by the American Law Institute. The UNIDROIT Principles are the work of scholars and did not involve governments. Like the American Restatements they are in a sense a private initiative but one given particular status by the fact that they were produced under the aegis of an international, intergovernmental organization and formally endorsed by its Governing Council.

The Principles, like the Restatements, do not have the force of law, since they are not issued by a lawmaker. Nevertheless, they are different in character from rules produced by such bodies of the International Chamber of Commerce, for the latter are essentially rules of *practice,* which do not necessarily reflect pre-existing usage but take effect by contractual incorporation. By contrast the Principles are designed as rules of law, and in that regard they have proved unexpectedly influential, blurring the distinction between *lex lata* and *lex ferenda.* They offer a set of rules produced and agreed by scholars representative of the main legal families of the world which, though deriving their inspiration from many legal systems, are not the rules of any one system and in various instances offer new solutions. Like the American Restatements they do not merely state common principles, they also somewhat extend them, as in the provisions relating to hardship[30] and change of circumstances.[31] They are a resource for those courts and arbitral tribunals who find them helpful—there have been numerous arbitral awards invoking them—and also provide a guide to legislatures seeking to codify or modernize their contract law. It may surprise some that the Principles not only defer to internationally mandatory rules but also contain mandatory rules of their own. I have explained elsewhere why the apparent paradox of including mandatory rules in non-binding Principles is not as strange as it might seem.[32] Finally, what the Principles demonstrate is that the formulation of international rules of general law, whether relating to international trade or otherwise, is best left to scholars, leaving governments and regional organizations such as the European Union to focus on more specific areas—for example, competition law, and consumer protection—where the rules are essentially mandatory rules or rules of public policy rather than dispositive provisions. Governments would have found it of little interest to engage in a project not intended to lead to a legally operative instrument, while business interests, which are essentially directed to ensuring that the

[30] Principles of International Commercial Contracts, Arts 6.2.1–6.2.3.

[31] Principles of European Contract Law, Art 6.111.

[32] Roy Goode 'International Restatements of Contract and English Contract Law' 1997-2 Uniform Law Review 231 at 246.

law facilitates transactions, have only a reduced role to play in principles of a general character covering an entire field of law.

## V. International Commercial Law Conventions

I come now to the final part of my lecture, the harmonization through international conventions. I want to consider two issues: the purpose and scope of harmonization; and resolution of the tensions arising in international lawmaking to which I briefly alluded earlier.

### A. The purpose and scope of harmonization

There are broadly two approaches to harmonization. One is that differences in national laws are *per se* undesirable, causing difficulties for business and for the operation of a common market, so that harmonization is a virtue in itself without further need for justification. Within the field of European Community law that approach appeared for a long time to be an article of faith of the European Commission and perhaps still is. The other approach, as regards commercial transactions, is that harmonization should be focused on what is needed to remove serious impediments to cross-border business. Both approaches are likely to carry with them improvements in existing legal regimes. Though a necessary start to a harmonization project is to engage in a comparative survey of existing laws and practices within the field of the project, it would be an exercise in futility merely to identify the lowest common denominators. What those engaged in any project are, or should be, concerned to produce is a set of rules designed to provide the most sensible answers to typical questions.

At the international level the desirability of uniform rules is perceived primarily in relation to international transactions, typically defined as transactions between persons having their places of business in different States. All UNCITRAL and UNIDROIT texts are focused on international situations. There is good sense in this approach. Legal systems vary widely in concepts, philosophy, and culture as well as in their institutional infrastructure. The sensitivity of sovereign States and their business communities to an interference with their domestic law is much less acute when confined to cross-border transactions, where the interests of foreigners have to be respected and where rules of law designed primarily for local dealings are not always well suited to an international environment. The position is otherwise in the case of regional harmonization, where it may be found desirable to harmonize business laws governing domestic as well as cross-border transactions in order to facilitate a common market and to provide a negotiating power in external relations which might otherwise be lacking. A prime example of regional economic integration is, of course, the European Union. Others include NAFTA, Mercosur and, more recently, OHADA. The international status of regional economic integration organizations has been enhanced by the recent practice of including in international commercial law conventions a provision enabling such organizations to assume the rights and obligations of a Contracting State on matters within the convention in respect of which they have had competence transferred to them by their sovereign Member States.[33]

Let me now examine the two purposes of harmonization in a little more detail.

## 1. *Uniformity for its own sake*

The substitution of a uniform, or broadly uniform, set of rules for the variety of rules provided by different national legal systems is said to increase legal predictability and reduce transaction costs. To the extent that domestic laws are dispositive there is little empirical evidence that they constitute a significant impediment to cross-border business and quite a strong view from industry that they do not. The business community is much more concerned with the consistency of decision-making—one of the attractions of English law, with its doctrine of judicial precedent—and with enforceability. The impact of differences in dispositive rules can easily be eliminated by contractual provisions which lay down a common set of rights and duties applicable in all relevant jurisdictions.

Yet even in the field of dispositive law it has been found convenient to have a uniform law as a gap-filler to deal with cases where the parties have dealt with each other informally without making a detailed agreement or where their written contract does not cover the point at issue. This is the primary function of Part III of the 1980 Convention on Contracts for the International Sale of Goods (CISG). CISG, which is again being considered for ratification by the United Kingdom, has become the central reference point for other private law harmonizing instruments, whether these take the form of international conventions, model laws or restatements such as the UNIDROIT Principles of International Commercial Contracts or the Principles of European Contract Law prepared by the Commission on European Contract Law. Yet CISG is very distinctive in at least two respects. First, as I have said, its provisions on the rights and duties of parties to a contract of sale are, with two exceptions, entirely dispositive. This feature is unique to CISG and is not to be found in any subsequent international convention. It is no doubt justified by the central importance of sale as an international transaction and by the fact that many international sales are concluded informally, so that it is useful to have a set of gap-filling rules. This same feature may also be used to explain the second feature of CISG, namely its relatively comprehensive character as regards the contractual aspects of sale. There are few, if any, other types of contract so central or so susceptible to informality as to justify such a massive statement of dispositive rules.

I doubt whether we shall ever again see the emergence of international conventions possessing these twin characteristics. Though many commercial law conventions incorporate some provisions as to the rights and duties of contracting parties in

[33] Convention on International Interests in Mobile Equipment 2001, Art 48; Convention on the law applicable to certain rights in respect of securities held with an intermediary 2002, Art 18.

the absence of contrary agreement, these tend to be ancillary to broader objectives. As I have said, the coverage of a complete field in core subjects such as the law of obligations and the law of property is best left to scholars, who possess both the technical expertise and freedom from political constraints. Outside the law of international sale, and perhaps even within it, uniformity in a general field is no longer seen as a sufficient end in itself; on the contrary, research by Professor Doreen McBarnet shows that practitioners welcome diversity because it gives them choice and the ability to achieve their primary objective, namely to secure the best legal regime they can for their clients.[34] Commercial lawyers here will remember the golden days of the so-called double dip, when the fact that a transaction characterized as a lease under English law was treated as a conditional sale under American law enabled both parties to obtain capital allowances.[35]

In any event the focus of interest has moved sharply from contract to property, since it is in the field of property rights, priorities, and insolvency effects that the deficiencies in national legal systems and their inadequacy to handle cross-border transactions are at their most acute.

## *2. Removal of specific impediments to cross-border business*

This brings me to the second objective of transnational commercial law, namely to clarify and improve rules which in national systems are non-existent, undeveloped, unclear, or unsuited to international transactions, and thereby remove impediments to cross-border trading which the parties cannot resolve by agreement under national law. Every commercial law convention since CISG has been motivated by this problem-oriented approach. This in turn has led to a growing boldness on the part of the harmonizing agencies who are now prepared to move into areas previously taboo, such as property rights, priorities, and even to a limited degree insolvency law. The focus is now on the rules to preserve the efficacy and finality of transactions and to reduce risk, including settlement risk. Property rights were excluded from CISG as too complex; priority issues were excluded from the UNIDROIT factoring convention for the same reason; insolvency was long considered a no-go area. All of this has changed. The Cape Town Convention on International Interests in Mobile Equipment, the Aircraft Equipment Protocol and the UN Receivables Financing Convention contain rules governing priority and the effects of insolvency; the Hague Securities Convention provides conflict rules primarily aimed at the proprietary aspects of dealings in securities held with an intermediary; and the current UNIDROIT project on substantive rules for securities held with an intermediary is a further example of an initiative designed to overcome problems created by the inadequacies of existing national legal systems.

[34] 'Transnational transactions: legal work, cross-border commerce and global regulation', in Michael Likosky (ed) *Transnational Legal Process: Globalization and Power Disparities* (CUP Cambridge 2002) 100 at 109–10.

[35] In the UK this loophole was subsequently closed by legislation.

The most ambitious problem-solving convention to date is without doubt the 2001 Cape Town Convention on International Interests in Mobile Equipment, which addresses the problem of taking and retaining rights *in rem* in assets such as aircraft objects, railway rolling stock, and space assets that are constantly moving from one jurisdiction to another or, in the case of satellites, are not on earth at all. The Convention creates an entirely new juridical institution, the international interest, covering the supply of aircraft objects, railway rolling stock, and space assets under security agreements and conditional sale and leasing agreements and, under the associated Aircraft Equipment Protocol, outright sales of aircraft. Nor is this all. The Convention further creates a means of perfecting such interests by registration in a new international register administered by a registrar under the aegis of a Supervisory Authority, thereby securing priority and protection in the event of the debtor's insolvency. And the aircraft equipment protocol has optional clauses dealing in detail with the creditor's right to remove aircraft equipment from the control of the insolvency administrator. The Convention is also interesting in that while it is primarily a private law convention, certain obligations are imposed on Contracting States, including the provision of a procedural regime for speedy interim relief. Nice questions arise as to a creditor's remedy in international law against a Contracting State which fails in this vitally important obligation.

Work in progress on the draft space protocol shows the complexity of issues relating to complex objects and the absolute necessity of substantial technical and technological input, which I have already demonstrated in relation to the Hague Securities Convention. Satellites are almost entirely one-purpose objects, so that the true value of the security lies in the associated payment and performance contracts rather than in the object itself; in other ways, space financing is project finance disguised as asset finance. There are many components that go into or are affixed to a satellite. The most prominent are transponders but there are other types of asset, including some not yet developed, which may need to become the subject of separate registrable interests even though it may be difficult to recover them separately from the satellite itself. This prospect of multiple and co-ownership registrations has to be addressed in legal rules which have yet to be developed.

These examples show that where the need is sufficiently pressing there are few, if any, no-go areas for private law conventions. At regional level the European Community has been in the vanguard of such an approach with its important directives on settlement finality[36] and financial collateral,[37] designed to avoid excessive formalism in the acquisition of rights in financial collateral and to safeguard security interests against rules of national insolvency law considered inimical to the smooth functioning of the securities market.

[36] Directive on Settlement Finality in Payment and Security Systems, 98/26/EC dated 19 May 1998.
[37] Directive on Financial Collateral Arrangements, 2002/47/EC dated 6 June 2002.

## B. The tensions arising in the preparation of international conventions

The preparation of international conventions is arduous and time-consuming and calls for immense patience, mutual respect, and a very great deal of hard work. Even where these qualities are present—as they usually are, particularly in drafting committees, which are the work horse of study groups and Diplomatic Conferences—tensions can arise which are not related to the quality of the work. Time permits me to mention only four of them.

The first arises from the fact that the sophistication of commercial law is directly related to the volume and diversity of business transactions. The greater the volume of business, the more diverse the instruments and the wider the range of problems that will be encountered by the business community and the courts. This in turn is a factor of the degree of freedom given to business people to make their own law and to devise their own instruments, structures, and governing rules. This *laissez-faire* approach is much less acceptable to civil law jurisdictions, particularly in the field of property law, where there are many rules which constitute a serious impediment to modern methods of dealing and finance. I refer in particular to strict formalities, a restricted view of admissible property rights, a requirement of specificity of subject-matter, a hostile attitude towards non-possessory security interests, difficulties with the concept of real rights in after-acquired property, the absence of effective perfection requirements and facilities, the lack of the trust except in attenuated form, and restrictions on resort to contractual self-help remedies.

In a highly developed financial centre whose laws embody a *laissez-faire* philosophy, there will be more solutions to a greater number of problems than in a jurisdiction which has a lower degree of commercial activity. It is an undisputed fact that although substantial volumes of business are transacted in many commercial capitals of the world, the leaders by a long margin are New York and London, the laws of whose countries are in consequence regularly chosen as the governing law by parties to contracts that have no necessary connection with the United States or England. And this creates a problem, because those from other jurisdictions, particularly the major civil law jurisdictions, rightly take pride in their own legal systems and do not wish to find the preparatory proceedings dominated by Anglo-American laws and lawyers. This is a point to which the English and Americans have to be particularly sensitive. My own experience of working with colleagues from a variety of countries, including France, Germany, Italy, the Netherlands, the Scandinavian countries, Japan, and China, is that they are very open-minded but find a number of concepts of the common law unfamiliar and requiring explanation, so that one has to proceed step by step in a process of familiarization. Some of the difficulties of civil law to which I have alluded in regard to property rights have begun to be resolved as a response to the needs of international commerce and finance and the desire of countries to ensure that their legal systems remain competitive, though the changes have been gradual and fragmented.

But the learning process is by no means one-way. The civilians have just as much to contribute as to receive. They bring with them a concept of system, a high degree of intellectual rigour, and a keen perception of the need to balance other interests against commercial interests. So they may feel that some proposed rules are too creditor-friendly and give insufficient weight to the interests of debtors, while other rules fail to take account of long-established legal traditions, such as rules restricting self-help. These sensitivities need to be respected and accommodated. The civilians also appreciate drafting that is not only accurate but elegant and light.

The second tension relates to new players on the international scene. There has long been a feeling that transnational law is dominated by developed countries and is then imposed on developing countries and new market economies, who may feel that their views are not being adequately considered. In most cases these concerns can be overcome by mutual respect and attentiveness to differing viewpoints and by ensuring that representatives of developing countries are included in study groups, working parties and drafting committees. Sometimes it helps if a State with well-developed laws is given a leadership role within its region. For example, at the Diplomatic Conference in Cape Town on the mobile equipment convention—a conference superbly hosted by the Government of South Africa—the African States, though representing and participating individually, were happy to entrust leadership of their interventions to South Africa, with very good results.

The third tension relates to the maintenance of a balance between pressure from commercial interests and respect for the rights of others. We have to face the reality that the business community, by virtue of its intimate knowledge of the workings of commerce and finance, is best equipped to identify the problems and to come up with solutions and international business organizations must be major players from the very outset of a harmonization project. At the same time we must ensure that other interests are respected, and where the balance is drawn is likely to vary from State to State. It is not the function of an international convention simply to reproduce provisions found in standard-term contracts. This is not always understood. There were some practitioners in the leasing industry who complained that the dispositive provisions of the UNIDROIT Convention on International Financial Leasing did not reflect the typical terms of a finance lease, with its hell-or-high-water clauses for payment of rent, its provisions for damages on termination for default, and the like. I pointed out that the function of any transactional law is to maintain a balance of interests. We do not frame our sales legislation to reflect sellers' standard terms of business. Similarly with leasing. If lessors want additional rights, they must do what they have also done, namely negotiate to have their own standard terms accepted.

There are various ways in which a balance may be achieved in the preparation of convention rules: a compromise approach to a proposed rule; the provision of variants, leaving it to each Contracting State to decide which it prefers; the insertion of provisions allowing a State to opt out of rules too much at variance with its legal traditions or limiting the application of rules to those States that opt into them.[38] All these techniques are to be found in the Mobile Equipment Convention, and there is

[38] Jeffrey Wool 'Rethinking the Notion of Uniformity in the Drafting of International Commercial Law: A Preliminary Proposal for the Development of a Policy-Based Unification Model' 1997-1 Uniform Law Review 46.

no doubt that they were in no small measure responsible for the fact that on the last day of the Diplomatic Conference no fewer than 20 States signed a Convention of 62 Articles and an Aircraft Equipment Protocol of 37 Articles—a total of 99 Articles in all and in my view a major achievement.

There is, however, a fourth form of tension that potentially arises from regional harmonization. Of particular significance is the exercise by the European Union of external competence in the negotiation and conclusion of international conventions. The subject is one of considerable complexity on which others are much better placed to speak than I am. I will therefore confine myself to two aspects, namely the way in which Community competence may influence negotiations for an international convention and the admission of the European Union to membership of international organizations such as UNIDROIT and The Hague Conference.

The relationship between regional commitments and international obligations is a matter of some delicacy. The European Union has to respect international law. On the other hand, Member States are not permitted to enter into international conventions on their own where these fall wholly or partly within the competence of the European Union, and in cases of mixed competence they must act in collaboration with the Union. The two international conventions previously mentioned—the 2001 Cape Town Convention and the 2002 Hague Convention—which enable the European Union to accede to them. In that event the EU has the rights and obligations of a Contracting State to the extent of its competence over matters governed by the convention, though it does not count as an additional Contracting State where numbers are relevant.

In participating in a Diplomatic Conference in a field in which the European Union has competence, Member States are not free to go their own way but are bound by any mandate from the Council and by any common negotiating position established pursuant to that mandate. Given that international conventions in the field of private commercial law not only require precision of thought and drafting but are increasingly technical in some of their aspects, it is important that Member States shall be able to make a meaningful contribution to the debates and to respond to constantly evolving argument. This can be achieved by the holding of co-ordinating meetings of Member States during the Diplomatic Conference, but it is essential, first, that the mandate given by the Council permits of reasonable flexibility and, second, that the Commission negotiators are properly briefed and have a full understanding of the legal as well as the policy issues. There is at least one instance where this was not the case and a serious problem was encountered which was resolved only by the speedy response of COREPER to representations from delegations.

Another issue relates to the stage at which Member States become subject to an inhibition on independent contributions to debates. I recall at least one instance of a meeting held prior to the Diplomatic Conference where the Presidency sought to assert that until the European Union had settled on a negotiating position on matters within its competence delegates from Member States should not participate in discussion of those matters. Adherence to such an injunction would, of course, have been disastrous, because it would have left all the running to delegates from outside Europe, leaving Europe effectively disenfranchised pending settlement of a common position. Fortunately the ruling was dropped after protests, and the meeting proceeded in the ordinary way. I think these incidents show the wisdom of Bismarck's famous remark that 'those who love laws and sausages should not ask how they are made'!

The issue of freedom of Member States to take part in pre-Conference discussions on draft conventions is to some extent linked to the question of EU membership of bodies such as UNIDROIT and The Hague Conference. This is now under discussion. Such membership is permitted by the UNIDROIT statute but not by the Hague statute, which would have to be amended. It would in my view be essential to be clear as to the implications of such membership for the ability of delegates, where participating as representatives of their governments rather than as individuals, to play their normal rule in examining drafts and proposing additions and amendments.

## VI. ENVOI

It is now time to draw the threads together and bring this talk to a close. We should modify the traditional *opinio juris* rule to make it easier to establish a binding international usage. We should recognise the strength of the desire to have recourse to sources other than national laws in determining disputes, while adhering to the concept that freedom of contract is in the last resort limited by what sovereign States will accept. In work on international conventions the participants should respect the sensitivities and respond to the tensions to which I have referred. International conventions should be clearly drafted and sharply problem-oriented and experts from the business sectors involved should be encouraged to participate actively in the work from the outset and to contribute their detailed expertise. But it is also necessary to have regard to fundamental values and to ensure a fair balance of competing interests, so that the policy of *laissez-faire* which is a central tenet of commercial law in common law jurisdictions is counter-balanced by a due respect for the safeguards to which civil law jurisdictions attach such importance. It is primarily for scholars and participating governments to bring this about.

International lawmaking is immensely time-consuming, but it is important that the time be found. As so often in his lifetime, the last word lies with Francis Mann:

> If I ask myself what is the most important lesson which my life teaches, the answer, I believe, is one that will come as a surprise to many; it is that there is time for everything or, in other words, nothing will have to remain undone on the ground that there is no time for it.[39]

[39] Unpublished autobiography, 204–5. I am indebted to Mr Richard Hart of Hart Publishing for lending me his copy of the autobiography.

# 21

# Is the *Lex Mercatoria* Autonomous?*

*Roy Goode*

Jan Hellner was a scholar of outstanding range and power. A leading authority in sales law, who played a prominent role in the reform of the Swedish Sale of Goods Act, he was equally at home in the fields of international sales and domestic and comparative law relating to insurance, tort, contract, and informatics. He spoke and wrote in English as elegantly and effortlessly as in his native Swedish and his annual *Julschrift*, with learned pieces in both languages, was a delight. In tribute to his international standing he was elected a corresponding fellow of the British Academy in 1991. Though he was direct in manner and reticent by nature, I recall with affection the warmth of his hospitality and visits to his flat where he had a splendid collection of glassware (later donated to Stockholm University) and objets d'art. He will be sadly missed.

## I. Introduction

### The theory of the modern *lex mercatoria*

There is no doubt of the influence of commercial practice on the development of commercial law. Judges do not decide cases in some legal vacuum; they are acutely sensitive to legitimate commercial needs and strive to give effect to new types of transaction which do not fit neatly into existing legal pigeon holes. It is therefore true to say that parties to commercial transactions are given a wide licence to 'make their own law'. This fact, coupled with the globalization of finance and commerce, has led several scholars of international repute to postulate not only a revival in modern form of the mediaeval *lex mercatoria* but its autonomous character in the sense of being a legal system independent of national laws. Early progenitors of the concept of the *lex mercatoria* were Berthold Goldman and Clive Schmitthoff. In a series of writings Goldman concluded that the *lex mercatoria* existed independently of national legal systems and constituted a legal system, though not a complete

* First Published in Juridisk Tidskrift (2000) 2 253. Reproduced with permission of the Stockholm Centre for Commercial Law, Stockholm University

one.[1] Schmitthoff, by contrast, regarded the *lex mercatoria* as rules of international origin fashioned by merchants but dependent on national laws for recognition,[2] a point often overlooked by commentators who invoke Schmitthoff's name to support a wholly autonomous law merchant. Since then a vast literature on the subject has developed.[3] A leading modern exponent of the autonomous nature of the *lex mercatoria* is Professor Gunter Teubner, who argues that contract is not only a source of law but the primary source and that while it requires recognition by other legal orders this is only a secondary consideration, for recognition is not constitutive of the existence of a legal order.[4] On this view the paradox of a self-validating contract—the so-called *contrat sans loi,* which most scholars reject[5]—is resolved by private externalization, that is, by referring conditions of validity not to a court or other tribunal established by the State but to private institutions created by the business community itself, most notably arbitration and arbitral organizations.[6] Others too ascribe the autonomous character of the *lex mercatoria* to self-supervision by the business community. Contracts may be enforced in various ways which do not involve recourse to national law or national courts. One such method is reference to an arbitral tribunal; another consists of sanctions imposed by trade associations, such as black lists, withdrawal of membership, and forfeiture of bonds.[7] Thus the evolution of the modern *lex mercatoria* is characterized by the declining role of the nation State, its laws and its institutions in the field of transnational commercial law, rules of national law giving way to those of a transnational legal system.

A transnational understanding of modern commercial law has an important effect on the doctrine of private international law. Neither the parties' agreement to have the lex mercatoria applied to their contract nor the application of this transnational commercial law by international arbitrators in the absence of a choice of law by the parties lead to a *'contrat sans loi'*. International arbitrators who apply the lex mercatoria do not act in a legal vacuum, nor do they render a decision in equity. Instead, they apply the rules and principles of transnational legal system, and their award will be respected by domestic courts.[8]

## What is the *lex mercatoria*?

A threshold problem is that there is no agreement on the nature and sources of the *lex mercatoria.* Some, such as Professor Ole Lando, equate it with transnational

[1] Berthold Goldman, *Lex Mercatoria,* Forum internationale No 3 (Kluwer, Deventer, 1983) 22.

[2] 'It is, therefore, wrong to attribute the character of international or supranational law to international trade law. It acquires its autonomous character by leave and licence of all national sovereigns. Its character is very different from public international law. Ultimately it is founded on national law ...' (Clive Schmitthoff, *Commercial Law in a Changing Economic Climate* (2nd edn, Sweet & Maxwell, London, 1981) 22.

[3] This is well described by Filip De Ly, *International Business Law and* Lex Mercatoria (North-Holland, Amsterdam, 1992), Chapter IV.

[4] Gunther Teubner, 'Global Bukowina': Legal Pluralism in the World Society', in *Global Law Without a State* (Ashgate, Aldershot, 1997), 3, 18–19.

[5] See further below, p. 338.

[6] Teubner (n. 4) 16–17.

[7] Klaus Peter Berger, *The Creeping Codification of the* Lex Mercatoria (Kluwer Law International, The Hague, 1999) 29.

[8] *ibid,* 113.

commercial law and thus treat all sources of uniform law as within its purview, including public international law, international conventions, general principles of law, rules of international organizations, customs and usages, and standard form contracts.[9] Others, like Goldman, consider the *lex mercatoria* to be '*a set of general principles and customary rules referred to or elaborated in the framework of international trade, without reference to a particular national system of law.*'[10] On this latter view the *lex mercatoria* does not include national or international legislation or other rules of law that are not customary in origin, but does include general principles of law.

Professor Klaus Peter Berger[11] clearly subscribes to the wide view propounded several years earlier by Lando. In his ambitious attempt to depict the *lex mercatoria* as a coherent order and integrated body of supra-national commercial law, Berger has compiled a list of what he describes as principles, rules, and standards of the *lex mercatoria.*[12] This consists of some 78 principles and rules common to a number of national legal systems or resulting from international restatements such as the UNIDROIT Principles of International Commercial Contracts. The list

> reproduces all those rules and principles of the lex mercatoria which have been accepted in international and arbitral contract practice together with comprehensive comparative references. The list unifies the various sources that have fostered the evolution of a transnational commercial legal system into one single, open-ended set of rules and principles[13]

The sources consist of arbitral awards, international conventions, civil codes and other national legislation, international restatements, and scholarly writings. However, most of the rules, even if originating in mercantile practice, have long since existed as rules of law common to many legal systems and subsist entirely independently of mercantile practice. Indeed, many of them are so general in character that on any particular issue it is scarcely possible to determine their application without reference to national law or to international restatements largely derived from the commonality of national laws. For example:

> *Rule 1 The parties are free to enter into contracts and determine their contents (principle of party autonomy)*

This principle originates in national laws. It is certainly a general principle in that it is common to most legal systems but it owes nothing to the practice of merchants, who cannot by their own fiat determine the validity of agreements they enter into.

> *Rule 2 A valid contract is binding on the parties. It can only be modified or terminated by consent of the parties or if provided for by the law ('pacta sunt servanda')*

Again, this is a general principle common to legal systems but it is the law, not mercantile practice, which determines the conditions in which a contract is or is not

[9] Ole Lando, 'The *Lex Mercatoria* in International Commercial Arbitration' (1985) 34 ICLQ 747, 748 ff.

[10] Berthold Goldman, 'The applicable law: general principles of law—the *lex mercatoria,* in *Contemporary Problems in International Arbitration* (ed Julian D M Lew, School of International Arbitration, Centre for Commercial Law Studies, Queen Mary College, London, 1986), 113, 116.

[11] Above, n 7. [12] *ibid*, 278 ff. [13] *ibid*, 210–11.

or ceases to be binding, and the manner in which it can be modified. A rule of this kind is of little help to arbitrators. The principle it expresses is no doubt common to most legal systems but its application varies widely from country to country, so that in any particular case it is likely to be necessary to refer to national law. Indeed, the concluding phrase 'if provided for by the law' shows how difficult it is to insulate contracts from rules of national legal systems.

*Rule 3 A valid contractual consent requires that the parties intend to be legally bound and that they have sufficiently identified the terms of the contract with respect to the subject matter*

This too is a general principle but it is one fashioned laboriously over centuries by courts of different legal systems who have wrestled with questions such as whether intention is to be ascertained subjectively or objectively, what factors vitiate consent, and what is entailed in the requirement of certainty of terms. It may be possible to avoid reference to national law by invoking, for example, the UNIDROIT Principles, but these are the product of the work of scholars and the merchant community played little or no part in their preparation.

Some of the rules were fashioned by specialists in private international law in order to produce a fair and reasonably predictable result. For example:

*Rule 26 Absent a choice of law by the parties, the contract is governed by the law with which the contract has the closest connection.*

This is a surprising rule to find in a set of rules of the *lex mercatoria*, for surely the characteristic of the latter is that it is transnational in character, so that reference to a national law is unnecessary. As has been pointed out by others, the purpose of the conflict of laws is antipathetical to the premise of the *lex mercatoria.*[14]

A number of the rules are not confined to commercial contracts or even to contracts at all. Two examples will serve to make the point:

*Rule 25 No one may derive an advantage from his own unlawful act*

This rule is not peculiar to commercial contracts or even to contract law. It applies equally in other contexts. For example, a person who murders another cannot benefit from that other's will—a well-established principle that has nothing to do with merchants or with the law of contract.

*Rule 55 Specialized laws prevail over general laws*

It is hard to see why this is to be considered part of the *lex mercatoria.* It is a general principle of construction of contracts, statutes, and international conventions which has no necessary connection with commerce at all.

Thus Berger's conception of *lex mercatoria,* like that of Lando, would seem to encompass the whole or substantially the whole of transnational commercial law by

[14] Lord Justice Mustill (now Lord Mustill), 'The New *Lex Mercatoria*: The First Twenty-five Years', in *Liber Amicorum for Lord Wilberforce* (ed Maarten Bos and Ian Brownlie, Clarendon Press, Oxford, 1987) 149, 154.

covering every principle and rule of commercial law that is not referable exclusively to any one legal system. In short, the concept of the *lex mercatoria* as law fashioned by merchants and administered by tribunals they establish has been broadened to encompass all rules, from whatever source, governing commercial transactions and common to several legal systems, including rules in the formulation of which the merchant has played no part and which have emerged not from mercantile tribunals but from decisions of national courts, enactments of national legislatures, or international restatements of scholars. The corollary, of course, is that what is done by transnational rules can usually be equally well done by reference to an applicable law national law.[15] If arbitral tribunals sometimes invoke transnational rules instead of the applicable law under conflict of laws rules it is not because the latter does not provide an answer but because of a concern to demonstrate neutrality or a perception that the relevant rule of the applicable law is in some way deficient or against the modern trend.

It is, of course, the prerogative of every writer to create his own dictionary. My own view is that it is useful to preserve the concept of *lex mercatoria* as a distinct subset of transnational commercial law consisting of the unwritten practices of merchants and financiers in international trade which are observed from a sense that they are intended to be binding,[16] for it is surely mercantile practice and the ability of merchants to 'make their own law' and to have it determined and applied by their own tribunals that is the hallmark of the *lex mercatoria* and distinguishes it from law emanating from parallelism in judicial decisions and rules embodied in international conventions and restatements.

On this basis I consider that there are good reasons for excluding from the *lex mercatoria* rules contained in international conventions and even codified usages such as the Uniform Customs and Practice for Documentary Credits issued by the International Chamber of Commerce. Even where such rules are customary in origin, their force is derived not from the custom of merchants but from the legally binding nature of contract, whether it be a contract entered into between States through adoption of a convention or between private parties through contractual incorporation of uniform rules promulgated by an international organization.

It is widely accepted that a fundamental characteristic of the *lex mercatoria* is that it derives its force from the spontaneously developed custom of merchants. But once embodied in a formal contract rules change their character. It ceases to matter whether they do, or ever did, truly reflect mercantile practice; they are binding because they represent the agreement of the parties. Moreover, it cannot be assumed that they embodied mercantile practice even at the time they were concluded. This is

[15] A point well made by Emmanuel Gaillard, 'Transnational Law: a Legal System or a Method of Decision-Making', in *The Practice of Transnational Law* (ed Klaus Peter Berger, Kluwer Law International, The Hague 2001) 53, 55.

[16] This is the *opinio juris* element of customary international law, a concept not free from controversy because it appears to be either superfluous or paradoxical (if the belief that the rule is binding is true it is unnecessary; if it is false then it is a strange basis for the binding nature of the rule). Space does not permit its discussion here. I have attempted an analysis elsewhere. See Roy Goode, 'Usage and Its Reception in Transnational Commercial Law' (1985) 46 ICLQ 1, 9–10.

because those engaged in the preparation of uniform rules are concerned to produce best results and not merely to reproduce but to improve existing rules. It is therefore inevitable that in some degree the product of their labours represents not what businessmen do now but what they ought to do in the future. It is thus the contract, recognized by law,[17] and not the practice of merchants, which gives normative force to the rules.

For the same reason, though at one time I thought it appropriate to treat general principles of law as part of the *lex mercatoria,* I would now exclude these, for while some of them may have originated in the custom of merchants they have acquired an independent status making it unnecessary to invoke mercantile practice, which must in any event give way to positive law.

I conclude that if the new *lex mercatoria* is indeed the product of spontaneous mercantile practice, then it is essentially customary in nature. So just as transnational rules in general are to be identified not by their content but by their sources,[18] so also the *lex mercatoria* is characterized not by rules which are necessarily distinct from those of national law but by the fact that they find their origins in commercial practice. This to some extent limits the utility of the *lex mercatoria* in that usage has to be established and it is much easier to establish a local trade usage than an international one. Where the usage is codified contracting parties may incorporate it into their contract but in so doing they change its status, because its binding force now derives from the contract, not from the usage, so that it becomes unnecessary to prove the usage. On the other hand, codified rules not incorporated into the contract may be evidence of pre-existing usage or lead to new usage.[19]

## II. To What Extent can Merchants 'Make Their Own Law'?

### Is contract law?

Let us begin with contracts. It is generally (though not universally) accepted that a contract cannot speak to its own validity but is dependent on satisfying certain external legal criteria. In other words, while parties who conclude a valid contract can fairly be said to be making their own law, they cannot themselves prescribe the conditions of validity. If the position were otherwise, parties to a private agreement could make up their own rules, however unfair or irrational. Moreover, a contract does not become independent of legal norms merely because it incorporates rules produced by an international organization, however august that organization might be. The status of such incorporated terms is in principle no different from that of other terms. Insofar as the contract is valid and binding this is because it meets the

[17] See below, p.340.

[18] Gaillard, above, n 15, who (at p. 55) finds the specificity of transnational rules to lie in the fact that they are not derived from any one legal system but from different legal systems.

[19] See below.

conditions set by the applicable law or, at the very least, conditions that fulfil some generally accepted standard.

But although contractually incorporated uniform rules promulgated by a body such as the ICC do not have any special status *as contract terms* they may either evidence pre-existing usages or bring about new usages. So when first introduced a new revision of the UCP *may* be evidence of pre-existing usage, though without further enquiry this can usually be demonstrated only insofar as they reproduce the effect of existing rules by which usage has been established. It should not be overlooked that uniform rules of this kind are designed to fulfil at least three different functions. First, they state existing usage where this is consistently adopted and is considered not to require change. Second, they introduce consistency into previously divergent commercial practices. Third, where considered appropriate they depart from existing usage in order to improve contract practice and make it more efficient. In this way they will establish new usages but only when they have gained general acceptance, a process which usually takes time. So we can reasonably assume that UCP 500, which was published some 13 years ago, partly reflected existing usages and partly introduced modifications or additions leading to new usages. Provisions in UCP 600 which alter the rules of UCP 500, for example, by abolishing the reference to reasonable time for presentation of documents, will be immediately binding on parties to contracts that incorporate them but will not be evidence of new usages, so as to be capable of being applied to contracts that do not incorporate them, until UCP 600 has been in force for some years and has become widely adopted, at which point they will acquire normative force.

## Is commercial practice law?

It is commonly asserted that commercial law is founded on the practices of merchants, which is true, and that commercial practice thus has normative force, which is not true. Commercial practice by itself is never sufficient to establish a legal norm. What is needed is an additional factor, observance of the practice from a sense of binding obligation, which converts the practice into a normative usage. It is true that the validity of a usage is itself dependent on conformity with certain basic conditions, for example that it is generally known, consistently adopted, reasonable, and in conformity with positive law. But what distinguishes usage from contract is that usage is generally recognized as a true source of law which may affect parties who have not agreed to it and may even be unaware of it.

The main reason why business practice is not by itself normative in character is that the parties may have adopted it not from a sense of obligation but for reasons of convenience, courtesy or goodwill. Normative trade usage, like a rule of customary international law, requires a conjunction of *usus* and *opinio juris*. Thus in an English case arising from the freeze imposed by the American authorities on transfers from and to accounts held by Libyan nationals it was held that while for practical reasons the method of withdrawing a Eurodollar deposit in London denominated in US dollars was by an inter-bank transfer through CHIPS in New York as the clearing system of the country in whose currency the account was denominated, a transfer which would be illegal under US law as the law of the place for performance, the evidence before the court did not establish any usage to that effect and the depositor, a Libyan bank, was entitled to withdraw its deposit in London in cash[20] or by other means not involving any action in the United States and therefore not susceptible to the US freeze in proceedings in an English court.[21]

## III. Is the *Lex Mercatoria* Autonomous?

This brings me at last to the central question posed by this paper: is the *lex mercatoria* as I have defined it an autonomous body of law? It is clear that it is not a complete legal system, but as I have pointed out elsewhere[22] that by itself would not disqualify it from being selected as the applicable law, for its rules might be sufficient to resolve the issue and to the extent that they are not reference can be made to some applicable national law. Is it nevertheless autonomous within its own limited sphere of application? Here I believe much confusion has been caused by imprecision in the use of the word autonomy. Insofar as this means that rules of the *lex mercatoria* are derived from mercantile practice, not from national law in the first instance, its use is unexceptionable. It is quite another thing to say that the *lex mercatoria* is unfettered by rules of national law. This is manifestly untrue and reflects a failure to distinguish *de jure* from *de facto* autonomy. It is undoubtedly the case that freedom of contract is everywhere controlled by national laws and that the validity of commercial usage is subject to externally imposed criteria. There are policy limits to what even commercial men may properly agree. One need only mention national and regional laws governing competition, financial services, drug trafficking and money laundering, to mention only a few. Even international commercial arbitration, which a number of scholars have asserted constitutes an autonomous system of decision-making, is not truly autonomous, a fact which is obvious when one considers that countries around the world have enacted legislation governing arbitration, that national courts control the validity and enforcement of arbitral awards and that international conventions such as the 1958 New York Convention on the recognition and enforcement of arbitral awards lay down clear rules relating to recognition and enforcement.

What is undoubtedly true, however, is that national laws give a wide degree of licence to contracting parties and cast a benevolent eye on rules produced by international organizations which are designed to ensure consistency of practice and to provide a fair balance of interests among the parties to contracts. Further, courts strive to give legal efficacy to transactions which promote economic activity and are seen to serve legitimate purposes, even where such transactions do not fit well with

[20] Which might have involved some practical difficulties in that the amount of the deposit was US$ 292 million!

[21] *Libyan Arab Foreign Bank v Bankers Trust Co* [1989] QB 728.

[22] Roy Goode, 'Usage and its Reception in Transnational Commercial Law' (1997) 46 ICLQ 1, 33.

established legal doctrine. For example, courts around the world have been exercised by questions relating to the validity of abstract payment undertakings, such as demand guarantees, which do not conform to traditional rules relating to *cause*, consideration, offer and acceptance, reliance, and the like, but which the courts nevertheless feel constrained to uphold in order not to damage markets or impede the creative activity of merchants and bankers. Moreover, arbitration as an institution undoubtedly enhances the concept of *de facto* autonomy of the *lex mercatoria* in that courts and legislatures have delegated a wide degree of freedom to arbitral institutions and tribunals in international arbitration as to the procedures tribunals adopt, the evidence they may receive, and the conflict rules and rules of law they may apply in the absence of a choice of law by the parties, so that tribunals not infrequently resort to non-national sources of rules based on judicial or legislative parallelism or on restatements of scholars such as the UNIDROIT Principles of International Commercial Contracts and the Principles of European Contract Law produced by the Commission on European Contract Law. To this one may add the fact that in most jurisdictions it is far less easy to have an arbitral award set aside than it is to have a judgment of a court successfully appealed.

We can therefore say that while from a legal perspective the *lex mercatoria* is autonomous in the sense that its source lies in the custom of merchants rather than in rules of national law, it is not insulated from such rules *as a matter of law*, being everywhere dependent on external criteria of validity and external control. On the other hand, the *lex mercatoria* enjoys a large measure of *de facto* independence in that the mercantile community and its arbitral institutions are largely free to go their own way within the overall limits of national, regional and international public policy.

## IV. The *Lex Mercatoria* as an Applicable Law

Can arbitral tribunals apply the *lex mercatoria* instead of the applicable law as determined by the rules of private international law? And can the *lex mercatoria* be selected as the applicable law?

### Application of the *lex mercatoria* by an arbitral tribunal

Whatever theoretical difficulties may be in the way of accepting the *lex mercatoria* as the applicable law, arbitral tribunals have on occasion applied it, so that even if they could equally well have reached the same result by reference to an applicable law it would be futile to deny their power to apply the *lex mercatoria* in making their awards. In practice this is unusual. Indeed, it is not unfair to say that the importance of the *lex mercatoria* in arbitration practice is in inverse proportion to the volume of literature devoted to it. But with a defined issue before it the tribunal may find no practical difficulty in identifying a rule that has gained common currency among legal systems or is contained in an international or regional restatement and in applying it to the case in hand.

## Choice as to the applicable law

Traditional theory has it that only the rules of a legal system can be designated as the applicable law, and that is generally considered to be the approach of the Rome Convention on the law applicable to contractual obligations, which provides that a contract shall be governed by 'the law' chosen by the parties rather than the broader 'rules of law', which has come to denote rules not necessarily derived from a national legal system. A sound policy reason for such an approach is not that a legal system is likely to be either complete or at any rate more complete and more clearly defined than rules based on mercantile practice, for as mentioned above those rules may be adequate to resolve the particular issue before the tribunal, but that they have not been subject to scrutiny and approval by governments and legislatures and therefore lack legitimacy. But under the influence of international arbitration practice attitudes have changed. Article 28(1) of the UNCITRAL Model Law on international commercial arbitration requires the arbitral tribunal to decide the dispute in accordance with 'such rules of law as are chosen by the parties as applicable to the substance of dispute', though in the absence of choice the tribunal is to apply 'the law' determined by the conflict of laws rules which it considers applicable.

However, it is important that the rules to be applied are reasonably ascertainable, and this can hardly be said to be true of the *lex mercatoria.* It is one thing for an arbitral tribunal, tasked with determination of particular issues and armed with the relevant facts, to apply *ex post* the rules that it considers appropriate, it is quite another for parties to prescribe the *lex mercatoria* as the applicable law in advance when they have no idea whether a dispute will arise or what the issues will be. It is thus not surprising to find strong opposition among practising lawyers to selection of the *lex mercatoria* as the applicable law because of its perceived lack of definition.[23]

A similar approach was taken by the European Commission in its draft Regulation ('Rome I') to replace the 1980 Rome Convention on the law applicable to contractual obligations. The Commission considered the *lex mercatoria* too uncertain in content to justify the status of an applicable law. By contrast, formulations adopted by groups of scholars from around the world or from the Member States of the European Community were free from this objection. There remained the question of legitimacy, which the Commission sought to address by providing in Article 3 that the parties could choose as the applicable law 'the principles and rules of the substantive law of contract recognised internationally or in the Community.' The Commission's Explanatory Memorandum stated that this:

> would authorise the choice of the UNIDROIT principles, the *Principles of European Contract Law* or a possible future optional Community instrument, while excluding the *lex mercatoria,*

[23] See Berger, 'The New Law Merchant and the Global Market Place', in *The Practice of Transnational Law*, above, n 15, 1–2, describing the results of a worldwide survey among attorneys active in international commercial law carried out by an American lawyer in 1995 which depicted of identifying the sources and content of the *lex mercatoria.*

which is not precise enough, or private codifications not adequately recognised by the international community.[24]

However, the proposal met with strong objections and was withdrawn. If recognition could not be secured for sets of principles widely publicized and discussed and frequently adopted by arbitral tribunals in international commercial arbitration, how much less likely it is that the *lex mercatoria* will ever be acceptable as a choice of law.

[24] Proposal for a Regulation of the European Parliament and the Council on the law applicable to contractual obligations (Rome I), Brussels, 15.12.2005, COM(2005) 650 final.

# PART IV
# DISPUTE RESOLUTION

In Chapter 22 I returned to the question what makes business practice binding before moving on to the disputed question of the extent to which, after arbitral proceedings have been determined and an award set aside by a court under the law of the seat of the arbitration agreed by the parties, the court of enforcement in another jurisdiction should feel free to disregard the order and grant enforcement. Whether the enforcing court is *entitled* to do this is not in dispute. The question is whether it should. In the article embodied in this chapter I argued that while there might be exceptional cases in which it would be right to allow enforcement, such as whether the proceedings leading to the setting aside order suffered from some gross irregularity, the enforcing court ought in general to respect the order made in the State of origin of the arbitral proceedings. I advanced many reasons for this, not the least of these being that if parties agree on the law that is to govern their arbitration, including rules of that law allowing awards to be reviewed and set aside, why should a party whose award has been set aside be free to disregard the *lex loci arbitri* to which he submitted by agreement and secure enforcement in another jurisdiction? It is fair to say that in most countries, France being a notable exception, orders of the court of origin will be respected. But the issue has generated enormous academic heat, if not always academic light.

Chapter 23, the 1991 Freshfields arbitration lecture, was concerned with a different subject, namely what seemed to me to be the excessive readiness of English courts to set aside arbitral awards or otherwise intervene in the arbitration. Disquiet over the loss of arbitration business by London because of this later led to the establishment of a government department committee of which I was a member and whose report led to the enactment of the Arbitration Act 1996. It was exceptionally well drafted by parliamentary counsel Geoffrey Summers—so much so that at a conference at King's College London there was a huge round of applause for Geoffrey Summers, surely unprecedented in the history of conferences on legislation! The 1996 Act successfully dealt with most of the issues to which my lecture had been devoted.

The penultimate essay in this Part examines the differences between litigation and arbitration not simply in terms of procedure but in their impact on substantive rights, particularly determination of the law applicable, the reference by arbitral tribunals to "rules of law", including non-national law and the *lex mercatoria*, the admissibility of evidence, and the impact of the New York Convention on the Recognition and Enforcement of Foreign Arbitrals rendering such awards far easier to enforce in another country than is the case with court judgments.

The substantive essays in this volume conclude with a reproduction of my 1997 Alexander lecture in which I drew attention to what seemed to me to be a growing culture of aggression and obstruction in the conduct of both litigation and arbitration, and expressed the view, which I still hold, that lawyers are allowed to play too great a role in the dispute resolution process, with greater planning in the pre-contract stage instead of an automatic choice of one form of dispute resolution over another when the parties have no idea in what context a dispute may arise and whether the particular resolution method selected is appropriate.

The final piece reproduces a tribute paid to my long-standing friend Professor Jacob Ziegel, an outstanding scholar who has, over a long life, influenced the shape of commercial and consumer law not only in Canada, where he spent his working life, but in other countries, through his writings, lectures, and work on committees, his long editorship of the Canadian Business Law Journal, and his remarkable series of annual workshops over a period of more than 40 years which attracted scholars from all over the world. He approached many issues from a comparative law perspective and his fierce intellectual curiosity manifested itself in his life-long love of scholarly disputation. Sadly ill-health has made it impossible for him to continue any of these activities. But he remains a warm-hearted friend, always concerned for others, not for himself. So I take this opportunity to salute him.

# 22

# The Role of the *Lex Loci Arbitri* in International Commercial Arbitration*

*Roy Goode*†

This article is concerned with the role of the *lex loci arbitri* in international commercial arbitration[1] and the extent to which judgments or orders made by a court of one state[2] should influence a foreign court of another state in which the arbitral award is sought to be enforced. Much has been written about the concept of international commercial arbitration as an autonomous, anational institution, the procedures of which are not subject to the constraints of national laws. If any excuse is needed for adding yet more to the literature on the subject, it is its relevance to the future development of international co-operation in cross-border dispute resolution.

## I. Introduction

### (a) The Genesis of the Autonomy Concept

The relationship between courts and private tribunals has not always been as benevolent as it is today. In England the central courts for centuries jealously guarded their domain, watchful of encroachments on their jurisdiction. Even among the courts themselves there were strenuous turf battles as each sought to enlarge its jurisdiction at the expense of others. One unfortunate victim of this rivalry was commercial law, which lost much of its international character as the common law courts gradually usurped the powers of those institutions most responsive to external influences, notably the ecclesiastical courts, the courts of Admiralty, and the merchant

* Originally published as R Goode: "The Role of *Lex Loci Arbitri* in International Commercial Arbitration" in Rose (ed.): *Lex Mercatoria: Essays on International Commercial Law in Honour of Francis Reynolds* (2000, Informa Law from Routledge). Reproduced by kind permission of the publisher.

† This article was written as a contribution to *Lex Mercatoria,* in honour of Professor Francis Reynolds, and is published here with kind permission of LLP.

[1] That is, the procedural law of the state where such an arbitration takes place.

[2] Hereafter 'the court of origin'.

courts. Similarly, arbitration was for a long time viewed with disfavour, being seen as a private dispute settlement mechanism designed to oust the jurisdiction of the courts and to substitute private adjudication for public decision-making. This hostility to the private process of arbitration was not confined to English courts but was a widespread phenomenon.

However, every action prompts reaction. The stricter the controls, the more vehement the demand for liberation. Ultimately, in England as elsewhere, pressures from the commercial community were not to be denied. Fierce judicial opposition to arbitration gradually gave way to a wary acceptance, but under the closest judicial scrutiny, and it is only in the last half of the twentieth century (and in England, only in the past two decades) that courts have finally come to terms with the fact that parties to arbitration agreements want privacy, confidentiality, and finality in the settlement of their disputes, and view judicial intervention in the arbitral process or in the review of awards as a measure to be taken only in exceptional circumstances. Since the parties had entrusted the determination of their dispute to an arbitral tribunal it was the arbitrators and the parties rather than the courts who should control the procedure, and it was not the courts but the arbitral tribunal which in the first instance should decide such matters as the validity of the contract in dispute and the extent of the tribunal's jurisdiction. Now we have gone further. Not merely have we adopted the principle that the arbitration clause is to be considered separate from the rest of the contract, so that the invalidity of the contract does not deprive the arbitral tribunal of jurisdiction, but our Arbitration Act 1996 provides that the tribunal may even adjudicate on the validity of the agreement to arbitrate.[3]

Though the Arbitration Act does not distinguish domestic from international commercial arbitration, it is the latter which has forced the pace of change. It is now almost universally accepted that disputes involving parties and arbitrators from different countries cannot be constrained by the same rules as govern courts. So in this country, as elsewhere, we now recognize that arbitrators are not bound by rules of procedure and evidence applied by courts; that they need not apply the conflict of laws rules of the forum to determine the applicable law and, in the absence of party choice, may apply whatever conflict rules they consider appropriate; and that courts should intervene during the arbitral process, and arbitral awards should be set aside, only in exceptional circumstances.[4] In these developments the UNCITRAL Model Law on International Commercial Arbitration has proved to have a much greater influence than at one time seemed likely, and the Arbitration Act 1996, unlike early versions of the draft Arbitration Bill prepared for the Departmental Advisory Committee on Arbitration, bears the strong impress of the Model Law.[5]

[3] Arbitration Act 1996, s. 30(1).

[4] The Arbitration Act 1996 recognizes three categories of case: want of jurisdiction, serious procedural irregularity, and error of law. The right of appeal in a case within one of the first two categories is mandatory; an appeal against an award on the ground of error of law may be freely excluded by agreement and, even where it is not, is subject to fairly stringent additional criteria.

[5] The Arbitration Act 1996 was drafted with a degree of clarity and user-friendliness unusual in modern parliamentary drafting. Indeed, this was so widely noted that at a major conference held at King's College London to examine the Act a compliment paid to the draftsman, Mr. Geoffrey Sellers, by

But these relaxations in judicial control in England and elsewhere came too late to stem the pent-up frustrations of certain leading international arbitrators, particularly French scholars, at what was rightly perceived to be an excessive judicial interference with party autonomy, which deprived parties to arbitration of the predictability, finality, and confidentiality to which they attached so much importance. Hence the movement, developed in particular by leading French scholars[6] and strongly supported by a number of other international authorities,[7] to promote the idea of international arbitration as something variously described as 'anational', 'stateless', 'delocalized', 'detached'.[8] By this was meant that in international commercial arbitration the arbitral procedure and any resulting award were autonomous, being unconnected to any national legal system and deriving their force solely from the agreement of the parties. Accordingly an arbitral award not only took effect from the time of its issue but from then on became the prospective beneficiary of the recognition laws of a putative foreign state of enforcement and was thus unaffected by any subsequent order made by the court of origin setting the award aside. In other words, at the very moment of its birth, produced by the consensual coupling of the parties in the arbitration process, the award took off and disappeared into the firmament, landing only in those places where enforcement was sought.

The rebellion against the constraints imposed by national law on the conduct of arbitration went hand in hand with a sustained assault on the conflict of laws and its central thesis that all disputes had to be determined in accordance with a national legal system which it was the function of the conflict rules to identify. Why, it was asked, should parties to an international contract be locked into a national law that in all probability was designed primarily for domestic transactions? Why should they not be free to have their substantive rights determined by customary commercial law (*lex mercatoria*) or by general principles of law or even by public international law? Why should they not be free to designate as the applicable law an international convention such as the Vienna Convention on Contracts for the International Sale of Goods 1980? Hence the drive for freedom of arbitral procedure from national laws was paralleled by a move towards resurrection in modern form of the medieval *lex mercatoria* as a supposedly free-floating, autonomous body of law which was neutral in character and obviated the need to resort to national legal systems and, in consequence, rules of private international law.

one of the speakers attracted thunderous applause from the audience—a reaction surely unprecedented in the annals of parliamentary drafting!

[6] Notably Professors Rene David, Berthold Goldman, and Philippe Fouchard. However, the idea first appears to have been suggested hy a Greek scholar, Professor Charambalos N. Fragistas. See F.A. Mann, 'Lex Facit Arhitrum', in *International Arbitration: Liber Amicorum for Martin Domke* (ed. Pieter Sanders), (The Hague, Martinus Nijhoff 1967) at p. 158.

[7] Including in particular Jan Paulsson and Professors Pierre Lalive and Arthur von Mehren.

[8] For an early example see Berthold Goldman, 'Les Conflits de Lois dans l'Arbitrage International de Droit Prive', (1963) 109 *Recueils des Cours* 351; and for a recent restatement Phillipe Fouchard, 'La portee internationale de l'annulation de la sentence arbitrate dans son pays d'origine' (1997) *Rev. de l'Arb.* 329.

The imagery of an autonomous *lex mercatoria* enforced by an anational arbitration procedure leading to a stateless award captured the Gallic imagination. As has so often happened in the history of ideas, it was the proponents of the new spirit of revolution who tended to make the running in arbitration literature, not simply because they expressed their ideas with elegance and force but because they were able to conjure up a picture of transnationality that seemed so much more exciting than the more down to earth approach of traditional scholars. And, as so often in the past, the attention given to these new doctrines has been in inverse proportion to their practical impact. Yet we owe a good deal to the advocates of the *lex mercatoria*, and to others involved in the development and formulation of international principles of contract, commercial law and arbitration procedure, for they have had considerable success in shifting the balance of decisional authority from the courts to the arbitrators and in freeing the hands of arbitral tribunals in international arbitration from constraints which parties and their lawyers undoubtedly found unduly irksome.

## II. The New York Convention

Before we discuss the opposing concepts of territoriality and party autonomy it is necessary to say a few words about the United Nations Convention on the Enforcement of Foreign Arbitral Awards 1958 (the New York Convention). The purpose of the Convention is to facilitate the international enforcement of arbitral awards. The New York Convention has been astonishingly successful, no fewer than 123 states having become parties to it. The two articles with which we are particularly concerned are Articles V and VII.

Article V provides that recognition and enforcement of a foreign arbitral award may be refused, at the request of the party against whom it is invoked, only if that party furnishes to the competent authority where the recognition and enforcement is sought proof of one of the matters listed in the ensuing paragraphs. Among these is the ground mentioned in paragraph (e), namely that the award 'has not yet become binding on the parties, or has been set aside or suspended by a competent authority of the country in which, or under the law of which, that order was made'. It is clear that Article V is mandatory only in precluding refusal of enforcement on grounds other than those set out in it. Proof of the existence of one of those grounds entitles the courts of a Convention state to refuse recognition and enforcement but does not oblige them to do so. Refusal is discretionary.[9]

[9] A great deal of ink has been spent on the significance of the word 'may' in the English text, as opposed to 'shall'. It is astonishing how many writers have concluded that the discretion to allow enforcement despite the existence of a ground for refusal in Article V exist, because the word 'shall' was not used. This can only be ascribed to unfamiliarity with the nuances of the English language. The discretionary effect of Article V would not have been changed one whit if the word 'shall' had been used, because it would have to be read not in isolation but in conjunction with 'only'. Thus the phrase would have become: 'Recognition and enforcement of the award shall be refused . . . only if . . .'. That means no more than that the courts of an enforcing state shall not/may not/cannot refuse enforcement unless one of the stated grounds for so doing exists. It does not imply that if such a ground does exist the court must not enforce the award. That construction would necessitate a phrase such as 'shall be refused if and only if'.

Under Article VII the provisions of the Convention are not to affect the validity of multilateral or bilateral agreements concerning the recognition and enforcement of arbitral awards entered into by the Contracting States 'nor deprive any interested party of any right he may have to avail himself of an arbitral award in the manner and to the extent allowed by the law or the treaties of the country where such an award is sought to be relied on'. One of the more remarkable features of the territoriality/party autonomy debate is that the protagonists on both sides invoke the New York Convention to support their position: the territorialists on the ground that numerous provisions of the Convention explicitly recognize the role of the *lex loci arbitri*;[10] the advocates of party autonomy and the statelessness of awards, on the ground that Article VII plainly establishes the right of enforcement states to allow enforcement of a foreign award which complies with their domestic law, despite its annulment by the court of origin, where that annulment is not a ground under the domestic law for refusal of recognition of the award. One thing seems clear, and that is that the New York Convention recognizes the important role of the *lex loci arbitri;* and while Article VII allows the *lex loci arbitri* to be bypassed, it certainly provides no warrant for the concept of a stateless award. On the contrary, it is strongly arguable that a stateless award would be not enforceable under the Convention. In the words of a leading authority on the Convention:[11]

> It is not only the legislative history of the Convention which seems to be contrary to the Convention's applicability to the 'a-national' award. The system and text of the Convention too appear to be against such interpretation. The Convention applies to the enforcement of an award made in another State. Those who advocate the concept of the 'a-national' award, on the other hand, deny that such award is made in a particular country *('sentence flottante' 'sentence apatride')*. How could such award then fit into the Convention's scope?

## III. Territoriality versus Autonomy

### (a) The Territoriality/Party Autonomy Spectrum

The traditional theory of territoriality is based on the general principle of international law that a state is sovereign within its own borders and that its law and

[10] See in particular Article 11(1) ('differences ... in respect of a defined legal relationship ... concerning a subject matter capable of settlement by arbitration', which is implicitly a reference to the *lex arbitri*); Article 11(3) (which requires a court to refer a dispute to arbitration under the arbitration agreement 'unless it finds that the said agreement is null and void, inoperative or incapable of being performed'—again matters to be determined under the *lex arbitri*); Article V(l)(a) (enabling the court to refuse recognition if it finds that the arbitration agreement is not valid under the law to which the parties have subjected it or, failing any indication thereon, under the law of the country where the award was made); Article V(l)(d) (composition of the arbitral tribunal not in accordance with the agreement of the parties or, failing such agreement, not in accordance with the law of the country where the arbitration took place); Article V(e), previously set out; Article VI (empowering the court of the state of enforcement to adjourn the enforcement proceedings if an application is pending before the competent authority of the country in which, or under the law of which, the award was made). The *lex loci arbitri* controls even if the *lex arbitri* is different. *See* infra, n. 25.

[11] Albert Jan van den Berg, *The New York Convention* of 1958 (Deventer, Kluwer Law and Taxation Publishers 1981) at p. 37. After 18 years Professor van den Berg's book is still the seminal work on the New York Convention.

its courts have the exclusive right to determine the legal effect of acts done (and consequently of arbitral awards made) within those borders. The concept of party autonomy in arbitration predicates that the binding authority of an award derives solely from the agreement of the parties, not from national law. However, neither of these two approaches embodies a single, homogenous concept. The scope of the territoriality principle varies according to the degree of respect the courts of a particular state are willing to accord to the decisions of courts of other states of competent jurisdiction. Similarly, there is no single concept of party autonomy. In fact, territoriality and party autonomy do not represent a sharp dichotomy but together occupy a spectrum, along which we can identify at least six possible, and at least four actual, models, arranged in ascending order of delocalization.

In the first model the law of the enforcing state *requires* its courts, in the absence of specified conditions, to refuse recognition and enforcement of an arbitral award that has been set aside by a court of competent jurisdiction. In other words, such law adopts the substance of Article V(e) of the New York Convention but as a mandatory, not a discretionary, provision. Examples of this model are the Italian Code of Civil Procedure and the Netherlands Private International Law Act. Article 840(5) of the former provides as follows:

> The Court of Appeal shall refuse recognition or enforcement of the foreign award if in the opposition proceedings the party against whom the award is invoked proves any of the following circumstances:
>
> (5) the award has not yet become binding on the parties or has been set aside or suspended by a competent authority of the State in which, or under the law of which, it was made.

Article 1076(1)(A)(e) of the Netherlands Private International Law Act is differently formulated but produces the same effect. Under this Article:

> If no treaty concerning recognition and enforcement is applicable, or if an applicable treaty allows a party to rely on the law of the country in which recognition or enforcement is sought, an arbitral award made in a foreign State may be recognised in the Netherlands and its enforcement may be sought in the Netherlands . . . unless:
>
> (e) the arbitral award has been set aside by a competent authority of the country in which the award is made.

Thus under both Italian and Dutch law the setting aside of the arbitral award in or under the law of the place where it was made makes it mandatory to refuse enforcement. These laws provide good examples of the strong form of territoriality.

In the second model it is recognized that within its own territory a state is sovereign and its courts have the exclusive right to adjudicate on the legality of acts done within that territory. What is said, however, is that laws and court decisions made within the state are not entitled to recognition *erga omnes*—which is clearly correct—but that for policy reasons the decision of a foreign court of competent jurisdiction setting aside an award will usually be respected by courts of the state of enforcement, subject to rights of impeachment in cases such as procedural unfairness or the obtaining of a judgment by fraud. States following this model generally adopt provisions in their arbitration laws which follow those of Article V of the New York Convention, with or without modification, and, like Article V, allow a discretion to enforce notwithstanding the order annulling the award. Examples are the English Arbitration Act 1996,[12] the Mexican Commercial Code,[13] the German Code of Civil Procedure,[14] and the Swiss Private International Law Act 1987.[15] The first two track the wording of Article V(l)(e); the German and Swiss legislation simply incorporates the provisions of the New York Convention by reference.

The third model is the same as the first except that under the laws of the enforcing state the grounds for refusal of recognition of a foreign arbitral award are more restricted than those of Article V and in particular do not include the setting aside of the award under the *lex loci arbitri.* The courts of such states are then permitted by Article VII of the New York Convention to recognize the right of the party obtaining the award to benefit from the more generous approach of the domestic law of the state of enforcement and, if the requirements of that law are met, to have the award enforced even though it has been annulled by the court of origin. Nevertheless, though the annulling order is not as such a ground for refusal of recognition, to the extent that it is based on grounds which have a counterpart in the domestic law of the enforcing state the courts of the state may be willing to hold that there is a conclusive, strong or at least *prima facie* presumption that such grounds have been established for the purposes of its domestic law. This approach reflects a traditional principle of the conflict of laws.

In the fourth model the law of the enforcing state, while still recognizing the concept of a *lex arbitri,* does not recognize an annulment order in the court of origin either as a ground in itself for refusing recognition of the award or as raising any kind of presumption that such an order establishes facts which would bring the case within an equivalent ground under the law of the enforcing state.

The fifth, and very intense, model is to be found in French legislation and in the jurisprudence of French courts, which have carried the delocalization principle to the point where an international award (by which is presumably meant an award in an international arbitration) is stateless and derives its force not from the *lex loci arbitri,* or indeed from any other national law, but solely from the will of the parties. This result, which needs a brief historical account, was reached only in stages. First came the decision in the *Gotaverken* case,[16] in which the Paris Court of Appeal declined jurisdiction to set aside an ICC award rendered in Paris on the ground that, while the arbitration had taken place in Paris, neither the parties nor the contracts had any connection with France and they had not designated French law—or, indeed, any law—as the procedural law apart from the procedural rules of the ICC, and that accordingly the award had no connection with the French legal order and

[12] See s. 103(2). [13] *See* art. 1462. [14] See s. 1061. [15] *See* art. 194.

[16] *General National Maritime Transport* Co. v. *Götaverken Arendal AB,* Court of Appeal, Paris, 21 February 1980, (1980) *Rev. de l'Arb. 107, (1981) 6 Y.B. Comm. Arb.* 221. For an excellent and balanced discussion, see Jan Paulsson, 'Arbitration Unbound: Award Detached from the Law of its Country of Origin' (1981) 80 *ICLQ* 858; and for a response, William W. Park, 'The *Lex Loci Arbitri* and International Commercial Arbitration' (1988) 82 *ICLQ* 21.

was not a French award. Meanwhile the Swedish courts, asked to recognize the award at a time when the challenge to it was still pending in the French courts, held that the award was binding, not under French law but by the agreement of the parties to be bound, an agreement recognized and enforceable under Swedish law, so that the mere fact that the award was being challenged in France was not a ground for suspending the recognition proceedings in Sweden. The judgment of the Paris Court of Appeal did not say in terms that arbitral awards in international arbitration were stateless, merely that on the facts there was no connection with the French legal order. But since courts of a state other than that of the seat of the arbitration are unlikely to take jurisdiction in the absence of agreement by the parties, the effect of the *Gotaverken* decision, if it were to be applied universally, is that, unless the parties themselves agree to submit to the procedural law of a particular state, the arbitral proceedings are not reviewable by any court other than the court of a state in which enforcement is sought. The next stage came in a series of cases[17] in which the Court of Cassation held that the setting aside or suspension of an award by a court did not deprive the party obtaining the award of his right to enforce it in France in the conditions permitted by French law. These decisions were plainly correct,[18] since while Article V of the New York Convention gave a discretionary power to the court of enforcement to refuse to recognize an award that had been set aside[19] by the competent authority of the state where it was rendered, Article VII expressly preserved the right of an interested party to rely on the more favourable provisions, if any, of that state's domestic law. The provisions of the French Code of Civil Procedure did not then, and the provisions of the New Code of Civil Procedure do not now, include as a ground for refusing enforcement of a foreign award the fact that it had been set aside by the court of origin. Accordingly up to this point, if criticism was to be made, it was of the restrictive approach of the French legislation rather than that of the French courts. Moreover, it seems that where the grounds for the foreign annulment are comparable to those contained in the French Code of Civil Procedure, French courts are nevertheless unwilling to recognize that they have any competence to treat the annulment order as raising a strong, or even *prima facie,* presumption that such grounds have been established for the purposes of French domestic law. The effect of

[17] *Pabalt Tikeret Sirketi* v. *Norsolor*, Cas. le civ. 9 October 1984, (1985) *Rev. de l'Arb.* 481; *Polish Ocean Line* v. *Jolasry,* Cas. le civ. 10 March 1998, (1998) *Rev. de l'Arb.* 255; *Hilmarton Ltd.* v. *Omnium de Traitement et de Valorisation (OTV)* Cass. le civ., 28 March 1994, (1994) *Rev. de l'Arb.* 827, the last of these involving an extraordinary judicial saga in a number of countries; *Arab Republic of Egypt* v. *Chromalloy Air Services,* CA Paris, 14 January 1997, (1997) *Rev.* de *l'Arb.* 895.

[18] The same cannot necessarily be said of that part of the reasoning of the Federal District Court for the District of Columbia in the American *Chromalloy* case denying *res judicata* effect to the decision of the Cairo Court of Appeal annulling an arbitral award rendered in Egypt. See *Chromalloy Air Services* v. *The Arab Republic of Egypt,* 989 F.Supp. 907 (1996), and the critical comment on this aspect of the case by Georgios Petrochilos (2000) *ICLQ* 856, and Eric Schwartz, 'A Comment on Chromalloy-Hilmarton *a l'americaine*' (1997) 14 *J. Int.Arb.* 125. For a recent review of these developments see Emmanuel Gaillard, 'Enforcement of Awards Nullified in the Country of Origin: The French Experience' in *Improving the Efficiency of Arbitration Agreements and Awards: 40 Years of Application of the New York Convention* (ed. Albert Jan van den Berg), (ICCA Congress Series No. 9, Deventer, Kluwer 1999) at p. 505.

[19] *Supra* n. 17.

the three decisions mentioned *supra* is thus that French courts will enforce an award which is enforceable under French domestic law even if it has been set aside or suspended under the *lex loci arbitri.*

Unfortunately, in *Hilmarton* the Court of Cassation, not content with relying on the provisions of its domestic law, appears to have gone out of its way to say, in effect, that judgments of the court of origin setting aside an arbitral award were of no significance whatsoever in France, for in an international commercial arbitration the award, though made in a particular state (in that case, Switzerland), was itself international and was thus 'not integrated into the legal system of that State'. Accordingly a decision of Switzerland's highest court annulling an award was entirely irrelevant to its enforceability in France. This has widely been seen as a regrettable and unnecessary (if surely unintended) affront to a foreign court of the highest standing. One commentator who is not unsympathetic to the internationalist approach has nevertheless observed:[20]

> Although consistent with a conception of international arbitration that has a noble and prestigious heritage in France, this presumption, I might timidly venture to ask, is nevertheless just a little bit presumptuous, is it not? For on what authority can a French court decide what does or does not form part of the Swiss legal order? I would have thought that this was a matter for Swiss legislators and courts, and not the French Court of Cassation, to decide.

A similar decision was by the Paris Court of Appeal in *Arab Republic of Egypt* v. *Chromalloy Air Services Ltd*:[21]

> The award made in Egypt is by definition an international award which, by definition, is not integrated into the legal order of that State so that its existence remains established despite its being annulled and its enforcement in France is not in violation of international public policy.

To this one might add: is it not paradoxical that French law, while declining to recognize the integration of a foreign award into the legal system of the *locus arbitri,* sees no difficulty in empowering French courts to set aside French awards in an international arbitration?

It been held that French courts will undertake the review of an award challenged before them by the losing party even if the court of origin had already dismissed a challenge on the same grounds.[22] Hence the position now reached in France is, in effect, that Article V of the New York Convention will rarely be applied and can for all practical purposes be regarded as a dead letter.

[20] Eric A. Schwartz (1997) 14 *J.Int.Arb.* 125, 131. The approach of the English courts has traditionally been rather different. 'For the English court to pronounce on the validity of the law of a foreign state within its own territory, so that the validity of that law became the *res* of the *res judicata* in the suit, would be to assert jurisdiction over the internal affairs of that state. That would be a breach of the rules of comity. In my view this court has no jurisdiction to do so' *(Buck* v. *Attorney-General* [1965] Ch. 745, 770, *per* Diplock J).

[21] 14 January 1997, (1997) *Rev. de l'Arb.* 395.

[22] *Unichips Finanziara* v. *Gesnouin (No. 3),* Court of Appeal, Paris, 1st Chamber, 12 February 1993, (1993) *Rev. de l'Arb.* 255.

Finally, we come to the most extreme delocalization model, adopted by the Belgian legislation, to the effect that no court in Belgium could set aside an award unless at least one of the parties was Belgian. As noted later, that law has been modified to allow the parties the choice whether to retain or to opt out of judicial review in Belgium. If they do, then the resulting award becomes truly stateless.

### (b) The Question to be Addressed

It is clear that a judgment of a court at the seat of an arbitration setting aside the arbitral award has no effect in another state except to the extent that the law of that state is willing to give effect to it. In some jurisdictions such a judgment may be treated as grounding a plea of *res judicata,* precluding the party who obtained the award from relitigating the issue of its validity. In others, the judgment does not attract the principle of *res judicata* but will nevertheless be respected in the absence of exceptional circumstances. In yet other jurisdictions, notably France, the annulling judgment will be regarded as of no significance whatever, being rooted in a legal order to which the award is not subject. The question for consideration, then, is not whether the courts of an enforcing state *must* respect the foreign judgment—which plainly is not the case—but rather whether as a matter of policy they *should.* Adoption of the latter course is necessarily inconsistent with the theory of the stateless award. It will be contended: first, that the arguments are overwhelmingly against the concept of the stateless award, not only from the viewpoint of legal theory but also in terms of policy, practicality, and the general legislative approach among states; secondly, that courts asked to enforce an award should, where permitted by their own law, defer to decisions of the court of origin under the *lex loci arbitri* in the absence of special circumstances; and, thirdly, that any legislative barriers to the adoption of such an approach should be removed. I hope to show that, apart from other considerations, the theory of the stateless award is riddled with inconsistencies. In particular, it is founded on party autonomy, yet the parties' choice of their procedural law is ignored; it is motivated by the desire to promote the concept of internationality in cross-border arbitration, yet its effect, at any rate under French law, is totally to ignore international considerations and to rely exclusively on national law; its proponents declare that an award is not integrated into the legal system under which the arbitration takes place, or any legal system, yet they simultaneously insist that the award is integrated into the legal system of the state of enforcement, recognizing that there has to be some court somewhere able to protect the parties against gross procedural unfairness or the exercise by arbitrators of a jurisdiction they do not possess.

## IV. The Central Role of the *Lex Loci Arbitri*

### (a) No Contract Without Law

One can begin with the simple proposition relating to substantive rights that a contract is not law, and no award can be binding simply by virtue of the parties' agreement to be bound. A contract depends for its force on recognition by law. The point was made by Dr Francis Mann in characteristically trenchant style in a passage from his seminal piece 'Lex Facit Arbitrum',[23] which has been cited on countless occasions but is worth repeating:

> No one has ever or anywhere been able to point to any provision or legal principle which would permit individuals to act outside the confines of a system of municipal law; even the idea of the autonomy of the parties exists only by virtue of a given system of municipal law and in different systems may have different characteristics and effects. Similarly, every arbitration is necessarily subject to the law of a given State. No private person has the right or the power to act on any level other than that of municipal law. Every right or power a private person enjoys is inexorably conferred by or derived from a system of municipal law which may conveniently and in accordance with tradition be called the *lex fori*, though it would be more exact (but also less familiar) to speak of the *lex arbitri* or, in French, *la loi d'arbitrage*.

The same is true of usage, whether domestic or international.[24] A usage is not law; it is effective only so far as recognized by municipal law as having binding force. Even an international trade usage must be established. The only difference between litigation and international arbitration is that in the former the usage, if not already established by law, will need to be proved to the satisfaction of the judge, and to be accepted by the judge as conforming to the legal prerequisites of a binding usage, if it is to be enforceable, whereas in an international arbitration a tribunal may feel free to infer the existence of usage without the same degree of stringency in requiring evidence or in applying legal criteria, confident in the knowledge that nowadays the judicial review of arbitral awards is severely restricted.

Even the most ardent advocates of party autonomy appear to accept that arbitration must act within some system of law. Their case is that the only relevant system is that of the state of enforcement. But this argument never gets off the ground, for it presupposes that the arbitral process works in a complete legal vacuum unless and until application is made to enforce the award as a foreign award. If that were so, then at the time of its rendering the award would have no legal underpinnings at all. It would undoubtedly be the product of the parties' agreement, under which they assented to be bound, but as stated earlier that assent is no more than an agreement, lacking any legal force unless accepted as binding by the relevant national law; and the only possible law is the *lex loci arbitri*.[25] Moreover, one may ask what, under the autonomy concept, is the status of the arbitral proceedings prior to the award. Do these too rest solely on the will of the parties? Such a contention has only to be stated for its absurdity to become obvious. A great many states around the world have now

[23] *Supra*, n. 6, at pp. 157, 160. *See* to similar effect in a conflict of laws context Horacio A. Grigera Naon, *Choice-of-law Problems in International Commercial Arbitration* (Tübingen, JCB Mohr (Paul Siebeck) 1992) at pp. 84, 85.

[24] *See generally* Roy Goode, 'Usage and its Reception in Transnational Commercial Law', (1997) 46 *ICLQ* 1.

[25] That is true even if the parties were unwisely to select as the curial law the law of a state other than that of the seat of the arbitration. The foreign curial law could be applied at the seat of the arbitration only so far as permitted by the *lex loci arbitri* and subject to the latter's own mandatory provisions.

enacted arbitration statutes designed to accommodate international arbitration. Are these to count for nothing? Are they simply instruments writ in water? What does it mean to say that the arbitral proceedings are not constrained by national laws when all over the globe we find national laws which do exactly that?

Belgium, in the hope of attracting more international arbitration, introduced what it thought would be a popular provision into its law excluding the power of Belgian courts to entertain an application for annulment of an award unless at least one of the parties to the dispute was Belgian.[26] This ingenious measure back-fired as the arbitration community came to see that its effect was to leave parties who wanted judicial assistance or had good grounds for annulment with nowhere to go.[27] Faced with this criticism[28] Belgium followed the lead of the Swiss Private International Law Act,[29] and changed its law to give the parties the option to exclude judicial review by agreement. So also did Sweden.[30] However, it appears that in Swiss arbitrations most foreign parties, following the advice of leading commentators on the Swiss Private International Law Act, have not availed themselves of that exclusion option.[31] This strongly suggests that most parties do not wish to take themselves wholly outside a legal framework in settling their disputes through arbitration.

### (b) Respect for Party Autonomy

The theory of the stateless award is grounded on the notion that the will of the parties should be respected and that it is this, not a *lex arbitri,* which gives binding force to an award. It is worth reminding ourselves of the terms of the arbitration clauses in the cases referred to above. In *Gotaverken* the arbitration clause provided that disputes were to be referred to arbitration and this was to take place in Paris under the ICC Rules. These stated that the rules governing the procedure were to be those resulting from the ICC Rules themselves, and, where they were silent, any rules which the parties (or failing them, the arbitrator) might settle, and whether or not reference was thereby made to a municipal procedural law to be applied to the arbitration. So in this case the effect of the arbitration clause was neutral; the ICC Rules contemplated that the parties or the arbitrator could, if they wished, resort to municipal law, but that they would not necessarily do so. In *Norsolor*[32] the position was the same except that ICC Court fixed Vienna as the place of arbitration. By contrast in *Hilmarton*[33] the arbitration clause specifically provided that the arbitration 'shall take place in Geneva under the law of the Canton of Geneva'. If the theory of the stateless award is based on the overriding effects of party autonomy, how was the

[26] Judicial Code, art. 1717(4).

[27] It is an accepted principle that while an enforcing court may refuse to recognize a foreign award, only the court of origin has power to annul it.

[28] *See, e.g.,* William W. Park, 'National Law and Commercial Justice: Safeguarding Procedural Integrity in International Arbitration', (1989) 63 *Tulane L. Rev.* 647.

[29] Private International Law Act, art. 192(2).

[30] Arbitration Act 1999, s. 51.

[31] Bruno Leurent, 'Reflections on the International Effectiveness of Arbitration Awards' (1996) 12 *Arbitration International* 269, 273.

[32] *Supra* n. 17.

[33] *Supra* n. 17.

French Court of Cassation able to find that the *Hilmarton* award was not integrated into the Swiss legal system, to which the parties had expressly subjected the arbitral proceedings? In *Chromalloy*[34] the arbitration clause provided that 'both parties have irrevocably agreed to apply Egypt [sic] Laws and to choose Cairo as the seat of the court of arbitration'. We may note the use of the word 'seat' rather than 'place', emphasizing the intention to choose Egypt as the place with which the arbitration was to have its juridical link. Again, one may ask, on what basis could the Court of Cassation disregard the express choice of the parties and instead determine that the award was not integrated into the Egyptian legal system? It seems that the principle of party autonomy is being used with a high degree of selectivity. The award derives its force from the agreement of the parties, but their decision to select a stated national law to govern the proceedings leading to the award is to be ignored![35]

### (c) The Protection of Legitimate Expectations

A fundamental purpose of the conflict of laws, and the reason why national courts are ready in appropriate cases to apply a foreign law to a dispute and to recognize and enforce judgments of foreign courts, is to protect the legitimate expectations of the parties to the dispute, who would suffer injustice if their reasonable reliance on the applicability of the law having the closest connection to the matters in issue were to be frustrated.[36] Where the parties have, expressly or by implication, selected a curial law, then to deny legal effect to that selection is not only to undermine the very principle of party autonomy on which the theory of the stateless award is based, but to frustrate their legitimate expectations. Of course, one of the tenets of the delocalization concept is that in international arbitration we should seek to dispense with reliance on conflict of laws rules altogether, since these are seen as merely perpetuating a national, rather than transnational, approach to the determination of disputes. Still, they have to face the question: what about party autonomy? Several answers have been propounded.

#### *(i) The choice of seat is often* a *matter of mere convenience*

This is a *canard* of long standing. It is doubtful whether it was ever true. Francis Mann, for example, wrote more than 30 years ago that choice of the seat 'is usually far from fortuitous, but made for good and well-understood reasons and purposes'.[37] More recently, it has been said that:

> The seat is typically fixed in a place where neither party has a place of business, e.g. the shores of Lake Leman. That location is not selected for its hotel facilities or charming setting, but

[34] *Supra* n. 18.

[35] It should be observed that we are here speaking not merely of a choice of venue, and the implications to be drawn from this, which are examined *infra*, but explicit choice of the procedural law (in *Hilmarton*) or of the seat *(Chromalloy)*.

[36] *Dicey and Morris on the Conflict of Laws* (2000, 13th ed.), para. 1-006.

[37] 'Lex facit arbitrum' (*supra* n. 6) at p. 163.

essentially because of the parties' confidence in the neutrality of the forum, the quality of the Swiss Private International Law (FSPIL) and the competence of Swiss jurists, arbitrators and judges (the same applies to Paris, London, Stockholm and other places).[38]

### *(ii) The choice of seat is often determined not by the parties but by the arbitral institution they have selected*

This is true but not to the point. Parties choose an arbitral institution because of their confidence in its ability to administer the arbitration and to make a sensible decision on the selection of the seat in the light of relevant factors, including the adequacy of the legal regime governing international commercial arbitration.

### *(iii) The choice of seat is often governed by the desire for neutrality*

This is also true, but if anything reinforces the argument that the parties have given serious thought to the choice of seat. It is fanciful to suppose that they would be happy to select as the seat any place that happened to be convenient and neutral.

### *(iv) The role of the arbitral tribunal is transitory and the seat has no necessary connection with the dispute*

This may be true but proves too much, for it fails to explain why as a matter of principle or policy the law of an enforcing state should necessarily have any greater claim to recognition than the *lex loci arbitri*. There may be at least as much contact with the forum state as with the enforcement state, which may have no link with the parties or the transaction whatsoever and is involved merely because of the fortuitous existence of assets of the respondent within its jurisdiction. Consider the following:

A German corporation and a French corporation enter into a contract under which the German corporation agrees to construct a plant in Milan for the French corporation. Any disputes are to be determined by an arbitral tribunal having its seat in Zurich and established in accordance with the arbitration rules of the Zurich Chamber of Commerce. The German corporation has its principal place of business in Berlin but other substantial places of business in Stockholm and Milan. It also has significant investments in New York but does not carry on any trading activity in the USA. The French corporation has its principal place of business in Paris but conducts substantial business activity in Milan and The Netherlands. It has no points of contact with the USA. The contract is made in Milan and is to be performed there. The French corporation, alleging that the plant did not comply with the contract specifications, invokes the arbitration clause. An award is made in favour of the French corporation but is set aside by the Swiss courts. The French corporation then applies to a US federal court in New York to enforce the award.

[38] Leurent, (1996) 12 *Arbitration International* 269, 272.

Of all the states connected to the dispute, the USA is the one whose link is the most tenuous. There are far more points of contact with the other states: France, Germany, Italy, Sweden, and The Netherlands. For neutrality none of these is chosen; the parties consciously choose Switzerland, having confidence in the Swiss legal environment governing international commercial arbitration. On what basis can it be said that in terms of policy New York law has a stronger claim to consideration than Swiss law? But for the fact that the German company had assets in New York there would be no ground whatsoever for New York courts even to entertain jurisdiction. The reason why it has to be given jurisdiction is, of course, that if it were not the successful claimant would have no way of reaching the assets. But that is simply a consequence of state sovereignty and power and has little to do with the question what law should be applied by the New York court.

The delocalization theory undermines the concept of party autonomy in another sense. If, following annulment of the award, the parties engage in a fresh arbitration, appointing the same or a new panel of arbitrators, and pursue the proceedings to a second award, why should not the consensual basis of the new arbitration proceedings, and the implicit acceptance of the nullity of the original award, be respected?[39] Why should the will of the parties be disregarded? And if it is conceded that it should not be disregarded, we are left with the farcical position of two separate, and possibly conflicting, awards covering the same dispute, both of them having to be treated as valid under the theory of delocalization.

### (d) Finality

Another fundamental purpose of the conflict of laws is to help bring finality to disputes involving an international element. That is why English courts have traditionally declined to re-examine the judgment of a foreign court of competent jurisdiction in the absence of special reasons for so doing. *Interest reipublicae ut sit finis litium.*[40] The territorial approach, in insisting that the validity of an arbitral award is governed by the *lex loci arbitri,* has the great merit of subjecting the question of validity to a single decision at the court of origin. By contrast, denial of the function of a *lex loci arbitri* may involve litigation in every country in which the respondent has assets, and even within a single country may entail the case being taken up through a two-tier or even three-tier hierarchical chain and then, where the highest court acts as a court of cassation, being sent back again to a new lower court for a fresh determination. One has only to look at the history of the litigation in some of the cases referred to *supra* to see the disastrous consequences of this. In *Hilmarton*[41] the Swiss award was taken through the hierarchy of courts in Switzerland and France, where the absurd position was reached that an award which had been set aside in Switzerland was granted exequatur by the Court of Appeal of Versailles; a second award resulting from fresh arbitration proceedings produced a different result but

[39] This fact situation also raises the question of estoppel, discussed *infra.*

[40] *Dicey & Morris, supra* n. 36, para. 14-110.

[41] *Supra* n. 17.

was in turn granted exequatur by the Versailles Court of Appeal; and the Court of Cassation, which had to do its best to resolve the muddle, made a decision which necessarily upheld one award (the first) and rejected the other. Ultimately the case ended up in English litigation, after which it was settled. In *Chromalloy*[42] the contract gave rise to proceedings in Egypt, France, and the USA. So much for finality! As more than one commentator has pointed out, this is not delocalization, it is multilocalization.[43]

### (e) Avoidance of Multiple Jeopardy

Closely linked to the conflict of laws policy of promoting finality is its separate policy of avoiding double jeopardy. *Nemo debet vis vexari pro eadem causa.*[44] The effect of refusal to acknowledge any place for the *lex loci arbitri* is that the respondent against whom an award is made, having battled successfully through his own courts to have it set aside, is then faced with the prospect of having to relitigate the identical issues before the courts of every country in which he has assets. This can only be described as oppressive.

### (f) Economic Efficiency

The exposure to a multiplicity of proceedings in a number of different countries also undermines what should be one of the purposes of international commercial arbitration, namely to promote economic efficiency in the handling of the dispute. A concept which provokes multiple lawsuits in different jurisdictions induces profligacy and the wasteful use of resources.

### (g) Estoppel

It is a general principle of law that a contracting party who pursues a particular course of conduct on which the other party reasonably relies cannot subsequently be allowed to follow a course which is inconsistent with the position he previously took. This principle of estoppel (reflected in civil law jurisdictions in the maxim *non concedit venire contra factum proprium*) has many manifestations. For example, in litigation an English court will take as its starting point the fact that a foreign judgment against a party by a court of competent jurisdiction creates an estoppel *per rem judicatam* precluding that party from relitigating the issue in England except where there are strong grounds to impeach the judgment, e.g. that it was obtained by fraud. In arbitration a similar principle prevails. Thus it is widely accepted that a person who participates in arbitration proceedings and against whom an arbitral award is

[42] *Supra* n. 18.

[43] See, *e.g.*, Pierre Mayer, 'The Trend Towards Delocalisation in the Last 100 Years', in *The Internationalisation of International Arbitration: The LCIA Centenary Conference* (ed. Hunter, Marriott and Veeder), (London/Dordrecht/Boston, Graham & Trotman/Martinus Nijhoff 1995) at p. 46.

[44] *Dicey and Morris, supra* n. 36, para. 14-110.

made cannot in general invoke a ground for attacking the validity of the arbitration agreement or the jurisdiction of the tribunal which he did not advance before the tribunal itself.[45]

One of the problems with the concept of the stateless award is that it fails to respect this well-established principle of estoppel. A party against whom an award is made decides to challenge it in the courts of the seat of the arbitration. If he is unsuccessful, why should he be allowed a second—or a third or fourth—bite at the cherry in proceedings before a court or courts elsewhere? Why, having embarked on a challenge under the *lex loci arbitri,* should he not be required to accept the outcome? Let us take the argument a step further. An arbitral award is set aside at the court of the seat. Thereupon the claimant institutes fresh arbitration proceedings in the same place. Why, having done this, should he be allowed simultaneously to enforce the first award in a foreign country? Why does not his institution of the second arbitral proceedings constitute an acceptance of the invalidity of the earlier award and an election to pursue his claim through the new proceedings?

## (h) *Inconsistency* of *Judgments of Foreign Courts*

A further consequence of the statelessness of an arbitral award is that it gives rise to the strong possibility of conflicting decisions of different foreign courts. This is surely a strange way of promoting the internationality of arbitration. Take the case where, after the annulment of an award, the claimant institutes fresh arbitration proceedings and is again successful but this time secures an amount only half of that given in the first award. What happens then? Is he to have the option to go back to the first, annulled, award? The present position would seem to be that the claimant can enforce the larger award in France and countries which follow the approach of French law but is restricted to the smaller award in countries which do not follow the French line. This hardly seems the best way of promoting predictability or uniformity in international arbitration.

There is another problem which is potentially even more acute. In the legal systems of some countries (which included Germany until it amended its arbitration law) the effect of annulment of an award is not to leave the way open for a fresh arbitration but to restore the ordinary competence of the courts, so that a fresh proceeding by way of action rather than arbitration becomes admissible. That proceeding may lead to a judgment which is required to be recognized and enforced elsewhere under bilateral or regional conventions, such as the Brussels Convention on Jurisdiction and the Enforcement of Judgments in Civil Matters. So, for example, the annulment of an award in one such state will have no effect in France, the courts of which would apply its own arbitration law to enforce the award, while those same courts would at the same time be duty bound to recognize and enforce the judgment upholding the claim in the post-annulment litigation. Of course, a

[45] For a recent English decision to this effect see *Westacre Investments Inc. v. Jugoilnport-SDRP Holding Co. Ltd.* [1999] 3 All ER 864.

solution would have to be found, and would be found, but why create the problem in the first place?

### (i) The Privileged Status of Arbitration Agreements

Another important factor overlooked by the protagonists of the stateless award is that a written arbitration agreement is not like an ordinary contract. Around the world it is given special, and highly prized, privileges. In the first place, a valid agreement to arbitrate invoked by a party against whom court proceedings are instituted effectively halts the proceedings. This is mandatory for the courts of states parties to the New York Convention[46] and is also specifically provided in the UNCITRAL Model Law.[47] Secondly, the parties and their arbitrator have much more freedom in the conduct of the arbitration than national judges. They need not follow rules of procedure or evidence prescribed for actions by the *lex fori,* nor are they required to apply the conflict rules of the *lex fori* in determining the applicable law in the absence of party choice. Thirdly, judicial review of an arbitral award is very much more restricted than an appeal against a judgment. Fourthly, an arbitral award can be enforced in the country of the award as if it were a judgment without the need for an action on the award. Finally, under the New York Convention and conventions with similar objectives[48] an award made in one state can be enforced in all other Contracting States[49] where the conditions set by the convention and any implementing legislation are satisfied. This is a hugely important privilege, which is much more extensive in geographical scope than that accorded to judgments of courts.

These privileges derive from national laws and international conventions, not from contract. How can parties to an arbitration claim the benefit of such laws and conventions and simultaneously ascribe the binding force of the arbitral award exclusively to their mutual will? If it is the case that the agreement to arbitrate is the sole source of the binding nature of the award, then let the parties be bound by the consequences attaching to any normal contract, namely that the sole method of enforcement is by an action on the award and that the resulting judgment will not enjoy the finality of an arbitral award or the benefit of the New York Convention.

### (j) Comity and Co-operation

If the courts of other countries followed the example of the French courts it is clear that Article V of the New York Convention would become a dead letter. No court would have any regard for the decisions of foreign courts setting aside an award; all

[46] Article 11(3). [47] Article 8(1).

[48] For example, the European (Geneva) Convention on International Commercial Arbitration 1961 and the Inter-American (Panama) Convention on Arbitration 1975.

[49] Assuming, in the case of the New York Convention, that the state of origin is a Contracting State or that the state of enforcement has not made a declaration under Article 1(3) limiting its obligation to the enforcement of awards made in another Contracting State.

courts would take refuge in their own arbitration law. Such an approach is subversive of the very internationality which the theory of statelessness is proclaimed to advance. Moreover, it is incompatible with the mutual courtesy and respect which each state and its courts are expected to show to other states and their courts as regards laws and decisions made by the latter within their respective jurisdictions. The principle of comity embodying such notions of mutual courtesy and respect has had varying impact at different stages in its history. At one time it was thought to be the basic principle upon which the conflict of laws rested. Later it was downgraded to a more subsidiary role as state courts came to the view that comity as such did not provide a reliable basis for deciding when to exercise self-restraint in the face of proceedings and judgments in foreign courts. Yet there are now indications that the concept of comity is regaining ground. In England, for example, one reason why it is invoked is to avoid jurisdictional conflicts. That is why English courts, in granting worldwide *Mareva* injunctions (now 'freezing orders'), are careful to stipulate that enforcement abroad requires the approval of the requisite foreign court:

> The jurisdiction to make such orders is now firmly established. It is exercised with caution and a sufficient case to justify its exercise must always be made out; but such orders are nowadays routinely made in cases of international fraud and the conditions necessary in order to preserve international comity and prevent conflicts of jurisdiction have become standardised.[50]

That is why also they have regard to considerations of comity in cross-border insolvency cases.[51] But the case can be put even more strongly. We have now moved beyond the concept of self-restraint and towards active international co-operation in civil procedure. This has come about through a variety of means: legislation, of which again insolvency law provides an example;[52] judicial activism, particularly in the field of cross-border insolvency, where independently of legislation judges of national courts sought ways to assist their counterparts in foreign countries; and the work of international organizations (such as UNCITRAL and the International Bar Association) in promoting cross-border collaboration in specific fields, such as cross-border insolvency,[53] and in civil proceedings generally.[54] For the world of international arbitration to revert to a system in which each state paid regard only to its own laws, and each court only to judicial decisions within its own jurisdiction, would severely impede the cause of international co-operation in dispute resolution. The internationalization of arbitration does not depend on, and is not promoted by, the concept of statelessness, which the courts of enforcing states adopting such a concept never see as applying to their own enforcement orders; on the contrary, all the concept achieves is a fragmentation of decision-making as each court focuses

[50] *Credit Suisse Fides Trust SA* v. *Cuoghi* [1998] QB 818, 824, *per* Millett LJ.

[51] See *e.g., Re Paramount Airways Ltd.* [1993] Ch 223; *Jyske Bank (Gibraltar) Ltd.* v. *Spjeldnaes* [1999] 2 BCC 101.

[52] Insolvency Act 1986, s. 426.

[53] See *e.g.,* the UNCITRAL Model Law on Cross-Border Insolvency 1997.

[54] *e.g.* the American Law Institute Project on Transnational Rules of Civil Procedure, in which international organizations such as UNIDROIT have been invited to participate.

exclusively on its own powers and refuses to countenance a proper law for courts of the seat of the arbitration.

### (k) Disappearance of the Raison d'Etre for Disregard of the Curial Law

Finally, the main cause of the reluctance of courts of enforcement states to defer to rulings of courts of origin, namely the hostility of local courts in a number of jurisdictions to the concept of arbitration and their assertion of excessive jurisdiction over arbitral proceedings and awards, has largely (though not entirely) disappeared as state after state has departed from its traditional arbitration rules and enacted legislation along the lines of the UNCITRAL Model Law. As one authority has rightly commented, if Member States of the European Communities had sufficient confidence in each other's courts to ratify the Brussels and Lugano Conventions providing for the mutual recognition and enforcement of judgments, why should they not have the same confidence in judgments of courts of other states setting aside arbitral awards?[55]

## V. Conclusion

The objections to the concept of the stateless award are overwhelming and should now be universally accepted. None of the arguments in favour of the stateless award has explained why, apart from *force majeure,* the courts of an enforcement state should be considered to have a prerogative denied to others. If, which is not suggested, there is to be a single court the judgments of which are in principle to have effect *erga omnes,* it should be the court of the seat. France is almost alone in its advocacy of the stateless award and is believed to be unique in not even allowing its courts to invoke the setting aside of an award in the court of origin as a ground for refusing recognition and enforcement in France. French scholars and French courts have over the years made an immense contribution to the liberalization of international commercial arbitration. Faced with widespread opposition to the concept of the stateless award they could perform a further and signal service to international arbitration by gracefully withdrawing from their present approach, which is seen in most countries as a step too far. This change of direction would itself be an act of leadership, not of defeat, and would help to restore the transnational character of international commercial arbitration.

The most appropriate solution is that based on fulfilling the twin objectives of satisfying legitimate expectations and fostering international co-operation among courts. Article VII of the New York Convention is here a stumbling block in that it encourages states to bypass Article V and invoke their own laws. That is damaging

[55] J.-F. Poudret, 'Quelle solution pour en finir avec l'affaire Hilmarton? Reponse à Philippe Fouchard' [1998] *Rev. de l'Arb.* 7, 14–15. See also Klaus Peter Berger, *International Economic Arbitration: Studies in Transnational Economic Law,* vol. 9 (Deventer, Kluwer Law and Taxation, 1993) at pp. 96–7. See also William W. Park, 'Duty and Discretion in International Arbitration', (1999) 93 *AJIL* 805, 813.

to the process of internationalization which the Convention itself has done so much to foster. A strong case can be made for amending Article VII of the Convention by restricting its scope to treaties entered into by the enforcing state removing that part of Article VII which enables a party to invoke the more favourable provisions of the law of enforcement—and by leaving courts of enforcing states to rely on the discretion already available to them under Article V, a discretion which itself should be exercised with caution.[56] This should go hand in hand with a self-denying precept of legislatures and courts to the effect that, while the court of enforcement must inevitably have the last word to cater for exceptional cases, in principle judgments of courts of the seat enforcing, suspending or annulling an award should be respected, as should findings of fact by such courts. Obviously there will be such exceptional cases, e.g. fraud discovered only after the judgment, but adherence to the general principle is essential if we are to respect party choice, to avoid the cost, inconvenience and risk of inconsistent decisions resulting from a multiplicity of proceedings, and to foster rather than damage mutual respect and co-operation among courts of different states.

[56] Albert Jan van den Berg, 'Residual Discretion and the Validity of the Arbitration Agreement in the Enforcement of Arbitral Awards under the New York Convention of 1958', in *Current Legal Issues in International Commercial Arbitration* (ed. Chang *et al.*), (University of Singapore 1997) at pp. 335-6, noting that the discretion to allow enforcement despite a ground for refusal under Article V was designed to cater for two situations, namely minor procedural irregularity and failure to raise before the arbitral tribunal the objection to the tribunal's jurisdiction advanced as a challenge to the award before the court of enforcement.

# 23

# The Adaptation of English Law to International Commercial Arbitration*

*Roy Goode*[1]

The U.K. Department of Trade and Industry Advisory Committee on Arbitration, established some years ago under the chairmanship of Lord Justice Mustill and now chaired by Lord Justice Steyn, is currently engaged in work on a new Arbitration Act.[2] It is therefore an opportune time to examine the extent to which English law adequately accommodates international commercial arbitration.

The high regard in which English law and English courts are held in other jurisdictions is amply attested by the regularity with which parties to contracts having no significant connection with England select English law as the governing law and English courts to determine their disputes. But we must constantly guard against arrogance or complacency. We live in a highly competitive world. The City of London may at present be pre-eminent as a financial centre but we cannot take it for granted that this will continue. We may feel that our laws and procedures are superior to those of other States but if we cut ourselves off from outside influence we may discover sooner than we think that our ideas have become outmoded, that they are no longer seen to be responsive to the needs of the international business community.

It is salutary to reflect that a mere seventeen years ago we were almost the only developed jurisdiction that still retained the concept of absolute sovereign immunity; that a mere twelve years ago we were still applying a procedure unique to this country, the special case stated, in international as well as domestic arbitration,

* Originally published as Roy Goode, 'The Adaptation of English Law to International Commercial Arbitration'. *(1992) 8 Arbitration International 1*: 1–16.

[1] Norton Rose Professor of English Law in the University of Oxford, Fellow of St. John's College, Oxford. This is a revised and slightly expanded reproduction of the Freshfields Arbitration Lecture delivered at Queen Mary and Westfield College, University of London, on 5 June 1991. Though the writer is a member of the Department of Trade and Industry Advisory Committee on Arbitration the views expressed here are purely personal and should not be taken as indicating the Committee's current thinking. I should like to express my thanks to my research assistant, Miss Regina Asariotis, for all her assistance in gathering sources for the lecture here reproduced.

[2] A privately financed project made possible through the initiative and labours of Mr. Arthur Marriott and his team and proceeding under the direction of a Bill Sub-Committee chaired by Mr. Martin Hunter, whose firm so generously supports the lecture series referred to above.

and only the steady loss of business made us think again; that even today our law is unable to comprehend something as basic as the creation of an international organisation under international law except so far as it has become localised by English legislation; and that foreigners trading on our swap markets are expected to investigate the power of local authorities to engage in market operations.[3]

The fact is that whilst we are not impervious to foreign influence we are not very good at doing the influencing ourselves. Though we make major contributions to the preparation of international conventions we are usually the last major State rather than the first to ratify. Thus while some three dozen States, including many major jurisdictions, have ratified the Vienna Convention on Contracts for the International Sale of Goods, we remain reluctant to concede that anything could possibly be better than our century-old Sale of Goods Act[4] and we conveniently ignore the fact that for every sale contract governed by English law there are several others that are governed by foreign law available only in a foreign language to which the common law has made no contribution, leaving our nationals much more exposed than they would be under the Convention, for which there is an official English text and comprehensive commentaries in English.

So while others might look to us for leadership we are all too often followers rather than leaders, with the result that when issues of interpretation of a Convention arise our courts are late in the field and their ability to influence thinking in other jurisdictions is correspondingly reduced.

## I. The Needs of Foreign Parties Arbitrating in England

Contracting parties carrying on business in different States not infrequently choose the law of a third State to govern their contract and the curial law of that State to control the arbitration. The principal reason is to avoid one party being given what is perceived to be the undesirable advantage of arbitrating under his own law and his own country's arbitration rules with which he and his lawyers are likely to be much more familiar than their foreign counterparts. The parties thus submit themselves to the law of and to arbitration in a country for whose law and administration they may in a general sense have the highest regard but whose history, culture, traditions, language, method of contracting, legal reasoning and rules of substantive law and procedure are quite different from their own. Indeed, their two countries may have much more in common with each other than with the selected third State.

What, then, do such parties expect when they come to arbitrate in a foreign land? One thing they may reasonably expect is that the arbitrator will have regard to the international character of the transaction. They may have chosen English law, but does that mean English law as applied in all its detail to domestic transactions? An international transaction is not the same as a domestic transaction and a dispute

[3] *Hazell v. Hammersmith and Fulham London Borough Council* [1991] 2 W.L.R. 372.

[4] The current Act is, of course, the Sale of Goods Act 1979 but for the most part this re-enacts the Sale of Goods Act 1893.

between two foreigners is not the same as a dispute between two Englishmen. We can reasonably suppose that when they invoke English law they envisage English law applied with a broader brush and with an eye to established international usage and the need to accommodate the particular factors that are peculiar to transactions involving a foreign element.

So also with rules of procedure and evidence. When foreigners pay us the courtesy of arbitrating in England, we like to think they have a perception of English arbitration procedure as embodying highly developed principles of fair play and natural justice; but does it follow that they also intend to submit themselves to the very same rules of procedure and evidence that are applied in all their particularity to purely domestic disputes? Again, I would suggest not. Foreign parties are entitled to assume that the arbitrator will have regard to procedures and modes of proof appropriate to the arbitration of an international commercial transaction.

It is against this background that I turn to consider English arbitration law as it affects transactions involving a foreign element.

## II. The Rules of English Law Governing International Commercial Arbitration

The old law merchant, a diffuse and uncodified body of trade usage, was international in character, was founded on good faith and was largely free from the technicalities of national law. In England its application was not dependent on contract; in relation to dealings between merchants it was recognised by statute and by the courts as not only normative but superior to dispositive law. Its administration was informal, flexible and fast. Special privileges and protections were conferred on merchants from overseas. Eventually it was supplanted by national law, which localised international transactions through the development and application of conflict of laws rules and to a high degree subjected arbitration to the rules of evidence and procedure applicable to litigation.

To what extent does modern English law make special accommodation for international commercial arbitration? It cannot be denied that we have made some moves in the right direction. Our rules of public policy are applied somewhat less stringently to transactions with a foreign element; and in the case of non-domestic agreements to arbitrate outside the special categories of admiralty cases, insurance and commodities we make it easier to exclude appeals to the courts. Moreover, by enacting the New York Convention we have removed in the case of non-domestic arbitration agreements the discretion normally enjoyed by our courts to refuse a stay of proceedings by reason of an agreement to arbitrate.[5]

How far have we gone beyond this? Dr. Gilles Wetter, an eminent Swedish authority well disposed to this country and its institutions has observed perceptively that:

[5] Arbitration Act 1975, s. 1.

London is the *locale* of the greatest number of international arbitrations in the world. Yet the vast majority of these are viewed by the arbitrators, counsel and the parties as wholly domestic in character in the sense that the proceedings are indistinguishable from those which take place between two English parties. In Sweden, to the contrary, arbitrations in which at least one party is non-Swedish are treated as being multi-dimensional, in recognition of the particular requirements and problems inherent in transnational disputes.[6]

The force of this observation may be seen from the following propositions of English law which are believed to be tolerably accurate:

(1) An arbitrator cannot, by ruling on his own jurisdiction, preclude a pre-award ruling by the court as to whether he has jurisdiction.

(2) An arbitrator cannot adjudicate on the validity of the agreement containing the arbitration provision under which he was appointed.

(3) An arbitrator is obliged to observe the rules of evidence applicable to ordinary litigation except so far as the parties otherwise agree.

(4) An agreement purporting to confer on an arbitrator power to decide a case *ex aequo et bono* has no legal effect.

(5) A party can, with leave of the High Court, appeal from an award on grounds which include an error of law on the face of the award, except where the parties have exercised their right to make an exclusion agreement.

Every single one of these propositions of law, designed for domestic arbitration, appears equally applicable to international arbitration, except that the exclusion agreement can in the latter case be made in advance of the dispute, whereas in a domestic arbitration it is valid only if made after the dispute has arisen. And on each proposition English law is quite out of line with the prevailing approach in other major jurisdictions. Of course, this does not necessarily mean that we are wrong. To the contrary, we have it on what was previously the highest political authority that in international matters the United Kingdom is the only one in step, the sole observer of the true faith! As it happens, I believe this to be true of the first proposition. But we need to look at each of them more closely. The five propositions will be considered under two broad heads, the limits of arbitral power and the availability of judicial review.

## (a) The Limits of Arbitral Power

### *(i) The arbitrator's power to determine his own jurisdiction*

Much has been written about Kompetenz-Kompetenz and a brief comment will suffice. The arbitrator's power to determine his own jurisdiction is subject to judicial intervention not only after his award but before it. This is the particular characteristic

6 'Choice of Law in International Arbitration Proceedings in Sweden' (1986) 2 *Arbitration International* 294 at p. 298.

of the English law rule on Kompetenz-Kompetenz, and with one qualification it is sensible, for it avoids expense and it is flexible, the court retaining a discretion to refuse to intervene where it considers it more expedient for the arbitrator to give his award first.

The qualification is that this power should be limited to direct jurisdictional issues, as opposed to those which arise indirectly through an attack on the validity of the agreement pursuant to which the arbitrator was appointed. That should be dealt with by accepting the arbitrator's power to determine questions affecting the validity of the agreement.

### *(ii) Arbitrator's jurisdiction to rule on the validity of the agreement*

Where English law is not merely particular but peculiar in the popular sense is in the situation where there is a dispute as to the very existence or validity of the agreement relied on as containing the agreement to arbitrate. This is not in truth a question of Kompetenz-Kompetenz at all, but a quite distinct question whether an arbitrator has power to adjudicate on the validity of the agreement containing the clause pursuant to which he was appointed. English law adheres to the perceived logic of the proposition that if the agreement of which the arbitration clause forms part is invalid the reference to arbitration is necessarily invalid.

In taking this stance English law is isolated. The essential question is the intention of the parties. In general, it is to be assumed that they intend to confer on the arbitrator power to determine the validity of the contract between them, so that only if the agreement to arbitrate is itself vitiated does the arbitration fall to the ground. Even without the well established doctrine of separability the logic of the English position would be arid and unhelpful. In the law of contract we find nothing inherently illogical in allowing a party to exclude the other's right to rescind for misrepresentation, even though the clause excluding rescission forms part of a contract which upon rescission would be rendered retrospectively null and void. In the conflict of laws we see no great difficulty in the proposition that the law to be applied to determine the validity of a contract is the law which would be applicable if the contract were in fact valid, a principle now embodied in the Rome Convention which we have enacted. If we can swallow the camel of these particular circularities, why should we strain at the gnat of autonomy of an arbitration clause? Of course, the assumed separate agreement is notional but there is no harm in that; the concept of separability is simply a device to give effect to the presumed intention of the parties that the arbitrator's remit is to include, where necessary, a ruling on the validity of the substantive agreement.[7]

[7] The most recent decision is the judgment of Steyn J. (as he then was) in *Harbour Assurance Co. (UK) Ltd.* v. *Kansa General International Insurance Co. Ltd.* [1992] 1 Lloyd's Rep. 81, in which he indicated that had he not felt constrained by prior authority he would have held that the arbitrator was entitled to rule on the question of the initial illegality of the agreement.

### (iii) *Observance of rules of evidence*

On the need to follow rules of evidence that magisterial work, Mustill and Boyd, has the following to say:

> It is widely believed that an arbitrator, merely because he is an arbitrator, is empowered to act on evidence which would not be strictly admissible in a Court of Law. This is not so. Arbitrators are bound by the law of England, and the rules regarding admissibility of evidence are part of that law.[8]

Even for domestic arbitrations such a rule lacks merit. One of the reasons why parties opt for arbitration is informality and a commercial approach to the determination of their dispute. The notion that they intend the rules of evidence for litigation to be applied in all their rigour is surprising indeed. In the case of international arbitration such a rule has nothing in its favour. The English law of evidence possesses a most unfortunate tendency to rigidity in the formulation of rules which fly in the face of experience and are alleviated only by the robust good sense of our trial judges.

Three examples will suffice. We have a parol evidence rule, a rule greatly eroded by exceptions and so complex and circular in character that our Law Commission finally decided not to recommend its abolition because it was impossible to say what it meant![9] We have a rule against hearsay evidence, also subject to numerous exceptions, which if properly applied would exclude a good deal of both oral and documentary evidence upon which ordinary businessmen rely. We have rules for the interpretation of contracts which, so the House of Lords has ruled not once but several times, render evidence of pre-contract negotiations and post-contract behaviour absolutely inadmissible for the purpose of construing a contract,[10] though we all know that such evidence regularly surfaces in agreed bundles of documents placed before the court and is often the most reliable guide to the meaning of the contract.

Now if we in England wish to tie ourselves hand and foot by rules of this kind in domestic legislation, so be it. But why, in an international arbitration, should we expect foreign parties accustomed to business evidence and to relaxed evidential rules in their own countries, to be circumscribed by our arcane jurisprudence on evidence? The mediaeval courts of common law, which were notoriously strict in their approach to evidence, were nevertheless content to tolerate and recognise the informality of the merchant courts in the reception of evidence. How ironic if we in the closing years of the 20th century, when the volume of international trade has reached unparalleled levels, should now impose a more severe regime than our predecessors of the Middle Ages!

The only requirement should be that the arbitrator acts fairly and in conformity with natural justice.

[8] *Commercial Arbitration* (2nd edn., London 1989), p. 352.

[9] *Law of Contract: The Parol Evidence Rule* (Law Com. No. 154, Cmnd. 9700, 1986).

[10] *James Miller & Partners* v. *Whitworth Street Estates (Manchester) Ltd.* [1970] A.C. 583; *Prenn* v. *Simmonds* [1971] 1 W.L.R. 1381; *Schuler AG* v. *Wickman Machine Tools Ltd.* [1974] A.C. 235.

### *(iv) Decisions* ex aequo et bono

English courts have always set their faces against giving legal effect to an award based on an arbitration agreement by which the arbitrator is empowered to decide the case *ex aequo et bono*. The reason ascribed to this rule is that such an agreement negates an intention to create legal relations, so that there is no contract and thus no award that the law can recognise.[11] As I have pointed out elsewhere,[12] this conclusion is based on a decided *non sequitur*. The fact that the parties wish the award to be arrived at otherwise than by recourse to rules of law does not mean that they intend to deny legal force to the undertaking to arbitrate on the resulting award, merely that the arbitrator may apply non-legal criteria in reaching his decision. Mr. Steward Boyd QC has argued powerfully that if this is what the parties want there is no reasonable basis upon which to deny it to them.[13]

> . . .there is a widespread and growing appreciation of the extent to which arbitrators in other jurisdictions are permitted to decide in accordance with principles which are not those of any one fixed system of law, but an amalgam or distillation of many systems of law, or indeed no recognised system of law at all. What principle of English public policy, it may be asked, would require the English courts to refuse to recognise and enforce a foreign award made in accordance with such principles if it is valid in accordance with the law of the country by which the arbitration is governed? And if there is no such principle of public policy precluding enforcement of such an award made abroad, should not such an award be equally enforceable if made in England under English arbitration law?

## (b) The Availability of Judicial Review

I now turn to an issue which is both complex and controversial: the judicial review of an arbitral award.[14] Prior to the Arbitration Act 1979 the special case stated procedure and a fairly liberal post-award appeal regime provided endless opportunity for dilatory tactics, and the resultant loss of foreign business became so noticeable that legislative action had to be taken. The 1979 Act abolished the special case stated procedure and introduced provisions design to curb appeals on a point of law.

[11] *Orion Compania Espanola de Seguros* v. *Belford Maatschaapij voor Algemeene Verzekringen* [1962] 2 Lloyd's Rep. 257, *per* Megaw J. at p. 264; *Deutsche Schachtbau-und- Tiefbohrgesellschaft mbH* v. *Ras Al Khaimah National Oil Co.* [1987] 2 Lloyd's Rep. 246, *per* Sir John Donaldson M. R., at p. 253. In the latter case the Master of the Rolls, in whose judgment the other members of the court concurred, concluded that in an arbitration under the ICC Rules, which allow the arbitrators, in default of a choice of law by the parties in their contract, to determine the proper law by the rule of conflict they consider appropriate, the arbitrators were perfectly entitled to select as the proper law 'a common denominator of principles underlying the laws of the various nations governing contractual relations' (*ibid.*, at p. 254). The decision generated much debate but is plainly in accordance with principle. The parties themselves could have selected an amalgam of the rules of different legal systems; the ICC Rules gave the arbitrators the same freedom.

[12] *Commercial Law* (London, 1982), p. 975.

[13] '"Arbitrator not to be bound by the Law" Clauses' (1990) *Arbitration International* 122, at p. 123.

[14] For an excellent comparative survey, see Adam Samuel, *Jurisdictional Problems in International Commercial Arbitration: A Study of Belgian, Dutch, English, French, Scandinavian, US and West German Law* (Zürich, 1989).

Under section 1 of the Arbitration Act 1979 an appeal on a question of law arising out of an arbitral award lies to the High Court with the consent of all the parties or, in the absence of a valid exclusion agreement, with leave of the court.[15] Leave is not to be granted by the High Court 'unless it considers that, having regard to all the circumstances, the determination of the question of law concerned could substantially affect the rights of one or more parties to the arbitration agreement.'[16] That is the sole constraint on the court's power to grant leave to appeal in non-exclusion cases, and does not by itself provide a great deal of encouragement to those who favour finality or predictability in arbitration. It has been left to the courts to give effect to the perceived will of Parliament substantially to reduce judicial review of arbitral awards.

As the result of the 'guidelines' laid down by the House of Lords in *The Nema*[17] and *The Antaios*[18] and a spate of ensuing case law the factors relevant to the issue now appear to include the following: whether the situation is 'one-off' or repeat; whether, in the former case, it is of limited interest or raises an important point of principle; whether the dispute depends upon the interpretation of contracts or clauses in general use in a particular trade; whether determination of the point of law by the court would add significantly to the clarity and certainty of English commercial law; whether the circumstances in which the reference was made suggest that the parties attached importance to the speed and finality of the decision; whether it is clear, probable or merely possible that the arbitrator has gone wrong in law, noting, however, that the degree of certainty of error required varies according to the first two factors mentioned and has been expressed in a wide variety of judicial expressions. To quote again from Mustill and Boyd:

> Thus it is said that the award must be 'obviously wrong on a mere perusal'; that it must be 'clearly wrong'; that the judge 'would need a good deal of convincing the arbitrator was right'. Leave would, however, be given if the judge received the decision 'with very considerable surprise.' It is not enough, however, to show 'very considerable doubt.' On the other hand the bare word 'wrong' has also been employed. No doubt other expressions can and will be used in the future. We suggest that it is unprofitable and indeed misleading to attempt a reconciliation. These turns of phrase reflect the reaction of the court to a particular award, in relation to a particular question of law, and they show that the principles of the exercise of the discretion are not confined to rigid categories.[19]

The learned authors continue:

> . . .Other factors may have a powerful influence on the exercise of the discretion: more powerful, on occasion, than the judge's estimate of the general utility of a decision. Thus, if the way in which the reference was brought into existence and conducted was such as to suggest that both parties wished for a speedy resolution of the dispute, or if the parties deliberately abstained from asking for a reasoned award, it is less likely that leave will be given . . . . Conversely, if the arbitrator is asked to make a reasoned award, this will be some evidence that the desire for speed and finality was not paramount.[20]

[15] Arbitration Act 1979, s. 1(3). [16] *Ibid.*, s. 1(4). [17] [1981] 2 Lloyd's Rep. 239.
[18] [1985] A. C. 191. [19] *Op. cit.*, at p. 607. [20] *Ibid.*

Finally, we are told that:

> Since the Nema did not purport to lay down exclusive criteria for the grant of leave to appeal, other factors will on occasion have to be taken into account.[21]

The analysis of the case law to the end of 1988 takes up no fewer than nine pages of commentary in the latest edition of Mustill and Boyd[22] and the flow of cases has continued unabated. Not one of the factors to which I have alluded appears anywhere in the 1979 Arbitration Act; it is pure judge-made law, a robust and sensible approach to an indeterminate statutory provision. But how far is it law at all? In the *Aden Refinery* case Mustill L. J. pointed out that the guidelines themselves were not intended to be immutable but were subject to adaptation or refinement to meet varying or unforeseen circumstances. On the other hand those passages in *The Nema* and *The Antaios* which dealt with the *spirit* in which judges should approach the discretionary power conferred on them (namely to be consistent with the intention of Parliament to secure finality) were authoritative pronouncements which judges should observe.

This brings us to the question of appeals to the Court of Appeal which require leave of the High Court *and* a certificate that the question of law is of general public importance or is one which for some other special reason should be considered by the Court of Appeal. Subject to these conditions it was until recently generally assumed that such an appeal was governed by the *Nema* guidelines. Then it was realised that this postulated the trial judge giving leave to appeal on the ground that the decision he had rendered only moments before was almost certainly wrong! Hence the ruling in *Geogas SA v. Trammo Gas Ltd.*[23] that the relevant test was not whether there was a strong prima facie case that the judge was wrong but whether the question of law certified by the judge was worthy of consideration by the Court of Appeal, which involved an assessment whether there was sufficient doubt about the correctness of the decision to warrant such consideration, whether the decision of the Court of Appeal would add significantly to the clarity and certainty of English commercial law or whether for some other reason the Court of Appeal should consider the question of law.

If one were asked by foreign parties negotiating a contract whether if they chose English arbitration and the rules of natural justice, procedure and jurisdiction were to be followed, they could rely on the award being final, one's answer would have to be: 'God only knows!' Let me emphasise once again that this is not the fault of the judiciary. To the contrary our courts have laboured mightily to promote finality and restrict judicial review but they have been hampered by the almost total absence of meaningful criteria in the legislation and have thus had to make bricks with precious little statutory straw.

Where, then, does this leave us? The parties to a contract, who have chosen arbitration in order to secure informality, finality and confidentiality, find all their expectations frustrated because the judge considers that an issue of law in their

[21] *Ibid.*, p. 608. [22] *Ibid.*, pp. 600–9. [23] [1991] 2 W.L.R. 794.

private dispute raises questions of general importance which will help *other* parties in *future* cases and will add to the clarity and certainty of English commercial law. Now I am perfectly happy to accept the underlying premiss that English commodity associations and English arbitrating parties share a burning enthusiasm to enrich English jurisprudence—or that if they do not, then they jolly well should! But why should foreign parties be exposed to the delay, the expense and the breach of confidentaliality involved in an appeal to the court? Why should such parties have to face the uncertainty of a procedure so utterly dependent on judicial discretion? Why, in short, should parties to an international commercial arbitration be served up as cannon fodder for the English legal system? As that great lawyer Lord Devlin sardonically remarked: 'The next step would, I suppose, be a prohibition placed on the settlement of cases involving interesting points of law.'[24] If there is indeed a general interest in the authoritative determination of a particular issue there should be no difficulty in organising an agreed test case in litigation or arbitration. If no two parties can be found who are willing to initiate a test case, it suggests that the point is not of such interest after all—except, perhaps, to the academics and the judges!

It might be argued that the parties' inferred desire for finality is outweighed by the interests of the State in having authoritative rulings on points of major importance in English commercial law and in maintaining a watchful eye over arbitrators, so that they are aware of the prospect of judicial review if they overstep the mark. But even if such a standpoint were at one time tenable it has now been fatally undermined by the provisions of the 1979 Act permitting exclusion agreements—the clearest possible statutory acknowledgment that in international arbitrations, at least, there is no fundamental principle of public policy at stake which necessitates the preservation of judicial review against the wishes of the parties.

We ought not to expect foreigners to be familiar with our rules on exclusion agreements when drafting their contracts. Nor should the onus be on the parties to prove a desire for finality, when such desire is the norm rather than the exception. We should emulate the law of other countries, both those who have adopted the UNCITRAL Model Law and those who have not, in restricting judicial review to fundamental and clearly defined grounds.[25] Such an approach is not peculiar to civil law systems. It has been adopted by Australia and Canada and also by the United States, where what has to be shown is not mere error of law but 'manifest disregard for the law.' It is noteworthy that the Rules of our own London Court of International Arbitration expressly exclude judicial review.

## III. Towards a Transnational Commercial Law

I have earlier remarked on the way in which English law localises international commercial transactions, converting them to the status of domestic transactions. This is

[24] *The Judge* (Oxford, 1979), at p. 106.

[25] See K.P. Berger, 'The Modern Trend Towards Exclusion of Recourse Against Transnational Arbitral Awards: A European Perspective,' 12 Fordham Int. L.J. 605 (1989).

not in itself surprising, for it is the conventional approach of the conflict of laws. You select the conflict rule and then apply the law ascertained by that rule. What tends to be overlooked is the necessary third enquiry: is that law, according to its own terms, to be applied as if it were a domestic transaction or do the foreign elements qualify its application or even exclude it entirely? Even if the spatial reach of the rule of domestic law is limited only by the conflict of laws rules of the forum—an assumption which in my view tends to be made too readily and without adequate consideration of the policy of the *lex fori*—it does not follow that it must be applied in exactly the same way to an international transaction as to a domestic one. Yet it remains the case that when English lawyers speak of international trade law they do not mean the *international* law of trade, they mean the *national law* governing international trade transactions.

In recent years there has been an increasingly strong reaction against the domestication of international contracts. It is interesting to note, for example, that even though French lawyers believe even more passionately in the quality and good sense of their law than we do in ours, yet French courts were among the first to declare that it was not appropriate to apply French conceptions of *ordre public* to international transactions. This reaction against the domestication of international contracts is one we do well to observe, for in my belief it is the motive force which impels lawyers whose vision transcends national boundaries to urge recognition of a new *lex mercatoria*.

It was my friend and colleague the late Professor Clive Schmitthoff, the doyen of international trade law scholars, who is credited with propounding the new transnational law merchant,[26] and his ideas were picked up and developed by others.[27]

Much has been written about the *lex mercatoria*,[28] a concept of which English lawyers, in their pragmatic way, have tended to be somewhat dismissive. Indeed, they are not alone, for there is world-wide controversy not only as to the scope of the *lex mercatoria*[29] but as to its very existence. Let me say at once that I do not myself

[26] Clive M. Schmitthoff, 'The Law of International Trade, its Growth, Formulation and Operation,' in *The Sources of the Law of International Trade* (ed. Schmitthoff, London, 1964).

[27] The most notable exponent being the distinguished French scholar Professor Berthold Goldman. See B. Goldman, 'Frontières du droit et *lex mercatoria*,' (1964) IX Archives de philosophie du droit 177 and, for a more recent exposition, *Lex mercatoria* (1983) Forum Internationale, lecture 3. See also Aleksander Goldštajn, 'The New Law Merchant' [1961] J.B.L. 12 and 'Reflections on the Structure of the Modern Law of International Trade,' in *International Contracts and Conflicts of Laws* (ed. Petar Šarčević, London, 1990), Chapter 2.

[28] With particular reference to international commercial arbitration and the conflict of laws. See, for example, Ole Lando, 'The *Lex Mercatoria* in International Commercial Arbitration' (1985) 34 I.C.L.Q. 747; F. A. Mann, '*Lex facit arbitrum*' in *International Arbitration: Liber Amicorum for Martin Domke* (ed. P. Sanders, The Hague, 1967); M. Mustill, 'The New *Lex Mercatoria*: The First Twenty-five Years,' in *Liber Amicorum for the Rt. Hon. Lord Wilberforce* (ed. Bos and Brownlie, Oxford, 1987), reprinted, with minor amendments, in 4 Arb. Int. 86 (1988).

[29] The wide view of the *lex mercatoria* equates it with transnational commercial law, by which is generally meant that set of rules, from whatever source, which governs international commercial transactions and is common to a number of legal systems. Such commonality may derive from uncodified international trade usage, from codifications of that usage exemplified by the ICC's Incoterms and Uniform Customs and Practice for Documentary Credits, from standard-term contracts which have acquired international currency, from common principles established in different jurisdictions (whether independently or by the adoption in a particular jurisdiction of a principle developed by the courts

believe in a body of customary international commercial law as an independent legal norm 'floating in the transnational firmament', to use the graphic words of Sir Michael Kerr when rejecting the concept of a stateless arbitration procedure.[30] It is clear that uncodified international trade usages,[31] so far as identifiable, are capable of being given normative force by a national or supranational legal system and to that extent constitute a modern *lex mercatoria*. But the usages which are said to constitute the *lex mercatoria* do not penetrate a contract or a legal system merely by being there. They have to be triggered by a legally adoptive act—express or implied contractual incorporation, adoption by legislation or self-executing Convention or reception by the courts of a national or supranational legal system. Until so adopted they exist merely as facts, not as normative rules. No party can be required to have imposed upon him rules for which he has not contracted and which neither emanate from a national or supranational legal system nor have received the imprimatur of that system. Even the normative effect of the old law merchant was dependent upon its acceptance into national legal systems, an acceptance everywhere qualified by certain preconditions grounded on public policy.

I am not unaware of the strong, though far from universal, body of opinion which holds that even without the authority of the contract an arbitrator is free to apply the conflict rules he considers appropriate and to disregard the curial conflict rules, a subject authoritatively examined by Dr. Lew in his much cited work on the applicable law in arbitration.[32] This, of course, makes it much easier to recognise the arbitrator's right to apply a floating *lex mercatoria*. But the adoption of conflict of laws Conventions, and in particular the Rome Convention on the law applicable to contractual obligations, makes it increasingly difficult to detach arbitration from national conflict of laws rules, for such Conventions require the application of a national law (unless the parties otherwise agree) and the Conventions themselves form part of transnational commercial law.

Nevertheless it is clear that the *lex mercatoria* is a source to which, so far as its rules can be identified, national judges are entitled to resort by receiving them into their own legal system. We ourselves have done it quite recently when we drew on prevailing foreign legal doctrine to abandon our theory of absolute sovereign

of a different jurisdiction) and by a variety of international instruments such as Conventions, model laws and model rules. There is, of course, no magic in labels; but the concept of the *lex mercatoria* as an autonomous anational body of law can have no significance in relation to judicial decisions, legislation or operative Conventions, nor to contracts effective under a national legal system. The anational corpus of law contended for must therefore be international customary law; but in identifying international custom it is legitimate to look to all sources providing evidence of practice, including Codes and Conventions.

[30] *Bank Mellat v. Helleniki Techniki SA* [1984] Q.B. 291, at p. 301.

[31] When customary international trade usages become codified, as in the case of the various sets of rules promulgated by the International Chamber of Commerce, their status tends to change, in that they typically take effect by express contractual incorporation or, in some countries, by legislative adoption. But even in a transaction where they have not been effectuated in one of these ways they may be referred to as the best evidence of current usage.

[32] Julian Lew, *Applicable Law in International Commercial Arbitration* (New York, 1978).

immunity in favour of the modern theory which requires the court to distinguish *acta jure imperii* from *acta jure gestionis*.[33]

Thus we ought not to be dismissive of the *lex mercatoria*, for it is a resource which, with the huge growth in harmonising Conventions, codifications of trade terms and trade usages, and other harmonising measures, will increasingly be drawn upon by our civilian colleagues. As Redfern and Hunter rightly point out:[34] 'There *is* evidence of a unified international standard in the practice of many modern forms of commerce.'

I believe it to be important that as part of the European market we do not allow ourselves to become isolated from current thinking merely because ours is a common law tradition. When our courts decide to jettison a long hallowed principle as running counter to generally modern thinking, then, while in form they merely declare what the law is now seen to be, the reality is that they are exercising a power to create a new rule. Similarly, when they reach out to the doctrine or jurisprudence of other jurisdictions to find a solution to a problem which our own case law has not had occasion to address, they are acting creatively in admitting into English law that which has become received wisdom elsewhere. In so doing they are not applying some anational norm floating in a jurisprudential vacuum; they are applying English law as reinterpreted in the light of internationally recognised principle and practice. And if it is open to a national judge to draw on external influences to interpret national law, why should it not be equally open to an arbitrator, whose function is to apply a national law as if he were a judge?

## IV. The Adaptation of English Commercial Law to International Commercial Arbitration

What I have attempted to demonstrate is the importance of sensitivity to international trends in the application of domestic law to international transactions and international commercial arbitration. We take pride in the fact that English has now become the *lingua franca*. Yet perhaps we should pause to ask ourselves this question: when an English company seeks to break into the French market, to whom will the French award their contracts? To the Englishman, whose language they well understand; or to the Italian, who speaks French? So also in the field of commercial law and commercial arbitration. We in England have much to be proud of in our legal tradition, in particular, the adaptability of our substantive commercial law and the high calibre of our judicial and arbitral institutions. If we are at fault it is not, I believe, in anything fundamental but rather in a certain procedural conservatism, a failure in our arbitration law to match the sensitivity of our substantive law to the needs of the market, coupled with a degree of imperviousness to external influence

[33] *I Congreso del Partido* [1983] 1 A.C. 244.

[34] *Law and Practice of International Commercial Arbitration* (London, 1986) at p. 90. This passage has not, however, been reproduced in the second edition (London, 1991).

which is inimical to our legal development. In the result our arbitration law is rigid where it should be flexible and uncertain where it should be predictable.

It is almost everywhere the rule that an arbitration clause is to be treated as independent of the contract of which it forms part. That is a rule we should adopt. It is widely recognised that an arbitration agreement can confer on an arbitrator power to reach a legally binding decision *ex aequo et bono*. We should do likewise. We should also refrain from imposing on arbitrators the shackles of English rules of evidence which are alien to other legal systems. All that is required is that the arbitrator should observe the agreement of the parties and the rules of natural justice. Finally, we should emulate other States in restricting judicial review to clearly defined categories—want of jurisdiction, impropriety, procedural unfairness, manifest disregard of the law, public policy requirements[35] and the like—and to cases where the parties themselves opt for judicial review. The clarification of English commercial law, whether for the enrichment of our jurisprudence in general or for the benefit of future contestants in particular, is not in my view a proper ground for destroying the privacy and finality of the dispute resolution procedure for which the parties have opted. Other countries do not find it necessary to permit judicial review in such cases; what is so special about English arbitration that we should find it necessary to act differently?

I have expressed the view that there is nothing fundamentally wrong with English arbitration law. But in restating its principles and rules in a new Arbitration Act we must draw on the inspiration of the UNCITRAL Model Law (which as Lord Justice Steyn has so rightly observed is one of the most remarkable achievements of UNCITRAL[36]) to liberate ourselves from the shackles which fetter our freedom of movement in international commercial arbitration. By showing ourselves receptive to the practices of international arbitrators and to the trends of thought of our civil law friends and colleagues we do not diminish the influence of the English common law and its tried and tested institutions; rather we strengthen it, so that instead of merely responding belatedly to approaches that have become commonplace elsewhere in Europe, instead of being a reluctant follower along trails blazed by others, we can ourselves influence not only the development of international commercial arbitration but, more fundamentally, the evolution of transnational commercial law.

[35] Which should be applied from a transnational rather than a domestic viewpoint. See generally, Pierre Lalive, 'Transnational (or Truly International) Public Policy and International Arbitration' in *Comparative Arbitration Practice and Public Policy in Arbitration* (ed. P. Sanders), ICCA Congress Series No. 3, VIII the International Arbitration Congress, New York 1986, 257.

[36] 'Towards A New English Arbitration Act,' (1991) *Arbitration International* 17, at p. 18.

# 24

# Litigation or Arbitration? The Influence of the Dispute Resolution Procedure on Substantive Rights*

*Roy Goode*†

Allan Farnsworth was one of the world's great contract and commercial lawyers. His textbook and separate casebook on contract law became classics, displaying enormous scholarship and extraordinary industry. So too did the American *Restatement (Second) of Contracts,* of which he was the Reporter. Allan is a huge loss to the Columbia Law School, where he laboured in the vineyards for over half a century. But his absence will also be keenly felt elsewhere, not least at UNIDROIT,[1] where he served with distinction as a member of the Governing Council for two decades and was a major influence in the shaping of the UNIDROIT Principles of International Commercial Contracts as a member of the Working Group so admirably chaired by Professor Michael Joachim Bonell. Allan had a gift for succinctly capturing the commercial realities underlying rule-making. Writing of dispositive contract rules applicable in default of contrary agreement by the parties, he commented:

> Some default rules are intended to spare parties the cost of negotiating and drafting by providing the rules that they would probably have agreed upon had they taken the time to do so .... But many default rules have a different purpose. They are *not* the rules that the parties would probably have agreed upon; they are instead rules that will induce the parties—often one of the parties—to negotiate a more suitable rule for the particular transaction.[2]

* Originally published as Roy Goode, "Litigation or Arbitration? The Influence of the Dispute Resolution Procedure on Substantive Rights", 19 Pace Int'l L. Rev. 53 (2007). Reproduced by kind permission from the publisher.

† Emeritus Professor of Law in the University of Oxford and Emeritus Fellow of St. John's College, Oxford.

[1] The International Institute for the Unification of Private Law, an international intergovernmental organization based in Rome and devoted to the unification of private law at the international level.

[2] E. Allan Farnsworth, "An American View of the Principles as a Guide to Drafting Contracts", in *UNIDROIT Principles for International Commercial Contracts: A New Lex Mercatoria?* 87 (1995).

This would have been the perfect answer to complaints by certain sectors of the leasing industry that the provisions of the 1988 UNIDROIT Convention on International Financial Leasing did not reflect the typical terms of a financial lease.

Allan was much in demand as an arbitrator in international commercial arbitrations, where his commercial grasp and trenchant style quickly demolished untenable propositions. I was once privileged to be invited by him and his co-arbitrator to be the Chairman of a tribunal in an arbitration in which they were engaged. The applicable law was that of the State of Illinois and the procedure, was governed by the arbitration rules of the Arbitration Institute of the Stockholm Chamber of Commerce. The American party sought to have a substantial volume of evidence excluded on the ground that it contravened the Illinois parol evidence rule. Allan gave a snort of derision—and that was the end of the argument!

This short piece has no pretensions to profundity; it is written simply as a brief tribute to an outstanding scholar who could have written it so much better himself.

## I. Introduction

Much has been written on the relative merits of litigation and arbitration. Advantages claimed for the latter are party selection of the tribunal, privacy, confidentiality, party control of the procedure, finality, speed, and cost reduction. In relation to the first five of these, the claims are justified, though with the caveat that confidentiality and finality may be undermined by judicial review, whilst in the case of international commercial arbitration, at least, it is often far from the case that the proceedings are quicker and less expensive than litigation.[3] What is interesting, however, is that in the decision whether to select litigation or arbitration as the mode of dispute resolution, the focus is almost exclusively on procedure and on the exclusion or restriction of judicial review. Relatively little attention has been paid to the potential impact of the choice of arbitration on the determination of substantive rights in international disputes. In particular, regard should be had to: (1) the determination of the applicable law, (2) the application of "rules of law", (3) the effect of failure to apply the applicable law correctly or at all, (4) the impact of a more relaxed approach to the admissibility of evidence, and (5) recognition and enforcement of a foreign arbitral award. Of course, the restriction of judicial review remains an important factor to be taken into consideration.

[3] Whereas in judicial proceedings court fees are usually modest and no payment has to be made for the judge or the use of the courtroom, in the typical case involving a panel of three arbitrators the parties will be responsible for their travel costs, hotel accommodation, fees of the arbitrators, hire of rooms for the hearing and, in the case of an institutional arbitration, the fees of the institution administering the arbitration. Moreover, dates have to be fixed which accommodate the diaries of the three members of the arbitral tribunal, lawyers on both sides, the parties themselves, and witnesses. This can result in substantial delays before the case is heard.

## II. The Impact of Institutional Rules

In evaluating an arbitration clause providing for institutional arbitration—for example, arbitration under the aegis of the International Chamber of Commerce or the London Court of International Arbitration—it is all too easy to overlook the impact of the institutional rules by which the parties agree to be bound when submitting their request for arbitration. These rules, though primarily directed to the appointment of the arbitral tribunal and the conduct of the arbitration, may also contain important provisions which directly or indirectly affect substantive rights. For example, the determination of the applicable law, the power of the tribunal to draw on non-binding rules as sources of rights, the admissibility of evidence, and the exclusion of judicial review may be affected. Therefore, institutional rules may, in various ways, expand the power of the tribunal and limit the circumstances in which its award may be set aside or refused recognition.[4]

## III. Determination of the Applicable Law

In cases involving a foreign element, the national judge frequently[5] has to determine what law governs the issue or issues before the court. For that purpose he is obliged to apply his own country's rules of private international law. The trend in arbitration is towards giving the arbitral tribunal greater freedom. This may be enshrined in legislation on arbitration or in institutional rules. Thus, under some of these rules, an arbitral tribunal, while obliged to respect party choice of law, may in the absence of such choice determine the law applicable to the substance of the dispute in accordance with the conflict rules it considers applicable[6] or appropriate.[7] Not all jurisdictions are quite so liberal. For example, where the seat of the arbitration is in Switzerland, section 187(1) of the Swiss Private International Law Act 1987 requires the arbitral tribunal to decide the case in accordance with the rules of law[8] with which the case has the closest connection. This is the approach taken by several other jurisdictions. In neither case, however, is the tribunal required to apply the conflict rules of the seat of the arbitration itself. This distinguishes the position of an arbitral tribunal from that of a national judge. So the applicable law as determined by an arbitral tribunal may well be different from that determined by a judge under national

[4] *See infra* Parts VI, VII.

[5] But not always, because foreign law may not have been pleaded or because on the point at issue the laws of the different states may be the same.

[6] *See, e.g.,* Uncitral Model Law on International Commercial Arbitration, art. 28(2) (1994); UNCITRAL ARBITRATION RULES, art. 33(1) (1998); Arbitration Act, 1996, 23, § 46(3) (Eng.).

[7] *See, e.g.,* International Chamber of Commerce (ICC) Rules of Arbitration, art. 17(1) (Jan. 1, 1998) [hereinafter ICC Rules of Arbitration]; LCIA Arbitration Rules, art. 22(3) (1998).

[8] As to "rules of law", see *infra* Part IV.

conflict of laws rules and may produce an entirely different outcome. However, in all these cases the tribunal must reach the applicable law through a conflicts rule. But some jurisdictions allow the tribunal to determine the applicable law directly without going through a conflicts rule.[9]

## IV. The Application of "Rules of Law"

The traditional conflict of laws doctrine is that only the law of a state can be selected to govern a transaction or issue. On this basis, a national court, unless otherwise empowered by its own law, cannot directly apply the *lex mercatoria* or rules based on a combination of national laws or non-binding rules of law, such as the UNIDROIT Principles of International Commercial Contracts (PICC) or the Principles of European Contract Law (PECL), though these may well serve as a reference point for the court in deciding in which direction its national law should develop. It is generally considered that the 1980 Rome Convention on the law applicable to contractual obligations,[10] in its references to "law", applies only to the legal system of a state, not to non-binding rules of law. However, the impetus in international commercial arbitration to free arbitral tribunals from the shackles of national law and enable them to draw on sources offering the best solutions to modern problems has led increasingly to the acceptance of "rules of law". These legal rules are drawn from a number of legal systems and are evolving as transnational rules, general principles or *lex mercatoria,* including formulations in non-binding instruments such as the PICC and PECL. The ICC Rules of Arbitration provide for the application of rules of law in the following terms:

> The parties shall be free to agree upon the rules of law to be applied by the Arbitral Tribunal to the merits of the dispute. In the absence of any such agreement, the Arbitral Tribunal shall apply the rules of law which it determines to be appropriate.[11]

There has been an increasing number of references to the UNIDROIT Principles in ICC awards, and in several of these cases the Principles have been directly applied as rules of law or as evidence of custom or usage or to supplement the applicable law.[12]

[9] *See Fouchard, Gaillard, Goldman on International Commercial Arbitration* at 1552–3 (Emmanuel Gaillard & John Savage eds., 1999).

[10] Now being converted into an EC regulation, an early draft of which would have empowered the parties, instead of choosing the law of a state, to "choose as the applicable law the principles and rules of the substantive law of contract recognised internationally or in the Community." *See* Proposal for a Regulation of the European Parliament and the Council on the Law Applicable to Contractual Obligations (Rome I), com (2005) 650 final (15 December 2005), 4.2. This provision, which would have allowed choice of the PICC and the PECL as the applicable law, proved too controversial and has been dropped.

[11] ICC Rules of Arbitration, *supra* note 7, art. 17(1).

[12] *See* UNIDROIT Principles of International Commercial Contracts: Reflections on Their Use in International Arbitration, A Special Supplement to the ICC International Court of Arbitration Bulletin (Int'l Chamber of Commerce 2002); Emmanuel Jolivet, *The UNIDROIT Principles in ICC Arbitration, in* UNIDROIT Principles: New Developments and Applications, ICC International Court of Arbitration Bulletin 2005 Special Supplement (Int'l Chamber of Commerce 2006).

The concept of rules of law is seen as more responsive than national law to the needs and practices of international commerce and the identification of best solutions to given problems. The UNCITRAL Model Law,[13] the Washington Convention,[14] and the arbitration laws of a number of legal systems, including English law,[15] permit the parties to choose rules of law but, in the absence of choice, require the tribunal to apply "law" in the traditional way. Certain other systems, including French law, are more liberal, and empower the tribunal to apply the rules of law it considers appropriate.[16] Either approach gives the arbitrator a wider degree of freedom than that enjoyed by a judge applying national law and may lead to the application of rules different from that which the judge would apply and, in consequence, to a different result. So again, the choice of arbitration as the dispute resolution mechanism may affect not only the procedure to be followed, but the substantive result of the case.

## V. Evidence

The admissibility of evidence in proceedings before a court is governed by the law of evidence, which may impose constraints on what can be admitted. Thus, many common law systems have or have had rules excluding the admissibility of hearsay evidence,[17] secondary evidence, such as a copy of a document when the original is available,[18] and parol evidence.[19] Though in modern times rules of this kind are of reduced importance, they may nevertheless from time to time operate to exclude evidence which, if admitted, might have led to a different outcome of the case. Arbitrators, however, are not bound by such rules except so far as the parties themselves agree to apply them. In practice, the strong tendency in arbitration is not to apply exclusionary rules but to evaluate the weight, rather than the admissibility, of evidence. Article 34(2)(f) of the English Arbitration Act leaves it to the tribunal to decide whether to apply strict rules of evidence (or any other rules) as to the admissibility, relevance or weight of any material (oral, written, or other) sought to be tendered.

[13] UNCITRAL Model Law on International Commercial Arbitration, art. 28(2) (1994).

[14] Convention on the Settlement of Investment Disputes Between States and Nationals of Other States, International Center for Settlement of Investment Disputes, Washington 1965 thereinafter Washington Convention]. *See infra* Part VI.

[15] Arbitration Act, 1996, 23, § 46(1)(b) (Eng.). This does not use the phrase "rules of law" but, after referring to the law chosen by the parties, empowers the tribunal, if the parties so agree, to decide the dispute in accordance with "such other considerations as are agreed by them or determined by the tribunal", which goes even wider than rules of law and enables the parties to give the tribunal power to decide *ex aequo et bono.*

[16] New Code of Civ. Pro., art. 1496.

[17] An out-of-court statement offered in evidence to show the truth of the facts asserted in the statement.

[18] The so-called "best evidence" rule.

[19] Extrinsic evidence adduced to add to, contradict or vary the terms of a written contract. The parol evidence rule was traditionally formulated as one which excluded oral (parol) evidence but in fact applies to any evidence, written or oral. The rule is subject to numerous exceptions and has little to commend it.

Again, the significance of any applicable institutional rules should not be overlooked. So Article 25(6) of the UNCITRAL Arbitration Rules provides that the arbitral tribunal shall determine the admissibility, relevance, materiality, and weight of the evidence offered, and similar provisions are to be found in Article 34(1) of the ICSID Arbitration Rules, Article 22(1)(f) of the LCIA Arbitration Rules, and Article 20(6) of the American Arbitration Association International Rules.

## VI. Restrictions on Judicial Review of an Arbitral Award

One of the undoubted advantages of arbitration is the greater degree of finality that results from an arbitral award than from a court judgment. It is much harder to have an arbitral award set aside or varied in court proceedings than it is to have a judgment upset or modified on an appeal to a higher court. Thus in principle it is not a ground for setting aside an award that the tribunal was guilty of errors of fact. However, under US law, an award may be set aside for "manifest disregard of the law", that is, an intentional disregard of the law agreed by the parties or found by the tribunal to be applicable, where, if the law had been applied, it would have led to a different result,[20] whilst English law allows an appeal on the grounds of want of jurisdiction, serious procedural irregularity and error of law, though in this last case only if the parties agree or the court gives leave (which it cannot do unless various conditions are satisfied) and the right of appeal has not been excluded by agreement.[21]

A distinctive feature of arbitration under the Arbitration Rules of the International Centre for the Settlement of Investment Disputes (ICSID) is that ICSID awards, though subject to an internal annulment procedure by an *ad hoc* committee appointed in accordance with Article 52(3) of the Washington Convention, are immune from judicial review in every Contracting State.[22]

## VII. Recognition and Enforcement of Awards

While there are only limited arrangements in force for the international recognition and enforcement of judgments in civil cases,[23] the position is otherwise in the case of international commercial arbitration, which is governed by the

[20] In a recent decision, the Eleventh Circuit Court of Appeals reviewed the "manifest disregard of the law" standard and held that the case fell far short of what was required to show a breach of that standard: *B L Harbert Int'l LLC v. Hercules Steel Co.*, 441 F.3d 905 (11th Cir. 2006); *see also* Eric D. Dunlop, *Setting Aside Arbitration Awards and the Manifest Disregard of the Law Standard*, 80 FLA. B.J. 51 (2006).

[21] Arbitration Act, 1996, 23, §§ 67–69 (Eng.).

[22] Washington Convention, art. 53(1). The grounds for annulment are laid down in art. 52(1) and are very restricted.

[23] Within the European Community mutual recognition and enforcement are provided by Council Regulation (EC) No 44/2001, Dec. 22, 2000 (commonly known as "Brussels I") on the recognition and enforcement of judgments in civil and commercial matters. Outside the European Community, recognition and enforcement are dependent on bilateral treaties.

United Nations Convention on the Recognition and Enforcement of Foreign Arbitral Awards,[24] which has been ratified by no fewer than 137 states. Under the Convention, a party receiving an arbitral award in one state is entitled, on complying with the requisite formalities, to have the award recognized and enforced in another state, provided that state is a party to the Convention.[25] Such recognition and enforcement may be refused only in the restricted circumstances laid down in Article V.[26]

## VIII. Implications for the Drafting of Arbitration Agreements

I have often felt that insufficient attention is given to dispute resolution clauses, which tend to be treated as boilerplate. Typically, the parties opt either for litigation in a selected forum under an exclusive or non-exclusive jurisdiction clause or for arbitration, often under institutional rules, by arbitrators appointed pursuant to those rules or some other given procedure. However, at the time of their agreement the parties may not be well placed to predict in advance the form of dispute resolution best suited to their case. It would often be preferable to specify an interim procedure, such as negotiation followed by a mechanism to determine the most appropriate means of resolving the dispute. But whatever procedure is agreed upon, it is important, when drafting the dispute resolution clause, to take into account the different ways in which, as described above, the choice may impact on the parties' substantive rights.

So when an arbitration clause is being drafted the parties need to consider to what extent they wish either to expand or to constrain the powers of the arbitral tribunal. In particular, should the tribunal be free to have recourse to soft law embodied in non-binding rules either to supplement or to supplant the otherwise applicable law? Should the parties consider the inclusion of an express provision dispensing with strict rules of evidence rather than leaving themselves in the hands of the arbitral tribunal? Should they not ensure, when adopting institutional rules, that there are no default rules which need to be excluded or varied? Moreover, in fixing the seat of the arbitration, the parties need to consider the law of the intended forum governing judicial review and the extent to which they are content to have any award subjected to an appeal to the courts in accordance with that law.

There is one final point. In some jurisdictions, such as France, the courts consider that an award in an international commercial arbitration is autonomous in character, so that where, for example, the seat of the arbitration is Switzerland, a French court is nevertheless entitled to enforce an arbitral award that has been set aside by Switzerland's highest court because the award, being international, is not

[24] United Nations Convention on the Recognition and Enforcement of Foreign Arbitral Awards, June 10, 1958, 330 U.N.T.S. 38.

[25] *Ibid.* arts. III, IV.

[26] However, a state, when signing, ratifying or acceding to the Convention, may declare that it will apply the Convention only to awards made in the territory of another Contracting State. *Ibid.* art. I(3).

"integrated into the legal system" of Switzerland.[27] The parties need to consider whether, in the interests of preserving the finality of the award, which as noted earlier is one of the key attractions of arbitration, they should agree that no application will be made in a foreign court to enforce an award set aside under the *lex loci arbitri.*

[27] *Hilmarton Ltd. v. Omnium de Traitement et de Valorisation (OTV),* Cass. le civ., Mar. 23, 1994, 1994 REV. ARE. 327. *See also Pabalt Tikeret Sirketi v. Norsolor,* Cass. le civ., Oct. 9, 1981, 1985 REV. ARE. 431; *Polish Ocean Line v. Jolasry,* Cass. le civ. Mar. 10, 1993, 1993 REV. ARE. 255; *Arab Republic of Egypt v. Chromalloy Air Services, CA,* Paris, Jan. 14, 1997, 1997 REV. ARB. 395. *See* Roy Goode, *The Role of the Lex Loci Arbitri in International Commercial Arbitration, 17* ARB. INT. 19, 32–3 (2001) (provides a detailed criticism of the concept of delocalization of the award reflected in these decisions).

# 25

# The End of An Era: A Tribute to Jacob Ziegel*

After an astonishing 35 years as Editor-in Chief of the C.B.L.J., during which time he contributed to and oversaw the content of no fewer than 52 of the Journal's 54 volumes, Professor Jacob Ziegel, who recently suffered a stroke from which he is steadily recovering, has now been compelled to hand the reins to his friend and colleague Professor Tony Duggan, while Jacob himself becomes Editor-in-Chief Emeritus.

Jacob stepped into the shoes of his distinguished predecessor Frank Iacobucci, in September, 1978, which marked the first issue of the third volume, bringing to the Journal a vast knowledge of commercial and consumer law and an impressive track record of teaching—at Saskatoon, McGill, Osgoode Hall, and, finally, Toronto—and scholarly publication. Always supportive of the work of younger colleagues, Jacob made it his business to welcome the widest range of contributors to the C.B.L.J.: leading legal figures and young scholars, law teachers, practitioners, judges, and others. This rich diversity of contributors was one of the key factors in establishing the Journal's reputation for sharp and concise analysis combined with a focus on current decisions and legislative developments in commercial law.

And he led by example. An endless series of articles, papers, textbooks, case books, and case notes of the highest quality flowed from his pen. His range has been enormous, covering all aspects of commercial and consumer law, including personal property security, personal and corporate insolvency, consumer credit, and partnership and company law, not only in Canada but in a range of other jurisdictions, in particular, the United States, the United Kingdom, and the British Commonwealth. Nor is this all. He has taken a keen interest in the system for appointments to the judiciary, about which he has written critical comments.

Through his teaching, writings, work on legal committees, and general involvement in legal developments he has made a major contribution to Canadian jurisprudence and played a highly influential role in the evolution and analysis of the Canadian Personal Property Security legislation. Jacob was very active at the international level, and was a founder member of the International Academy of Commercial and Consumer Law.

* Reproduced from Roy M. Goode: *The End of an Era: A Tribute to Jacob Ziegel*, (2013) 54 C.B.L.J 319, by permission of Canadian Business Law Journal Inc. and Thomson Reuters Canada Limited.

Jacob's love of disputation and his intense intellectual curiosity manifested itself in a series of interrogations of those of us who thought we were experts, only to find, frustratingly, that we were unable to answer his questions on the history of this rule, the policy of that rule, or even the legal conundrums he periodically posed. His fame as a scholar led to invitations to give lectures and seminars, and speak at conferences, all around the world, and everywhere he went his warmth and immense capacity for friendship resulted in an ever-widening circle of friends and admirers.

All this was not enough to absorb Jacob's inexhaustible energy. In 1970 he set up the first of a long series of annual workshops on commercial and consumer law. This rapidly became one of *the* events in the year in the commercial law world, attracting scholars, judges, and practising lawyers from many countries. His retirement in 1993 was purely notional. The Journal continued to flourish under his leadership, the workshops went on unabated. The 2010 workshop celebrated an astonishing 40 years of organisation by Jacob. At the conference dinner, a commemorative medal, designed by a well-known Canadian sculptor, was presented to Jacob amid acclamation from all his friends and colleagues; and to mark this 40th annual workshop, volume 50 of the C.B.L.J. was devoted to a collection of commemorative essays. Jacob has now retired in a real sense. We salute this illustrious scholar, esteemed colleague, and warmest of friends, we thank him for his great contribution to the world of law and we wish him well.

Sir Roy Goode<br>Emeritus Professor of Law, Oxford University

## APPENDIX

# Roy Goode: Publications 1962–2018

### BOOKS

*Hire-Purchase Law and Practice* (Butterworths, 1st edn. 1962, 2nd edn. 1970, supplement 1975).

*Hire-Purchase and Conditional Sale: A Comparative Survey of Commonwealth and American Law* (jointly with Professor Jacob S. Ziegel) (British Institute of International and Comparative Law 1965).

*Introduction to the Consumer Credit Act 1974* (Butterworths 1974).

*Sweet & Maxwell's Commercial Law Statutes* (ed.), Sweet & Maxwell, 1979

*The Consumer Credit Act: A Students' Guide* (Butterworths 1979).

*Consumer Credit Legislation* (Butterworths, looseleaf) (original author, and now General Editor with assistant editors).

*Commercial Law* (Penguin Books and Allen Lane 1982, reprinted with minor revisions 1985, reprinted Pelican Books 1986, many subsequent reprints; 2nd edn. 1995, reprinted with minor revisions 1996; hardback edn. published by Butterworths 1998; 3rd edn. Penguin Books 2004, hardback LexisNexis 2004, 4th edn. (ed. Ewan McKendrick), 2009, hardback LexisNexis, 2010 paperback Penguin Books 2010, 5th edition (ed. Ewan McKendrick), hardback LexisNexis 2016, paperback Penguin Books 2016.

*Legal Problems of Credit and Security* (Sweet & Maxwell and Centre for Commercial Law Studies, 1st edn. 1982, 2nd edn. 1988, 3rd edn. 2003, 4th edn. (ed. Louise Gullifer) 2008, 5th edn. (ed. Louise Gullifer) 2013, 6th edn. (ed. Louise Gullifer) 2017.

*Payment Obligations in Commercial and Financial Transactions* (Sweet & Maxwell and Centre for Commercial Law Studies 1983), 2nd edn. (ed. Charles Proctor) 2009, 3rd edn. (ed. Charles Proctor and Victoria Dixon) 2016.

*Proprietary Rights and Insolvency in Sales Transactions* (Sweet & Maxwell and Centre for Commercial Law Studies, 1st edn. 1985, 2nd edn. 1989), 3rd edn. (ed. Simon Mills) 2010.

*Consumer Credit Law* (reproducing in revised and expanded form Division I of *Consumer Credit Legislation*) (Butterworths 1989).

*Principles of Corporate Insolvency Law* (Sweet & Maxwell and Centre for Commercial Law Studies, 1st edn. 1990, 2nd edn. 1997, 3rd edn. 2005, 4th edn. hardback and paperback, Sweet & Maxwell, 2080, 5th edn. (ed. Kristin van Zwieten) 2018.

*Guide to the ICC Uniform Rules for Demand Guarantees* (1CC Publications 1992).

*Commercial Law in the Next Millennium, the 1997 Hamlyn Lectures* (Sweet & Maxwell 1998), translated into Italian (Giuffre 2003).

*Official Commentary on the Convention on International Interests in Mobile Equipment and Aircraft Protocol* (UNIDROIT, 2003, also reproduced in 2002-2 Uniform Law Review 353; revised edn. 2008, 3rd edn. 2013).
*Official Commentary on the Convention on International Interests in Mobile Equipment and Rail Protocol* (UNIDROIT 2008, 2nd edn. 2014).
*Official Commentary on the Convention on International Interests in Mobile Equipment and Space Protocol* (UNIDROIT 2013).
*Transnational Commercial Law: International Instruments and Commentary* (with Herbert Kronke, Ewan McKendrick, and Jeffrey Wool) (Oxford University Press 2004, 2nd edn. 2012).
*Transnational Commercial* (two-volume student text, with Herbert Kronke and Ewan McKendrick) (OUP 2007, 2nd edn. 2015).
*Explanatory Report on the Hague Convention on the Law Applicable to Certain Rights in Respect of Securities Held with an Intermediary* (with Professors Hideki Kanda and Karl Kreuzer, assisted by Dr. Christophe Bernasconi) (Martinus Nijhoff 2005, 2nd edn. (format change only) Hague Conference 2017).
*Guide to the ICC Uniform Rules for Demand Guarantees, URDG 758* (with Georges Affaki) (ICC Services Publications 2011).

## CONTRIBUTIONS TO ENCYCLOPAEDIC WORKS

*Halsbury's Laws of England* (4th edn.), 'Bills of Sale, and Reissue' in vol. 4(1) 1992.
*Encyclopaedia of Forms and Precedents* (4th edn.), vol. 4, 'Bills of Sale'; vol. 10, 'Hiring and Hire-Purchase'.
*The Dictionary of National Biography 1986–1990* (Clive Schmitthoff).
*Palgrave's Dictionary of Economics and the Law*, 'Instalment Credit Agreements'.

## BOOKS AND JOURNALS EDITED

*Commercial Law Bulletin 1984–86* (Sweet & Maxwell).

*Consumer Credit Legislation* (Butterworths, looseleaf, relaunched as *Goode's Consumer Credit Law and Practice*).

*Commercial Operations in Europe* (with K.R. Simmonds) (Sijthoff 1978).

*Consumer Credit* (Sijthoff, 1978, for United Kingdom National Committee of Comparative Law and Faculty of Laws, Queen Mary College).

*Electronic Banking: The Legal Implications* (ed.) (Institute of Bankers and Centre for Commercial Law Studies 1985).

*Conflicts of Interest in the Changing Financial World* (ed.) (Institute of Bankers and Centre for Commercial Law Studies 1986).

Group Trading and the Lending Banker (ed.) (Institute of Bankers and Centre for Commercial Law Studies 1988).

*Commercial and Consumer Law* (with Ross Cranston) (Oxford University Press 1993).

*Goode's Consumer Credit Law and Practice* (General Editor and contributor), a five-volume looseleaf previously entitled *Goode's Consumer Credit Legislation* and relaunched under its new title in December 1999 (Butterworths).

*Goode's Consumer Credit Reports*, a three-volume looseleaf set of reports (Butterworths launched 1999).

## ARTICLES, PAPERS AND CONTRIBUTIONS TO EDITED WORKS

'Some Problems of Hire-Purchase Law' (1962) 112 LJ 35, 216, 231, 251; (1963) 113 LJ 116, 229.

'Hire-Purchase Law' (Notes of a Lecture delivered at the Law Society's Hall on 22 April 1965, Law Society 1965).

'The Ideal Instalment Credit Law' (Address to the European Federation of Finance House Associations, Edinburgh 1966).

'The Legal Regulation of Lending' (Paper presented at a conference on Instalment Credit by the British Institute of International and Comparative Law 1968, and published as chapter 3 of *Instalment Credit* (ed. Aubrey L. Diamond) (Stevens 1970).

'Is Article 9 of the Uniform Commercial Code Exportable? An English Reaction' (Presented jointly with Professor L.C.B. Gower at a conference on Comparative Commercial Law, McGill University 1968, and comprising chapter 22 of *Aspects of Comparative Commercial Law* (ed. Jacob S. Ziegel and William Foster) (McGill University and Oceana Publications 1969).

'Recent Legislative and Judicial Trends in England' (Presented at a conference on Comparative Commercial Law, McGill University 1968, and comprising chapter 10 of *Aspects of Comparative Commercial Law* (ed. Jacob S. Ziegel and William Foster (McGill University and Oceana Publications 1969).

'A Credit Law for Europe?' (Inaugural lecture delivered at Queen Mary College 1973, published as revised and expanded in (1974) ICLQ 227).

'The Consumer Credit Act 1974' (1975) Camb LJ 79.

'The New Face of Consumer Credit Law, Obiter' Queen Mary College Law Society Journal Summer 1976, 13.

'The Right to Trace and Its Impact in Commercial Transactions' (1976) 92 LQR 360, 528.

'Security for Payment in Export and Import Transactions' (jointly with Ulrich Drobnig), published in *Commercial Operations in Europe* (with K.R. Simmonds) (Sijthoff 1978).

'Reflections on Credit Law' The Three Banks Review, March 1978, 26.

'Inalienable Rights?' (1979) 42 MLR 553

'Equipment Leasing in England' (Paper presented at the conference of the German Society of Comparative Law, Lausanne, 1979, and published in *Leasingvertrage im Handelsverkehr* (ed. Wolfgang von Marschall) (Alfred Metzner 1980).

'Introductory Survey' in *Consumer Credit* (Sijthoff, 1978, for United Kingdom National Committee of Comparative Law and Faculty of Laws, Queen Mary College).

'The Secured Creditor and Insolvency under English Law' (Published in a special issue of *Rabels Zeitschrift* 1980 on *Securities and Insolvency* (ed. David E. Allan and Ulrich Drobnig) (J.C.B. Mohr 1980).

'The Death of Insolvency Law' (1980) 1 Co Law 123.

'The Bank's Right to Recover Money Paid on a Stopped Cheque' (1981) 97 LQR 254.

'Reservation of Title: The EEC's Faulty Approach' (1980) 1 Co Law 185.

'Is the Law Too Favourable to Secured Creditors?' (Paper presented at the Twelfth Annual Workshop on Commercial and Consumer Law, University of Toronto, and published in (1983–84) Can Bus LJ 53.

'Some Concepts of English Commercial Law: A Reappraisal' (1982) Cambrian Law Review 14.

'Usury in English Law' (1982) 1 Arizona Journal of International and Comparative Law 38.

'Creditors' Rights: The Cork Proposals' (1983) Co Law 51.

'Twentieth Century Developments in Commercial Law' (1983) 3 Legal Studies 283.

'Truth in Lending: The Purposes and Principles of Rate Disclosure' (Paper presented at the 1983 Course of the Centre d'Etude et de Recherches Européenne, Luxembourg, July 1983, and published in *Consumer Protection* (Editions UGA 1984)).

'The Protection of the Consumer in Credit Transactions: Some Dilemmas for the Lawmaker (Paper presented at the above Course and published in *Consumer Protection* (Editions UGA 1984)).

'The Modernisation of Personal Property Security Law' (1984) 100 LQR 234.

'A Uniform Law on International Factoring' (Contribution to *Unification* (essays in honour of Professor J.G. Sauveplanne) (Kluwer 1984).

'Electronic Funds Transfer as an Immediate Payment System' (Published in *Electronic Banking: The Legal Implications*).

'Harmonisation of Commercial Law: Policies and Problems' (The Dr. Mary Shore Jones Memorial Lecture delivered at the University of Liverpool, 4 March 1983 and reproduced in (1985) Revista de la Facultad de Derecho de Mexico 215).

'The Legal Implications of Electronic Banking' (Paper presented at a conference of the International Bar Association Business Section, Amsterdam 1986).

'The Recovery of Judgment Debts in the County Court: Some Preliminary Results' (with Roger Cotterrell, Bob Davies, Hugh Gravelle and Jane Phipps) in *Debtors and Creditors* (ed. Iain Ramsay, Professional Books 1986).

'Ownership and Obligation in Commercial Transactions' (The first Mary Oliver Memorial Address to the Mansfield Law Club, 1987, published in (1987) 103 LQR 433).

'Concepts of Payment in Relation to the Expropriation and Freezing of Bank Deposits' [1987] 2 JIBL 80.

'The Legal Aspects of International Factoring' in *Factoring-Handbuch* (ed. K.F. Hagenmüller, 2nd edn 1987, Fritz Knapp Verlag) 149.

'Conclusion of the Leasing and Factoring Conventions – I' [1988] JBL 347.

'Conclusion of the Leasing and Factoring Conventions – II' [1988] JBL 510.

'Penalties in Finance Leases' (1988) 104 LQR 25.

'The Changing Face of Banking and Finance: Some Legal Implications' (The second Falconbridge Lecture, delivered at Osgoode Hall Law School, York University, Canada, 1987, published in (1989) 27 Osgoode Hall LJ 359).

'The Codification of Commercial Law' (1988) 14 Monash L Rev 135.

'Guarantees, Rites, Rights and Rewrites' [1988] 5 JBL 249.

'Security: A Pragmatic Conceptualist's Response' (1989) 15 Monash U L Rev 361.

'The Creation of a Single European Banking Market' (Paper presented at the European Finance Symposium, Antwerp, November 1988, published in European Affairs, Special Issue on the European Finance Symposium, 1989, 283, 'Uncertainty About Reciprocal Treatment').

'The Academic Stage of Legal Education: A Non-Vocational View' [1988] Gazette, 30 March, 12.

'The Codification of Commercial Law' (Seventeenth Wilfred Fullagar Memorial Lecture, delivered at Monash University 1988, published (1988) 14 Mon LR 135).

'The Banker's Duty of Confidentiality' [1989] JBL 269.

'The English Floating Charge' in *Lectures on the Common Law* (Kluwer 1989), delivered as one of the Tilburg-Leiden Lectures.

'The Banker's Duty of Confidentiality' [1989] JBL 269.

'The Teaching and Application of Fundamental Concepts of Commercial Law' (Paper presented at the fourth Biennial Meeting of the International Academy of Commercial and Commercial Law, Melbourne, 1988, published in *Essays on Comparative Commercial and Consumer Law* (ed. Donald B. King) (Fred B, Rothman & Co. 1992) and, in modified form, in (1991) 25 Law Teacher 200 as a memorial lecture for Professor Clive Schmitthoff.

'Legal Questions [of Electronic Data Interchange] and Problems to be Overcome' (with Eric Bergsten) in *Trading with EDI—The Legal Issues* (ed. Thomsen and Wheble) (IBC Financial Books 1989).

'1992: The Insolvency Implications for Banks' in *1992: The Legal Implications for Banks*, ed. Ross Cranston, Chartered Institute of Bankers and Centre for Commercial Law Studies 1989). Revised and published in *The Single Market and the Law of Banking* (ed. Ross Cranston) (Lloyds of London Press 1991).

'The Concept and Implications of a Market in Commercial Law', the 33rd Lionel Cohen Lecture, delivered at the Hebrew University of Jerusalem 1990, published in (1990) 24 Is LR 185, also published in [1991] LMCLQ 177.

'Liabilities on Insolvency' in *Banks—Liability and Risk* (ed. Ross Cranston) (Lloyds of London Press 1990).

'Property and Unjust Enrichment' in *Essays on Restitution* (ed. A. Burrows) (Oxford University Press 1991).

'Abstract Payment Undertakings' in *Essays for Patrick Atiyah* (ed. P. Cane and J. Stapleton) (Oxford University Press 1991).

'The Adaptation of English Law to International Commercial Arbitration' (1992) 8 Arbitration International 1, the Freshfields Arbitration Lecture delivered at Queen Mary and Westfield College, June 1991.

'The Concept of 'Good Faith' in English Law' (1992) Centro di stui e ricerche di diritto comparato e strainero, Saggi, Conferenze e Seminari, no. 2.

'The European Law School' (1993) 13 Legal Studies 1 (The Presidential Address to the Society of Public Teachers of Law at the University of Oxford, September 1992).

'The Recovery of a Director's Improper Gains: Proprietary Remedies for Infringement of Non-Proprietary Rights' in *Commercial Aspects of Trusts and Fiduciary Obligations* (ed. Ewan McKendrick) (Oxford University Press and Norton Rose M5 Group 1992).

'Reflections on the Harmonisation of Commercial Law' 1991-I Uniform Law Review 54, also published in *Commercial and Consumer Law* (ed. Ross Cranston and Roy Goode) (Oxford University Press 1993) a paper delivered at the 5th Biennial Meeting of the International Academy of Commercial and Consumer Law at the University of Oxford, August 1990.

'Practical Questions Relating to the UNIDROIT Convention on International Financial Leasing' in *Uniform Commercial Law in the Twenty-first Century* 106, Proceeding of the Congress of the United Nations Commission on International Trade Law, New York, 18–22 May 1992, a paper presented at the Congress.

'Defining and Protecting the Pension Promise' (1994) 121 Journal of the Institute of Actuaries 161, the 1993 Jubilee Lecture delivered at the Staple Inn Actuarial Society, November 1993.

'Occupational Pensions: Securing the Pension Promise' (1995) 9 Denning LJ 15, the Royal Bank of Scotland Lecture 1994.

'The Future of the Pension Trust' Hind Lecture, Nottingham, 1994.

'Charges over Book Debts: A Missed Opportunity' (1994) 110 LQR 592.

'Abstract Payment Undertakings and the Rules of the International Chamber of Commerce' (39 Saint Louis University Law Journal 725 (1995).

'Abstract Payment Undertakings in International Transactions' 22 Brooklyn Journal of International Law 1 (1996).

'The Exodus of the Floating Charge' in *Corporate and Commercial Law* (ed. David Feldman and Frank Meisel), a Festschrift for Professor Robert Pennington (1996) chapter 10.

'The Draft UNIDROIT Convention on International Interests in Mobile Equipment' in *Festkrift till Jan Ramberg*, Juristförlaget 1996, 151–63.

'The Nature and Transfer of Rights in Dematerialised and Immobilised Securities' (Paper delivered at the Oxford Law Colloquium 1995 published as chapter 7 of *The Future for the Global Securities Market* (ed. Fidelis Oditah) (Clarendon Press 1996) and reproduced in (1996) 4 JIFBL 167 and Capital Markets Forum Annual 1997.

'Usage and Its Reception in Transnational Commercial Law' (Paper presented at the 8th Biennial Conference of Commercial and Consumer Law and reproduced in

*New Developments in International Commercial and Consumer Law* (ed. Jacob S Ziegel) (Hart Publishing 1998) and in (1997) 46 ICLQ 1.

'International Restatements of Contracts and English Contract Law' 1997-II Uniform Law Review 231.

'Insolvent Trading under English and Australian Law,' (1998) 16 Corporate & Securities LJ 70–5, a paper presented at a conference at the University of Melbourne on 18 September 1997.

'The Protection of Interests in Movables in Transnational Commercial Law' in Uniform Law Review 1998-2/3, *Uniform Law Studies* in memory of Malcolm Evans, 453–65.

'Transcending the Boundaries of Earth and Space: The Preliminary Draft UNIDROIT Convention on International Interests in Mobile Equipment' 1998-I Uniform Law Review 64.

'Security in Cross-Border Transactions' 33 Texas International Law Journal 47 (1998), a paper presented at a conference at the University of Texas at Austin 1996.

'Dispute Resolution in the Twenty-First Century' *Arbitration*, February 1998, the 1997 Alexander Lecture.

'Proprietary Rights and Unsecured Creditors', in *The Realm of Company Law* (ed. Barry A.K. Rider 1998), a Collection of Papers in Honour of Professor Leonard Sealy, 183, also published in *Law at the Centre: The Institute of Advanced Legal Studies at Fifty* (ed. Barry A.K. Rider) (Kluwer Law International, 1999) chapter 12.

'Charge-backs and Legal Fictions' (1998) 114 LQR 178.

'Security Entitlements as Collateral and the Conflict of Laws' Butterworths Journal of International Banking and Financial Law, Special Supplement, September 1998, 22–8.

'The Changing Nature of Security Rights' in *Emerging Financial Markets and Secured Transactions* (ed. Joseph J. Norton and Mads Andenas) (Kluwer Law International 1998) 1.

'Proprietary Restitutionary Claims' in *Restitution: Past, Present and Future* (ed. Cornish et al.) (Hart Publishing 1998), 63–77.

'Security Interests in Movables under English Law' (Paper presented at the 25th Comparative Law Conference of the German Society of Comparative Law, Jena, March 1996, published in *Mobiliarsicherheiten: Vielfalt oder Einheit* (ed. Karl F. Kreuzer) (Nomos Verlagsgesellschaft 1999), 43–74.

'The Preliminary Draft UNIDROIT Convention on International Interests in Mobile Equipment: The Next Stage' 1999-2 Uniform Law Review, 265–74.

'Commercial Law and the Scottish Parliament', 4 Scottish Law and Practice Quarterly 81–92, reproducing a lecture delivered at the David Hume Institute, Edinburgh, on 25 November 1998, also published as Hume Occasional Paper No 57, David Hume Institute 1999.

'International Restatements and National Law' in *The Search for Principle*, a collection of essays in honour of Lord Goff (ed. William Swadling and Gareth Jones) (UNIDROIT and Kluwer Law International 1999) 45–58.

'The UNIDROIT Draft Mobile Equipment Convention: A Confluence of Legal Concepts and Philosophies' in *Mélanges en L'Honneur de Denis Tallon* (Société de Législation Comparée 1999) 69.

'A New International *Lex Mercatoria*?' (1999 Cassel Lecture), (2000) 2 Juridisk Tidskrift 253–68.

'The Role of the *lex Loci Arbitri* in International Commercial Arbitration' in *Lex Mercatoria: Essays on International Commercial Law in Honour of Francis Reynolds* (ed. Francis D. Rose, LLP 2000) 245–70, also published in (2001) 17 Arbitration International 19.

'Battening Down Your Security Interests: How the Shipping Industry Can Benefit from the UNIDROIT Convention on International Interests in Mobile Equipment', the 1999 Donald O'May Lecture [2000] LMCLQ 161–91.

'The Private Finance Initiative and Security for Payment under English Law' (Paper presented at a conference of the Association Sorbonne-Oxford on 6 July 2000 at the Sorbonne, and published in (2002) 54-1 Revue International du Droit Comparé 41.

'The Role and Influence of Non-Binding Rules in the Development of Transnational Commercial Law', a contribution to *Propos Impertinents de Droit des Affaires: Mélanges en l'Honneur de Christian Gavalda* (Dalloz, May 2001).

'Insularity or Leadership? The Role of the United Kingdom in the Harmonisation of Commercial Law' (2001) 50 ICLQ 751, reproducing the COMBAR Lecture 2000, 30 November 2000.

'The Mobile Equipment Convention' in *Cross-Border Security and Insolvency* (ed. Michael Bridge and Robert Stevens) (Oxford University Press 2001) 225.

'The Cape Town Convention on international interests in Mobile Equipment: A Driving Force for International Asset-Based Financing' 2002-1 Uniform Law Review 3.

'Assignment Clauses in International Contracts' (2002) International Business Law 389.

'Arbitration—Should Courts Get Involved?' (Paper presented at the Irish Annual Circuit Court Conference, Adare, on 13 April 2002 and published in (2002) 2 Judicial Studies Institute Journal 33).

'The Private Finance Initiative and Security for Payment under English Law' 2001-1 Revue Internationale de Droit Comparé 41.

'Europe and English Commercial Law' in *The British Contribution to the Europe of the Twenty-First Century* (ed. B.S. Markesinis) (Hart Publishing 2002) 15.

'Are Intangible Assets Fungible?' in *Themes in Comparative Law: Essays in Honour of Bernard Rudden* 97 (ed. Peter Birks and Arianna Pretto) (Oxford University Press 2002), reproduced with amendments in (2003) LMCLQ 379.

'International Interests in Mobile Equipment: A Transnational Juridical Concept' (2003) 15 Bond Law Review 9 (Special Issue: Festschrift for David Allan and Mary Hiscock) 1.

'Contract and Commercial Law: The Logic and Limits of Harmonisation' Ius Commune June 2003 1, the 2003 Wiarda Lecture, reproduced in *International Contract Law* (ed. F Willem Grosheide, Ewoud Hondius, and Katharina Boele-Woelki) (Intersentia 2004) 309.

'Harmonised Modernisation of the Law Governing Secured Transactions: General-Sectorial, Globa-Regional' 2003 VIII Unif l Rev 341.

'Developments in the International Harmonisation of Laws Governing Security Interests in Movables' (Paper presented at a conference of central bank legal experts in Hong Kong on 5 and 6 February 2004).

'The International Interest as an Autonomous Property Interest' (2004) European Review of Private Law 18.

'The Harmonization of Dispositive Contract and Commercial Law—Should the European Community be Involved?' in *Denationalisierung des Privatrechts?* (ed. Eva-Maria Kieninger, Mohr Siebeck 2005) 19.

'Interests in Securities Held with an Intermediary' in *From Government to Governance—The Growing Influence of Non-State Actors on the International and European Legal System—2003 Hague Joint Conference on Contemporary Issues of International Law* (ed. W.P. Heere) (TMC Asser Press 2004) 244.

'Rule, Practice and Pragmatism in Transnational Commercial Law' (2005) 54 ICLQ 539.

'The Avoidance of Transactions in Insolvency Proceedings and Restitutionary Defences' in *Mapping the Law: Essays in Memory of Peter Birks* (ed. Andrew Burrows and Lord Rodger of Earlsferry) (Oxford University Press 2006) chapter 16.

'The Hague Convention on the Law Applicable to Indirectly Held Securities: A Market-Oriented Approach to the Conflict of Laws' in *Beyond Borders: Perspectives on International and Comparative Law,* Symposium in Honour of Hein Kötz (ed. Florian Faust and Gregor Thüsing) (Carl Heymanns Verlag 2006) 63.

'The Case for the Abolition of the Floating Charge' in *Company Charges: Spectrum and Beyond* (ed. Joshua Gezler and Jennifer Payne) (Oxford University Press 2006) chapter 2.

'Removing the Obstacles to Commercial Law Reform', 13th Blackstone lecture, published in (2007) 123 LQR 602.

'Litigation or Arbitration? The Influence of the Dispute Resolution Procedure on Substantive Rights' 19 Pace Int l Rev 53 (Spring 2007).

'Is the *Lex Mercatoria* Autonomous?' in *Commercial Challenges in the 21st Century: Jan Hellner In Memoriam* (Iustus Förlag 2007) 73.

'Contractual Prohibitions against Assignment' in *Rationality in Company Law: Essays in Honour of D D Prentice* (ed. John Armour and Jennifer Payne) (Hart Publishing 2009) 355, republished in [2009] LMCLQ 300.

'Earth, Air and Space: The Cape Town Convention and Protocols and their Contribution to International Commercial Law' (Contribution to *Tom Bingham and the Transformation of the Law,* a collection of essays in honour of Lord Bingham (ed. Mads Andenas and Duncan Fairgrieve) (Oxford University Press, 2009) 649

'Transnational Commercial Law and the Influence of the Cape Town Convention and Aircraft Protocol' (2011) 50 Can Bus LJ 186.

'Perpetual Trustee and Flip Clauses in Swap Transactions' (2011) 127 LQR 1.

'Proprietary Liability for Secret Profits—A Reply' (2011) 127 LQR 493.

'Flip Clauses—The End of the Affair?' (2012) 128 LQR 171.
'The Priority Rules under the Cape Town Convention and Protocols' (2012) 1 The Cape Town Convention Journal 95.
'From Acorn to Oak Tree: The Development of the Cape Town Convention and Protocols' (2012) 17 ULR 599.
'The Cape Town Convention and Protocols and the Conflict of Laws' in *A Commitment to Private International Law*, a collection of essays in honour of Hans van Loon (ed. the Permanent Bureau of the Hague Conference, Intersentia, 2013) 221.
'The End of an Era: A Tribute to Jacob Ziegel' (2013) 54 Can Bus LJ 319.
'The Treatment of Intangible Assets under the Cape Town Convention and Protocols (2013) 2 Cape Town Convention Journal 41.
'Security Interests in Mobile Equipment: Lawmaking Lessons from the Cape Town Convention' (2014) 35 Adelaide Law Rev 59.
'The Assignment of Pure Intangibles in the Conflict of Laws' [2015] LMCLQ 289.
'*Force majeure* under URDG 758' in *The Age of Uniform Law: Essays in Honour of Michael Joachim Nonell to Celebrate his 70th Birthday* (UNIDROIT 2016) 689.
'Private Commercial Law Conventions and Public and Private International Law: The Radical Approach of the Cape Town Convention 2001 and its Protocols' (2016) 65 ICLQ 523, reproducing the 2016 Inaugural Roy Goode Lecture in Commercial Law delivered at the Inner Temple 1 March 2016.
'Reforming the Law of Secured Transactions in Jersey' (with John Rainer) in *Secured Transactions Law Reform* (ed. Louise Gullifer and Orkun Akseli) (Bloomsbury 2016) 207.
'Security Interests in Investment Securities under Jersey Law' (2017) Jersey and Guernsey Law Rev 7.
'La Convention du Cap relative aux guaranties internationals portant sur des matériels d'équipement mobile at son protocole aéronautique' in *Le Droit du financement des aéronefs* (ed. Cyril-Igor Grigorieff and Vincent Correia) (Bruylant 2017) Part III, chapter 2.
'Asset Identification under the Cape Town Convention and Protocols' [2018] 81 L & Contem Problems 135 (2018).
'The Power to Dispose under the Cape Town Convention and Aircraft Protocol' [2018] CTCJ 2.
Numerous smaller articles, case notes, papers, reviews, etc., in academic and practitioner journals, national press, and elsewhere.

# Index

The manufacturer's authorised representative in the EU for product safety is Oxford University Press España S.A. of el Parque Empresarial San Fernando de Henares, Avenida de Castilla, 2 – 28830 Madrid (www.oup.es/en or product.safety@oup.com). OUP España S.A. also acts as importer into Spain of products made by the manufacturer.

www.ingramcontent.com/pod-product-compliance
Lightning Source LLC
LaVergne TN
LVHW011903200926
848484LV00002B/515
* 9 7 8 0 1 9 8 8 2 5 8 1 4 *